Psychopathology of Childhood

(PGPS-95)

Pergamon Titles of Related Interest

Related Journals*

Pergamon General Psychology Series

Editors

Arnold P. Goldstein, Syracuse University
Leonard Krasner, SUNY at Stony Brook

Psychopathology of Childhood

A Clinical-Experimental Approach
Second Edition

Steven Schwartz, University of Queensland
James H. Johnson, University of Florida

PERGAMON PRESS

NEW YORK · OXFORD · BEIJING · FRANKFURT
SÃO PAULO · SYDNEY · TOKYO · TORONTO

U.S.A.	Pergamon Press Inc., Maxwell House, Fairview Park, Elmsford, New York 10523, U.S.A.
U.K.	Pergamon Press plc, Headington Hill Hall, Oxford OX3 0BW, England
PEOPLE'S REPUBLIC OF CHINA	Pergamon Press, Room 4037, Qianmen Hotel, Beijing, People's Republic of China
FEDERAL REPUBLIC OF GERMANY	Pergamon Press GmbH, Hammerweg 6, D-6242 Kronberg, Federal Republic of Germany
BRAZIL	Pergamon Editora Ltda, Rua Eça de Queiros, 346, CEP 04011, Paraiso, São Paulo, Brazil
AUSTRALIA	Pergamon Press Australia Pty Ltd., P.O. Box 544, Potts Point, N.S.W. 2011, Australia
JAPAN	Pergamon Press, 5th Floor, Matsuoka Central Building, 1-7-1 Nishishinjuku, Shinjuku-ku, Tokyo 160, Japan
CANADA	Pergamon Press Canada Ltd., Suite No 271, 253 College Street, Toronto, Ontario, Canada M5T 1R5

Library of Congress Cataloging in Publication Data
Schwartz, Steven,
　　Psychopathology of Childhood
　　Reprinted 1987, 1988
　　(Pergamon general psychology series; 95)
　　Includes bibliographies and indexes.
　　1. Child psychopathology. I. Johnson,
James H. (James Harmon), 1943–　　. II. Title,
III. Series, [DNLM: 1. Mental Disorders-in infancy
& childhood. 2. Psychopathology-in infancy &
childhood. WS 350 S399p]
RJ499.S47 1985　　618.92'8907　　85-9373
ISBN 0-08-030935-6

Printed in Great Britain by A. Wheaton & Co. Ltd., Exeter

To our wives Carolyn and Theda
and our children
Seth, Tricia, & Gregory Schwartz and Jamie & Trey Johnson

CONTENTS

PREFACE

When the first edition of this book was published in 1981, the field of childhood psychopathology was just beginning to develop into a specialty area within clinical psychology. As we write this preface, a scant 4 years later, we are struck by how much the field has grown. There are new specialist journals, international meetings, doctoral and post-doctoral training programs, and a general level of concern with the area greater than we could have hoped for 4 years ago.

Perhaps the biggest area of growth has been in research. Scientists and clinicians at universities, clinics, and hospitals have devoted themselves to the problems of children with such fervor that much of the research cited in this second edition was not yet published when the first edition was written.

The amount of new work published in the last 4 years demanded that much of the second edition be rewritten rather than simply updated. Relatively few pages from the first edition remain unchanged. Some topics have been given less space, but most have received increased coverage. In addition, many new topics (e.g., child advocacy, child temperament, noncompliance) have been added. We have also tried to provide students with a greater appreciation of the importance of developmental variables in child psychopathology. Clinical case examples have been added to give readers a better picture of how the various syndromes manifest themselves in chil-

dren. Although a great deal of clinical material has been added, the focus remains, as in the first edition, on research.

For many the term *research* brings to mind the image of laboratory workers in white coats, of shiny brass instruments and confusing statistical formulae. This view of research is much narrower than the one portrayed in this book. Research in the present context is conceived broadly as any scientific investigation into the nature and treatment of childhood psychopathology. Research may take place in clinics, schools, and hospitals, as well as laboratories. It may proceed from many different theoretical orientations and use many different methods. It may employ many subjects or consider the behavior of only one individual under controlled conditions. Many of the investigations described in this book do, however, share certain common features — a preference for rigorous thinking, the willingness to make assumptions available to public scrutiny, and the belief that the ultimate value of research will be its practical applicability to solving the psychological problems of children.

In writing this book we have not given equal attention to all of the literature in the field. We have been biased in favor of those views of the etiology and treatment of psychopathology that have been put to experimental test. Consequently, a larger portion of this book is devoted to work in behavioral and, to some extent, cognitive psychology than to the presentation of psychoanalytic views, although analytic and other views are considered. In addition, we have tended to devote more space to research programs than to single experiments that have not been replicated or followed up. Throughout, we have tried to present a coherent picture of the current state of knowledge of childhood psychopathology.

Because psychologists, psychiatrists, neurologists, pediatricians, and educators have all made contributions to our understanding of child psychopathology, this book is rather broad in scope. For ease of exposition we have organized the book around traditional topics, but our discussion reflects modern rather than traditional theorizing. We have also attempt-

ed to emphasize the role of developmental factors, as an understanding of their contribution is essential to understanding abnormal child behavior.

Although we do not expect that all our readers will be psychologists, we have assumed that they will have a basic background in psychology. Advanced undergraduates, graduate students, and professionals in such areas as psychology, psychiatry, and special education are our intended audience.

We hope this book will provide readers with a picture of the current state of knowledge about child psychopathology, and perhaps motivate some to join us in the attempt to learn even more.

ACKNOWLEDGMENTS

We are indebted to many people without whose help this second edition could have never been completed. Our colleagues, assistants, secretaries, students, patients, and families have all contributed directly or indirectly to this volume. Their expertise has added much to the quality of this book and their support has made its writing a more enjoyable task. We specifically wish to thank Terri Sheldon, Judy Brown, Bob Aber, and Jenny Doelling for their help in researching and/or proofreading the manuscript. We also wish to express a special note of thanks to Jerry Frank and the staff at Pergamon Press. Their expertise has added much to the quality of the book and their support throughout this project has been appreciated.

This second edition was written while one of us (S. Schwartz) was on the faculty of the University of Queensland and, for a time, Visiting Professor at Stanford University and while the other (J. H. Johnson) was on the faculty of the University of Florida. The assistance of these institutions, as well as the financial support of the Australian Research Grants Scheme, is gratefully acknowledged. Finally, it should be noted that this edition, like the first, was truly a joint effort, with both authors contributing equally to the finished product.

1 PSYCHOPATHOLOGY OF CHILDHOOD: A HISTORICAL, THEORETICAL, AND METHODOLOGICAL FRAMEWORK

The following cases are taken from the files of a busy clinical child psychologist.

Sarah

An excessively skinny 16-year-old girl, Sarah was referred by her family doctor because he was concerned by her severe weight loss. About 6 months before the referral, Sarah (who was 5 ft. 5 in. tall and had never been fat) felt that her 115 lb made her unattractive, and she decided to diet in order to lose weight. She began reasonably enough; first she avoided sweets, then all carbohydrates. But progress was too slow for her, so she also eliminated starches and meat from her diet. Fruit went next. At the time of her referral, she was down to a few carrots each day. Sarah's weight dropped to 85 lb, she had trouble sleeping, and became irritable and depressed. She also stopped having menstrual periods. Despite her weight, Sarah still felt she was too fat and needed to diet. If her dieting continued, her condition could become life threatening.

Simon

Simon's mother brought him to the psychologist because, try as she might, she could not get him to stop wetting the bed. Despite various interventions (praise, reward, even spanking), Simon has never been dry for more than a few nights in a row in all his 10 years. Simon rarely wets himself during the day and never in the company of other children. Investigations have uncovered no medical reason for his problem. In most other ways, Simon's behavior is perfectly normal, although his mother reports a tendency toward temper tantrums whenever he is thwarted.

Vivian

Vivian's parents sought psychological advice when their formerly quiet but "normal" daughter began having a variety of "strange experiences," which often took the form of voices only she could hear. The voices told her how to cast "spells" that could stop birds from flying and how to change the weather merely by moving her hand. Vivian also started walking through doors backwards so that

1

she could see any "devils" sneaking up behind her. Vivian's aunt lived out her days in a mental hospital, and her mother feared that "bad blood" had infected her 13-year-old daughter as well.

One does not need to be a trained psychologist to realize that these three children have quite different problems. Any psychologist who hopes to intervene effectively must be able to recognize these differences and implement treatment programs suited to the particular child. But Sarah, Simon, and Vivian represent only a small sample of the diverse problems seen in clinical practice. As will be described in this book, today's clinical-child psychologists are being asked to cope with many different behavioral difficulties, and the list becomes longer all the time. Although most of the disorders treated by clinical-child psychologists are described in this book, their diversity makes it difficult to see the entire field in a unified light. The purpose of the present chapter is to provide a general structure into which later, more specific discussions may be incorporated.

Although it seems obvious to modern readers that Sarah, Simon, and Vivian have problems, this was not always the case. For most of recorded history, psychological disorders were either ignored or attributed to supernatural forces. The first section of this chapter reviews the history of psychopathology with a specific focus on children's problems. It will be shown that attitudes toward psychological problems change as society changes and that these attitudes are as important as new scientific discoveries in determining how children are treated.

Although changes in social values affect the way psychological problems are viewed, it is the thesis of this book that studying psychopathology is (or should be) a scientific enterprise. The second section of this chapter is concerned with theories of psychopathology and the third with how theory and experimentation interact to advance our knowledge of child psychopathology.

Understanding children's behavior requires consideration of their developmental level.

Children are developing organisms; their behavior changes over time. Behaviors appropriate to one developmental stage may not be appropriate to another. Bedwetting, for example, is far less serious in a 4-year-old than in a 10-year-old like Simon. Vivian's experiences might also be less of a concern if she were 10 years younger. The importance of the developmental variable is discussed in the fourth section of this chapter.

Many influences combine to produce disordered behavior. Simon's bedwetting problem may be largely the result of poor training—a faulty habit. But this is not likely to be the sole cause of Vivian's problem, which may well have a genetic as well as a learning component. Sarah's difficulty is also most likely the result of several interacting factors, including hormonal ones. The final section of this chapter reviews the various etiological factors in childhood psychopathology.

CHILDHOOD PSYCHOPATHOLOGY FROM ANCIENT TO MODERN TIMES

Science, like most other important intellectual endeavors, thrives on precise description and measurement. A person's state of mental health, however, is a completely different sort of fact than a person's weight, height, or blood pressure. This is true not only because of the differences between physical and mental measurements, but also because mental health, unlike pounds and inches, is both subjective and relative. A yardstick indicates a value for height that anyone familiar with rulers will agree upon, but such is not the case for the diagnostic instruments most often used in the field of psychopathology. Unlike reading yardsticks, judgments about mental health are heavily influenced by the context in which they are made. Behavior that is perfectly normal in one situation may be viewed as pathological in another. The treatment of the mentally disturbed is also a function of cultural attitudes. This can best be illustrated by examining the history of mental illness and its treatment.

Psychopathology Prior to the 18th Century

References to what is known today as "mental illness" can be found even among prehistoric artifacts. (The term *mental illness* is used here in a neutral manner to refer to disorders of behavior, cognition, or affect. It does not imply any specific etiological model.) Early man, however, made no distinction between physical disease and psychological disorders. All disease was thought to be caused by spirits, and mental disease was thought to be caused by spirits inhabiting the brain. It is likely that for prehistoric man only relatively severe deviations were noted as disease, as opposed to the broad categories employed today.

Among the early accepted treatments for brain disease was trephining, in which a circle of bone was chipped from the skull to allow the demons inside to escape. Archeological evidence indicates that some patients survived trephining, and it is even conceivable that patients suffering from excessive pressure within the skull improved as a result of the procedure. Thus, the treatment may have been effective, but for the wrong reasons — an occurrence by no means unusual even today.

The belief in demonology and unseen forces was challenged as early as 400 B.C. by Hippocrates. During a time of great advances in the sciences and the humanities under the Greek and Roman civilizations, Hippocrates suggested that mental illness (again, defined relatively narrowly by today's usage) was caused by diseases of the brain and should be treated no differently from other diseases. Comforting and relaxing treatments for mental disorders were favored by Hippocrates and his students and were administered in a humanitarian way by both the Greeks and Romans.

Although the Arab civilizations continued to accept the teachings of ancient Rome, the Middle Ages brought the return of demonology to Europe. It is beyond the scope of the present discussion to cover all the factors involved in the breakdown of civilization during the Dark Ages. It is sufficient to note that the destruction of the economic system and the resulting decline in commerce and trade led to a loss of belief in the social order and a renewed sense of helplessness and superstition. Almost anything that could be construed as "different" was suspect. For example, any hint of a lack of faith in the religious orthodoxies of the time or any objection to the mores of the community could be interpreted as mental derangement. In the Middle Ages, for the first time, the definition of mental illness was broader than that used today. Frequently, authorities used the accusation of demonic possession as a means of keeping power and controlling their enemies. This technique is still common in some countries, where the term *mentally ill* is reserved for political enemies, and is not entirely unheard of in the United States (Szasz, 1965).

In the Middle Ages, the deranged were turned over to the clergy and the feudal secular powers, who combined to punish the "agents of the devil" by burning them at the stake or otherwise disposing of them. For more than 10 centuries, thousands were burned as witches; the practice did not completely die out until the 18th century.

The many dangers of medieval life and the uncertainties of existence led to aberrations of behavior appropriate to that precarious time. For example, a curious phenomenon known as Saint Vitus's Dance would sometimes engulf the population of an entire village. The inhabitants would throw off their clothes, roll on the ground, bang their heads, and scream incessantly — a form of mass hysteria not likely to occur on such a scale today, particularly in Western cultures. On the other hand, it is equally likely that many of the aberrations that modern psychiatrists encounter were never heard of then. Whatever mental illness is, it is certainly not culture-free.

The psychological problems of children were largely ignored by our medieval ancestors. In fact, the entire notion of childhood as a separate developmental stage was foreign to them (see Kessel & Seigel, 1983, for essays dealing with the "invention of children"). Ariès (1962) describes how the artifacts of the Middle Ages (paintings, sculpture, biographies, etc.) portray children as little adults differing from adults only in size and strength. There were no special children's games or literature; children were mainly a labor resource easily exploited by stronger adults. Ariès speculates that high mortality made parents wary of becoming too attached to their children.

There is no doubt that childhood mortality was high; as late as 1750 the odds were still three to one against a child making it past age 5 (Kessen, 1965). But this was not the whole story. Children continued to be exploited for centuries after parents began viewing them as different and precious. Poverty insured that few families could afford the luxury of non-working children. It was not until the 19th century that the Society for the Prevention of Cruelty to Children was founded — an offshoot of the *older* Society for the Prevention of Cruelty to Animals. Even as recently as 1959, the United Nations found it necessary to issue a resolution confirming that human rights belong to children, not just to adults.

The early part of the 18th century witnessed the decline of demonology, but unfortunately this did not lead directly to more enlightened treatment of those considered mentally ill. Patients were still abused, locked in cellars, kept in chains, and whipped. In the field of psychopathology, treatment, as well as diagnosis, is related to the social milieu. More humane treatment developed slowly in the 18th century, primarily because the culture changed slowly. By far the greatest progress was made in the two countries whose culture, marked by revolution, was changing faster than average: the United States and France. Although no great advances in medical or psychiatric knowledge occurred, the changing social climates of both nations made the time ripe for a new attitude toward psychological disorders. Both France and America had revolted against monarchies and elitist societies. Democracy and social egalitarianism were the declared order of the day. The introduction of new hospitals for the "insane" stemmed directly from the belief that the government had a responsibility to provide for the welfare of all citizens. The French and American revolutions and the separation of church and state were responsible for important changes in the attitude toward the treatment of mental illness.

This is not to say that the medical profession was not changing as well. The physicians of the 18th century still largely believed in the physical basis of mental illness and often with good reason. By the end of the century, a physical etiology had been established for many derangements of behavior — alcoholic psychosis, senile psychosis, and general paresis. Even the notorious "mad hatters" of *Alice in Wonderland* fame were found to exhibit their irrational behavior as a result of nervous system damage caused by the mercury used in treating the felt from which hats were manufactured.

Unfortunately, for the majority of cases, hypothetical diseases of the brain proved quite difficult to discover. Despite valiant attempts and numerous autopsies of deranged patients, physiological bases for most mental illnesses were not forthcoming. As a consequence, a number of physicians began to think in terms of "functional" mental illnesses, those that are purely "psychological" in origin. It is these functional illnesses that most people associate with mental illness today.

Child Psychopathology in the Modern Era*

Toward the end of the 18th century, the study of the problems of childhood began in earnest. The influences that can be directly credited with the increase in interest in children were not, interestingly enough, the same influences that affected the study of adult psychopathology. In fact, child psychopathology was not fully recognized as a legitimate specialty by the mental health field until fairly recently (Gardner, 1976). The study of child psychopathology has its roots in neither adult

---

*Parts of this discussion were drawn from the volume edited by Lowery (1948).

psychiatry nor pediatrics, but in education, psychology, and the social sciences.

Education

Perhaps the seminal worker in the modern era in the field of early childhood education was Pestalozzi (1895). Much influenced by Rousseau, Pestalozzi attempted to develop a philosophy and method of education that would reflect accurately the ideas of that famous philosopher. Pestalozzi's educational goal was to help children develop their innate powers of observation and perception. To this end, Pestalozzi felt the curriculum should include not just lectures, but also field trips and active participation by the children in the educational process. Pestalozzi's ideas were carried forward by Froebel (1903), who, as the founder of the first kindergarten, succeeded in applying new "discovery" methods of education to the very young child. The rapidity with which the idea of kindergartens spread throughout Europe is rather surprising, considering how radically different Pestalozzi's and Froebel's ideas of education were from prevailing practices. Prior to their work, most educational practice derived from the belief that children were not born with the faculties necessary for learning and moral development and that these qualities needed to be inculcated in children from without, often by the use of force. The change in attitude toward childhood education mirrored changes in society as much as it did new discoveries in the field of education. Optimism about the essential nature of man was on the rise in 19th-century Europe and America, making the time ripe for new ideas.

The first kindergarten in the United States was begun by Elizabeth Peabody in Boston in 1860, and the first public school kindergarten was established in St. Louis 13 years later. By the turn of the century, kindergartens could be found in most parts of the country. One of the salutary effects of the development of kindergartens and the widespread acceptance of Pestalozzi's approach to education was the new availability of a population of young children to study. Research into child behavior became important because more information was needed to design new curricula, and because children began to be of interest in their own right. One of the most influential of the early students of child development was Herbart (1901), who introduced the idea that children pass through various stages of development, each with its characteristic problems and accomplishments. The idea of developmental stages is encountered repeatedly in the field of child development.

The influence of educators then, was one of the first formative factors in the development of modern child psychology. And as the development of children came to be viewed as important and interesting, their problems began to be viewed with interest as well.

Mental Retardation

Another important influence on the developing field of child psychopathology was the increasing concern with the care and treatment of the mentally retarded. Although the retarded were an identifiable group in the writings of most early educators, psychologists, and psychiatrists, it was in the 19th century that the problem of mental retardation was brought into the mainstream of psychology. A beginning date of sorts was the year 1880, when a boy was found in the woods near Aveyron, France, who appeared to have had no contact with other human beings for some years. Because of his manner and his inability to communicate, he was called a "savage" or "wild boy." Jean Itard (see Itard, 1932), a French psychologist, undertook to apply the new educational ideas already described to the task of rehabilitating the "wild boy." Itard's work, although largely ineffective, led to an interest in helping "idiots," as the mentally retarded were called at that time. A pupil of Itard's, Séguin, began to treat the mentally retarded in Paris' famous Bicêtre Hospital. His work culminated in his famous treatise on the education of the mentally retarded (1866), which quickly became the recognized source in the field.

Taking Séguin's lead, schools for the mentally retarded were established throughout

Europe and the United States. These early institutions began as experiments and were primarily educational institutions rather than asylums. It was hoped that, after training, the pupils could be returned to their homes. Later this optimism gave way to the more pessimistic belief that for most of these children, custodial care would have to be provided for life.

In recent years, this pessimism has once again given way to a more optimistic view of what can be done to aid the mentally retarded in finding a useful place in society (see Vitello & Soskin, 1985). These new developments are discussed in considerable detail in Chapter 8. A natural outgrowth of attempts to educate the mentally retarded was the development of measures to assess intellectual functioning and the intense study of children's cognitive development.

Intelligence Testing

Understanding and measuring intelligence has been a long-standing interest of psychologists. However, it was not until Darwin's influential theory of "survival of the fittest" that human abilities began to be systematically studied.

Galton (1862), Darwin's cousin, was one of the first modern scientists to investigate individual differences in mental functioning. Convinced of the heritability of human traits and influenced by the philosophical notion that all knowledge comes through the senses, Galton believed the most able individuals were those who possessed the most acute senses. He began his investigation by designing numerous tests to measure simple sensory discriminations (i.e., visual acuity and tone discrimination). But his attempts to measure cognitive ability through perceptual-motor tasks did not succeed in differentiating the gifted from the mentally retarded. In retrospect, it is easy to see why Galton's theory was wrong. His attempts to measure intellectual prowess were undermined by the much greater extent to which he was measuring motor and sensory functioning.

Interest in intelligence was revived as a subject for psychology by the work of Alfred Binet at the beginning of the 20th century. Binet's early work on human abilities closely resembled that of Galton, in that he was concerned largely with physical attributes and simple sensory discriminations. It was not until he was commissioned by the French government to study mental deficiency in the Paris school system that his work took a more practical turn. Binet temporarily abandoned the theoretical approach of Galton and turned from investigating the "elements" of human ability to the development of an overall index of intellectual functioning. The only theoretical assumption Binet made was that the *relative* mental ability of an individual (with respect to others in a population) was constant over time. Binet realized that to produce a socially useful instrument, his tests had to tap various aspects of intelligence, for example, the knowledge of facts, reasoning, and language ability. One of his most far-reaching contributions was his assumption that the types of tasks used to measure intellectual ability need only satisfy the criteria of agreeing with current and future academic success. Thus, any task was considered useful if it could be shown to predict later academic accomplishments. In 1905, Binet completed his first test, which consisted of 30 items reflecting a child's ability to understand and reason with objects common in his or her cultural environment. Test items were clustered by age levels and increased in difficulty from those that could easily be solved by the very young to those that were difficult for the average adult. In a later revision Binet introduced the concept of mental age, which was defined as the highest age level at which a child could perform adequately. Some items from the American version of Binet's test appear in Table 1.1.

Binet's test of intelligence had a tremendous impact and strongly influenced the field of applied psychology and the study of children. His method of discriminating those children who could benefit from normal school experiences from those who lacked the capacity to advance was rapidly emulated by psy-

TABLE 1.1. SAMPLE ITEMS FROM STANFORD-BINET INTELLIGENCE SCALE.

Age	Name of Item	Description
2	Form Board	Child must place a circle, triangle, and square in correct place on board.
3	Picture Vocabulary	Ten of 18 line drawings must be named.
4	Picture Identification	Child must point to the correct object in response to questions.
7	Copying	Copies three pictures of diamonds.
8	Vocabulary	Defines eight words from a longer list.
9	Digits Reversed	Repeats four digits in backward order.

Source: Terman & Merrill (1973).

chology clinics, the armed forces, and industry. The success of Binet-type tests in various settings greatly increased the influence of applied psychology in subsequent human-ability research. Since Binet's day, efforts to improve the predictive power of IQ tests have succeeded to an impressive degree. Indeed, we have probably reached the maximum predictive power attainable, given the usual restrictions on time and expense. This concentration on predictive validity has, however, overshadowed attempts to explicate intelligence as a theoretical construct.

The atheoretical nature of intelligence tests has led to their frequent misuse. They have been used to label national and racial groups inferior and otherwise serve political ends (Kamin, 1974). Misuse was caused as much by the social climate as by practitioners and test designers. For example, the depression of the 1930s and the immigration waves of the late 19th century and early 20th century frightened many people, who feared their jobs would be lost to cheaper labor. As a result, in some quarters, "scientific proof" of the inferiority of this or that immigrant group was eagerly welcomed.

For our purposes, it is interesting to note that at the same time that intelligence tests were being developed and refined, another group of investigators was studying cognitive development in the laboratory and clinic.

Cognitive and Social Development

One can hardly list the large number of pioneering workers whose investigations of child development set the stage for much of modern developmental psychology. Among the early notables was William Stern (1930), who, in addition to having popularized the term *intelligence quotient*, attempted to relate intelligence testing to what was then known about child development. This combination of psychometric and experimental methods was also the hallmark of Arnold Gesell (Gesell & Thompson, 1938), whose group put together the most complete picture of child maturation ever attempted.

One of the most influential psychologists to turn his attention to the problems of child development was G. Stanley Hall, who, as chairman of the psychology department at Clark University, exerted an extraordinary influence on the development of 20th-century academic psychology. In 1891, Hall founded the *Pedagogical Seminary*, the first scholarly journal devoted to child development. Before moving to Clark, he was also the founder of the Illinois Society of Child Study, the first of its kind in the United States. Although many of Hall's ideas are out of date today, he influenced many psychologists who followed him in the scientific study of childhood. Among his students were Goddard, who for many years worked with the mentally retarded at the Vineland School in New Jersey, and Louis Terman, who more than anyone else, was responsible for the American acceptance of Binet's scales and who initiated the largest longitudinal study of "genius" ever attempted, which continues to this day (Terman & Oden, 1959).

The United States government has also been an active supporter and contributor to the field of child study. It sponsors periodic conferences on children, supports a great deal of research through its agencies (The Children's Bureau, the Office of Child Development, the National Institute of Child Health and Human Development), and publishes the *Infant Care Bulletin*, which is widely read.

A review of past and current issues of the *Bulletin* shows clearly how changes in the cultural and social climate exert a strong influence on child rearing. In early issues, for example, self-stimulating behaviors such as thumb sucking and masturbation were thought to present a potential danger, and parents were advised to stop children from engaging in these behaviors, lest they run the risk of permanent damage. By the 1920s, these prohibitions were deemphasized. Instead, bowel training and feeding became of preeminent importance, and parents were told to be rigid, stick to a schedule, and train early. The most recent editions of the *Bulletin* put relatively little stress on prohibitions and see self-stimulatory behavior as not only harmless, but actually beneficial in helping the infant to learn about his world. Parents are advised not to rush bowel training and to be flexible rather than rigid about feeding. Similar patterns may be seen in the *Bulletin's* advice about pacifiers, which have been damned as well as praised over the years. Table 1.2 shows some changes in the *Bulletin's* attitude toward several aspects of child rearing, indicating a consistent trend toward greater permissiveness in child-rearing practices. This trend cannot be directly related to scientific discoveries of the last 60 years, but is more likely the result of cultural changes that have emphasized permissiveness in most aspects of conduct.

No discussion of the field of child study would be complete without mention of the work carried out at the Institute Jean Jacques Rousseau in Geneva, Switzerland, by the late Jean Piaget and his students. The idea of stages in cognitive development was carried to its logical conclusion by Piaget, who used a naturalistic method to study the growth of cognitive and moral processes in the child. After a period of neglect, experimental psychologists turned to Piaget's work as a guide to the study of children. His influence has never been so widespread or so important as it is now, and it promises to remain so in the foreseeable future. We will return to Piaget's work later in this chapter.

The study of child development, growing out of the need to solve such practical problems as how to best design instructional curricula and the treatment of the mentally retarded, soon became an area of scientific interest. The work of various students of child development has exerted a strong influence on the field of modern psychopathology, and in many ways their findings constitute the data base upon which psychopathologists have attempted to build their theories of abnormal behavior.

Mental Hygiene and Child Guidance

An important influence on the present status of child psychopathology had its beginnings in an autobiographical book, *A Mind that Found Itself*, written by Clifford Beers (1908). Beers, whose psychiatric hospitalization convinced him of the need for a world-wide movement to aid the mentally ill, wrote his book with the hope of mobilizing public sentiment, and it was an almost immediate success. With the aid of the publicity generated by his story, Beers was able to enlist the help of many important people, and the mental hygiene movement was born. The movement's goals — to raise the standards of care, educate the public about mental illness, and prevent mental illness — quickly expanded to include support for the training of mental health workers.

TABLE 1.2. CHANGES IN ATTITUDE TOWARD COMMON CHILDHOOD BEHAVIORS AS REFLECTED IN THE INFANT CARE BULLETIN.

Severity in the Handling of:	From 1914 to 1921	From 1921 to 1929	From 1929 to 1938	From 1938 to 1942–45	From 1942–45 to 1951	From 1951 to Present
Masturbation	Decreases	Decreases	Constant	Decreases	Constant	Decreases
Thumb sucking	Constant	Decreases	Constant	Decreases	Decreases	Decreases
Weaning	Increases	Increases	Constant	Decreases	Constant	Decreases
Bowel training	Increases	Increases	Decreases	Decreases	Decreases	Constant
Bladder training	Increases	Decreases	Decreases	Decreases	Decreases	Constant

Source: Adapted from Wolfenstein (1953). © 1953 by the *American Orthopsychiatric Association* and reprinted by permission.

The profession that benefited the most from the support of the mental hygiene movement was psychiatric social work, which became very important because of the mental hygiene movement's concern with the problems of children. Because an orientation toward families and their operation within the cultural milieu was believed helpful in dealing with children, social workers were seen as offering an expertise unobtainable elsewhere. Children's problems were looked at not only from the point of view of treatment, but also as a way of learning about the etiology of mental disorders and their possible prevention. The emphasis on early detection and treatment of problems inevitably created a need for diagnostic and treatment facilities. It was for these reasons that child guidance clinics developed.

The recognized leader in this field was William Healy, who established what is now known as the Institute for Juvenile Research in Chicago in 1909. An earlier clinic had been established as part of a research project in Philadelphia by Lightner Witmer, but it was Healy who put together the various features that later became known as the child guidance clinic. Healy's clinic was originally established to aid the Cook County courts in dealing with adolescents who were to be tried as delinquents. Disposition of these cases often depended on emotional, intellectual, and social factors in the child's background, and Healy's clinic was established to provide this sort of information. Although the purpose of the clinic was to diagnose and evaluate cases referred by the courts, treatment recommendations were frequently made as well.

Healy's clinic presented a unique model, because it included not only physicians but psychologists (who served largely as mental testers) and social workers (whose major tasks involved home visits). The interdisciplinary model of the Healy child guidance clinic reflected the important role of individual traits and social influences on behavior; it is a model still frequently encountered in child clinics today. Healy's work with delinquents and his later work at the Judge Baker Guidance Center in Boston ensured that his ideas would receive wide attention. Child guidance clinics soon began to develop throughout the country. With the encouragement of the mental hygiene movement and the public at large, clinics began to see younger and younger children. Planned consultations with social agencies and treatment were added to the clinics' diagnostic and evaluation functions. Public education about mental hygiene and child rearing also became important tasks of child guidance clinics.

Although adult psychiatry was growing both in stature and influence, most psychiatrists had little influence on either child guidance centers or, interestingly, the mental hygiene movement. An important exception was Adolph Meyer.

Meyer emigrated to the United States at the end of the 19th century to accept a position at the state hospital in Kankakee, Illinois. As his interests turned more toward psychiatry, Meyer moved to Worcester State Hospital in Massachusetts, where he came into contact with G. Stanley Hall at nearby Clark University. At Worcester, and later at the

Phipps Clinic in Baltimore, Meyer was a pioneer in setting standards for the professional training of psychiatrists. Although influenced by Freud and largely responsible for the introduction of psychoanalytic ideas into American psychiatry, Meyer remained eclectic in his approach, looking for progress in psychiatry not only in the work of Freud and his followers, but also in the work of physiologists and behavioral psychologists. Meyer showed an early interest in the mental hygiene movement and in the problems of children, and emphasized the importance of preventive work, psychiatric social work, mental hospitals, and multidisciplinary clinics. His theory of psychobiology stressed the importance of the patient as a person and the need to study the patient's whole life history, capacities, and traits to fully understand his or her problems. Much of what Meyer wrote about is now considered common sense; in fact, it is so much a part of psychiatry that he is often denied the credit he deserves. His approach toward working with children, enlisting the help of social agencies, schools, and social workers, is basic to the way the problems of children are treated today.

From these beginnings a field of study and clinical work devoted to the problems of children began to develop. It finally crystalized with the founding of the American Orthopsychiatric Association in 1924. From the outset, the organization included psychologists and social workers as well as psychiatrists. Today there are many organizations and specialty groups concerned with the treatment of children's problems, but the philosophy described thus far has held strong: a focus on early intervention, prevention, and the need for interdisciplinary cooperation in child study is still the rule.

Education, psychology, psychiatry, and social work have all influenced the field of child psychopathology. Today each field exerts its influence through clinical practice and research. In the next section, the main theories influencing research and practice are described.

MAJOR THEORETICAL INFLUENCES IN CHILD PSYCHOPATHOLOGY

As noted earlier, defining abnormal behavior in childhood is not simple. It requires a knowledge of child development, as well as a sensitivity to cultural values and social norms. Over the years several general approaches to conceptualizing childhood behavior disorders have developed; some have been elaborated to the stage where they can be considered general theories. These theories serve to organize data about behavior disorders and to offer explanations for their etiology. But this is not all: Good theories also make new predictions and suggest useful areas for further research.

Although theories vary in their scope, testability, and usefulness, following one or another is ultimately a matter of preference. Clinical psychologists are free to choose whichever theory they feel most valuable, but this choice should always remain tentative. New data should lead to the revision of theories. If theories (or clinicians) are resistant to new data, then the theories will serve to blind practitioners rather than illuminate them. The following discussion reviews the major theories in the field of child psychopathology.

Psychoanalysis

More than in any other area of abnormal psychology, Freud's theories have influenced the study of child psychopathology. Very early in his writings, Freud emphasized the importance of childhood experiences and emotions in shaping adult personality. If the problems of adults could be traced back to early experiences, understanding child development was obviously important: The more that is known in this area, the greater the probability that future problems can be avoided. Once again, the importance of prevention in the field of child psychopathology is emphasized. Freud, of course, contributed not only a theory, but also a method of treatment. He first applied his method—although by mail—in the famous case of Little Hans reported in 1909. It was not until 10 years later, however, that other published reports of the use of psychoanalysis with children began to appear. Melanie Klein (1932) was the first to use free play (play therapy) with children, which she saw as a substitute for the free associations obtained in adult psychoanalysis. She encouraged children to play and interpreted the meanings of their activities in much the same way that an adult's free associations might be interpreted. Anna Freud (1928), on the other hand, felt that a somewhat different approach was most appropriate with children, whose problems lie in the present rather than in the past. Because children's problems are inextricably intertwined with their experiences at school and home, she recommended enlisting the cooperation of parents and teachers in the treatment of children.

A large number of psychoanalysts and psychoanalytically inclined psychologists and social workers have made contributions to the field of child psychopathology. Because much current theorizing in the area of abnormal child behavior is still derived from a psychoanalytic perspective, a more detailed exposition of the theory is necessary. [For an even more detailed but still accessible description of psychoanalytic theory, see Freedman, Kaplan & Sadock (1976).]

Freud and Psychoanalysis: Background

Freud was born in what is now Czechoslovakia; he and his family moved to Vienna when he was 4 years old. He completed medical school at the University of Vienna, but his major interest was in research rather than clinical practice. In order to pursue this interest, he joined the Institute of Cerebral Research, but low wages and anti-Semitism eventually led him into private practice. Nonetheless, he remained committed to theory and research, and even after the development of psychoanalysis, Freud was less interested in curing patients than in developing a theory of personality.

Freud soon became taken with the new approaches to emotional problems pioneered at the end of the 19th century by Jean Charcot and Joseph Breuer. Charcot, a famous French physician, treated patients who presented neurological symptoms without manifest neurological disease (hysterics) with hypnosis; Breuer emphasized a cathartic approach in which he had patients talk about their problems in order to deal with pent-up emotions thought to be related to their difficulties. Both of these men strongly influenced Freud. He favored Breuer's talking approach, but after his relationship with Breuer broke down (because of Freud's emphasis on the role of unresolved sexual conflicts in the development of hysteria), Freud proceeded on his own to develop psychoanalytic theory and psychoanalysis. He was a prolific author, and his work attracted numerous students. He exerted an important influence on psychiatry and on psychology as well. Freud's influence reached its high point with his lectures at Clark University at the invitation of G. Stanley Hall.

Freud's theory developed not out of the laboratory, but out of the clinical situation. Listening to his patients, Freud tried to construct a theory that would explain their behavior and, potentially, all of human behavior. He was a committed determinist who felt that no behavior was accidental—not even slips of the tongue—and that all behavior could be explained, given enough data. Freud's theory is not easily subject to experimental test, however. Scientific verification of psychoanalysis has still not been accomplished today. Nevertheless, Freud's efforts to organize and explain the totality of human behavior remain the most ambitious ever attempted. Their influence, particularly in the area of abnormal psychology, is still quite strong and is likely to remain so.

Personality Structure: Consciousness

Mental functioning, for Freud, takes place at more than one level. In an arrangement that has been likened to an iceberg, only the smallest part of mental functioning—the exposed tip of the iceberg—is available to awareness. Another somewhat larger part of the iceberg lies immediately below the surface. This is the preconscious, which contains material that is not in immediate consciousness but is available when needed. Thus, although it may require some mental effort, we can usually recall information, such as a telephone number, that resides in the preconscious. By far the largest part of the iceberg, the unconscious, lies deep beneath the surface and is usually out of awareness. Here are contained traces of past experiences, current impulses and desires, and the basic biological instincts. In the unconscious, thoughts and wishes are permitted to run free without the constraints of civilized society. Unconscious material may sometimes reach consciousness (in dreams, for example), but when this occurs the material is usually experienced as "foreign."

Personality Structure: Three Aspects

Psychoanalytic theory divides personality into three interacting parts: the id, the ego, and the superego.

At first, only the id exists. It contains the immediate and important needs (hunger, thirst, sex) and demands their immediate satisfaction. The demand for immediate satisfaction (known as the pleasure principle) is often impossible to meet, and wish-fulfilling fantasies (primary process thinking) are instituted as a temporary solution. These fantasies, however, do not satisfy real biological needs; this is the ego's job. The ego allows the individual to come to terms with the real world and fosters the development of behaviors that permit needs to be met within the constraints of civilized society. The ability to test reality and to work toward a goal (secondary process thinking) allows the individual to satisfy important needs without violating the demands of reality. The superego is, in a sense, an optional personality characteristic. One can exist without it, and indeed, individuals are thought to vary in the extent of its develop-

ment. The superego consists of an internalized moral code more or less similar to the familiar conscience. At times, the pleasure demands of the id conflict with the superego. In these situations, it is the ego that strikes a compromise between the id and the real world. The relationships between the various aspects of personality and consciousness are illustrated in Figure 1.1.

Personality Dynamics: Energy

Freud, who saw the organism as a complex energy system, included as a central feature of his theory the notion of psychic energy. This energy was assumed to be derived from the instinctual desires of the id. Among those instincts considered most prominent were the life instincts that have as their goal the survival of the individual (hunger, sex) and the death instinct, along with its derivative, aggression. Energy derived from the life instincts (libido) and death instincts was thought to drive activities such as thinking, remembering, the workings of the ego and superego, and other important psychological functions.

Stages of Psychosexual Development

From a psychoanalytic point of view, early life is crucial in setting the stage for later personality. The child must face a series of conflicts with the world, each of which requires some kind of adjustment. The oral stage, which comes first, centers around the child's pleasure at sucking, eating, and later, biting. If for some reason the child is frustrated at this stage, "fixation" will result. Some libidinal energy will remain at the oral stage, and the individual will need to incorporate things; that is, the individual will continue to require satisfaction of oral needs. If fixation occurs later in the oral stage, the individual may become someone who abuses others verbally.

The next stage, the anal stage, represents the first challenge from civilization to the primary process, pleasure-seeking id. Defecation, a reflexive, pleasurable activity, must be

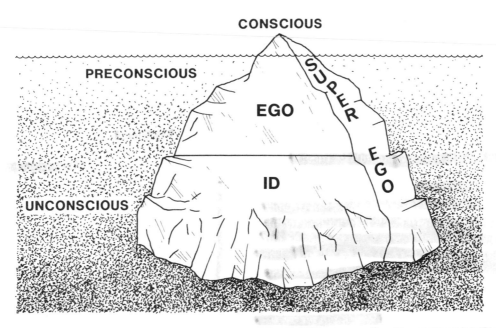

CONSCIOUS

PRECONSCIOUS

EGO

SUPER EGO

ID

UNCONSCIOUS

FIGURE 1.1. Freud referred to personality as similar to an iceberg. Only a very small part is conscious. A somewhat larger part is preconscious — available to conscious awareness with some mental effort. But by far the largest part of personality is unconscious, unavailable to the individual without massive psychoanalytic effort.

regulated according to the demands of society when toilet training begins. Fixation at this stage could result in conformity (slavish adherence to society's demands) or cruelty and temper (a refusal to bow to society).

Next, an even more threatening conflict between the child's natural urges and the demands of civilized society develops during the phallic stage. Now it is the genitals that are the site of pleasurable feelings, and it is at this point that the Oedipal conflict occurs. Males are forced, through fears of castration, to repress their desires for their mothers and to identify with and pattern themselves after their fathers. Although a similar process occurs for females, its resolution is not as clear. The outcome of all of this turmoil during the phallic stage of development has implications for much later social and sexual behavior. It also marks the birth of the superego, which incorporates the moral code of the child's parents.

The final stage of development, the genital stage, sees the development of interpersonal skills, friendships, and other social attachments. A fully developed personality requires the successful passage through all psychosexual stages.

Anxiety and Mechanisms of Defense

Anxiety, an affective state involving unpleasant feelings of dread and fear, may arise from a variety of sources. When anxiety is troublesome, some relief may be obtained by the use of defense mechanisms, which operate unconsciously and involve some distortion of reality. Among the principal defense mechanisms are repression, or unconscious forgetting of threatening, anxiety-producing material; projection, or seeing anxiety as caused by external sources rather than oneself; and reaction formation, which avoids anxiety-provoking impulses by expressing the presence of precisely the opposite feeling. In general, defense mechanisms can be ordered along a continuum of increasing distortions of reality. Some defenses require little distortion and therefore are not considered unhealthy (rationalizing the failure to obtain a coveted new job by saying that it would have been too much work, for example), whereas others (denial of actual events) involve a great deal of distortion and are decidedly unhealthy.

Psychoanalysis and Its Heirs

Modifications to psychoanalytic theory have been made by neo-Freudian theorists during the past 50 years (see Greenspan & Lourie, 1982). The trend has been away from reliance on biological instincts as the main determinant of personality development and toward a greater role for social determinants. The role of the ego has been strengthened as well. In its general orientation and basic philosophical position, however, psychoanalysis remains very much unchanged. It also currently remains the sole example of a global psychological theory designed to account for the totality of human behavior. Psychoanalytic contributions to the study of child psychopathology have been of enormous influence, and these contributions will be discussed throughout this book. Now, however, we turn to another important trend in the history of child psychopathology, which, for historical as well as theoretical reasons, is known as behaviorism.

Behaviorism

Unlike psychoanalysis, there is no generally agreed-upon theory called behaviorism. As a point of view, however, behaviorism and its modern descendants present the most important alternative to psychoanalytic theory.

Watson and Behaviorism: Background

Unlike psychoanalysis, behaviorism arose not in the clinic but in the psychological laboratory. Early 20th-century psychology was concerned with the study of consciousness through introspection. Trained subjects, for example, were asked to report their conscious experience when exposed to the color blue. Controversies about whether thoughts always involve images and the precise content of consciousness preoccupied academic psychology, but psychology's experimental method, introspection, was incapable of providing data sufficient to resolve these disputes. Within this environment, John B. Watson's *Psychology as the Behaviorist Views It* (1913) sounded a call for change. Watson criticized academic psychology for its obsession with consciousness and its use of introspection. In his own words:

> Psychology as the behaviorist views it is a purely objective branch of natural science. Its theoretical goal is the prediction and control of behavior. Introspection forms no essential part of its methods, nor is the scientific value of its data dependent upon the readiness with which they lend themselves to interpretations in terms of consciousness. (p. 158)

Watson's belief that psychology could safely ignore consciousness is not difficult to understand, considering that the approach he was proposing was developed out of studies of animal learning, where consciousness was a largely unnecessary construct.

Watson's work served to move psychology's focus away from studying the contents of consciousness and toward the study of learning. What stimuli controlled which responses became the dominant question, and two types of learning began to generate a great deal of research.

The first type was initially investigated by Ivan Pavlov, the Russian physiologist, at the beginning of the 20th century. Originally interested in the physiology of the digestive process, Pavlov, who used dogs as experimental subjects, discovered that some physiological reactions (such as salivating in response to the smell of meat) could be brought under the control of previously neutral stimuli (see Figure 1.2).

In the famous case of the infant Albert, Watson and Raynor (1920) demonstrated the relationship between classical conditioning and the development of fears. Albert, an 11-month-old infant, was shown a white rat and at first showed no fear of the animal. But a fear was created by striking a steel bar near

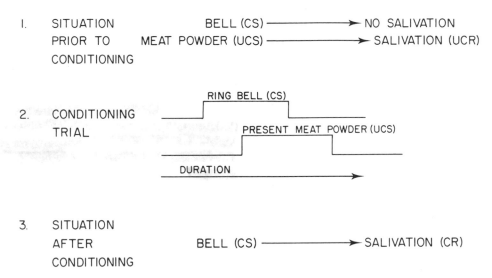

FIGURE 1.2. Pavlov's demonstration of classical conditioning: (a) Before conditioning the bell does not elicit salivation, but the meat powder does; (b) Conditioning takes place by pairing the CS and UCS; (c) After conditioning the CS elicits the CR (salivation).

Albert, causing a loud noise, each time he reached for the rat. The loud noise (UCS) produced fear (UCR), which ultimately was associated with the rat (CS). This study, a classic in psychology, has also been cited in some textbooks as evidence for stimulus generalization and deconditioning, neither of which was actually demonstrated (Harris, 1979).

The second type of learning, instrumental conditioning, draws from the work of Edward Thorndike's "law of effect": Behavior that is followed by pleasant consequences will be repeated, whereas behavior followed by unpleasant consequences or the absence of reinforcement will be discouraged (see Figure 1.3). This basic approach has been widely applied in the work of B. F. Skinner and will be explored in great detail in various chapters in this book.

Other behaviorists (e.g., Dollard & Miller, 1950; Hull, 1943) and other approaches to learning (modeling or learning by imitation)

have also received considerable attention and continue to influence work even today. What is interesting to note is that from the outset, behaviorism and the developing field of child psychopathology had some deep affinities.

Watson, for example, worked at Johns Hopkins University, where he grew to be an admirer of Adolph Meyer. Like Meyer, he emphasized the importance of mental hygiene. Although he agreed that the important personality characteristics were established in early childhood and that attitudes toward sex should be less repressive, he differed strongly with Meyer about the potential value of psychoanalysis.

The last 50 years have witnessed several attempts to reconcile psychoanalysis and behaviorism. The best known was Dollard and Miller's *Personality and Psychotherapy* (1950). Their translation of psychoanalysis into the terms of Hullian learning theory never became popular. Although Hullian learning theory has become a less important force in

OPERANT CONDITIONING

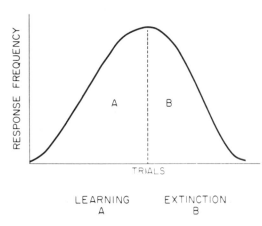

LEARNING   EXTINCTION
   A   B

FIGURE 1.3. Thorndike's law of effect. When a target response is followed by reinforcement, it is likely to be repeated (the learning half of the curve). Ultimately, the frequency levels off at the point when responding cannot occur any faster. When reinforcement no longer follows response, the frequency decreases until it eventually no longer occurs (extinction).

experimental psychology today, psychoanalysis retains its influence on the field of child psychopathology.

Behaviorism and Psychopathology

Currently, behaviorism plays an important metatheoretical role in the field of child psychopathology. Its philosophical approach, which stresses the importance of learning rather than unconscious conflicts and its emphasis on empirical verification, has had a profound influence on the thinking of many in the field. This metatheoretical influence is at least as important as the particular details of any behavioral theory.

Since the late 1950s, behavioral approaches to the treatment of psychopathology have developed rapidly and today claim a large number of adherents. The diversity and complexity of this work is illustrated in the discussions found throughout this book (see also Phillips & Ray, 1980). It should be kept in mind that the success of various forms of behavioral and psychoanalytic treatment does not mean that behavioral or psychoanalytic explanations for the etiology of various pathological conditions are correct, any more than the success of a particular tranquilizer in treating anxiety means that anxiety is caused by a lack of tranquilizers. The successful explanation and future prevention of emotional problems in childhood require direct knowledge of the variables responsible for pathological development. What we have learned thus far from behavioral studies, both successful and unsuccessful, is discussed in the remaining chapters of this book.

Social Learning Theory

Although derived from a largely behavioral base, social learning theory views individuals as active determiners of their own fates. In contrast to Watson or Skinner, who emphasize the importance of environmental stimuli and rewards, social learning theorists (and other "cognitive" behaviorists) focus on how children interpret their experiences. For example, children who perceive parental concern ("be careful playing") as a reflection of love have a different interpretation from children who view such concern as evidence that their parents lack faith in their abilities. Because interpretations take place internally, they are considered *cognitive*; because they involve interactions among individuals, they are considered *social*.

The person most closely identified with social learning theory is Albert Bandura (1977, 1981). Bandura, who has long argued that cognitions are an important aspect of any theory of human learning, emphasizes the important role that expectancies play in influencing behavior. By observing what happens to others, children learn what to expect in common social situations. For instance, a child who is scolded by the teacher for disrupting the class directly experiences the consequences (the teacher's wrath) of misbehavior. At the same time, the other children learn what to expect should they behave similarly. According to Bandura, such "vicarious learning" (usually known as modeling) is the method by which children learn many proper social behaviors; it can also be the source of deviant behaviors. Such "abnormal" behaviors could develop if the child is exposed to deviant models or inappropriate reinforcement.

Social learning theory is not concerned with personality traits of the sort found in other theories. Instead, the theory refers to generalized expectancies. Bandura (1977), for instance, describes *self-efficacy* as a belief in one's ability to successfully achieve desired outcomes. Individuals vary in their self-efficacy as a function of their past experience and the models to whom they are exposed. Those children with low self-efficacy avoid new challenges because they expect failure. They prefer not trying to failing. Those with positive views about their self-efficacy will keep on trying and perhaps even increase their efforts when faced with a challenge. According to social learning theory, effective psychological treatment often involves increasing an individual's feelings of self-efficacy.

Social learning theory provides a powerful framework within which to conceptualize psychopathology and psychotherapy. By taking into account interpretations as well as expectations, social learning theory recognizes the important role played by cognition in determining behavior. We will have more to say on the importance of cognitions later in this book when we discuss psychological treatment methods.

Biogenesis

Recent discoveries, particularly in the field of childhood psychoses, have renewed interest in the biological substrate of psychopathology. This has now reached the point where it may almost be considered a theoretical orientation. Neglect of biochemical hypotheses during a large part of this century is quickly being corrected.

Biochemical and physiological experiments have been conducted from several theoretical viewpoints. These vary in complexity from those that depend on a "let's look and see what happens" approach (investigating whether there are EEG abnormalities among juvenile delinquents, for example) to those derived from sophisticated theories of brain functioning. Obviously, the latter approach is preferable, but even elaborate models of brain functioning are not, by themselves, adequate for understanding psychopathology. Just as an understanding of computers, for example, depends not only on an understanding of electronics (hardware), but also on what the particular program (software) is trying to accomplish, understanding child psychopathology depends on our knowledge of both brain functioning and psychological principles.

Developmental Psychopathology

As noted earlier, recent years have seen a renewal of interest in the developmental psychology of Jean Piaget and others. Clinical-child psychologists have been particularly interested in incorporating the findings of developmental psychologists into their theories because the "meaning" of a child's behavior changes as the child grows up. In addition, the effectiveness of a therapeutic intervention also depends on a child's developmental stage. Because of the importance of the developmental variable in child psychopathology (it is an integral aspect of all the models discussed in this section), it will be discussed in more detail later in this chapter. Before turning to this topic, however, we will first have a closer look at how scientific theories and experiments interact in the study of child psychopathology.

SCIENCE AND PSYCHOPATHOLOGY

Science: Philosophy and Method

In its most basic sense, the term *science* simply means knowledge. A particular science, then, is just one circumscribed branch of knowledge. Given this definition, most would agree that research in child psychopathology is largely a scientific enterprise. Unfortunately, many laymen, and many scientists as well, have adopted a rather different definition of science. For them, science involves a special sort of knowledge gathered in specific ways. The typical picture is drawn from laboratory-based experimentation, as in chemistry and the other physical sciences.

In the field of psychopathology, this emphasis on laboratory experimentation and statistical inference has, in some instances, stultified growth and led to a rift between those interested primarily in clinical work and those whose major commitment is to research. The result has been unfortunate for both. For the clinician needing help with patients' problems, the findings of experimental psychology have too often appeared irrelevant. For the experimentalist, detachment from the problems of the clinic has resulted in the loss of a fruitful source of hypotheses as well as a chance to test theories against the demands of the real world. The reasons behind this schism between experimentalists and clinicians are many and complex. Among the most important, however, is the confusion of science with a particular philosophy and method. This is not unusual in the historical development of scientific disciplines.

Science develops through an evolutionary (some might say revolutionary) process. At various periods during the development of a discipline, a particular method, theory, or orientation is dominant. Often research techniques associated with this theory become deified, and scientists become quite conformist in their behavior. Such periods last until a change takes place, when some widely accepted theory is replaced by a new and incompatible one. In the physical sciences, men such as Copernicus, Newton, and Einstein were responsible for drastic changes of this sort. Thomas Kuhn (1962, 1974), a well-known philosopher and historian of science, has referred to the changes in outlook that periodically assault scientific domains as "changes in paradigms." A paradigm is defined as the conceptual framework within which a scientist works, a set of basic assumptions (often implicit) that specify which phenomena require study, which concepts are legitimate, and which scientific methods will be used to collect data. As should be clear, a shared paradigm allows scientists to communicate with one another and, to a large extent, defines a scientific discipline. Shared paradigms, however, are not without their limiting aspects. One problem is that a paradigm will have a strong influence on how facts are interpreted; that is, the same facts may mean different things to investigators operating under different paradigms. For example, the movement of the planets prior to Copernicus seemed to support the pre-Copernican view that the earth was the center of the universe. Today, of course, the same planetary movements corroborate a very different point of view.

The fact that a paradigm may bias the way facts are interpreted is very important in the field of child psychopathology, where there are a variety of paradigms and, as one might expect, many ways of viewing the same problem. Moreover, not all paradigms are equally worthwhile. For example, whereas all theories are ultimately likely to be at least partly wrong, the quality of *falsifiability* (the ability to be disproved) is an important characteristic of a good theory. From this viewpoint, a theory such as psychoanalysis suffers because its hypotheses are very difficult to disprove. Philosophers of science (Lakatos & Musgrave, 1970, for example), have also stressed that theories must not just lag behind facts, explaining them as they emerge, but must pose new questions and predict new facts not as yet uncovered. As an example of how a paradigm may influence research and treatment, let us consider the relatively common problem of childhood bed-wetting or enuresis. [This discussion represents an extension of the example provided by Yates (1970).]

Paradigm Clash: Enuresis and the Question of Models

Enuresis is not an uncommon problem. Depending on how it is defined, at some point in childhood, 3 to 20% of children wet their beds often enough to disturb their parents

(American Psychiatric Association, 1980). With a problem of this magnitude, it is not surprising that there exists a great deal of literature on the subject. For our present purpose, two major aspects of this literature will be contrasted: the psychodynamic view and the behavioral view.

From a psychodynamic (psychoanalytic) point of view, enuresis is usually thought to be an overt symptom of some underlying problem. Some conflict, probably unconscious, is said to give rise to this symptom, which, in turn, is held to symbolically represent the underlying problem, often thought to be sexual in nature. Thus Fenichel (1946) writes:

> Infantile (nocturnal) enuresis is a sexual discharge. Urinary excretion originally served as an autoerotic activity which gave the child urethral-erotic wetting (and cutaneous) satisfaction. . . . Between the infantile autoerotic wetting and the later symptom of enuresis, there was a time of masturbation; and the enuresis represents a substitute and equivalent of suppressed masturbation . . . (p. 232)

Other psychoanalytic writers have proposed similar interpretations. No matter what the specific interpretation, however, most psychodynamic theorists would agree that enuresis is merely symptomatic of an underlying disturbance. From this viewpoint, treatment of the symptom, even if it is successful in stopping bed-wetting, is futile. Because symptomatic treatment leaves the underlying conflict unresolved, other symptoms are expected to develop to take the treated symptom's place (symptom substitution). Effective treatment is thought to require the uncovering and resolution of the unconscious conflicts responsible for the child's symptom.

In the behavioral view, enuresis is not a symptom of underlying emotional conflict, but a habit deficiency. That is, ordinary toilet training requires that the child learn to respond to bladder stimulation not with the reflexive response of elimination, but with a complicated series of steps that culminate in going to the toilet. If this complex series of responses is not learned, enuresis results. In some cases this habit deficiency is due to poor toilet training. In others, it may be due to psychophysiological factors. It is not unlikely that in certain other cases it may result from intense psychological stress that interferes with the learning of this complex task. Generally, however, behaviorists view enuresis as a relatively isolated habit pattern that is not reflective of a hidden emotional disturbance. (Needless to say, both behaviorists and psychoanalysts take a developmental perspective. Neither would consider bedwetting in a 2-year-old as serious as bedwetting in a 12-year-old.)

Unlike psychodynamic practitioners, behaviorists do not believe that traditional forms of psychotherapy, dealing with underlying causes, are particularly useful in the treatment of enuresis. Instead, they focus on conditioning therapies and the learning of appropriate behaviors. In this regard, it has been shown that, in the absence of physical etiology, enuresis can be effectively dealt with through the application of learning procedures (Schaefer, 1979). Further, such treatment typically does not result in symptom substitution, as the analytically oriented clinician would suggest. In fact, enuretic children often have numerous problems resulting from their "symptom" (children make fun of them; their mothers become angry with them), and the elimination of bed-wetting often appears to lead to a general overall improvement in functioning, rather than to symptom substitution. (The treatment of enuresis will be considered further in a later chapter.)

From the above comparison, one can see that these two paradigms, the psychodynamic and the behavioral, differ fundamentally in their conceptualization of even so common a problem as childhood enuresis, as Table 1.3 illustrates.

The clash between psychodynamic and behavioral viewpoints is obvious as one pursues the study of child psychopathology. These differences constitute not only different theories, but separate models or conceptualizations of psychopathology.

The psychodynamic approach to the psychopathology of childhood is one example of a *medical model* of psychopathology. Most, if

TABLE 1.3. MAIN FEATURES OF HABIT DEFICIENCY
AND SYMPTOM THEORIES OF ENURESIS.

HABIT DEFICIENCY THEORY (Behavioral Model)

Process of normal continence development
Failure to establish response of sphincter inhibition sufficiently strongly.

Etiology of enuresis
In majority of cases: Absence of environmental conditions ordinarily
necessary for learning to occur and/or low level of conditionability.
In minority of cases: Presence of condition ordinarily inimical to efficient learning or productive of breakdown of previously established
linkages (e.g., "nervous tension").

Treatment of choice
Conditioning by special apparatus, plus, in minority of cases, ancillary
drug treatment or removal of conditions inimical to efficient learning.

View of psychotherapeutic treatment
Useless in majority of cases. Possibly useful in minority of cases to reduce
nervous tension.

SYMPTOM OF EMOTIONAL DISTURBANCE THEORY
(Psychodynamic Model)

Process of normal continence development
No specification of process.

Etiology of enuresis
Psychological conflict or stress. Symptom of emotional disturbance of
general character in majority of cases.

Treatment of choice
Psychotherapy to remove underlying emotional disturbance.

View of conditioning treatment
Symptomatic treatment, useless as only treatment. Likely to be positively
harmful, through production of emotional crisis or substitute symptom
formation.

Source: Adapted from Lovibond, (1964). © 1964 Pergamon Press and reprinted by permission.

not all, texts dealing with psychopathology
devote substantial space to discussions of the
medical model (even though they do not all
use the term in exactly the same way). These
discussions will not be repeated in detail here.
A brief overview, however, is necessary for
the reader to fully appreciate the current state
of the field.

Nineteenth-century medicine made great
inroads in the conquest of disease. Physiological correlates of abnormal behavior patterns
were sought and sometimes found, as in the
case of general paresis. Psychiatrists, trained
as physicians (not, as is commonly supposed,
in psychology) adopted the medical approach
that seemed to work so well for physical ill-

ness in their work with disordered behavior.
Thus, various pathological behaviors were
thought to be symptomatic of diseases for
which specific etiologies and cures could be
found.

Although it seems likely that the medical
model is quite appropriate for conceptualizing
some of the problems to be dealt with in this
volume, it seems equally clear that a psychological model will prove to be as important
in conceptualizing many other psychopathological problems of childhood. Psychodynamic
formulations, such as the one described earlier for enuresis, incorporate the important
aspects of the medical model by analogy.
While rejecting the notion of physical cause,

they retain the idea that behavioral problems are mere symptoms of underlying conflict. Moreover, they argue that symptomatic treatment, ignoring the underlying conflict, is doomed to failure, with symptom substitution the inevitable result.

Although no one can deny the relationship between physiology and certain behavioral disorders, there are numerous behavioral problems for which no organic cause has been or is likely to be found. In these cases, the application of the medical model is inappropriate. To the extent that deviant behaviors may result from learning experiences, the application of the medical model by analogy, as in the psychodynamic formulation, may also be of limited value.

As was suggested earlier, the psychological or behavioral model views psychopathology as understandable in terms of learning history and those current environmental factors that elicit and maintain behavior. It may be noted, however, that in actuality there is no such thing as the behavioral model; indeed, there are many behavioral points of view. However, they do share some common qualities. All view abnormal behavior as learned, and all emphasize the importance of environmental as opposed to intrapsychic determinants of behavior. As illustrated earlier in the example of enuresis, deviant behaviors may be a function of a deviant learning history, thwarted motivation, physiological disturbances, or some combination of all three. From a behavioral perspective, the study of psychopathology, then, is seen as no different from the study of behavior in general and includes concepts from the areas of learning, perception, information processing, and cognition. Analogies from other disciplines, for example from medicine, are not generally part of the behavioral model. At present these two points of view, the medical model (largely psychoanalytic) and the behavioral model (largely based on conditioning) account for most of the work in the field of child psychopathology, although researchers and clinicians bring various combinations of views to their work.

In many ways, the view of the behaviorist has proved enormously fruitful in the study of child psychopathology. In other ways, it has been limited. Without depreciating the often impressive accomplishments of behaviorally oriented psychologists, it should be noted that behavioral views have only just begun to incorporate important research findings from other areas of human experimental psychology.

Today experimental psychology is largely the study of cognition, but the study of human cognition has only had a limited impact on child psychopathology. However, information theory, psycholinguistics, computer analogies and simulations, and the study of cognition in general do have implications for the field of psychopathology in general and for child psychopathology specifically. Behavior therapists have begun to incorporate cognitive approaches into their clinical procedures (Mahoney, 1977; Meichenbaum, 1979; Reid & Hresko, 1981). We will have occasion in many parts of this book to make reference to this work.

Theories, Experiments, and Knowledge

Scientific theories vary in several important ways. Some (psychoanalytic theory, for instance) are broad and extensive; they attempt to account for many facets of behavior. Other theories are more circumscribed. Theories also vary in their complexity, consistency, and usefulness, but there is one characteristic that all truly scientific theories must share — testability. The predictions of a scientific theory must be open to empirical test. Otherwise, the theory cannot be confirmed or refuted. A belief in untestable theories is an act of faith, not science.

Many aspects of psychoanalysis are not refutable. One problem is that psychoanalytic terms are not always clearly defined nor are they tied to a method of measurement. Thus, different researchers may use different definitions of the same theoretical construct. In addition, many psychoanalytic predictions are too vague to be testable. A fixation at the anal stage, for example, is supposed to produce either conformity or noncomformity and either very orderly or excessively sloppy personalities. Even if it were possible to ascertain whether a child had been fixated at the anal stage (no easy task in itself), the theory predicts almost all possible outcomes and cannot, therefore, be refuted. No matter what the outcome, the theory is always correct.

Assuming a theory makes clear, testable predictions, it is then up to scientists to devise some way of testing them. Various research strategies may be used in studying the same general problem areas. For example, individual differences in the way children solve problems can be investigated in highly controlled laboratory settings involving relatively simple behaviors such as discrimination learning or other kinds of conditioning. (Discrimination learning tasks are not simple in terms of the psychological processes involved, but they are probably less complex than most classroom learning.) The same phenomena may also be studied in naturalistic settings, such as classrooms, where the dependent variables are real-life behaviors. Each approach has its advantages and disadvantages. Knowledge gained in artificial laboratory settings may not apply when other influences, such as those present in the classroom, are permitted to operate. On the other hand, the uncontrolled variables of the real world may make results difficult to interpret. Experiments involve a trade-off between control and generalizability. It is up to experimenters to decide whether they will use artificial laboratory situations, where many extraneous variables can be controlled, but where the lack of generality is always a problem, or naturalistic settings, where interfering variables are not controlled, but where generalizability may be increased.

A special type of naturalistic research with a long history in clinical psychology is the *case study*. Case studies — intense studies of single children (or families) — serve an indispensable role in clinical research. The first mention of many of the disorders discussed in this book (early infantile autism, Tourette's syndrome, and many others) occurred in case studies. In fact, more research hypotheses in the field of child psychopathology have been drawn from case studies than from theoretical predictions. Examples of case studies appear throughout this book. Although they are important sources of research hypotheses, case studies are limited as research tools because they are difficult to generalize to other children and other situations. It is never possible to know whether the unique aspects of a case are responsible for any observations. So, although case studies are useful sources of research hypotheses, controlled research is required to test these hypotheses. Research, however, can take many forms.

Correlational versus Experimental Methods

Correlational methods are more common than experimental methods in the study of child psychopathology. Many of the variables of interest, such as mothering techniques or early infantile backgrounds, are not open to experimental manipulation, and in these instances correlational methods are often used. For example, different patterns of mothering may be identified in different subject populations, and the consequent personality development of the children studied. The correlations, if any, between mothering techniques and the subsequent personality development of these children are then calculated. Even if such correlations are found to be significant, however, we cannot ascertain the direction of this relationship. That is, although it might often be intuitively clear that it was the mother's personality that led to the child's particular behavior patterns, the opposite relationship — the child's behavior affecting the mother — is also a possibility. Even a third possibility exists: Namely, a genetic disposition or some other variable may be responsible for the personality of both the mother and child. (These three possibilities are illustrated in Figure 1.4.) Correlational findings do not, therefore, imply that one variable caused a change in another; it is always possible that some third variable is responsible for the ob-

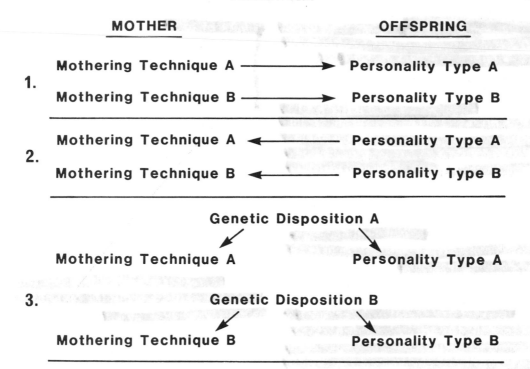

MOTHER   **OFFSPRING**

1.
Mothering Technique A ⟶ Personality Type A

Mothering Technique B ⟶ Personality Type B

2.
Mothering Technique A ⟵ Personality Type A

Mothering Technique B ⟵ Personality Type B

Genetic Disposition A

Mothering Technique A   Personality Type A

3.   **Genetic Disposition B**

Mothering Technique B   Personality Type B

FIGURE 1.4. Three possible explanations for a correlation between mothering techniques and personality types. In panel 1, mothering techniques are shown to produce personality types. In panel 2, the personality type of the offspring is shown influencing the mother's choice of mothering technique. In the third panel, both mothering technique and personality type are produced by a third factor, a genetic disposition that affects both mother and offspring. Of course, all three relationships can be operating simultaneously, and in the real world, they usually are.

served relationship. The old caveat that correlation does not imply causation cannot be reiterated too often.

To obtain information concerning causal relationships, it would seem desirable to conduct experimental research whenever possible — where a specific variable of interest is manipulated by the experimenter and the effects of this variable on behavior are observed. Unfortunately, many important issues in development and child psychopathology cannot, for ethical or practical reasons, be studied in this manner. Here a correlational approach, in spite of its limitations, may be the only practical one.

Experimental methods, like correlational ones, can take many forms, but all share a common format. An *independent variable* is manipulated by the experimenter, and measurements are taken on some *dependent varia-*

ble. For example, an experimenter who wishes to study the effect of diet on hyperactivity could assign children to different diets (independent variable) and observe the effect of each diet on the childrens' activity level (dependent variable).

Cross-Sectional versus Longitudinal Research

The fact that a child is a developing organism strongly influences research techniques. Particularly important is the need to separate deviant from normal development and the need to make research as ecologically valid (generalizable to real-life situations) as possible.

Because development occurs over time, investigators have insisted that children of different ages be investigated in order to determine to what extent their behavior reflects developmental processes. This *cross-sectional* strategy requires that children be randomly selected from each of several age levels. The performance of each age group is compared, and inferences about systematic age changes are made. The disadvantage of this technique is the difficulty of obtaining comparable children in each of the successive age groups. Moreover, no two age groups are ever exposed to exactly the same environmental variables, and these environmental variables may result in changes other than the ones of interest. A second approach, consistent with the concept of development, is the *longitudinal* method, which involves repeated observations of the same children over time. This method insures the comparability of the sample because the same children are considered at each age level. The effects of changes in the culture are not controlled by this method because specific events can modify behaviors at particular ages; statistical techniques may be used to isolate these effects, however. In some cases particular variables of interest can be investigated either cross-sectionally or longitudinally. In others, one or the other technique is preferable. The ideal, of course, would be to use both and thereby provide convergent validation for theoretical findings. Unfortunately, the expense of doing longitudinal research has often precluded the use of this approach (for excellent examples of this approach, however, see Nicol, 1985).

Some investigators have tried to avoid the expense of longitudinal research by doing retrospective studies, in which individuals who display particular behaviors or who have received a similar diagnosis are identified and their pasts explored in order to determine whether they experienced specific events during their youth. This strategy is a difficult one to implement. Recollections are often vague or inadequately recorded, and because individuals are chosen in the first place because they display a given syndrome, the bias toward reporting pathological events in childhood is uncontrolled — and a difficult problem to deal with. Prospective longitudinal research, although methodologically superior, is not easy to do. Finding groups of people who are willing and able to cooperate over long periods of time and following them as they change location is not only expensive, but demands a great deal of scientific effort and dedication.

A variety of research strategies applicable to child psychopathology are described by Kendall and Finch (1979).

Interaction of Theory and Research

Research hypotheses can come from anywhere — some are derived from theoretical predictions, others from observing clinical cases. No matter where a hypothesis comes from, it must be confirmed scientifically if it is to be considered valid. As already noted, not all hypotheses can be tested in laboratory experiments; some can only be examined naturalistically. In either case, however, the studies must be carefully controlled.

Controlled studies are those in which extraneous factors are eliminated, allowing the experimenter to attribute any results to a specific variable or variables. For example, a study of a new drug's effectiveness in helping autistic children must involve more than merely giving the drug to some autistic children and noting improvements in their behavior. For one thing, some children may improve by themselves, drug or no drug (that is called spontaneous remission). In addition, simply receiving the extra attention involved in drug administration may beneficially affect the children's behavior. High hopes for the drug on the part of the person administering it and on the part of parents and teachers might cause them to behave differently toward the children, thereby affecting the outcome. The only way to determine whether the drug itself is effective is to include a control group in the experiment. The control group should also be comprised of autistic children, but instead of the drug they receive an inactive substance (a placebo). No one directly involved in the experiment knows which children are getting the drug and which are receiving the placebo. The rationale for this approach is that because the control group also experiences the extra attention involved in drug administration, as well as any benefits derived from the high expectations of parents and teachers, any difference between the two groups must be caused by the drug itself.

Even carefully controlled research may be open to more than one interpretation. When this happens, theories and hypotheses must be modified and sometimes abandoned altogether. Research involves a continual interaction between theory and data, in which few theories can be expected to remain unchanged forever.

For example, Zajonc (Zajonc & Bargh, 1980a; Zajonc & Markus, 1975) presented a theory to explain data indicating that first-born children have higher IQs than later-born children. This theory, called the confluence model, asserts that intellectual development depends on a family's average intellectual level. If two parents with average IQs of 100 have a baby (whose intellectual level is assumed to be 0), the family's intellectual environment is said to be 67: $(100 + 100 + 0)/3$. If another child is born when the first reaches an intellectual level of 40, the family's intellectual environment decreases to 60: $(100 + 100 + 40 + 0)/4$. With each additional child, the family's intellectual level decreases, reducing the intelligence of later-born children. Of course, if the children were spaced widely apart, the situation would be quite different, as the family's intellectual level would have recovered before the next child was born.

Although the confluence model was able to explain many findings in the literature, there were some anomalies in the data. For example, in a large Dutch study, "only" children were not found to have the highest IQs, although they should according to the Zajonc theory because their families have the highest intellectual level. To explain this, Zajonc introduced a teaching hypothesis, which states that because only children do not have younger children to teach, their IQs are lower than they would ordinarily be. Teaching, he assumed, improves IQ scores. (Although the

"teaching hypothesis" was developed after the fact, it is still testable, at least in theory.) In this manner, the researcher modified his theory on the basis of the available data. Other modifications followed (Zajonc, Markus, & Markus, 1979).

Although the confluence model won wide recognition, some studies failed to support it (see Ernst & Angst, 1983), and Zajonc, himself (Zajonc & Bargh, 1980b) found that for the Scholastic Aptitude Test (SAT), the number of children in the family showed virtually no correlation with test scores.

Because the number of children in a family is related to social class (lower social class families have more children), religion (Roman Catholic families have more children), and many other factors, it is possible that the relationship between IQ and birth order simply reflects these other factors rather than those hypothesized by the confluence model. The data analyzed by Zajonc came from large surveys including thousands of subjects. Even with great care, it is difficult to control all extraneous factors. By far the best way to test the confluence hypothesis is to examine individual families. In each family, first-borns should have higher IQs than later-born children. By examining individual families, differences between families in social class, income, religion, and so on are controlled, and the effect of birth order on IQ can be studied directly. Studies of individual families have found that birth order has little or no effect on IQ (Ernst & Angst, 1983; see also, Price, Walsh, & Vilberg, 1984), suggesting that large-scale surveys may indeed be confounded by extraneous factors.

The confluence hypothesis can be said to have passed through several stages. Its initial formulation accounted for much available data, but it soon had to be modified to account for new findings. Further modifications followed. Finally, the results of other studies (some actually older than Zajonc's work) indicate that the confluence model may be incorrect — between-family differences may have been confused with within-family differences. There is no reason to believe that this is the last word on the subject. Additional research and analyses are continuing, and further modifications of the model are to be expected. Indeed, the confluence model will be mentioned again later in this book. The history of the confluence model is an excellent example of the interplay between hypothesis and research, an interaction that continually brings us closer to understanding the psychological factors influencing behavior.

Research Ethics

Researchers, who are primarily motivated by curiosity and a search for truth, must also consider the social context in which they live and work before planning their studies. Whether an experiment is concerned with animals or people, there are ethical obligations to which all scientists must adhere. Professional organizations like the American Psychological Association have formulated ethical standards for their members (American Psychological Association, 1981), and books on this topic have also appeared (Diener & Crandall, 1978). Probably the most important ethical problem in the field of child psychopathology is the issue of *informed consent*. A basic tenet in most research guidelines is that subjects must voluntarily consent to participate in a study. In order to do this, subjects must be accurately informed of all potential risks and benefits, and they must have the capacity to make a mature judgment.

Voluntary consent, in this context, means more than merely asking a subject to participate. Children asked by their teachers, prisoners asked by prison officials, and soldiers asked by their officers may all feel they must agree to participate even though participation is supposed to be voluntary. In such situations, it is usually best if recruiting requests come not from someone in authority, but directly from the experimenter. When the experimenter is someone directly involved in the subject's life, extra care must be taken to insure that participation is truly voluntary.

Informed consent not only requires that subjects be informed of all potential risks and benefits, but that such information is presented in a way they can understand. If the subjects are children, their guardians must be informed. Subjects also have a right to learn the outcome of the research.

The requirement that subjects have the capacity to volunteer is particularly important in research with children. Capacity is a legal term. Children, who are *legally* minors, lack the legal capacity to decide for themselves. They can only participate in research with their guardian's consent (of course, the child must agree as well). The mentally retarded, psychotics, and certain others who also lack legal capacity cannot participate in research without the consent of those responsible for their care.

Even when informed consent is obtained, experimenters must determine whether their research is really worth doing. Morally, the best decision rule is one that involves a comparison of risks and benefits. Research in which the benefits to the individuals involved or to some other group do not outweigh the risks to the subjects is difficult to justify.

Finally, research subjects deserve confidentiality. Data that can be used to identify subjects should never be released without their consent.

Perhaps the most important difference between the fields of adult and child psychopathology is that children are still developing. In the next section, we examine several crucial developmental themes and show the importance of the developmental variable in child psychopathology.

THE DEVELOPMENTAL VARIABLE IN CHILD PSYCHOPATHOLOGY

Children are constantly changing. Change may be systematic or erratic, but it is inexorable. Often children are described as being in a particular developmental stage. For example, Freud's personality theory and Piaget's theory of cognitive development both use the idea of stages to indicate important changes in behavior as a function of development.

This use of the term *stage* should not be confused with the vaguely defined phases that children are supposed to pass through (the "terrible twos," for example). Stages are only of interest when they are discontinuous, that is, when they are clearly differentiated from what came before and what follows. Piaget's theory, for instance, posits different mental structures and new ways of thinking about the world at different developmental stages.

Child development is usually considered to be a series of more or less orderly changes leading ultimately to a mature individual. Unfortunately, as many professionals working in the field of psychopathology have come to know, progress through developmental stages is often erratic. When a child fails to negotiate a particular stage adequately, the result is likely to be the sort of problems described in this book. In addition, slow or erratic development may have important consequences for later adjustment. A child much older than the others in a classroom may have trouble developing social relationships, and a child who fails to develop physically may find it hard to relate when everyone else enters puberty.

In recent years, clinical-child psychologists have come to realize the importance of the developmental variable in child psychopathology. As noted earlier, the same behaviors (enuresis, magical thinking, negativism) can be normal in children at one stage of development and abnormal in children at another developmental level. Indeed, some psychologists have suggested that child psychopathology can best be understood as normal development gone awry (Wenar, 1982).

Some childhood psychopathologies are reflected in developmental delays (normal but slow development); others in deviations from normal development. Moreover, what appears to be the same problem may have different origins in different children. For example, a child with a specific learning problem may be suffering from inadequate instruction, neurological damage, anxiety about being evaluated, poor vision, distractibility, or some combination of all five of these problems. Clearly, describing psychopathology as normal development gone awry is not enough. We must also be able to specify the precise nature of the developmental disturbance, the factors causing it, and the way these factors interact before we can say that we understand a particular psychopathology.

Developmental trends are discussed throughout this book in their appropriate contexts. For instance, intellectual development is discussed in the chapter dealing with mental retardation and intellectual disorders, moral development appears in conjunction with conduct disorders, and the development of attachments is discussed in the chapter dealing with the most serious attachment problems—the pervasive developmental disorders. In this way, we can best show how developmental trends combine with etiological variables to produce specific psychopathologies. The present section provides an overview of the most important developmental themes.

Physical Development

The most noticeable manifestations of child development are changes in a child's size and appearance. During the first two years, physical maturation and motor development are very rapid (see Table 1.4). Growth slows down during the preschool and early primary school years, only to speed up again at puberty. Throughout childhood, girls are closer to their final height than boys (Smart & Smart, 1977). Manual dexterity improves during the primary school years (as any teacher of handwriting can testify), although some children become awkward again during early adolescence. Adolescence ushers in another period of rapid growth; it is also when children mature sexually. During adolescence, children develop a self-image that may color their self-concept and affect their behavior for years to come. Not only does physical attractiveness influence acceptance among one's peers (Cavior & Dokecki, 1973), it can even influence a teacher's academic evaluations (Clifford, 1975). At one time, there was little that could be done to change a child's height or physical

TABLE 1.4. EARLY MOTOR DEVELOPMENT IN CHILDREN.

Age Range	Ability Demonstrated by Child
Birth to 4 weeks	Lifts head off bed while on stomach
6 weeks to 3½ months	Touches hands together in front of body
2½ to 4 months	Grasps object placed in fingers
2 to 5 months	Rolls over
5 to 8 months	Sits without support when placed in sitting position
5 to 10 months	Stands while holding on to something
7 to 10 months	Picks up small object using thumb and finger
9 to 13 months	Stands alone momentarily
10 to 14 months	Stands alone well
7½ to 13 months	Walks while holding onto something
11 to 15 months	Walks without assistance

Source: Adapted from U.S. Department of Health and Human Services (1980).

appearance. However, new developments in cosmetic surgery and in synthesizing growth hormones are beginning to offer many new alternatives to those whose physical development could be a potential cause of psychological problems (Baxter, Martial, & Hallwell, 1979).

Cognitive Development

Although newborns are more competent than most adults realize (Turner & Helms, 1983), their knowledge of the world is extremely limited. By interacting with their environment, newborns begin to learn about the world and, as a consequence, about themselves. This is what is known as cognitive development. Although much of what the young child learns comes from the environment, it is wrong to think of children as passive recipients of information. Cognitive development involves more than learning from experience; it also involves active information-seeking on the part of the child. As the child develops, biological maturation produces new abilities that can be used to help learn about the world. Cognitive development, then, can best be viewed as an interaction between environmental and maturational factors. The child's maturational level determines what can be learned at a particular developmental stage; the environment determines whether it will be learned. For example, from the age of 1 or so, children are biologically ready to learn a language, but whether they will learn one depends on being exposed to language users.

Research in neurobiology has strongly substantiated the interactive nature of cognitive development. The nervous systems of young children (and other organisms) have been found to be quite "plastic"; their development depends on environmental experiences. For example, animals raised without ever being exposed to certain visual patterns are later unable to learn to make visual discriminations (Rieson, 1960). Environmental characteristics early in life have also been found to influence brain anatomy in adulthood (see Cotman & Nieto-Sampedro, 1982; Rosenzweig, 1976).

The notion of an interaction between maturation and the environment is central to Piaget's (1963) theory of cognitive development. According to Piaget, cognitive development involves passing through a series of stages, each of which requires some modification in the way children think. The ages at which the various stages are reached differs from child to child, but the order is thought to be fixed. The first stage is called *sensorimotor* and lasts from birth to approximately age 2. During this stage, the child learns from the environment, primarily by manipulation, listening, and seeing. Children in the sensorimotor stage have not developed the ability to think about objects they cannot physically see, hear, and touch. In fact, they have no notion of object permanence. For them, an object that cannot be perceived or manipulated no longer exists. Only when children begin to realize that things exist "out there" in the real world can they understand that they are also a separate part of the world. This realization comes slowly toward the end of the second year, as the child develops the capacity to use language as a means of assigning labels to symbols. Once children develop the concept of object permanence, they are ready to move to the next stage of cognitive development, the *preoperational stage*.

The preoperational stage, which begins at age 2 and lasts for about 5 years, is characterized by the development of language and the ability to symbolize. It is no longer necessary for the child to perceive an object in order to think about it; symbolization permits the child to think about things even when they are not present. Although this is an advance over the sensorimotor stage, children in the preoperational stage are still intuitive thinkers. Con

sider, for example, Piaget's famous "conservation" experiments. When preoperational children watch water being poured from a short, wide container into a long, narrow one, they insist that there is now more water, even though no additional water has been added. They think this way because, intuitively, they believe tall containers should hold more than short ones; that is, they associate taller with greater. In Piaget's terminology, the children fail to "conserve" the quantity of water as it changes in appearance. A typical conservation demonstration is illustrated in Figure 1.5. It is not until the next stage, the *concrete-operational stage*, that children begin to conserve quantity and to reason logically about the world.

The concrete-operational stage lasts for about 4 years and is marked by an ever-growing ability to reason symbolically. Thinking in this stage, however, still tends to be concrete. Children do not reach the full potential of logical thought until they enter the *formal-operational stage* sometime in their teenage years. Recent work in the Piagetian tradition suggests that there may even be further stages beyond the formal operational stage (Commons, Richards, & Armon, 1983).

Piaget's stage theory is not the only way to look at intellectual development. As will be seen in later chapters, psychometricians, cognitive psychologists, and others have also de-

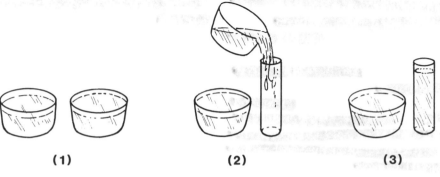

(1) (2) (3)

FIGURE 1.5. An illustration of Piaget's famous conservation demonstration. Preoperational children shown the two glasses in step 1 agree that they hold equal amounts of water. In step 2, children observe the water being poured from one of the short containers into a long, narrow one. In step 3, the children are once again asked whether the two containers hold equal amounts of water. They answer "no" because the container on the right is taller, a quality they associate with greater.

veloped important models of intellectual performance. Piaget's model was described here, however, because it emphasizes the importance of the interaction between the child as a developing organism and the environment in determining intellectual performance. As the child matures, environmental inputs take on new meanings, meanings they could not have had before the child was ready to appreciate them. In a reciprocal fashion, environmental inputs actually shape the development of the nervous system. Although some of the details of Piaget's theories may prove to be incorrect, no other theorist has challenged the notion that cognitive development requires the interaction of both environmental and organismic factors.

Language Development

How children acquire language remains problematic, but the acquisition sequence and its relation to stages of development is fairly well known. At birth children have only a small number of actual vocalizations in their repertoire; their verbal behavior is little more than crying and grunts. After 3 months or so, other vocalizations occur, often referred to as babbling. As the child grows, vowels become even more prominent, and consonant sounds are very much in the minority. This gradually changes during the first year, with consonant sounds finally becoming more frequent toward the end of the year. Interestingly, the initial sounds uttered by babies are the same in all cultural groups and languages.

The age at which babies speak their first word is hard to determine because babble often sounds like words. The average appears to be about 60 weeks, although the range is considerable. What is certain is that by around the end of the first year, active use of language has begun. The baby's ability to understand language is usually far in advance of the ability to produce language. First words are usually one-word sentences in which a single word appears in a variety of contexts and elicits many different responses from adults. For example, depending on how it is uttered, the word "doggie" may be a simple declarative ("It's a doggie"), a question ("Is it a doggie?"), or a demand ("I want a doggie"). The baby's vocabulary, of course, increases rapidly from the time the first word appears, although once again it should be emphasized that throughout language development, children understand considerably more words than they use. One-word sentences quickly give rise to two-word sentences and the acquisition of a rather primitive grammar. The early sentences consisting of two words are sometimes divided into a pivot word and an open word. This two-word "pivotal" grammar is the fore-runner of later language development. Two-word sentences at 2 years generally develop into much longer sentences and a rudimentary adult grammar by the age of 5. At about age 6, a child's ability to manipulate syntactical structures seems to be complete, although vocabulary will continue to develop throughout life.

The question of how language is acquired has long occupied psychologists and linguists. Not too long ago, the most widely held theory was that of Skinner (1957), who sees language developing in the same way as any other instrumental (operant) behavior, a position that brings language acquisition into line with other types of conditioning without requiring additional constructs. Skinner's general argument is that certain kinds of words and intonations are strengthened through reward and gradually are made to occur in appropriate situations by the process of discrimination learning. This view presumes that language consists only of chains of words and, for this reason, has come under considerable criticism; language tends to be considerably more complex than a model of simple chains of single verbal responses would allow.

The basic problem stems from a focus on the single word as the basic building block of language. In linguistics, the pronunciation of a word, a word's meaning, and a word's syntactic role in a sentence can often only be determined by a prior general analysis of the sentence in which it appears. On the other hand, any theory that depends on the strengthening of associations between single, sequential words will have difficulty explaining the meaning of words in sentences. There is a great deal of evidence to support the contention that single words or randomized sequences of words are very different from words organized into sentences. In addition, the production and comprehension of language occurs at a rate that is too fast to allow the repeated transmission of signals from ear to brain that would be required by any theory of language that depends on connections between single words (see Lashley, 1950).

Perhaps the biggest drawback to studying individual words is that connected discourse is more complex than the sum of the meanings of its constituent words. The order of words is as important in determining their meaning (a "baby buggy" is not the same thing as a "buggy baby," for instance) as are the rules of syntax. Even when the meanings of all the individual words in a phrase are clear, the meaning of the utterance as a whole will still depend on how the various words are put together. Therefore, the order of words and the grammar of English sentences need to be considered in any theory about how language is acquired and understood. Moreover, there is a large biological component to the development of language. Among the factors pointing to a role for biology in language development are the regular sequence of language acquisition; its uniform beginning between the first 18 and 28 months of life; the synchronization with other functions clearly attributable to physical maturation (see Table 1.5); and the indications of a critical period for language acquisition. The notion of a critical period for language acquisition has been most vigorously put forth by Eric Lenneberg (1967). The strong influence of maturation and the comparative ease with which children learn foreign languages both support the notions of a biologically influenced critical period for language development.

If the Skinnerian view is to be rejected, what can it be replaced with? The general answer has been that children learn not a series of associations between words, but a set

TABLE 1.5. LANGUAGE DEVELOPMENT SEQUENCE.

Age (Months)	Language Development
0–3	Cooing sounds begin.
4–6	Repeats and imitates sounds, babbles.
7–20	Goes from babbling to words, names, familiar objects, one-word sentences (e.g., "Go").
21–36	Language acquisition period. Vocabulary expands to around 900 words. Produces 2–3 word sentences. Begins to ask questions.
37–48	Vocabulary develops to 1,500 words, and sentences average 5 to 6 words in length (but longer sentences are also common). Begins to tell stories, draw analogies, and refine grammar.
61–72	Vocabulary of 2,500 words is used in sentences averaging 6 to 7 words in length. Can use metaphor and complex grammatical forms.
72–132	Adult grammar becomes common as well as adult accents. Vocabulary continues to grow.

Source: Adapted and summarized from several sources.

of rules. This point of view originated from the work of linguist Noam Chomsky (1965). Because linguistic behavior is creative (except for occasional clichés), unique, and novel, an adequate explanation of language must account for this originality; previous experience and conditioning provide no basis for dealing with a behavior that is occurring for the first time. According to Chomsky, a set of basic rules (grammar) is used to generate language. These rules develop during language acquisition, and they are relatively independent of the meaning of words (semantics). Chomsky (Caplan & Chomsky, 1980) has postulated the existence of innate neurophysiological structures that underlie language development — an idea that is closely related to Lenneberg's notions of language development.

When Chomsky suggests that language learning may be innate, he doesn't mean that children are born knowing a language. Obviously, the language we learn to speak depends upon where and by whom we are raised. Instead, Chomsky means that our brains have evolved so that they are specialized to learn language, just as other parts of our brains are specialized for visual perception or the control of motor movements. In the same sense that birds are born with an innate tendency to learn to fly, people are born with the neurological and muscular equipment necessary to learn a language. But no language will be learned without exposure to language users. Both biological equipment and appropriate environmental experience are necessary.

To summarize the discussion thus far: The traditional position was that language is acquired by a form of serial learning. A language consisting of serially organized strings of words, however, does not reflect language as it is actually used. Linguists have pointed out that language development occurs too rapidly to provide the number of conditioning trials necessary to master a language in the way described by traditional theories. These conditioning theories also cannot handle the creative quality of language. Even the speed of talking argues against a conditioning view. The strong maturational component of language is not taken into consideration by such theories, nor is the fact that individuals can produce and understand astronomically large numbers of sentences, the great majority of which are unique and original.

In response, a new type of theory has developed, whose key idea is that a child learns (through a combination of biological maturation and experience) not a series of relationships among words, but a series of rules used to understand and create language. This rule system, called grammar, includes what is necessary for understanding the relationships of different syntactical patterns, transforming one sentence into another, and various other principles. Which view one adopts, the traditional conditioning view or one based on grammar, is closely related to how one will interpret language deficits. If one accepts the conditioning theory, this deficit may be viewed as the result of faulty learning. If, on the other hand, language is regarded as depending on

biological prerequisites, one might favor psychophysiological theories.

We shall return to the question of language development later in this book and merely mention here that language disorders are receiving increasing attention from those interested in psychopathology. Language development represents another area in which biological maturation and experience interact during development.

Moral Development

According to Piaget, moral development, like cognitive development, can be viewed in terms of a series of stages (Kohlberg, 1976; Piaget & Inhelder, 1969). Young children have a very rigid moral code that delineates which acts are right and which are wrong. Typically, this moral code is applied to all situations without regard to extenuating circumstances. Young children tend to judge the severity of wrongdoing by its physical consequences (taking three cookies is worse than taking one), and they believe in punishment for its own sake. In the earliest stage of moral development, then, the child is primarily concerned with whether behavior will be rewarded or punished. As the child gets older, this focus on the consequences of behavior gives way to a slavish conformity to accepted standards. Morality is judged by reference to what is expected of a "good child." Finally, sometime in adolescence, an ethical sense develops. Moral rules are not rigidly enforced but become flexible. Punishment and reward are no longer absolutes but are altered to fit the circumstances. Kohlberg's stages are summarized in Table 1.6.

Later in this book, we will have reason to refer again to moral development and to look in more detail at how parents and peers serve as models for children's moral development.

Social Development

In a way, this entire book is concerned with social development. Behavior disorders, by their very nature, are defined by reference to

TABLE 1.6. LEVELS OF MORAL DEVELOPMENT.

Level	Moral Code
I	Some acts are "right," others "wrong." No consideration of extenuating circumstances.
II	Adherence to standards for role-appropriate behavior. Behave as a stereotyped "good boy" or "good girl."
III	Principles of moral equity determine behavior. Rewards and punishments vary to fit the circumstances.

Source: Adapted from Kohlberg (1976).

a particular culture. What is considered normal in some places (and times) may be considered abnormal in others. Behavior-disordered children are almost always those who, for one reason or another, fail to behave in the ways demanded by their culture.

All societies have expectations for the way their members are supposed to behave. Often these expectations are based on social roles; there is a father role, a mother role, a student role, and so on. As children develop, they adopt different roles, going from the dependent infant role, to the inquiring toddler, to the semi-independent teenager. A failure to adopt new roles or to behave in role-appropriate ways is likely to be viewed by society as a sign of a behavior disorder.

The process by which children are trained to adopt social roles is known as socialization. Socialization takes place in many contexts and is largely a matter of providing proper models for children to emulate (and rewarding them for doing so). Although socialization is clearly a matter of learning, it would be wrong to discount biological influences. Indeed, the emerging field of sociobiology is concerned solely with unraveling genetic influences in social behavior (Lumsden & Wilson, 1983).

The first relationships formed by the newborn infant set the stage for later social development. For this reason, the formation of the mother-infant bond (and the importance of this bond) has received considerable research attention (see Sluckin, Herbert, & Sluckin,

1983, for an up to date review). We shall have reason to examine this research carefully in later chapters. For now, we wish to note that children appear to go through a series of stages in the development of attachments (Schaffer & Emerson, 1964). In the first stage (which lasts from birth to about the middle of the first year), children respond equally to all adults, even strangers. They have no attachment to specific people. During the next 6 months, the child forms a strong attachment to a specific individual (usually the mother). The child shows signs of stress when the attached individual departs and is soothed when they are reunited. As the attachment is formed, strangers begin to be feared; their presence provokes distress in the child. The second year of life sees the formation of additional attachments (to fathers, babysitters, grandmothers, and so on), but the initial attachment remains strongest.

Early attachments have an influence on later social relations, but there are several theories about just how the socialization process operates. Several socialization theories are described in this section.

According to McCandless (1976), there are five major theories of socialization. *Humanism*, as a theory, provides only vague descriptions of how the socialization process takes place, offering the philosophical position that if people are free and loved, they will become socialized. Humanists optimistically emphasize the positive aspects of people, ignoring abnormal behavior.

The *cognitive-developmentalists*, whose work we have already mentioned, emphasize a natural progression through stages. As we have already seen, moral and cognitive development can be viewed as a series of discontinuous stages. For those holding such views, socialization only requires that the child be permitted to interact with the environment in a relatively unfettered way. Biological and psychological maturation, and the passing through stages, will take care of the rest (see Overton, 1983, for a collection of essays on the relationship between social and cognitive development).

The *psychoanalytic* theory of socialization has also been touched on earlier. Classical psychoanalysis views children as instinct-ridden, pleasure-seeking organisms. Socialization, from this viewpoint, involves learning to subjugate one's instinctual desires in order to get along in the world. Psychoanalysts, like cognitive-developmentalists, also make use of the concept of stages. Each psychosexual stage poses a new socialization problem. By resolving each of these problems, the child learns to rely on the reality principle instead of the pleasure principle. A failure to negotiate a resolution to the problems presented by each psychosexual stage is thought by psychoanalysts to be the root of later behavior disorders. In recent years, psychoanalysts have tended to emphasize the importance of social forces in personality development (Greenspan & Lourie, 1982).

The fourth socialization theory described by McCandless, *self-theory*, emphasizes the role of a child's self-image in the socialization process (see Bandura, 1981, for one version of self-theory). According to this point of view, children respond to reinforcers from the environment as a function of how consistent reinforcement is with their self-image. For example, children with poor self-images may reject some reinforcers because they feel undeserving ("I'm not really worthy of this reward"), whereas children with strong group identities may only respond to group specific rewards. Urban gang members, for example, may only respond to those rewards that increase prestige in the gang. Self-theory asserts that socialization depends on children receiving "appropriate" reinforcers for desired behaviors. In this way, the theory is compatible with McCandless' fifth theory, *behaviorism*.

Behaviorism views socialization as a learning process in which children are reinforced for behaving in role-appropriate ways. There has always been a range of opinion among behaviorists as to how malleable children are. Watson (1928), for example, looked upon children as blank slates upon which anything could be written:

Give me a dozen healthy infants, well-formed, and my own specialized world to bring them up in, and I'll guarantee to take any one at random and train him to be any type of specialist I might select — doctor, lawyer, artist, merchant-chief, yes, even beggarman and thief. (p. 82)

Today, most behaviorists believe that organismic variables (differences among children) have at least some influence on socialization. An important aspect of the socialization process from the behavioral viewpoint (and from most other theories as well) is a change in the nature of reinforcers as children develop. Whereas young children are sensitive to tangible reinforcers (food, drink, and so on), the socialization process in older children is controlled largely by social reinforcers (esteem, prestige, position, love). By adulthood, when socialization is supposed to be complete, social reinforcement may actually be self-administered. That is, adults reinforce themselves for behaving in socially appropriate ways. As we will show in the chapter on pervasive developmental disorders, a failure to respond to social reinforcers not only makes socialization difficult, it can produce severely deviant behavior.

Growth, Development, and Psychopathology

The preceding overview of developmental themes illustrates perhaps the most important point to be learned by any student of psychopathology — development is an interactive process. Infants are not born tabula rasa (blank slates), as the philosopher John Locke once thought, nor do they experience the world as a "blooming buzzing confusion," as the famous psychologist William James described it. Infants are more competent than either knew. Babies inherit a set of capacities that helps them to develop in a specific environment. They bring into the world a capacity for social attachments, for learning, and even for language. Moreover, their nervous systems display a degree of plasticity; they can be modified by experience. Physical, cognitive, moral, language, and even social development are dependent on the interaction of biological, psychological, and social factors. As we shall see in later chapters, failures in any of these areas (genetic disease, psychological deprivation, deviant subcultures, to name just three) can result in behavior disorders.

The present discussion has focused on developmental themes. In the next section, we show how certain etiological factors in child psychopathology are related to development.

ETIOLOGICAL FACTORS IN CHILD PSYCHOPATHOLOGY

As should be clear from the preceding discussions, behavior disorders in children are determined by a variety of factors interacting in a complex fashion. There are some exceptions, of course. For example, one form of mental retardation, Down's Syndrome (mongolism), is known to result from a genetic accident at the time of conception. Maternal illnesses during pregnancy (rubella, for instance) can also produce disordered children. These single-cause syndromes are very much the exception, however. Most of the disorders described in this book have no single cause; their etiology derives from the complex interaction of biological and social variables.

The etiologies of the various disorders described in this book (as far as they are known) are discussed in the appropriate chapters. Thus, the causes of intellectual disorders are covered in the chapters dealing with mental retardation and specific learning disabilities, the etiology of early infantile autism is discussed in the chapter on pervasive developmental disorders, and so on. In this section, we provide a general overview of some of the most important etiological factors in child psychopathology.

In order to emphasize once again the importance of the developmental variable in child psychopathology, our discussion of etiological factors is organized along developmental lines. We begin with genetic factors then go on to prenatal influences, followed by factors operating in infancy and early childhood, and end with etiological factors that exert their influence in later childhood.

Genetics and Child Psychopathology

Sigmund Freud once said "Biology is destiny." Although he meant that personality is strongly determined by whether one is born male or female, his statement has much wider applicability. We are all biological organisms, and biology plays an important role in determining how we behave. Some readers may find the concept of biology influencing behavior somewhat startling. Although everyone admits that biological factors determine appearance, many feel that personality and behavior patterns are solely the result of life experience. Nothing could be further from the truth. Human behavior results from both biological and environmental influences acting together. In this section, we focus on the way biological traits are transmitted and what happens when something goes wrong.

Humans, like all other living things, evolved over millions of years. The evolutionary process is guided by three major influences: *genetic variability, adaptation,* and *selection.* Genetic variability is an attribute of every species. It means that each member of a species differs slightly in its genetic endowment. Except for identical twins, no two people have the same genetic endowment. This is why people do not all look alike and, to some extent, why they behave differently. Sometimes genetic variability leads to characteristics that give the organism an edge over others. This adaptive advantage is passed to succeeding generations. In evolutionary terms, those displaying adaptation are selected for survival. Eventually, if selection goes on for many generations, only those showing adaptation will survive; the others will have disappeared.

Evolution does not simply involve changes in appearance. Species-specific behaviors evolve also. Ethological research has shown that in animals, at least, many complex behaviors are, in fact, the product of an evolutionary process. These behaviors are usually called instincts to indicate that they are inherited. Once again, the truth is more complex. In an article entitled "How an Instinct is Learned," Hailman (1969) shows how biological influences interact with environmental factors to "teach" herring gull chicks to peck at an adult's bill. In the wild, chicks are only fed when they peck at the adult's bill; if they fail to peck, they will die. But how do they learn to peck in the first place? Hailman attempted to find out by constructing wooden models of adult herring gulls and exposing baby chicks to the models rather than to live adults. Adult gulls have yellow beaks with a red spot on the lower end. Hailman's models had red spots in several places. Hailman found that on the first day after hatching, pecking was governed by the red spot. That is, babies pecked at the red spot even if the spot were painted on the adult's forehead instead of its beak. After a few days, however, pecking was more likely to occur on spots on the beak. Because pecking the beak led to feeding, it appears that birds who have a biological instinct to peck the red spot modify their behavior as a function of their experience — they learn only to peck at red spots on adults' beaks.

Nesting and reproductive behavior in birds has also been shown to result from a combination of biological drives and external factors such as day length, presence of a mate, social status, and even the weather (Wingfield, 1983). When birds reach puberty, they tend to migrate to a breeding area. Although such birds are able to reproduce, they will not do so unless their hormonal systems receive certain environmental cues. For example, before procreation, males must establish a territory, something they will not do unless they have higher than average levels of the sex hormone testosterone. But what increases testosterone levels in the first place? The answer is social cues. The presence of a female or a rival male raises testosterone levels. In a reciprocal fashion, the male's presence influences the female's sexual development. In a labora-

tory experiment, recorded male songs played to female canaries accelerated ovarian development, stimulated nest building, and increased blood levels of sex hormones compared to control birds who did not hear the recordings. Even the weather plays a role in bird reproduction. The amount of daylight influences blood levels of sex hormones. In unusually rainy seasons, when skies are overcast, birds have lower levels of sex hormones and mate later than in sunny seasons.

What has all this to do with people? After all, humans have an enormous capacity to adapt to their environment and culture. John Watson (1928), as we have already seen, thought he could make babies into any type of person he desired. However, neither he nor his behaviorist descendants have ever actually been able to substantiate this claim. Humans are biological organisms; they inherit a potential for various types of behavior. Like other organisms, human biology interacts with experience to produce behavior. People, of course, differ from other animals (otherwise laboratory rats would be writing scholarly papers about B. F. Skinner), but they share one important characteristic in common — their behavior is made up of a combination of biological dispositions and environmental experience.

Although most modern scientists believe that human behavior is the result of an interaction between genetic endowments and experience, the relative importance of each is a matter of some controversy. Sociobiologists (Lumsden & Wilson, 1983; Wilson, 1975) tend to view a great deal of human behavior as largely genetic in origin. In some ways, their position represents the opposite extreme to John Watson's. Critics of sociobiology emphasize the importance of experience in shaping human behavior. The question of which is more important — nature or nurture — will be returned to many times in this book. In most instances, it will be found unanswerable; one must understand both nature and nurture to help troubled children.

Everyone reading this book knows that genetic endowments are transmitted from generation to generation through the genes. Each of us has about 50,000 genes living on 23 pairs of chromosomes in each of our millions of cells. One member of each chromosome pair is inherited from our mothers, the other from our fathers, thus ensuring the genetic variability noted earlier. With one exception, each human being has a unique collection of genes. The exception is identical twins. Identical twins are produced when a fertilized egg (called a *zygote*) splits to form two individuals (hence, *monozygotic* twins). Not all twins are monozygotic. Fraternal twins are produced by the simultaneous fertilization of two eggs. Such twins are called *dizygotic* and are no more similar genetically than any pair of siblings.

There are certain abnormalities that have been traced to particular chromosome aberrations. Down's Syndrome, for example, has been traced to the presence of a third chromosome where there should be only two. Down's Syndrome and other genetic abnormalities will be discussed in more detail later in this book. For now, however, it is important to note that many traits influencing behavior are thought to be polygenic (influenced by many genes). These traits are often studied using epidemiological methods.

Pedigree analysis is an old method for studying the role of heredity in determining behavior. The technique involves examining family trees for instances of a particular behavior or trait. This was the method used by Galton (1869) in his study of genius. Although a possible source of hypotheses, pedigree analysis has one important drawback: It leaves environmental influences uncontrolled. It is impossible to determine whether a trait is the result of inheritance or merely the fact that various people all grew up in the same family environment.

A more scientific approach uses adoption studies to examine the effects of heredity and environment on behavioral traits. Children adopted into new families at birth may experience different environments from those of their natural families. If these children resemble their biological relatives more close-ly than their adoptive ones, the effects of heredity are said to outweigh environmental influences. Of course, the logic of this approach requires that the natural and adoptive environments be different, otherwise any correlations between adopted children and their natural relatives could be the result of the similarity in environments. As we shall see in later chapters, it is often difficult to ensure that natural and adoptive environments are uncorrelated.

The best way to study behavioral genetics in humans capitalizes on the identical genetic make-up of monozygotic twins. Twins who are more similar on some behavioral trait than other siblings in the same family are thought to be reflecting the influence of their identical heredity, because their environment is more or less the same. Similarly, twins raised apart for some reason, who show differences from one another on some behavioral measure (IQ tests, for example), are thought to demonstrate the importance of environment, as their genetic endowments are identical. Several behavior genetics research strategies are illustrated in Table 1.7.

We review a variety of genetic studies in this book. Although such research is often controversial, we will find evidence for at least some genetic influence on intelligence, schizophrenia, depression, and several other behavior disorders described in this book. The presence of a genetic influence does not mean that psychological methods of intervention are doomed to failure. It is important to keep

TABLE 1.7. SOURCES OF VARIABILITY IN BEHAVIOR-GENETICS STUDIES.

Type of Study	Permitted to Vary	Controlled
Identical twins raised apart	Environment	Genetic endowment
Adopted children	Genetic endowment	Environment
Identical twins vs. other siblings	Genetic endowment	Environment

in mind the important distinction between *genotype* (genetic endowment) and *phenotype* (observed appearance or behavior). Just as one can inherit a genotype for black hair and produce a phenotype of blond hair (all it takes is a bottle of bleach), it is possible to influence behavioral genotypes by various means to produce new phenotypes. (It may soon even be possible to influence genotypes directly now that genes are being created artificially, Baxter et al., 1979.)

We began this discussion of genetic factors with Freud's maxim, "Biology is destiny." We can now see that this is something of an overstatement. Our biology is partly responsible for what we are, but it acts in combination with the environment to produce phenotypic differences. It is more accurate to say that biology and experience interacting in complex ways determine our destiny.

Prenatal Etiological Factors

Before World War II, 65 of every 10,000 births ended in the mother's death. Today, the comparable figure is 2 in 10,000. Infant mortality has also decreased. Nevertheless, in America today, 14 infants still die in childbirth for every 1,000 live children born (The World Almanac, 1983). This infant mortality rate is higher than that of many other western countries. For every child that dies, of course, many others are born damaged. Some of these children may exhibit behavioral disorders later in life.

Although the fetus is protected from most harmful influences by the placental barrier and the tough uterine walls, it is not entirely safe. Poisons and drugs taken during pregnancy can affect the developing fetus. In the 1960s, thousands of pregnant women who took thalidomide (a sedative drug) gave birth to severely deformed children. Nuclear fallout following the atomic explosions at Hiroshima and Nagasaki had similar effects. Sometimes, a drug's harmful effects may not become obvious for many years. For example, DES (a synthetic female hormone) was used widely in the 1960s to prevent miscar-

riages. Now it appears that females whose mothers received DES during pregnancy have a higher than average incidence of cervical cancer (Berger & Goldstein, 1980).

Women addicted to narcotics during pregnancy produce addicted babies who must undergo withdrawal during the first few days of life. There is also a "fetal alcohol syndrome" (Streissguth, 1976) found in children of alcoholic mothers. Such children evidence various growth deficiencies and facial deformities and are likely to have a high mortality rate. Even smoking has an effect on the unborn infant. Smoking mothers have more miscarriages and lower birth-weight children (Butler, Goldstein, & Ross, 1972). Although much of the evidence for the effects of various substances taken during pregnancy on the newborn child is correlational (no one is quite sure how smoking and birth weight are connected, for instance), expectant mothers should be extremely careful about what drugs and other potentially harmful substances they consume during pregnancy.

Maternal nutrition during pregnancy is also an important variable in child development. Poor nutrition can lead to birth complications, retarded development, and even abnormal behavior among offspring (Winick, 1979). In developed countries, most maternal diets are sufficient to ensure at least the physical health of the fetus. As we shall show in the chapter on mental retardation, even severely restricted diets, although producing low birth-weight infants, have little effect on the intelligence of offspring.

Maternal age and the number of previous children born to a mother can affect the course of pregnancy and even infant mortality. Down's Syndrome, for example, is more common in mothers over 35 than in younger women (Mikkelsen & Stene, 1970). In addition, first-born children and last-born children tend to be more vulnerable than those born in between, although this finding may also be related to maternal age (young mothers and older mothers tend to have more problem pregnancies than mothers in their twenties). Some maternal infections can be transmitted to the newborn during pregnancy (Sever, 1970). Syphilis, for example, can be passed from mother to child and may be responsible for various fetal abnormalities. This is a relatively uncommon problem in western countries, where pregnant women can be treated with penicillin. Toxoplasmosis, a mild parasitic infection in adults, can wreak havoc on the unborn fetus, causing mental retardation, blindness, and even death. Rubella (German measles) contracted during the first part of pregnancy can also result in mental retardation, blindness, and other birth complications. Mass immunization programs are quickly reducing this risk, however.

Maternal illnesses such as diabetes, atypical births, and even a mother's anxiety level can affect her unborn child. All of these factors will be addressed again in various chapters of this book. Although each of these prenatal etiological factors is important and serious, they are becoming less common as health care, nutrition, and immunization programs improve. It probably should be emphasized, just as a matter of balance, that most fetuses make it through pregnancy completely unscathed.

Etiological Factors in Infancy and Early Childhood

Complications of delivery can sometimes result in the types of disorders studied in this book. For example, some babies are born with their umbilical cords wrapped around their necks. Oxygen may be cut off temporarily. If the oxygen deprivation is severe enough, brain damage may result. There are other possible causes for oxygen deprivation (known as anoxia) during delivery, but the widespread use of fetal monitors has diminished their frequency considerably.

For one reason or another, some children are injured during the delivery process. They, and infants unlucky enough to inherit metabolic deficiencies, are at risk of developing some of the behavior disorders described in this book. In addition, diseases such as meningitis, which produce high fevers, may lead to brain damage and subsequent intellectual and emotional problems. Head injuries also play a role. The list of all the possible accidents and diseases that can affect normal development is long and tragic. We will not mention them all here; many will be discussed in later chapters. For now, it is sufficient to mention that illness, particularly if it is chronic and accompanied by prolonged hospitalizations, can produce behavioral problems.

Social influences early in life can also be etiological factors in behavior disorders. We have already mentioned the importance of the attachments that begin to form during the first year of life. A failure to develop social attachments can lead to serious behavior disorders.

Birth order has already been mentioned in connection with the confluence hypothesis. Although different psychological traits are thought to characterize children born first from those born later in the family, many of these traits have not been substantiated by careful research (Ernst & Angst, 1983). We will return to the subject of birth order in several places later in this book.

Another important etiological factor in many childhood problems is poverty. Indeed, poverty begins to affect children even before they are born. Impoverished women in developing countries have poor nutrition and produce low birth-weight babies (Lechtig et al., 1975). Low birth-weight children are more vulnerable to many illnesses of early childhood than their heavier siblings. Poverty also affects the way young children develop after birth. Poor food, inadequate medical care, and overworked, harrassed parenting all take their toll on the young child. Many of the children seen by clinical-child psychologists come from the poorest section of society. Later in this book, in the chapter dealing with prevention, we will describe several attempts to combat poverty's effects.

Over the past 50 years, divorce has become increasingly common not only in America, but in all western countries. (The trend is vividly depicted in Figure 1.6.) The divorce rate in America more than doubled between 1960

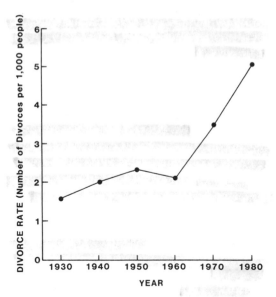

FIGURE 1.6. American divorce rates 1930–1980 per 1,000 people. Source: Adapted from the World Almanac, 1983, p. 955.

and 1980 (The World Almanac, 1983); many of these broken families included children. Researchers have estimated that half of all children born today will spend at least a few years with only one parent (Glick & Norton, 1977). Although there are differences in degree, divorce is almost always accompanied by marital and family conflict. Not infrequently, children are asked to choose sides in a battle that they cannot win. In addition, divorce frequently results in financial difficulties, thus adding the effects of poverty to those of emotional upheaval (Goetting, 1981).

Divorce exerts its strongest emotional effect on young, preschool-age children, who may become excessively demanding and dependent on the parent they remain with (Wallerstein & Kelly, 1975). Some children, blaming themselves for their parent's break-up, have become depressed. Primary-school-aged children may have similar reactions to their parents' divorce, often accompanied by feelings of anger and resentment (Wallerstein & Kelly, 1976). Even adolescents, who are beginning to adopt independent lives, may have problems adjusting to family break-up (Waller-

stein & Kelly, 1974). Various types of counseling and psychotherapy have been developed to aid divorced families; many of these are discussed in Chapter 10. Divorce or loss of a parent through death can produce a child who is particularly at risk for developing a behavior disorder. Such at-risk children require special interventions, which are described in Chapter 11.

Another social problem with important implications for childhood psychopathology is child abuse. Each year, thousands of children are physically or sexually abused, and thousands more are neglected (poorly fed, clothed, or supervised). Some of these children sustain temporary physical and emotional damage, but many bear permanent scars, and several thousand actually die each year (Broadhurst, Edmunds, & MacDicken, 1979). Although there are legal distinctions between neglect, abuse, and sexual abuse, these distinctions are sometimes difficult to make in practice (Starr, 1979). In some societies (Sweden for one), it is now considered abusive to spank a child, whereas in England and British Commonwealth countries, the traditional headmaster's cane remains the punishment expected by misbehaving school boys. Of course, when neglect or physical abuse reaches extremes, it does not require a lawyer to identify that a problem exists. A survey carried out by Gelles (1978) in the United States indicated that 8% of the parents interviewed had kicked, bitten, or hit their children with closed fists and that 3% had either threatened or actually used a gun or knife on their children. Most people would agree that such acts constitute extreme abuse.

Abusive parents have not been found to be suffering from psychiatric disorders (or at least these disorders are no more common among them than the population at large), nor are they confined to the lowest social classes. Many are well-educated middle-class parents (Starr, 1979). One characteristic that does seem common to many child abusers is a history of being abused themselves as children (Cicchetti, Taraldson, & Egeland, 1978). There is also some indication that abusive parents may be uninformed about children's behavior and may have unrealistic expectations about the effects of discipline. For example, they may expect that scolding or spanking should stop an infant from crying. When such interventions prove ineffective, they may lose control and increase the punishment (Garbarino, 1977). Abusive parents have frequently been found to be going through periods of stress (divorce, unemployment) and to have few close friends to help them ride out these rocky periods. Although some writers (see Green, 1982) have suggested that children with certain characteristics are more likely to be abused than others (parents often abuse only one of their children), these assertions are difficult to substantiate. After all, the children are being studied *after* they have been abused. There is no way of knowing whether any special characteristics they exhibit brought on their abuse or whether these behaviors developed as a result of being abused. There do, however, appear to be more premature, mentally retarded, handicapped, and deformed children among the abused population than we might expect on a statistical basis alone (Friedrich & Boriskin, 1976).

Early identification of abuse, parental counseling, and parental education programs have all been instituted to try and reduce the incidence of child abuse (see Belsky, 1980, for a review). In 1977, a new journal, *Child Abuse and Neglect*, was founded to keep pace with the rapidly growing research in this area. These programs will be discussed further in a later chapter. For now, we turn our attention to etiological variables operating primarily in later childhood.

Etiological Factors in Late Childhood and Adolescence

Although older children and adolescents can also contract disease and suffer accidents, the most important etiological variables in this age group are social in nature. Two influences are particularly important, the development of peer relationships and the capacity for useful work.

Late childhood and adolescence marks the emergence of adult-style groups. These can range from informal crowds of friends to rigidly formal street gangs with their own specific rules of conduct. Membership in such groups can bring prestige and, of course, a sense of acceptance. Moreover, group (or gang) norms help the insecure adolescent by prescribing what clothing to wear, what language to use, and so on. Conformity to group norms and peer pressure have their maximum influence in the adolescent years.

One important peer group influence revolves around exposure to addictive substances. Alcohol and cigarette use is particularly common in America. Approximately one-half of all high school students have tried both (Abelson, Fishburne, & Cisin, 1977). Although alcohol consumption appears to run in families (Zucker, 1976), a child's first exposure to cigarettes, alcohol, and drugs is often through a peer-group member. In a sense, experimenting with these substances has become a normal part of growing up. Although many people still hold the view that addicts are psychologically disturbed individuals, recent research indicates that there is little correlation between psychiatric symptoms (depression or anxiety, for example) and substance abuse (Kellam, Brown, Rubin, & Ensminger, 1983). Needless to say, there are multiple factors influencing drug use, but there is no doubt that peer-group pressure plays an important role.

Peer relationships also provide a way for teenagers to begin relating to the opposite sex. Hormonal changes at puberty ensure that both boys and girls take a strong interest in sex. Sexual information is exchanged through interactions with same-sexed group members, and the heterogeneous make-up of most groups also provides sexual partners for experimentation. Mentally retarded, handicapped, and other "different" children often have difficulty fitting into such groups. The result can be social isolation, low self-esteem, and a failure to develop normal interpersonal relationships.

Conformity to peer-group standards is one of several important factors in the etiology of juvenile delinquency. As will be shown in the chapter on delinquency later in this book, at least one subgroup of delinquents performs their antisocial acts in accordance with the norms of their deviant (gang) subgroup.

In addition to peer relationships, late childhood and adolescence are also the periods when work begins to become important. Although children are accustomed to performing required tasks in the classroom, they now must give serious thought to the work they will be doing for the rest of their lives. To a great extent, their self-identities will be wound up in their ability to perform useful work. As children approach adulthood, work takes on increasing importance. It is not just something done for money; it gives the individual a feeling of competence, usefulness, and self-esteem.

The importance of the capacity to work on psychological well-being (at least among males) is illustrated by a recent study reported by Vaillant and Vaillant (1981). They found that for their sample of 456 men, the capacity to work (measured by income, job satisfaction, and the ability to remain employed) is highly correlated with global measures of mental health. More importantly, they found that teenagers who held part-time jobs, performed regular household tasks, or worked on extracurricular school projects were less likely to develop behavior disorders than those who did not show this capacity for work. Children who, for one reason or another, fail to develop a capacity for work are likely to develop behavior disorders at later stages of life.

SUMMARY

This book is an attempt to organize and synthesize current work in the field of child psychopathology, taking into consideration the development of the child. Although much of the work in this area is cross-sectional in nature, a good deal is known about child development, and, where possible, an attempt has been made to integrate what we know about developmental processes with what is known

about psychopathology and learning in general. Armed with a knowledge of scientific paradigms, models of psychopathology, and the major developmental themes and etiologies, the careful reader will try to consider, when reading the remaining chapters in this book, what paradigm research workers and clinicians are employing when they discuss various psychopathological problems, as well as the influence of such paradigms on the interpretation and conduct of research. In addition, the conclusions various investigators draw from research must also be carefully evaluated. When considering the research presented in this volume, one should ask:

1. What paradigm is the researcher working from?
2. Are adequate controls employed in the research?
3. Is the author making causal interpretations from essentially correlational data?
4. Has the author considered the role of developmental factors?

It should also be noted that research does not take place in a vacuum. Indeed, social forces and historical forces are always influencing the conduct of research and the interpretations drawn from research. Before the 18th century, conditions that today would be called psychopathological were thought to be the result of either demonic possession or diseases of the brain. Although the treatment of the "insane" varied from harsh and punitive to comforting and humanitarian, depending on the prevalent social climate, it was not until the 18th century that the study of psychopathology became a legitimate and recognized branch of the medical and psychological sciences.

Child psychopathology as a field grew out of a number of 19th-century influences. Interestingly enough, adult psychopathology and pediatrics were not the most important of these influences. Instead, new trends in education, the care of the mentally retarded, intelligence testing, developmental psychology, and the emergent mental hygiene movement were the most important formative influences. Today, a variety of theoretical approaches mark the field of adult psychopathology, whereas child psychopathology is largely under the influence of three: psychoanalysis, various behavioristic orientations, and a renewed interest in biochemical and neurological abnormalities.

This book is organized around the specific problem areas commonly observed and studied by psychologists and others interested in child psychopathology. Chapter 2 is an overview of assessment procedures employed by clinicians working with children and a consideration of issues related to the classification of psychopathological conditions. Common behavioral problems of childhood are discussed in Chapter 3. Next, various forms of child psychopathology will be considered. For each disorder or group of disorders, a discussion of its history, the various theories advanced to explain it, and the research bearing on these theories is presented and related to general historical and scientific trends. This is followed by a consideration of various treatment approaches to child psychopathology, in which research into the effectiveness of individual, group, and family approaches to treatment is reviewed. Finally, the prevention of psychopathology is considered. Throughout, a historical developmental perspective integrates the discussion.

SUGGESTED READINGS

Beers, C. (1908). *A mind that found itself.* New York: Longmans, Green. The book that gave birth to the mental hygiene movement.

Lane, H. (1976). *The wild boy of Aveyron.* Cambridge, MA: Harvard University Press. Professor Itard's famous experiment with the "wild boy" and its influence on modern concepts of intellectual development are described.

Lumsden, C. J., & Wilson, E. O. (1983). *Promethean fire.* Cambridge, MA: Harvard University Press. The sociobiological viewpoint of cultural development in easy to understand terms.

Kendall, P. C., & Finch, A. J., Jr. (1979). Strategies for research in child psychopathology. In A. J. Finch, Jr. & P. C. Kendall (Eds.), *Clinical treatment and research in child psychopathology* (pp. 3–34). New York: SP Medical and Scientific Books. A review and description of experimental and correlational strategies in child psychopathology research.

Annis, L. F. (1978). *The child before birth.* Ithaca, NY: Cornell University Press. Everything you will ever want to know about prenatal development.

Turner, J. S., & Helms, D. B. (1983). *Lifespan development* (2nd ed.). New York: Holt, Reinhart, & Winston. A comprehensive, readable textbook dealing with development through the lifespan.

2 ASSESSMENT AND CLASSIFICATION OF CHILD PSYCHOPATHOLOGY

Regardless of theoretical orientation, most clinical-child psychologists would agree that assessment is a necessary prerequisite for the successful treatment of psychological disorders. The specific nature of the procedures employed, the goals of assessment, and the ways assessment information is used, however, will vary depending upon the clinician's model of psychopathology. For example, assessment procedures may be employed in an attempt to determine the personality characteristics of the child and the underlying nature of his or her psychological problems so that the cause of the disorder can be determined and treated. Or assessment procedures can be directed toward observable behaviors rather than underlying causes. In the latter case the clinician may focus on the specific behaviors that have led to the child's referral, the context in which these behaviors are displayed, and the factors in the child's natural environment that reinforce and maintain these problem behaviors. Thus, although most clinicians view assessment as important, they approach it in different ways with different goals in mind.

Clinicians have also devoted much attention to the classification of psychopathological disorders, motivated in part by the assumption that specific syndromes exist and

that these disorders have specific, determinable etiologies. Further, it has been assumed that in order to effectively treat an individual, a proper diagnosis must be made. Over the years several approaches to classification have been proposed. As will be seen, certain of these schemes are more relevant to the classification of child disorders than others.

This chapter will attempt to provide an overview of the typical assessment procedures used with children. We will also consider several approaches to the classification of abnormal child behavior and the advantages and shortcomings of each. The chapter will consider both more traditional approaches and newer approaches to behavioral assessment with children.

INTERVIEWING THE PARENT AND CHILD

The child and his or her parents are two important sources of information about a child's behavior. Information is also often obtained from the school, if the child is of school age, from the referral source (if other than the parent or school), and perhaps from the child's physician. From information provided by these informants (possibly supplemented by the results of psychological testing or other assessment data), the clinician attempts to ascertain whether the child is behaving normally or abnormally, given his or her age and present environment and the nature of those factors that may contribute to the child's difficulties should it be determined that some type of psychopathology is being displayed.

In this section we will briefly consider two sources of information commonly used in child assessment: the parental interview and the child interview. This will be followed by a discussion of psychological testing as a supplement to interview data.

Parental Interview

An interview with the child's parents is often the starting point in child assessment. The parents are, in many cases, the first to note the child's problem and have often been in a unique position to observe the child's development and behavior in a variety of contexts. As a result they are often able to provide more detailed information than could be obtained by simply observing the child in the clinic or even in the home. In those instances where the parents may have had less opportunity to observe their child and are unable to provide needed information (as a result of both the mother and father working long hours, frequently being away from home, and so forth) the parental interview may be supplemented by obtaining information from other caretakers as well.

In the interview with the parent (or other caretaker) the clinician may attempt to obtain information concerning the specific nature of the child's problem behaviors, the duration of these behaviors, the nature of precipitating events, the situations in which the problem behaviors occur, how the child's behaviors are responded to by others, and previous attempts to deal with the problem. Additionally, the clinician may try to get information about the child's developmental history (e.g., the age at which the child sat up, crawled, walked, started to speak, was toilet trained), medical history (e.g., pregnancy or birth complications, injuries, illnesses), school perform-

ance, and peer and family relationships. During the interview the clinician often seeks to determine parental attitudes toward discipline and child rearing, parental expectations of the child, and possibly the extent to which parents' attitudes and behaviors may relate to the child's problems.

Although information from parents is useful, it must be kept in mind that parental reports are not infallible and may be subject to bias. Parents may neglect to mention things that might be considered important by the clinician if such information reflects negatively on them, or they may simply not be careful observers of their children and therefore unable to provide certain types of information. In other instances parents may be so involved in their child's problems that they cannot view the child's behavior objectively. These factors make it necessary to carefully consider information obtained from parents and supplement it with data from other sources.

Despite the important role of the parental interview in child assessment, there has been little research in this area. One early study was conducted by Graham and Rutter (1968), who described an interview procedure for use by clinicians and researchers designed to elicit information from the parents concerning the child's behavior during the previous year. In the first part of the interview (open-ended), mothers were simply asked whether they felt their child displayed any problems of behavior or "nervous" troubles. If the answer was no, the interviewer proceeded to the second part. If a problem was reported, the mother was asked whether there were additional problems, and further information concerning each of the problems reported was obtained (for example, whether the problem was worse than that displayed by most children of her child's age, what attempts had been made to deal with the problem, what the mother perceived to be the cause of the problem, what made the problem better or worse, how frequently the behavior occurred, where it occurred, etc.).

The second portion of the interview (structured) involved asking the mother 36 questions concerning the occurrence of specific problem behaviors thought to be of clinical importance. For example, mothers were asked whether the child displayed specific fears, antisocial behavior, evidence of hyperactivity, bed-wetting, or other problems. For each problem reported, the interviewer attempted to get more detailed information similar to that obtained in the open-ended portion of the interview.

This interview procedure was used with 268 mothers of 10- and 11-year-old children, selected as possibly displaying psychological problems (36 mothers were interviewed a second time at a later date). In each case responses to each of the 36 questions asked in the structured portion of the interview were rated on a 4-point scale: no abnormality; dubious or trivial abnormality; definite slight abnormality; or definite marked abnormality. Ratings of overall degree of disturbance, as indicated by responses to the structured portion, were also made on this same 4-point scale. Employing this procedure, Graham and Rutter were able to obtain data concerning the reliability of ratings and the degree of correspondence between data obtained in the open-ended and structured portions. They found that when two clinicians independently rated the same structured interview responses for overall degree of maladjustment, a correlation of .81 was obtained, suggesting a high level of agreement and that global ratings of maladjustment are quite reliable when based on similar interview information. Ratings of degree of maladjustment in specific areas (hyperactivity and antisocial behavior, for example), based on responses to the 36 individual items, were found to be quite unreliable, however. Judges' ratings of overall level of maladjustment, based on responses obtained from mothers in two different interviews, were also relatively inconsistent ($r = .64$). The authors noted that mothers often failed to spontaneously report problems that were later elicited during the more structured phase of the interview. Also, mothers who were interviewed twice displayed considerable inconsistency in their spontaneous reporting of problem behaviors; in many instances problems were spontaneously reported in one interview and not mentioned at all in the other. Mothers were also found to be unreliable in their perceptions of the degree of disturbance displayed by their children. Graham and Rutter noted that the correlation between parent ratings of overall degree of maladjustment obtained during the first and second interviews was only .43.

The results of this study indicate that information elicited from a structured interview can be used by clinicians to make reliable judgments of overall level of maladjustment, but that mothers are often inconsistent in their perceptions of their child's problems and may often fail to report significant information in open-ended interviews. It seems, then, that in order to get the most information possible concerning specific problem behaviors, a combination of the structured and open-ended interview format may be the most useful approach. The usefulness of a structured interview format with parents has also been demonstrated by Herjanic, Herjanic, Brown, and Wheatt (1975).

The quality of the information obtained in the parental interview may also be enhanced through the use of behavior problem checklists, which may be obtained from parents prior to the interview. Such measures (which will be discussed in more detail in a later section) typically ask the parent to indicate which of a wide range of problem behaviors are displayed by the child and to rate the intensity of these behaviors. Armed with this data prior to the interview, the interviewer may use the parents' responses as a basis for obtaining further information about those behaviors reported as problematic. Because behavior problems checklists assess a wide range of behaviors in a structured way, they may (if followed up on in the interview) play a role in assessment similar to that of the structured interview described in the Graham and Rutter study cited above. Indeed, LaGreca (1983) has suggested that the lack of attention given to parental interviews in the literature probably relates to the development of various parent-report checklists for obtaining structured information regarding child behavior.

The Child Interview

In addition to the parental interview, an interview with the child may often be helpful. With younger children who lack well developed verbal skills, this interview is frequently conducted in a playroom where the child can both talk with the interviewer and engage in various play activities. In addition to gaining information by observing the child's overt behaviors (e.g., how easily he or she separates from the parents or interacts with the interviewer) and through talking with the child, many clinicians assume that the child's play may symbolically reflect personality characteristics and that observations of play activities may provide insights into the nature of the child's problems. Thus, using an alligator puppet to chew on the head of a doll, similar in apparent age and sex to the child's younger brother or sister, may be interpreted as evidence of sibling rivalry. Or the constant selection of toys like guns and knives over other play materials may be viewed as indicating hostility and aggressive tendencies. Although it is plausible that useful information may be gained through the observation of children's playroom behavior, relatively little information is available regarding the reliability and validity of data obtained in this setting.

With older children and adolescents, the interview is more likely to take the form of a verbal interchange between the child and the interviewer. It should be noted that, although important at any age, the development of rapport and the maintaining of cooperation on the part of the child are especially important with this age group. Given that children often end up in mental health settings, not because they desire help, but because their behavior has become a source of concern for others, cooperation with the interviewer is not something that can be taken for granted. Many children are quite resistant until they learn that the interviewer is a person they can trust, who wishes to help, who is accepting of their behavior, and who is not just an ally of their parents or other adults who find their behavior unacceptable. In other instances the lack of cooperation may not represent resistance on the part of the child so much as anxiety over having to deal with an authority figure about issues that may be sensitive and distressing to discuss. In either case, special attention must be given to the issue of relationship development as well as facilitating a verbal interchange that will lead to obtaining meaningful information regarding the child's problems. For an excellent overview of useful interview techniques, see Kanfer, Eyberg, and Krahn (1983).

Although the specific type of information one attempts to obtain in the interview is likely to vary depending on the nature of the presenting problem, the amount of information available from other sources, and other factors, a range of topics are frequently dealt with. Table 2.1 lists a number of areas often touched on in the child interview and provides examples of the types of information about which one might wish to inquire.

Although clinical interviews with children, as well as parents, have traditionally been conducted in an open-ended manner, increased attention has recently been given to the development of structured interview formats for use with younger age groups. This approach is perhaps best illustrated by the Child Assessment Schedule (CAS), developed by Hodges and her colleagues (Hodges, Kline, Fitch, McKnew, & Cytryn, 1981; Hodges, Kline, Stern, Cytryn, & McKnew, 1982a; Hodges, McKnew, Cytryn, Stern, & Kline 1982b).

The CAS is a structured interview that consists of two parts. Initially the child is asked a number of questions (approximately 75 in all) covering a range of topics dealing with activities, hobbies, school, friends, family, fears and worries, mood, self-concept, bodily concerns, anger, disordered thought, and the like. The child's responses to each of these is scored by the interviewer to indicate the degree to which various characteristics

TABLE 2.1. CONTENT AREAS FREQUENTLY ASSESSED IN CHILD INTERVIEWS.

Area	Examples of Specific Content
All Ages	
Referral problem	What does the child think the main problem is? Does the child see the referral problem as a problem? What does the child think will help?
Interests	What does the child like to do (in spare time)? What does the child like to do alone? with friends? with family members?
School	What does the child like best about school? Least? How does the child feel about his or her teachers? What kinds of grades does the child get in school?
Peers	Who does the child like to play with? Who are the child's friends? What do they like to do together? Who does the child dislike?
Family	How does the child get along with his or her parents? What do they do that the child likes? That makes the child angry? How does the child get along with his or her brothers and sisters? What do they do that the child likes/dislikes?
Fears/Worries	What kinds of things is the child afraid of? What kinds of things make the child nervous, jumpy? What kinds of things does the child worry about?
Self-Image	What does the child like/dislike about himself or herself? What can the child do well, relative to peers? How would the child describe himself or herself?
Mood/Feelings	What kinds of things make the child feel sad? happy? How often do these feelings happen? What kinds of things make the child feel mad? What does he or she do when mad?
Somatic concerns	Does the child have any headaches or stomachaches? Or other kinds of body pains? How often does this happen? What does the child usually do?
Thought disorder	Does the child hear things or see things that seem funny or unusual? Describe them.
Aspirations	What would the child like to do for a living when he or she gets older? What are other things the child would like to do when older?
Fantasy	What kinds of things does the child daydream about? What kinds of things does the child dream about? If the child could have any three wishes, what would they be?
Adolescents	
Heterosexual relations	Is the adolescent involved in any dating activities? What kinds of dating activities? Are there any restrictions on the adolescent's dating activities? How does he or she feel about them?
Sex	What kinds of sexual concerns does the adolescent have? What are his or her attitudes toward premarital sex? Do these conflict at all with parents' views? Is the adolescent adequately informed about contraception?
Drug/Alcohol use	What kinds of things has the adolescent ever used to get "high" (e.g., pills, alcohol, pot, glue)? Are other friends involved in these activities?

Source: LaGreca (1983). © 1983 John Wiley and Sons. Reprinted by permission.

are descriptive of the child. It should be noted that although the interview contains a large number of questions, these are grouped according to natural topics of conversation. This enables the interviewer to obtain the necessary information within the context of an ongoing discussion rather than requiring the child to respond to a large number of isolated questions that might damage rapport. This portion of the interview usually lasts from 45 minutes to 1 hour. Examples of questions and scoring criteria for Part 1 of the CAS are presented in Table 2.2.

Part 2 of the interview is made up of 53 items, which the interviewer responds to after the completion of the interview. These items relate to such areas as activity level, motor coordination, insight, emotional expressiveness, interpersonal interactions, speech and thought processes, and so forth (see Table 2.3).

Information derived from the CAS can be viewed in two ways. Qualitatively it can be used to provide information regarding specific problem areas. As the content areas tapped by the CAS are reflective of DSM-III (the currently accepted scheme for classifying psychological disorders) diagnostic criteria, it is also possible to obtain a diagnostic impression.

Several types of information have been presented regarding the adequacy of the CAS. Research has demonstrated adequate inter-rater reliability (e.g., different interviewers can agree on the scoring of interview items). Correlations between raters have generally exceeded .90 regardless of whether the total score or subscale scores are considered. Data derived from the interview has been shown to successfully discriminate between such groups as psychiatric inpatients, psychiatric outpatients, and normal controls (Hodges et al., 1982b). Other findings also suggest that indices of psychopathology derived via this interview correlate well with parent-report measures of child problems. Taken together these findings seem to provide reasonable support for the usefulness of the CAS as both a clinical and research tool.

Despite finding support for the reliability and validity of structured interview methods like the CAS, there is relatively little information regarding the validity of the less structured interview methods and playroom-interaction procedures that are often used in clinical settings.

PSYCHOLOGICAL TESTING IN CHILD ASSESSMENT

Psychological tests most commonly used in child assessment include developmental tests (designed to assess deviations from normal cognitive, motor, or social development — usually in infants), intelligence tests (which are usually used with somewhat older children to assess general cognitive and/or performance abilities), achievement tests (which document knowledge in specific school-related areas), and personality measures (both objective and projective in nature), which are designed to assess various personality characteristics and provide clues as to the presence, type, and/or nature of any psychopathology that the child may display. In the following sections, we will briefly consider the general nature of several of these better-known assessment procedures.

Developmental Assessment

The Bayley Scale

The Bayley Scale of Infant Development (Bayley, 1969) is an individually administered measure that is designed to assess the developmental level of children between the ages of 2 and 30 months. The measure consists of some 244 items, graded in terms of developmental level, which tap both cognitive (163 items) and motor development (81 items). An associated 30-item Infant Behavior Record, which is completed after testing, is also provided to assess aspects of behavioral style (e.g., cooperativeness, fearfulness, activity level, endurance, reactivity, etc.). Examples of items included in the Mental and Motor scales are presented in Table 2.4.

Administering the Bayley takes about 45 minutes to 1 hour. When scored it yields a

TABLE 2.2. EXAMPLE OF QUESTIONS ON PART I OF THE CAS.

Questions	Response Items	Response Categories				
		No (False)	Yes (True)	Ambiguous	No Response	Not Applicable
Sample from "Fears and Anxieties"						
Most people are afraid of something: What are you afraid of? Does this fear keep you from doing anything?	Indicates s/he had fears which are excessive. If true: check all that apply	——	——	——	——	——
	a. Indicates that fears keep him/her from performing adequately.	——	——	——	——	——
	b. Fear is of a bizarre nature (i.e., does not reflect age-appropriate reality testing).	——	——	——	——	——
	c. Fears are associated with a panic attack.	——	——	——	——	——
Sometimes kids have nervous or jumpy feelings. Do you have these kinds of feelings a little, a medium amount, or a lot of the time?	Indicates anxiety a lot of the time.	——	——	——	——	——
	Check here if anxiety is characterized by any of the following:					
(If child indicates presence of a lot of anxiety, ask:) Can you describe what your anxious feelings are about?	a. Chronic worry about the future (anticipatory anxiety).	——	——	——	——	——
	b. Worry about being perfect.	——	——	——	——	——
	c. Precocious concerns.	——	——	——	——	——

Soruce: Hodges et al. (1982b). © 1982 American Academy of Child Psychiatry. Reprinted by permission.

TABLE 2.3. EXAMPLE OF ITEMS ON PART II OF THE CAS.

Questions	Response Items	Response Categories				
		No (False)	Yes (True)	Ambiguous	No Response	Not Applicable
Impressions about quality of interpersonal interactions	Difficulty separating from parental figure or attachment figure.	—	—	—	—	—
	Stubborn, oppositional.	—	—	—	—	—
	Argumentative, belligerent, provocative.	—	—	—	—	—
	Quality of rapport seems superficial (e.g., not interested in rapport).	—	—	—		
	Appears to lack concern for feelings of others, including lack of appropriate guilt and remorse.	—	—	—		
	Appears manipulative and exploitative (e.g., does not extend self for others unless there is obvious immediate advantage to him/her).	—	—	—		
	Excessively conforming or approval-seeking.	—	—	—	—	—
	Difficulty in establishing rapport and seems to be due to shyness as opposed to hostility, avoidance of specific issues, or thought disorder.	—	—	—	—	—
	Quality of rapport is superficial, secondary to serious impairment in relating interpersonally ("feel like there is a wall between you and your patient").	—	—	—		

Source: Hodges et al. (1982b). © 1982 American Academy of Child Psychiatry. Reprinted by permission.

TABLE 2.4. SAMPLE ITEMS FROM THE BAYLEY SCALE AT SIX AGE LEVELS.

Approximate Age	Mental Scale	Motor Scale
2 months	Recognizes mother	Elevates self by arms
4 months	Turns head to sound of rattle	Sits with slight support
6 months	Looks for fallen spoon	Sits alone for 30 seconds or more
12 months	Turns pages of book	Walks alone
24 months	Names three objects	Walks on a line
30 months	Understands three prepositions	Walks on tiptoe, 10 feet

Source: Adapted from Bayley (1969).

Mental Development Index and a Psychomotor Development Index. These measures allow one to determine the degree to which a child differs from others of his or her age in terms of mental and motor development and to estimate the child's level of functioning in these areas. This measure is not only useful in testing very young children, but it may also be of value in assessing very low functioning children (whose abilities may lie in the 2 to 30 month range) that are performing at a level below that assessed by standard intelligence measures. Whereas scores derived from the Bayley Scales are similar to those of other developmental measures, in that they are poor predictors of later intellectual functioning (McCall, Hogarty, & Hurlburt, 1972), the measure is valuable as a screening device, as low scores and uneven performance (between scale scores) may suggest serious problems of development (Achenbach, 1982). For a brief overview of information on the validity and reliability of this measure, see Goldman, Stein, and Guerry (1983). All things considered, the Bayley is probably the best of the available infant development measures.

Minnesota Child Development Inventory (MCDI)

The MCDI (Ireton & Thwing, 1974) differs from the Bayley in that it is completed by the child's mother instead of being individually administered. It also taps a broader age range, being suitable for children less than a year and up to age 6. The test consists of 320 yes-no items that ask about behaviors related to various areas of development (e.g., motor development, language development, personality, and social development). When scored the MCDI yields developmental age-equivalents on eight different scales (see Figure 2.1). Generally, a score that is below the average obtained by children who are 30% younger than the child tested (e.g., 8.5 months for a 1-year-old; 17.5 months for a 2-year-old) is seen as suggesting developmental retardation.

The MCDI would seem useful as a brief developmental *screening* measure and as a supplement to a parental interview. It is important to note that completion of the MCDI requires an approximate eighth-grade reading level, suggesting that the measure may not be useful with cases where parents are poorly educated. Given that the MCDI relies solely on maternal reports, it is necessary to supplement the measure with individually administered tests in those cases where serious developmental delays are suggested.

Miscellaneous Developmental Measures

In addition to the two measures described here, there are other developmental scales that are also used in clinical practice. Included here are measures such as the Denver Developmental Screening Test (Frankenburg, Dodd, & Fandal, 1973), the Illinois Test of Psycholinguistic Abilities (Kirk, McCarthy, & Kirk, 1968), and the McCarthy Scales of Children's Abilities (McCarthy, 1970). Of special

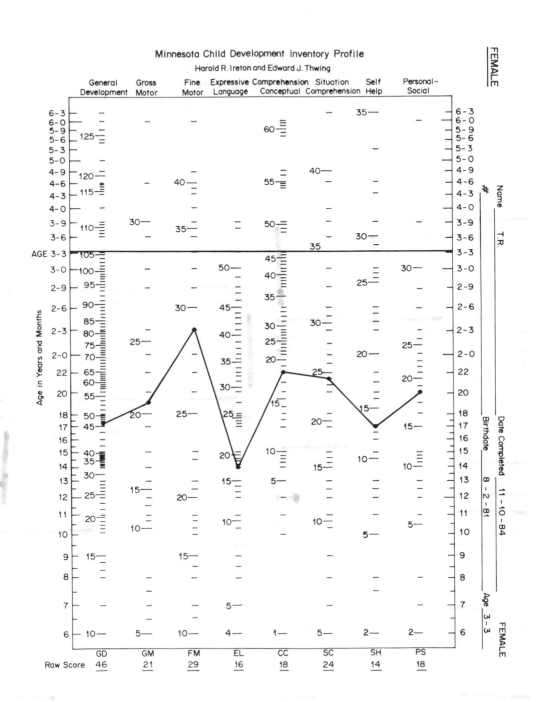

FIGURE 2.1. MCDI profile of a developmentally delayed child. Source: © 1974 by H. R. Ireton and E. J. Thwing; reproduced by permission.

note are the McCarthy Scales, as these measures appear to take up where the Bayley leaves off in providing a developmental measure of children's abilities across the 2½- to 8½-year age range. This measure allows one to obtain scores in three major areas (verbal, perceptual-performance, and quantitative), which together yield a General Cognitive Index, as well as separate scores reflective of memory and motor abilities. As with the Bayley, this scale is well constructed and appears to provide an adequate index of development over the age range for which it is intended. Despite these positive attributes, the McCarthy has not been as widely used as the Bayley. This may be related to the fact that there are well-established measures of intelligence, which are suitable for children in this age range, and that measures for IQ are seen as more useful than a General Cognitive Index, although for all practical purposes this index seems to be a measure of intelligence (Goldman et al., 1983). Although not as widely used, it should be noted that a number of the McCarthy subscales can be quite useful as supplements to intelligence tests in providing more detailed measures of memory and motor skills when an assessment of abilities in these areas is important.

Intellectual Assessment

The Stanford-Binet

The present-day Stanford-Binet intelligence scale is an outgrowth of the early work of Alfred Binet mentioned in Chapter 1. Binet, with his colleague Theodore Simon, developed the first measure designed to predict subsequent school performance. This test was introduced into the United States in a modified form by Stanford psychologist Terman in 1916. There have been two subsequent revisions (Terman & Merrill, 1937, 1960) and a collection of additional norms (Terman & Merrill, 1973), although questions have been raised regarding the representativeness of this normative data (Goldman et al., 1983). A third extensive revision of the measure is currently underway.

The Stanford-Binet is an individually ad-

ministered test, designed for individuals 2 to 18 years of age, although it is sometimes administered to those over 18 as well. It is composed of test items arranged according to age level, with item difficulty increased as a function of age. At each level items represent tasks typically accomplishable by average individuals of that age. Although the test contains various types of items, it appears to be heavily loaded with items tapping verbal abilities, particularly at the upper age levels. Therefore, the Stanford-Binet may be regarded primarily as a verbal test of intelligence (Garfield, 1974). Representative tasks presented at some of the younger age levels may be found in Table 2.5.

The Stanford-Binet has been widely used by clinicians in the assessment of intelligence among normals, in the assessment of mental retardation, and in research. The research literature and psychometric properties of this scale have been well summarized by Sattler (1982). Suffice it to say that the Stanford-Binet is one of the more well-standardized and respected tests of intelligence.

The Wechsler Intelligence Scales for Children

A second popular intelligence test developed for use with children is the Wechsler Intelligence Scale for Children-Revised (Wechsler, 1974), or the WISC-R as it is more commonly called.

A feature unique to the WISC-R is the grouping of items into specific subtests that make up separate verbal and performance scales. Whereas the Binet is largely a verbal test of intelligence and yields only a single score, the WISC-R taps both verbal and performance abilities and yields three values: a verbal IQ, a performance IQ, and a full-scale IQ.

The verbal and performance IQ scores reflect the contribution of various subtests, each of which taps various abilities. Verbal scales sample the degree to which children have acquired general information from their environment, their ability to master concepts, think abstractly, and concentrate, as well as their judgment and memory. The perform-

TABLE 2.5. STANFORD-BINET TASKS AT SELECTED AGES.

Year 2	Placing a circle, square, and triangle in the appropriate three holes of a form board. Identify several parts of the body (hair, mouth, feet, ear, nose).
Year 5	Finish an incomplete drawing of a man. Fold a paper triangle in a manner similar to that modeled by the examiner.
Year 8	Answer several specific questions about a story that has been read by the examiner. Indicate how a number of objects are similar and different.
Year 12	Give definition for a number of words (orange, envelope, puddle). Repeat five digits backward.
Year 13	Repeat sentence read by examiner. Give definition for a number of abstract words (connection, obedience, revenge).

Source: Adapted from Terman & Merrill (1973).

ance tests tap attention to detail, visual-motor skills, and planning ability, as well as other attributes. A listing of the verbal and performance subtests of the WISC-R and a brief description of each is presented in Table 2.6.

Unlike the Stanford-Binet, the WISC-R does not group items according to age levels but arranges subtest items, measuring a particular skill, according to difficulty level. Testing on a subtest typically ends when a specified number of items are missed. The WISC-R, unlike the Binet, permits the examiner to not only compare the child's verbal and performance abilities, but also to evaluate performance on the various subtests and determine particular areas of strength or weakness. For a useful clinical guide to the interpretation of the WISC-R, see Kaufman (1979).

Not only has the WISC-R been widely used in clinical practice, but an additional scale, the Wechsler Preschool and Primary Scale of Intelligence (WPPSI), has also been developed (Wechsler, 1967). This scale, which is similar to the WISC-R, is designed for children in the 4 to 6½-year age range. An overview of the development of these scales and research related to them may be found in the previously cited reference by Sattler (1982).

The Wechsler Scale in Personality Assessment

It has been widely assumed that the Wechsler scales may be used not only for purposes of intellectual evaluation, but also in personality assessment. It has been suggested that individuals give information concerning their personality characteristics and possibly the nature of their psychological problems by their responses to certain subtest items. For example, the response "me" to the vocabulary item "nuisance" may be judged to provide insight into the child's self-concept. Likewise, the child who responds to the comprehension item "What is the thing to do when you cut your finger?" with "Die" or "Bleed to death" might be viewed in a very different light from the child who gives a more appropriate response, such as "Wash it and put a Band-aid on it." Additionally, bizarre responses that have little to do with the item presented may give reason to suspect the presence of more serious forms of psychopathology. Further examples of such an approach to interpretation have been presented by Glasser and Zimmerman (1967).

It has also been suggested that useful information can be obtained from a scatter analysis of the Wechsler scales. This involves analyzing the pattern of subtest scores, for example, the differences between verbal and performance IQ scores or the degree to which scaled scores on specific subtests deviate from the mean verbal or performance subscale score. According to clinical lore, the relative superiority or inferiority of performance on various subtests may be related to personality and type of psychopathology. Examples of test patterns thought to be associated with specific disorders have been presented by Wechsler (1958) and Matarazzo (1972). Whereas scatter analysis was initially presented by Wechsler as a way of interpreting the Wechsler Adult Intelligence Scales, this approach has also been applied to children's test records by many clinicians.

In considering evidence regarding the validity of the WISC-R in personality assessment, it would appear that there are relatively few methodologically sound studies that provide support for the use of scatter analysis in personality assessment, and few studies have even attempted to explore the validity of analyzing the content of test responses, the approach illustrated earlier (Gittelman, 1980; Gittelman-Klein, 1978). Although the Wechsler Scales appear to be quite adequate as IQ measures, their value in personality assess-

ment remains to be demonstrated (Sattler, 1982).

Miscellaneous Tests of Intelligence

In addition to the Stanford-Binet and the Wechsler Scales, which are the two most well-established measures, there are a variety of *nonverbal* measures that have been developed to assess cognitive functions thought to be reflective of intelligence. Included here are the Peabody Picture Vocabulary Test (Dunn & Dunn, 1981), the Columbia Mental Maturity Scale (Burgermeister, Blum, & Lorge, 1972), the Leiter International Performance Scale (Leiter, 1969), and the Test of Nonverbal Intelligence (Brown, Sherbenow, &

TABLE 2.6. VERBAL AND PERFORMANCE SUBTESTS OF THE WISC-R.

VERBAL SUBTESTS

Information: 30 questions arranged in ascending order of difficulty. Taps information that might be acquired by the person from his environment. (How many days are in a month? What is the day that comes after Tuesday?)

Comprehension: 17 questions that tap adequacy of judgment or common sense. (What should you do if a friend has lost something?)

Arithmetic: 18 problems arranged in order of difficulty, which must be calculated mentally within time limits.

Similarities: 17 items that require the child to indicate similarities between various items. (In what way are a candle and a match alike?)

Vocabulary: 32 words that the child is asked to define. Items are arranged in order of difficulty. (Boat, infection, anomaly.)

Digit span: A series of digits of differing lengths, to be repeated either forward or backward.

PERFORMANCE SUBTESTS

Picture completion: 26 pictures that have an important part missing. Child is required to indicate the missing part.

Picture arrangement: 13 picture sequences (similar to those seen in comic strips) that are cut up into segments. The task is to arrange these picture so they tell a story, within time limits.

Block design: The child is presented with a number of cards with two-dimensional designs on them and asked to reproduce these designs with multicolored blocks within time limits.

Object assembly: Consists of cut-up pictures of a girl, a horse, a face, and a car. These are presented in random order, to be assembled within time limits.

Coding: Consists of presenting the child with a standard set of symbols, each of which is associated with a number. With this standard to look at, the child is to match appropriate symbols with a random list of numbers. Timed.

Mazes: A number of mazes presented in a booklet. Child must trace the way from the starting point to the goal within time limits.

Source: Adapted from Wechsler (1974).

Dollar, 1982). Although many of these tests do not tap the range of abilities assessed by the Binet or the WISC-R, they may at times be useful in the assessment of handicapped children who display impaired language skills.

An additional, recently developed measure of general intelligence that should be mentioned is the Kaufman Assessment Battery for Children (K-ABC). This measure, developed by Kaufman and Kaufman (1983), represents a combined intelligence and achievement measure, suitable for children 2½ to 12½ years of age. Like the WISC-R, this measure is composed of a range of subtests, each related to various abilities, which are combined to derive more general scores. Among these more general scores are a Mental Processing Composite Index (which provides a global estimate of intellectual functioning) and an Achievement Index (which assesses the child's knowledge of facts, language concepts, and various school-related skills such as arithmetic, reading, and vocabulary). Although relatively new, the developers of the measure have provided extensive data in support of its validity and reliability. As the measure provides both an index of intellectual functioning and achievement level, one might predict that the K-ABC will be well received by professionals in educational settings and those who work with children displaying academic related problems.

Intelligence, Social Class, and Bias

Controversy has surrounded the use of intelligence tests from their inception to the present (see Kamin, 1974). In the past some of this controversy has involved the overly political use of IQ tests, for example in congressional immigration hearings in which some immigrants were labeled mentally retarded because of their low scores on tests such as the Stanford-Binet. Other objections have been raised to the tests' possible cultural bias. This bias is indisputable and is traceable to the tests' original purpose — the prediction of school performance. Insofar as school performance is related to social and cultural factors, the tests will be similarly biased in order to be valid predictors (Anastasi, 1967). Despite findings that some instruments like the K-ABC may be less influenced by cultural factors than certain other intelligence tests (Kaufman & Kaufman, 1983), attempts to eliminate cultural bias in intelligence tests have not been totally successful. The influence of this bias should always be kept in mind.

Achievement Testing

Wide Range Achievement Test (WRAT)

The WRAT (Jastak & Jastak, 1978) has been widely used by psychologists, as it is quick to administer (as part of a larger test battery) and provides achievement scores in important school-related areas. It consists of three subjects (reading, spelling, and arithmetic) and is suitable for use with individuals ranging in age from 5 years to adulthood. Reading is assessed through letter recognition and pronouncing words, spelling through copying marks that look like letters, writing one's name and dictated words, and arithmetic through a timed test (10 minutes) that may involve counting, reading numbers, and solving oral and written problems. When scored the measure yields standard scores, percentile ranks, and grade ratings for each of the three areas. The WRAT is popular because it usually requires less than a half-hour to administer, and because it is assumed to provide adequate estimates of achievement level in the three areas assessed.

Despite the popularity of the WRAT, questions have been raised regarding its adequacy. These center around several issues, including a less than representative normative sample, the fact that the test may seriously underestimate achievement levels and that it provides an overly restrictive sampling of abilities in certain areas (Sattler, 1982). In considering these issues, it would appear that the test's use should be restricted to those instances where the clinician needs only the roughest of estimates regarding achievement level. Any recommendations or decisions regarding school placement, areas in need of remediation, and the like should be based on a more detailed assessment.

The Peabody Individual Achievement Test (PIAT)

The PIAT (Dunn & Markwardt, 1970) is an individually administered screening measure that requires anywhere from 30 to 45 minutes to give and that is appropriate for individuals ranging in age from 5 to 18 years. It provides measures of mathematics, reading recognition, reading comprehension, spelling, and general information, as well as an overall achievement index. When scored it yields grade and age equivalents as well as percentile ranks for each of the measures. Although the PIAT would appear to be more well standardized and generally to have more to recommend it as an achievement screening measure than the WRAT (Goldman et al., 1983), potential limitations include the fact that the test relies heavily on an answer-recognition format (having children indicate which of several answers is correct), thus providing little information concerning factors that may have actually contributed to a poor performance on a specific test. This would seem to be most problematic with the mathematics and spelling subtests, although one might note that the use of a recognition approach for assessing reading may also be a less than optimal way of assessing the child's actual ability to read material such as that dealt with in the school setting.

Miscellaneous Measures of Achievement

In addition to the measures just described, there are a range of other achievement tests that are also worth noting. Some are individually administered tests. Included here are the achievement scales of the Woodcock-Johnson Psycho-educational Battery (Woodcock & Johnson, 1977), which provide achievement measures in the areas of science, social science, humanities, and written language, in addition to the more frequently covered areas of reading and mathematics. It may also be recalled that the Kaufman Assessment Battery for Children (Kaufman & Kaufman, 1983) also includes measures of achievement (e.g., expressive vocabulary, arithmetic, reading/decoding, etc.) as part of the overall test battery. Other measures have been designed for group administration. Among these are the Stanford Achievement Tests (Madden, Gardner, Rudman, Karlsen, & Merwin, 1973) and the Metropolitan Achievement Tests (Psychological Corporation, 1978), both of which have been widely used in school settings.

It should be emphasized that in this section we have focused on screening tests, designed to assess the child's general level of performance in a number of areas. There are other tests that provide information concerning the child's performance in more restricted areas as well as diagnostic information related to those factors that may contribute to specific academic disabilities. Such tests may also provide useful information regarding possible remedial approaches. These, however, are more often used by educational specialists than by psychologists.

Personality Assessment: Projective Methods

Over the years a variety of assessment procedures have been developed that may be classified as projective techniques. These include the Rorschach test, the Thematic Apperception Test (TAT), the Draw-A-Person test (DAP), and sentence-completion tests of various types. All of these instruments are similar in certain respects. First, they use relatively unstructured materials as test stimuli. Second, the development of each of them has been based on what has been referred to as the projective hypothesis: that an individual presented with an unstructured stimulus attempts to impose his or her own structure, and in doing so reveals personality characteristics and the nature of his/her conflicts in the response (Sundberg, 1977). It is also normally assumed that projective techniques tap deeper levels of personality than do more structured personality tests. In fact, it was once assumed that these techniques could actually provide a sort of x-ray view of the personality. A more detailed discussion of the basic assumptions underlying the development of projective techniques has been presented in a now classic article by Frank (1939).

In the following sections we briefly discuss several popular projective techniques and illustrate how they are used clinically. Special attention will be given to the use of these techniques with children.

The Rorschach

The Rorschach is probably the most popular of the projective techniques (Lubin, Wallis, & Paine, 1971; Sundberg, 1977). It has been used clinically with both adults and children and has been the subject of numerous research studies.

The Rorschach test stimuli consist of 10 inkblots. Half of these are achromatic, whereas the other half include colors to a greater or lesser degree. An inkblot similar to those used in the Rorschach is presented in Figure 2.2.

Administration of the test involves presenting the 10 Rorschach cards, one at a time, re-

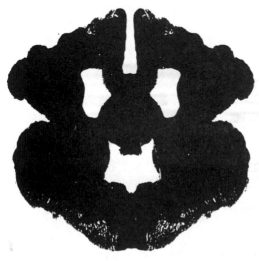

FIGURE 2.2. Inkblot similar to those of the Rorschach test.

questing that the individual say what he or she sees or what the inkblot looks like. The examiner records these responses verbatim, indicating the length of time before the first response and specific behaviors the person may engage in (turning the card, looking at the back of the card, etc.). Responses to each of the 10 cards are obtained in this way. This portion of the testing is known as the "free association" phase. In a second phase, referred to as the "inquiry," an attempt is made to determine where and why the person saw what was reported in free association. The person is again presented with the cards, one at a time, and his/her responses are read back. The testee is then asked where on the blot he or she saw the response (inquiry for location). The examiner then inquires about the determinant of the response (what made the person see what he or she saw): Was the response based on the shape or the outline of the blot (form), or did the response result from the specific color of the blot? In other cases, the response may have been influenced by the shading of the blot, and in still others perceived movement may have contributed to the response. This inquiry to assess the location and determinants of responses is conducted for each of the responses to each of the 10 cards.

After all this data is obtained, the Rorschach may be scored using any one of several scoring systems. The most widely used are those of Beck (Beck, Beck, Levitt, & Molish, 1961), Klopfer (Klopfer, Ainsworth, Klopfer, & Holt, 1954) and Exner (Exner, 1974, 1978; Exner & Weiner, 1982), although others have also been developed. Some of the more common scoring categories are presented in Table 2.7.

In addition to the scoring categories shown in Table 2.7, the Rorschach record may be scored for the number of popular responses (P), number of original responses (O), and for various types of content, for example human content (H), human detail (Hd), animal responses (A), anatomy responses (At), and sexual content (Sex). It might be noted that be-

TABLE 2.7. COMMON RORSCHACH SCORING CATEGORIES.

Category	Proposed Significance
R	Refers to the number of responses given to the ten inkblots, which may be quite variable. For example, obsessive individuals may give numerous responses, while severely depressed and withdrawn individuals may give relatively few.
W	The number of responses based on the entire blot, rather than a portion of it. This score is thought to be related to organizational ability, and has sometimes been associated with intelligence.
D	The person who has a high D score tends to base responses on only a portion of the blot. D refers to the use of larger details; in some scoring systems the symbol Dd may be used to refer to excessively small details. High D and Dd values are often associated with obsessive-compulsive features.
F	Reflects the percentage of responses based on the shape or form of the blot. F responses are scored to indicate whether they are good (F +) or poor (F −) form, reflecting the extent to which the percept actually fits with the shape of the part of the blot responded to. A large number of F − responses (responses that seem unrelated to the blot) have often been associated with "poor reality testing" and more serious psychopathology, while a number of F + responses is often thought to be related to "good ego strength."
C	Reflects the degree to which responses are determined by the color of the blot, and is thought to relate to the degree of emotional expressiveness displayed by the testee.
M	Refers to responses determined by perceived movement. High scores on this variable have been associated with introversion, tendencies toward internalization, degree of inner control, an active imagination, and fantasy activity.

cause scoring the Rorschach can be a very time-consuming task, formal scoring is often replaced by a more informal qualitative analysis of the test record, with an emphasis on content.

Along with the many publications concerning the use of the Rorschach with adults, several authors (Exner & Weiner, 1982; Francis-Williams, 1968; Halpern, 1960; Levitt & Truumaa, 1972) have focused on the use of the test with children and adolescents. As Halpern (1960) has noted, several factors must be taken into account when testing children. For example, with very young children it is necessary to give the inquiry about the responses immediately after they are given, rather than waiting until the free association phase is completed, because responses may be forgotten by the child if a delayed inquiry procedure is used. Halpern also pointed out that with children it is essential that developmental factors be taken into ac-

count, noting that the frequency of various responses may vary depending on the age of the child. For example, the percentage of good form responses (F + ; see Table 2.7) seems to vary with age. Although a poor form level in an older individual is often thought to reflect disturbance, a lower F + percentage in early childhood is to be expected. Additionally, the percentage of animal and human responses also changes with increasing age. A young child may give many animal responses and relatively few human responses; older children, however, typically give a higher percentage of human responses, and a high percentage of animal responses may be considered a sign of immaturity. Age norms for various types of Rorschach responses have been provided by Exner (1978) and Exner and Weiner (1982). The Exner and Weiner reference also provides the most comprehensive information available regarding the use of the Rorschach with children.

*The Thematic Apperception
Test (TAT)*

The TAT was first introduced by Morgan and Murray (1935) and has been since widely used with both adults and children. The TAT test stimuli consist of 30 cards. Twenty-nine of the cards depict various scenes, usually people engaging in various activities. One card is blank, providing the most unstructured stimulus possible. These cards are marked on the back to indicate their appropriateness for use with male and female children and adults. A sample TAT card appears in Figure 2.3.

Standard testing procedure calls for the administration of 20 cards. Many clinicians, however, give fewer than this number, often selecting only those they feel are likely to provide information especially useful in a given case. The person taking the test is asked to take the cards, one at a time, and make up a story about the scene depicted on the card, indicating what is happening in the scene, what the people are thinking or feeling, and what the outcome of the story will be. These stories are recorded verbatim.

Although several scoring systems for the TAT have been developed (Varble, 1971), they have mainly been used in research, and in actual clinical practice the test is seldom scored. When the test is used clinically, an attempt is usually made to determine whether there is consistency in the themes — dependence, aggression, guilt — reflected in the various stories. Clinicians also usually try to determine which of the figures on the card the storyteller-subject identifies with. This is usually the major character in the story, often referred to as the "hero" in the TAT literature. It is often assumed that statements concern-

FIGURE 2.3. Card 1 of the TAT. Source: Reprinted by permission of Henry A. Murray, Thematic Apperception Test, Cambridge, MA: Harvard University Press. © 1943 by the President and Fellows of Harvard College; renewed 1971 by Henry A. Murray.

ing this figure, his relationship to the environment, and his perceptions of the world are related to how the storyteller perceives himself and his environment. In an analysis of a TAT record, the clinician might ask questions such as: How adequate is the hero? Is he easily pushed around, or is he assertive? Is he successful or unsuccessful in what he attempts to do? How does he deal with and perceive authority figures and members of the opposite sex? Does he control his environment, or is he controlled by it? Does he see the environment as hostile and threatening or supportive? Additionally, the clinician will note the degree to which stories depart from the actual pictures on the cards and the extent to which stimulus elements not depicted on the cards are introduced into the stories.

In addition to the TAT, a similar test designed specifically for use with children has been developed. The Children's Apperception Test (CAT), which is based on the notion that children more readily identify with animals than human figures (Bellack, 1975), uses pictures of animals engaging in various activities as test stimuli. As with the TAT, the testee is requested to make up a story about the scene and to include information similar to that requested with the TAT. To date, the research on this measure has failed to provide support for the assumption that children more readily identify with animal figures (French, Graves, & Levitt, 1983) and provides little reason to select it over the TAT in testing children.

The Draw-A-Person Test

Administration of the Draw-A-Person (DAP) Test simply involves asking the testee to draw a picture of a person and then to draw another person of the opposite sex after the first drawing is completed. It is assumed that the testee projects into these drawings his or her own body image and reflects the nature of underlying conflicts, anxieties, and other personality characteristics.

This technique was first popularized by Machover (1949) in her monograph *Personality Projection in the Drawing of the Human Figure*, in which a variety of interpretive

hypotheses associated with specific drawing characteristics were presented. Other authors (Buck, 1948; McElhaney, 1969) have also suggested interpretive guidelines for analyzing figure drawings. Attention is often given to the sex of the first figure drawn, as this is thought to be indicative of the sex with which the person identifies. Placement on the page has also been considered to be of interpretive significance. Placement in the upper left corner of the page has been associated with anxiety, placement in the lower half of the page with depressive features. Another characteristic regarded as significant is size: Small drawings are associated with characteristics such as depression, withdrawal, anxiety, and poor self-concept, and large drawings with aggressiveness and feelings of grandiosity. Finally, it is often assumed that the specific content of the drawings is related to personality characteristics. In this regard, shading and erasures have both been considered to be conflict indicators, with their specific location indicative of the area of conflict. Excessively detailed drawings have been associated with obsessional characteristics, and strongly detailed eyes and ears have been associated with paranoid features. These examples are only a few of the numerous interpretive hypotheses that have been associated with characteristics of human figure drawings.

Although the Draw-A-Person Test was first employed with adults, it has also been widely used with children. Machover (1960) has considered in detail the developmental aspects of children's figure drawings, and Koppitz (1969) has published a book dealing exclusively with children's drawings that also focuses on developmental variables.

Miscellaneous Projective Techniques

In addition to the techniques already mentioned, many other projective tests have been developed. These include sentence completion tests (Forer, 1950; Holsopple & Miale, 1954; Rotter & Rafferty, 1950; Stein, 1947), the House-Tree-Person test (Buck, 1948), the Kinetic Family Drawing Test (Burns & Kaufman, 1970), as well as such procedures as the Rosenzweig Picture-Frustration Test (Rosenzweig, 1960), the Blacky Pictures Test (Blum, 1960) and the Tasks of Emotional Development (Cohen & Weil, 1971). The use of play (Murphy & Krall, 1960) and puppetry (Woltmann, 1960) as projective techniques has also been proposed. Additionally, the Bender Gestalt test, which has been most often used as a screening test for brain damage (see Chapter 5) has been employed by some in personality assessment (Hutt, 1977; Lerner, 1972).

Interpretation of Projective Techniques

In the preceding sections, projective techniques commonly used with children have been described with an emphasis on providing a general idea of how they might be interpreted when used clinically. It should be pointed out, however, that the interpretations suggested here serve only to illustrate how such hypotheses *might* be generated from projective test data and do not provide guidelines for test interpretation. Most clinicians would agree that the interpretation of projective tests is a complex matter involving the integration of data obtained from various sources, and that there is no one-to-one relationship between specific test "signs" and personality characteristics.

Validity of Projective Techniques

A review of the extensive research on the validity of projective techniques is beyond the scope of this chapter. However, there are several reviews of research related to the use of these measures with both adults (Klopfer & Taulbee, 1976) and children (French et al., 1983; Gittelman, 1980; Gittelman-Klein, 1978) that may be recommended.

Global statements concerning the validity of projective techniques with children are difficult to make and ignore many important issues (not the least of which is that many of the studies upon which conclusions might be based are less than adequate methodologically). Nevertheless, it can be stated that the research literature generally fails to support the validity of these techniques. Indeed, Gittelman (1980), after reviewing the literature on projective techniques with children, suggested that the current status of such tests can be summarized succinctly: "sometimes they tell us poorly something we already know" (p. 434). Despite these disappointing research findings, many who are involved in applied clinical work would argue that these tests provide useful information, at the level of the individual clinical case, and continue to use them in clinical assessment.

Personality Assessment: Nonprojective Methods

Not all personality measures are of the projective variety. Indeed, some employ very structured stimuli, requiring the person to respond to a range of items that tap specific characteristics or that discriminate between individuals who do and do not display various forms of psychopathology. Two examples of objective tests used with younger age groups are the Minnesota Multiphasic Personality Inventory and the Personality Inventory for Children.

The Minnesota Multiphasic Personality Inventory (MMPI)

The MMPI is perhaps the most well-known example of an objective personality measure (Palmer, 1983). Since its development by Hathaway and McKinley (1943) it has been widely used with both adults and adolescents. The measure itself consists of 566 true-false items. When scored, it yields values on three validity scales (designed to determine whether respondents have consciously distorted, misunderstood questions, or otherwise failed to give a valid test record) and a total of nine clinical scales (assessing the similarity of the testees' responses to those of various clinical groups), as well as a scale assessing social introversion-extraversion. A listing of the MMPI scales and a brief description is presented in Table 2.8.

When scored, the values derived from the scales are plotted on a profile sheet, as in Figure 2.4. Interpretation of the MMPI involves a consideration of the pattern of scores and the total profile, rather than of simply the elevation of individuals' scale scores. Guides to the interpretation of the MMPI have been published by Graham (1977), Marks, Seeman, and Haller (1974), and Duckworth (1979). Additional sources (Dahlstrom, Welsh, & Dahlstrom, 1972, 1975) also provide useful information on the general nature of the test, research related to the validity and reliability of the scale and its clinical use.

Although the MMPI has often been employed in the assessment of adolescents, it is generally not considered appropriate for use with individuals below the age of 13 or so (French et al., 1983) and only then if the person can read above the sixth-grade level (Ward & Ward, 1980). Adolescent norms provided by Marks et al. (1974) are useful when using the MMPI with these younger age groups.

The Personality Inventory for Children

With the exception of scales designed to measure specific personality characteristics, inventory measures have not been widely used with preadolescents, and even these measures have not been used with very young children. This is due to the fact that children at younger age levels usually do not display the reading

---

TABLE 2.8. SCALES OF THE MMPI.

VALIDITY SCALES

?	Total number of unanswered items.
L	(Lie) 15 items designed to detect tendency to be deliberately evasive in responding.
F	(Frequency or infrequency) 64 items seldom answered in the scored direction by normals (less than 10% of the time). High scores may suggest failure to understand items, atypical response set, or exaggeration of existing difficulties.
K	(Correction) 30 items designed to detect defensiveness in responding.

CLINICAL SCALES

Scale 1	(Hypochondriasis) 33 items reflecting abnormal concern with bodily functions.
Scale 2	(Depression) 60 items related to moodiness, apathy, pessimism, feelings of hopelessness, slowing of thought and action.
Scale 3	(Hysteria) 60 items assessing the tendency to use conversion reactions as a way of dealing with stress or solving conflicts.
Scale 4	(Psychopathic deviate) 50 items reflecting antisocial acting out, disregard for social customs, emotional shallowness, and an inability to learn from punishment.
Scale 5	(Masculinity-Feminity) 60 items related to masculine and feminine interests.
Scale 6	(Paranoia) 40 items related to abnormal suspiciousness, delusional beliefs, feelings of persecution.
Scale 7	(Psychasthenia) 48 items reflective of obsessions, compulsions, abnormal fears, guilt and indecisiveness.
Scale 8	(Schizophrenia) 78 items related to feelings of alienation, poor family relations, unusual perceptions, unusual thoughts and behavior.
Scale 9	(Hypomania) 46 items assessing increased activity level, elated mood, excitement, overactivity, and flight of ideas.
Scale 0	(Social introversion) 70 items related to shyness, lack of interest in people, and insecurity in social situations.

Source: Adapted from Dahlstrom, Welsh, & Dahlstrom (1972).

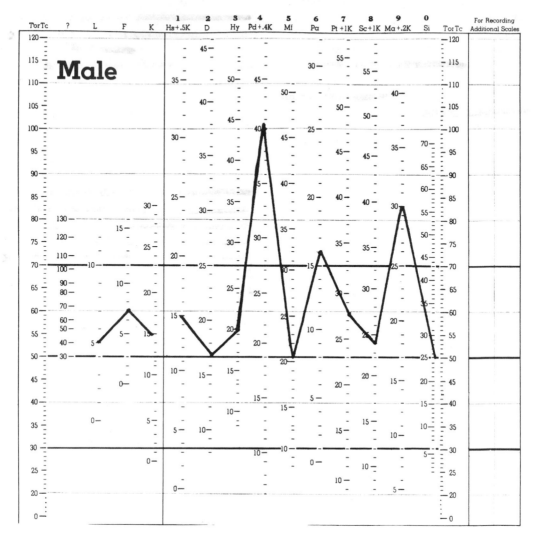

FIGURE 2.4. MMPI profile of a male subject suggestive of antisocial behavior. Source: Profile sheet © 1966 by the Psychological Corporation and reproduced by permission.

skills necessary to respond to such tests. As a result, there have been relatively few attempts to develop self-report inventories for younger age groups. One measure that has managed to circumvent this problem by employing the parent rather than the child as the respondent is the Personality Inventory for Children (PIC). This measure, developed by Wirt, Lachar, Klinedinst, and Seat (1977), is composed of 600 true-false items, descriptive of child and family characteristics, and can be used with children ages 3 through 16 (although the norms are better for children over

5). When completed, this measure can be scored to yield values on a variety of scales. Three of these are presented as validity scales and are designed to detect defensiveness on the part of the parent in responding to the measure. The PIC also yields values on 12 clinical scales that provide information concerning the nature of child psychopathology and personality characteristics. (For a clinical interpretive guide to the PIC, see Lachar & Gdowski, 1979.) A listing of the various PIC scales and a brief description of each is presented in Table 2.9. Also obtainable are scores on 17 supplemental scales. Included here are measures of variables such as asocial behavior, introversion-extraversion, aggression, somatization, reality distortion, and sex-role orientation, among others.

Whereas the PIC is a newer test than many of those already discussed, the scale has a long history, with its original development dating back to the late 1950s. The results of a number of validity and reliability studies appear to provide at least preliminary support for its use in child personality assessment (Lachar, Gdowski, & Snyder, 1984; Wirt et al., 1977). For a more detailed discussion of the PIC as well as a critique of its usefulness, see Wirt and Lachar (1981) and Achenbach (1981).

Miscellaneous Measures

Along with the MMPI and PIC, there are many other inventory-type measures that have been developed to assess specific personality characteristics. Examples include measures such as the Children's Depression Inventory (Kovacs, 1981), The Children's Manifest Anxiety Scale (Castenada, McCandless, & Palermo, 1956), the State-Trait Anxiety Inventory for Children (Spielberger, 1973), and the Nowicki and Strickland (1973) Locus of Control Scale for Children, among others. (For an overview of a number of these specific measures, see Goldman et al., 1983.)

One additional measure that adopts a parent-report format is the Parenting Stress Index (PSI), developed by Abidin (1983). Its inclusion in this section is somewhat arbitrary, because it is not strictly a child personality measure, but one that assesses child characteristics, along with parental and situational variables. It consists of 150 items (to be completed by the mother) that are designed to assess sources of strain on the parent-child relationship that can lead to dysfunctional behavior. The measure yields a Total Stress score as well as Child, Mother, and Situational/Demographic Domain scores.

TABLE 2.9. SCALES OF THE PIC.

Scale Name	Description
VALIDITY AND SCREENING SCALES	
Lie	Assesses tendency to deny child's behavior problems
F	Assesses deviant response sets (e.g., random responding)
Defensiveness	Assesses parent's defensiveness about child's behavior
Adjustment	Screening scale to identify general psychological maladjustment
CLINICAL SCALES	
Achievement	Identifies children who are underachievers despite adequate intelligence
Intellectual screening	Identifies children whose problems relate to impaired intellectual functioning
Development	Assesses below-average intellectual and physical development
Somatic concern	Assesses frequency of illness, physical complaints, and general somatic difficulties
Depression	Assesses various behaviors thought to be indicative of childhood depression
Family relations	Measures family effectiveness and cohesion
Delinquency	Assesses tendency toward delinquent behavior
Withdrawal	Assesses degree of withdrawal from social contact
Anxiety	Measures various manifestations of anxiety
Psychosis	Designed to detect children displaying psychotic symptoms
Hyperactivity	Designed to detect children considered to be "hyperkinetic"
Social skills	Assesses effectiveness in social relationships

Source: Adapted from Wirt, Lachar, Klinedinst, & Seat (1977).

Child Domain scores reflect the degree to which children display a range of characteristics that make them problematic for parents to deal with. These characteristics are reflected in a number of subscales: child adaptability, acceptability of the child to mother, child demandingness, child mood, distractibility/activity level, and mother reinforced by the child. Mother Domain scores reflect sources of strain on the parent-child system related to maternal functioning. Subscales included within this domain are maternal depression, maternal attachment, restrictions imposed by parental role, maternal sense of competence, social isolation, realistic attitudes toward children, relationship with husband, and maternal health. Scores in the Situational/Demographic domain reflect problematic socioeconomic circumstances and major life events that may be a source of stress. Because this measure not only assesses a range of child characteristics, but also other variables that may combine with these to result in significant parent-child difficulties, it would seem to be a useful addition to the literature. For a detailed discussion of the development, validity, and reliability of the PSI, see Abidin (1983).

Child Assessment: An Overview of Nonbehavioral Methods

As was noted in the preceding sections, child assessment involves obtaining information of various types from several sources, including the child, the child's parents, and possibly others, such as school personnel and the family physician. The types of information obtained may include both interview and test data. An attempt is made to integrate this data in such a way as to determine the nature, severity, and possible treatment approaches to the child's problem.

It must be stressed that the assessment of childhood disorders is a complex undertaking that demands an abundance of clinical skill and sophistication. Among other things, it requires a thorough knowledge of personality theory and child psychopathology, an awareness of what normal child development involves, and an ability to interpret data from any test instruments employed. Finally, successful assessment also requires a great deal in the way of integrative ability. Most clinicians would be quite uncomfortable making judgments about a child based on specific test responses or from specific tests used in isolation; likewise, interview data would seldom be considered apart from other types of information. Instead an attempt is made to integrate the data obtained from the interview, from various psychological tests, and from other sources in order to develop a comprehensive picture of the child and the nature of his or her difficulties.

BEHAVIORAL APPROACHES TO CHILD ASSESSMENT

Thus far we have focused on more traditional approaches to child assessment, but this is not to imply that assessment is less important from a behavioral point of view. Indeed, adequate assessment is considered an essential prerequisite for effective behavioral treatment. Behavioral approaches to assessment do, however, differ from more traditional methods in a variety of ways. Several dimensions along which these approaches differ are highlighted in Table 2.10.

Unlike those approaches that view test data simply as a *sign* of underlying personality characteristics, conflict, or traits, behavioral assessment methods involve fewer assumptions: Here the focus is on behavior itself. Data obtained in behavioral assessment is viewed as a *sample* of how the child is likely to respond in various situations in the natural environment (Goldfried & Kent, 1972). The focus of assessment is on determining the nature of the behaviors that have led the child to be considered deviant or maladaptive and the nature of those environmental factors that elicit and/or maintain these behaviors. Behavioral assessment is not limited to obtaining pretreatment data, as is often the case with

TABLE 2.10. COMPARISONS BETWEEN BEHAVIORAL AND TRADITIONAL APPROACHES TO ASSESSMENT.

	Behavioral	Traditional
I. Assumptions		
1. Conceptions of personality	Personality constructs mainly employed to summarize specific behavior patterns, if at all	Personality as a reflection of enduring underlying states or traits
2. Causes of behavior	Maintaining conditions sought in current environment	Intrapsychic or within the individual
II. Implications		
1. Role of behavior	Important as a sample of person's repertoire in specific situation	Behavior assumes importance only insofar as it indexes underlying causes
2. Role of history	Relatively unimportant, except, for example, to provide a retrospective baseline	Crucial in that present condition seen as a product of the past
3. Consistency of behavior	Behavior thought to be specific to the situation	Behavior expected to be consistent across time and settings
III. Uses of data	To describe target behaviors and maintaining conditions	To describe personality functioning and etiology
	To select the appropriate treatment	To diagnose or classify
	To evaluate and revise treatment	To make prognosis; to predict
IV. Other characteristics		
1. Level of inferences	Low	Medium to high
2. Comparisons	More emphasis on intraindividual or idiographic	More emphasis on interindividual or nomothetic
3. Methods of assessment	More emphasis on direct methods (e.g., observations of behavior in natural environment)	More emphasis on indirect methods (e.g., interviews and self-reports)
4. Timing of assessment	More ongoing (prior, during, and after treatment)	Pre- and perhaps post-treatment, or strictly to diagnose
5. Scope of assessment	Specific measures and of more variables (e.g., of target behaviors in various situations; of side effects, context, and strengths as well as deficiencies)	More global measures (e.g., of cure or of improvement) but only of the individual

Source: D. Hartmann, B. Roper, & D. Bradford (1979). © 1979 by Plenum Publishing Co. Reprinted with permission.

traditional approaches, but is continually employed throughout treatment to evaluate the effectiveness of treatment procedures.

A number of authors have noted that the basic information necessary for a behavioral analysis can be summarized by the acronym SORC. S refers to those stimuli that elicit maladaptive behavior or that may serve as discriminative stimuli for the occurrence of such behavior. These stimuli relate to those situations or events that are antecedents of problem behavior(s). O refers to those organismic variables that may influence behavior: physical handicaps, other biological variables, cognitions, and so on. R denotes the response characteristics of behaviors judged to be problematic. Here special attention is given to assessing the frequency, duration, and/or intensity of these behaviors, with behavior being broadly defined to include overt responses, cognitive-verbal behaviors, and psychophysiological responses. Finally, C refers to the consequences of the individual's behavior, those events both positive and negative that follow the behavior of interest and may increase or decrease its frequency (Kanfer & Saslow, 1969, 1976; Ollendick & Hersen, 1984).

Methods of Child Behavioral Assessment

Behavioral Interviewing

To obtain the information required in an SORC analysis, behaviorists employ a wide variety of procedures. Perhaps the most common procedure is an interview with the parents or some other informant. Although much of the information sought may be quite similar to that obtained in nonbehavioral interviews (e.g., physical and developmental history, current problems, family and peer relationships, etc.), the behavioral interview is characterized by its greater focus on specific aspects of child behavior and on environmental factors that may contribute to the child's problem. This greater degree of specificity is suggested by the brief interviewer guidelines presented in Table 2.11.

As Ullmann and Krasner (1975) have noted, the focus of the behavioral interview should be on "what" questions: *What* behaviors, occurring in *what* situations, with *what* consequences, cause a problem for the child? These types of questions are useful in pinpointing the specific nature of the problem behaviors displayed and in obtaining *preliminary* information regarding possible controlling variables. Here, as with other types of interviews, important information may be uncovered regarding parents' expectations and the degree to which they are motivated to obtain treatment for their child. For a more general dis-

cussion of the role of the interview in child behavioral assessment, see Gross (1984).

Parent-Report and Self-Report Measures

Although useful information regarding the nature of the child's behavior may be obtained in the interview, this is usually supplemented by information provided by the child and/or his parents. Several types of self- and parent-report measures are used to provide this additional data.

Behavior-problem checklists are often used to provide data that may serve as a starting point for the interview. These measures typically provide a listing of various child behaviors (e.g., "cries a lot," "has nightmares," "is overly active," "has trouble concentrating," "hits others," etc.) to which the parents respond by checking those behaviors displayed by their child and rating them as to their frequency or intensity. Examples of such measures include The Behavior Problem Checklist (Quay, 1977), the Child Behavior Checklist (Achenbach & Edelbrock, 1983), and the Eyberg Child Behavior Inventory (Eyberg & Ross, 1978; Robinson, Eyberg, & Ross, 1980). These measures may be quite useful, because they provide a quick and structured format for obtaining information regarding a wide range of problematic child behaviors. [For an overview of this approach see McMahon (1984).]

Behaviorists also frequently use child self-report measures designed to assess specific problem areas. Included here are measures such as the Children's Manifest Anxiety Scale (Castaneda et al., 1956), the State-Trait Anxiety Scale for Children (Spielberger, 1973), and the Children's Depression Inventory (Kovacs, 1981), which were discussed earlier. Another example of a widely used self-report measure is the Fear Survey Schedule for Children (Scherer & Nakamura, 1968). As its name suggests, this measure was developed to assess childhood fears. It consists of a listing of some 83 different stimuli capable of eliciting fear responses (e.g., "taking a test," "the sight of blood," "snakes," "high places," "look-

TABLE 2.11. POINTS TO CONSIDER IN INITIAL CARETAKER INTERVIEW.

The interview consists both of the culturally prescribed social behavior greeting (polite interaction, and farewell) and of questions aimed to detect and explore behavior problems. The interviewee must be made at ease and helped to feel comfortable when discussing problematic situations, and must be encouraged to provide all of the relevant information possible. The interviewer must convince the interviewee of his or her sympathetic interest in the welfare of both the child and the adult caretakers. Social skills are a necessity for an effective interviewer. The following description of interview components has been adapted, with permission, from Iwata, Wong, Riordan, Dorsey, and Lau (1982).

1. Clinician greets the client and chats briefly to make the client feel at ease. If necessary, the clinician should introduce herself and explain that she is a student, which program she is in, and what educational institution she attends.

2. Asks for needed biographical information regarding the child, such as age, grade in school, name of school, siblings, marital status of parents, etc.

3. Asks interviewee to describe the child's major behavioral problems, and inquires about other types of problems with academic work, social behavior at home and at school, relations with adults, relations with siblings, classmates, and other peers, health problems regarding sleep, eating, or elimination, speech problems, and any others volunteered by the interviewee.

4. Requests interviewee to rank the major problems in priority.

5. Asks interviewee to provide an example of the problem in behavioral terms.

6. Asks for additional specific instances and noninstances of the problem.

7. Summarizes interviewee's description as a particular, observable, and quantifiable behavior, and asks for feedback on accuracy of description.

8. Determines possible origins and frequency and concomitants of the target behavior. When and where did interviewee first notice the problem? What other events or responses appear to covary with the target behavior? What times, places, events, or persons are associated with occurrence of the problem?

9. Identifies current consequences. What happens after the behavior occurs or not, and who provides these consequences?

10. Asks for description of any prior attempts to deal with the problem. How successful were they?

11. Summarizes discussion of the problem, requests confirmation, and asks for additions, if any.

12. Asks interviewee to specify criteria for successful problem solution in order to determine the treatment goal.

13. Asks for description of child's strengths and skills, and for potential reinforcers. . . .

14. If feasible, conducts direct observation of child and interviewee interacting in order to help confirm target behavior and treatment goal selection.

15. Describes potential treatment program and solicits interviewee reactions and suggestions.

16. Describes referral possibilities in the community, if appropriate, and alternative sources of help for the child.

17. Schedules next appointment for review of treatment plan and possibly for further information from interviewee.

18. Thanks interviewee for her time, escorts her from the room, and bids her farewell.

Finally, a word of caution: Don't become too formal and mechanical in an effort to perform superprofessionally as an interviewer. Remember these suggestions by Holland (1970, p. 71): "(This) guide does not suggest the use of a mechanical gathering of information devoid of the rhythm and pace found in the counseling experience. The points covered in the guide are logical in nature and are not intended to place artificial constraints on the counselor or the (interviewee). Neither are they intended as substitutes for the more traditional skills of a sensitive ear or a judicious tongue."

Source: Gelfand and Hartmann (1984). ©1984 Pergamon Press and reprinted by permission.

ing foolish"), which the child rates according to the degree of fear each elicits. A final example of such a measure (which nicely illustrates how the format of a measure may be simplified for use with young children) is provided by the Children's Inventory of Anger (CIA), developed by Nelson and Finch (1978). In this measure the child is asked to respond to each of 71 items by rating the amount of anger experienced in response to each situation described by the item (see Figure 2.5). Responses are made on a 4-point scale (1 = "I don't care"; 4 = "I'm furious"), with each the points on the scale being illustrated by faces suggesting varying degrees of anger. Although more research is needed, it is noteworthy that

the CIA has been found to display high test-retest reliability (e.g., similar scores are obtained when children are tested over time), and scores derived from the measure are significantly related to external criteria such as peer-rated anger. See Finch and Rogers (1984) for a review of reliability and validity findings related to these and other self-report measures employed in child behavioral assessment.

Assessment Through Direct Observation

As data derived from parent-report and self-report measures are potentially subject to bias, behaviorally oriented clinicians have often

Sample CIA items.

1 2 3 4	(46)	Your sister breaks your favorite toy after you have asked her not to play with it.	
1 2 3 4	(47)	Your parents won't give you a "yes" or "no" answer but say "we'll see" when you want to plan on doing something.	
1 2 3 4	(48)	Your parents make you eat something you hate (e.g., spinach) in order to "clean your plate."	
1 2 3 4	(49)	You tell your mom that you don't have any homework but she makes you study anyway.	
1 2 3 4	(50)	The bus driver takes your name for acting up on the bus, but everybody else was acting up too.	
1 2 3 4	(51)	You have to go to bed at 9:30 even in the summertime, and your friends get to stay up until 10:30 or 11:00.	
1 2 3 4	(52)	Your mom says that you have to do your homework as soon as you get home before you can go out to play.	
1 2 3 4	(53)	You get lost at the shopping center, and, when you finally find your parents, your dad is mad and screams at you.	

FIGURE 2.5. Sample items from the Children's Inventory of Anger. Source: Finch & Rogers (1984). © 1984 by Pergamon Press and reproduced by permission.

favored the direct observation of child behavior. Observational measures have been of several types. Some have taken the form of comprehensive coding systems designed to assess a range of child behaviors in particular settings. Others have been developed to tap more restricted areas of behavior. Measures have also varied from those that assess behaviors in naturalistic situations (e.g., the home, school) to those that obtain behavioral data within the context of the clinical setting. Overviews of observational approaches and factors to consider in their use have been provided by LaGreca (1983) and Barton and Ascione (1984).

One example of more complex behavioral observation systems was developed by Wahler, House, and Stambaugh (1976). This system, which was designed to allow trained raters to make behavioral observations in the home or school, provides for the objective coding of a range of specific parent (or teacher) and child behaviors. Examples of categories considered within the system are aversive and nonaversive instructions (by parent or teacher), positive or aversive attention (by parent or teacher), and a range of child behaviors such as sustained attention, sustained play, compliance, opposition, eye contact, and social interaction. In each case the coding of behaviors is facilitated by providing raters with objective descriptions of the behaviors to be assessed. As a second example,

Freeman and her colleagues (Freeman, Ritvo, & Schroth, 1984) have developed a broad-based behavioral coding system specifically for use with autistic children (The Behavioral Observation System for Autism—BOS). In this system, trained raters observe autistic children in a playroom setting (through a one-way mirror) and rate them with regard to the occurrence of 67 behaviors. Examples include "body rocking," "covers ears," "hand flapping," "sniffs objects," "eye contact," "shows communicative speech," "ignores examiner," "shows echolalic speech," and "is mute." Each of the 67 behaviors are rated on a 4-point scale (0 = does not occur; 1 = occurs rarely but at least once; 2 = occurs moderately but not continuously; 3 = occurs continuously). Observations are made during nine 3-minute observation periods. In addition to these coding systems Patterson and his colleagues (see Patterson, Cobb, & Ray, 1973; Reid, 1978) have also developed a detailed observational system that has been widely used for assessing parent-child interactions within the home.

In addition to the broad-based coding systems, like the ones just described, other observational approaches have focused on specific classes of behavior. An example is the Preschool Observation Scale of Anxiety—POSA (Glennon & Weisz, 1978), which focuses specifically on overt behaviors reflective of anxiety (see Table 2.12). An additional example

---

TABLE 2.12. SAMPLE ITEMS FROM THE PRESCHOOL OBSERVATION SCALE OF ANXIETY.

1. Physical complaint: Child says he or she has a headache, stomachache, or has to go to the bathroom.
2. Expression of fear or worry: Child complains about being afraid of or worried about something; must use the word "afraid," "scared," "worried," or a synonym.
3. Cry: Tears should be visible.
4. Scream.
5. Nail-biting: Child actually bites his or her nails in the testing room.
6. Lip-licking: Tongue should be visible.
7. Trembling lip.
8. Rigid posture: Part of body is held unusually stiff or motionless for an entire 30-sec interval.
9. Avoidance of eye contact: Examiner should have clear trouble making eye contact with the child.
10. Fearful facial expression.

Source: Adapted from Glennon & Weisz (1978).

of this more restricted type of observational assessment is the Behavioral Avoidance Test (BAT), which is often used in the assessment of adult and child phobias (Lang & Lazovik, 1963). In the BAT, the child might be brought to a room that contains the feared stimulus (a dog, for example), which is some distance from the child (e.g., the other side of the room). The child may then be asked to engage in a number of behaviors that bring him or her into closer and closer proximity with this stimulus. The child might be asked, for example, to step closer and closer to the cage containing the dog. If the child gets as far as the cage, he or she might be asked to put a hand on top of the cage, open the cage, put a hand in the cage, pet the dog, let the dog out of the cage, and so on. Here the child would be observed to determine how close he or she actually comes to the dog and for observable signs of anxiety that might be associated with his or her approach to the animal.

It might be pointed out that whereas the observational procedures described here are quite applicable for use in applied clinical work, they have been most often used within the context of research studies. This may relate to the fact that observational measures often require special training in the use of behavioral codes and that they are not seen as cost-efficient for use with individual cases. This would seem to be especially true of the more broad-based measures that have been described. It would seem less true of measures such as the BAT and the POSA, which appear to be quite suitable for use with individual cases.

Finally, it should be noted that whereas observational methods usually rely on trained individuals to make observations, this is not always the case. In clinical practice, parents are often used as observers. Here the parent may be asked to record, in some objective and systematic manner, the frequency, duration and/or intensity of specific child behaviors, and perhaps the situation in which these behaviors occurred and the consequences of the behaviors. Although not as objective as data obtained from unbiased observers, par-

ents' observations of relevant child behaviors and the antecedents and consequences of these behaviors in the home environment can be a useful supplement to other assessment information. Having parents keep records of relevant child behaviors over the course of treatment may also be useful in those instances (and there are many) where practical reasons make it difficult to have trained raters make repeated observations in the home.

Assessing Treatment Outcome

As was noted earlier, behavioral assessment does not end with obtaining the information necessary for treatment planning, but continues throughout treatment. Behavior therapists, probably more than any other group of clinicians, have managed to effectively integrate clinical treatment with research. Thus, an attempt is made to assess the degree to which the child displays particular problem behaviors and to monitor behavior changes correlated with the introduction of treatment procedures. Single-subject experimental designs are used to demonstrate a functional relationship between treatment contingencies and behavioral change. Each case becomes a mini-experiment that systematically tests the effects of a specific treatment approach on a specific individual with a particular problem in a systematic manner.

Reversal Design
(ABAB design)

The reversal or ABAB design is probably the most frequently employed single-subject design. Initially it involves collecting baseline data on some target behavior (the behavior one is attempting to change) until a relatively stable baseline is obtained (A phase). In the second phase, (B), treatment contingencies (reinforcement, punishment, extinction, etc.) are applied. During this phase, data on the target behavior continue to be collected so that changes correlated with the introduction of the treatment variable can be assessed. It might be noted that observed change in this second phase provides no evidence that the change is due to treatment, as such changes might be due simply to the passage of time, other changes in the environment, or a whole host of extraneous variables. Additional manipulations are therefore necessary to establish a functional relationship between treatment contingencies and behavior change. The third phase of the reversal design (A2) is the first step in obtaining information about a functional relationship. In this phase treatment contingencies, introduced in phase B, are removed and conditions approximating those of the baseline period (A) are reinstated. Behavior continues to be monitored, and during this phase a return of the target behavior to the pretreatment or baseline level may be noted. Because in most cases the goal is not only to establish a meaningful relationship between the introduction of treatment and behavior change, but also to bring about a positive behavior change in the person being

treated, treatment contingencies are again introduced (B2 phase) to accomplish this result. An illustration of behavior change associated with the systematic introduction and removal of contingencies within a reversal design is presented in Figure 2.6.

If a systematic relationship between the application and removal of treatment procedures and behavior change can be demonstrated, it may be reasonably assumed that the observed change is due to the treatment procedures employed and not to other variables.

Multiple Baseline Design *Know*

There are instances where the use of the reversal design is either not possible or undesirable. For example, if a given treatment procedure with an autistic child resulted in a marked reduction or cessation of self-destructive behaviors, or if treatment reinstated eating in

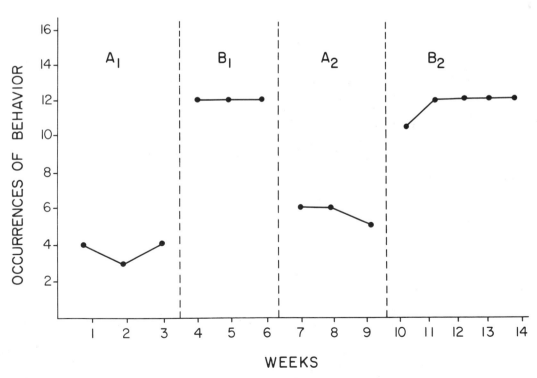

FIGURE 2.6. Hypothetical behavior change occurring within an ABAB (reversal) design: A_1 = baseline, B_1 = introduction of reinforcement contingent on hypothetical behavior, A_2 = return to baseline conditions, B_2 = reintroduction of reinforcement contingencies.

a patient whose life was threatened due to anorexia nervosa, one would certainly not want to reverse these effects. In other cases, when desirable change has been brought about in the school or in the home, teachers and parents are, understandably, often reluctant to allow a reversal of these effects. The multiple baseline design may be used effectively in such instances, where reversal is not possible, but systematic evaluation of the effects of treatment is still desired.

In the most widely used form of the multiple baseline design, measures are obtained on two or more behaviors that are thought to be relatively independent of one another. After stable baselines are obtained, treatment contingencies are applied to one of the behaviors. During this second phase, changes occurring in the treated as well as other nontreated behaviors are monitored. If behaviors have been well chosen (that is, if they are not controlled by the same contingency) and if treatment effects are due to the contingencies applied and not other variables, one might expect to find

that change occurs in the treated behavior but not in the untreated behavior(s). After change in the first (treated) behavior occurs, the therapist may then wish to systematically apply the treatment procedures to the additional behaviors on which baseline measures had been obtained to determine if changes in these behaviors occur immediately after the introduction of treatment procedures. Regarding the logic of this design, Baer, Wolf, and Risley (1968) comment that "the experimenter is attempting to show that he has a reliable experimental variable in that each behavior changes maximally only when the experimental variable is applied to it" (p. 94). Here the term *experimental variable* refers to the treatment designed to modify the specific behavior under consideration. An example of behavioral change associated with a multiple baseline design is presented in Figure 2.7.

It may be noted that whereas single-subject designs such as those described here are clearly associated with an operant approach to behavior modification, they are also ap-

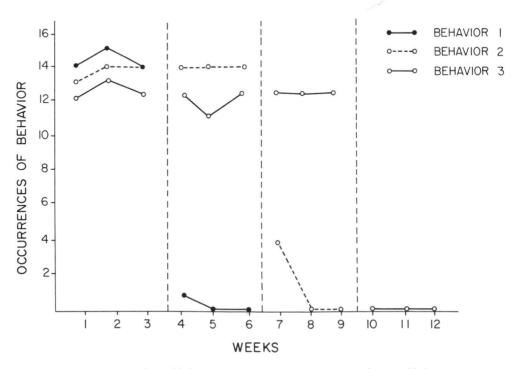

FIGURE 2.7. Hypothetical behavior change due to contingent punishment of behaviors occurring within a multiple baseline design.

propriate for evaluating other types of behavioral treatments as well. For more detailed discussion of these and other single-subject designs, see Barlow and Hersen (1984) and Kazdin (1982b, 1983).

CLASSIFICATION OF CHILD PSYCHOPATHOLOGY

In 1883 Emil Kraepelin, a German psychiatrist, published an influential psychiatry text in which he presented what was probably the first classification system of mental disorders. Since that time much attention has been focused on the classification of psychological problems, and a variety of alternative systems have been proposed. This interest in classification has been based, in part, on the notion that specific syndromes or disorders exist and can be defined in terms of a particular cluster of symptoms. Additionally, it has been assumed by many that classification of some sort is necessary, as it is only after proper diagnosis that one can select an appropriate course of treatment. In the sections to follow we will consider current approaches to classification, with an emphasis on childhood disorders, as well as their limitations and the pros and cons of classification in general.

The American Psychiatric Association Classification System: DSM-III

The most widely accepted diagnostic nomenclature is embodied in the most recent edition of the American Psychiatric Associations's *Diagnostic and Statistical Manual of Mental Disorders* — DSM-III (American Psychiatric Association, 1980). An outline of this classification scheme is presented in Table 2.13, with emphasis on childhood disorders.

DSM-III would seem to have a number of advantages over earlier versions of this scheme. First, DSM-III contains more than four times as many categories specific for use with children and adolescents than did DSM-II (American Psychiatric Association,

1968). It is thus a much more comprehensive system for classifying childhood disorders. A second notable feature is that it provides more objective diagnostic criteria for making diagnostic judgments. The greater degree of specificity can be illustrated by comparing DSM-II and DSM-III with regard to guidelines for diagnosing one condition: Overanxious Reaction of Childhood. According to DSM-II, "This disorder is characterized by chronic anxiety, excessive and unrealistic fears, sleeplessness, nightmares and exaggerated, autonomic responses. The patient tends to be immature, self-conscious, grossly lacking in self confidence, conforming, inhibited, dutiful, approval seeking and apprehensive in new situations and unfamiliar surroundings" (APA, 1968, p. 48).

As can be seen, no guidelines are given concerning how many of the above characteristics must be present or the degree to which they must be manifest for this diagnosis to be considered appropriate. In contrast, the diagnostic criteria for this same disorder are presented in DSM-III as follows:

A. The predominant disturbance is generalized and persistent anxiety or worry (not related to concern about separation), as manifest by at least four of the following:
   1. Unrealistic worry about future events.
   2. Preoccupation with the appropriateness of the individual's behavior in the past.
   3. Overconcern about competence in a variety of areas (e.g., academic, athletic, social).
   4. Excessive need for reassurance about a variety of worries.
   5. Somatic complaints, such as headaches or stomachaches, for which no physical basis can be established.
   6. Marked self-consciousness or susceptibility to embarrassment or humiliation.
   7. Marked feelings of tension or inability to relax.
B. The symptoms in A have persisted for at least 6 months.
C. If 18 or older does not meet the criteria for Generalized Anxiety Disorder.
D. The disturbance is not due to another

TABLE 2.13. OUTLINE OF DSM-III CLASSIFICATION SYSTEM
WITH EMPHASIS ON CHILD AND ADOLESCENT DISORDERS.

I. *Disorders usually arising in childhood or adolescence*

   A. *Mental retardation*
      Mild
      Moderate
      Severe
      Profound

   B. *Attention deficit disorder*
      With hyperactivity
      Without hyperactivity
      Residual type

   C. *Conduct disorder*
      Undersocialized, aggressive
      Undersocialized, nonaggressive
      Socialized, aggressive
      Socialized, nonaggressive
      Atypical

   D. *Anxiety disorders of childood or adolescence*
      Separation anxiety disorder
      Avoidant disorder of childhood or adolescence
      Overanxious disorder

   E. *Other disorders of infancy, childhood, or adolescence*
      Reactive attachment disorder of infancy
      Schizoid disorder of childhood or adolescence
      Elective mutism
      Oppositional disorder
      Identity disorder

   F. *Eating disorder*
      Anorexia nervosa
      Bulimia
      Pica
      Rumination disorder of infancy
      Atypical eating disorder

   G. *Stereotyped movement disorders*
      Transient tic disorder
      Chronic motor tic disorder
      Tourette's syndrome
      Atypical tic disorder
      Atypical stereotyped movement disorder

   H. *Other disorders with physical manifestations*
      Stuttering
      Functional enuresis
      Functional encopresis
      Sleepwalking
      Sleep terror

   I. *Pervasive developmental disorders*
      Infantile autism
      Childhood onset pervasive developmental disorder
      Atypical pervasive developmental disorder

   J. *Specific developmental disorders (Axis II)*
      Developmental reading disorder

(continued)

mental disorder such as Separation Anxiety Disorder, Avoidant Disorder of Childhood or Adolescence, Phobic Disorder, Obsessive-Compulsive Disorder, Depressive Disorder, Schizophrenia, or a Pervasive Developmental Disorder (APA, 1980, pp. 56–57, with permission).

In addition to DSM-III's greater objectivity, it also relies much less on psychoanalytic assumptions and terminology than did earlier versions. This tendency toward increased objectivity and a greater focus on behavior was intended to enhance the reliability of the system and make it more palatable to individuals of diverse theoretical orientations.

An additional advantage of the DSM-III scheme involves its use of a multiaxial classification system. This provides for the classification of persons along several independent dimensions. To illustrate, the individual is first classified in terms of the major psychiatric syndrome displayed (see Table 2.13). Next it is determined whether there is any accompanying personality disorder (in the case of adults) or developmental disorder (in the case of children). Third, the presence of any physical disorder that might be of significance is noted. Fourth, the individual is classified with regard to the degree of psychosocial stress experienced during the previous year. Finally,

TABLE 2.13. *(continued)*

Developmental arithmetic disorder
Developmental language disorder
Developmental articulation disorder
Mixed specific developmental disorder
Atypical specific developmental disorder

II. *Organic mental disorders*
(e.g., senile and presenile dementias, substance-induced organic disorder, other organic brain syndrome)

III. *Substance use disorders*
(e.g., alcohol abuse, barbiturate abuse, other substance abuse)

IV. *Schizophrenic disorders*
(e.g., disorganized, catatonic, paranoid, undifferentiated, residual)

V. *Paranoid disorders*

VI. *Psychotic disorders not elsewhere classified*
(e.g., schizophreniform disorder, brief reactive psychosis)

VII. *Affective disorders*
(e.g., manic disorders, depressive disorders, mixed cyclothymic disorder)

VIII. *Anxiety disorders*
(e.g., phobic disorders, obsessive compulsive disorder, generalized anxiety disorder)

IX. *Somatoform disorders*
(e.g., conversion disorder, psychogenic pain disorder)

X. *Dissociative disorders*
(e.g., psychogenic amnesia, multiple personality)

XI. *Psychosexual disorders*
(e.g., transsexualism, gender identity disorder of childhood, sexual sadism, psychosexual dysfunction)

XII. *Factitious disorders*
(e.g., factitious illness with physical or psychological symptoms)

XIII. *Disorders of impulse control not elsewhere classified*
(e.g., pathological gambling, kleptomania)

XIV. *Adjustment disorder*
(e.g., adjustment disorder with depressed mood, with anxious mood, with mixed emotional features)

XV. *Psychological factors affecting physical condition*

XVI. *Personality disorders (Axis II)*
(e.g., dependent, passive-aggressive disorder)

XVII. *Conditions not attributable to mental disorders*

Source: Adapted from American Psychiatric Association (1980). © 1980 American Psychiatric Association. Reprinted by permission of the publisher.
*The section on childhood disorders (Section I) lists conditions usually manifest in childhood or adolescence. According to this scheme, any appropriate adult diagnosis (Sections II–XVII) can also be used with children.

the person is categorized in terms of the highest level of adaptive functioning displayed during the previous year. (Classification on Axes I through III make up the official diagnosis, Axes IV and V are reserved for use in specific clinical and research settings.) A summary of this multiaxial system is presented in Table 2.14.

The potential advantage of this multiaxial approach to classification is that it provides for the diagnosis of conditions other than those reflected in the individual's presenting problem and ensures that he or she will be assessed along a variety of dimensions.

Given the greater degree of objectivity, the increased number of diagnostic categories relevant to children and adolescents, and its multiaxial approach to classification, DSM-III would seem to be a significant improvement over its predecessors. The advantages of this system have been considered in detail by Cantwell (1985), Spitzer, Williams, and Sko-

TABLE 2.14. SUMMARY OF DSM-III MULTIAXIAL CLASSIFICATION SYSTEM.

Axis Dimension Considered	Specific Classification Procedure
I Psychiatric syndrome displayed	Listing of psychiatric diagnosis as presented in classification system
II Personality disorder (adult) Developmental disorder (children – adolescents)	Listing of any personality or specific developmental disorder displayed in addition to primary psychiatric diagnosis
III Physical disorders	Listing of any current physical disorder which may be of etiological significance or may be significant in the overall management of the individual
IV Psychosocial stressors	Severity of psychosocial stressors, rated from none to catastrophic
V Level of adaptive functioning	Rating of the individual's highest level of adaptive functioning during the past year, considering specifically areas of social relations, occupational functioning, and use of leisure time. Rating of adaptive functioning on scale ranging from 1 = superior to 7 = grossly impaired.

Source: Adapted from American Psychiatric Association (1980). ©1980 by the American Psychiatric Association. Reprinted by permission of the publisher.

dol (1980), and Rutter and Shaffer (1980). But it must be emphasized that the actual value of DSM-III can only be determined by research into its reliability and validity. Although research findings will be considered in later sections, it may be noted here that initial studies with children have generally failed to document the degree of reliability that might be expected given the emphasis on objective diagnostic criteria (Mattison, Cantwell, Russell, & Will, 1979; Werry, Methven, Fitzpatrick, & Dixon, 1983). Questions have also been raised regarding the validity of the various diagnostic categories included within the system.

Despite the positive aspects of DSM-III, it has been criticized on several counts. One criticism has to do with basic assumptions upon which the system is based. DSM-III is derived from a traditional medical model of psychopathology and the assumption that there are, in fact, a variety of mental disorders that can be defined in terms of a specific constellation of symptoms and that reflect underlying psychopathology of some sort. This assumption is not likely to be shared by many behaviorally oriented clinicians, who tend to focus on the assessment of specific patterns of maladaptive behavior and their environmental correlates, rather than on underlying disorders or clinical syndromes such as those referred to in DSM-III (see Harris & Powers, 1984). A second issue of concern for many clinicians has to do with the range of difficulties included within DSM-III under the heading of mental disorders, which are implicitly considered to be a subset of medical disorders (Garmezy, 1978; Nathan, 1979; Schacht & Nathan, 1977). For example, conditions such as reading disabilities, arithmetical disabilities, and articulation problems are all considered as diagnostic categories. As Harris (1979) has noted, the issue is not whether such conditions pose problems for the children who display them and their parents, but whether such conditions can be legitimately considered as mental disorders. Of concern here is the possible effect that defining such problems as mental disorders may have for children who are so diagnosed. The issue is an important one, for there is evidence that in some cases being labeled "ill" or "disordered" may have an undesirable effect on how others react to an individual and perhaps on his or her self-concept. If a child is labeled as having a diagnosable disorder because of reading, arithmetic, or articulation problems, might this not be potentially damaging and lead to additional difficulties — as a result of the labeling itself? It would be argued by many that there is no empirical basis for considering problems such as these mental disorders and that to do so is a serious disservice to children who show evidence of such problems.

The GAP Classification System

A second major classification system has been developed by the Group for the Advancement of Psychiatry (1966) specifically for use with children and adolescents. The GAP nomenclature covers a broad range of childhood problems, including neurotic, personality, psychotic, and psychophysiological disorders and developmental deviations, among others. Provision is also made for the separate diagnosis of several forms of child psychosis: autism, interactional psychotic disorder (symbiotic psychosis), schizophreniform psychotic disorders (childhood schizophrenia), and psychoses of adolescence. A unique feature of the GAP system is the inclusion of a Healthy Response category, which serves to "emphasize the need for the assessment of positive strengths in the child whenever possible and to avoid so far as possible the diagnosis of healthy states by the exclusion of pathology" (GAP, 1966, pp. 219–220). Under this heading would be considered behaviors that are related to specific developmental stages or that represent normal responses to situational stress in the absence of psychopathology.

The limitations of the GAP system are similar to those that have plagued earlier versions of the DSM system, in particular a reliance on subjective psychoanalytic terminology in the description of child disorders. It is likely that the subjectivity of these descriptions contributes significantly to diagnostic unreliability of this system.

Although the DSM and GAP classification systems are the two that have received the most attention in the clinical literature, a variety of others have been proposed. Space limitations preclude a discussion of these other systems, but it is noteworthy that a total of 23 different schemes have been outlined by the Group for the Advancement of Psychiatry (GAP, 1966). Most of these have not been widely used with children, however.

Multivariate Approaches to Classification

Most traditional approaches to classification have been based on clinical observation and assume the existence of various types of disorders, each defined in terms of a particular constellation of symptoms. However, it is possible to take a more empirical approach to assessing patterns of maladaptive behavior. To do so, a multivariate statistical approach may be employed.

Multivariate approaches to classification have most often involved the use of factor analytic procedures. These initially involve obtaining some index of the behavioral characteristics of a large number of subjects. For example, a behavior problem checklist might be used to determine, for each individual, which of a large number of behaviors are or are not displayed. Through a factor analysis of this data for a large sample of individuals it is possible to determine the correlations between the occurrence or nonoccurrence of each behavior and every other behavior. One can, then, through appropriate statistical techniques, determine clusters of behavioral characteristics that are highly intercorrelated and seem to be commonly found together. Assuming an adequate sampling of behavioral characteristics and an adequate sample, this approach is assumed to allow the determination of major patterns of childhood behavior.

In reviewing some 55 factor analytic studies of this type, Quay (1984) found a total of seven behavioral dimensions that have been replicated in as many as 10 separate studies. A listing of these "syndromes" and several characteristics associated with each is presented in Table 2.15. It may be noted that these factors, for the most part, can be grouped under the broader general heading of *Internaliz-*

TABLE 2.15. EMPIRICALLY DERIVED DIMENSIONS OF BEHAVIOR
REPLICATED IN MORE THAN TEN STUDIES

Behavioral Dimension	Associated Characteristics
CONDUCT DISORDER	Disobedient, defiant Fighting, hitting Destructiveness Uncooperative, resistant
SOCIALIZED AGGRESSION	Has "bad" companions Truant from school Loyal to delinquent friends Steals in the company of others
MOTOR OVERACTIVITY	Restless, overactive Overtalkative Excitable, impulsive Squirmy, jittery
ATTENTION PROBLEMS	Poor concentration, short attention span Daydreaming Preoccupied, stares into space Impulsive
ANXIOUS-DEPRESSED WITHDRAWAL	Anxious, fearful, tense Shy, timid, bashful Depressed, sad, disturbed Feels inferior, worthless
SOMATIC COMPLAINTS	Stomachaches Vomiting, nausea Headaches Elimination problems
PSYCHOTIC DISORDER	Bizarre, odd, peculiar Incoherent speech Visual hallucinations Strange ideas and behavior

Source: Adapted from Quay (1984) and reprinted by permission of the author.

ing-Externalizing syndromes, which serves to distinguish between fearful, inhibited, and overcontrolled (internalizing) and aggressive, antisocial, and undercontrolled (externalizing) disorders. For a more detailed discussion of the internalizing-externalizing dimensions as they relate to empirical approaches to classification, see Achenbach (1966) and Achenbach and Edelbrock (1983).

These findings would seem to have implications for the validity of existing classification systems such as DSM-III. Quay (1984) has noted, for example, that while there is some correspondence between these empirically derived syndromes and certain DSM-III diagnostic categories (see Table 2.16), most categories have no empirically derived counterpart (also see Achenbach, 1980).

Although the failure to find empirically derived matches for many DSM-III child/adolescent categories raises legitimate questions regarding the validity of the DSM-III system, it is important to note that multivariate studies have not systematically assessed the entire range of DSM-III criteria (as these have only recently been developed), and many have not sampled children who could be reasonably expected to display the range of pathology reflected in the system. It is likely that the most adequate tests of validity will come from empirical studies that assess the full range of behaviors reflected in DSM-III criteria while also employing a broad sample of clinic cases that display diverse manifestations of child psychopathology.

Reliability of Diagnostic Judgments

A fundamental question regarding existing classification systems is the reliability of diagnostic judgments based on them. That is, can two or more clinicians, using a given system, arrive at a similar diagnosis after independently assessing the same individual? In years past a number of studies have been conducted to answer this question. Most of them have involved the use of either DMS-I or DSM-II with adults (Beck, Ward, Mendelson, Molk, & Erbaugh, 1962; Sandifer, Pettus, & Quade,

1964; Schmidt & Fonda, 1965), although at least one study was done with children, using the GAP system (Freeman, 1971). The results of these studies suggested that reliable judgments could be made only if broad diagnostic groupings were considered (organic, psychotic, neurotic). Judges were often found to disagree about more specific diagnoses. These findings provided little support for the value of these classification systems.

In view of the negative results found with the GAP and earlier DSM systems, there has been considerable interest in determining whether a greater degree of reliability will be found with DSM-III. Indeed, this would be expected given the increased focus on behavior and more objective diagnostic guidelines that are provided. Several studies have provided information regarding the reliabil-

TABLE 2.16. EMPIRICALLY DERIVED COUNTERPARTS TO DSM-III CHILD
AND ADOLESCENT CATEGORIES.

DSM-III Category	Empirically Derived Dimension
ATTENTION DEFICIT DISORDER	
With Hyperactivity	ATTENTION PROBLEMS WITH MOTOR EXCESS
Without Hyperactivity	ATTENTION PROBLEMS WITHOUT MOTOR EXCESS
CONDUCT DISORDER	
Undersocialized, Aggressive	CONDUCT DISORDER
Undersocialized, Nonaggressive	
Socialized, Aggressive	SOCIALIZED AGGRESSION
Socialized, Nonaggressive	
ANXIETY DISORDERS	
Separation Anxiety Disorder	
Avoidant Disorder	
Overanxious Disorder	ANXIOUS-DEPRESSED WITHDRAWAL
OTHER DISORDERS	
Reactive Attachment Disorder	
of Infancy	
Schizoid Disorder	
Elective Mutism	
Oppositional Disorder	
Identity Disorder	
PERVASIVE DEVELOPMENTAL DISORDER	
Infantile Autism	PSYCHOTIC DISORDER
Childhood Onset Pervasive	
Developmental Disorder	PSYCHOTIC DISORDER

Note: Only those empirically derived factors that have been replicated in at least ten studies are listed. Quay has noted two additional "weakly replicated" dimensions, "Social Ineptness" and "Schizoid-Unresponsiveness," which relate to the DSM-III categories of Avoidant Disorder and Schizoid Disorder, respectively.
Source: Adapted from Quay (1984) and reprinted by permission of the author.

ity of the DSM-III child and adolescent categories.

Cantwell and his colleagues (Cantwell, Mattison, Russell, & Will, 1979; Mattison et al., 1979) have conducted a series of studies to compare DSM-II and DSM-III with regard to diagnostic judgments with children. In these studies diagnostic judgments were based on information provided in written case history material on a number of child clinic cases. These studies suggest that diagnostic judgments of children using the two systems are equally reliable. For example, in the Mattison et al. (1979) study, the average interjudge agreement was 57% for DSM-II and 54% for Axis I (clinical psychiatric syndrome) of DSM-III. Reliability figures related to other axes of the DSM Multiaxial system seem to support this general approach. Overall interjudge agreement on Axis II (developmental disorder) was 78%, and agreement on Axis III (nonmental medical disorder) was 90%. Agreement on Axis IV (severity of psychosocial stressors) was 63%. Finally, clinicians agreed on their ratings of degree of impairment in adaptive functioning (Axis V) 64% of the time.

More recently, Werry et al. (1983) have assessed reliability in a more naturalistic setting. Here clinicians were asked to make diagnostic judgments on a total of 195 children admitted to a large child psychiatry inpatient unit. Independent diagnoses of each case were made based on detailed information presented at a case conference held within a week after the child's admission. Kappa coefficients (which indicate the percentage of agreement among judges when corrected for chance) were used to indicate level of agreement for major diagnostic categories (e.g., Anxiety Disorders of Childhood and Adolescence) and subcategories (e.g., Separation Anxiety Disorder). Reliability findings for the various DSM-III child/adolescent and adult categories (which were used with these children) are presented in Table 2.17.

Assuming a Kappa coefficient of .70 to reflect an acceptable level of reliability (Spitzer, Forman, & Nee, 1979), these figures seem

TABLE 2.17. RELIABILITY OF DSM-III DIAGNOSTIC CATEGORIES WITH CHILDREN AND ADOLESCENTS.

Diagnostic Category	Degree of Agreement (Kappa)
I. Child/Adolescent Categories:	
Mental Retardation	.62
Mild	.62
Attention Deficit Disorder (ADD)	.76
ADD With Hyperactivity	.73
ADD Without Hyperactivity	.05
Conduct Disorder	.53
Undersocialized, Aggressive	.57
Undersocialized, Nonaggressive	.18
Socialized, Aggressive	−.04
Socialized, Nonaggressive	.32
Unspecified Subtype	.40
Anxiety Disorder of Childhood and Adolescence	.67
Separation Anxiety Disorder	.72
Avoidant Disorder	.05
Overanxious Disorder	.65
Other Disorders of Childhood and Adolescence	.39
Schizoid Disorder	.37
Oppositional Disorder	.39
Identity Disorder	.28
Eating Disorder	.91
Anorexia Nervosa	1.00
Other Disorders with Physical Manifestations	.91
Enuresis	.96
Encopresis	.91
II. Adult Categories:	
Organic Mental Disorders	.89
Delirium	1.00
Substance Abuse Disorder	1.00
Other, Mixed, Unspecified	.62
Other Specified	.02
Schizophrenic Disorders	.70
Paranoid type	.16
Undifferentiated	.35
Psychotic Disorders (not elsewhere classified)	.47
Schizophreniform	.19
Atypical Psychosis	.05
Anxiety Disorders (Adult)	.91
Simple Phobia	.27
Obsessive Compulsive	.94
Atypical	.27

TABLE 2.17. (continued)

Diagnostic Category	Degree of Agreement (Kappa)
Factitious Disorders	.05
With Psychological Symptoms	.05
Somatoform Disorder	.49
Somatization	.11
Conversion Reaction	.37
Psychogenic Pain	.50
Adjustment Disorder	.23
With Depressed Mood	.67
With Anxious Mood	− .04
With Mixed Emotional Features	.06
With Disturbances of Conduct	.05
With Mixed Disturbance of Emotions and Conduct	.20
III. Other Codes	
Malingering	− .10
Parent Child Problem	.22
Unspecified Disorder	.28
No Axis I Diagnosis	.41

Note. Several DSM-III diagnostic categories are not listed, since the frequency of occurrence of these diagnoses was too low to compute reliability. Source: Adapted from Werry, Methven, Fitzpatrick, & Dixon (1983).

to suggest adequate levels of reliability for a number of the major diagnostic categories, but that the reliability for most subcategories is unacceptably low. In considering these findings, Werry et al. (1983) suggest

> while the major categories appear robust and could well be tidied up with a little effort, our results suggest that the subcategories have serious problems. . . . If other studies can confirm our results, a great deal of work will need to be done in the area of diagnostic criteria themselves and/or in the data-collection process in child psychiatry to justify the continued existence of subcategories. (p. 353)

Taken together, these findings along with others (American Psychiatric Association, 1980), suggest that moderate to high levels of agreement can be obtained between cli-

nicians using Axes II through V of the multiaxial system, thus providing some evidence for the usefulness of the multiaxial approach. Findings with regard to Axis I judgments are somewhat more disappointing, especially when the reliability of DSM-III subcategories is considered. Although more research is needed, the available findings provide reason to question the reliability of many of the DSM-III diagnostic categories.

On the Problem of Classification

In addition to those who have become dissatisfied with existing classification systems because of their inadequacies, there are other clinicians who argue against the idea of classification and labeling in general. (For an overview of issues related to the classification of children, see Hobbs, 1975.) These arguments take several forms. Some clinicians contend that classification typically results in a *loss* of information about the individual, because classification of any sort involves considering only a small portion of the individual's actual behavior, and characteristics not considered relevant to the classification system may be overlooked. The DSM-III classification system's multiaxial approach is to some extent a response to this criticism. With this approach, individuals are not only assessed in terms of their major psychological disorder, but information is obtained about other personality or developmental problems as well as physical and social variables. Even in more complex systems such as DSM-III, however, much information is lost in the process of classification. The important issue is whether this lost information is relevant to the decisions that are to be made concerning the patient.

A second significant criticism of classification is that placing individuals in specific diagnostic categories gives the impression that they are qualitatively different from so-called normals. Many clinicians who believe that some degree of continuity exists between normal and abnormal behavior would argue that categorization gives the false impression of discontinuity (Davison & Neal, 1974).

A third criticism is that the application of a diagnostic label may have an effect on the way others react to the person so labeled. As Ullmann and Krasner (1975) have pointed out, the very fact that a person is given a diagnosis may influence the behavior of the labeler and therefore the type of treatment and progress of the person who has been labeled: A diagnosis may become a self-fulfilling prophecy. Additionally, several studies (Langer & Abelson, 1974; Temerlin, 1968) strongly suggest that the application of labels has a significant effect on the way other individuals respond to the person who has been labeled. The potentially deleterious effect of labeling is strikingly illustrated in the remarks of a former mental patient:

> I had little idea of how dehumanizing and humiliating the hospital would be for me. My parents were told by the attending physician upon my leaving the hospital that my diagnosis was schizophrenia. My label seemed to be the focal point of their debasing behavior. After that, I had partly lost my right to stand among humanity as human — and that for some people I would be forever-more something of a subhuman creature. (Anonymous, 1977, p. 4)

Statements such as this, along with research findings, show that the act of diagnosis and labeling is not an inconsequential one.

Finally, there are behaviorally oriented clinicians who claim that classification is unnecessary and largely unrelated to treatment in many instances. It is argued, for example, that it makes little difference to the choice of treatment whether a child is diagnosed as autistic or schizophrenic, because the basic task is to determine the specific nature of the child's behavioral excesses or deficits and find ways to remedy them. On the other hand, in support of classification it might be argued that if autism and schizophrenia are in fact separate conditions, research related to their etiology cannot progress unless separate groupings of children with these diagnoses are made; aside from treatment, classification may be important in defining relevant populations for purposes of research.

In general, although some categorization of behavior is inevitable and may be of value for purposes of research and communicating with other professionals, the labeling of individuals may have undesirable effects that should be given serious consideration in clinical practice.

SUMMARY

We have considered several approaches to the assessment of child psychopathology. It was noted that traditional approaches to child assessment typically involve both parent and child interviews and the giving of various psychological tests. Both open-ended and more structured interviews have been employed. Although each has advantages, there is evidence that a somewhat structured approach to interviewing, whereby various areas of child behavior are systematically assessed, may yield more reliable information. Psychological tests that are often used include developmental measures (such as the Bayley scales), intelligence tests (such as the Binet and WISC-R), achievement tests (such as the WRAT and PIAT), and a variety of projective and objective personality tests.

The more widely used projective tests include the Rorschach, the TAT, the Draw-A-Person test, and sentence completion tests of various types. All are based on what may be referred to as the projective hypothesis, the assumption that when a person is presented with an unstructured stimulus of some sort, an attempt will be made to impose structure on the stimulus situation, and that in doing so the individual will reveal aspects of his or her personality and perhaps the nature of any psychopathology. More objective tests commonly used with children and adolescents, including the MMPI and the Personality Inventory for Children, are more empirical in nature, employ a more structured format (true-false questions), and are commonly assumed to tap a level of personality closer to awareness than do projective techniques. An adequate assessment involves an integration of information derived from various sources in a way that allows the clinician to develop an adequate picture of the child and his or her difficulties.

Behavioral assessment differs from more traditional approaches in a number of respects. Rather than trying to assess personality characteristics or the nature of an underlying psychological disorder, behavioral assessment, as the term implies, focuses on behavior itself. An attempt is made to assess the specific nature of the behaviors that are viewed as maladaptive, the environmental circumstances in which they occur, and the consequences of these behaviors for the individual. This assessment may be accomplished through the use of behavior-problem checklists, behavioral interviews, self-report measures, or by observing the child's behavior in the natural environment. A noteworthy feature of behavioral assessment is that it is conducted not only prior to therapy, but throughout treatment, in order to assess the effectiveness of the intervention procedures employed.

Along with their emphasis on assessment, psychologists, psychiatrists, and other mental health professionals have been interested in the classification of psychopathology. A third revision of the most widely used classification system, the American Psychiatric Associations's *Diagnostic and Statistical Manual of Mental Disorders*, has recently been published, which differs from earlier versions of this popular diagnostic scheme in that it is more objective and focuses on relevant physical and social variables in addition to the specific nature of the individual's "mental disorder." The degree to which this system, DSM-III, represents a significant advance over earlier versions of this classification scheme is not yet clear.

Regardless of the classification scheme employed, there are clinicians who argue against the process of classification on several grounds.

The two most prominent arguments are that classification is unrelated to intervention and that providing an individual with a diagnostic label may have undesirable effects, and in particular may negatively influence how others respond to the person being labeled. In spite of such problems, some degree of classification is inevitable and may be useful for research, administrative, and communication purposes.

SUGGESTED READINGS

Greenspan, S., & Greenspan, N. P. (1981). *The clinical interview of the child*. New York: McGraw-Hill. A well-done introduction to the child interview, written from a psychodynamic perspective.

Goldman, J., Stein, C. L., & Guerry, S. (1983). *Psychological methods in child assessment*. New York: Brunner/Mazel. In addition to providing a rather thorough discussion of assessment-related issues, provides a wealth of basic information about a wide range of psychological tests.

Ollendick, T. H., & Hersen, M. (1984). *Child behavioral assessment: Principles and procedures*. New York: Pergamon Press. An excellent collection of individually authored chapters that deal with all aspects of child behavioral assessment.

Hobbs, N. (1975). *Issues in the classification of children*. San Francisco: Jossy-Bass. Contains a variety of papers on various aspects of classification, focusing on childhood disorders.

Cantwell, D. P. (1985). Organization and use of DSM-III. In D. Shaffer, A. A. Ehrhardt, & L. L. Greenhill (Eds.). *The clinical guide to child psychiatry*. New York: The Free Press. A good overview of the DSM-III system as it is used with children and adolescents, with a discussion of both its strengths and weaknesses.

3 COMMON DEVELOPMENTAL PROBLEMS

It should be obvious that children can manifest a variety of psychopathological conditions. Some, such as autism, pervasive developmental disorder, and mental retardation, are characterized by severe impairments in both behavior and cognition. Others, often considered to be psychosomatic or psychophysiological in nature, are not only distressing, but sometimes pose a threat to life. Still other conditions such as child anxiety and affective disorders can result in levels of psychological distress that seriously disrupts the lives of both the child and his/her parents.

In addition to these conditions there are a variety of other, typically less severe childhood difficulties that not infrequently come to the attention of the child clinician. Included here are problems associated with normal toilet training, childhood fears, social withdrawal, thumbsucking, nightmares, and other behaviors such as temper tantrums, aggressivity, and noncompliance. Further, some children, almost from birth, display temperament characteristics that cause them to be more difficult to care for than other children. In this chapter we will briefly discuss a variety of problem behaviors of this type. But first, it would seem necessary to consider the prevalence of behavior problems in the normal child population as well as the criteria one might use in distinguishing simple problems of development from child psychopathology.

BEHAVIORAL PROBLEMS IN NONCLINICAL POPULATIONS

The best-known study of problem behaviors in nonclinical children is a large-scale longitudinal study conducted by MacFarlane, Allen, and Honzik (1954) that examined developmental problems experienced by children age 21 months to 14 years. Table 3.1 shows the proportion of children found by the study to display specific problems at various age levels. As can be seen, a fairly high percentage of these normal children displayed behaviors that are often considered pathological in nature, or at least symptomatic of underlying difficulties. With some exceptions, it can be seen that problem behaviors tended to decline with age, suggesting that they frequently resolve themselves as the child grows older.

Behavior problems among normal children was also the subject of a cross-sectional study conducted by Lapouse and Monk (1958, 1959, 1964), in which the mothers of 482 children age 6 to 12 were interviewed regarding problem behaviors of their children. The proportion of children within this age group found to show behavior problems is presented in Table 3.2. Consistent with the findings of MacFarlane, Allen, and Honzik (1954), Lapouse and Monk found age to be highly corre-

TABLE 3.1. INCIDENCE OF SELECTED PROBLEM BEHAVIORS
AT FOUR AGE LEVELS.

		Percent of Problem Incidence			
Problem	Sex	Age 3	Age 5	Age 10	Age 14
Disturbing dreams	B	29	20	33	6
	G	29	29	47	4
Nocturnal enuresis	B	18	8	11	11
	G	31	10	6	0
Soiling	B	4	3	0	0
	G	0	0	0	0
Tics and mannerisms	B	0	5	0	0
	G	4	5	0	0
Nail biting	B	8	8	18	33
	G	10	17	32	22
Thumb sucking	B	18	5	0	0
	G	35	19	6	0
Excessive activity	B	37	46	26	11
	G	33	35	15	0
Speech problems	B	24	18	11	0
	G	18	8	3	4
Lying	B	14	49	15	6
	G	12	42	12	0
Stealing	B	12	10	4	0
	G	18	4	0	0

Source: MacFarlane, Allen, & Honzik (1954) © 1954 University of California Press and reprinted by
permission.

lated with the occurrence of problem behaviors; with older children showing less evidence of behavioral difficulties than younger children.

Further findings in line with these two studies were obtained by Werry and Quay (1971), who had teachers, rather than parents, rate children for the presence of behavioral difficulties. In their sample of kindergarten through third-grade children, a high frequency of behaviors such as temper tantrums, disruptiveness, attention seeking, overactivity, and fearfulness was observed. Achenbach (1978) has also reported a fairly high frequency of problem behaviors in normal children as have Crowther, Bond, and Rolf (1981).

DEVELOPMENTAL PROBLEM OR PSYCHOPATHOLOGY?: A DEVELOPMENTAL PERSPECTIVE

How is one to think of those behaviors that MacFarlane et al. (1954), Lapouse and Monk (1959), and others have found to occur so frequently in the general population? Are these behavior problems to be viewed as psychopathological or simply as difficulties associated with normal development? Such questions are of importance, as child clinicians are often consulted by parents of children who show these kinds of behavioral difficulties. A major question expressed by these parents frequently has to do with whether the child's behavior is normal or abnormal. How do we make this decision?

In discussing developmental factors as they relate to childhood psychopathology, Wenar (1982) has urged that we define all child psychopathology as deviant development as "normal development gone awry" (p. 198). From this perspective, child behaviors are considered pathological only if they represent a departure from normal developmental processes.

Wenar cites several developmental criteria that may be used in judging whether behaviors are normal or abnormal. Two of these have to do with whether the behavior in question represents a *fixation* or *regression* in behavior. Fixation here refers to behaviors that continue beyond the age where they are considered appropriate. Wetting the bed, for example, might be considered quite normal for a 3-year-old but abnormal for a child of 7. Regression refers to a child having initially achieved an appropriate level of development in some area only to revert back to behaviors characteristic of an earlier age. Staying with the problem of bed-wetting, the child who

TABLE 3.2. INCIDENCE OF SELECTED PROBLEM BEHAVIORS
IN A SAMPLE OF CHILDREN AGES 6 TO 12.

Behavior	Percent of Problem Incidence
Fears and worries: 7 or more present	43
Wetting bed within the past year	
All frequencies	17
Once a month or more	8
Nightmares	28
Temper loss	
Once a month or more	80
Twice a week or more	48
Once a day or more	11
Overactivity	49
Restlessness	30
Stuttering	4
Unusual movements, twitching, or jerking (tics)	12
Biting nails	
All intensities	27
Nails bitten down (more severe)	17
Grinding teeth	14
Sucking thumb or fingers	
All frequencies	10
"Almost all the time"	2
Biting, sucking, or chewing clothing or other objects	16
Picking nose	26
Picking sores	16
Chewing or sucking lips or tongue or biting inside of mouth	11

Source: Lapouse & Monk (1959). © 1959, *American Journal of Orthopsychiatry* and reprinted with permission.

was toilet trained at age 4, but starts wetting the bed again at age 6, would be seen as having regressed. Bed-wetting, which was considered normal at an earlier age, would now be seen as reflecting psychopathology.

Psychopathology may also be suggested by the *failure* of the child to display behaviors that are expected at a given age. Not displaying communicative speech at age 3 or 4 would be an example. This absence of well-developed speech would not be judged pathological at 18 months, as most children are not verbally facile at this point in their development. Likewise, deviant development might be suggested by an *exaggeration* of otherwise normal behaviors. Mild fears and aggressive behavior are to be expected in young normal children and in this mild form are not generally viewed as deviant. On the other hand, incapacitating fears and violent displays of aggression would be seen at pathological because of the extreme nature of these responses. Sometimes, on rare occasions, a child's behavior may be judged abnormal because it is seen as *qualitatively* different from behavior normally seen at any age. Here Wenar cites, as examples, the failure of certain children to engage in exploratory behaviors and the negative response of other children to environmental stimulation. Such responses are to be contrasted with the tendency of normal children to engage in environmental exploration and to seek out stimulation.

Given a knowledge of normal child development, including information concerning the frequency of occurrence of various child behaviors at various age levels, it should be possible to use developmentally based criteria such as these to make reasonable judgments regarding the normality-abnormality of child behaviors.

From a developmental perspective, there seem to be several reasons for considering the difficulties discussed in this chapter as common developmental problems rather than disorders. First, these problems are quite common in the normal child population. Second, in their usual form, they are less severe than most other conditions discussed in this book.

Third, they are usually somewhat transient, often declining with increasing age. Finally, these problems are most often reflected in one specific problem behavior (or type of behavior) rather than in a constellation of symptoms, as is the case in most psychological disorders. This is not to say that such behaviors may not become a source of concern if they occur to an extensive degree or continue beyond the age where they are developmentally appropriate. In such instances professional help in dealing with these more serious problems may be in order.

THE TEMPERAMENTALLY DIFFICULT CHILD

From the first weeks or months of life children show differences in responding to their environment. Some children display behaviors that make parenting relatively easy, whereas others like Brian, the child depicted in Figure 3.1, display behavioral styles that may challenge the coping skills and patience of even the most adequate of parents.

The most extensive work related to these early differences in responding has been conducted by psychiatrists Alexander Thomas and Stella Chess and their colleagues as part of the New York Longitudinal Project (Thomas, Chess, & Birch, 1968; Thomas & Chess, 1977, 1984). This study has now spanned a period of almost 25 years and has provided data regarding both temperament and measures of adjustment on well over 100 children at different age levels. In their early work Thomas et al. were able to define a total of nine dimensions of child behavior that differentiated among children as young as 2 to 3 months of age and that were assumed to reflect biologically based temperament characteristics. A listing of these nine dimensions and examples of associated behavior is presented in Table 3.3.

Although these investigators delineated nine temperament dimensions in all, they found several of these to cluster together so as to define three general temperament groups. "Easy" children were seen as displaying regular pat-

FIGURE 3.1. Brian

As soon as Brian came home from the hospital, his parents knew they had their hands full. Brian did not sleep nearly as much as his parents had thought he should, and the timing and duration of his naps were very unpredictable. Some nights he would go to bed at a reasonable hour and wake up only a couple of times. Other nights (and there were many more of these) the parents were up a large part of the night trying to get him back to sleep, often without much success. Brian's grandmother commented that he obviously had his days and nights mixed up. Feeding was not much better. Brian's mother had hoped to get him on a schedule where he would be fed every 2 or 3 hours so she could plan her day. Brian would have nothing to do with this schedule, often crying until fed at varying times throughout the day and night.

Brian's parents found that it was not just the lack of sleep and the uncertain nature of his eating habits that were troublesome. They were bothered by the fact that Brian seemed to cry much more than other children. Not only did he cry a great deal at night, but he cried when he was wet, when he was soiled, and whenever anyone except his mother or father picked him up. The parents report that his crying was intense and that they often feared they would not be able to soothe him when he became upset. Commenting on the fact that Brian seemed to have a lot of trouble dealing with what seemed to be routine activities, the parents indicated that even after 4 months he still was not used to his bath, resisted being diapered, and would not let even close relatives hold him without becoming upset. During these first few months Brian's parents consulted their pediatrician on several occasions to see what they were doing wrong.

Although Brian and his parents made it through this difficult time, his mother and father both report that, even at age 10, he still shows behaviors that bear a resemblance to these earlier ways of responding. They note, for example, that Brian still goes to bed at a different time each night and awakens at varying times in the morning. Sometimes he is awake before anyone else gets up. Other times he is hard to awaken for school. His mother indicates that he remains very unpredictable regarding his eating habits, still demanding to eat on his own schedule. In addition to these characteristics, Brian still seems to adapt poorly to new situations. On one occasion he is said to have become quite upset when going on his first Cub Scout camping trip, crying because he was homesick for most of the first day or so. His mother stated that he also had a lot of problems adjusting to a new school that he is now attending. He is said to be very intense emotionally and to often become upset easily. In this regard his father related how Brian frequently would tear up an entire page of homework if he made even a small mistake and that he often broke down and cried when faced with tasks that he thought he just couldn't do.

Commenting on the nature of Brian's behavior, his parents report that dealing with him has taken a great deal of effort, as he is more difficult to handle than other children they know. His mother suggested that the most difficult part of all was her constant feeling that if she was a better mother she wouldn't have problems with him. She noted that the only thing she had found to work was to try to be flexible in her dealings with him and give him time to deal with new situations on his own terms.

TABLE 3.3. DIMENSIONS OF TEMPERAMENT AND REPRESENTATIVE BEHAVIORS AT TWO MONTHS AND FIVE YEARS OF AGE.

Temperamental Quality	Rating	Two Months	Five Years
Activity Level	High	Moves often in sleep. Wiggles when diaper is changed.	Leaves table often during meals; always runs.
	Low	Does not move when being dressed or during sleep.	Takes a long time to dress; sits quietly on long automobile rides.
Rhythmicity	Regular	Has been on 4-hour feeding schedule since birth. Regular bowel habits.	Falls asleep when put to bed; bowel movement regular.
	Irregular	Awakes at a different time each morning. Size of feeding varies.	Food intake varies; so does time of bowel movement.
Distractibility	Distractible	Will stop crying for food if rocked. Stops fussing if given pacifier when diaper is being changed.	Can be coaxed out of forbidden activity by being led into something else.
	Not Distractible	Will not stop crying when diaper is changed. Fusses after eating, even if rocked.	Seems not to hear if involved in favorite activity; cries for a long time when hurt.
Approach/Withdrawal	Positive	Smiles and licks washcloth. Has always liked bottle.	Entered school building unhesitatingly; tries new foods.
	Negative	Rejects cereal the first time. Cries when strangers appear.	Hides behind mother when entering school.
Adaptability	Adaptive	Passive during first bath; now enjoys bathing; smiles at nurse.	Hesitates to go to nursery school at first; now goes eagerly; slept well on camping trip.

Dimension	Level	Example (infancy)	Example (later childhood)
	Not Adaptive	Still startled by sudden, sharp noise; resists diapering.	Has to be hand led into classroom each day; bounces on bed in spite of spankings.
Attention Span and Persistence	Long	If soiled, continues to cry until changed. Repeatedly rejects water if he wants milk.	Practiced riding a two-wheeled bicycle for hours until he mastered it. Spent over an hour reading a book.
	Short	Cries when awakened but stops almost immediately. Objects only mildly if cereal precedes bottle.	Still cannot tie his shoes because he gives up when he is not successful. Fidgets when parents read to him.
Intensity of Reaction	Intense	Cries when diapers are wet. Rejects food vigorously when satisfied.	Rushes to greet father. Gets hiccups from laughing so hard.
	Mild	Does not cry when diapers are wet. Whimpers instead of crying when hungry.	Drops eyes and remains silent when given a firm parental "No." Does not laugh much.
Threshold of Responsiveness	Low	Stops sucking on bottle when approached.	Always notices when mother puts new dress on for the first time. Refuses milk if it is not ice cold.
	High	Is not startled by loud noises. Takes bottle and breast equally well.	Does not hear loud, sudden noises when reading. Does not object to injections.
Quality of Mood	Positive	Smacks lips when first tasting new food. Smiles at parents.	Laughs loudly while watching television cartoons. Smiles at everyone.
	Negative	Fusses after nursing. Cries when carriage is rocked.	Objects to putting boots on. Cries when frustrated.

Note. The dimensions underlined make up the "Easy-Difficult" continuum.
Source: Adapted from Thomas, Chess, & Birch (1970). © 1970 *Scientific American*, Inc. and reproduced by permission.

terns of elimination, eating, and sleeping. They tended to approach and adapt readily to new situations. They showed primarily positive emotional reactions that were usually mild in intensity. "Slow-to-warm-up" children were characterized as having a low activity level, as slower to adapt than the easy child, and as having a tendency to withdraw from new situations. Although they may show negative moods, the intensity of their emotional response is usually fairly low. The "difficult" child, on the other hand, was described as irregular in terms of eating, sleeping, and elimination patterns, as slow to adapt, and with a tendency to withdraw, rather than approach, new situations. He or she was also seen as frequently exhibiting high intensity negative emotional reactions. It is not surprising that the behavior of these children often becomes a source of concern for their parents, as children may not only display these difficult characteristics in infancy, but throughout childhood as well. Fortunately, there seem to be fewer children who fall into the difficult child category than would be characterized as easy or slow-to-warm-up. For example, Thomas et al. (1968) found that of 141 children assessed in their original sample, only about 10% were classified as difficult (30% were considered easy, 15% slow-to-warm-up, and the remainder did not fall into any of these three groups).

Contributors to Child Temperament

Although the factors that contribute to temperamental differences in childhood are not fully understood, it is often assumed that they are of a biological origin. Supportive of this position is the fact that differences in temperament can be seen almost from birth, the implication being that if differences exist before the child is subject to significant socialization experiences, they may be assumed to be of constitutional origin. Tentative support for the role of biological factors comes from twin studies that have compared monozygotic (MZ) and dizygotic (DZ) twins in terms of temper-

ament. Findings from such studies suggest that, at least with regard to some temperament dimensions, MZ (identical) twins are more similar than are DZ (fraternal) twins (Torgersen, 1982). Assuming that same-sex twins experience roughly similar environments and that the major differences between MZ and DZ twins have to do with genetic similarity (and this may be a big assumption), these results support the notion that genetic factors make a contribution to the child's temperamental make-up. That biological factors may be of importance is also suggested by the fact that Bell and Waldrop (1982) have documented a relationship between temperament and minor physical anomalies. These minor physical anomalies are slight deviations in the child's physical make-up (small or large head circumference, fine electrostatically charged hair, slightly malformed ears, the absence of ear lobes, high steepled palate, curved fifth finger, wide gap between first and second toes, etc.) that are reflective of deviant embryological development. Finding significant relationships between indices of temperament and such anomalies strongly suggests that there may be factors (genetic or teratogenic) that may impact on embryological development so as to influence both physical development and child behavior. Although the results of studies such as these provide some tentative support for the assumption that temperament is biologically based, environmental factors are almost certainly of major importance in shaping the way temperament is displayed as the child gets older. Relevant to this point are the findings of Cameron (1978), who has demonstrated changes in temperament over time that were correlated with parent characteristics. More research into those variables that may contribute to temperament differences in children is clearly needed.

Correlates of Difficult Temperament

Even though children with difficult temperament characteristics are seen less frequently than children with other types of temperament make-up, much of the research in the area has focused on the difficult child. This emphasis probably relates to the fact that these children can be so problematic for parents and to the common belief that difficult temperament places the child at risk for later psychopathology. Early findings concerning this latter issue were provided by Thomas et al. (1968), who found that 70% of the difficult children in their study developed behavior problems in later childhood or adolescence. Only 18% of the easy children developed such problems. A recent follow-up of these same individuals in adulthood has likewise documented a significant relationship between child temperament (age 3–5) and adult psychiatric disorder. Other studies have also provided support for a significant relationship between difficult temperament and child adjustment (Earls, 1981; Graham, Rutter, & George, 1973; Johnson, Basham, & Gordon, 1984; Scholom, Zucker, & Stollack, 1979; Webster-Stratton & Eyberg, 1982). Despite the fact that significant correlations between childhood temperament and adjustment problems have been reasonably well documented, one must note that the strength of this relationship is not sufficient for temperament measures to be used with confidence as predictors of later behavioral disorders.

Temperament and Environment: The "Goodness-of-Fit" Model

Rather than assuming temperament to have a strong direct influence on later behavior, workers in the area (see Thomas & Chess, 1977) have advocated a goodness-of-fit model. From this perspective, it is the degree of "fit" between the child's temperament and his/her environment that determines the likelihood of later psychopathology, rather than temperament per se. Thus, it is suggested that a child with difficult temperament characteristics might develop significant problems if raised by parents who are rigid, demanding, and intolerant of his or her behavioral individuality but that such problems might not

develop if this same child were raised by parents who were more flexible in their style of parenting. Although research designed to test this model is just beginning to appear (see Plomin, 1983 for an overview), the results of such studies seem to provide general support for the interactive effects of child temperament and parental behavior.

Difficult Temperament: A Final Note

Even though there are a range of questions regarding the most appropriate ways of assessing temperament (e.g., parent questionnaires, teacher questionnaires, behavioral observations), the factors that contribute to varying temperament characteristics, the stability of temperament across age levels, and the degree and type of interaction between temperament and environment, there is sufficient data to suggest that temperament is an important contributor to child behavior. In considering the importance of temperament, however, it should be noted that difficult temperament is not to be equated with child psychopathology. This is not to minimize the fact that the behaviors of the difficult child may become a significant source of concern for many parents, who may find these behaviors difficult to deal with and who may benefit from learning how to relate to this type of child in a way most likely to lead to a favorable outcome.

DEVELOPMENT OF BLADDER AND BOWEL CONTROL

Of the various developmental tasks of childhood, toilet training is perhaps the one that causes greatest concern for the largest number of parents. Parents often have questions regarding the age at which they should begin toilet training, how to go about it, and frequently worry if their child is not trained as early as his/her playmates. Despite these concerns, most children develop control over urination and defecation without any serious problems and within normal age limits.

Children vary a great deal in the age at which control over urination and defecation are attained. Of course, lack of control is the rule with infants and very young children. By the age of 3 years, however, most children have achieved daytime bladder control (Christopherson & Rapoff, 1983). By the age of 4 or 5, roughly 75 to 80% of children develop nocturnal control over micturition (Schaefer, 1979).

Control over defecation tends to occur earlier than control over urination. According to Erickson (1978), almost 70% of all 2-year-old children and over 90% of all 4-year-olds have such control. Lapouse and Monk (1959) estimated, however, that as many as 7% of children ages 4 to 8, and 4% of children ages 9 to 12 may not be completely trained. Although the exact age will vary from one child to the next, the figures cited here suggest that one might reasonably expect a child to display bladder control (both day and night) by the age of 4 or so, and to show control over defecation perhaps a bit earlier.

Because successful toilet training can only be accomplished given a certain degree of cortical maturation (Yates, 1970), attempts at training should not begin too early. If the child is not sufficiently mature to control the reflexive acts of defecation and urination, the time spent in early training may be wasted; further, the child may become frustrated by demands that cannot be met.

Two years is often suggested in the medical literature as the age at which toilet training should begin. Research conducted by Madsen, Hoffman, Thomas, Korpsak, and Madsen (1966), however, indicates that under proper conditions, successful toilet training can be accomplished at an earlier age. Madsen et al. compared the effectiveness of several behavioral approaches to toilet training with a total of 70 children who had not previously been trained. In one condition parents were asked to reward their children for spending increasing amounts of time sitting on a potty chair, and then to reward the child with edibles when the child eliminated appropriately. No consequences followed accidents. In a second condition parents used a "buzzer pants" device with their children. Here special training pants were fitted with a buzzer apparatus that emitted a sound whenever the child urinated or defecated. When the sound occurred, parents were to take their child immediately to the potty chair. In a third condition parents used the buzzer pants apparatus and also rewarded the child for successful elimination in the toilet. Two control conditions were a maturation control group, where parents made no attempt at toilet training, and a group of parents who were instructed simply to proceed with whatever toilet training approach they thought best; here no information was given concerning training methods.

All three groups displayed a significant decrease in accidents. The reward and the reward-plus-buzzer-pants groups also showed a significant increase in appropriate toileting behavior. Apparently a toilet training approach that involves reinforcement for appropriate elimination can be of value in training normal children. Particularly interesting is that no negative consequences of any kind were necessary for successful training. Another finding of interest is the effectiveness of the program with children of varying ages. Children participating in the program were divided into four age groups: 12 to 14 months, 16 to 18 months, 20 to 22 months, and over 24 months. Although the reinforcement procedures described here were effective with the three older groups (especially those over 24 months), they were much less effective with children in the 12- to 14-month group. All three older age groups differed significantly from this younger group. Thus, even though children can be successfully toilet trained prior to the age of 2 and perhaps as early as 16 months or so in some cases, it is probably not advisable to attempt toilet training with children as young as 12- to 14-months. Consistent with the results of this study, which support the usefulness of a positive approach to the toilet training of normal children given a sufficient level of maturity, Table 3.4 presents a number of general guidelines that may be useful for parents in dealing with the issue of toilet training.

Although the nature of the approach is perhaps more intense than would be appealing to most parents, Foxx and Azrin (1973) have also described another approach for toilet training normal children that is based on principles of modeling and reinforcement. The rapid effectiveness of this approach is suggested by the title of the book describing the procedure: *Toilet Training in Less Than a Day* (Azrin & Foxx, 1974). This procedure is generally used with children who are a bit older than those involved in the Madsen et al. (1969) study. It should also be noted that more recent research with this approach suggests that parents may have difficulty carrying out the program on their own without consultation and that some aspects of the training may elicit strong emotional reactions on the part of the child (Matson & Ollendick, 1977).

As the figures presented at the beginning

TABLE 3.4. SOME GENERAL GUIDELINES FOR TOILET TRAINING NORMAL CHILDREN.

DO'S

- Look for signs that the child is ready for training (e.g., goes a night without wetting, wakes up dry from nap, seems uncomfortable when wet or dirty), so as to not begin training too early (the longer one waits to begin training, the shorter the time it will take to get results).

- Allow child to observe other family members using the toilet and suggest that the child do the same. Capitalize on modeling effects.

- Use a "potty chair." It's more comfortable, less fearful, and requires less involvement on the part of parents for the child to use than the regular toilet.

- Switch to training pants instead of diapers to indicate to the child that you believe he/she is ready to be trained — treat this as a sign of growing up.

- Try to anticipate the need to go to the toilet. Take to the toilet if you observe signs of the child needing to go, such as squirming, grimacing, etc. Verbally praise any success and suggest that the child should go to the bathroom whenever he/she needs to.

- Give the child reminders to use the toilet. Ask the child at regular intervals if he/she needs to go. Reward success.

- Establish a schedule to take the child to the toilet at regular times (e.g., after meals, before and after naps). Encourage the child to sit on potty chair and to try to eliminate at these times. Reward success with praise or tangible reinforcers.

- Expect the child to have some accidents, which should generally be ignored. Expect gradual progress rather than instant success.

DO NOT'S

- Do not use punishment, shaming, or guilt induction for accidents. These are likely to make the problem worse. Further, they are likely to negatively influence the child's view of himself/herself.

- Do not insist that the child sit on the potty for more than 5 minutes or so. You don't want the child to develop negative attitudes toward the toileting situation.

- Don't restrict fluids before bedtime, as this can result in bladder-neck irritation, which may result in the urge to urinate when the bladder is less full than normal.

- Don't worry about night wetting once daytime training has been accomplished. Children typically begin to sleep through the night without wetting when they are sufficiently mature. Praise dry nights when they begin to happen.

- Don't worry if the child is a bit later than other children in being trained. Don't compete with other parents in terms of toilet training. There is much variability in the normal age at which bladder and bowel control can occur.

Adapted from Schaefer (1979) and presented by permission of the author.

of this section would suggest, most children attain bladder and bowel control by the age of 4 or 5. Although this is usually accomplished without a great deal of parental effort, training may be facilitated by taking a low-key approach such as that suggested by the guidelines presented in Table 3.4. However, for reasons that are presently not entirely clear, a small number of children fail to develop adequate control by the age of 5 or so. The terms *enuresis* and *encopresis* are used to denote the failure to develop bladder (enuresis) and bowel (encopresis) control by this age. These conditions are discussed in some detail in Chapter 7.

CHILDHOOD FEARS

Fears are a common problem of childhood. A large proportion of normal children not only display specific fears at some time during their early years, but also frequently show evidence of multiple fears. Lapouse and Monk (1959), for example, found that of 482 children ages 6 to 12, 43% displayed seven or more fears intense enough to be reported by their mothers. A variety of other studies (Jersild & Holmes, 1935; MacFarlane et al., 1954) have also documented the prevalence of fears in the normal child population. These fears take many forms, from fears of specific concrete stimuli (animals, strangers, water) to those involving somewhat more abstract situations (getting lost, death, being kidnapped). Certain fears are especially common, but the range of stimuli that can elicit fear in young children is extremely broad. Though both boys and girls frequently display such fears, they seem to be somewhat more commonly reported by girls, at least among older children (Bauer, 1976).

The development of childhood fears and phobias has been explained from a variety of perspectives, and these are considered in detail in Chapter 6. In brief, however, it seems that one source of children's fears relates to direct learning experiences with specific stimuli. The classic experiment by Watson and Raynor (1920), illustrating the classical conditioning of a fear response in a young child,

little Albert, by pairing an aversive stimulus (noise) with a neutral stimulus (rat), presented an analogue of this process. Because in most instances it is not possible to determine a specific conditioning incident that could account for the child's fear, it is usually assumed that other factors must also be involved. Regarding these other factors, it appears that many fears develop as the result of children observing models (e.g., parents, peers) who themselves display fear responses, thus resulting in the vicarious acquisition of fear. It would also seem that many fear responses (however they initially develop) are maintained because they are reinforced by the environment. In this regard it may be noted that avoidance responses may be reinforced, as such behaviors serve to reduce and/or avoid the anxiety associated with feared objects or situations that the child might otherwise encounter. It would also seem likely that certain dimensions of childhood temperament, such as those discussed earlier, may predispose the child to develop fear reactions (S. B. Johnson, 1985). One might speculate that dimensions such as adaptability, approach/ withdrawal, intensity of reaction, and threshold of responsiveness (Thomas & Chess, 1977) may be especially relevant in this regard. Finally, it is likely that developmental factors make a significant contribution to childhood fears. Here the child's level of cognitive development appears to relate not only to the development of fears, but also to the nature of fear displayed, with younger children showing more fears of concrete stimuli and older children showing fears of more imaginary objects (see Figure 3.2), as their cognitive skills and capabilities for imagination develops (Schroeder, Gordon, & Hawk, 1983).

The fears of childhood are often quite transient in nature. To use the words of Emmelkamp (1982) "they are a passing episode in a normal developmental process" (p. 2). As was noted earlier, MacFarlane et al. (1954) found that common fears declined with increasing age; so did Lapouse and Monk (1964). More recently Crowther, Bond, and Rolf (1981) have also provided data that support this

FIGURE 3.2. A Case of Childhood Fear

Grace, an attractive 5-year-old girl, is described by her parents as having developed normally in all respects and as presently doing well in kindergarten. Although initially a bit shy when meeting new people, Grace's parents indicate that she has a large number of friends and seems to be well liked by her peers. They report no major problem behaviors.

In discussing Grace's development the parents note that one problem area which they had experienced within the last year was her hesitancy to sleep in her own room at night. Grace's mother indicated that her daughter would frequently wake up in the night, call for the mother to come and get her and take her to the parents' bed. On several of these occasions, Grace has commented on the fact that she is afraid that a monster might be outside her bedroom window. Several times Grace has asked to change her room to another one that does not have a window.

In trying to make sense of Grace's fears the mother indicated that only the bottom half of the windows in Grace's room are covered (by very sheer curtains), that there are several large bushes just outside, and that there is a streetlight just a short distance away. She and her husband have concluded that at night the vague forms of the bushes stand out against the streetlight to appear suspiciously monster-like when seen through the sheer curtains. In commenting on the resolution of the problem, the parents noted that buying shades to completely cover the windows at night had done much to alleviate the problem, although Grace still sometimes seems fearful if the shades are not drawn.

view. Although not all studies have found children's fears to be this transient (see Eme & Schmidt, 1978), many do seem to disappear without intervention. Thus, mild fears may be appropriately viewed as a normal accompaniment of childhood, rather than as necessarily pathological. This would seem especially true for so-called stage-specific fears, which have been reported to be most prominent at certain age levels. A listing of several common childhood fears and the ages at which they typically appear is presented in Table 3.5.

Given that mild childhood fears are so common and that in many cases they tend to disappear spontaneously with increasing age, it would seem that unless they result in serious distress, there is no compelling reason to involve the child in formal treatment, although procedures such as modeling and *in vivo* desensitization have been found to be quite effective in dealing with normal fears as well as phobias (Morris & Kratochwill, 1983). Obviously, if the fear becomes excessive and does not resolve itself over time, or if it creates a serious problem for the child, intervention should be considered. Here the distinction between a fear and a phobia needs to be clearly made, because phobic disorders often require some form of treatment. In this regard it might be noted that fear is typically viewed as an essentially normal response to some objective source of danger; phobias, on the other hand, are usually described as fears that are excessive, beyond voluntary control, that cannot be explained or reasoned away, are not age or stage specific, persist over an extended period of time, and result in maladaptive avoidance behavior (Miller, 1983; Miller, Barrett, & Hampe, 1974). A discussion of childhood phobias is presented in Chapter 6.

SOCIAL WITHDRAWAL

Learning to relate in a satisfying manner to peers and adults is a major developmental task of childhood. Although this aspect of so-

TABLE 3.5. COMMON CHILDHOOD FEARS AT VARIOUS AGE LEVELS.

0–6 months:	Loss of support, loud noises;
7–12 months:	Fear of strangers, fear of sudden, unexpected, and looming objects;
1 year:	Separation from parent, toilet, injury, strangers;
2 years:	A multitude of fears including loud noises (vacuum cleaners, sirens/alarms, trucks, and thunder), animals (e.g., large dog), dark room, separation from parent, large objects/machines, change in personal environment;
3 years:	Masks, dark, animals, separation from parent;
4 years:	Parent separation, animals, dark, noises (including at night);
5 years:	Animals, "bad" people, dark, separation from parent, bodily harm;
6 years:	Supernatural beings (e.g., ghosts, witches, "Darth Vader"), bodily injuries, thunder and lightning, dark, sleeping or staying alone, separation from parent;
7–8 years:	Supernatural beings, dark, fears based on media events, staying alone, bodily injury;
9–12 years:	Tests and examinations in school, school performance, bodily injury, physical appearance, thunder and lightning, death, dark (low percentage).

Source: Morris & Kratochwill (1983). © 1983, Pergamon Press and reprinted with permission.

cialization may pose no problem for most children, some are hesitant to interact with others and appear shy, introverted, and socially withdrawn. That this is a relatively common problem is suggested by the results of a retrospective study by Zimbardo, Pilkonis, and Norwood (cited in Gelfand, 1978), which indicated that as many as 25% of high school and college students report having been shy most of their lives. Crowther et al. (1981) have provided additional data that indicate that a fairly high percentage of preschool age children are described by teachers as bashful, as avoiding contacts with others, and as having difficulty interacting with peers. Prevalence figures for children showing these characteristics are presented in Table 3.6.

Being shy or socially introverted would not typically be considered abnormal, but the failure of a child to interact with ease in social situations may be a source of concern for parents, especially if they themselves do not display such difficulty and see gregariousness as a positive personality characteristic.

It is not clear why some children tend to be shy, bashful, and withdrawn and others are more outgoing. Several factors may be involved. First there is some evidence that genetic factors may be involved, at least to some degree. Eysenck (1956), for example, found evidence for the heritability of introversion-extraversion, indicating that some children may be predisposed to be more socially introverted than others. Secondly, it seems not un-

TABLE 3.6. PREVALENCE RATES OF MODERATE TO HIGH LEVELS OF BEHAVIORS REFLECTIVE OF SOCIAL WITHDRAWAL IN MALE AND FEMALE PRESCHOOLERS AT FOUR AGE LEVELS.

Behaviors	2		3		4		5	
	M	F	M	F	M	F	M	F
Bashful/Avoids Contact With Others	42.9	27.3	25.5	19.3	22.6	23.8	14.6	16.0
Overly Afraid of Everyday Situations and People	21.4	18.2	8.3	12.1	9.4	8.1	7.6	3.1
Fails to Mix Freely With Others	00.0	9.1	17.0	13.8	19.3	17.3	15.6	13.4

Note. Figures represent prevalence rates per 100 cases, with cases displaying moderate and high levels of these behaviors being combined (High = teachers' ratings of almost all the time to several times per day; Moderate = once per day to several times per week).
Source: Adapted from Crowther, Bond, & Rolf (1981).

likely that the introverted behaviors seen in some children may represent the behavioral manifestations of temperament characteristics such as those considered earlier in this chapter. Of relevance are the findings of Johnson et al., (1984) suggesting that difficult temperament is related to variables such as social withdrawal, anxiety, and lowered levels of social skills. In a related vein, it is clear that with some children the hesitancy to interact with others may relate to anxiety associated with such interaction, perhaps resulting from previous learning experiences. Children may feel anxious about being made fun of or fear being bullied by other children, for example. Social withdrawal may also result from the child's failure to acquire social skills necessary for interacting in a smooth manner with others. Thus, in addition to the possible role of genetic and/or temperament factors, social introversion may relate to the child's anxiety over interacting with others, to a failure to acquire specific social skills, or a combination of these.

It would follow from this that attempts to increase appropriate social interactions should be directed toward reducing any anxiety and teaching appropriate social skills, if a skill deficit seems to be a contributing factor. It has been demonstrated that modeling experiences, in which socially withdrawn children view progressively closer and closer social interactions between various peer models and other persons, are capable of increasing the social interactions of such children (O'Connor, 1969). It is probable that this approach not only vicariously extinguishes anxiety associated with social interactions, but also teaches socially appropriate ways of interacting with others. The value of operant procedures in increasing social interaction in young children has also been demonstrated by Allen, Hart, Buell, Harris, & Wolf (1964). Considering these and other studies, Gelfand (1978) has concluded that

> symbolic modeling and shaping procedures have proved effective in increasing social participation rates among shy and withdrawn children. Effective modeling demonstrations have presented peer models as initially highly similar to the unskilled observers but as increasingly assertive and successful. There is some evidence that even brief symbolic modeling treatments can have long lasting effects, but are particularly likely to effect long term improvement when combined with shaping and contingency management programs. (p. 345)

In other words, although modeling of social interactions may be useful in increasing the social participation of withdrawn children, the additional positive reinforcement of these behaviors may encourage the long-term maintenance of these interactions. For a more detailed discussion of approaches to social skills training that may include such components, see Cartledge and Milburn (1980), Combs and Slaby (1977), and Michelson, Sugai, Wood, and Kazdin (1983). An additional approach that involves using peers as change agents in dealing with withdrawn classmates has also been presented by Strain and Fox (1981).

TEMPER TANTRUMS

Not infrequently parents are confronted with a child who responds to frustrating situations by displaying tantrum behaviors. The child may cry, scream, hit, pound the floor, or engage in a variety of other behaviors designed to show his/her displeasure with the situation. Although temper tantrums are fairly common among normal children it is not surprising that parents often seek help in dealing with them, especially when they occur frequently.

Although the causes of temper tantrums vary, in many cases they are elicited by frustrating situations and maintained by the consequences that follow and are contingent on the tantrum. The following example illustrates a common occurrence. Consider a mother in a supermarket with her young child. The child eyes a candy bar and asks the mother for it. The mother refuses, and the child begins to escalate demands for the candy. After becoming quite vocal about wanting the candy and again being denied, the child throws a full-fledged tantrum. The tantrum behavior is likely to be quite aversive to the parent. Not only are the crying and other tantrum behaviors unpleasant in their own right, but the mother may be embarrassed, feeling that others in the store may think that she is not a good mother, that she can't control her child, and so forth. Given this situation, one not too unlikely outcome is that the mother gives in and buys the candy for the child. It is obvious that in this instance the parent is reinforcing the child for tantrum behaviors, and thereby increasing the probability that the child will throw a tantrum on future similar occasions. From a different perspective it will be noted that there is some payoff for the mother as well. Because giving in to the child most likely terminates the tantrum, the mother's behavior may be negatively reinforced (i.e., strengthened) because the behavior (giving in to the child) results in the cessation of an aversive state of affairs (child's tantrum behavior). This creates an increased probability that the mother will give in to her child on future similar occasions. Thus, tantrums can be elicited or initiated by some frustrating state of affairs, and may then be maintained as a result of the consequences they elicit from others in the environment. Although there is little research bearing on this issue, because it is recognized that many behaviors are learned vicariously, it seems likely that tantrum behavior in some older children may be learned by observing models who display tantrum behavior and the consequences that follow these behaviors.

If this account of tantrum behaviors is accurate it might be expected that temper tantrums can be dealt with by the application of learning principles. This is in fact suggested by the results of several studies. One classic example of a behavioral approach to this problem is illustrated in a case study by Williams (1959); which is considered in detail in Chapter 10. In brief, the case involved a 21-month-old child who exhibited severe tantrum behaviors upon being put to bed if the parents left the room. The magnitude of the problem

was such that the parents often had to spend up to 2 hours in the child's room each evening. Based on the notion that the child's behavior was being maintained by the attention elicited from the parents, an extinction program was undertaken. The parents were instructed to put the child to bed and, after assuring themselves that the child was all right, to leave the room and not return even though the child might continue to scream and cry. Although the child cried in excess of 45 minutes on the first night, tantrum behavior was eliminated by night 10.

Time-out procedures have also been used with temper tantrums. Although time-out can be accomplished in various ways, all time-out procedures are based on the assumption that if the child is removed from a reinforcing situation as soon as a behavior occurs and before it can be rewarded, the problem behavior will be decreased. For example, in a situation where a child's tantrums are being reinforced by attention from others, time-out would involve removing the child from the situation as soon as a tantrum occurred. This would be done in a matter of fact way, without discussing the tantrum with the child, so as to not further reinforce the behavior (assuming that the use of time-out had previously been discussed with the child). The child might then be placed in a "time-out" room (e.g., some room that is safe, nonscary, but essentially devoid of reinforcers) or in some other non-reinforcing location (e.g., facing a corner) for a short period of time (usually 10 minutes or less). As these contingencies are implemented and tantrums are no longer followed by reinforcement, a decrease in tantrum behaviors would be expected. Several studies have provided evidence that time-out procedures are indeed effective in reducing temper tantrums (Patterson and Brodsky, 1966; Wahler, 1969). Yet although time-out procedures may be effective when used appropriately, many behavioral clinicians see the need to combine them with positive reinforcement for more appropriate behaviors, so that the child would be taught more appropriate responses as well as how not to behave.

AGGRESSIVE BEHAVIOR

In temper tantrums the child displays behaviors that are quite aversive but pose no threat to others. In other instances, the child who is frustrated may become upset and behave aggressively toward others — hitting, shoving, biting, scratching, kicking, taking objects away from others — or display other types of behaviors. This must be dealt with by almost all parents at one time or another and is a common source of concern.

Clarizio and McCoy (1983) emphasized that learning how to handle aggression appropriately is an important aspect of the socialization of the child. They point out that although it is important to teach the child not to be unduly and inappropriately aggressive toward others, it is also important not to deal with aggressive behavior so harshly that its expression is totally inhibited, for the healthy derivatives of aggression, such as assertiveness and competitiveness, are necessary for effective functioning in our society. Thus, learning to deal with aggression appropriately is an important task of early childhood. It would appear that although high rates of aggressive behavior are less frequently seen, most children show aggressive behavior to some degree. Prevalence data for moderate to high levels of aggressive behavior in young children is presented in Table 3.7.

TABLE 3.7. PREVALENCE RATES FOR MODERATE TO HIGH LEVELS OF AGGRESSIVE BEHAVIOR FOR MALE AND FEMALE PRESCHOOLERS AT FOUR AGE LEVELS.

Sex/Age	Two	Three	Four	Five
Male	28.5	39.4	26.8	24.7
Female	9.1	27.6	12.6	11.0

Note. Figures represent prevalence rates per 100 cases, with cases displaying moderate and high levels of aggressiveness (struggles/picks fights with others) being combined (High = teachers' ratings of almost all the time to several times per day; Moderate = once per day to several times per week).
Source: Adapted from Crowther, Bond, & Rolf (1981).

Given that aggressive behavior is fairly frequent among young children, it is logical to ask why children behave this way. What causes a child to hit another, to verbally abuse another, or to shove another child aside to take a toy? Over the years many theories of aggression have been proposed. Because an excellent overview of these theories has been presented by Bandura (1973), only a brief discussion of major views will be presented here.

Adherents to a psychoanalytic point of view have often viewed aggression as resulting from instinctual drives (Gillespie, 1971). Others have seen aggressive behavior as a reaction to the frustration associated with the blocking of goal-directed behavior (Dollard, Doob, Miller, Mower, & Sears, 1939). Still others (see Bandura, 1973) have adopted a social learning perspective that has focused on the vicarious learning of aggressive behaviors (through the observation of aggressive models) and on the maintenance of these behaviors by social reinforcement. A full discussion of research related to these theories is beyond the scope of this book, but available research seems to provide greatest support for the social learning point of view, which claims that modeling (observational learning) and reinforcement are of primary importance in the development and maintenance of aggression. Of special interest are findings from reasonably well-controlled studies that suggest that an exposure to heavy doses of television violence during early childhood is significantly related to later aggressive behavior (Eron & Huesmann, 1984). There are also studies that support the notion that frustration may be related to aggression in some instances. As Bandura (1973) noted, however, "frustration or anger arousal is facilitative but not a necessary condition for aggression" (p. 58). Little evidence is presently available to support the psychodynamic position.

A major concern of individuals confronted with an aggressive child is not so much the cause of this behavior, but how to deal with it. Research concerning the modification of aggressive responses provides some useful guidelines in this regard. It has been demonstrated, for example, that it is possible to reduce aggressive behaviors by exposing observers to nonaggressive models or having them observe models whose aggressive behaviors are disapproved of or punished (Bandura, 1973; Kirkland & Thelen, 1977). In some cases simply ignoring aggressive behavior and thus not reinforcing it through attention may serve to decrease it. Brown and Elliott (1965) showed that it is possible to reduce both physical and verbal aggression in an entire nursery school class by not attending to aggressive behavior while rewarding cooperative behavior.

Sometimes it is difficult to extinguish aggressive behavior by simply ignoring it. This may be because attention is not the reinforcer that maintains the behavior. And even if it is, whereas the teacher or parent attempts to ignore such behaviors, the child may be reinforced by the attention received from classmates if at school or from siblings if at home. In other instances, where the aggressive behavior could result in harm to other children, it is simply not possible or appropriate to ignore it. In these cases time-out procedures, such as those described in the section on temper tantrums, may be appropriate. The usefulness of this type of approach has been demonstrated by Tyler and Brown (1967) and Firestone (1976), among others. Taken together, the literature suggests that a useful way of dealing with aggressive behavior is to eliminate reinforcement for aggressive responses and subsequently reinforce more appropriate behavior, especially those behaviors that are incompatible with aggression (cooperative play for example).

A word of caution is in order concerning the use of physical punishment in attempts to reduce aggressive behavior, because it might seem that the application of such aversive consequences contingent on aggression would reduce aggression. In fact, physical punishment for aggression may *increase* rather than decrease aggression (Bandura & Walters, 1959). One reason may be that the person who uses physical punishment to control child behavior may be themselves serving as a model of aggressive behavior for the child.

NONCOMPLIANCE

Parents frequently complain that their children do not mind. They may not do things that the parent asks them to do (e.g., cleaning their room), or they may not *stop* doing things that the parent asks them not to do (e.g., picking on little brother). Further, they may not adhere to basic rules that the parents may have established (e.g., putting their feet on the sofa when they have been previously told not to).

Such problems with compliance are frequently found among children referred to mental health settings. Indeed, there are a number of studies that suggest that among children referred to clinics for behavioral problems, noncompliance is the most frequent presenting complaint (Forehand & McMahon, 1981). Seriously noncompliant behavior is also seen, along with heightened levels of aggression and other antisocial behaviors, in conduct disordered children (see Chapter 9). In its milder forms however, this behavior is often seen in nonclinical children and is viewed by some as simply one aspect of the young child's attempts to develop independence. As such it is viewed as a normal aspect of child development (Campbell, 1983).

That noncompliance is a common problem in normal children is suggested by Crowther et al. (1981), who, in addition to other information, obtained teacher ratings of noncompliance on over seven hundred 2- to 7-year-old children attending day care. Table 3.8 presents prevalence figures for both boys and girls at each of four age levels. As can be seen, a high percentage of 2- to 3-year-old children show moderate to high rates of noncompliance. Although noncompliance seems to decline with age, even at age 5 a substantial number of children show moderate to high levels.

Although the range of factors that may contribute to noncompliant behavior have not been fully delineated, it would appear that at least two classes of variables are involved. Included here are the antecedents and consequences of noncompliance. An important antecedent is the way that requests

TABLE 3.8. PREVALENCE RATES OF MODERATE
TO HIGH LEVELS OF NONCOMPLIANCE FOR
MALE AND FEMALE PRESCHOOLERS
AT FOUR AGE LEVELS.

Sex/Age	Two	Three	Four	Five
Male	57.2	42.5	26.2	17.3
Female	54.6	31.6	17.1	14.7

Note. Figures represent prevalence rates per 100 cases, with cases displaying moderate and high levels of noncompliance (refuses to do something when asked) being combined (High = teachers' ratings of almost all the time to several times per day; Moderate = once per day to several times per week).
Source: Adapted from Crowther, Bond, & Rolf (1981).

for compliance are presented to the child. Consequences have to do with what happens (or does not happen) to the child after noncompliance occurs.

Citing research studies documenting a relationship between type of parental requests and lowered levels of compliance, Forehand and McMahon (1981) note five types of commands (presented in Table 3.9) that typically result in poor compliance.

In contrast to the often ineffectual commands presented here, there are others that are likely to be more effective. Such commands typically display the characteristics presented in Table 3.10.

In addition to a relationship between type of command given and compliance, rate of compliance has also been shown to correlate with the number of requests made of the child; the more requests, the lower the rate of compliance (Forehand & Scarboro, 1975). Such findings suggest that parents would do well to avoid giving indiscriminate commands as a force of habit and restrict their commands to those behaviors that are clearly of importance.

Noncompliance also relates to the consequences that follow failures to comply. As with aggressive and tantrum behavior, discussed in the preceding sections, noncompliance appears to be increased and maintained as a result of the reinforcement of this behavior by the child's environment. This reinforcement may take a variety of forms. For example, the child may derive positive rein-

forcement as a result of the parental attention given when he or she fails to comply (e.g., extended discussions related to why the child did not comply; pleading with the child to do what he or she was asked, etc.). Alternatively, the child may be negatively reinforced for noncompliance, in that a failure to comply with the parents' requests may allow the child to avoid engaging in the requested behavior, which may be viewed as aversive by the child. Consistent with this formulation, several behaviorally oriented approaches directed toward modifying the consequences of noncompliant responses have been shown to be useful. Research has demonstrated that noncompliance can be reduced both by reinforcing compliance and by punishing noncompliant behavior through the use of time-out procedures (Scarboro & Forehand, 1975). Also, taking into account the importance of both the antecedents and consequences of noncompliance, Forehand and McMahon (1981) have developed a comprehensive treatment program for dealing with seriously noncompliant behavior. This approach includes training parents in social learning principles, in using appropriate commands, social reinforcement, and time-out procedures in dealing with the behavior itself, as well as training in self-control. Preliminary research on the effectiveness of this program has provided support for the usefulness of this general approach. Although involvement in such an intensive program is not likely to be necessary for dealing with the level of noncompliance seen in most normal children, this would seem to be a valuable treatment approach for use in those cases where the problem is exaggerated. Certain aspects of this program (e.g., the emphasis on making appropriate commands; the emphasis on reinforcing compliance when it occurs) may also serve as useful guides to parents in dealing with subclinical levels of noncompliance on a more informal basis.

THUMBSUCKING

Thumbsucking is yet another relatively common behavior of infants and young children. To illustrate, Brazelton (1956) found evidence

TABLE 3.9. TYPES OF COMMANDS THAT CONTRIBUTE TO LOW LEVELS OF COMPLIANCE.

CHAIN COMMANDS: These are a series of commands strung together, which may require the completion of several unrelated activities (e.g., "Pick up the blocks and put them in the box, then make your bed and put the dirty clothes in the hamper"). Depending on the age of the child, chain commands may result in an information overload with a resultant failure of the child to comply.

VAGUE COMMANDS: These directives do not specify observable behaviors to be performed by the child and, as such, present an ambiguous situation for the child. Classic vague commands include "be careful," "watch out," and "be a good boy." Although the parent probably has some specific behaviors in mind when issuing these commands (e.g., "Don't run into the street" or "Don't hit your brother"), the child has not acquired a long enough learning history to associate these vague directives with specific behaviors.

QUESTION COMMANDS: These are perhaps the most problematic type of commands for parents. At issue here is the subtle discrimination between a request and a command. A request implies that the receiver has the option of choosing whether to do as the requester has asked. Commands are directives in which the parent expects the child to follow though on instructions. This is relatively straightforward. However, this discrimination is blurred in adult-adult interactions. Most commands and requests to adults are phrased in a question format (e.g., "Would you work this weekend?"). Parents then use the same type of phrasing with their children when they give a command. They are usually surprised when they say to their 6-year-old, "Would you like to take your bath now?" and he or she says no. It is important to stress that requests themselves are not inappropriate. Rather, it is when the parent expects compliance to a command but phrases it as a request that it becomes problematic.

"LET'S . . . " COMMANDS: These are commands stated in such a fashion as to include the parent ("Let's pick up the toys"). If the parent intends to assist the child in the activity, then this is an appropriate form of instruction. However, parents often use this to trap the child into beginning an activity. The parent has no intention of becoming involved. The child feels tricked, and the typical result is an uncompleted task and another round of escalation in the coercive cycle.

COMMANDS FOLLOWED BY A RATIONALE OR OTHER VERBALIZATIONS: A rationale for a parental command is quite appropriate, especially with older children. However, the rationale should precede the command. For example, the parent might say, "We're having company tonight and I'd like the house to look nice, please put away the toys in your room." In contrast, when the parent provides the rationale *following* the command, she or he is inadvertently obscuring the actual directive and increasing the likelihood that the child will not comply. It is not unusual for parents to get sidetracked when giving a rationale after a command and to completely forget the original command.

Source: Adapted from Forehand & McMahon (1981). © 1981, Guilford Publishing Co. and reprinted by permission.

TABLE 3.10. CHARACTERISTICS OF COMMANDS THAT INCREASE COMPLIANCE.

COMMANDS THAT ARE SPECIFIC AND DIRECT: The parent should first get the child's attention. The parent should call the child's name and pause until eye contact is established. The voice should be firm (but not angry) and slightly louder than usual. This is to provide a discriminative cue to the child that a command, as opposed to a request or other type of verbalization, will follow. The command should be phrased as a "do" command rather than a "stop" command if at all possible, since the former tells the child what is expected. ("Do" commands are also easier for the parent to provide appropriate consequences.) The parent should say exactly what is meant without excessive verbalization, and the command should be phrased in language the child can understand. If appropriate, gestures may be used to explain the command (e.g., pointing to the cupboard in which the toy should be placed).

COMMANDS PRESENTED ONE AT A TIME: The parent should only give one directive at a time. If there are several tasks that he or she desires to be completed, a separate command should be issued for each one.

COMMANDS SHOULD BE FOLLOWED BY A WAIT OF 5 SECONDS: The parent should not issue additional directives or any other verbalizations until the child initiates compliance or until 5 seconds have passed. This wait helps to avoid many of the problems associated with certain of the ineffective commands presented in Table 3.9.

Source: Adapted from Forehand & McMahon (1981). © 1981, Guilford Publishing Co. and reprinted by permission.

of this behavior in approximately 90% of a sample of normal infants. Although thumbsucking usually peaks before age 2, it may continue throughout the preschool years (Schroeder et al., 1983). Indeed, the previously cited study by Lapouse and Monk (1959) found that 10% of children as old as 6 to 12 displayed this behavior to some extent and that in 2% the behavior was clearly excessive. It is when thumbsucking continues to occur at these later ages and appears to be excessive that it typically becomes the concern of parents.

Few clinicians would consider thumbsucking a major psychological problem. It is, in some cases, viewed as symbolic of underlying conflict by individuals of a psychoanalytic orientation, but there seems to be little evidence that children who suck their thumbs are emotionally disturbed (Davidson, 1970).

Because thumbsucking is common in infancy, tends to decline with increasing age, and seems unrelated to the presence of psychological problems, it would appear to be a behavior of little significance, except insofar as it elicits unfavorable comments from others, in the case of older children. Although this view may be appropriate in many cases, thumbsucking can be a significant source of difficulty because of its dental effects. Thumbsucking, especially if it is excessive and persists beyond the age of 5 or so, can result in severe malocclusion of the teeth that may ultimately require treatment by a dentist or orthodontist. Thus, with young children (under 5 or so) thumbsucking poses no major problem. Because of the possible dental effects some sort of intervention may be warranted with certain older children.

Davidson (1970) noted that a variety of home remedies have been employed to deal with thumbsucking, the most popular of which involves applying bitter-tasting substances of various types to the thumb. An operant approach has been used by Baer (1962), who demonstrated that thumbsucking could be reduced in a 5-year-old boy by allowing the child to watch cartoons initially and then making termination of the cartoons contingent on thumbsucking. A somewhat similar approach (but one that also involved other elements such as reinforcement for not engaging in thumbsucking and reminders not to engage in this behavior by siblings) has also been used successfully by Clowes-Hollins and King (1982). Cohen, Montey, and Williams (1980) have also reported the elimination of thumbsucking in a 10-year-old by use of self-monitoring procedures that required the child to record instances of the behavior.

Probably the most successful treatment of this problem involves the use of a palatal crib (Wright, Schaefer, & Solomons, 1979). This is a crib-shaped device made of wire that covers the roof of the mouth and can be cemented to the teeth to keep it in place. It is likely that the palatal crib removes an important reinforcer of thumbsucking, namely the stimulation produced by this activity. The device breaks the suction between the roof of the mouth and the thumb and reduces or eliminates stimulation of the palate by the thumb. The effectiveness of this procedure is clearly borne out by research by Haryett, Hansen, and Davidson (1967), which reported the palatal crib effective with 100% of the children receiving this form of treatment. Because of the expense involved, however, its use is usually restricted to cases where dental problems threaten to be the likely outcome of this behavior.

NIGHTMARES

A final problem that deserves at least brief mention is nightmares. Nightmares are relatively common in the normal child population. Lapouse and Monk (1959) found some 28% of normal 6- to 12-year-olds to be bothered by them to some degree. Nightmares seem to be most common between the ages of 3 and 7, gradually decrease in frequency with age, and seem to be experienced equally often by males and females (Hartmann, 1980). They usually occur during the latter part of the night during REM (rapid eye movement) sleep, when dreaming of all types is most common.

With nightmares the child may wake up screaming or crying because he or she has had a "bad dream." The dream often involves being chased, attacked, seeing a loved one harmed, or experiencing some sort of major catastrophe (Hartmann, 1980). Despite being scared, when awakened the child is usually coherent, oriented, recognizes those around him, and is able to provide a vivid account of the dream (Bakwin & Bakwin, 1972). Although the child may want the parent to remain in the bedroom for a while or go to the parents' bed, fearfulness usually subsides quickly with parental reassurance.

Nightmares, which are common, can be distinguished from the much less common pavor nocturnus or night terror. With night terrors, parents may be awakened to find the child disoriented and sitting up in bed or moving about the room screaming and apparently terrified. Although the child is not fully awake the eyes may be open, as though staring at something, and the child may show distorted facial features, heavy breathing, profuse perspiration, and other signs of extreme distress. The child may run helplessly about the room screaming that something is after him or her, clutching at the parents, and begging for help, although perhaps not recognizing them. In other instances, what the child says may be quite incoherent. These episodes, which may last for up to 15 or 20 minutes, are followed by peaceful sleep and complete amnesia for the contents and occurrence of the episode (Kanner, 1972). Night terrors are most common in early childhood and are rarely seen beyond the age of puberty (Kanner, 1972). That sleep terrors are different from nightmares is suggested by their occurring at a different time during the night, usually during the first 2 hours after going to bed (during non-REM sleep), by the fact that the child does not awaken during or after the distressing episode, and that there is no recollection of the event.

The causes of nightmares are not well-known. Stress, emotional strain, excitement, and overstimulation have all been suggested as contributors (Bakwin & Bakwin, 1972). It has also been suggested that they are most likely to occur in extremely sensitive children

who tend to get their feelings hurt easily (Hartmann, 1980). More analytically oriented writers (see Kessler, 1966) have suggested that nightmares are the result of anxiety-laden impulses breaking through the ego's defenses during sleep. Perhaps even less is known about the causes of night terrors, although the role of stress has been implicated, and there is some suggestion that immaturity of the nervous system may be a contributing factor (Bakwin & Bakwin, 1972).

Occasional nightmares are not usually seen as pathological in nature. As noted earlier, they are relatively common in normal children and can usually be dealt with by simply comforting the child when a nightmare occurs. Generally, nightmares (and night terrors) do not require treatment, as they usually are not so severe as to cause major problems in other areas and most often show spontaneous remission (Knopf, 1984). However, should the problem become especially severe or chronic in nature, treatment should be considered.

SUMMARY

Although this book focuses largely on childhood psychopathology, many children display behavioral difficulties of a less serious nature. Several studies, for example, have found that children in the general population often display behaviors such as fearfulness, nightmares, bed-wetting, thumbsucking, restlessness, lying, minor speech problems, disobedience, impulsivity, stubbornness, aggressiveness, and temper tantrums. Because of the frequency of these problems in the normal population and their tendency to decrease with increasing age, it seems appropriate to view such difficulties as problems of development rather than as indicators of psychopathology. In this chapter we have considered several such developmental problems as they are manifested in essentially normal children.

It was noted that almost from birth, children differ in terms of temperament characteristics (e.g., their style of responding to the environment). They vary in the tendency to approach or withdraw from new situations, the speed with which they adapt to these situations, and their regularity in terms of eating, sleeping, and elimination. They show differences in the degree to which they display positive or negative emotions and in the intensity of their emotional responses. Children also show variation in terms of activity level, attention span, distractibility, and in their threshold of responsiveness. It is commonly assumed that these are biologically based characteristics that may be influenced by socialization experiences.

Although a range of temperament dimensions have been discussed in the literature, the focus of many workers in the area has been on the "temperamentally difficult child." This child, whose behavior is characterized by irregularity, high intensity negative moods, and a tendency to avoid and adapt slowly to new situations, not only poses a significant problem in parenting, but may be at risk for the development of later psychopathology.

Two significant developmental tasks of childhood involve the development of bladder and bowel control. Although the development of such control is dependent on both cortical maturation and learning, most children attain control without too much difficulty by the age of 4 or 5. There is some evidence that toilet training can be facilitated through the use of behavioral procedures that emphasize positive reinforcement for appropriate toileting behavior. It is important, however, not to begin such a program too early, as it may be ineffective if the child is not sufficiently developed and may lead to frustration on the part of both parent and child.

Also among the more common problems of childhood are fears of various objects and situations. Some are relatively age or stage specific, whereas others are unique to the individual child. Many of these fears are quite transient and disappear spontaneously in a matter of weeks or months without any form of treatment. The causes of childhood fears are not totally understood, but classical conditioning, operant learning, and observational learning explanations have all been proposed. It is possible that genetic and/or temperament factors may also be involved. It was noted that although most childhood fears are relatively mild and short-lived, more severe fears or phobic conditions are seen in children as well as adults. In these instances treatment may be necessary.

In addition to fears, some children show problems with social avoidance. They may be hesitant to interact with others, appearing shy, introverted, and socially withdrawn. This social withdrawal may relate to a variety of factors, including, perhaps, temperamental make-up, anxiety over social interactions, and/or the exhibiting of social skills deficits. The use of modeling procedures has been shown to be of value in increasing the social behaviors of such children, although more work is needed to assess the long-term effects of this approach.

Temper tantrums, aggressive behavior, and problems with noncompliance are also relatively common in young children. These behaviors, although different, appear to be elicited by specific environmental stimuli (often the behavior of others) and maintained by the consequences that follow them in the natural environment (often the reactions of others). Each of these can be effectively dealt with through the use of behavioral methods.

Traditionally, thumbsucking has been considered a sign of psychological conflict and a symptom of emotional difficulties. Evidence for this point of view, however, is nonexistent. Thumbsucking, although common in very young children, tends to decline with age. If it continues past the age of 5 or 6, the major consequence is likely to be malocclusion of the teeth, although it can also provoke teasing and other negative reactions, thus creating secondary difficulties for the child. The primary effects, however, seem to be physical rather than psychological in nature.

The final developmental problem considered in the chapter was nightmares. Here it was noted that occasional nightmares (which were distinguished from sleep terror episodes) are experienced by many children and are not usually considered pathological unless the problem becomes severe or chronic in nature, in which case professional consultation may be necessary. The occasional nightmare can usually be dealt with by simply providing support and reassurance for the child when the nightmare occurs. In most instances, the problem resolves itself spontaneously.

SUGGESTED READINGS

Wenar, C. (1982). Developmental psychopathology: Its nature and models. *Journal of Clinical Child Psychology, 11*, 192–201. Discusses the ways in which developmental factors should be taken into account in considering child psychopathology.

Plomin, R. (1983). Childhood temperament. In B. Lahey & A. Kazdin (Eds.), *Advances in clinical child psychology: Vol. 6.* New York: Plenum. An excellent overview of the concept of child temperament and research related to temperament characteristics.

Forehand, R., & McMahon, R. (1981). *Helping the noncompliant child.* New York: Guilford Press. Presents a comprehensive program for dealing with noncompliant children.

Miller, L. C. (1983). Fears and anxiety in children. In E. Walker & M. Roberts (Eds.), *Handbook of clinical child psychology.* New York: Wiley. Chapter provides a good general coverage of childhood fear and anxiety disorders.

Schaefer, C. E., & Millman, H. (1980). *How to help children with common problems.* New York: Van Nostrand Reinhold. A useful source dealing with ways of dealing with common behavioral difficulties.

4 PERVASIVE DEVELOPMENTAL DISORDERS AND SCHIZOPHRENIA

Despite early doubts about their very existence, today little question remains that behavior disorders of major proportions occur in childhood and adolescence. The disorders described in this chapter — the pervasive developmental disorders and schizophrenia — are the most serious psychopathological conditions occurring in childhood. They are marked by fundamental personality disturbances, deviations in relationships with people, and distorted thinking, perception, and affect. In the past, it was not uncommon for all of these disorders to be referred to as childhood schizophrenia. With the realization that there are actually several different major developmental disorders, only one of which is similar to adult schizophrenia, diagnostic practices have become more specific.

Three types of disorders, each with different distinguishing characteristics, will be discussed in this chapter. The first, early infantile autism, almost always makes its appearance before 30 months of age. The second, childhood onset pervasive developmental disorder, (which, like autism, is considered under the general DSM-III category of pervasive developmental disorders) occurs after a period of normal development, usually between the ages of 3 and 12. The third disorder, schizophrenia, typically develops in late childhood or early adolescence, but may begin as early as 7. This chapter discusses the diagnosis, etiology, and treatment of these conditions. Where possible, research findings supporting theoretical explanations for these disorders are described.

EARLY INFANTILE AUTISM

Background

It has been nearly 40 years since Leo Kanner's (1943) article "Autistic Disturbances of Affective Contact" first appeared. Kanner's article described in detail the characteristics and family background of 11 children who displayed a unique syndrome later dubbed early infantile autism. Although conditions similar to autism (the term *infantile* is often dropped) had been described earlier (DeSanctis, 1908), Kanner's article sparked a strong interest among scientists and clinicians in understanding and treating this disorder. This interest continues unabated today. Between 1970 and 1980, over 1,100 articles dealing with autism were published in scientific journals (DeMyer, Hingtgen, & Jackson, 1981), and each year brings three or four new books on the subject. Obviously, we will not be able to review all of this work here. Instead, we focus where possible on confirmed findings and controlled research with a bias toward more recent findings.

Because, in many instances, treatment is predicated on knowing the nature of a child's difficulties, accurate classification plays an important role in child psychopathology. Diagnostic precision is no less important to the researcher. If the experimenter fails to follow careful selection procedures, important findings may be obscured by the presence of many different disorders among the subject population. Unfortunately, the diag-nosis of autism has not always been carefully applied (Ramondo & Schwartz, 1981). In the past, autism has been variously employed as a synonym for all pervasive childhood disorders, equated with childhood schizophrenia, considered to be a type of mental retardation, and treated as a separate diagnostic entity. Because of its importance, the first topic we discuss is diagnosis. Figure 4.1 contains a case description of an autistic child. This case illustrates most of the behaviors thought to characterize autism; it will be referred to throughout the following discussion.

FIGURE 4.1. An Autistic Child

Both Robert and his wife Susan were 26 when Mark, their first child, was born. Despite his youth, Robert had already achieved eminence as an attorney, and it was generally agreed that he was well on his way to a successful legal career. Robert met Susan in college where both were honor students. Susan, who is considered intelligent and pretty, gave up a promising career in mathematics when she married Robert. Neither Robert nor Susan know of any "mental illness" in their respective families, but Susan's brother did have a language disorder as a child. Both come from healthy family backgrounds and are in excellent health themselves.

Susan's pregnancy was unremarkable, and there were no complications at the time of Mark's delivery. For the first 6 months he appeared to be a normal, healthy baby. At about 6 months, Susan consulted a pediatrician because she was distressed by Mark's frequent and prolonged crying spells. During these episodes, neither cuddling nor rocking seemed to console him. These crying periods gradually disappeared during the year and were all but gone by Mark's first birthday.

Although Susan voiced no other concerns to her doctor until Mark was over 2, in retrospect, she can recall some things that appeared odd to her. For example, she remembers that although he smiled and enjoyed being tickled, Mark never seemed to anticipate being picked up when she approached. Not once can she recall Mark's stretching out his arms to her as she neared his bed. In addition, despite Mark's attachment to a pacifier (he would complain if it were mislaid), he showed little interest in toys. In fact, Mark seemed to lack interest in anything. He rarely pointed to things and seemed oblivious to sounds. (Both Robert and Susan can recall being concerned about Mark's hearing.) Mark spent much of his time repetitively tapping on tables, seemingly lost in a world of his own.

Perhaps these behaviors should have brought some positive action from Robert and Susan. Mark, however, was their first child. Not only did they have no other children with which to compare him, but since his health was good, his appearance attractive, and his various developmental milestones (crawling, walking) only slightly behind schedule, they had little basis to suspect that Mark was not a normal, healthy child.

After his second birthday, Mark's behavior began to trouble his parents enough for them to seek professional advice. Mark, they said, would "look

Description and Diagnosis

With the important exception of his apparent improvement, Mark's development followed a course characteristic of most autistic children. Unfortunately, for the majority the prognosis is poor, and their lives are most likely to be lived out in desperation at home or in an institution.

The DSM-III diagnostic criteria for infantile autism appear in Table 4.1. As may be seen, when he was 2 years old, Mark met all of these criteria. In addition, he displayed other behaviors (excellent memory, for instance) that are not included in the DSM-III.

In the following discussion, we look at the DSM-III criteria (and some of Mark's other behaviors) in more detail.

Onset Before 30 Months of Age

The DSM-III defines autism as a syndrome beginning before 30 months of age. This definition is not arbitrary, but based on many clinical observations as well as research. Kolvin (1971), for example, in a study conducted in England, found that the onset of the pervasive developmental disorders in childhood reaches a zenith prior to 3 years. (Actually, Kolvin referred to "childhood psychoses," a

FIGURE 4.1. (continued)

through" people or past them but rarely at them. He could say a few words but did not seem to understand speech. In fact, he did not even respond to his own name. Mark's time was occupied examining familiar objects, which he would hold in front of his eyes while he twisted and turned them. Particularly troublesome were Mark's odd movements — he would jump, flap his arms, twist his hands and fingers, and perform all sorts of odd facial grimaces, especially when he was excited — and what Robert described as Mark's "rigidity." Mark would line objects up in rows and scream if they were disturbed. He insisted on keeping objects in their place and would become extremely upset if Susan attempted to rearrange the living room furniture. Mark also insisted on following a daily routine and reacted strongly if any activity (his bath, for example) were rescheduled.

This portrait of Mark at age 2 remained reasonably accurate for the next 3 years. Slowly, beginning at age 5, Mark began to improve. Although his speech consisted primarily of echoing back words and phrases that he had heard, by the age of 5 he began to learn to communicate this way. When hungry, he would reproduce the phrase, "Do you want dinner?" The pronoun may be inappropriate, and the phrase merely a question he had been asked many times in the past, but his meaning was clear. Mark's rote memory for spoken language was actually quite remarkable. He could recall long verbal sequences and repeat them in accurate detail. At about this time, Mark's musical ability became increasingly apparent. He liked to listen to records and sometimes he would even sing along. Here again, his unusual memory helped him to reproduce long sequences.

Mark's speech continued to develop for the next 2 years. Occasional spontaneous utterances began to make their appearance. Today, at age 7, Mark is able to communicate verbally but only with great effort. His social development has also improved, and even his insistence on sameness in his environment and his routines has decreased. Mark attends a normal public school where he is in a special education class. He engages in various activities (particularly music) but he does not play directly with other children. His health is excellent, he is still considered quite attractive, and there is every reason to believe that he will continue to improve.

Source: Adapted from Wing (1966).

TABLE 4.1. DSM-III CRITERIA FOR
INFANTILE AUTISM.

A. Onset before 30 months of age.
B. Pervasive lack of responsiveness to other people (autism).
C. Gross deficits in language development.
D. If speech is present, peculiar speech patterns such as immediate and delayed echolalia, metaphorical language, pronominal reversal.
E. Bizarre responses to various aspects of the environment: e.g., resistance to change, peculiar interest in or attachments to animate or inanimate objects.
F. Absence of delusions, hallucinations, loosening of associations, and incoherence, as in schizophrenia.

Source: American Psychiatric Association (1980). © 1980 by the American Psychiatric Association and reprinted by permission of the publisher.

category that included autism, schizophrenia, and the other pervasive developmental disorders. Although the term *psychosis*, which was commonly used at the time Kolvin was writing, suggests the severity of these disorders, there is really no connection between autism and any of the adult psychoses.) The incidence of these disorders drops after this and does not peak again until early adolescence. Data similar to Kolvin's have been reported by Makita (1966) working in Japan and by Prior, Boulton, Gajzago, and Perry (1975), whose work was conducted in Australia. The relationship between the incidence of pervasive developmental disorders (and schizophrenia) and age across several studies is illustrated in Figure 4.2.

Not only are there two distinct ages when serious disorders develop, but the two groups of children have also been found to differ in many ways. For example, Prior et al. (1975), using a behavioral checklist, reported 29 statistically significant differences between "early" and "late onset" children (including symptoms, course, and family history). We will have more to say on the differences between early and late onset children later in this chapter. For now, the important point is that only the early onset children are likely to have all of the other DSM-III criteria for autism. In other words, confining the diagnosis of autism only to children whose problems appear before 30 months ensures that autism remains a relatively homogeneous category. Sometimes the age at which a child's problems began is difficult to determine (Harper & Williams, 1974). Retrospective reports are notoriously biased; some parents cannot recall accurately when troubling behaviors first occurred. Nevertheless, the usefulness of the criterion cannot be denied. Children whose disorder first manifests itself after the age of 2½ are probably not autistic.

Pervasive Lack of Responsiveness to Other People

Mark's behavior toward others as a young child was quite typical for an autistic child but very different from normal children. By the middle of their first year, most normal children begin to show attachments to important people in their environment (Schaffer & Emerson, 1964). These "specific" attachments are quite noticeable; the infant shows signs of distress whenever the attached individual (usually the mother) departs and is comforted

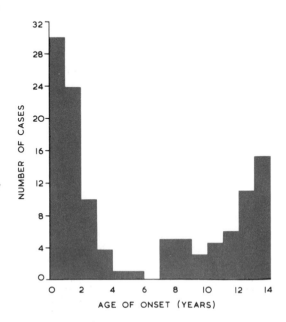

FIGURE 4.2. Incidence of pervasive developmental disorders and schizophrenia in childhood. Source: Rutter (1974). © 1974 by the British Medical Association and reproduced with permission.

by the same individual's return. There are, of course, other signs of attachment in addition to distress upon separation. Cuddling, hugging, wanting to be near the attached individual, and even looking at the attached person are all signs of attachment.

Quite a lot has been written by psychologists, social workers, and doctors on the general subject of attachment and the more specific topic of maternal bonding. A good review of work in the area of bonding can be found in Sluckin, Herbert, and Sluckin (1983). Although there is some controversy about how and when attachments form, there seems little doubt that autistic children do not develop them (Rutter, 1978a). Mark, for example, behaved in a manner frequently reported by the parents of autistic children. He never anticipated being picked up when his parents approached his bed. Autistic children have also been described as not adapting their posture to their mothers' upon being picked up; in essence, they are not "cuddly" (Wing, 1976). Kanner (1943) emphasized the autistic child's "aloneness." In fact, the term *autism* is derived from a Greek word meaning *self*. Autistic children are alone within themselves; they do not relate to others. A tendency to look through people rather than at them, a failure to respond to their names, and sometimes a low sensitivity to pain all combine to reinforce the impression that autistic children are aloof.

As will be seen later in this chapter, the failure of autistic children to develop attachments has sometimes been taken to indicate that their parents somehow failed to foster a proper relationship. But the available evidence contradicts this view. Kubicek (1980), for example, analyzed a filmed interaction between a mother and her 16-week-old-child 2 years before the child was diagnosed autistic. As a control, Kubicek was fortunate to have a similar filmed interaction between the same mother and the child's fraternal twin brother. Kubicek's analysis indicates that the boy who was later diagnosed autistic differed in several ways from his brother. For example, he used fewer facial expressions, avoided social give-and-take, and failed to provide any positive feedback to his mother (he didn't respond to her gestures, attempts to play, etc.). In this case, at least, it appeared to be the child who was thwarting the formation of an attachment rather than the mother.

Gross Deficits in Language Development, Peculiar Speech Patterns, Echolalia, Metaphorical Language, and Pronominal Reversal

A language disturbance is always associated with infantile autism. About 50% of autistic children, particularly those who are severely intellectually handicapped, never gain any useful speech. Even those who develop speech produce peculiar utterances unlike those of other language-disturbed children (Schwartz, 1981; Tager-Flusberg, 1981a). In fact, autistic language is deviant from the very beginning—a peculiar form of infant babble (Bartak, Rutter, & Cox, 1975).

Often the first speech produced by autistic children is the meaningless echoing of words spoken by other people. Echolalia may be immediate or delayed and may involve pronominal reversal (substituting "you" for "I", for example). Echolalia also occurs among non-autistic mentally retarded children, although it seems to be more common among autistics (Hermelin & O'Connor, 1970). Autistic children rarely speak spontaneously, and when they do, their utterances are characterized by such abnormalities in grammatical construction as dropping prepositions, conjunctions, and pronouns (Wing, 1969). Their use of words is also unusual, often involving curious metaphors and odd expressions. Although autistic children appear to have normal articulation, they do not use the expressive-intonational features of speech such as stress and pitch very well (Simon, 1976).

In his review of language disabilities in autism, Schwartz (1981) concluded that autistic children have a special linguistic coding disability (see also, Tager-Flusberg, 1981a, 1981b). That is, they appear to have adequate rote memory for language (a necessity for delayed echolalia), but seem unable to appreciate its meaning. This deficiency cannot, by the way, be construed as a developmental failure. Autistic children are not merely children who are slow to develop language; their peculiar language marks a true deviation from normal development (Rutter, 1978b). Interestingly, autistic children do seem able to learn to gesture, mimic others, and even communicate to a degree through sign language (Bonvillian, Nelson, & Rhyne, 1981).

Although the DSM-III emphasizes the language deficit in autism, psychological research indicates that autistic children have a fundamental cognitive deficit as well. In one early study, Hermelin & O'Connor (1965) found that autistic children could learn to discriminate between two visual stimuli (respond to one but not the other) when these stimuli differed in brightness (they could learn to choose between a bright light and a dim one) or size (they could learn to choose between a big stimulus and a little one). But the children had great difficulty learning to disciminate between arrows pointing in different directions. This study suggested that autistic children have a special problem using conceptual cues, such as direction, in learning. When learning is based solely on sensory qualities (brightness, size), they perform adequately. However, when meaning is required (knowing the difference between left and right in the case of the arrows), their performance deteriorates. Many subsequent studies have reinforced this finding (see Hermelin & O'Connor, 1970; Schwartz, 1981). For example, autistic children have been found not to use the "meaning" of a jigsaw puzzle when arranging the pictures. They can put puzzles together as well when the pieces are upside down as when the picture side is visible. Even their memory feats appear to be accomplished without regard to meaning. For instance, unlike normal or mentally retarded children, autistic children do not have better memories for meaningful sentences than for random word strings. It is as if meaning is of no use to them in organizing their memories. These and other similar findings have led many writers to conclude that there is a fundamental cognitive deficit in autism. Autistic chil-

dren appear unable to link meaning to sensory experience or to use it in their cognitive processing.

Bizarre Responses to Various Aspects of the Environment

Kanner (1951) maintained that an obsessive insistence on the preservation of sameness is one of the most important autistic signs. Autistic children, he claimed, try to keep things in a particular place and to maintain routines. Any novel stimulus or change in routine may result in a "catastrophic reaction" (a screaming infantile tantrum). Mark showed such reactions whenever the living room furniture was rearranged or his bath rescheduled.

A preoccupation with mechanical objects is also a common autistic symptom. Some children collect objects and show great distress if one is lost. These objects are usually used in strange, stereotyped ways (Prior & Macmillan, 1973). For example, a child may tap an object repeatedly or spin things around for long periods. Stereotyped body movements such as rocking, whirling, and hand waving have also been associated with autism.

Absence of Delusions, Hallucinations, and Incoherence

This criterion is included solely to differentiate autism from another serious disorder, schizophrenia. Autistic children do not appear to have hallucinations (abnormal sensory experiences), delusions (peculiar ideas), or even normal daydreams. Indeed, their fantasy life is probably impoverished when compared with other children (Rutter, 1979; Ungerer & Sigman, 1981). We shall return to the question of differentiating autism from schizophrenia later in this chapter.

Additional Characteristics of Autistic Children

Although not included in the DSM-III diagnostic criteria, several other factors have historically been associated with autism. For example, Wing (1976) described their sad facial expressions and a tendency toward self-mutilation. These characteristics, however, are not as commonly observed as those discussed so far. One intriguing and frequently noted autistic attribute is what Kanner referred to as "good cognitive potential." Despite serious mental retardation in most autistic children, some display special abilities, particularly in the area of music, art, arithmetic, and memory (see Figure 4.3 for an example). Their behavior in this respect mirrors that of children known as *idiot savants* ("retarded scholars"). Although many if not all idiot savants are probably autistic (Lester, 1978), the relationship does not hold in reverse. The majority of autistic children do not show any special intellectual or artistic abilities.

FIGURE 4.3. Sometimes autistic children can demonstrate special abilities in certain areas. In this case, an autistic girl had extraordinary drawing ability. Source: Selfe (1977). © 1977 Academic Press (London) and reprinted with their permission.

Demography

Based on observations of their educational achievement, Kanner (1943, 1965) suggested that the parents of autistic children are remarkably intelligent. This observation was important because most serious psychological disorders (schizophrenia, for example) appear more commonly among the poorly educated, lower social classes. Reviewing the literature available at the time, Rimland (1964) concluded that Kanner's observations were accurate. However, it is possible that highly intelligent and well-educated parents may simply be more likely to seek psychiatric help for their autistic children than poorly educated parents. In other words, Kanner may simply have been reporting the educational level of the people who consulted him rather than the education level of the parents of autistic children in general. Although a reasonably well-designed epidemiological study by Treffert (1970) controlled for "referral biases" without substantially altering Kanner's observation, additional studies (DeMyer et al. 1973; Schopler, Andrews, & Stropp, 1979) suggest that the earlier observations may have been biased in subtle ways. Two recent studies (Gillberg & Schaumann, 1982; Tsai, Stewart, Faust, & Shook, 1982) confirm that when selection factors are held constant, no particular relationship between autism and social class was found. (This finding, of course, still differentiates autism from schizophrenia, which is more common among the lower social classes.)

Although autism does not appear related to social class and parental education, it may differ slightly from culture to culture. For example, Lotter (1978) found that autistic children in several African countries, although similar to their American and European counterparts, are much less likely to engage in some types of stereotyped behavior. Nevertheless, a syndrome very much like autism appears to occur in most cultures and countries.

Also unlike schizophrenia, autism is not found to run in families. Although there is some increased probability of finding a second autistic child in a family where one has been diagnosed, the increased probability is only about 2% (Rutter, 1968). (Although small, this is still 50 times the probability of finding autism in the general population.) Several cases of autism in identical twins have been reported (Folstein & Rutter, 1978), and there is also a tendency for language defects to be more common in the families of autistic children (Rutter, Bartak, & Newman, 1971).

Kanner always maintained that autism is a rare disorder. As of 1958, he reported having seen about 20,000 children in his clinical practice, only 150 of whom were autistic. Because Kanner was widely recognized as an eminent authority, he received many referrals in which autism was the suspected diagnosis. Autistics, therefore, may have been overrepresented in Kanner's practice, making his numbers unrepresentative of the population at large. Epidemiological studies have, indeed, found the incidence of autism to be lower than Kanner's experience. Wing, Yeates, Brierly, and Gould (1976) reviewed prevalence studies from several countries, concluding that the disorder occurs in 4 or 5 out of every 10,000 children aged under 15 years. Although these numbers are valuable in suggesting that autism is a rare condition, it should be noted that accurate figures of incidence have always been difficult to obtain because epidemiological surveys often suffer from the lack of diagnostic precision endemic to the field.

Autism occurs more frequently among boys than girls. Estimates for the predominance of boys over girls range from 2.5 autistic boys for every girl (Lotter, 1967) to 4.95 boys for every girl (Ando & Tsuda, 1975). Among Kanner's first 100 autistic cases, 80 were boys and only 20 were girls. It has also been reported that autism is more prevalent among children who, like Mark, are first-born, although recent research findings indicate that this is an oversimplification (Tsai & Stewart, 1983). Autistic children also seem more likely to be the fourth child born in a family. It should be noted that birth order data are notoriously difficult to interpret (Ernst & Angst, 1983).

Differential Diagnosis

Although it would appear, based on the discussion so far, that diagnosing autism is a rather easy matter, in practice it has proven quite difficult (see Table 4.2). The major diagnostic problem faced by scientists and clinicians is differentiating autism from other diagnostic entities with which it shares some common features.

Mental Retardation

Many different conditions may result in mental subnormality. Therefore, it is strange that the DSM-III considers mental retardation an independent diagnostic category (see Rutter & Shaffer, 1980, for a discussion of this point). Nevertheless, although mental retardation is present in most autistic children, they may be differentiated from nonautistic mentally retarded children by their aloofness, their need to maintain sameness, their failure to play with other children, their bizarre speech, and, sometimes, by their special abilities. These behaviors are not characteristic of the nonautistic mentally retarded.

Deafness

It is sometimes difficult, by observation alone, to differentiate autism from deafness, because autistic children often appear unresponsive to auditory stimuli. Children suffering auditory handicaps, however, rarely display the full complement of autistic symptomatology. Some diagnostic difficulties may occur, however, when an autistic child is also deaf. In such cases, it is not easy to determine whether the child is merely unresponsive, as autistic children often are, or truly deaf. Some of the similarities and differences between autistic, mentally retarded, and sensory handicapped children are illustrated in Table 4.3.

Schizophrenia

In the past, schizophrenia was frequently confused with infantile autism. The reason for this confusion lay more in the vagueness inherent in much of psychiatric practice than in any similarities between the two disorders.

TABLE 4.2. AGREEMENT BETWEEN PAIRS OF DIAGNOSTICIANS ON THE DIAGNOSES ASSIGNED TO 445 CHILDREN SHOWING SEVERE BEHAVIOR DISORDERS.

First Diagnosis	Second Diagnosis								
	Autistic	Infantile autism or early infantile autism	Childhood schizophrenia	Emotionally disturbed or mentally ill	Brain damaged, neurologically damaged	Retarded	Psychotic (symbiotic psychosis), etc.	Deaf or partly deaf	Total
Autistic	33	5	53	18	23	51	10	7	200
Infantile autism or early infantile autism	1	10	6	—	4	6	—	2	29
Childhood schizophrenia	17	3	1	2	8	1	—	—	32
Emotionally disturbed or mentally ill	12	2	4	2	9	13	3	—	45
Brain damaged or neuro-logically damaged	14	3	2	5	4	15	—	1	44
Retarded	21	2	6	18	16	5	2	2	72
Psychotic (symbiotic psy-chosis), etc.	4	—	1	1	2	2	—	—	10
Deaf or partly deaf	4	1	—	2	—	5	1	—	13
Total	106	26	73	48	66	98	16	12	445

Source: Rimland (1971). © 1971 by Plenum Publishing Company and reprinted with permission.

TABLE 4.3. IMPAIRMENTS OF FUNCTION AND SECONDARY BEHAVIORAL PROBLEMS IN AUTISTIC AND OTHER HANDICAPPED CHILDREN TWO TO FIVE YEARS OF AGE.

	Speaking Autistic (n = 20) %	Mute Autistic (n = 7) %	Partially Blind and Deaf (n = 15) %	Mentally Retarded (n = 15) %	Normal Controls (n = 25) %
Impairments in:					
Response to sound	85	86	93	20	0
Comprehension of speech	100	100	93	(67)	4
Use of speech	100	NR	NR	40	32
Pronunciation	85	NR	NR	73	0
Right-left orientation and copying skilled movements	75	NR	NR	NR	40
Visual perception	95	85	100	27	0
Understanding and use of gestures	55	85	60	7	0
Abnormalities of behavior:					
Preference for proximal senses	100	85	87	47	28
Stereotyped movements	95	100	93	20	4
Social withdrawal	95	85	(53)	13	0
Attachment to objects and routines	100	100	(60)	7	20
Irrational fears and lack of real fear of danger	100	100	80	40	20
Lack of play	95	100	87	27	0
Socially embarrassing behavior	90	86	73	27	28
Lack of nonverbal skills	0	43	93	73	12

*All values represent the percentage of children in each group with abnormal scores. Values underlined denote no significant differences from those for speaking autistic children. Values in parentheses denote significantly less abnormality than in autistic children but significantly more than in the control group. NR = not rated; some groups were not rated on certain items because they were too handicapped to show the necessary behavior.
Source: Adapted from Wing (1969).

In fact, autistic children are not much like schizophrenics. Their speech, although abnormal, is not like that of schizophrenics (see Schwartz, 1981, 1982), and they do not grow up to become schizophrenic. Rimland (1971) points out that the courses of the two conditions differ in other respects as well. Autism is present at birth or within 30 months, whereas schizophrenia has its onset later in childhood or early adolescence, preceded by a period of normal development. Autistic children are frequently described as healthy and good-looking, whereas schizophrenic children are often sickly and undistinguished physically. Schizophrenic children are not described as failing to anticipate being picked up from their beds, nor do they require the maintenance of sameness. In addition, as already noted, schizophrenia is correlated with lower social class membership, whereas autism appears independent of social class. We will have more to say on the differences between autism and schizophrenia later in this chapter.

Autistic-like Syndromes

An epidemiological study by Wing (1981) makes it clear that autism is one among many similar impairments in children. Indeed, the DSM-III provides not only for autism, but also for other childhood onset pervasive disorders (discussed later in this chapter) and also for atypical pervasive disorders that share some but not all of autism's characteristics. Clearly, diagnosing autism requires careful attention to the DSM-III criteria if confusion is to be avoided. Several attempts to develop diagnostic instruments (tests) for differential diagnosis have been made. These will be discussed after we mention several other diagnostic problems.

Other Problems in Differential Diagnosis

Some overt sign of central nervous system dysfunction is present in about half of all autistic children (Rutter, 1978b), and a number appear to develop epileptic-type seizures in adolescence (Lotter, 1974). This does not necessarily mean the remaining children are free of organic damage. Common neurological diagnostic techniques are not always sensitive to many subtle organic deficits, and some children who appear normal may later turn out to be brain damaged. The majority of researchers working in the field believe that autism is at least in part a neurological disorder.

In the past, a different sort of diagnostic problem resulted from a tendency to employ vague, undefined terms when describing autistic behaviors. Writers passionately argued about whether autistic children had "disturbed body images" or whether they "lacked object relations" (Ward, 1970). Because these terms have no mutually agreed-upon definitions, these disagreements have never been resolved. Today, these arguments are of historical rather than scientific interest. When diagnosis is limited to objective criteria such as those used in the DSM-III, fewer diagnostic disagreements occur.

Diagnostic Instruments

Perhaps the first attempt to develop an instrument for diagnosing childhood autism was made by Bernard Rimland. In his book *Childhood Autism*, Rimland (1964) presented an experimental questionnaire, designed to be completed by parents, which he hoped would help identify the "classical" autistic syndrome. Experience soon showed this checklist, called form E-1, in need of revision. A revised scale, form E-2, was used widely by researchers and clinicians to differentiate autistic children from others with autistic-like symptoms. Based on this work, form E-2 has now been joined by form E-3. Table 4.4 contains some items from Rimland's scale and some characteristic response patterns.

Although scores on Rimland's checklist have been found to agree with diagnoses made by Kanner (see Rimland, 1971) and even to differentiate between children with a blood platelet abnormality associated with autism and those with normal blood platelets (Boullin, Coleman, O'Brien, & Rimland, 1971), it has not always been successful in differentiating autistic from nonautistic children (Rutter, 1978c). Rating scales for diagnosing autism have also been introduced by Freeman, Ritvo, Guthrie, Schroth, and Ball (1978), as well as by Schopler, Reichler, DeVellis, and Daly (1980). There is even a multifactor Autism Screening Instrument for Education Planning being sold commercially (Krug, Arick, & Almond, 1982). After reviewing the literature on diagnosis, Parks (1983) concludes that none of the checklists introduced so far is clearly superior, indicating that more work is needed in this area. For a recent review of the literature on assessing autistic children, see Baker (1983).

Prognosis

A study by DeMyer and her colleagues (DeMyer, Barton, DeMyer, Norton, Allen, & Steele, 1973) reported a follow-up of 85 autistic boys and 35 girls, as well as a control

TABLE 4.4. SAMPLE ITEMS FROM FORM E-2 AND RESPONSE PERCENTAGES FROM GROUPS
OF AUTISTIC AND AUTISTIC-TYPE CHILDREN.

Item	Autistic*		Nonautistic*	
	Speaking (n = 65)	Mute (n = 35)	(n = 230)	Key
Did you ever suspect the child was very nearly deaf?				
1 Yes	77	94	54	(+)
2 No	23	6	46	(−)
	100	100	100	
(Age 2–5) Is he cuddly?				
1 Definitely, likes to cling to adults	2	2	20	(−)
2 Above average (likes to be held)	8	8	18	(−)
3 No, rather stiff and awkward to hold	90	88	56	(+)
4 Don't know	0	2	6	
	100	100	100	
(Age 3–5) How skillful is the child in doing fine work with his fingers or playing with small objects?				
1 Exceptionally skillful	71	75	33	(+)
2 Average for age	6	9	23	(−)
3 A little awkward, or very awkward	15	8	33	(−)
4 Don't know	8	8	11	
	100	100	100	
(Age 3–5) How interested is the child in mechanical objects such as the stove or vacuum cleaner?				
1 Little or no interest	19	9	23	(−)
2 Average interest	4	0	21	(−)
3 Fascinated by certain mechanical things	77	92	56	(+)
	100	100	100	
(Age 3–5) Does the child get very upset if certain things he is used to are changed (like furniture or toy arrangement, or certain doors that must be left open or shut)?				
1 No	4	2	29	(−)
2 Yes, definitely	87	86	41	(+)
3 Slightly true	9	12	30	(−)
	100	100	100	
(Age 3–5) Does the child typically say yes by repeating the same question he has been asked? (Example: You ask, "Shall we go for a walk, honey?" and he indicates he does want to by saying, "Shall we go for a walk?")				
1 Yes, definitely, does not say yes directly	94	12**	22	(+)
2 No, would say "yes" or "OK" or similar answer	0	3	8	
3 Not sure	4	6	8	
4 Too little speech to say	2	79	62	
	100	100	100	

*All values are expressed as percentages.
**Not applicable to the mute group.
Source: Rimland (1971). © 1971 by Plenum Publishing Company and reprinted with permission.

124

group of 36 children. Diagnostic measures taken at the time of initial evaluation included psychiatric examinations, a language evaluation, psychological testing, physical and neurological exams, and laboratory studies. In addition, the children's parents were interviewed. Seven years later, patients and families were again interviewed and the children were retested. At this follow-up, only a few autistic children used speech more complex than that required to ask for immediate needs. In addition, every autistic child with any communicative speech was echolalic. The autistic children were also found to have social problems. They tended to be loners and were often judged to be seriously out of touch with their social environment. Most of the autistic children were functioning below the educable mentally retarded level.

Other follow-up studies have provided information concerning the status of autistics in adulthood. Reviewing several studies, Ornitz & Ritvo (1976) summarized the findings as indicating that roughly 75% of autistic children are likely to be regarded as mentally retarded throughout life and that anywhere between 7 and 28% develop seizures prior to age 18. These authors, like DeMyer et al. (1973), report that even those autistics who

improve continue to display serious interpersonal problems.

Longitudinal studies of autistic (and other severely disturbed) children into adolescence and adulthood have been published and reviewed by DeMyer et al. (1981). The findings of their review are illustrated in Table 4.5. As can be seen, from 5 to 20% of autistic children eventually reach the borderline of normality. Sixteen to 27% have a fair outcome, and 60 to 75% have a very poor outcome. In many cases, a good prognosis is related to cognitive functioning (particularly language ability) early in life (Lotter, 1974). Specifically, children who have useful communicative abilities at about age 5 are much more likely to improve than those without such abilities. Improvement is also associated with neurological status. Children with gross organic dysfunction are less likely to improve than those with minimal neurological deficits.

That some children have a less pessimistic fate is suggested by Kanner (1971). In a paper titled "How Far Can Autistic Children Go in Matters of Social Adaptation?" Kanner noted that of 96 patients diagnosed by him as autistic before 1953, 11 were judged as success stories in adulthood. Kanner indicated that

TABLE 4.5. PROGNOSIS FOR AUTISTIC
AND OTHER PERVASIVELY DISABLED
CHILDREN – SUMMARY OF SIX STUDIES.

Outcome Criterion	Percent of Children Reaching Criterion
Overall Outcome	
Good	5–19
Fair	16–27
Poor	55–74
Specific Criteria	
Develop Normal Speech	6–16
Develop Some Speech	46–51
No Speech	32
In Age-Appropriate School Grade	0–10
Gainfully Employed	0–18
Long-Term Institutionalization	42–48

Note: Numbers refer to range of findings across six studies. Source: Adapted from DeMyer et al. (1981).

3 of the 11 had received college degrees and that 3 others had received a junior college education (the remainder received varying levels of education ranging from training in a sheltered workshop to the completion of high school). Eight of the 11 lived alone (the others lived with their families), and all were employed. Their occupations ranged from helper in a pharmacy to bank teller. Although these 11 autistic individuals all showed the ability to function in society, none had ever contemplated marriage, and as a group, they continued to display problems in developing close relationships. Although these findings demonstrate that some autistic children have a more favorable future than others, it should be kept in mind that the majority are destined for lives of little hope.

Etiology of Autism: Research and Theory

Despite a multitude of hypotheses by theorists who have implicated everything from smothering, symbiotic mothers to difficulties in perceptual integration, a satisfactory explanation for autism has yet to be proposed. In the following discussion, the various hypotheses will be divided into two classes: those that see autism's etiology as primarily psychological and those that view autism as rooted in a biological defect. It should be kept in mind that some theorists attempt to combine the two views. In these cases, assignment to one of the two categories is somewhat arbitrary.

Psychogenesis

For a long time, the dominant view among psychiatrists and psychologists held autism to be the result of psychological and emotional factors. Although there has been some dispute over precisely which psychological factors are important, most psychogenic theorists have focused on disturbances in the mother-child relationship.

Maternal Personality. Kanner, although not himself a psychogenic theorist, has given comfort to that view with his emphasis on parental personality characteristics. In his writings, he has, on occasion, referred to the "refrigerator parent" who behaves in a cold, detached manner. Hypotheses based on some sort of emotional malfunction between parent and child are most often associated with Bettleheim (1967). Although it is true that Bettleheim's definition of autism is much broader than the one given in the DSM-III, his views are reflective of many others. From Bettleheim's point of view, autistic behavior results from a "denial of self" in defense against a destructive (particularly maternal) environment. Variations on this theme have been proposed by Edelson (1966), who sees the autistic child as reacting to a perceived loss of motherly love, and Speers and Lansing (1964), who attribute autism to a variety of causes including unresolved maternal dependency conflicts.

Environmental Deviance. In contrast to the views of Bettleheim and other psychodynamic theorists, Ferster (1961) applied Skinner's operant conditioning approach to an analysis of autistic behavior. Ferster's essential idea is that the autistic child's early environment somehow failed to reinforce proper behavioral patterns. The children, having learned few social behaviors, engage in repetitive, self-stimulatory behaviors because these have been directly reinforced through their immediate environmental effects.

Psychogenesis and Organic Dispositions. Psychogenic hypotheses are not incompatible with the idea that some children display an organic disposition to develop autism. In fact, it seems logical for psychogenic theorists (Bettleheim, 1967; Tinbergen & Tinbergen, 1983) to postulate that some children are predisposed to develop autism in response to experiences that other children weather without harm. Needless to say, merely stating that such a predisposition exists does not constitute an explanation. To be useful, the theory needs to describe the nature of the predisposition and the mechanism by which it leads to autism. Often these hypothesized dispositions are vaguely specified and poorly conceptualized. In such cases, progress in understanding autism is retarded rather than advanced.

Psychogenesis: Status of the Hypothesis. Psychogenic hypotheses are, on the whole, not of the calibre generally required of scientific theories because they tend to share implicit assumptions that are never put to test. For example, many psychogenic theories assume that maternal overprotection, deprivation, or some other practice can lead to the disturbances evidenced by autistic children. Putting aside, for a moment, the question of whether or not the mothers of autistic children really do behave differently from other mothers, there is good evidence suggesting that maternal practices of any kind cannot produce autism. This evidence comes from studying children raised in poorly run orphanages from birth. Despite extremely low levels of adult interaction, these children show no greater incidence of autism than does the population at large (Hermelin & O'Connor, 1970; Hingtgen & Bryson, 1972). If lack of maternal affection and coldness are in any way responsible for autism, one would expect the syndrome to flourish in such institutions.

It should also be emphasized that even if autism had been found common in such institutions, there would still be reason to doubt the validity of most psychogenic theories. There exists no acceptable evidence that the mothers of autistic children differ from other mothers in either personality or in the way they relate to babies (Cox, Rutter, Newman, & Bartak, 1975; Koegel, Schreibman, O'Neill, & Burke, 1983; McAdoo & DeMyer, 1978). In fact, autistic children usually have normal siblings.

Criticism thus far has been directed at those psychogenic hypotheses that implicate maternal personality as the primary etiological factor. Similar criticisms also apply to Ferster's environmental view. There is absolutely no evidence that the early environment of autistic children is markedly different from that of other children. Indeed, the

presence of normal brothers and sisters argues strongly against such a notion. Kubicek's (1980) analysis of the filmed interaction between a mother and her twin sons mentioned earlier suggests that it was the baby later diagnosed as autistic who failed to provide reinforcement for his mother rather than the other way around.

There seems little use to pursue further the notion that autism is psychogenic in origin. In at least one important way, the demise of psychogenic hypotheses will have a salutary effect: Guilt feelings engendered in the parents of autistic children whose lives have already been heavily burdened by the child's condition will be lessened, and as a consequence their families will forgo much unnecessary suffering.

Biogenesis

Biogenic theories appear in various guises and range from those that seek a genetic component in autism to neurological and even biochemical theories. Despite this lack of unanimity, there is good reason to suspect that some form of biological explanation is more likely to explain autism than any psychogenic theory. First, autism's presence so soon after birth makes any psychogenic hypothesis inherently unlikely. Moreover, the sex ratio (more boys than girls) seems consistent with a biogenic defect. The presence of autistic-like behavior among children with known brain damage, the remarkable similarity of one autistic child to another, the finding that autism and congenital rubella are related (Chess, 1971), the relationship between autism and exposure to toxic chemicals (Coleman, 1976), and the higher than average incidence of pregnancy and birth complications in the histories of autistic children (Deykin & MacMahon, 1980) all argue strongly in favor of a biogenic explanation. In this section, several important biogenic approaches will be discussed.

Genetics. Although autism does not run in families in the same way as hair color, there is a greater chance of finding a second autistic child in a family where one has been diag-nosed than in the population at large (Ritvo, Ritvo, & Brothers, 1982). Moreover, cogni-tive, particularly language, disorders also ap-pear more commonly in the families of autis-tic children (August, Stewart, & Tsai, 1981). Although these findings are clearly suggestive, it is still unclear precisely what role inherit-ance plays in autism. Some researchers feel that perhaps a subgroup of autistics inherited their disorder (Ritvo et al., 1982), whereas others (Folstein & Rutter, 1978, for example) believe that only certain autistic deficits (pri-marily the language disorder) are inherited. A third possibility is that what is inherited is not autism but some other trait that indirect-ly results in autism. For example, a decreased resistance to viruses might explain the rela-tionship between autism and congenital ru-bella mentioned earlier. This last possibility is consistent with Folstein and Rutter's (1978) finding that autism does not always occur in both members of a pair of monozygotic twins. If autism were purely inherited, then both twins should be affected. If, however, what is inherited is an indirect vulnerability to cer-tain viruses (or other environmental dangers), then only those children exposed to the dan-ger would develop autism.

Neurology. The most obvious way to study the brains of autistic children is directly, by examining them. Darby (1976) reviewed all reported cases of autopsies on children diag-nosed autistic (or psychotic) and found that many showed evidence of neuropathology, although no consistent pattern was discov-ered. On the other hand, a brain bank set up specifically to study the brains of autistic persons has so far found no neuropathology in the three brains they have examined (Rit-vo, 1983). Because most autistic children do not die young, it is possible that those whose brain's show neuropathology are a special group not typical of the majority.

Electrophysiological studies permit brain functioning to be studied without intruding into children's heads. Studies using electro-encephalographs (EEGs) have been reviewed

by Piggott (1979) and DeMyer et al. (1981). Two basic types of studies have been con-ducted: ongoing EEG studies that record electrical activity from one or more brain sites over a specified period of time and event-related potential studies (ERPs), which repre-sent the brain's responses to specific stimuli. Abnormalities in EEGs and ERPs have been reported among autistic children, but so far no one has been able to find an abnormality unique to autism.

One hypothesis that is based partly on the findings of EEG studies holds that autistic children suffer from a chronic state of under-arousal (Rimland, 1964). The concept of arousal or activation is a common one in many areas of psychology. In its simplest form, it refers to a dimension that varies from sleep to states of high tension. During wak-ing hours, most people find themselves some-where between these two extremes. It is pos-sible, however, that some individuals differ markedly from the norm and are chronical-ly under- or overaroused. Although there is some direct EEG evidence (Hutt, Hutt, Lee, & Ounstead, 1964) and some indirect evidence (Hutt & Hutt, 1970) indicating that autistic children may be chronically overaroused, the hypothesis remains speculative and not wide-ly accepted.

Although electrophysiological recordings are gross measures that provide only an in-direct view of brain structure or functioning, it is possible using sophisticated techniques to isolate abnormalities to specific brain areas. Tanguay and Edwards (1982) argue that this new work indicates a dysfunction in the primitive parts of the brain (the brainstem) of autistic children. This hypothesis, too, awaits further confirmation.

Hauser, Delong, and Rosman (1975) found structural defects in the brains of autistic chil-dren using the pneumoencephalograph (an x-ray procedure that permits soft brain tissue to be visualized). More recently, investigators have used computer-assisted tomography (CT scans) instead of the pneumoencephalograph to visualize brains. CT scans use computer-controlled x-rays to produce relatively clear views of successive layers of brain tissue. Four studies using CT scans to study the brains of autistic children were reviewed by Rapoport and Ismond (1982). The studies varied in how the autistic children were selected, the way the CT scans were read, and the adequacy of the control group (one had no control group at all). This last point is particularly important, because (for ethical reasons) it may be impossible to form a truly normal control group. Thus, although some of the studies indicated brain abnormalities among autistic children, the reliability and validity of these findings are still to be determined. New techniques for visualizing the brain using radioactive tracers and magnetic resonance (see Rapoport & Ismond, 1982) may help unravel some of the still unanswered questions.

Some writers have suggested that autistic children have defects in the left cerebral hemispheres of their brains (Prior, 1979). Growing out of early work with epileptic patients whose cerebral hemispheres were surgically severed (Levy-Agresti & Sperry, 1968), the notion that the two cerebral hemispheres are differentially specialized for cognitive processing has become both popular and well-known. Early theories distinguished the two hemispheres on the basis of the type of stimulus each is specialized to process. The left hemisphere, it was thought, dealt with verbal materials, whereas the right was specialized for spatial and other nonverbal materials. More recent theories of hemispheric specialization have deemphasized the role of the stimulus, opting instead for hemispheric differences in cognitive processing strategies (see Bradshaw & Nettleton, 1983). The theory that autistic children have deficient left hemisphere functioning is based on the following logic: Autistic children all have some sort of language deficit, language is a function of the left cerebral hemisphere, therefore autistic children must have something wrong with their left hemispheres.

Several lines of evidence have been cited in support of this hypothesis. Blackstock (1978, Experiment 1), for example, argues

that autistic children's preference for music over speech indicates heightened right hemisphere and decreased left-hemisphere functioning. Others have cited better spatial than verbal IQ performance, excessive left handedness, and dichotic listening studies (in which the children appear to show an advantage for materials presented to the left ear) as supporting left-hemisphere dysfunction among autistics (see McCann, 1981, for a review of this literature).

Two important difficulties with this research (in addition to the typical problems in diagnosing autism) are the problems in providing adequate control groups and the nature of the "laterality" measures themselves. Adequate control groups should at least include a group of mentally retarded children (to control for any effects of low intelligence) and probably a language-impaired group as well. Even when suitable controls are incorporated into the experimental design, however, the problem of adequate measures remains. Many of the tasks taken to indicate left or right brain functioning have low reliability and validity (Schwartz & Kirsner, 1984). For this reason, it is possible to alter the outcome of laterality experiments simply by changing small aspects of the procedure (Schwartz & Kirsner, 1982).

A recent experiment with important implications for the left-hemisphere dysfunction hypothesis was reported by Arnold and Schwartz (1983). Their experiment used a dichotic listening task in which materials were presented to one or the other ear over stereo headphones, and the children indicated which ear they "heard first." A bias toward one ear was taken as indicating better performance in the opposite hemisphere. That is, left-ear bias meant better performance in the right hemisphere, whereas a right-ear bias indicated left-hemisphere superiority. Three groups of children were studied: an autistic group, a group of language-impaired children, and a group of normal children. The results of this experiment are summarized in Table 4.6. As may be seen, the language-impaired children showed a left-ear (right hemisphere) advan-

TABLE 4.6. COMPARISON OF EAR
ADVANTAGE SCORES.

	Language-impaired	Autistic	Non-language-impaired
	.0625	.0417	0
	− .3750	0	.1431
	− .3958	.0625	.0481
	0	.2708	.1018
	− .0417	.0833	.1656
	− .0625	− .0833	.4974
	− .1458	.2292	0
	− .0833	.1042	.0971
Mean	− .1302	.0886	.1316

Note: A negative score indicates a left ear advantage. Scores can range
from − 1 to + 1. Source: Arnold & Schwartz, (1983).©1983 Plenum
Publishing Co. and reprinted with permission.

tage as might be expected, because language disability is often correlated with left-hemisphere dysfunction. The autistic children, however, could not be distinguished from the normals. These results provided no support for the notion that autistic children have poorly functioning left cerebral hemispheres. Fein, Humes, Kaplan, Lucci, & Waterhouse (1984) reached a similar conclusion after reviewing the literature.

Biochemistry. Over the past 10 years, there have been many attempts to discover possible biochemical abnormalities in autistic children. Although many different possibilities have been pursued, most attention has been devoted to serotonin, one of many chemicals that permit nerve cells to communicate with one another. Serotonin serves as a neurotransmitter, permitting messages to travel across neurons. Several studies have found elevated serotonin levels in the blood platelets of autistic children (see DeMyer et al., 1981). Unfortunately, nonautistic children have also been found to have higher than average serotonin levels, and some autistic children have perfectly normal levels. Thus, high serotonin levels cannot be considered a "marker" (biochemical abnormality) unique to autism. The possibility that autism, in at least some

children, can be treated by lowering serotonin levels will be addressed later in this chapter.

Biogenesis: Current Status. Although psychogenic theories were at one time more common than biogenic views, the trend today is definitely in the other direction. A great deal of research activity has focused on hypothesized genetic, neurological, and biochemical defects of autistic children. Although the results of these experiments are still tentative, the findings are beginning to converge. Autistic children appear to have a congenital vulnerability that may be inherited or, perhaps, acquired as an accident of birth. The result of this vulnerability is a language disability and an inability to form normal human attachments. Although there are no clear-cut biochemical or neurological markers unique to autism, new biochemical and imaging techniques hold promise for identifying such markers in the not too distant future.

Treatment of Autism

Psychotherapy

Autistic children have been treated with just about every known psychological and biochemical therapy. Traditionally, psychoanalytically oriented psychotherapy was recommended for autism. A report by the Research Task Force of the National Institute of Mental Health (1975) summarizing the results of many years of research, concludes, "Psychotherapy with autistic children of the kind designed to provide insight has not proved effective and in the light of our knowledge about autism is unlikely to do so" (p. 207). Nevertheless, there are still advocates of this type of therapy, most prominently Bettleheim (1967), who believes that autistic children should be removed from their homes to a special school (because the real world is too threatening) and treated by a nondemanding therapist who allows them to behave in any way that they desire. It should be remembered that Bettleheim's definition of autism is more general than the one given in the DSM-III. The effectiveness of his treatment for Kanner's syndrome children remains undemonstrated.

In addition to psychotherapy, some writers have suggested "body stimulation" as a method for treating autistic children (Des-Lauriers & Carlson, 1969). Group therapy, sensory isolation, and sundry other therapies have also been recommended at one time or another. None have made much difference in the lives of autistic children.

Behavior Modification

The most widely employed treatment method for autism today is behavior modification. Behavior modification (often implemented as part of special educational programs) has made it possible for autistic children to learn various skills and has led to significant improvements in social behavior (see Steffen & Karoly, 1982, for examples). Largely because of the introduction of behavior modification techniques, the prognosis for autistic children has improved. In contrast to early pessimistic views, therapists are now reporting success in working with autistic children, even mute ones. It is difficult to disagree with Ross and Pelham (1981), who state in their recent review " . . . behavior modification is at this

time the treatment of choice for autism" (p. 272). A more detailed discussion of specific behavior modification procedures appears in Chapter 10.

Although behavior modification has proven useful, it is by no means a panacea. Early high hopes for what can be accomplished through behavior modification have had to be toned down as research findings have failed to replicate the dramatic gains claimed by early workers. For example, in the 1960s it was thought possible to produce usable spoken language in autistic children by "reinforcing" certain behaviors and suitably altering their environment (Hewett, 1965). Twenty years, and dozens of studies later, Howlin (1981) concludes her review of behavioral language training by stating:

> The evidence from language intervention studies with autistic children suggest that the effects of training are limited by the inherent linguistic abilities of the children involved. . . . If autistic children have the essential prerequisites for language development, operant techniques can be useful in teaching them to use these skills more appropriately for purposes of communication. . . . However, in the case of autistic children who are profoundly handicapped in both comprehension and expressive skills, as well as in their play and social development, operant techniques are unlikely to result in the acquisition of communicative speech. (1981, p. 100–101)

Another area in which early claims have proved to be overstated is in the area of selective attention. A number of studies have indicated that autistic children exhibit stimulus overselectivity, which may account for many of their difficulties in complex learning and the development of social skills (Koegel & Wilhelm, 1973; Lovaas, Koegel, & Schreibman, 1979). Stimulus overselectivity occurs when a child is conditioned to respond to a multidimensional stimulus but only learns to respond to one of the stimuli. Because many learning situations consist of multiple stimuli that are presented simultaneously by a therapist, teacher, or other agent, the autistic child is clearly at a disadvantage by being unable to respond to more than one dimension. Overselective attention has been used to explain why some autistic children fail to acquire appropriate conditioned responses; that is, why they fail to associate unconditioned stimuli with neutral conditioned stimuli. This, in turn, may explain their lack of normal conditioned behaviors. A normal child, for example, learns to associate its mother with pleasure-producing stimuli such as food. This occurs because the child generalizes its positive response to food to the other stimuli in the feeding environment, one of these being the mother. Overselective children may fail to make the connection between food and the food provider and therefore fail to develop the usual affectionate feelings for their parents.

The overselectivity hypothesis has become a widely used explanation for many of the problems of autistic children, and training programs have been developed to help children become less selective (Schreibman, 1975). Early reports notwithstanding, studies by Edwards, Shigley, and Edwards (1976) and Litrownik, McInnis, Wetzel-Pritchard, and Filipelli (1978) suggest that overselectivity is not universal among autistic children. Indeed, it now appears that overselectivity is a function of mental age rather than autism (see also, Schover & Newsom, 1976). In other words, overselectivity is found among nonautistic mentally retarded children. Because these children do not display autistic behaviors (a failure to form social relationships, for example), it seems unlikely that overselectivity is responsible for all peculiar autistic behaviors, and training designed to reduce overselectivity will not make much difference in modifying many autistic behaviors.

Pharmacology

At one time or another, just about every kind of drug has been administered to autistic children. Often, at least in the beginning, drugs are reported to be effective in reducing some autistic symptoms only to be found ineffec-

tive later on. The problem is that most of these drugs were initially given to children in a relatively uncontrolled fashion. When the drugs are compared with placebos, most autistics show no significant improvement. There are some exceptions, however. Haloperidol, a drug used with adult schizophrenics, appears to improve learning ability in autistic children (Campbell, Anderson, Small, Perry, Green, & Caplan, 1982), and large doses of certain vitamins may also lead to improvement in some autistic symptoms (Rimland, Callaway, & Dreyfus, 1978).

The most recent pharmacological approach to autism is derived from the finding reported earlier that some autistic children have higher than average levels of serotonin in their blood platelets. Geller, Ritvo, Freeman, and Yuwiler (1982) reported a preliminary pilot study in which three autistic children with elevated serotonin levels were given fenfluramine (a diet drug), which reduces serotonin levels. They noted that not only did the children's serotonin levels fall, but many autistic symptoms also improved. When drug administration ceased, the children's serotonin levels rose again, and behavior deteriorated. This initial success led to a nationwide, multi-center study that will eventually include over 100 autistic children. A preliminary report concerning 14 autistic children has already appeared (Ritvo, Freeman, Geller, & Yuwiler, 1983). The report confirms that fenfluramine does reduce serotonin levels while also improving autistic functioning on a variety of social and intellectual indices. Interestingly, improvements were noted even among those autistic children who did not have elevated serotonin levels. Further clarification of the relationship between fenfluramine, serotonin, and autistic behavior will be forthcoming as the study continues.

Autism: Present and Future

Forty years of research into the nature of autism have brought a great many insights into the syndrome. First, it seems clear that although autism represents a fairly reliable diagnostic category, there are many other children who display some, but not all, of the autistic behaviors. The challenge of developing more reliable and valid diagnostic instruments has been taken up by experimenters. Today, there are several valuable diagnostic instruments, and they are continuing to be refined.

Although research has proceeded from many theoretical viewpoints, both psychological and biological studies seem to be converging on similar findings. Autistic children have a cognitive deficit that prevents them from using meanings or symbols in their language, which is either nonexistent or a peculiar echoing devoid of all meaning. Although the exact nature of this cognitive deficit is not yet known, some combination of genetic vulnerability and environmental nervous system insult is strongly suspected. The finding that some autistic children may have high levels of serotonin also suggests a central nervous system disorder. The possibility that there may be more than one etiology for autism and even more than one type of autism (genetic versus nongenetic, for example) seems increasingly likely as research findings mount up. Figure 4.4 summarizes some of the possible etiologies of the autistic syndrome.

Two important issues for the future are the increasing number of autistic adults and the prevention of autism. In the past, great efforts have been devoted to teaching autistic children. Although many autistic children do learn some skills, most reach adolescence and early adulthood still requiring help and assistance. Unfortunately, few preparations have been made. Adolescents must learn to deal with their awakening sexuality, their awareness of being different, and they must also learn a new set of social skills. Providing the training and facilities necessary for autistic adolescents and adults presents an important challenge to those working in the field of child psychopathology (Mesibov & Schopler, 1983).

Although recent research with drugs like fenfluramine holds promise for ameliorating autistic symptoms, no drug is likely to effect a cure. Preventing the syndrome from developing in the first place is the only way to really control autism. If the genetic mechanism is ever unraveled, genetic counseling will become a possibility. Similarly, the discovery of a unique biological marker for autism will also aid in prevention. Although still a long way off, new biological and psychological research findings suggest that the possibility of preventing autism has never been closer.

CHILDHOOD ONSET PERVASIVE DEVELOPMENTAL DISORDER

Background

Although Kanner's early observations suggested that autism is a unique syndrome, it became clear rather early on that there were many children who displayed some but not all autistic symptoms. As we described earlier in this chapter, diagnostic instruments have been designed to try and separate those children who are classically autistic from others who are similar. These efforts have met with varying degrees of success—it is not always easy to separate the classic autistic syndromes from other pervasive developmental disorders.

Some of these not-so-classic children have been described in the literature. DeSanctis (1908) described a condition he called dementia praecocissima, which he assumed was a psychosis like schizophrenia occurring in young children. Heller (1930) wrote about a syndrome he called dementia infantalis and also thought of it as a sort of schizophrenia. Margaret Mahler (1968), on the other hand, put the emphasis on mother-child interactions when she described a disorder called symbiotic psychosis. Mahler thought that these children failed to develop beyond the normal symbiotic infant-mother relationship of early childhood and therefore showed panic whenever they were separated from their mothers. Finally, some writers have referred to the disintegrative psychoses that de-

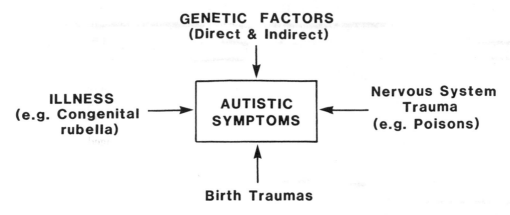

FIGURE 4.4. Possible etiological factors in autism. Different factors may produce similar behaviors in different autistic children.

velop in early childhood after a period of normal development (Rutter, 1972a). These children show a deterioration in social skills and loss of intelligence sometimes accompanied by strange mannerisms.

Although each writer concentrates on specific details, these syndromes do tend to overlap one another, and many share autistic characteristics as well. In an attempt to clarify some of these relationships, Wing (1981) and her colleagues undertook an epidemiological study in the London borough of Camberwell, where there were 35,000 children under the age of 15. Wing and her team set out to identify every child seen by any agency (medical, social, or educational) for any sort of problem. This meant identifying each child sent for speech therapy, seen by a pediatrician for a health problem, and so on. They identified 914 children this way. Each of these children was screened in order to identify anyone who was either mentally retarded or had one or more of the signs associated with pervasive developmental disorders (including autism). Of the 914 children, 163 fit either or both of these criteria. Out of these, 17 had the classic autistic syndrome. This turns out to be 4.9 per 10,000, which agrees very well with the incidence estimates given earlier.

However, Wing and her colleagues also found another 57 children whose behavior could be described as peculiar. These children, presumably, could have received one or more of the diagnoses described above. Because it is not yet possible to differentiate these diagnoses very well, the DSM-III places them all in a single category called Childhood Onset Pervasive Developmental Disorder. This diagnostic category is clearly a heterogeneous one. Some of the children who receive this diagnosis are the victims of a childhood illness. For example, a normal child may contract encephalitis leading to brain damage and wind up with a pervasive developmental disorder (Corbett, Harris, Taylor, & Trimble, 1977), or sometimes the problem begins after a head injury. For other children, no organic etiology can be discovered (although one is usually expected). The inclusion of this diagnosis in the DSM-III does not imply that the children have a single disorder. It merely acknowledges that there are severe developmental disorders of childhood other than autism.

Description and Diagnosis

The DSM-III criteria for childhood onset pervasive developmental disorder appear in Table 4.7. As may be seen, the first criterion calls for a failure to develop social relationships. Although the children may display the same asocial tendencies exhibited by autistic

TABLE 4.7. DSM-III CRITERIA FOR CHILDHOOD ONSET PERVASIVE DEVELOPMENTAL DISORDER.

A. Gross and sustained impairment in social relationships, e.g., lack of appropriate affective responsivity, inappropriate clinging, asociality, lack of empathy.
B. At least three of the following:
   (1) sudden excessive anxiety manifested by such symptoms as free-floating anxiety, catastrophic reactions to every-day occurrences, inability to be consoled when upset, unexplained panic attacks
   (2) constricted or inappropriate affect, including lack of appropriate fear reactions, unexplained rage reactions, and extreme mood lability
   (3) resistance to change in the environment (e.g., upset if dinner time is changed), or insistence on doing things in the same manner every time (e.g., putting on clothes always in the same order)
   (4) oddities of motor movement, such as peculiar posturing, peculiar hand or finger movements, or walking on tiptoe
   (5) abnormalities of speech, such as questionlike melody, monotonous voice
   (6) hyper- or hypo-sensitivity to sensory stimuli, e.g., hyperacusis
   (7) self-mutilation, e.g., biting or hitting self, head banging
C. Onset of the full syndrome after 30 months of age and before 12 years of age.
D. Absence of delusions, hallucinations, incoherence, or marked loosening of associations.

Source: American Psychiatric Association (1980).©1980 by the American Psychiatric Association and reprinted by permission of the publisher.

children, inappropriate clinging (of the type described by Mahler) can also be taken as a sign of improper social relationships. Wing (1981) even suggested that a failure to develop normal social relationships underlies all of the pervasive developmental disorders.

As can be seen, the second criterion is merely a list of bizarre behaviors that have been associated with developmental disorders beginning early in life. As far as we can tell, the requirement that at least three be present for a diagnosis is purely arbitrary and not based on any research findings.

The third criterion, onset after 30 months of age and before age 12, is meant to distinguish these disorders from autism and, presumably from schizophrenia, which usually first occurs in late childhood or early adolescence. This criterion apparently ignores Kolvin's (1971) findings described earlier, indicating that schizophrenia may begin as early as 8. In any event, as depicted in Figure 4.1, very few disorders develop between 30 months and 12 years of age, making childhood onset pervasive disorders even rarer than autism.

The final DSM-III criterion is almost identical to the final criterion for autism. It is included in order to exclude any children suffering from schizophrenia.

Interestingly, despite the heterogeneity of the diagnostic category, the DSM-III also includes a diagnostic category called atypical pervasive developmental disorder. This final category is meant to include all those who do not fall into the autistic or pervasive disorder categories. Presumably, this category would include those children who have, say, only one or two of the bizarre behaviors described in criterion B in Table 4.7. We see little value in multiplying diagnostic categories this way and predict that this diagnosis will not be used very often.

Etiology and Treatment

The heterogeneous nature of the illness insures that there is no single etiology for the pervasive developmental disorders, although most cases are thought to have an organic basis. Because they are rare, little is known about family patterns or any predisposing factors. Like autism, the disorders appear to occur more commonly among boys than girls.

As in autism, the treatment of choice for the behavioral deficits evidenced by these children is behavior modification. Of course, drug treatment is also useful in dealing with specific symptoms. As of yet, there is no cure, nor is there likely to be one until the various etiologies are sorted out.

SCHIZOPHRENIA

Background

Although the term *childhood schizophrenia* was once used as a synonym for all of the serious problems of childhood, today's usage is much more specific. In fact, the DSM-III makes no provision for the diagnosis childhood schizophrenia, classifying schizophrenia in childhood as no different from any other type of schizophrenia. This marks a large step forward in the field of childhood psychopathology. Not only is there likely to be far less diagnostic confusion, but separating schizophrenia from the other pervasive disorders has also, as we shall show, clarified several etiological questions as well.

Symptoms similar to those associated with schizophrenia have been recorded throughout history; however, the disorder's recent history is generally taken to begin with observations made in the 19th century that certain individuals tended to develop a progressive, deteriorating mental disorder beginning in adolescence, which is characterized by loose associations, disturbed thinking, and inappropriate affect. The syndrome was originally referred to as dementia praecox, but this was soon replaced with the term *schizophrenia* by the psychiatrist Bleuler (1950). Although schizophrenia translates literally to mean "split personality," the term does not refer to the rare multiple personalities so popular with movie writers and the press. The "split" referred to in schizophrenia is among parts of the same personality. Schizophrenics suffer from a loosening of associations (evidenced by odd jumps from one idea to another) and disorganized behavior. Actually, Bleuler referred to the schizophrenias, reflecting his belief that schizophrenia is not a homogeneous disorder but actually a group of disorders that share certain features.

Diagnosis and Description

The DSM-III diagnostic criteria for schizophrenia appear in Table 4.8. These criteria are the same whether the disorder begins in childhood or later in life. The first criterion lists the recognized schizophrenic behaviors. In this list, delusions refer to bizarre thoughts and hallucinations or to odd sensory experiences (hearing sounds when there are none, seeing things that aren't there). Historically, most writers have emphasized the dramatic schizophrenic symptoms such as hallucinations and delusions as being the most important features of schizophrenia. Bleuler, however, considered these secondary features, focusing instead on what are called the four "A's": associations, affect, autism, and ambivalence.

TABLE 4.8. DSM-III DIAGNOSTIC CRITERIA FOR A SCHIZOPHRENIC DISORDER.

A. At least one of the following during a phase of the illness:
   (1) bizarre delusions (content is patently absurd and has no possible basis in fact), such as delusions of being controlled, thought broadcasting, thought insertion, or thought withdrawal
   (2) somatic, grandiose, religious, nihilistic, or other delusions without persecutory or jealous content
   (3) delusions with persecutory or jealous content if accompanied by hallucinations of any type
   (4) auditory hallucinations in which either a voice keeps up a running commentary on the individual's behavior or thoughts, or two or more voices converse with each other
   (5) auditory hallucinations on several occasions with content of more than one or two words, having no apparent relation to depression or elation
   (6) incoherence, marked loosening of associations, markedly illogical thinking, or marked poverty of content of speech if associated with at least one of the following: (a) blunted, flat, or inappropriate affect (b) delusions or hallucinations (c) catatonic or other grossly disorganized behavior
B. Deterioration from a previous level of functioning in such areas as work, social relations, and self-care.
C. Duration: Continuous signs of the illness for at least six months at some time during the person's life, with some signs of the illness at present. The six-month period must include an active phase during which there were symptoms from A.

Source: American Psychiatric Association (1980).©1980 by the American Psychiatric Association and reprinted by permission of the publisher.

In schizophrenia, the associative links between thoughts break down, resulting in bizarre, rambling language and illogical thinking. In addition, affect (or emotions) become inappropriate. Patients behave autistically; that is, they become self-absorbed (this should not be confused with infantile autism). Finally, ambivalence is expressed in uncertain affect and behavior. When these symptoms occur together, the result is an individual unable to organize logical, consistent behavior or to interact with others in an effective manner.

It should be obvious from Table 4.8 that DSM-III criterion A-6 refers to Bleuler's four A's. It should also be clear that schizophrenia is a very broad category. For example, the first criterion requires the individual being diagnosed to have exhibited one of six behaviors sometime during a phase of the illness. Because only one behavior is required, it is possible to classify two individuals as schizophrenic, even though they do not have the same symptoms. For example, incoherent speech (criterion A-6) can be the basis for the first person's diagnosis, whereas grandiose delusions (criterion A-2) can be the reason the second person is diagnosed schizophrenic. Both have the same diagnosis, although they don't actually have the same symptoms. It is probably no surprise that this approach to diagnosis has come under heavy criticism (see the exchange of comments in Schwartz, 1982).

In addition to the behaviors in criterion A, the DSM-III requires that two other criteria be met. The individual must show a deterioration from a higher level of functioning and must have displayed the behavior or behaviors in criterion A for at least 6 months.

Often individuals who meet the criteria for schizophrenia pass through a *prodromal* phase prior to developing their disorder. This prodromal phase is characterized by social isolation, peculiar behavior (talking to oneself, for instance), or bizarre ideas. This phase is viewed as a precursor of the full-blown schizophrenic illness.

The DSM-III also includes criteria for diagnosing various schizophrenic subtypes. These include a disorganized type (marked mainly by incoherent or disorganized speech); a cat-atonic type, in which the major disturbance is motor rather than cognitive (patients take on strange postures, for instance); a paranoid type, in which delusions (usually persecutory) are the main symptoms; and finally an undifferentiated type, which means just what it says.

Although the various subtypes (and a few others that are not even in the DSM-III) are used in psychiatric practice, there is some doubt about how reliable these diagnoses are. (It is impossible to write about schizophrenia without mentioning the frequently lamented unreliability of the schizophrenic diagnosis.) Some writers have even gone so far as to assert that schizophrenia does not exist, calling it merely society's moral judgment of aberrant behavior (Sarbin & Mancuso, 1980). However, a disorder resembling schizophrenia has been described in just about every culture in the world. Moreover, studies of interrater agreement have found a fair degree of reliability for the diagnosis of schizophrenia, if not for the subtypes (see Schwartz, 1982, for a review).

Figure 4.5 presents the case history of a child diagnosed schizophrenic. As may be seen, the child, John, meets all of the DSM-III criteria. The case illustrates why it is no more necessary to have a special category of childhood schizophrenia than it is to have a category of, say, middle-age or old-age schizophrenia.

John's history and behavior include many of the characteristics associated with schizophrenia in children. For example, early development may be apparently normal. However, once the disorder begins to develop, the child's behavior becomes increasingly bizarre. Preoccupation with objects, such as John's fascination with mailboxes, may grow into compulsive rituals, and early fears may develop into delusions of persecution later on (Kolvin, 1971; Kydd & Werry, 1982). The children typically show a limited range of emotions (blunt affect) and sometimes experience hallucinations (although auditory hallucinations like John's are more rare). Periods of remission may be followed by relapses, with the general trend being a continuation

FIGURE 4.5. A Schizophrenic Child

John's first visit to the clinic at age 9 took place at the suggestion of his pediatrician. John's mother, Sandra, sought the pediatrician's help because of her son's increasingly peculiar behavior. She felt that there was something terribly wrong with him because he did not talk and act like other children his age. As examples of John's odd behaviors, Sandra described his fondness for flushing toilets and his fascination with barber shops. He liked to visit them and stare at the barbers at work. John knew the location of about ten different barber shops. Sandra also reported that John stayed home a great deal. When he was around other children their games seemed to frighten him. ("He was always a sensitive child," she said.) John likes to inspect mailboxes, which he calls "loaders," and whenever the opportunity arises he likes nothing better than playing around a mailbox, touching it, and talking to it. Whenever he passes a mail box, he asks to stop and see "the loader."

John's difficulties appear to have begun when he was about 7, although Sandra at one time thought she noted odd behaviors somewhat earlier, when John's younger sister, Helen, was born. His infancy, on the other hand, was quite typical. He anticipated being picked up and reached for his bottle and his mother. He was friendly, would look at people, and began smiling before he was 3 months old. He took his first unassisted step at about 1 year and began talking shortly after that.

John's father, also named John, works as a laborer for the city water department. A quiet, introverted man, John Sr. has no history of "mental illness," but his sister, John Jr.'s aunt, has been hospitalized several times with a diagnosis of schizophrenia.

An interview with the boy showed him to be almost completely without interpersonal contact. He ignored the interviewer and spent most of his time playing aimlessly and talking to no one in particular. He did not respond to directions and did not play with toys in a creative fashion. Although he occasionally answered questions directly, his interest could not be held for very long. John's physical appearance was noted to be rather poor. He was a sickly looking child who suffered from frequent colds and minor illnesses. A physical examination was unremarkable, except for an abnormal EEG (the abnormality appeared to be located in the left side of the brain).

Beginning at age 10, John and his family were seen for dynamic psychotherapy for several years. During that time, John showed periods of improved behavior when he was able to go to a special school. However, during his teenage years, John's bizarre behavior returned. In addition to his other symptoms, he developed auditory hallucinations. Several times he heard voices hatching a plot against him. John was hospitalized several times before he was 20, but each time, his behavior improved enough for him to be sent home. Now, in his early twenties, John lives in a sheltered half-way house with several other patients and a counselor. He receives medication, which appears to reduce his symptoms, although the chances of future flare-ups serious enough to require rehospitalization remain high.

of the disorder throughout adulthood (Rutter, 1972). As may be seen, the characteristic symptoms are similar to those of adult schizophrenics — delusions, hallucinations and altered mood — and unlike those associated with autism.

Demography

Kolvin's (1971) study, which we have mentioned several times in this chapter, described 33 cases of schizophrenia beginning before 15 years of age in a London sample. Kydd and Werry (1982) found 15 schizophrenic children under the age of 16 treated in a New Zealand hospital over a 10-year period. Ten percent of these children had one or more parents who were also diagnosed schizophrenic. This is approximately the same percentage found for adult schizophrenics. Both Kolvin and Kydd and Werry found that schizophrenic children were most likely to come from lower social class backgrounds. This may be contrasted with the findings reported earlier for infantile autism, in which mental illness was found to be rare in family backgrounds, and there was no social class bias. There is also a much higher probability of finding a second schizophrenic child in a family where one has already been diagnosed than of finding a second autistic child in similar circumstances (Hanson & Gottesman, 1976). One similarity between schizophrenia in childhood and autism is the sex ratio. Kolvin found boys to outnumber girls in his sample of schizophrenic children by a ratio of 2.5 to 1 (although Kydd and Werry found approximately the same number of schizophrenic boys and girls). Unlike autism, however, the incidence of schizophrenia in girls rises with age, until the ratio becomes about equal among adult schizophrenics (Miller, 1974).

Early Development

No clear relationship between pregnancy or birth complications and schizophrenia has been established. But there is a tendency for schizophrenic children to be below average in birth weight (Mednick & Schulsinger, 1968), suggesting perhaps that early pre- and perinatal factors may contribute to the later development of schizophrenia.

As in the case of John, early development of schizophrenic children is fairly normal. The autistic characteristics of failing to show anticipatory posturing, the desire to maintain sameness, and stereotyped movements are not generally noted. On the other hand, schizophrenic children may display unusual behaviors of another type. They may be anxious and prone to the development of fears, and they may display periods of hyperactivity (Offord & Cross, 1969). Recent evidence suggests that children who later develop schizophrenia may also be more distractible and less able to focus their attention (Erlenmyer-Kimling, Cornblatt, & Golden, 1983). Determining which children display behaviors indicative of later schizophrenia (that is, which children are at risk to develop schizophrenia) plays an important role in prevention. We shall have more to say on the topic of prevention later in this book.

Prevalence

Cases of schizophrenia in childhood are very rare; it took Kolvin many years to collect a sample of 33, and Kydd and Werry could only find 15 cases over a 10-year period. Because of some of the problems in definition already alluded to, it is impossible to obtain accurate estimates of schizophrenia's prevalence in childhood and adolescence. About 3 to 4 children in 10,000 (Neale and Oltmanns, 1980) is a rough approximation.

Prognosis

Fewer clear conclusions can be drawn about the prognosis for childhood schizophrenia than for autism. Once again, this is the result of the regrettable tendency to lump children with different disorders together in many early studies. When some attempt is made to separate out schizophrenic children, the prognosis turns out to be poor but somewhat better than for autism. Kydd and Werry found that approximately two-fifths of schizophrenic children were in remission at the time of their follow-up.

Differential Diagnosis

As was noted earlier, the term *childhood schizophrenia* has been used so often as to be almost meaningless. Schizophrenia, whether occurring in children, adolescents, or adults should be kept separate from other disorders with which it shares some features.

Mental Retardation

Most individuals who develop schizophrenia fall in the low average range of intelligence (see Rutter, 1972a). It is sometimes difficult to measure the IQ of a schizophrenic child (or an autistic child, for that matter) because they may not cooperate in the testing. But like autistic children, schizophrenic children can usually be differentiated from nonschizophrenic mentally retarded children because of their idiosyncratic behaviors. Delusions, hallucinations, and blunt affect are not usually associated with mental retardation.

Infantile Autism

There are several important ways in which schizophrenia differs from autism. (Most of these points were originally noted by Rimland, 1964.)

1. *Age of onset*: Autism begins before 30 months of age. Schizophrenia begins after a period of normal development. Referring again to the distribution of "age of onset" depicted in Figure 4.2, the two peaks in the distribution represent autism (early onset peak) and schizophrenia (the late onset peak), respectively.
2. *Health and appearance*: Autistic children are often described as good-looking and physically healthy, whereas schizophrenic children are sickly and undistinguished physically.
3. *Infant responsiveness*: Unlike autistics, schizophrenic children are rarely described as failing to anticipate being picked up or looking through people.

4. *Need to preserve sameness*: A hallmark of autism, this symptom is not normally present in schizophrenia.
5. *Language disorder*: The peculiar language of autism — echolalia, pronominal reversal — is not commonly found in schizophrenia. Schizophrenic language is characterized by peculiarities in thought (Schwartz, 1982).
6. *Family background*: Schizophrenia is more common among working class families and seems to run in families. Autism does not appear to have a social class bias and only weakly runs in families.
7. *Idiot savant performance*: Pockets of superior achievement have not typically been associated with schizophrenia.

Although some of these distinctions may in fact become somewhat blurred in actual practice, the virtues of considering schizophrenia as separate from autism and childhood onset pervasive developmental disorders are illustrated in Table 4.9. It is clear from the table that late onset disorders resemble adult forms of schizophrenia, whereas early onset disorders resemble pervasive developmental disorders (including autism), suggesting that the two peaks in Figure 4.2 represent differing types of psychopathology.

Etiology of Schizophrenia: Research and Theory

A satisfactory explanation for schizophrenia has yet to be found. Although biogenic explanations have become increasingly common, they still have not converged on a single cause for schizophrenia. Since schizophrenia may occur as a reaction to unusual stress (on the battlefield, for instance), many theorists have concluded that some combination of life stress and biological vulnerability is necessary to develop schizophrenia.

Psychogenesis

As noted for autism, the dominant view for many years was that schizophrenia is the result of psychological and emotional causes. Although once again, the precise psycholog-

TABLE 4.9. A COMPARISON OF EARLY ONSET AND LATE ONSET DISORDERS WITH ORGANIC PSYCHOSES AND ADULT SCHIZOPHRENIA.

Symptom	Organic Psychoses	Childhood Disorder Early Onset	Childhood Disorder Late Onset	Adult Schizophrenia
Aloneness	+	+	−	−
Retardation	+	+	−	−
Males outnumber females	+	+	+	−
Stereotyped behavior	+	+	+ / −	+ / −
Pronominal reversal	−	+	−	−
Echolalia	+ / −	+	−	−
Onset before three	+ / −	+	−	−
Delayed speech	+ / −	+	−	−
Motor anomalies	+	+	−	−
Perceptual anomalies	+	+	−	−
Abnormal EEG/seizures	+	+	−	−
Remissions	−	−	+	+
Disordered thought	−	−	+	+
Hallucinations	−	−	+	+
Inappropriate emotions	−	−	+	+
Improved with drugs	−	−	+	+

Source: Adapted from Hanson & Gottesman (1976). © 1976 Plenum Publishing Co. and reprinted by permission.

ical factors were a matter of disagreement, most psychogenic theorists focused on disturbed mother-child and family interactions.

For example, the "schizophrenogenic" mother who is said to produce schizophrenia in her child by various means has been a common character in the literature. It has not always been easy to demonstrate that such mothers exist, however. Many studies rely on the memories of the schizophrenic patients themselves, and variables correlated with emotional problems such as socioeconomic level, marital dissatisfaction, and so forth have frequently been left uncontrolled when studying maternal personality.

As a result of hypotheses such as Bateson's notion of the "double-bind" (Bateson, Jackson, Haley, & Weakland, 1956), a great deal of attention has been given to the role of family interaction and communication patterns in producing schizophrenia. A double-

bind is said to exist when an individual receives two mutually contradictory messages; one cannot obey the first command without violating the other. Such messages occur in almost everyone's life. For example, someone buys you two shirts for your birthday; you wear one the next morning and the gift-giver says, "Don't you like the other?" It is not really clear how such messages lead to schizophrenic behavior. Why, for example, should a double-bind result in someone having hallucinations?

The nature of communication patterns in the families of schizophrenic and normal children has been studied repeatedly, but the results of these studies are difficult to interpret. Even when differences have been found between normal and schizophrenic families, it is often impossible to tell what came first, faulty interaction patterns or schizophrenia. That is, it is not clear whether abnormal interactions caused a family member to develop schizophrenia or whether having a schizophrenic in the family produces abnormal interaction patterns. To illustrate: Mishler and Waxler (1968) found parents to be rigid in their responses to their schizophrenic child but not to other, healthy children in the family. This, they suggested, means that parental rigidity is a response to their schizophrenic child's behavior, not the cause of it. A general review of the studies of family interaction patterns in normal and disturbed families (some of whom had schizophrenic children) may be found in Jacob (1975). More recent work in this area is described in Field, Goldberg, Stern, and Sostek (1980). In addition to work on interaction patterns, some studies claim to have found differences in the personalities of parents of schizophrenic and nonschizophrenic children (Singer & Wynne, 1965), but these findings are also controversial (Hirsch & Leff, 1971).

Although disordered family communication patterns and "schizophrenogenic" mothers are not easily identified, there is good evidence for the role of psychological factors of some sort in the onset and course of schizophrenia. Research by Brown, Birley, and Wing (1972) suggests that schizophrenic breakdowns are usually preceded by significant psychological stress. Because only some individuals respond to psychological stress by developing schizophrenia, it would appear that stress, although perhaps necessary, is not in itself sufficient to cause schizophrenia.

Biogenesis

Genetics. Although it is possible to find disagreements in the literature, the vast majority of those writing on this subject feel that there is a substantial genetic component in schizophrenia (Buchsbaum & Haier, 1982). Identical twins have higher concordance rates (the likelihood of a second twin having schizophrenia once one is diagnosed) than fraternal twins do, and adopted schizophrenic children are likely to have schizophrenic biological but not adoptive parents (see Kendler, 1983, for

a review). An important paper by Hanson and Gottesman (1976) reviewing the literature on the genetics of autism and childhood schizophrenia concluded that early onset disorders (beginning before age 5) are not genetically transmitted, but those beginning in later childhood are inherited in a manner similar to adult schizophrenia. Things are complicated a bit by the results of Folstein and Rutter (1978), who found that although autism itself does not appear to have a strong genetic basis, language disturbances may be more common in the families of autistics than in the population at large. It should be noted that although the genetic basis of schizophrenia seems fairly clear, the concordance in identical twins even when raised together is not perfect, once again suggesting a role for nongenetic, experiential factors in the etiology of schizophrenia.

Biochemistry and Neurology. The hypothesis that left-hemisphere brain functioning is disturbed in schizophrenia has received a fair amount of attention and, like the same hypothesis in autism, has not gone very far (Schwartz & Kirsner, 1984). Problems in the reliability and validity of laterality measures continue to plague this field.

The search for a biochemical marker for schizophrenia has also been widespread and arduous. Differences in neurotransmitter activity, enzyme levels, and metabolism have all been associated with schizophrenia, but as yet no single marker has been identified (Buchsbaum & Haier, 1982; Kety, 1979). Although the trend is toward focusing on biochemical and neurological markers for schizophrenia, the likelihood is that some interaction between a genetically transmitted vulnerability and psychological stress is responsible for schizophrenia. Because both the disposition and the stress can vary along a continuum of severity, it is distinctly possible that some children (those with a strong predisposition) may become schizophrenic in the face of only minimal stress, whereas others may require a fair amount of stress before becoming schizophrenic. The notion that stress and genetics interact to produce schizophrenia is known as the *diathesis-stress* theory.

Treatment

Psychotherapy of practically every type, from group to individual from play therapy to primal screams, has been offered to schizophrenic children and their families. The evidence for its effectiveness, although stronger than for autism, is hardly overwhelming. As in autism, the psychological treatment of choice is behavior modification.

Drug treatment has been more successful for schizophrenia than for the other pervasive disorders of childhood. Psychotropic medications such as the phenothiazines (major tranquilizers) appear to relieve some schizophrenic symptoms, thereby permitting schizophrenics to live outside hospitals and even to participate in behavioral treatment programs. Because many of these drugs block the formation of the neurotransmitter dopamine, researchers have hypothesized that an excess of dopamine may be at least partly responsible for schizophrenia. Research designed to clarify the relationship between neurotransmitters and schizophrenia is currently underway (Buchsbaum & Haier, 1982). If this research does reveal specific markers for schizophrenia, not only will treatment be improved, but we may also be able to prevent schizophrenia from developing in the first place by identifying vulnerable individuals. This approach to prevention is discussed further in a later chapter.

Schizophrenia: Current Status

It is generally agreed by virtually everyone working in the field today that schizophrenia in childhood is little different from schizophrenia in adults. Starting later in childhood than autism, is shares few characteristics with autism and many with adult schizophrenia. Although there is a strong genetic component in schizophrenia — and there is a likelihood that a biological marker will soon be identified — there also appears to be a psycholog-ical stress factor operating as well. Schizophrenia does not develop unless the biological predisposition and some source of stress are both present. Drug treatment is helpful in reducing symptoms, but behavioral interventions are usually necessary to modify unwanted behaviors.

SUMMARY

The pervasive developmental disorders of childhood (and schizophrenia in children), although quite rare, have received a great deal of research and clinical attention over the past 40 years. In the beginning, a lack of rigor tended to blur the distinctions between the various disorders and slowed progress in understanding them. Today, however, most clinicians and researchers acknowledge the merit of distinguishing between autism, which is present at birth or within the first 30 months, childhood onset pervasive developmental disorders, which share some features with autism but begin somewhat later, and schizophrenia, which does not typically occur until late childhood or early adolescence. All three disorders share features in common, but they may be distinguished by their age of onset, family characteristics (schizophrenia has a strong genetic component, for example), and idiosyncratic symptoms, such as the desire to maintain sameness, which characterizes autism but is rarely found in other disorders.

Psychogenic theories dominated the field for many years. They attempted to account for the various autistic and schizophrenic symptoms as reactions to deviant environments or as the result of a destructive maternal personality. These notions have received very little research support and are now declining in popularity. This is particularly true in the case of autism, where biogenetic explanations are most compelling. Although the precise nature of the biological deficit in autism has not yet been identified, it seems almost certain that autism is the direct result of some biochemical (or neurological) dysfunction. Schizophrenia in childhood is similar to schizophrenia in adults. Unlike autism, schizophrenia appears best explained as the outcome of a genetic vulnerability coupled with environmental stress of some kind. Research has begun to clarify the nature of this genetic disposition and of the source of psychological stress. If biological markers are discovered, the door will be open not only to curing autism and schizophrenia, but also from preventing their occurrence in the first place.

SUGGESTED READINGS

Greenfield, J. A child called Noah. (1973). New York: Paperback Library. A parent's view of what it is like to have an autistic child.

Rapoport, J. L., & Ismond, D. R. (1982). Biological research on child psychiatry. *Journal of the American Academy of Child Psychiatry, 21,* 543–548. A brief review of progress in biochemical and neuroanatomical research into the causes of child psychopathology.

DeMyer, M. K., Hingtgen, J. N., & Jackson, R. K. (1981). Infantile autism reviewed: A decade of research. *Schizophrenia Bulletin, 7,* 338–451. A review of all relevant research in the area, with reference to earlier research as well.

5 PSYCHOPATHOLOGY AND BRAIN PATHOLOGY

In earlier chapters, we noted that neurological damage has been implicated in the etiology of several behavior disorders, including infantile autism and schizophrenia. In a later chapter, we shall show that various forms of mental retardation also reflect central nervous system (CNS) dysfunction. Because the evidence for organic factors in some childhood psychopathologies is presented in appropriate places throughout this book, the present chapter reviews the general effects of brain damage on childhood behavior as well as several specific syndromes. We begin with a summary of the prenatal and postnatal factors that may result in neurological impairment. This is followed by a discussion of neurological assessment and a consideration of specific syndromes. The final section focuses on attention deficit disorder, a problem that has received much attention in recent years.

ON THE HETEROGENEITY OF NEUROLOGICALLY IMPAIRED CHILDREN

Although it is common to refer to brain damaged or neurologically impaired children as if they comprise a homogeneous group, brain-damaged children can be quite different from one another. (The term *brain damage*, although widely used, has no specific meaning. It can refer to anatomical lesions or disturb-

ances in function. We use the term here for convenience and recognizability, with the understanding that it can refer to virtually any form of neurological dysfunction.) In this section we discuss some of the causes of neurological dysfunction as well as several factors influencing how brain damage affects behavior.

Etiological Factors

As described in Chapter 1, many influences in a child's prenatal and postnatal environment *may* result in neurological impairment. Brain damage can even result from accidents associated with the birth process itself. Prenatal factors include maternal illnesses (rubella, for instance), maternal malnutrition, radiation exposure (x-rays, for example), and the use of toxic drugs during pregnancy. Even maternal stress during pregnancy may lead to complications and neurological impairment in the newborn. Prematurity, particularly when the newborn has a very low birth weight, has also been associated with neurological impairment. Teenage mothers appear to have a particularly high incidence of premature infants.

Delivery room physicians usually make a quick assessment of the newborn using what is known as the *Apgar Score*. Named after the anesthesiologist Virginia Apgar, the procedure is quite simple and quick. A numerical value from 0 to 2 is assigned to each of five dimensions: heart rate, respiration, muscle tone, response to stimulation, and skin color. A score of 10 is perfect. Lower scores require investigation, and extremely low scores, 3 or 4 for example, mean the infant may require intensive care.

Complications of the birth process that may result in CNS damage include a difficult passage through the birth canal, breech delivery, instrument delivery, and accidental twisting of the umbilical cord. Each of these complications can disrupt the oxygen supply to the brain, a condition known as *anoxia*. When the normal oxygen supply is disrupted, brain cells may be damaged or destroyed. If the damage, resulting from anoxia or other trauma, is extensive the child's later development will be affected. One especially severe result can be cerebral palsy, a motor disorder resulting from early brain damage, that may or may not be associated with mental retardation.

The first signs of cerebral palsy are usually a delay in motor development and abnormal reflexes. As the infant develops, *spasticity* (difficulty in making voluntary movements of the arms and legs) usually becomes apparent. Some children with cerebral palsy also have great difficulty speaking. The relationship between cerebral palsy and mental retardation is discussed further in Chapter 8. For now, it remains to be said that although children with cerebral palsy may have communication difficulties as well as all of the other problems associated with having a severe handicap, there is no necessary connection between their condition and either mental retardation or psychological disorder. Children with cerebral palsy, who have been given the opportunity, have grown up to live full and productive lives.

Events occurring postnatally can also sometimes result in neurological damage. In fact, the most frequently cited causes of severe head injuries in young children are automobile accidents and child abuse (Robinson & Robinson, 1976). Ingestion of various toxic substances such as lead-based paint, cleaning fluids, insect poisons and other household chemicals can also lead to brain damage, as can brain tumors, both benign and malignant. Finally, a variety of diseases (encephalitis and meningitis, for example) can produce CNS damage. So, too, can a high fever (although how high is a matter of some debate). It is undeniable that the factors mentioned so far can produce serious CNS dysfunction. The evidence relating certain other possible causes to brain damage is less clear. For example, although maternal drug abuse and maternal stress during pregnancy have been implicated in the development of brain dysfunction in newborns, there is insufficient evidence to conclude that these factors *invariably* result in brain injury or deviant behavior. Similarly, although animal research (Winick, 1970a, 1970b) suggests that maternal malnutrition can affect both the number and size of brain cells in newborns, there is far less evidence documenting the effects of maternal malnutrition on brain development in human offspring, even though it is assumed that malnourished mothers *may* give birth to neurologically impaired children.

Brain Damage and Behavior

In addition to the multitude of potential causes, there are several additional variables influencing how brain damage manifests itself in a particular child. An important one is the age of the child at the time of injury. Brain damage occurring prior to or at birth can have different effects from damage sustained later in childhood, when specific cognitive skills may already be developed. As Robinson and Robinson (1976) point out, however, the precise relationship between the child's age at the time of injury and the injury's behavioral consequences are unclear:

> There is some controversy whether a given degree of brain injury early in life results in greater or less impairment than "equivalent" damage in adulthood. During the period when organs are emerging and growing most rapidly, they are most vulnerable. This fact

argues for greater susceptibility of the fetus and infant, who are undergoing the highest rates of growth and differentiation. . . . The individual who has enjoyed a period of intact development prior to the injury has established some normal patterns and also has a backlog of experience upon which to draw. On the other hand, there is the possibility that the immature brain may be able to make adjustments or compensations which are impossible in the older person and that cells which are still undifferentiated at the time of injury may take over functions of the damaged ones. (pp. 217–218)

Evidence relevant to the "age" issue was provided by Boll (1973). Boll assessed differences among children who sustained brain damage at birth, those who suffered a brain injury after 2 to 4 years of normal development, those whose neurological impairment was incurred after 5 to 7 years of normal development, and a fourth group of children who never incurred brain damage. The mean age of all the children at the time of the study was approximately 7 years. All of the children received an intelligence test and a neuropsychological test battery developed specifically to detect brain damage. Not surprisingly, the children with no history of brain damage performed better on all measures than the other children. But there were also differences among the brain-damaged groups. Specifically, children whose brain injury occurred after 5 years of normal development had superior intelligence test scores to those whose neurological impairment occurred after only 2 years of normal development. This latter group, in turn, was superior to those children brain damaged from birth. On the neuropsychological test, all brain-damaged children showed similar motor abilities, but those with longer periods of normal development showed superior abstract thinking, problem solving, and verbal skills.

Boll concluded that his results indicate that children who enjoy longer periods of normal development prior to brain injury show less severe cognitive deficits than children who sustain brain damage early in life (see also,

Boll, 1978), but there are some contradictory findings. Schneider (1979), for instance, found no relationship between age of injury and psychopathological behavior in a study of children ranging from preschool age through adolescence. To complicate matters further, there is evidence that — for some functions at least — damage early in development may be less harmful than later brain injury. For example, Lenneberg (1967) argues that early damage to the brain areas responsible for language can be compensated for by other brain areas, whereas later injury to the same language areas may result in permanent impairment.

There is evidence, then, for every possible position. Boll concludes that early brain damage is worse than later injury, Lenneberg sees things the other way around (for language, at least), and Schneider argues that age may not even be an important variable. What's more they may all be right! As Teuber (1975) argues, the various parts of the brain become "committed" to specialized functions at different stages of development. From this viewpoint, the extent of the behavioral problems caused by a brain injury depends not only on when, but also on where in the brain the injury occurs.

Unfortunately, it is usually impossible to localize early brain damage to a specific area. In such cases, brain damage is said to be *diffuse*. Later in life, accidents generally produce more localized *lesions* (a lesion is any type of brain injury). In general, diffuse brain damage tends to result in more pervasive symptoms and greater behavioral and intellectual impairment than localized lesions, but once again the evidence is contradictory and there is room for disagreement (Werry, 1979c).

Damage to specific brain areas is often localizable by observing which psychological functions are disrupted. For example, lesions in the left side of the brain (in the left cerebral hemisphere, to be precise) frequently result in some form of language disorder, whereas right hemisphere lesions often interfere with tasks requiring spatial analysis. These relationships, however, are true mostly for adult patients with acute brain damage (a blow to the head, for instance). Localization of function is not quite so specific in children or among adults with diffuse damage. In addition, localization is often made difficult by so-called "silent" brain sites. Damage to these areas does not seem to result in any specific behavioral symptoms.

It should be clear that brain damage is far from a unitary construct. The child's age at the time of injury, the location of the lesion, even the cause of the damage varies from child to child, and each of these factors exerts an influence on whether (and how much) the child's behavior will be affected. It is also important to remember that brain damage and behavior both occur in an interpersonal context. A brain-damaged boy who appears very anxious around his peers may be showing the effects of brain damage, or he may be reacting to a difficult family situation or both. Indeed, some children actually receive their brain damage at the hands of abusing parents. In such cases, it is difficult if not impossible to determine whether the brain injury or the family situation is responsible for any behavior disorder. As indicated earlier in this book, all behavior is the result of an interaction between biological and psychosocial variables. The behavior of brain-damaged children is no exception.

ASSESSING BRAIN PATHOLOGY

A variety of procedures have been used to assess the presence and nature of brain damage in children, including developmental histories, psychological tests, neurological examinations, electroencephalograms, computer axial tomography, and other new imaging methods. Each of these assessment approaches is discussed in this section.

Developmental History

In cases of suspected brain damage, clinicians always seek information concerning the child's developmental history, with special emphasis on factors in the child's background that may result in brain damage. Questions typically focus on the child's general health, pregnancy or delivery complications, and early illnesses and injuries. In addition, the clinician also determines at what age the child reached important developmental milestones such as sitting up, walking, speaking, and bladder and bowel control. Although a positive history may provide additional reasons for a clinician to suspect that a child is brain damaged, it is never a sufficient basis, by itself, to diagnose brain damage. This is because there is no one-to-one relationship between the above-cited factors and the occurrence of neurological dysfunction. Likewise, an unremarkable history does not completely rule out brain damage, as parents frequently have difficulty recalling significant details of their child's development. As Werry (1979c) notes, developmental histories are the least useful yet most often used of all diagnostic procedures.

Psychological Tests

Psychological tests of brain function are all based on the idea that neurological damage often results in disordered behavior. In other words, because successful test performance depends on one or more parts of the brain functioning adequately, then poor performance must reflect a defect in brain functioning. Brain-damage tests (called neuropsychological tests) are part of a long tradition in psychology; they mark the latest attempt to outline relationships between brain anatomy and behavior.

Scientists have been trying to relate behavior to brain structures for thousands of years. In the modern era, brain localization research began when a Viennese doctor named Franz Joseph Gall developed a science called *phrenology*. Gall assumed that the shape of the skull reflects the size and shape of the underlying brain. He thought that each bump on the head reflected a separate brain "structure" and that each brain structure was responsible for a different personality characteristic (called *faculties*). For example, bulging eyes were thought to reflect a large frontal lobe (so large, it pushed out the eyes). Because the frontal lobe (the part of the brain directly behind the forehead) was supposed to be the part of the brain concerned with memory, Gall concluded that all people with bulging eyes had good memories.

Phrenologists soon mapped out entire heads assigning a characteristic to each bump. Although popular for many years, phrenology eventually died out mainly because exceptions to the phrenological rules became too frequent. Instead of localizing traits in different parts of the brain, Gall's successors looked for brain functions instead. That is, they assumed the brain did not have areas specialized for different faculties but for different cognitive and motor operations. Rather than brain centers specializing in love or envy, modern neuropsychologists look for areas concerned with language, spatial synthesis, and other cognitive functions.

There are several commercially available and widely used neuropsychological test batteries. Although these tests have many users, some neuropsychologists believe that standardized tests are a mistake and that a flexible, probing attitude is necessary to understand brain-behavior relationships (Luria, 1965; Walsh, 1978). Controveries in this field are too complex to go into here, but one point should be noted: Few neuropsychological tests have been standardized for use with young children. In clinical practice clinicians frequently use tests designed for other purposes as tests of brain damage. For example, clinical lore holds that specific response patterns on the Rorschach Ink Blot Test or the Wechsler Intelligence Scales may suggest organic dysfunction. Like most clinical lore, there probably is some rationale for this belief, but the validity of these tests for diagnosing brain damage is highly suspect.

An additional measure that has also been used with children is the Bender Gestalt Test (Bender, 1938). This test consists of nine geometric designs, presented sequentially, which the child is required to draw exactly as they appear. An example of one design appears in Figure 5.1.

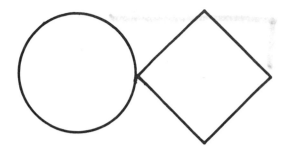

FIGURE 5.1. An example of the Bender Gestalt test figures. Source: Bender (1938). © 1938 American Orthopsychiatric Association. Reprinted by permission.

Specific characteristics of the patient's reproductions (whether the designs are drawn upside down, distorted, etc.) are supposed to be associated with neurological impairment. One important problem with this test is that young children have difficulty drawing the designs even when their brains are perfectly normal. In other words, drawings that are normal for children at one developmental stage may suggest brain damage in older children and adults. In order to make the test usable with young children, Koppitz (1964, 1975) devised a "developmental" scoring system for the Bender Gestalt Test that takes developmental level into account. Koppitz has gathered normative data for children aged 5 to 10 and has provided information regarding variables assumed to discriminate between brain-damaged and normal children in this age range. Evidence for this claim is sparse, however.

Although many clinicians rely on the Bender Gestalt, it should really be thought of as a screening device. Poor performance on tests such as the Bender Gestalt (there are other similar instruments) may lead clinicians to entertain brain damage as a hypothesis, but without further corroborating data, test performance alone is insufficient to make a diagnosis.

A problem with each of the brain-damage tests described here is that they examine only single (or very few) brain functions. An exception is the Reitan-Indiana Neuropsychological Battery For Children (Reitan, 1964), which examines a variety of functions and has been standardized on children from 9 to 14. Instead of simply measuring drawing ability or memory, the test examines both, as well as abstract categorization, tactile recognition, and a variety of other abilities. Because brain damage can affect a variety of different functions, such tests have a better chance of pinpointing problems than other, single-function tests. For a more detailed discussion of child neuropsychological assessment see Rourke, Bakker, Fisk, and Strang (1983).

Neurological Exam

A standard neurological examination entails looking for certain neurological signs that are indicators of neurological dysfunction. "Hard" signs are generally those associated with faulty reflexes. A failure to produce a patellar reflex (knee jerk) or the presence of a Babinski reflex (turning up the toes when the bottom of the foot is stroked) are both hard neurological signs. Neurologists also check the response of the eye pupils to light and assess whether there is any restriction in the visual field ("blind spots," for example). Loss of sensation in any part of the body or loss of function are also hard neurological signs.

In addition to hard signs, there are "soft" signs whose presence suggests neurological dysfunction. For example, children who have difficulty touching their noses with their index fingers are displaying a well-known soft sign — poor motor coordination. Unlike the hard signs, soft signs are not consistently related to any neurological lesion (Wender, 1971). Also, in contrast to the hard signs, which generally indicate severe, localized neurological impairment, soft signs are usually thought to reflect immature neurological development.

Electroencephalographic Assessment of Brain Damage

The electroencephalogram (EEG) is widely used to assess brain activity in children suspected of having neurological impairment.

The procedure involves placing two or more electrodes on the child's scalp and recording the electrical activity in the underlying areas. Abnormal brain function is indicated by unusual electrical activity patterns in one or more areas of the brain. Although the ongoing EEG is widely used in clinical neurology to detect gross pathology, it does have certain limitations. First, because the electrodes are placed on top of the head, abnormalities in deep structures of the brain may not show up (Brazier, 1964). Second, EEG use with children is complicated by the finding that roughly 10 to 20% of otherwise normal children display what can be considered to be abnormal EEG records, calling into question the discriminative validity of the procedure (Feuerstein, Ward, & Le Baron, 1979).

In addition to the ongoing EEG, it is also possible to use electrical recording equipment to monitor the brain's response to various environmental stimuli. Whenever a stimulus (say a light or a sound) is presented to an individual, the brain produces a characteristic response. This response is called an *event related potential* or ERP. Normally, the ERP is lost in the ongoing EEG record because of the brain's background activity, but by averaging over a series of stimulations, the ERP can usually be identified. Recent years have seen substantial interest in studying ERPs in children; several books reviewing this work have recently been published (Chiarenza & Papakostopoulos, 1982; Rothenberger, 1982). By measuring the brain's response to visual and auditory stimuli, ERPs have been used to detect visual disorders and deafness in very young and mentally retarded children who cannot be tested by normal means. Recently, there has been a great deal of interest in studying cognitive processes using ERPs (Gaillard & Ritter, 1983). Although this work is just beginning to filter into childhood problems, it holds promise for increasing our understanding of brain functioning in neurologically impaired children (Friedman, Erlenmeyer-Kimling, & Vaughan, 1982).

In the past, a major problem with EEGs and ERPs was traceable to the use of only a few recording leads. The "resolution" of an

EEG depends on the number of recording leads used. The fewer the leads, the coarser the picture of underlying brain functions. Recent developments in computer analysis and computer graphics have made it possible to record from many leads simultaneously and to display the results graphically in the form of a computer drawn picture of the brain such as that seen in Figure 5.2 (Buchsbaum et al., 1981). Computerized mapping systems are presently expensive. However, new developments in microtechnology should cause the price to fall. As such systems become more widely used, the value of the EEG in pinpointing neurological dysfunction should increase.

Imaging Techniques

Because neurological impairment is usually related to anatomical damage, assessment techniques that allow clinicians to visualize the brain are useful in making diagnoses. Although multiple channel EEG maps are certainly ways of drawing images of brain *activity*, imaging methods have traditionally relied on visualizing brain *structure* through x-rays. In the past, the most common procedures for forming brain images were skull x-rays, pneumoencephalograms, and angiograms. Because brains are comprised of soft tissue, they don't x-ray very well, making typical skull films less than satisfactory. The pneumoencephalogram and angiogram are ways of outlining the brain's ventricles (cavities) and blood vessels, respectively. The pneumoencephalogram involves forcing air into the brain's ventricles; the angiogram requires that radioactive dye be injected into the cerebral arteries. Although these procedures produce reasonably clear images, they carry a greater risk than EEGs, neurological exams, or skull x-rays and are typically useful only for detecting gross abnormalities (Werry, 1979c).

Today, the traditional methods have been largely replaced by a new imaging procedure, *computerized axial tomography* (CT scans). CT scans use computer-driven x-ray machines to produce exceptionally detailed images of the brain's surface as well as various brain levels below the surface (Bories, 1978). CT scans make it possible to localize lesions at any level of the brain without interference from overlying brain structures. Unlike the traditional imaging methods, CT scans are noninvasive and therefore much safer. An even newer imaging method, nuclear magnetic resonance (NMR), has been introduced in recent years. It involves using giant magnets to detect activity in the nuclei of cells. Like CT scans, NMR is noninvasive, and it produces even clearer images.

Except for EEG and ERP maps, the imaging techniques described so far produce a static picture of brain anatomy. Although they are useful in detecting structural or anatomical deficits, they do not give much information about brain function. That is, there may be children whose brains look anatomically normal but do not function normally. EEG maps can give some information about brain function, as can another new imaging method called positron emission tomography (PET scans). PET images are produced by introducing radioactive glucose (brain cells exist by metabolizing glucose) into the cerebral artery and recording the rate at which the glucose is metabolized in various parts of the brain. Increased metabolism in any brain area means more brain activity in that area. By comparing patients with normals, it is possible to determine whether brain function is abnormal. Because PET scans are very expensive and involve introducing radioactive substances into the brain, they have not been used very much with children. For now, the cheapest and safest way to draw images of brain function is with EEG maps.

Neurological Assessment Today

Until very recently, the neurological assessment of children was pretty much a hit or miss affair. Writing in 1972, Werry described the situation as follows:

The diagnosis of brain damage or dysfunction, unless gross, depends on a group of

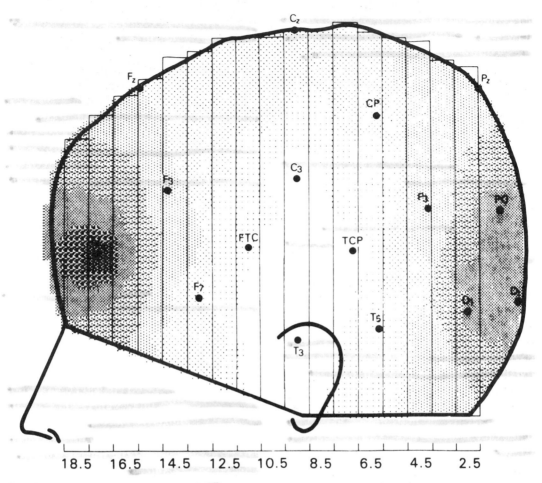

FIGURE 5.2. An example of a brain activity map produced by simultaneously recording brain electrical activity from many electrodes. The darker regions represent areas of greater activity. Source: Buchsbaum et al., 1982.

medical, historical and psychological measures, most of which are of low or untested reliability, which discriminate poorly between normal and brain damaged populations, and which apparently measure a variety of unrelated functions instead of a homogeneous variable "brain damage." . . . Under the circumstances the diagnosis of brain damage or dysfunction in the majority of children with behavior disorders is little more than an enlightened guess. (pp. 88–89)

Although today's situation has improved markedly (see Feuerstein et al., 1979), there are still no infallible indicators of brain damage in children. For this reason, the various assessment procedures described in this section are usually used in combination. For example, a child referred for psychological evaluation because of learning and behavioral problems may be given a battery of psychological tests. If these suggest the possibility of neurological dysfunction, the next step may be referral to a pediatric neurologist, who gives the child a neurological examination and may also order an EEG, skull films, and even a CT scan. The preponderance of evidence would be used to make a diagnosis and suggest treatment. A diagnosis is almost never made on the basis of one assessment device alone.

Thus far, we have been concerned with the general issues of definition and assessment. We have shown that brain damage is a heterogeneous category and that assessment involves converging evidence from many sources. In the remaining sections of this chapter, we describe several syndromes encountered in clinical work with children that are thought to result—at least in part—from neurological dysfunction. We begin with developmental language disorder.

DEVELOPMENTAL LANGUAGE DISORDER

Background

The DSM-III provides a category of problems called specific developmental disorders. These include developmental reading disorder, developmental arithmetic disorder, developmental articulation disorder, and developmental language disorder (as well as mixed and atypical developmental disorders). The presence of these categories in the DSM-III is controversial, as the children involved may have no real signs of psychopathology (Rutter & Shaffer, 1980). Nevertheless, there are sufficient children with each of these problems to warrant their inclusion in this book. The present section focuses on developmental language disorders; discussion of the other specific developmental disorders may be found in the chapter on intellectual disorders and learning disabilities.

Lesions to the cerebral cortex in adults (after a stroke, for instance) can be severely disabling and may result in language deficits. Language problems are particularly likely when a lesion occurs in the region of the brain specializing in language (the left hemisphere in 95% of adults). Language disorders acquired this way are referred to as *aphasia*, and they may take several different forms. The individual may have trouble understanding spoken language (receptive aphasia), expressing thoughts verbally (expressive aphasia), naming things (nominal aphasia), or repeating words (conduction aphasia). Pure cases are rare, however, and in most instances affected individuals show deficits in two or more of these functions. Many aphasic patients regain their language within 6 months or so of

their accident, but others never recover (Lenneberg, 1967). Those who regain language do so fairly rapidly.

Observations of children have revealed that some children have language deficits very similar to those found in adult aphasics. However, there is often no evidence for brain lesions among these children nor is the recovery pattern the same as in adult aphasics. In fact, because young children, at least, are still in the process of developing language in the first place, it is not even clear that talking about recovery or aphasia is even sensible. Moreover, most children with language deficits eventually develop adequate language, but they do so slowly over long periods of time. Because of these differences between adults and children, the DSM-III opted for the term *developmental language disorder* to describe children with language deficits rather than the older, misleading term, *childhood aphasia*.

Diagnosis and Description

Description

The DSM-III identifies three types of language disorders. The most severe, the failure to develop any language at all, is virtually always the result of profound mental retardation. The second type of language disorder, acquired language disabilities, are those clearly resulting from head trauma or neurological disorder after language has developed. The third type, delayed language acquisition, is known as developmental language disorder. Although the implication is that developmental language disorders differ from the acquired disorders, this is not always the case. In fact, most cases of developmental language disorder are probably also the result of neurological damage that has somehow missed being diagnosed.

The DSM-III differentiates between receptive and expressive language disorders more or less along the same lines as adult aphasia. Expressive disorders are marked by an inability to express oneself using spoken language, whereas the receptive type involves deficits in language comprehension. No special provision is made for nominal or conduction disorders. Instead, these are subsumed within the two types. The DSM-III criteria for developmental language disorder appear in Table 5.1; the case history of a language disordered child can be found in Figure 5.3.

Prevalence

The prevalence of expressive deficits in children has been estimated to be about 1 in every thousand children, with the receptive disorder being somewhat rarer (APA, 1980). Often language disorders appear to run in families (Folstein & Rutter, 1978).

Differential Diagnosis

The DSM-III differentiates developmental language disorders from mental retardation. In the latter, there is a general lowering of intelligence, whereas in the language disorders, nonverbal intelligence is unaffected. These children should also be differentiated from hearing impaired children. The latter, but not the former, have abnormal hearing tests. Although language disorders occur in autism, schizophrenia, and the other pervasive devel-

opmental disorders, they are always a secondary part of the syndrome. Developmental language disorders differ from acquired aphasia in that the latter occurs after normal language has developed, whereas the developmental disorders precede language development. In essence, then, developmental language disorder is a diagnosis made when a child's language problem cannot be attributed to mental retardation, deafness, or a severe emotional disturbance.

There are several commercially available tests designed to assess children's language functioning. One of the most thorough is the *Clinical Evaluation of Language Functions* (CLEF) described by Semel and Wiig (1980). The CLEF measures 13 aspects of receptive and expressive language as well as conceptual thinking.

It should be noted that language disorders are never due to disorders of the speech mechanism (lips, tongue, teeth, or vocal cords). Communication problems resulting from damaged speech mechanisms are classified as articulation disorders, as are all other pronunciation difficulties, even those not caused by any organic defect.

A type of articulation disorder that is classified separately in the DSM-III is stuttering. The DSM-III defines stuttering as "frequent repetitions or prolongations of sounds, syllables or words or frequent, unusual hesitations and pauses that disrupt the rhythmic flow of speech" (APA, 1980, p. 79). Stuttering usually starts when language begins, at 2 to 3 years of age, but many stutterers produce normal speech until age 5 or 6 when they enter school. The relationship between the onset of stuttering and age suggests that the stress of starting school may contribute to the development of the disorder; indeed, stutterers have been found to stutter more in stressful situations. Stuttering runs in families and is 4 times as common in boys as in girls. Through the years, a variety of explanations, both psychogenic and biogenic, have been offered to explain stuttering, and numerous, sometimes horrible, treatments have been tried (see Yates, 1970). Although there is still no de-

---

TABLE 5.1. DSM-III CRITERIA FOR
DEVELOPMENTAL LANGUAGE DISORDER.

Expressive Type
A. A failure to develop vocal expression (encoding) of language despite relatively intact comprehension of language.
B. Presence of inner language (the presence of age-appropriate concepts, such as understanding the purpose and use of a particular household object).
C. Not due to mental retardation, childhood onset pervasive disorder, hearing impairment, or trauma.
Receptive Type
A. Failure to develop comprehension (decoding) and vocal expression (encoding) of language.
B. Not due to hearing impairment, trauma, mental retardation, or childhood onset pervasive developmental disorder.

Source: APA (1980). © American Psychiatric Association (1980) and reprinted with permission.

FIGURE 5.3. A Case of Developmental Language Disorder

Donna, a 5-year-old girl, was seen by a child-clinical psychologist because of problems she was having in school. She was in the middle of her kindergarten year but still had no friends and was continually fighting with other children and disobeying her teacher. Several times, Donna's parents were called into school to meet with the teacher, but the misbehavior continued. Frequently, the teacher had the feeling that Donna did not comprehend what was expected of her. Moreover, her spoken language was very difficult to understand. Donna is presently in good health, and all developmental milestones occurred on schedule. Her mother does report, however, that Donna had "convulsions" in the past.

The psychological assessment took a long time. Donna would not allow her mother to leave the office and often appeared not to understand the psychologist's directions. When asked to put a row of beads on a string, she just tied the string in a knot and lined the beads up in a row. Donna said very little and what she said was difficult to follow. For example, in response to the command, "Point to the truck," Donna replied, "Truck go." Donna seemed to prefer gestures to speech and would use these whenever she could.

finitive answer to what causes stuttering, many behaviorally oriented speech therapists have been able to produce more articulate speech among stutterers (Van Riper, 1978).

Prognosis

As shown in Table 5.2, the severity and course of a language disturbance depends on when it began. In general, the effects of acquired brain lesions on subsequent language development are more severe among older than young children (Lenneberg, 1967). The reason for this relationship appears to be the decreasing ability of the nonlanguage cerebral hemisphere to take over language functions in older children. Prognosis also appears more favorable for those children with minimal or no signs of brain damage (normal EEGs, and so on) than for those with grossly abnormal neurological records.

Treatment

Speech therapy (which is usually based on behavioral principles) is the treatment most often prescribed for children with language or articulation disorders. Reviews of therapeutic approaches to childhood language disorders can be found in Van Riper (1978). Although the evidence clearly supports the efficacy of these approaches, there are some who feel that children's language disorders may improve with or without therapeutic interventions (Lenneberg, 1967). There is less doubt about the usefulness of speech therapy for the articulation disorders and stuttering (see Azrin & Nunn, 1974, for example).

Elective Mutism

Periodically, children are referred to psychologists because they refuse to speak under certain circumstances — usually to strangers or to teachers at school. Most often these children are found to speak to specific people (parents, siblings, sometimes friends). For this reason, the condition has become known as *elective mutism*. The label implies that the child chooses to be silent in certain situations; it should not, therefore, be applied to children with aphasia, hearing loss, or some other reason for not speaking. Elective mutism is not strictly a language disorder. Although there is no agreement as to its exact etiology, most writers believe the condition is anxiety

TABLE 5.2. LANGUAGE DEVELOPMENT AND MATURATION.

Age	Usual language development	Effects of acquired lateralized lesions	Physical maturation of central nervous system	Lateralization of function	Equipotentiality of hemispheres	Explanation
Months 0–3	Emergence of cooing	No effect on onset of language in half of all cases; other half has delayed onset but normal development	About 60–70% of developmental course accomplished	None: Symptoms and prognosis identical for either hemisphere	Perfect equipotentiality	Neuroanatomical and physiological prerequisites become established
4–20	From babbling to words					
21–36	Acquisition of language	All language accomplishments disappear; language is reacquired with repetition of all stages	Rate of maturation slowed down	Hand preference emerges	Right hemisphere can easily adopt sole responsibility for language	Language appears to involve entire brain; little cortical specialization with regard to language, though left hemisphere beginning to become dominant towards end of this period.
Years 3–10	Some grammatical refinement; expansion of vocabulary	Emergence of aphasic symptoms; disorders tend to recover without residual language deficits (except in reading or writing). During recovery period, two processes active: diminishing aphasic interference and further acquisition of language	Very slow completion of maturational processes	Cerebral dominance established between 3–5 years but evidence that right hemisphere may often still be involved in speech and language functions. About ¼ of early childhood aphasias are due to right hemisphere lesions.	In cases where language is already predominantly localized in left hemisphere and aphasia ensues with left lesion, it is possible to reestablish language, presumably by reactivating language functions in right hemisphere	A process of physiological organization takes place in which functional lateralization of language to left is prominent. "Physiological redundancy" is gradually reduced and polarization of activities between right and left hemisphere is established. As long as maturational processes have not stopped, reorganization is still possible.

156

11–14	Foreign accents emerge	Some aphasic symptoms become irreversible (particularly when acquired lesion was traumatic)	An asymptote is reached on almost all parameters. Exceptions are Myelinization and EEG spectrum	Apparently firmly established, but definitive statistics are not available	Marked signs of reduction in equipotentiality	Language markedly lateralized and internal organization established irreversibly for life. Language-free parts of brain cannot take over except where lateralization is incomplete or had been blocked by pathology during childhood
Midteens to Senium	Acquisition of second language becomes increasingly difficult	Symptoms present after 3–5 months post-insult are irreversible	None	In about 97% of the entire population language is definitely lateralized to the left	None for language	

Source: From Lenneberg, E. *Biological Foundations of Language*, © 1967 by John Wiley and Sons. Reprinted by permission of the publisher.

based (see Sluckin, 1977, for example). Some cases have been found to respond well to behavioral interventions. For a current review of the behavioral treatment of this condition see Labbé and Williamson (1984).

TOURETTE'S DISORDER

Although psychiatrist Georges Gilles de la Tourette first described a syndrome characterized by sudden involuntary movements, apparently uncontrollable utterances (often obscene), and multiple tics as long ago as 1885, the syndrome that today bears his name was largely ignored until fairly recently. In the past 25 years however, case reports, literature reviews, and original research have appeared with increasing frequency, and the disease is being diagnosed much more often than in the past. In fact, the number of known cases and the number of scientific papers on the condition have doubled in the past 10 years (Friedhoff & Chase, 1982).

Description and Diagnosis

The DSM-III diagnostic criteria for Tourette's syndrome appear in Table 5.3. As may be seen, these criteria emphasize motor movements and vocal tics. The syndrome differs from other brain-damaged induced movement disorders (called *apraxias*) in two important ways, however. As indicated by criterion D, Tourette's sufferers can inhibit their symptoms through voluntary effort, although not for very long. Furthermore, their symptoms vary in severity, sometimes even disappearing for weeks at a time (criterion E). A case description taken from Tourette's original article appears in Figure 5.4.

Description

Tourette's syndrome usually begins between 2 and 15 years of age (Shapiro, Shapiro, Brown, & Sweet, 1978). Boys are 3 times more likely to be afflicted than girls. Although there are individual differences, the first symptoms are usually facial tics, excessive eye blinking,

TABLE 5.3. DSM-III DIAGNOSTIC CRITERIA FOR TOURETTE'S DISORDER.

A. Age at onset between 2 and 15 years.
B. Presence of recurrent, involuntary, repetitive, rapid, purposeless motor movements affecting multiple muscle groups.
C. Multiple vocal tics.
D. Ability to suppress movements voluntarily for minutes to hours.
E. Variations in the intensity of the symptoms over weeks or months.
F. Duration of more than one year.

Source: APA (1980). © American Psychiatric Association, 1980, and reprinted with permission.

grimacing, or sniffing movements. As the disease progresses, the sufferer begins to produce head movements, neck and shoulder jerking, arm flinging, foot stamping, and other peculiar movements. Eventually all Tourette patients produce odd verbalizations. Coughing, shouting, sniffing, barking and, in more than half the patients, obscene speech (called *coprolalia*) have been reported. Some patients bang their heads or otherwise engage in self-destructive behavior. The tics come and go and are frequently replaced by new ones (Shapiro & Shapiro, 1982).

Etiology

The tics and verbalizations associated with Tourette's syndrome are only partly under voluntary control. Because they seem to worsen when the patient is under stress and improve when the patient is relaxed, the symptoms have often been thought to reflect an emotional disorder (Shapiro, Shapiro, Brown, & Sweet, 1978). This view is reinforced by the absence of tics during sleep. Although it seems clear that stress plays a role at least in exacerbating symptoms, most current research has focused on the neurochemistry of the illness. The discovery that a haloperidol, a drug used to treat schizophrenia, suppresses Tourette's symptoms in more than half the patients has led to the hypothesis that Tourette's patients may have an excess of the chemical dopamine. (Haloperidol reduces dopamine

FIGURE 5.4. The Case of Madame de D. by Gilles de la Tourette

Madame de D., presently age 26, at the age of 7 was afflicted by convulsive movements of the hand and arms. These abnormal movements occurred above all when the child tried to write, causing her to crudely reproduce the letters she was trying to trace. After each spasm, the movements of the hand became more regular and better controlled until another convulsive movement would again interrupt her work. She was felt to be suffering from overexcitement and mischief, and because the movements became more and more frequent, she was subject to reprimand and punishment. . . .

As the disease progressed, and the spasms spread to involve her voice and speech, the young lady made strange screams and said words that made no sense. However, during all this she was clearly alert and showed no signs of delerium or other mental problems. Months and years passed with no real change in her symptoms. It was hoped that with puberty these might naturally abate, but this did not occur. The young lady was therefore sent to Switzerland under the care of a doctor who specialized in the treatment of nervous disorders, relying primarily on milk baths as his form of therapy. . . . At the end of the year when this young woman left Switzerland and returned home, she was calm, beaming with freshness, and showing only rare and isolated muscle jerks around her mouth and neck. She married during this period . . . she was greatly disappointed, for the disease suddenly reappeared . . . her uncontrolled convulsive movements, which except for 18 to 20 months of abatement had lasted 18 years of her life, now returned, and rather than waning, they in fact seemed to be progressing.

Her examination showed spasmodic contractions that were continual or were separated only by momentary intervals of time. . . . The movements involved . . . the muscles of the upper arms, the finger muscles and those of the face, and the muscles involved with sound production and articulation. . . . In the midst of an interesting conversation, all of a sudden without being able to prevent it, she interrupts what she is saying or what she is listening to with horrible screams and with words that are even more extraordinary than her screams. All of this contrasts deplorably with her distinguished manners and background. These words are for the most part offensive curse words and obscene sayings . . . the more revolting these expressions are, the more tormented she becomes.

Source: Goetz & Klawans (1982, pp. 2–3). © Raven Press, 1982, and reprinted with permission.

levels.) This hypothesis is further supported by evidence that compounds known to increase dopamine levels tend also to increase the severity of the tics. Because dopamine functions in the nervous system as a neurotransmitter (a chemical that permits nerve cells to communicate), many neurologists believe that Tourette's disorder is primarily one of nerve cell communication.

Prevalence

The prevalence of Tourette's disorder is unknown. Attempts to estimate the number of sufferers have been hampered by sampling problems, unclear diagnostic criteria, and the rarity of the disease. There seems to be unanimity among both clinicians and researchers, however, that the syndrome is underdiagnosed.

A few years ago, a television show (*Quincy, M. E.*) screened an episode concerned with Tourette's disorder, releasing a flood of previously undiagnosed cases. Many of those who came forward after seeing the show had suffered from the syndrome all of their lives never knowing it had a name.

Research and Treatment

Tourette's syndrome is so rare that most doctors have never seen a case. Nevertheless, the disorder has received a great deal of research attention. This interest, which is out of proportion to the syndrome's incidence, results from the opportunity presented by the disorder to study the interplay of stress and biochemical factors (neurotransmitters) in producing the symptoms.

One apparent finding of recent research is that Tourette's appears to run in families and may be more frequent among some ethnic groups, East European Jews, for example (Shapiro et al., 1978). Like most severe child psychopathology, it is also more common among males. Schizophrenia has been noted in the families of Tourette's patients. Interestingly, both disorders respond to haloperidol. Coprolalia (surely, Tourette's most peculiar symptom) has also been noted among aphasic and schizophrenic patients (Lenneberg, 1967). There is presently no explanation for this symptom, although it has been noted that stress makes it worse.

Although stuttering is not a major symptom of Tourette's disorder, it has sometimes been noted. Moreover, there are marked similarities between Tourette patients and severe stutterers. For example, both produce facial tics and grimaces particularly in emotionally arousing situations, both improve when relaxed, and both may be helped by haloperidol (Rosenberger, Wheeldeen, & Kalotkin, 1976). If stuttering were found to be more common in the families of Tourette's patients, this would further reinforce the relationship between the two and perhaps shed additional light on the role of neurotransmitters in neurolinguistic disturbances.

Although other drugs have been shown to be useful, the treatment of choice for Tourette's syndrome remains haloperidol. Unfortunately, the drug's side effects can often be quite severe. The development of safer drugs has been hampered by the small market. Developing new drugs costs millions of dollars; not surprisingly, drug companies are reluctant to invest this money in drugs that are unlikely to recoup their investment. Recently, however, the U.S. Congress passed an "orphan drug bill," which guarantees government assistance to companies developing useful, but commercially questionable new drugs. The availability of this money makes it likely that more specific drugs for Tourette's syndrome will be developed (see Borison et al., 1982, for a review of new pharmacological approaches to treating Tourette's disorder).

Traditional psychodynamic psychotherapy has not proven useful for Tourette's disorder (Shapiro et al., 1978). Behavior therapy has been widely applied to Tourette's disorder with only marginally better results. Shapiro et al. (1978) reviewed 31 studies involving many different behavioral techniques. Although small sample sizes, varying types and lengths of treatment, and different follow-up periods make it difficult to derive firm conclusions, Shapiro et al. estimated that only 20 to 25% of Tourette's patients were treated successfully. Until better treatments are developed, some combination of pharmacological and behavioral treatment seems most likely to help Tourette's patients. Some idea of where these treatments may come from can be gained from the articles in the special edition of the *Journal of the American Academy of Child Psychiatry* (March, 1984) devoted to Tourette's.

SEIZURE DISORDERS

Background

Certain forms of brain injury are capable of damaging brain cells, making them discharge irregularly, thereby causing convulsions or seizures. These seizures can take varying forms; all involve some disturbance in consciousness, but only some are accompanied by disturbed motor behavior. Some seizures are transient reactions to illness (a high fever can trigger one) or to toxic substances (some drugs can cause seizures). They occur once and are not repeated. When seizures occur regularly, the term *epilepsy* is often used to describe the condition. Epilepsy is not a DSM-III diagnosis, because by itself, it does not necessarily reflect any psychopathology. Nevertheless, seizures do occur in children often enough to warrant discussion in this chapter.

Diagnosis and Description

There are several varieties of epileptic seizures. The most common and dramatic are called *grand mal* (literally, "very bad") seizures. These occur in about 60% of all cases of epilepsy (Sands & Minters, 1977). Grand mal seizures consist of four phases. The first phase is called the *aura*, during which the individual has sensory experiences (the person sees light flashes or smells odd odors) or unusual muscle sensations (tingling, twitching). The aura is a sort of warning to the patient that a seizure is about to begin. Unfortunately, most children do not appear to have an aura, and only one-half of adult epileptics report these preseizure warning experiences (Sands & Minters, 1977). The aura is followed by the *tonic* phase, in which the person loses consciousness, and the muscles contract violently. The person may fall to the ground, cry out, and lose bladder and bowel control. In some cases, the epileptic can turn blue from lack of oxygen. The next phase of a grand mal seizure, the *clonic* phase, consists of jerks and twitches as the muscles repeatedly contract. Foaming at the mouth can also occur. If not protected, patients can bite their tongues or smash their heads. The final phase, the *coma*, can last an hour or more and may be followed by bewilderment, fatigue, headache, and amnesia for the whole seizure experience.

In addition to grand mal seizures, children sometimes show *petit mal* ("less bad") seizures. These typically involve transient disturbances of consciousness without the extensive muscular involvement seen in grand mal seizures. Petit mal seizures typically occur without any warning and usually last only a few seconds. They may be recognized by the person concerned or the casual observer as short lapses in attention accompanied by muscular twitching and a fluttering of the eyelids. In a given patient, from 1 to 100 petit mal seizures can occur each day. The seizures usually begin between the ages of 4 and 8 and disappear by age 18 or so, at which time a significant portion (about two-thirds) of sufferers begin to display seizures of the grand mal type (Noyes & Kolb, 1968).

A third type of epilepsy described in the medical literature is called *psychomotor epilepsy*. It is the rarest of the three types, occurring in only 1 of 10 epileptic children. Although the exact manifestations may vary, psychomotor epilepsy almost always involves trance-like episodes lasting a few minutes to a few hours during which the sufferer appears confused and incoherent. Hallucinations may occur. During a psychomotor seizure children may smack their lips, make chewing movements, pick at their clothes, and so on. Some individuals may carry out coordinated sequences of movements, taking off their clothes or even attacking others (although this is rare) and be unable to recall anything once the seizure is over.

Although these are the major types of seizures, there is a great deal of individual variability in their exact manifestations, depending on the part of the brain in which the abnormal discharges occur, the extent of the damage, and the degree to which the abnormal discharges spread to other parts of the brain (Noyes & Kolb, 1968).

Prevalence

Lubar and Shouse (1977) report that 1 in every 250 people is diagnosed as epileptic. Slightly more males than females receive the diagnosis, and in 75% of cases, seizures begin before the age of 20 (Sands & Minters, 1977). Epilepsy is clearly a disorder originating in childhood, although it may often continue into adulthood.

Etiology and Treatment

Some cases of epilepsy can be traced back to specific causes, such as a blow to the head or a childhood illness such as meningitis. Such cases are referred to as *symptomatic* epilepsy, meaning that the seizures are symptoms produced by underlying brain damage. For many children, however, no specific cause for their seizures can be found. Such children are said to have *idiopathic* epilepsy. Idiopathic epilepsy tends to occur earlier in life than symptomatic epilepsy. At least half of all sufferers fall into the idiopathic category (Boll, 1978).

Treatment for epilepsy has been both psychological and medical. Medical treatment involves the use of drugs to control seizure activity. The most commonly used drugs are sedatives such as phenobarbital and specific anticonvulsants such as Dilantin or, more recently, Tegretol and Clonopin. More than 75% of patients have their seizures controlled by these medications (Sands & Minters, 1977). Some attempts to help epileptics control their seizures with biofeedback have also been reported (Lubar & Shouse, 1977). Intractible cases have sometimes been helped by surgery. Although it has sometimes been suggested that psychotherapy is of value in dealing with epilepsy, it is not of any use in controlling seizures. However, there is more to being epileptic than having seizures. Anxiety about when a seizure may occur, fear of developing relationships, resentment about being different, and having to take drugs all become part of the chronic sufferer's life. Thus, although there does not seem to be a specific epileptic personality disorder (see Herman & Whitman, 1984, for a recent review), it does seem possible that family and individual counseling could be useful in dealing with the depression and anxiety that accompany any chronic illness.

ATTENTION DEFICIT DISORDER AND HYPERACTIVITY

Background

The childhood problem known today as attention deficit disorder (ADD) has been a controversial subject for many years. Debates about whether the syndrome exists, its relationship to other disorders, and what happens to the children after they grow up have filled the clinical literature, with most issues remaining unresolved (Loney, 1983). One thing appears certain, however: ADD children do not comprise a homogeneous grouping.

ADD children have received a variety of diagnostic labels over the years. At one time or another, the disorder has been called the Strauss syndrome, hyperactive child syndrome, hyperkinetic syndrome, and, most recently, attention deficit disorder. The condition has been described in numerous review articles in the psychological, psychiatric, and pediatric literature (the reviewers do not always reach the same conclusions); the children have also been the subject of numerous articles in popular magazines and the press.

The historical origins of ADD were reviewed by Strother (1973) and by Ross and Ross (1976), who note that it originated from the early work of Alfred Strauss and his colleagues (Strauss & Kephart, 1955, for example). In a series of studies, Strauss and his coworkers attempted to isolate characteristics that would discriminate between groups of mentally retarded children with and without brain damage. A number of psychological and behavioral markers were found to be reliably associated with brain damage. These included hyperactivity, aggressiveness, impulsiveness, and distractibility. Strauss argued that these markers could also be used to diagnose brain damage in ambiguous cases, even when there was no clear-cut evidence of neurological impairment. Of the various markers, hyperactivity was given special status as the most valid indicator of brain damage (Ross & Ross, 1976).

A moment's reflection reveals that Strauss's

reasoning was completely circular. In effect, he was arguing that hyperactive children are brain damaged *because* they are hyperactive. Nevertheless, his basic premise has been accepted by many clinicians working with children displaying behavior problems. Doubtless, the acceptance of Strauss's view was spurred in part because children with documented cases of brain damage were often hyperactive. Nevertheless, it is incorrect to believe that all hyperactive children (a term, as we shall see, that is not easily defined) have brain damage. An important aspect of Strauss's work was the concept of minimal brain damage. Because many hyperactive (or distractible or impulsive) children had no sign of brain damage other than their hyperactive (or other problem) behavior, it became common practice to consider such children minimally brain damaged (Strother, 1973).

Over the years, additional behavioral markers were added to the ones emphasized by Strauss. Minimally brain-damaged children were not only hyperactive, impulsive, and distractible, they were also said to have short attention spans, emotional lability, perceptual-motor deficits, and poor coordination. Often, these signs were associated with specific learning deficits and equivocal neurological symptoms (soft signs) (Lambert, Windmiller, Sandoval, & Moore, 1976). Some writers called minimal brain damage the hyperkinetic syndrome, emphasizing hyperactivity more than other markers (Laufer & Denhoff, 1957).

Despite its popularity, the minimal brain damage/hyperkinetic syndrome was always highly controversial, mainly because no evidence was produced that such children were actually brain damaged. Even worse, a number of factor analytic studies failed to find significant relationships among the markers said to define the disorder. As a result, many began to question whether the syndrome even exists (Loney, 1983; Ross & Ross, 1976).

Most of the problems surrounding minimal brain damage and hyperkinesis were definitional ones. For one thing, diagnostic criteria were inconsistently applied. Some clinicians insisted that restlessness, distractibility, impulsivity, and a short attention span were essential criteria for a diagnosis, whereas others included perceptual difficulties, conceptual deficits, and learning disorders among their diagnostic criteria; still others saw features such as aggressive and acting-out behavior as significant diagnostic criteria (Campbell, 1976). Given these varying views regarding the essential characteristics of the disorder, it is not surprising to learn that different investigators using different diagnostic criteria and studying different children produced inconsistent results.

Into this confused situation, came the DSM-III. Its predecessor, the DSM-II, contained a diagnosis called hyperkinetic reaction of childhood. This diagnosis, however, was considered too narrow, and the DSM-III has replaced it with one called attention deficit disorder. The new diagnosis represents an attempt to have researchers focus on inattention rather than hyperactivity, as well as to remove implications that the syndrome is *always* the result of brain damage. In redefining hyperactivity as attention deficit disorder, the DSM-III recognizes the fact that for children having trouble in school, it is not always activity level that is the main obstacle. Although the DSM-III has led to more uniform diagnostic procedures, we shall see that diagnostic difficulties linger on. In this section we will use the term ADD rather than the older terminology. However, because most research has focused on hyperactivity rather than attentional deficits, it will often be necessary to revert to the older terms.

Diagnosis and Description

Figure 5.5 describes the story of Stanley, a boy who was ultimately diagnosed as having an attention deficit disorder with hyperactivity. The DSM-III also makes provision for a diagnosis of attention deficit disorder without hyperactivity, a condition that may or may not exist (Maurer & Stewart, 1980; Rutter & Shaffer, 1980).

The DSM-III diagnostic criteria for attention deficit disorder with hyperactivity appear in Table 5.4. According to the prefatory remarks, the criteria must be applied selec-

FIGURE 5.5. Attention Deficit Disorder in a Young Boy

Stanley was referred to a clinical child psychologist at the request of his teacher who, in her own words, "had enough." At 7 years of age, Stan required almost constant supervision to keep him from disturbing the other children in his class. The teacher says that Stan is unable to concentrate on schoolwork for more than a few minutes at a time and seems always to be moving. Even when in his seat, he fidgets around enough to disturb his neighbors.

Stan's mother reports that he is very active at home as well. He never seems to stick to any task for any length of time. Stan's mother also indicates that his judgment is very poor. He often wanders off without saying where he is going, frequently fails to return home at the proper time, and cannot be relied upon to complete his chores (or any other task). Stan has an older and younger brother but is unable to play with them because he will not stick to the rules of a game or concentrate for very long periods. Stan intrudes into conversations and games and seems unable to inhibit his impulses. He also has temper tantrums that come and go rapidly.

During the psychological assessment, Stan was able to maintain his seat but not his attention. He gave up on the IQ test task easily and frequently changed whatever conversational subject the examiner introduced. Although he admitted that he was not doing well in school, he did not feel that his behavior was responsible.

tively, taking into account the child's developmental stage. It is also important to note that the symptoms may not always be present and are more likely to be noticed at school than at home. The criteria are meant to apply to children between the ages of 8 and 10.

Diagnostic Problems

Although the DSM-III criteria represent a great improvement over previous diagnostic schemes, and the criteria appear to be objective, important definitional problems remain. First, although the DSM-III emphasizes that ADD is a developmental disorder and that a child's developmental level must be taken into account when applying the diagnostic criteria, the normative data necessary to do this are unavailable (Ross & Pelham, 1981). For example, criterion C(2), "has difficulty sitting still or fidgets excessively," assumes that there is a commonly agreed upon definition of fidgeting that can easily be applied by diagnosticians. Furthermore, it assumes that clinicians know how much fidgeting is "excessive" at

various developmental stages. Unfortunately, neither of these assumptions is true. In order to apply this criterion with reasonable reliability, we would first have to conduct normative studies under standardized conditions, observing children of different ages using an objective definition of "fidget." These studies would yield norms for the various criterion behaviors, which could then be used to determine whether a child deviates enough from other children at the same developmental stage to be considered to have an attention deficit disorder. The importance of developing appropriate norms is illustrated by Werry and Quay's (1971) report that teachers of 8-year-old boys classify 43% as having short attention spans!

Vague definitions and the important influence of context (some children show their disorder at school but not at home) are the main reasons why parents, teachers, and clinicians often fail to agree about which children suffer from ADD or hyperactivity (Sandberg, Wieselberg, & Shaffer, 1980). Furthermore, there are enormous differences in the frequency with which the syndrome is diagnosed in different countries. Rutter (1982) estimated that American clinicians are 50 times more likely to diagnose a child as ADD (or hyperactive) than their British counterparts, who seem to prefer to label such children as conduct disordered. Because conduct and attentional disorders often occur together (Sandberg et al., 1980), it is difficult to tell them apart, although some have tried (see Trites & Laprade, 1983, for example).

In addition to the lack of adequate definitions and norms, there is also some question about the accuracy of some of the DSM-III diagnostic criteria. For example, criterion A(3), "easily distracted," does not agree with empirical research findings reported by Douglas and Peters (1979). In their experiments, hyperactive children were found no more distractible than nonhyperactive children (see also, Lynn, Mirkin, Lanese, Schmidt, & Arnold, 1983).

TABLE 5.4. DSM-III DIAGNOSTIC CRITERIA: ATTENTION DEFICIT DISORDER WITH HYPERACTIVITY.

The child displays, for his or her mental and chronological age, signs of developmentally inappropriate inattention, impulsivity, and hyperactivity. The signs must be reported by adults in the child's environment, such as parents and teachers. Because the symptoms are typically variable, they may not be observed directly by the clinician. When the reports of teachers and parents conflict, primary consideration should be given to the teacher reports because of greater familiarity with age-appropriate norms. Symptoms typically worsen in situations that require self-application, as in the classroom. Signs of the disorder may be absent when the child is in a new or one-to-one situation.

The number of symptoms specified is for children between the ages of eight and ten, the peak age range for referral. In younger children, more severe forms of the symptoms and a greater number of symptoms are usually present. The opposite is true of older children.

A. *Inattention. At least three of the following:*
   1) Often fails to finish things he or she starts
   2) Often doesn't seem to listen
   3) Easily distracted
   4) Has difficulty concentrating on schoolwork or other tasks requiring sustained attention
   5) Has difficulty sticking to a play activity

B. *Impulsivity. At least three of the following:*
   1) Often acts before thinking
   2) Shifts excessively from one activity to another
   3) Has difficulty organizing work (this not being due to cognitive impairment)
   4) Needs a lot of supervision
   5) Frequently calls out in class
   6) Has difficulty awaiting turn in games or group situations

C. *Hyperactivity. At least two of the following:*
   1) Excessively runs about or climbs on things
   2) Has difficulty sitting still or fidgets excessively
   3) Has difficulty staying seated
   4) Moves about excessively during sleep
   5) Is always "on the go" or acts as if "driven by a motor"

D. *Onset before the age of seven.*

E. *Duration of at least six months.*

F. *Not due to schizophrenia, affective disorder, or severe or profound mental retardation.*

Note: DSM-III also provides for a diagnosis of attention deficit disorder without hyperactivity (same criteria, except child is judged never to have displayed signs of hyperactivity, Criterion C) and for the diagnosis of attention deficit disorder, residual type (child once met criteria for attention deficit disorder with hyperactivity, but hyperactivity is no longer present).
Source: American Psychiatric Association (1980), © 1980 American Psychiatric Association. Reprinted by permission.

Diagnostic Instruments

There have been several attempts to develop diagnostic checklists for assessing attention deficit (and related) disorders. Some checklists are meant to be completed by parents, others by teachers (Goyette, Conners, & Ulrich, 1978; Routh, Schroeder, & O'Tuama, 1974). Although norms have been provided for these scales, definitions of the various behaviors are not given. Consider the rating scale contained in Table 5.5. Item 5 requires the rater to make a judgment about whether the child is "restless or overactive." Because different people have different definitions of what constitutes restless behavior,

TABLE 5.5. A RATING SCALE FOR ASSESSING HYPERACTIVITY IN CHILDREN.

Item	Not at All	Just a Little	Quite a Bit	Very Much
1. Sits fiddling with small objects				
2. Hums and makes other odd noises				
3. Falls apart under stress of examination				
4. Coordination poor				
5. Restless or overactive				
6. Excitable				
7. Inattentive				
8. Difficulty in concentration				
9. Oversensitive				
10. Overly serious or sad				
11. Daydreams				
12. Sullen or sulky				
13. Selfish				
14. Disturbs other children				
15. Quarrelsome				
16. "Tattles"				
17. Acts "smart"				
18. Destructive				
19. Steals				
20. Lies				
21. Temper outbursts				
22. Isolates himself from other children				
23. Appears to be unaccepted by group				
24. Appears to be easily led				
25. No sense of fair play				
26. Appears to lack leadership				
27. Does not get along with opposite sex				
28. Does not get along with same sex				
29. Teases other children or interferes with their activities				
30. Submissive				
31. Defiant				
32. Impudent				
33. Shy				
34. Fearful				
35. Excessive demands for teacher's attention				
36. Stubborn				
37. Overly anxious to please				
38. Uncooperative				
39. Attendance problem				

Source: Adapted from Conners (1969), and presented by permission of the author.

it is not clear that two judges who describe a child as "quite restless or overactive" both mean the same thing. Perhaps this is the reason why the various checklists tend not to agree with one another (Wallender & Conger, 1981). There is simply no substitute for norms based on behavioral observations.

In addition to checklists, direct behavioral observations, electromechanical devices (designed to measure a child's movements), and standard psychological tests (intelligence tests) have all been used to assess ADD. Reviewing all of these methods, Wallender and Conger (1981) conclude that only a few are reliable and that there is very little between-test agreement. That is, the tests do not identify the same children as being hyperactive or attention disordered. They suggest that ADD may be multidimensional rather than a single entity.

The notion that ADD may be multidimensional receives further support from studies attempting to produce diagnostic criteria using multivariate (mainly factor analytic) procedures, most recently by Loney (1983). These studies suggest that there are probably two subtypes: an aggressive type of attentional disorder, in which the child has many interpersonal difficulties, and a nonaggressive attentional disorder, in which poor academic performance is the major problem. Neither the DSM-III nor the commonly used diagnostic instruments make this distinction.

Prevalence

Most published reports suggest that attention deficit disorders (defined in many ways) occur fairly frequently. Cole (1975) cites estimates by the U.S. Federal Office of Child Development suggesting that 3% of elementary school children display at least some of the characteristics associated with ADD. Wender (1971), using the terminology *minimal brain dysfunction*, puts the incidence at 5 to 10% of school-aged children; some studies go as high as 20% (see Whalen & Henker, 1980). The problem appears more common among boys than girls, with the sex ratio varying from 3 to 1 to 9 to 1 (Campbell, 1976;

Lambert, Sandoval, & Sassone, 1978; Trites, Dugas, Lynch, & Ferguson, 1979).

Prognosis and Follow-up

A major question concerning children diagnosed ADD (or hyperactive) is what happens to them as they grow older. Although clinical lore (and many writers) suggest that the problems (particularly hyperactivity) decrease with age, follow-up studies indicate that most children are not so lucky. Their problems persist, making the ultimate prognosis less than favorable. For example, Weiss, Minde, Werry, Douglas, and Nemeth (1971), in a 5-year follow-up of children with a diagnosis of minimal brain dysfynction, found that although their hyperactivity decreased over time, the children continued to display serious problems in attention, concentration, and underachievement. Huessy and Cohen (1976) found that by adolescence, 50 to 70% of hyperactives have failed at least one school grade and many have failed two. Hoy, Weiss, Minde, and Cohen (1978) reported that "hyperkinetic" children upon reaching adolescence displayed problems of sustained attention, performed less well on visual-motor tasks, exhibited more reading problems, and rated themselves lower in self-esteem than did a group of normal adolescents. Other studies (Mendelson, Johnson, & Stewart, 1971; Minde et al., 1971) suggest a similar outlook.

There have not been many follow-up studies of attention-disordered children through adulthood, but some writers have suggested (on the basis of retrospective studies) that antisocial adults may have been hyperactive as children (Robins, 1979). One study of particular interest was reported by Borland and Heckman (1976), who compared male hyperactive children with their nonhyperactive brothers over a 25-year period. The hyperactive children were found to have poorer school records and to have a lower socioeconomic status in adulthood. Although no longer hyperactive, the formerly hyperactive children were described as nervous, restless adults who easily lost their tempers. These men were also found to change jobs more often than their brothers and to perceive their work as more boring. Psychiatric problems were also more common among the hyperactive group than among their brothers, although none were reported to be incapacitated by these problems.

Follow-up findings, taken as a whole, suggest that although motor activity levels may decline as the attention-disordered child grows older, many problems remain to affect their lives even as adults.

Etiology and Research

As noted above, attention deficit disorders were originally thought to always result from brain dysfunction (albeit *minimal* brain dysfunction). Not surprisingly, therefore, much research attention has been devoted to determining the relationship between organic factors and attentional disorders. In general, this research has failed to demonstrate any one-to-one relationship between the symptoms of attention deficit disorder and any specific neurological impairment. Some children with clear-cut brain damage are neither hyperactive nor unable to sustain attention whereas a large proportion of those children who do display these behaviors have no independent evidence of brain injury. Studies using EEGs, for instance, have been unable to distinguish reliably between hyperactive and other children (Dubey, 1976).

Studies of soft neurological signs have suggested that whereas attention-disordered children as a group may display more of these signs than "normal" children, they do not display more of these signs than other children seen in clinics (e.g., the mentally retarded). In addition, studies of the specific factors that might be expected to cause brain damage in children (pregnancy and birth complications, for example) have found these to be only weak predictors of later hyperactivity or attention deficits (Firestone & Prabhu, 1983). Studies attempting to find a role for biochemical factors in attention deficit disorder have also failed to find significant differences between attention-disordered and other children seen in psychiatric clinics. Dubey (1976) concludes:

The evidence taken as a whole does not strongly support the notion that organic factors play a significant role in the behavior problems of most hyperkinetic children. The results from biochemical studies and studies of severe pregnancy and birth complications are clearly negative; results from electroencephalographic and neurological studies are conflicting; . . . as such, the assumption that a hyperkinetic child suffers from minimal brain dysfunction or any other biological deviations is unwarranted in the absence of unequivocal data. For *most* hyperkinetic children, such data is unavailable. (p. 362)

In the years since Dubey wrote, a great deal of additional research has been devoted to uncovering organic deficits in attention-disordered children. Unfortunately, we are no closer to identifying specific biochemical or neurological markers for ADD than we were in 1976. The present situation is aptly summarized by Rutter (1982) as follows:

. . . the hypotheses are varied, the empirical findings contradictory and inconclusive; and such differences as have been found serve to differentiate hyperkinetic from normal children and not from those with other psychiatric disorders. (p. 30)

Lead Poisoning

Prompted by a variety of published reports suggesting a history of lead poisoning in attention-disordered children, David (1974) undertook an investigation designed to reveal the relationship between lead levels and hyperactivity. David assumed that even in the absence of a history of lead poisoning, many children, especially those from low income areas, might show nontoxic but high lead levels in their blood. (Lead ingestion most frequently results from eating flakes of lead-based paint peeled from the woodwork and walls of dilapidated houses.)

In David's study, children were divided into four groups: Those for whom a "probable" organic basis for their behavior could be determined on the basis of a medical history; those for whom a "possible" organic cause was suspected; those with a clear history of lead poisoning; and a group for whom no specific etiology could be determined. The lead levels of all four groups were compared with those of a control group consisting of nonhyperactive children. Hyperactive children with no known organic etiology were found to have significantly higher lead levels than the control children, as did children with a history of lead poisoning and children with "possible" organic etiologies. Only children with known ("probable") organic etiologies for their symptoms had similar lead levels to the controls. This finding strongly suggests a relationship between lead levels and at least one symptom of ADD—hyperactivity. More recent research by David, Hoffman, Sverd, and Clark (1977) provides additional support for the relationship between blood lead levels and attention deficit disorder. Because lead levels can also be increased by breathing automobile fumes (many older cars still use lead-based gasoline) or living near lead smelters, it is possible that children other than those living in older, poorer neighborhoods may also be suffering from the effects of lead poisoning.

Minor Physical Anomalies

A series of studies conducted by Waldrop and her associates (Waldrop & Goering, 1971; Waldrop, Pederson, & Bell, 1968) also provides support for the role of biological factors in ADD. Waldrop and Goering (1971) examined the relationship between the frequency of minor physical anomalies thought to reflect accidents during embryological development and later hyperactivity. These anomalies consisted of physical defects that might go unnoticed by the casual observer, such as deviations in head circumference, misshapen ears, deviation of the mouth (high palate, furrowed tongue), curved fifth finger, third toe larger than second toe, and so on. Waldrop and Goering found that in boys there was a significant relationship between the frequency of these anomalies and hyperactivity—the more anomalies the greater the hyperactivity. Firestone and Prabhu (1983) as well as Gillberg, Carlstrom, and Rasmussen (1983) have reported similar findings.

Studies by Rapoport and her coworkers (see Rapoport & Ferguson, 1981, for a review) have also found a relationship between minor anomalies and later hyperactivity. They also reported that children with many anomalies become hyperactive at a younger age than those with fewer anomalies, and their mothers reported pregnancy complications more often than those with low scores. Interestingly, Rapoport and her colleagues found the number of physical anomalies to be more or less unrelated to EEG abnormalities or the presence of neurological signs. As Ross and Pelham (1981) point out, this appears to contradict the major reason for studying anomalies in the first place—namely, that anomalies are related to neurological dysfunction. If anomalies are unrelated to neurological functioning, then it is not clear why they should predict attention deficit disorders. Moreover, the relationships found between anomalies and hyperactivity, although statistically significant, are nevertheless small, making them only weak predictors of later hyperactive behavior.

Physiological Arousal and Responsiveness

Although studies of ADD children reveal that most do not show evidence of any specific neurological impairment, a number of investigations conducted during the past several years have been designed to test the possibility of more subtle psychophysiological differences between attention-disordered and other children. These studies have used many measures—cardiac responses, blood pressure recordings, galvanic skin responses, EEGs, ERPs—and have examined ADD and control children at rest and under varying degrees of stimulation. The findings of these studies were reviewed by Hastings and Barkley (1978) and by Ross and Pelham (1981). Few differences between ADD and control children were found during the resting state, but the attention-disordered children were slower to respond to stimulation, displayed a smaller physiological response to stimulation, and were also quicker to habituate. Based on these findings, researchers hypothesized that although attention-disordered children do not appear to be over or underaroused when resting, they may be less responsive to stimulation than other children.

Zentall (1975), based on these and other similar findings, suggested that ADD children (specifically those that are hyperactive) have a lower than optimal state of arousal and engage in extra activity in order to increase their level of stimulation. In other words, hyperactivity is a way of seeking stimulation. This hypothesis is certainly plausible, and it may also explain the value of stimulant drugs in treating hyperactivity (see the following), but it is surely not the whole explanation for attention deficit disorders. First of all, the results are not entirely consistent; some studies have even reported that attention-disordered children are over rather than underaroused. In addition, it is not unusual for arousal indices to fail to correlate with one another (see Gualtieri, Hicks, & Mayo, 1983). Arousal mechanisms appear too complex to support a one-dimensional theory of ADD.

Attention Deficits

Because the DSM-III has shifted the emphasis from hyperactivity to disordered attention, it is worthwhile examining research concerned directly with the nature of the attentional deficits in ADD and hyperactive children. We have already mentioned a study by Douglas and Peters (1979) that failed to find hyperactive children more distractible than nonhyperactive children. They did find, however, that hyperactives do have some difficulty sustaining attention over time. Because many of the children studied by Douglas and Peters were also learning disabled, it is difficult to say whether hyperactivity itself or learning disability accounted for their findings. In any case, as Ross and Pelham (1981) note, many hyperactive children appear able to watch television for long periods; thus, they do appear able to sustain their attention in certain circumstances. Perhaps their failure to do so in the experimental situation reflects a motivational (performance) deficit rather than a capacity deficit. Further research on the precise nature of the attentional deficit in ADD is currently underway. These studies should begin to clarify the current rather unclear situation.

Genetics

Studies concerned with the genetics of ADD are reviewed by Cantwell (1976) and McMahon (1980). At least two studies (Cantwell, 1972; Morrison & Stewart, 1971) found a higher incidence of hyperactivity in the relatives of hyperactive children than in the population at large. Moreover, close relatives were also found to have higher than average rates of alcoholism, sociopathy, and other psychiatric problems. Studies of hyperactive children who have been adopted (Cantwell, 1975; Morrison & Stewart, 1973) have not found these higher incidences among adopted parents and relatives, suggesting a genetic contribution to hyperactivity. The high concordance rates for twins (when one twin is diagnosed, the other has a higher than average chance of also being hyperactive) (Lopez, 1965) and a similar high concordance rate for general activity level in twins (Willerman, 1973) also suggest a possible genetic component. Each "genetic" study can be criticized for methodological flaws, but taken together, the evidence does appear to suggest some role for genetic factors in ADD (McMahon, 1980).

Etiology: A Final Note

To summarize this review of organic factors in ADD, it seems fair to say that studies have so far failed to provide evidence that attention-disordered children are brain damaged, minimally or otherwise. Nevertheless, investigations of the relationship between lead level and hyperactivity, psychophysiological findings, and the suggestive role of genetic factors indicate that perhaps subtle biological factors do play a role in the development of attention deficit disorders.

Treatment

The treatment of ADD, like everything else associated with it, has been the subject of much controversy. Drugs, educational interventions, behavior modification, and even diet have been suggested as possible treatments. The major approaches are reviewed here.

Pharmacological Treatment

Most children diagnosed as ADD or hyperactive are treated with stimulant drugs (Ritalin, Dexedrine, Cylert, Benzedrine). The literature dealing with pharmacological treatment has recently been reviewed by Barkley (1981), Rapoport (1983), Solanto (1984), and Whalen (1982). Although the diagnostic and definitional problems described earlier make it difficult to compare studies (it's hard to be certain that different investigators are actually studying the same children), it is estimated that 60 to 90% of hyperactive children respond favorably to stimulants (Whalen & Henker, 1976). The behavior most improved by stimulant drugs is the ability to sustain attention. Interestingly, the drugs do not necessarily reduce activity levels and have relatively little effect on academic performance. Rapoport (1983) calls the effects of stimulants on restless, hyperactive children "dramatic" and "the easiest clinical psychotropic drug effect to demonstrate" (p. 189).

Stimulants undoubtedly help the majority of ADD children, but no one really knows why. At one time, it was common to describe ADD children's response to stimulant drugs as "paradoxical," implying that unlike other people, ADD children are sedated rather than stimulated by the drugs (Wender, 1971). We know today that there is nothing paradoxical about ADD children's response to stimulants; the earlier beliefs were based on faulty observations. ADD children appear calmer when receiving stimulants because of their enhanced ability to attend and inhibit inappropriate behavior, but they are not sedated. Moreover, research comparing the reactions of ADD and normal children to stimulants reveals that both display strikingly similar responses, including increased attention and concentration

(Rapoport et al., 1978). Further research is necessary to clarify the precise mechanism by which stimulants exert their beneficial effect (see Solanto, 1984, for some recent ideas).

Although the beneficial short-term effects of stimulant treatment appear well documented, controversy surrounds their long-term benefits. Rapoport (1983) reviews several studies that followed hyperactive children for varying numbers of years. Most of these studies found no enduring improvements for children treated with stimulants. Even children who show a dramatic response to the drugs in the short term do not necessarily receive any long-term benefit. A possible exception to these pessimistic findings may be found in the results of a study by Loney, Kramer, and Kosier (1981). Loney et al. compared hyperactive children who had received stimulant medication with a matched group of control children who received behaviorally oriented counseling. Five years later, both groups had similar academic records, and their teachers found them equally active. However, mothers of children treated with stimulants rated them as better coordinated and considered them to have higher self-esteem than mothers of children who did not receive the drug. The drug-treated group also had fewer police contacts and drug-related problems.

An important drawback to the use of stimulants with children is the possible side effects of the drugs. As Werry (1978) observes, "it is seldom possible to produce a therapeutic effect with psychotropic drugs without simultaneously producing some unwanted effects" (p. 71). Loney and Ordona (1975) reported the side effects observed in a sample of 135 children treated with stimulant medication; their findings appear in Table 5.6. Several investigators have also reported that stimulant medications can retard growth (see Whalen, 1982). For this reason, many clinicians recommend "drug holidays" during school vacations to permit growth to catch up. In addition to these physical side effects, Whalen and Henker (1980) described what they called a drug's "emanative" effects. Children need to explain to their friends and themselves why they must take medication. One way of doing

TABLE 5.6. SIDE EFFECTS DURING
STIMULANT DRUG TREATMENT
OF HYPERACTIVE CHILDREN.

Side Effect Mentioned	Number of Children	Percent of Sample ($n = 135$)
Appetite reduction and/or weight loss	59	44
Sleep disturbance	43	32
Vomiting, nausea, "flu"	18	13
Headache, dizziness, fainting	17	13
Stomachache, cramps	12	9
More than one side effect	41	30
Only one side effect	52	39
No side effects	42	31

Source: From Loney & Ordona (1975), © 1975 by the American Orthopsychiatric Association and reprinted by permission.

this is to externalize responsibility for their behavioral problems ("I take the drugs because I cannot control myself"). Externalizing responsibility this way may make them less responsive to behavioral interventions.

It should be noted that although most ADD children are treated with stimulants, other pharmacological compounds have been tried. At one time or another, tranquilizers, antidepressants, and even antihistamines have been prescribed for ADD, by and large without much success (Werry, 1978).

A pharmacological approach that may be of use with selected ADD children was described by David, Hoffman, Sverd, Clark, and Voeller (1976). These investigators used lead-chelating (lead reducing) agents to reduce blood lead levels in 13 hyperactive children. All of these children had raised lead levels and no other known cause for their hyperactivity. The researchers reported improvements in the children, implying that lead-chelating agents may be of therapeutic value in treating hyperactive children with excessive lead in their systems.

Diet

Feingold (1975) put forward the controversial hypothesis that artificial food colorings and flavorings were responsible for hyperactivity in approximately 50% of children so diagnosed. Although professionals were wary about Feingold's claims, the public took to it right away. Before long, there were many children following the "Feingold diet" (a diet that eliminates colorings and other ingredients). Conners (1980) provides an interesting history of how Feingold's ideas were disseminated and how the diet became popular largely on the basis of anecdotal reports of its efficacy.

Controlled research on the Feingold diet was conducted in several research centers during the 1970s; this work is reviewed by Taylor (1979) and by Conners (1980). Both authors conclude that only a small proportion of hyperactive children are likely to be helped by the diet. Earlier claims that up to 50% of hyperactive children benefit were certainly overstated and most likely the result of a "placebo" phenomenon. That is, because early observations were uncontrolled (they were not double-blind), improvements attributed to the diet could have been due to expectancies on the part of the children and their parents that they would improve.

A recent review by Weiss (1982) reaches more favorable conclusions mainly by emphasizing positive findings at the expense of negative ones. Although a useful counterbalance to the more negative reviews, even Weiss cannot say what proportion of children are helped by the Feingold diet. For this reason, Weiss' favorable review does not alter Conners' conclusion concerning the question of whether there is anything of substance in Feingold's hypothesis. "Yes," Conners writes, "but not much and not consistently" (p. 107).

Psychological Treatment

O'Leary (1980), in a provocative article titled "Pills or Skills for Hyperactive Children" argues that terms like *hyperactivity* automatically imply brain damage and pharmacological treatment when what many children really need is to learn new behavioral habits. Although many would argue that the proper treatment for attention-disordered children is not an either-or question but merely a matter of what works (a point that will be returned to later), there is little doubt that many behavioral therapists look upon pharmacological treatment as potentially dangerous if not immoral. In its place they offer a variety of behavior modification techniques.

Cognitive behavioral approaches have been particularly popular (Bornstein & Quevillon, 1976; Kendall & Finch, 1978). The basic approach is to teach children a kind of "self-talk" in which they constantly remind themselves to pay attention to the task at hand. Although several studies support the efficacy of this approach, the usual diagnostic problems make it difficult to generalize their success to the entire population of ADD children.

Operant conditioning (contingency management) procedures have also been widely used to help ADD children (Ayllon & Rosenbaum, 1977). The aim of this approach is to reinforce attention to tasks and extinguish disruptive behaviors in classroom settings. Occasionally, parents as well as teachers are enlisted in order to help the new behaviors generalize beyond the classroom. These approaches can significantly reduce the troubling behaviors of ADD children. Much of this work is reviewed by Prout (1977) and by Mash and Dalby (1979).

A frequent criticism of behavioral approaches to ADD is that, like pharmacological treatment, they often seem to work only so long as the program is in effect. The problem of maintaining gains after behavioral programs end has still not been surmounted. On this score, Loney (1980) writes, "Drug treatments that last too long are decried; so are behavioral programs that don't last long enough. There seems little question that there are too many of both" (p. 38).

On the grounds that stimulant medications enhance conditionability, some researchers have argued that an optimum treatment would combine stimulants with behavior modification (Eysenck & Rachman, 1971). Although some writers seem to object to drugs on purely moral grounds (O'Leary, 1980), there are some research data to help answer the question of which treatment—drugs or behavior modification—is more effective. Gittelman et al. (1980) compared stimulant drug treatment with behavior modification and with a combination of behavior modification and drugs. Behavior modification alone was less effective than stimulants, but the combination of the two was most effective in helping the children. Unfortunately, but typical for this area of research, contradictory findings are also available (Kauffman & Hallahan, 1979).

Special Education

Educational approaches to treating ADD have, quite naturally, been designed to enhance the child's ability to benefit from classroom instruction by decreasing activity level and increasing attention. As Zentall (1975) observed, traditional approaches rest on certain assumptions made by Strauss concerning the nature of hyperactivity—namely, that hyperactive children are brain damaged, that they are unable to "screen out" incoming stimuli due to perceptual problems, and that overstimulation results in hyperactivity. Zentall pointed out that acceptance of this point of view has resulted in a "stimulus reduction" approach to the education of hyperactive children. Proponents of this approach (Cruikshank, Bentzen, Ratzeburg, & Tannhauser, 1961, for instance) recommend that classrooms for ADD children should be as devoid of stimulation as possible, with opaque windows, no bulletin boards, pictures, or excess furniture, and the walls, floor, and ceiling painted the same color. It has even been proposed that ADD children be placed in 3-foot-square cubicles in order to keep stimulation from other children to a minimum.

In a review of the literature concerning the validity of the stimulus-reduction notion and procedures, Zentall (1975) reported that studies comparing hyperactive children assigned to normal and stimulus-reduced environments have not shown the quieter environment to result in improved academic performance. Zentall has even suggested the opposite—that ADD children require increased levels of stimulation in order to bring them to their "optimum" level. This argument is similar to the one offered as an explanation for stimulant drugs. Zentall and Zentall (1976) provide data indicating that hyperactivity decreases with increased stimulation, thus lending some credence to this view. Additional research is necessary to determine what the optimum arousal levels are and how the stimulation approach may be integrated with classroom behavior modification programs mentioned earlier.

ADD: Current Status

It should be clear by now that hyperactivity and ADD are conditions about which there are more questions than answers. It is difficult to diagnose because many of the behaviors comprising the syndrome are not clearly defined, and it is closely related to other disorders, such as learning disability and conduct disorder. Many factors have been implicated in the etiology of ADD, but so far, no specific etiology has been uncovered. The same conclusion applies to treatment. Some combination of stimulant drugs and behavior modification appears most effective, but exactly what combination no one knows. It is also unclear why treatment effects do not last. Currently, research is going in several directions at once. Until clear diagnostic criteria are adopted by researchers in the field, the present confused situation is unlikely to improve.

SUMMARY

This chapter was concerned with the possible effects of neurological impairment on children's behavior and development. It was noted that brain damage may result from a variety of factors occurring prior to birth, during the birth process, or after birth and that such damage can manifest itself in a variety of

ways. Variables related to brain damage's behavioral effects include the child's age at the time of injury and the extent and location of the lesion. It was emphasized that although certain types of deficits have commonly been associated with brain damage, the variable influence of age, location, and extent of the injury suggest that brain damage should not be treated as a unitary construct and that there are few generalizations that apply to all brain-damaged children.

Many procedures are used to assess neurological impairment, including developmental histories, psychological tests, neurological exams, EEGs, and various imaging methods. Some of the newest imaging methods (CT scans and NMR, for instance) are able to produce images of brain sections without endangering the individual. There are even methods currently available to assess brain function as well as brain structure (EEG maps and PET scans). The availability of these new techniques has lead to an explosion in research on brain-behavior relationships.

Four syndromes that have been related to neurological dysfunction were also reviewed in this chapter. The first, developmental language disorder, was found to be similar to adult aphasia, but not the same thing. Developmental language disorders were differentiated from stuttering and other articulation disorders in which speech pronunciation rather than speech content is affected. Etiological theories and treatments were described.

Seizure disorders were discussed next. The various types of seizures were described as were common etiologies and treatments. The third syndrome discussed, Tourette's disorder, was seen to be a strange combination of motor tics and odd verbalizations that respond well to psychoactive drugs. The chapter ended with a discussion of attention deficit disorder and hyperactivity, the DSM-III name for what used to be referred to simply as hyperactivity or minimal brain damage. At one time, it was assumed that all ADD children suffered from some form of brain damage. Today, the picture is much more complicated. Etiological theories implicate many different causes, and the children receive a variety of treatments. Pharmacological treatments are particularly common, although they appear to work best in combination with behavior modification.

SUGGESTED READINGS

Rutter, M. (1983). *Developmental Neuropsychiatry*. New York: Guilford Press. An excellent edited text that contains many well written chapters dealing with factors that can contribute to child brain damage, child neuropsychological assessment, and organically based clinical syndromes.

Rothenberger, A. (Ed.). (1982). *Event-related potentials in children*. New York: Elsevier. A collection of papers describing how ERPs and EEGs are being used to understand brain-behavior relationships in children.

Friedhoff, A. J., & Chase, T. N. (Eds.). (1982). *Gilles de la Tourette Syndrome*. New York: Raven Press. A thorough review of this odd disorder.

Ross, A. O., & Pelham, W. E. (1981). Child psychopathology. *Annual Review of Psychology*, 32, 243–278. Over half of this chapter is devoted to reviewing the diagnosis, etiology, and treatment of ADD.

Ross, D. M., & Ross, S. A. (1982). *Hyperactivity: Research, theory and action*. New York: Wiley. An excellent text dealing with the etiology and correlates of childhood hyperactivity.

6 "NEUROTIC" BEHAVIOR DISORDERS OF CHILDHOOD: ANXIETY, AFFECTIVE, AND SOMATOFORM DISORDERS

I n this chapter several problems are considered that have traditionally been grouped under the heading of childhood neuroses. These disorders, while considered less severe than the pervasive developmental disorders discussed in Chapter 4, may nevertheless be quite disabling and problematic for both child and family.

The disorders to be considered include overanxious, avoidant, and separation anxiety disorders of childhood and adolescence as well as childhood phobias and obsessions and compulsions. Also discussed are childhood depression and conversion reactions. Various psychopathology texts (Adams & Sutker, 1984; Coleman, Butcher, & Carson, 1984; Turner & Hersen, 1984) have reviewed research related to such disorders in adults. The findings reported here, however, are in the main restricted to studies employing children as subjects, although results of studies with adults have been included when appropriate.

In the following sections we will briefly consider dynamic and behavioral conceptualizations of childhood neuroses, the similarities between these conditions, and the possible role of constitutional and family variables in their development. Later sections are devoted

to a more detailed consideration of specific disorders.

PSYCHODYNAMIC AND BEHAVIORAL PERSPECTIVES

A logical first question to ask when approaching this subject is to what does the term *neurosis* refer? Given the frequency with which this term is used, even outside of professional circles, it would seem that this question should be readily answered. Yet a review of the existing literature reveals marked differences of opinion, especially when the views of those subscribing to psychodynamic and behavioral models of psychopathology are contrasted. These differences can best be illustrated by surveying several descriptions of neuroses that have appeared in the psychopathology literature.

One traditional characterization of neurotic disorders was presented by the American Psychiatric Association in DSM-II, an earlier edition of their *Diagnostic and Statistical Manual of Mental Disorders*. Here it is noted that

Anxiety is the chief characteristic of the neuroses. It may be felt and expressed directly, or it may be controlled unconsciously and automatically by conversion, displacement, and various other psychological mechanisms. Generally, these mechanisms produce symptoms, experienced as subjective distress, from which the patient desires relief. . . . The neuroses, as contrasted with the psychoses, manifest neither gross distortion or misinterpretation of external reality, nor gross personality disorganization. (APA, 1968, p. 39)

A second description provided by the Group for the Advancement of Psychiatry (GAP, 1966) defines neuroses as

disorders based on unconscious conflicts over the handling of sexual and aggressive impulses which, though removed from awareness by the mechanism of repression, remain active and unresolved . . . anxiety acting as a danger signal to the ego, ordinarily sets into operation certain defense mechanisms, in addition to repression, and leads to the formation of psychological symptoms which symbolically deal with the conflict, thus achieving a partial though unhealthy solution. (pp. 229–230)

Kessler (1972), distinguishing between neurotic disorders and other problems of childhood, has written:

"Psychoneurosis" is sometimes synonymous with "emotional disturbance" mainly to differentiate both from "psychosis" which is more serious and from organic behavior disorders. Properly, a psychoneurosis is a special form of emotional disturbance, i.e., an *internalized conflict.* . . . If the symptomatic behavior is directly related to bad environment, or the result of deficient training, the child should not be diagnosed as having a psychoneurosis. . . . Psychoneurosis implies not only internalization but also conflict between different parts of the personality. (p. 277)

As can be seen, all three of these descriptions of neurotic behavior are based on a medical model of psychopathology, which sees symptoms as surface manifestations of underlying disorders or conflicts. Likewise, all reflect a psychodynamic conceptualization of personality functioning (see Chapter 1). From this position, neurotic symptoms are viewed as a compromise solution to reduce conflict between various aspects of the personality (id, ego, superego) over the handling of threatening impulses (usually of a sexual or aggressive nature). The symptoms are thought to symbolically reflect the nature of the unconscious conflict and function to protect the individual from anxiety arising from this conflict.

Not all clinicians would view child neuroses in this manner, however. Some use the term *neurosis* largely as a summary term referring to specific forms of maladaptive behavior (avoidance responses, compulsive behaviors, etc.), without subscribing to the notion of an underlying cause (e.g., *neurotic process*) of any sort. Behaviorally oriented clinicians, for example, tend to view neurotic behaviors as being largely the result of learning, arguing that these maladaptive modes of responding are learned according to the same principles that govern the acquisition of other behaviors (for example, classical conditioning, operant conditioning, observational learning). No underlying cause is seen as necessary to "explain" neurosis from this viewpoint, which considers maladaptive behavior to be more closely related to environmental factors than to intrapsychic processes. In fact, it is likely that most behaviorists would be hesitant to employ the term *neurosis* at all, except for purposes of communication, because they believe that this label conveys little useful information.

As this brief overview of psychodynamic and behavioral views of neuroses suggests, there are significant differences of opinion regarding the essential nature of neurotic behavior. These differences are especially apparent as they relate to etiology and the relative emphasis given to intrapsychic and environmental factors.

It is of interest that the developers of DSM-III (American Psychiatric Association, 1980) have attempted to come to grips with these differing views by suggesting the term *neu-*

rotic disorder be used only in the descriptive sense. In DSM-III

> the term neurotic disorder . . . refers to a mental disorder in which the predominant disturbance is a symptom or group of symptoms that is distressing to the individual and is recognized by him or her as unacceptable and alien (ego-dystonic); reality testing is grossly intact; behavior does not actively violate gross social norms (although functioning may be markedly impaired); the disturbance is relatively enduring or recurrent without treatment and is not limited to transitory reactions to stressors; and there is no demonstrable organic etiology or factors (p. 9–10)

Moreover, neurotic disorder, as used in DSM-III, does not imply any specific etiological process. This definition can be contrasted with the DSM-II characterization of the neuroses presented earlier, which relied heavily on a psychodynamic conceptualization of neurotic disorders. It is likely that the DSM-III approach will be more acceptable to individuals of diverse theoretical orientations. One additional point regarding DSM-III and neurotic disorders is worthy of note. Unlike earlier versions of this system, DSM-III does not group neurotic disorders under a single heading. This is not to suggest that such disorders were excluded. Rather, because of their diverse nature, the traditional neurotic subtypes are included under several different headings: anxiety disorders, affective disorders, somatoform disorders, dissociative disorders.

Here, consistent with DSM-III, the term *neurosis* will be used in a strictly descriptive sense to refer to a group of problems that share certain common characteristics, which will be described later. The term is used mainly to facilitate a discussion of these behavioral problems (which have traditionally been considered together) and does not in any way imply an adherence to a medical model of psychopathology, which has often been associated with this term.

GENERAL CHARACTERISTICS

Neurotic disorders of childhood may take several forms. However, although the specific behavioral manifestations of these disorders may differ, they are often thought to have certain common features. According to Davids (1973), for example, most clinicians would agree that a high level of anxiety is a major factor in most neurotic disorders. This is not to imply agreement as to what might be the source or specific role of anxiety, but simply that anxiety appears to be a prominent feature.

Kessler (1972) has written that a second feature, common to child neuroses, is that the child appears to suffer more than do others in the environment; that is, children with these disorders often seem apprehensive, unhappy, agitated, or fearful, or may display apparent impairment of physical functioning instead of "acting out" against the physical environment. Citing a study by Achenbach (1966), Kessler noted that there is some empirical basis for making a distinction between children classified as neurotic and those displaying other disorders.

In his study, Achenbach (1966) factor analyzed responses to a 91-item symptom checklist, using 600 male and female child psychiatric patients as subjects. The first principal factor defined in this analysis was a bipolar factor subsequently labeled Internalization-Externalization: Symptoms at the positive pole seemed to consist of problems with the "self," and symptoms at the negative pole appeared to involve conflict with the outside world. Symptoms displaying positive and negative loadings on this factor are presented in Table 6.1. As can be seen from this table, symptoms commonly associated with the term *neurotic disorder* (phobias, obsessions, compulsions, withdrawal, somatic complaints, etc.) all loaded on the internalizing end of this bipolar factor. This provides some empirical basis for grouping such childhood disorders together, because descriptors of these disor-

TABLE 6.1. EXAMPLES OF SYMPTOMS LOADING ON INTERNALIZATION-EXTERNALIZATION, FOR DISTURBED MALE AND FEMALE CHILDREN.*

Internalizing Symptoms		Externalizing Symptoms	
Males	Females	Males	Females
Phobias	Nausea	Disobedient	Disobedient
Stomachaches	Pains	Stealing	Lying
Fearful	Headaches	Lying	Stealing
Pains	Stomachaches	Fighting	Fighting
Worrying	Phobias	Cruelty	Running away
Withdrawn	Vomiting	Destructive	Swearing
Nausea	Diplopia	Inadequate guilt feelings	Quarrelsome
Obsessions	Refusing to eat	Vandalism	Threatening people
Shy	Obsessions	Truancy	Truancy
Vomiting	Fearful	Fire setting	Destructive
Compulsions	Withdrawn	Swearing	
Insomnia	Depression	Running away	
Crying	Dizziness	Temper tantrums	
Fantastic thinking	Crying	Showing off	
Headaches		Hyperactive	
Seclusive			
Apathy			

*Symptoms are presented in order of their factor loadings; those with loadings below .25 are not included.
Source: Adapted from Achenbach (1966).

ders appear correlated, and all involve an internalization rather than externalization of the problem. These findings led Kessler (1972) to conclude that "neurotic symptoms involve special inhibitions or demands which are imposed primarily on the self rather than acted out against others. This attribute, common to all the neuroses, provides a consensual basis for a major differentiation within the broad category of emotional disturbance" (p. 388). It may be noted that further support for this dimension of internalizing versus externalizing problems has been obtained in subsequent studies by Achenbach and his colleagues (see Achenbach, 1982; Achenbach and Edelbrock, 1983b) and that separate factors reflective of these two types of problems have also been found in multivariate studies conducted by other investigators (see Quay, 1984).

In general, then, childhood disorders traditionally referred to as neurotic appear to involve patterns of maladaptive behavior that are less severe and incapacitating than those commonly labeled psychotic, in that they do not typically involve a distortion of reality.

Neurotic disorders also are not thought to be the result of organic causes. Furthermore, these disorders are often characterized by high levels of anxiety, which may have an interfering effect on functioning. Finally, neurotic children display difficulties that seem to be primarily directed inwardly, toward the self, rather than outward, toward others.

The Role of Constitutional Factors

It is commonly thought that constitutional factors may play a role in the development of neurotic disorders. For example, Eysenck (1947, 1960) has suggested that neuroticism may be related to genetic factors and that certain individuals may be predisposed to the development of neurotic disorders (although it is assumed that genetic factors interact with environmental stress in producing their effects).

Studies investigating the relationship between indices of neuroticism in monozygotic (MZ) and same-sex dizygotic (DZ) twins are of interest on this score, because one would assume that if genetic factors are involved, MZ twins (who have an identical genetic endowment) would show a greater degree of concordance on measures of neuroticism than would DZ twins (who have only 50% of their genes in common). Correlations obtained from several of these studies, presented in Table 6.2, suggest that identical twins show a greater degree of similarity with regard to neuroticism than do fraternal twins. Although findings such as these suggest that genetic factors may play a role in neurotic disorders, McGuffin and Reich (1984) have argued that it is necessary to consider that genetic factors may contribute differently to specific disorders. These authors note that when MZ-DZ concordance rates are considered for specific neurotic disorders, fairly strong support is found for a genetic contribution in anxiety disorders. The role of such factors is less clear in other conditions, however.

Another factor that may be related to the development of child neurotic disorders is temperament (Dollinger, 1983). As was discussed in Chapter 3, children, from birth, display marked individual differences in responding to their environment (Thomas & Chess, 1977, 1984; Thomas et al., 1968). They may vary in activity level, degree of regularity in biological functions (e.g., sleep-wakefulness, patterns of eating and elimination), the degree to which they approach or withdraw from new situations, their adaptability to change, and their threshold of responsiveness. Differences are also seen in terms of their span of attention, distractibility, the degree to which they show predominantly positive or negative moods, and in the intensity of their emotional responses.

Because these individual differences are observed so early in life, they are often assumed to be biologically based. Support for this notion has come from twin studies that have suggested that at least certain temperament dimensions may have a significant genetic component (Torgersen, 1982). Still other studies (Bell & Waldrop, 1982) have documented a relationship between temperament and indices of deviant embryological development (e.g., minor physical anomalies), thus providing additional support for a link between temperament characteristics and biological factors. While environmental factors undeniably play a role in the manifestations of temperament (see Cameron, 1978), the available findings appear to provide some support for its constitutional basis (Rutter, 1982b).

As was indicated in Chapter 3, a number of these temperament characteristics (e.g., irregularity, withdrawal, unadaptability, negative mood, high intensity emotional responses) have been found to cluster together to define what Thomas et al. (1968) have referred to as the "difficult" child. Early work by Thomas and his colleagues demonstrated that difficult children were at significant risk for developing later psychological problems. Indeed, of the 141 children involved in the New York Longitudinal Study, 70% of those classified as difficult developed later psychological problems as compared to only 18% of those classified as easy. More recent work (Thomas & Chess, 1984) has suggested that these problems continued even into adulthood. Other research documenting a relationship between difficult temperament and psychological difficulties has been reviewed by Plomin (1983).

Relevant to the topic of neurotic or "internalizing" disorders are the results of a recent study by Johnson et al. (1984). In this study approximately 20 children, displaying difficult temperament characteristics, were compared with 20 children with easy temperament and a third group showing mixed temperament features. Temperament measures were ob-

TABLE 6.2. CORRELATION COEFFICIENTS BETWEEN MEASURES OF NEUROTICISM IN MONOZYGOTIC (MZ) AND DIZYGOTIC (DZ) TWINS REARED TOGETHER.

Investigator	MZ	DZ
Carter (1935)	.63	.32
Eysenck & Prell (1951)	.85	.22
Shields & Slater (1961)	.53	.25
Shields (1962)	.38	.11

tained when children were 3 to 4 years of age, and scores on the Personality Inventory for Children (see Chapter 2) were obtained 1 to 1½ years later. As the PIC provides scores reflective of various types of psychopathology, it was possible to assess not only whether difficult children showed higher scores on this measure, but the specific characteristics that differentiated between the groups as well.

Significant differences between difficult and easy children (and in some cases between difficult and mixed temperament children) were found on a number of PIC scales. Most relevant was the finding that difficult children displayed significantly higher levels of anxiety, depression, withdrawal, somatic concern, and poorer social skills. Although these difficult children were selected from the normal population and did not, at this age, show evidence of serious psychopathology, the fact that difficult temperament was found to be related to a range of internalizing problems suggests that difficult temperament characteristics may play a role in the development of neurotic disorders. Obviously, further research in this area is needed.

Although findings regarding the heritability of neuroticism and the possible link between temperament and neurotic disorder suggest that constitutional factors *may* play a role in the development of psychopathology, they are not inconsistent with an emphasis on environmental and social factors, for such variables may have a powerful effect on the phenotypic (behavioral) expression of any inherited predispositions. Based on their review of several longitudinal studies, Hetherington and Martin (1979) have suggested that if hereditary and temperamental predispositions do in fact exist, "they are modified by the child's life experiences, particularly those associated with early social interaction" (p. 255).

The Role of Family Variables

Over the years psychologists have displayed a more than casual interest in the role of the family in the development of psychopathol-ogy. Although much of the work in this area has been designed to investigate the relationship between family variables and schizophrenia, the role played by these variables in producing neurotic behaviors has also been of interest to clinicians and researchers alike. A review of studies in this area is beyond the scope of this chapter, but several published reviews of this literature are available (Frank, 1965; Hetherington & Martin, 1979; Jacob, 1975). By way of summary, Frank (1965) reviewed 40 years of research concerning family variables and psychopathology of various types, including neurotic disorders, and concluded:

> It seems apparent that the major conclusions that can be drawn from these data is that there is no such thing as a schizophrenogenic or a neurotogenic mother or family. At least these data do not permit the description of a particular constellation of psychological events within the home and, in particular, between mother and child that can be isolated as a unique factor in the development of one or the other kind of personality disorder. . . . Moreover, in many respects, it would be hard, on blind analysis, to distinguish the family which produced an emotionally disturbed child from that which produced the so-called normal or well adjusted child. (pp. 198–198)

Although these conclusions do not support the notion of a relationship between family variables and psychopathology, it might be noted that the early studies of family variables upon which these conclusions were based were often subject to methodological difficulties. Many focused specifically on mother-child variables without examining the role of other family members. Many involved retrospective reporting by parents of parent-child interactions as well as subjective assessment of child-rearing attitudes. Frank (1965) also pointed out that in many cases the procedures of employing and categorizing children into diagnostic groups may have left much to be desired, a factor that in and of itself might be expected to result in inconclusive findings across studies.

More recent studies of family variables have focused on direct observation of family interactions within the home and laboratory. This family interaction research has also progressed from research focusing on the simple recording of frequencies of various responses to the study of contingencies and the sequencing of behaviors within the interaction (Hetherington & Martin, 1979), tending to provide more useful information. Yet today, some 20 years after the Frank review, a causal relationship between family variables and various types of neurotic behavior has still not been demonstrated, although some relationships have been observed (as will be seen in later sections of this chapter).

It is true, of course, that it is especially difficult to demonstrate such a *causal* relationship. Even if relationships between family variables such as conflict, dominance, and rejection are found to be related to neurotic disorders, it is difficult to argue that such variables played a causal role; conflict within the family and so forth may also reflect the reaction of the family to the presence of a deviant child. Although intuitively it seems plausible, and even likely, that family variables play a significant role in the development of behaviors commonly referred to as neurotic, the problems inherent in this type of research have meant that this relationship is still to be convincingly demonstrated.

As a final comment, it seems important to note that studies seeking to find a direct link between family variables and child psychopathology may be seriously limited. It may be recalled (from Chapter 3) that workers in the area of child temperament (Thomas & Chess, 1977) have consistently argued that the "goodness-of-fit" between child temperament characteristics and parental behavior (or other aspects of the child's environment) is more predictive of later psychopathology than either temperament or family variables considered alone. Although research designed to test the goodness-of-fit notion is still in the early stages (Plomin, 1983), preliminary studies appear to provide support for studying the combined-interactive effects of child and family variables. In the future such an approach may prove to be the most useful way to investigate the role of constitutional and family variables as they relate to the development of neurotic disorders of childhood.

ANXIETY DISORDERS

DSM-III lists several disorders under the headings of anxiety disorders. Those most relevant to children and adolescents include overanxious disorder, avoidant disorder, separation anxiety disorder, phobic disorder, and obsessive-compulsive disorder. Prior to considering the nature of these conditions it should be pointed out that there are marked differences regarding what is known about them. This is due to the rarity of some conditions such as childhood obsessive-compulsive disorders. It also relates to the fact that some of these disorders are new to DSM-III and in some sense did not "exist" prior to the publication of this system. Thus, relatively little is known regarding children meeting the criteria for separation anxiety disorder and avoidant disorder (the same could be said for overanxious disorder, even though this category was included in DSM-II). These conditions can be contrasted with childhood phobias about which more has been written.

Overanxious Disorder

As indicated in Table 6.3 the clinical picture in overanxious disorder is one of generalized anxiety, excessive worrying, and fearfulness that is not related to any specific object or situation. In some instances the level of anxiety can be incapacitating.

Children with this disorder worry excessively about a wide range of things including possible injury, their ability to live up to expectations, being accepted by others, or they may be overly preoccupied and fearful of minor things such as routine visits to the doctor. They tend to be perfectionistic, often spending a great deal of time worrying about perceived inadequacies in their performance. Their heightened anxiety level may result in

TABLE 6.3. DSM-III CRITERIA FOR OVERANXIOUS DISORDER.

A. The predominant disturbance is generalized and persistent anxiety or worry (not related to concerns about separation), as manifested by at least four of the following:

1) unrealistic worry about future events.

2) preoccupation with the appropriateness of the individual's behavior in the past.

3) overconcern about competence in a variety of areas, e.g., academic, athletic, social.

4) excessive need for reassurance about a variety of worries.

5) somatic complaints, such as headaches or stomachaches, for which no physical basis can be established.

6) marked self-consciousness or susceptibility to embarrassment or humiliation.

7) marked feelings of tension or inability to relax.

B. The symptoms in A have persisted for at least six months.

C. If 18 or older, does not meet the criteria for Generalized Anxiety Disorder.

D. The disturbance is not due to another mental disorder, such as Separation Anxiety Disorder, Avoidant Disorder of Childhood or Adolescence, Phobic Disorder, Obsessive-Compulsive Disorder, Depressive Disorder, Schizophrenia, or a Pervasive Developmental Disorder.

Source: American Psychiatric Association (1980). © 1980, American Psychiatric Association and reprinted with permission.

FIGURE 6.1. Overanxious Disorder

> Jeremy, a third grader, is described by Miss Jones, his teacher, as an "up-tight perfectionist" who is concerned about doing *everything* just right. She notes that he can't deal with criticism and constantly seeks reassurance that he is doing things right. She indicated that on several occasions Jeremy has been referred to the school nurse because of his feeling dizzy, nauseous, and short of breath. No physical basis for these complaints has been found, even though he has also been evaluated by his pediatrician because of these symptoms. The nurse has suggested that when Jeremy is referred to her she can be sure that he is worried about something.
>
> Jeremy's mother states that this concern over the "correctness" of his behavior is also a problem at home, where he spends most of the time worrying about whether his homework is done correctly, whether other children will laugh at the clothes he wears, whether he may have said something to cause someone not to like him, or if he will get an invitation to someone's birthday party. The mother describes this behavior as being quite different from that of Jeremy's two younger brothers, who are "much more relaxed and don't worry even when they should."

physical symptoms such as headaches, dizziness, shortness of breath, upset stomach, and difficulties in sleeping (See Figure 6.1). In terms of associated characteristics, these children may appear "hypermature" because of their preoccupation with adult-like concerns and may display a variety of "nervous habits" such as nail biting, hair pulling, and the like (American Psychiatric Association, 1980).

Presently there is little information regarding etiological factors, prevalence, or effective treatments for this disorder. However, it is thought to be relatively common and to occur more frequently in boys, among first-born children, and in children from families where there are excessive demands for superior levels of performance. The disorder may have either a sudden or more gradual onset and may be exacerbated with increased levels of stress. It is further assumed that the disorder may persist into adulthood, possibly taking the form of a generalized anxiety or phobic disorder (American Psychiatric Association, 1980).

Although no suggestions have been provided regarding approaches to treatment, it would appear that behaviorally oriented anxiety-reduction techniques, such as those described in Chapter 10, may be of value. As performance pressures within the family have also been implicated as possible contributors,

it would seem that dealing with family-related variables should also be attended to in developing any treatment plan.

Avoidant Disorder

As can be seen in Figure 6.2, this condition is primarily reflected in a heightened level of anxiety experienced when the child comes into contact with strangers.

Although most very young children are fearful of strangers, avoidant disorder typically develops after an age where these fears are considered developmentally appropriate. The anxiety expressed is also much more extreme. Children with this disorder tend to be excessively timid and shy around those they do not know and may have difficulty even speaking to them. If pushed to interact they may cry and cling to the parent in an attempt to alleviate their fear and anxiety. These problems in relating to strangers may be contrasted with the close relationships the child may have with parents and his or her ability to get along well with those individuals who are well known. This fear of strangers may severely interfere with the child's peer relationships and the ability to function in those social settings where unknown children are present. Children with this disorder also tend to be

FIGURE 6.2. Avoidant Disorder

Tammy's mother indicates that she and her husband have become increasingly concerned over their daughter's behavior. The major problem they report is that Tammy appears to be excessively shy around strangers. When asked to elaborate the mother stated that Tammy's shyness was much more than is usually seen in 10-year-old girls. Tammy is said to avoid any situations where she might come into contact with a stranger. When approached by someone she doesn't know well, she is said to cling to one of the parents, become tearful, and appear frightened for no apparent reason. This behavior has become increasingly troublesome over the past year and is said to have gotten to the point where Tammy is hesitant to go shopping, to church, or any place with her parents where she might have to confront someone whom she doesn't know. The mother states that this behavior is really quite surprising, since Tammy relates well to everyone in the family, has several close friends, and does not seem at all shy except when strangers are around.

unassertive, lacking in self-confidence, and are frequently bothered by feelings of isolation resulting from their decreased level of social interactions.

Although no information is available concerning the prevalence of this disorder, it is said to be uncommon. No information is available regarding predisposing factors, sex ratio, or the prognosis of the disorder, although cases are said to range from those that remit spontaneously to those of a chronic nature (American Psychiatric Association, 1980).

As with overanxious disorder, there is little information concerning the most appropriate approach to take in treating this condition. However, an approach that combines anxiety-reduction techniques with the development of more adequate social skills (Michelson, Sugai, Wood, & Kazdin, 1984) would be worth pursuing.

Separation Anxiety Disorder

This condition, like avoidant disorder, involves anxiety associated with one particular area of functioning. In this case the anxiety relates to separation. As suggested in Table 6.5, this disorder is characterized by excessive anxiety experienced whenever the child is separated from his/her parents or some other person to whom he or she is closely attached. The anxiety here is much greater that the normal separation anxiety seen in very young children. Here, it can approach the level of a panic reaction and can be severely incapacitating.

Children displaying separation anxiety of this magnitude are often overly demanding of parents, cling to them, and refuse to let them out of their sight. They may refuse to stay overnight with friends, go to school, or go anywhere without their parents. Indeed, as will be seen later, this refusal to go to school may in some cases result in children being diagnosed (perhaps inappropriately) as school phobic. Children with this disorder frequently have accompanying fears of accidents, of getting lost, of being kidnapped, or of illness, monsters, or of other things that they might see as possibly separating them from their parents. Physical symptoms such as nausea, vomiting, headaches, and stomachaches may result from their heightened level of anxiety (see Figure 6.3). Except for problems with separation the child may show little evidence of other difficulties. For a more detailed discussion of the clinical manifestations of this disorder see Gardner (1985).

Although there has been little research on this specific disorder, it is said to be relatively common, to occur with approximately equal frequency in boys and girls, and to show some tendency to run in families. It may occur as early as preschool age, often after some major life stressor, and seems to develop most frequently (but not always) in children from "close-knit and caring" families. The typical course of the disorder is said to be one marked by exacerbation and remission over a period of years (American Psychiatric Association, 1980).

It was noted above that separation anxiety has been implicated as a factor in school phobia. In this context there has been a fair

---

TABLE 6.4. DSM-III CRITERIA FOR AVOIDANT DISORDER OF CHILDHOOD OR ADOLESCENCE.

A. Persistent and excessive shrinking from contact with strangers.

B. Desire for affection and acceptance, and generally warm and satisfying relations with family members and other familiar figures.

C. Avoidant behavior sufficiently severe to interfere with social functioning in peer relationships.

D. Age at least 2½. If 18 or older, does not meet the criteria for Avoidant Personality Disorder.

E. Duration of the disturbance of at least six months.

Source: American Psychiatric Association (1980). © 1980, American Psychiatric Association and reprinted with permission.

TABLE 6.5. DSM-III CRITERIA FOR SEPARATION ANXIETY DISORDER.

A. Excessive anxiety concerning separation from those to whom the child is attached, as manifested by at least three of the following:

1) unrealistic worry about possible harm befalling major attachment figures or fear that they will leave and not return.

2) unrealistic worry that an untoward calamitous event will separate the child from major attachment figure (e.g., the child will be lost, kidnapped, killed, or be the victim of an accident).

3) persistent reluctance or refusal to go to school in order to stay with major attachment figures or at home.

4) persistent reluctance or refusal to go to sleep without being next to a major attachment figure or to go to sleep away from home.

5) persistent avoidance of being alone in the home and emotionally upset if unable to follow the major attachment figure around the home.

6) repeated nightmares involving theme of separation.

7) complaints of physical symptoms on school days, e.g., stomachaches, headaches, nausea, vomiting.

8) signs of excessive distress upon separation, or when anticipating separation, from major attachment figures, e.g., temper tantrums or crying, pleading with parents not to leave (for children below the age of six, the distress must be of panic proportions).

9) social withdrawal, apathy, sadness, or difficulty concentrating on work or play when not with a major attachment figure.

B. Duration of disturbance of at least two weeks.

C. Not due to a Pervasive Developmental Disorder, Schizophrenia, or any other psychotic disorder.

D. If 18 or older, does not meet the criteria for Agoraphobia.

Source: American Psychiatric Association (1980). © 1980, American Psychiatric Association and reprinted with permission.

amount written regarding the role of separation fears in school refusal and some research on ways to reduce anxiety over separation. More dynamically oriented approaches to treatment have focused on determining the causes of the separation anxiety (which are often assumed to be the result of an overly protective mother communicating her own fears of separation to the child) and attempting to resolve these through individual or family therapies. Behavioral approaches involving in vivo desensitization have also been suggested as useful. Montenegro (1968), for example, has described the successful treatment of two cases of separation anxiety by gradually increasing the amount of time the children spent away from their mothers, while using eating to create a physiological state incompatible with anxiety. It should be noted, however, that although this desensitization approach appeared successful, such uncontrolled case reports provide little definitive information regarding effective treatments. Clearly more research on the treatment of this condition is needed. Separation anxiety and its relationship to school phobia will be considered further in the next section.

Childhood Phobias

Of all the problems of childhood, fears are among the most common. Fear of the dark, fear of strangers, and fears of animals are all found frequently in young children. Sometimes these fears are quite transient, often disappearing as the child gets older; in other cases fears are greatly exaggerated and do not go away, creating serious problems for the child and his or her parents.

In any consideration of childhood phobias one of the first problems to be addressed is that of distinguishing between fears and pho-

FIGURE 6.3. Separation Anxiety Disorder

Carrie, a 9-year-old female, was referred to the local mental health center by her school counselor because of her problems with school attendance. The counselor indicated that he perceived the girl's problem to be a fear of school and felt that she might be "school phobic." He reported that the problem seemed to begin about 2 months ago when Carrie seemed to become excessively anxious while at school for no apparent reason. She initially reported feeling sick to her stomach and later became quite concerned over being unable to get her breath. She stated that she was too nervous to stay at school and that she wanted her mother to come get her and take her home. Upon being called, Carrie's mother seemed extremely concerned and came to get her. The counselor indicated that a similar incident occurred the next day with Carrie ending up going home again. She had not returned to school since. The counselor reported having spoken to Carrie's mother over the phone, who stated that the family doctor was unable to find anything wrong with her daughter but that Carrie still resisted the idea of going to school.

At the time of the intake evaluation the mother indicated that she felt Carrie was just too nervous to go to school. She stated that she has encouraged her daughter to go to school on numerous occasions but that she seemed afraid to go and appeared to feel bad, so she had not forced her. In inquiring about Carrie's activities while not in school, the mother reported that she watched some TV and that the two of them found a lot of things to do together, such as visiting relatives or going shopping. When asked if Carrie went places by herself, the mother stated that Carrie didn't like to do that and that the two of them typically did most everything together. The mother went on to note that Carrie really seemed to want to have her (the mother) around all the time and tended to become upset whenever the two of them were separated.

When asked about factors that might contribute to Carrie's problems, the mother questioned whether the failure to go to school might be related to the death of Carrie's father (from cancer) 10 months ago. The mother noted that Carrie had been very close to her father and had taken his death very hard. Since that time she had seemed to become increasingly fearful of hospitals and ambulances and had become increasingly concerned over her mother's health. The mother stated that for the past 3 months she had been experiencing a very rapid heart beat and chest pains. A physical exam had suggested no physical problems, although the mother indicated that "doctors don't always find things that are wrong with you," noting that her husband had gone for a physical because of some symptoms and was told he was in good health only 3 months before the cancer that was causing the symptoms was found. The mother suggested that after thinking about it, she wondered if Carrie's hesitancy to go to school might be related to a fear that something might happen to her (the mother) while she (Carrie) was gone. This notion was partially confirmed by Carrie's statements that she was worried that her mother might die like her dad did and "then I wouldn't have anybody."

bias and arriving at a meaningful definition of phobic reactions. This distinction is not always an easy one, and previous attempts at definition have often been hampered by the fact that many writers have tended to define phobic reactions in terms of their own theoretical points of view.

Description and Diagnosis: Fears versus Phobias

Typically, fear has been considered a normal response to some objective source of danger. Fear may be expressed by physiological reactions, by verbal statements of fearfulness, and by avoidance of the feared situation (Lang, 1968; Morris & Kratochwill, 1983), and the response displayed is appropriate to the danger inherent in the feared situation. Phobias, on the other hand, are most often thought of as exaggerated fears; phobic individuals display fear of objects or situations that are not objectively a source of danger, or their fear of situations that normally arouse some fear is greatly out of proportion to the objective danger. Kessler (1966) characterized the differences between fears and phobias, using fear of dogs as an example, as follows:

> A school age child may express a dislike for dogs and be frankly uneasy if one is nearby; this is a reported fear. If the child is preoccupied with the possibility of encountering a dog and is in a constant state of anticipatory anxiety, he may not want to walk to school, visit friends, or leave home at all, to avoid seeing or hearing a dog. This is a phobia. (p. 235)

Thus, Kessler suggests, a major defining feature of phobias, as contrasted with normal fears, is that children with phobias are greatly preoccupied with the feared stimulus or situation.

In an overview of the various definitions of phobia that have been proposed, Berecz (1968) has indicated that most have focused on two descriptive characteristics: that the fear displayed is greatly out of proportion to the external stimulus, and that the person perceives the fear as being illogical. For pur-

poses of the present discussion, however, the definition originally proposed by Marks (1969) and elaborated upon by Miller et al. (1974) is the most adequate (and is consistent with DSM-III criteria for a simple phobia). According to this definition, a phobia may be considered a specific fear that

1. is out of proportion to demands of the situation
2. cannot be explained or reasoned away
3. is beyond voluntary control
4. leads to avoidance of the feared situation
5. persists over an extended period of time
6. is unadaptive
7. is not age or stage specific (p. 90)

This definition suggests the exaggerated nature of the fear, the inability of the individual to control the degree of fear displayed, the maladaptive nature of the fear, and the specific behavioral manifestations of the phobia (that is, avoidance of the feared object or situation). An example of such an exaggerated fear is presented in Figure 6.4.

Prevalence

Although there have been several studies that have provided data on the frequency of childhood fears (see Chapter 3), information on the prevalence of actual phobias is scarce. Considering figures derived from various sources, however, Kennedy (1983) has suggested that phobias occur in .5 to 1% of the general child population. Morris and Kratochwill (1983) have noted that prevalence rates among clinical referrals are usually found to be less than 8%.

Etiology: Psychoanalytic Perspectives

In 1909 Sigmund Freud published a case history in which he described the treatment of a 5-year-old boy, Little Hans, who displayed a phobia of horses. In this paper Freud presented the psychoanalytic position regarding the etiology and treatment of childhood phobic reactions, emphasizing a number of factors thought to be of etiological significance.

FIGURE 6.4. Jenny: A Case of Balloon Phobia

Jenny, a 6-year-old girl, was brought to the clinic by her mother, who had become increasingly concerned over Jenny's fearfulness. The major problem was that Jenny had recently become increasingly afraid of balloons and that this had begun to cause her serious difficulties in a number of situations. In discussing the problem with the mother it was determined that Jenny had a long history of being afraid of inflatable toys. The mother recalled that as early as age 2, Jenny frequently became upset when confronted with any toy that could be blown-up. In trying to determine whether Jenny had experienced some specific negative experience with inflatables that might account for the fear, the mother was unable to relate any such incident. She stated that these fears (which the parents dealt with by not having such toys in the house) had just gradually become more restricted to a fear of balloons, although the intensity of the fear seemed to have increased.

In describing Jenny's fear of balloons the mother appeared almost apologetic, indicating that in many ways a fear of such objects might seem quite insignificant. She noted, however, that there had been a number of instances where this fear had created significant difficulties for her daughter. In one instance Jenny, along with other children in her class, was asked to make papier mache animals by covering inflated balloons. Jenny became quite frightened, left the room, and refused to come back until the other children were through. On another occasion, Jenny and her mother attended a wedding where well-meaning friends of the groom filled the couple's car with balloons during the service. Upon walking the bride and groom to the car, Jenny became so upset she had to leave the area. The mother indicated that recently she and Jenny had to leave a parade Jenny was enjoying because she became so afraid of the balloons that were present and that there was one toy store in the local mall that Jenny refused to enter (or even walk past) because there was a balloon display at the entrance.

In speaking with Jenny, she indicated that she was "just afraid of them" (balloons). She was unable to identify exactly what about balloons she was afraid of, except that she became more afraid if they were full enough to pop. In assessing Jenny's reaction to actual balloons, presented in the clinic, she showed no signs of anxiety when presented with balloons that were not inflated, and only a small degree of anxiety when asked to blow up a balloon halfway. When presented with a fully inflated balloon blown up by the interviewer, however, she became increasingly upset, started to cry, asked for her mother, and indicated that she wanted to leave the room.

First of all, Freud suggested that the development of this phobia was intimately related to the child's attempts to deal with Oedipal strivings. It was assumed that Hans displayed strong feelings of sexual attraction toward his mother and that he also displayed feelings of jealousy and hostility toward his father, whom he viewed as possessing the mother and perceived as a rival for his mother's affections. Freud described the child as threatened by these hostile feelings (including death wishes) directed toward his father. Second, it was suggested that Hans feared castration by his father in retaliation for these unacceptable wishes. Faced with the anxiety arising from this conflict, the child was thought to have dealt with the conflict through various defensive maneuvers, including repression and projection. Freud suggested that the Oedipal conflict was repressed and the fear projected onto a specific object in the environment, horses in the case of Little Hans. From the analytic point of view, the phobic object chosen is thought to be symbolically reflective of the unconscious conflict that underlies the phobia (biting horse = castrating father). Employing such mechanisms is thought to be quite functional, in that they eliminate from awareness anxiety-arousing conflicts and attach the anxiety to some object in the environment that can subsequently be avoided.

Although this view of etiology is consistent with the basic tenets of psychoanalytic theory and reflects the ideas of a man who has had a profound impact on psychology and psychiatry, it must be regarded as somewhat speculative. To date little or no evidence, other than that obtained through case studies, has been provided to support his position.

Etiology: Behavioral Perspectives

Classical Conditioning. In an early study, already alluded to in Chapter 1, Watson and Raynor (1920) illustrated the possible importance of classical conditioning in the development of phobic behaviors. The two investigators observed the behavior of Little Albert, an 11-month-old child, in response to a live white rat. The rat initially failed to elicit any evidence of fear (rat = neutral stimulus). It was then demonstrated that by pairing subsequent approach behaviors toward the rat with a loud noise (unconditioned stimulus) the rat, which previously elicited no fear, came to evoke fear responses on the part of the child (rat = conditioned stimulus). Although a close reading of the original paper causes one to question whether the study really demonstrated classical or operant conditioning (the loud noise was presented contingent on orienting toward or approaching the rat), this experiment has been presented as an analogue of the development of phobias through classical conditioning.

Even though this classic study has been taken to suggest that fear *may* be learned through classical conditioning and that classical conditioning may provide a plausible explanation for some phobic responses, it cannot be concluded that all phobias are learned in this manner. Some investigators have failed in attempts to develop fear responses in a manner similar to that employed by Watson and Raynor, and others have not been able to find evidence that feared stimuli have been previously paired with aversive stimuli in the majority of phobic individuals (Johnson, 1985; Johnson & Melamed, 1979). Although the classical conditioning paradigm may provide a framework for understanding the development of some childhood phobias, at present there is insufficient evidence to assume that all, or even most, fears are learned in this way. It is likely that other factors are involved as well.

Observational Learning. Bandura (1971) has suggested that most behaviors learned through direct experience can also be learned vicariously, through the observation of others. From this perspective it would seem likely that phobic responses are learned in this way, as well as through classical conditioning. It seems reasonable that a child who observes parents or other family members displaying excessive fear and avoidance in response to certain stimuli or situations may likewise come to fear these same stimuli through vicarious learning. That vicarious learning of fear responses occurs is suggested by the results of an earlier study by Bandura and Rosenthal (1966). Observers viewed a model participating in a conditioning experiment where electric shock (apparently resulting in pain and arm withdrawal) was paired with a buzzer. Physiological recordings made on observers who had witnessed the model showed increased reactivity (suggestive of fear) to the buzzer, even though the observers had not been shocked themselves.

Although they do not provide direct evidence of the acquisition of phobias through observational learning, a number of studies have demonstrated that fearful children often have fearful parents and that parent and child often fear similar stimuli or situations (Johnson & Melamed, 1979). Although correlational data provided by these studies cannot be considered evidence of a causal relationship between fears of other family members and child phobias, the findings are consistent with the notion that fears may be learned in this manner.

Operant Conditioning. Several authors have suggested that it is likely that phobic avoidance responses may also be acquired and/or maintained through the process of operant conditioning (Johnson & Melamed, 1979; Miller et al., 1974). For example, a child who is initially apprehensive about going to school may state that he or she is afraid, ill, or cry and beg to stay home, and so forth. If these behaviors are frequently reinforced through parental attention and perhaps by permission to remain at home, and if the child is further reinforced in these behaviors by being allowed to engage in reinforcing activities while at home (e.g., play, watch TV), it is likely that the avoidance responses will continue. If allowed to remain at home over a period of time, it is also likely that the child may fall behind classmates and miss out on a variety of school-related experiences, putting the child in an even poorer position to cope with the school situation. The probable result is increased anxiety when confronted with the prospect of attending school and an even greater likelihood of avoidance responses.

It may also be the case that in some situations operant factors may be involved, along with classical conditioning or observational learning, in maintaining phobic behaviors. For instance, Mowrer (1956) hypothesized that avoidance responses might be maintained because of the anxiety-reducing nature of these behaviors; whereas the phobic behavior may have been acquired through classical conditioning (or modeling, perhaps), it may be maintained as a result of negative reinforcement. Other reinforcers in the natural environment often may also be involved in maintaining phobic behaviors originally acquired through classical conditioning or observational learning, implying that in the treatment of phobias one may need to deal not only with the phobic anxiety, but also with those contingencies in the child's environment that maintain avoidance responses after the anxiety has been eliminated.

Research

Classification of Child Phobias. One obstacle to the study of childhood phobias has been the absence of any meaningful classification system. In the past, phobias were often classified according to the feared object, largely by taking the Greek names for the phobic stimulus and attaching to it the word *phobia*, from the Greek *phobos*, meaning panic or terror. This practice has generated a large number of phobic labels, ranging from claustrophobia (fear of enclosed places) to phobophobia (fear of phobias). For a listing of some of these see Table 6.6. Obviously a potentially limitless classification based on the stimulus object is likely to be of little utility.

Miller et al. (1974) have sought to solve this problem with a new, albeit tentative, classification system based on the results of a factor analysis of responses to the Louisville Fear Survey Schedule (Miller, Barrett, Hampe, & Noble, 1972). Their analysis of parents' ratings of child fears yielded a total of three relatively independent factors: physical in-

TABLE 6.6. SELECTED PHOBIAS THAT
CHILDREN EXPERIENCE.

Technical Name	Phobia
Acrophobia	height
Agoraphobia	open spaces
Aichmophobia	sharp and pointed objects
Ailurophobia	cats
Arachnophobia	spiders
Anthrophobia	flowers
Anthropophobia	people
Aquaphobia	water
Astraphobia	lightning
Brontophobia	thunder
Claustrophobia	closed spaces
Cynophobia	dogs
Equinophobia	horses
Menophobia	being alone
Mikrophobia	germs
Murophobia	mice
Numerophobia	numbers
Nyctophobia	darkness
Ophidiophobia	snakes
Pyrophobia	fire
Thanatophobia	death
Trichophobia	hair
Xenophobia	strangers
Zoophobia	animals

Source: Morris & Krachowill (1983). © 1983 Pergamon Press
and reprinted with permission.

jury, natural events, and social anxiety. The authors proposed that the results of this analysis serve as a basis for the classification of childhood fears. Their classification scheme, with the 81 items of the Louisville Fear Survey Schedule listed under the appropriate headings, is presented in Table 6.7.

This scheme involves the three major categories derived from the factor analytic study plus a miscellaneous category. Each of the three major categories is subdivided; thus, physical injury items are subdivided into abstract and concrete situations, and natural events are divided into storms, the dark, enclosed places, animals, and other. In most cases subcategories are composed of several stimulus items. Miller and his coworkers (1974) explained that the specific subcategories were employed for various reasons. For instance, in the case of the physical injury

category, the distinction between abstract and concrete physical injury events may have implications for the type of treatment possible: Fears of stimuli listed under the concrete physical injury category might be dealt with using in vivo treatment procedures, but fears of stimuli in the abstract subcategory may need to be dealt with conceptually. Other subcategories were employed because of research findings suggesting differences between groups (for example, young and old school phobics), and still others were chosen largely on the basis of similarity of item content.

Miller et al. (1974) noted that a variety of stimuli loaded high on each of the factors derived from the factor analyses upon which the system was based. They indicate that this tendency "suggests an underlying dimensionality, which, in turn suggests that phobic objects do not occur randomly, but many are interrelated." Additionally, they suggest that,

for a given patient, treatment of one phobia within a dimension should reduce the aversiveness connected with other stimuli within that dimension. In addition, if factor analysis yields anything more than just phenotypes, the same treatment should be applicable to all phobias within a given dimension. (p. 93)

Although this classification scheme is presented as tentative, and although certain relevant hypotheses suggested by the authors await experimental verification (Morris & Kratochwill, 1983), it seems to be a reasonable potential remedy for the current absence of a readily available classification system.

Child Phobias and Other Deviant Behaviors

There are few well-designed studies relating childhood phobias to other characteristics. After perusing the literature related to personality characteristics of phobic children, Miller et al. (1974) concluded that there was no evidence for associating any particular personality characteristics with child phobias. More recent reviews of the literature (Morris & Kratochwill, 1983) suggest that significant

TABLE 6.7. CLASSIFICATION SCHEME FOR CHILDHOOD PHOBIAS.

I. Physical Injury	II. Natural Events	III. Social Anxiety	IV. Miscellaneous
A. *Abstract*	A. *Storms*	A. *School*	1. Dirt
1. War	1. Tornadoes, floods, earth-	1. Young (3–10)	2. Furry toys
2. Riots	quakes	(a) Type I	3. Sirens
3. Poisoned food	2. Lightning	(b) Type II	4. People who are old
4. Specific foods	3. Thunder	2. Old Age (11–22)	5. Crossing a street
5. Dying	B. *Dark*	(a) Type I	6. People who are ugly
6. Someone in family dying	C. *Enclosed places*	(b) Type II	7. Loud sounds, such as caps,
7. Seeing someone wounded	1. Bathrooms	B. *Separation*	firecrackers, explosions
8. Being wounded	2. Closets	1. Separation from parents	8. People in uniforms, police-
9. Someone in family get-	3. Elevators	2. Parts of house	men, mailmen, etc.
ting ill	4. Confined or locked up	3. Going to sleep at night	9. People of the opposite sex
10. Becoming ill	5. Strange rooms	C. *Performance*	10. Having bowel movements
11. Germs	D. *Animals*	1. Tests or examinations	11. Members of another race
12. Choking	1. Snakes	2. Being criticized	
13. Having an operation	2. Insects, spiders	3. Making mistakes	
14. Hospitals	3. Rats or mice	4. Reciting in class	
15. Hell	4. Frogs or lizards	D. *Social interactions*	
16. The Devil	5. Dogs or cats	1. Attending social events	
17. Breaking a religious law	6. Horses or cows	2. Making another person	
18. Being kidnapped	E. *Other*	angry	
19. Getting lost	1. Fire	3. Crowds	
20. Being adopted	2. Frightening thoughts or	4. Being touched by others	
21. Parents getting a divorce	daydreams	E. *Medical procedures*	
22. Going crazy	3. Ghosts	1. Doctors or dentists	
B. *Concrete*	4. Being alone	2. Getting a shot	
1. Flying in airplane	5. Nightmares	F. *Other*	
2. High places	6. Space creatures or mon-	1. Riding in a car or bus	
3. Deep water	sters		
4. Strangers	7. Faces at window		
5. Being seen naked	8. Masks or puppets		
	9. Sight of blood		
	10. People with deformities		
	11. Toilets		

Source: From Miller et al., (1974), © 1974 John Wiley and Sons. Reprinted by permission.

findings have also not appeared since that time. One study by Miller and his colleagues does, however, shed some light on the possible relationships between phobias and other forms of deviant behavior. Miller, Barrett, Hampe, and Noble (1972) compared 67 child phobic referrals with a matched sample of children drawn from the general population with regard to ratings on the Louisville Behavior Checklist, the School Behavior Checklist, and the Louisville Fear Survey Schedule. The results showed significant group differences on a number of variables tapped by the Louisville Behavior Checklist. Phobic children were found to differ significantly, in the undesirable direction, from normals on all measures (infantile aggression, hyperactivity, antisocial behavior, social withdrawal, sensitivity, fear, academic disability, immaturity, normal irritability, rare deviance, prosocial behavior). On the School Behavior Checklist, phobic children showed lower need achievement, more anxiety, greater academic disability, and were found to be less extraverted. And, as might be expected, several significant differences were found between these groups on the Fear Survey Schedule. Although not definitive, these results suggest that phobic children do not simply display this problem in isolation, but are likely to evidence a wide variety of other difficulties as well. These results, however, are in need of replication, as they seem to stand alone in the literature and are in contrast to findings suggesting few relationships between *fears* and deviant child behaviors (Lapouse & Monk, 1959).

School Phobia

School phobia is often considered separately from other phobias of childhood. Special attention has been given to this problem in the literature. Miller et al. (1974) report that the ratio of school phobia publications to published papers related to other types of child phobias is approximately 25 : 1, and separate theories of etiology have been proposed to account for this disorder.

As the name implies, school phobia is characterized by school avoidance. It is accompanied by anxiety and often by a variety of physical symptoms (abdominal complaints, nausea, vomiting). This disorder is to be distinguished from truancy, in which the child avoids school to participate in other activities away from home and school. Concerning this distinction, Kessler (1972) wrote that in the case of school phobia, "the child refuses to go to school and remains at home with the parents' knowledge, if not with their consent. Truant children, on the other hand, show no inclination to remain at home, and their whereabouts are unknown to their parents" (p. 409). School phobia may be considered a neurotic disorder, whereas truancy appears to be more closely associated with conduct disorders.

Prevalence and Demography. Although the true frequency of school phobia is not known, Weiner (1982) has suggested that a number of studies taken together indicate that 1 to 2% of children in the general school-age population and 5 to 8% of clinic referrals display this problem. He also notes that this disorder occurs with about equal frequency in males and females and may occur at any age, although peak referral rates are usually around the ages of 5 to 8 (early elementary school) and 11 to 14 (entry into junior or senior high school). Kessler (1972) has noted that school phobia seems to be most characteristic of the higher socioeconomic classes, although more data are needed on this point. Studies reviewed by Miller et al. (1974) generally support the notion that school phobias can occur at all IQ levels and are not restricted to those who are having academic problems.

Theoretical Views. Theoretical discussions of school phobia have centered around psychoanalytic and behavioral views. In addition to differences of opinion regarding etiology, there has also been much debate as to whether school phobia represents a fear of school, as the label suggests, or is more closely related to fear of separation.

Kelly (1973) characterized the psychoanalytic view this way:

> In general, psychoanalytic explanations stress the overdependency fostered by a mother who herself is often mildly neurotic and whose own dependency needs frequently are unresolved. The dependency creates repressed hostility in both the child and mother, and in the child especially a fear of separation. The dependency, fear, and hostility inhibit the ego development of the child, and the fear is displaced onto the school as the child anxiously clings to the mother in unresolved dependency. (p. 35)

Other analytically oriented theorists have argued that the fear is not of school at all and have conceptualized school phobia largely in terms of separation anxiety (Eisenberg, 1958; Johnson, 1957). They assume that school phobia does not involve fear of school so much as fear of separation from the parents, usually the mother, who may also display anxiety over separation and communicate this to the child. From this point of view the term *school phobia* would appear to be a misnomer (Kelly, 1973). The belief that this phobia is often reflective of separation anxiety is not restricted to individuals of a psychodynamic persuasion, but is shared by many behaviorally oriented clinicians as well.

Outlining one behavioral view of school phobia, Kelly (1973) has cited the position of Garvey and Hegreves (1968) as representative. From this point of view

> The child fears loss of his mother as a result of comments about leaving by the mother. . . . This fear becomes verbally conditioned to ideas about going to school, where he would "lose" his mother. As the fear of school becomes intense, he finally refuses to go. Staying at home has reinforcing properties in that it reduces fear and usually offers other rewards such as toys and affection. (p. 36)

It should be noted, however, that other behaviorists might emphasize different factors in the development of school phobia, such as conditioned anxiety in response to specific school-related stimuli.

Although many psychologists adhere to the notion that separation anxiety can play an important role in the development of what has been called school phobia, anxiety associated with school attendance and avoidance almost certainly occurs for a variety of reasons. It would be a mistake to label all school phobias as separation anxiety, Kessler (1972) has noted, because school phobias may also result from anxieties related to various aspects of the school situation, including fear of failure, fear of teachers, fear of classmates, and evaluation anxiety. On this issue Smith (1970) suggested that whereas separation anxiety might be characteristic of younger school phobics, older children's fears are more often specific to the school situation. It is obviously unwise to assume that all school phobias arise from the same causal factors and that the same form of treatment would be applicable to all children displaying this problem. The focus of treatment might be quite different depending on whether the child's fear is of separation from the parent or some aspect of the school situation itself. Careful assessment is a prerequisite for appropriate treatment.

Classification of School Phobias. Some attempts have been made to classify school phobias. For example, Kennedy (1965), in a widely cited paper, has provided criteria for distinguishing between two groups that he referred to as Type I (neurotic) and Type II (characterological) school phobics. These categories are roughly equivalent to the Acute (Type I) and Chronic (Type II) types described by other writers (see Weiner, 1982). Specific diagnostic criteria are presented in Table 6.8. According to Kennedy, classification as Type I or Type II school phobia is warranted if the child and his family display any seven of the ten characteristics listed.

Kennedy describes Type II school phobia as relatively rare, reporting that over an 8-year period only 6 cases had been seen at the

TABLE 6.8. DIFFERENTIAL SCHOOL PHOBIA SYMPTOMS.

TYPE I	TYPE II
1. The present illness is the first episode.	1. Second, third, or fourth episode
2. Monday onset, following an illness the previous Thursday or Friday	2. Monday onset following minor illness not a prevalent antecedent
3. An acute onset	3. Incipient onset
4. Lower grades most prevalent	4. Upper grades most prevalent
5. Expressed concern about death	5. Death theme not present
6. Mother's physical health in question (actually ill or child thinks so)	6. Health of mother not an issue
7. Good communication between parents	7. Poor communication between parents
8. Mother and father well adjusted in most areas	8. Mother shows neurotic behavior; father, a character disorder
9. Father competitive with mother in household management	9. Father shows little interest in household or children
10. Parents achieve understanding of dynamics easily	10. Parents very difficult to work with

Source: From Kennedy (1965). © 1965, American Psychological Association and reprinted by permission.

Florida State University Human Development Clinic, compared to over 50 cases of Type I school phobia. Kennedy noted that all of the six cases of Type II school phobia had families in which at least one parent was seriously disturbed. Two of the six children were considered schizophrenic, and two were diagnosed as having character disorders. School phobia was only one of these children's difficulties. In general they displayed serious problems suggestive of a relatively poor prognosis, in contrast to those diagnosed as Type I school phobics, who seemed to respond well to treatment. Indeed Kennedy (1965) described a treatment program involving the ignoring of somatic complaints (often displayed by children who are afraid to go to school), an early forced return to school, and reinforcement for school attendance that was reported to be effective in bringing about complete remission in 100% of 50 Type I cases seen for treatment.

Although this classification system appears to have interesting implications for understanding school phobia and for predicting treatment success, additional research regarding the correlates of these groups is needed, as little empirical research employing this system has been conducted.

Treatment of Childhood Phobias

Clinicians have utilized both analytic and behavioral approaches in the treatment of childhood phobias. Although little systematic research has been conducted to evaluate the effectiveness of analytic treatments, there are numerous case studies illustrating this approach (Freud, 1909; Bornstein, 1949; White, Hornsby, Boylston, & Gordon, 1972).

An early example of the behavioral approach was provided by Jones (1924), who described the elimination of a fear of rabbits in a young child by employing a combination of modeling and counterconditioning procedures (e.g., having the child observe other children interacting fearlessly with the rabbit and gradually bringing the rabbit closer and closer to the child while he was eating). More recent behavioral approaches to treatment have included desensitization (Croghan & Musante, 1975; Miller et al., 1972b; Montenegro, 1968; Wallick, 1979), emotive imagery (Boyd, 1980; Jackson & King, 1981), implosive therapy (Ollendick & Gruen, 1972; Smith & Sharpe, 1970), operant conditioning (Allyon, Smith, & Rogers, 1970; Neisworth, Madle, &

Goeke, 1975; Patterson, 1965), and modeling (Kirkland & Thelen, 1977). A discussion of these approaches and literature related to their effectiveness can be found in Chapter 10. Reviews by Graziano, DeGiovanny, and Garcia (1979), Johnson and Melamed (1979), Johnson (1985), and Morris and Kratochwill (1983) also provide good coverage of the research specifically related to the treatment of child phobias.

Childhood Phobias:
An Overview

Mild fears are common in childhood. They are often age or stage specific and are frequently transient in nature, disappearing with the passage of time without benefit of treatment. The expression of such fears is a normal aspect of development. Other fears are more severe: They are out of proportion to objective sources of danger, are beyond voluntary control, persist over an extended period of time, cannot be explained away, lead to avoidance behavior, and are not age or stage specific. These exaggerated fears, or phobias, can be quite disabling, creating a serious problem for both child and parent.

As with other neurotic disorders, clinicians of both a psychoanalytic and behavioral persuasion have proposed theoretical explanations to account for the development of phobias. Although the specific etiological factors related to phobia development are not completely understood, it seems likely that most childhood phobias can be explained in terms of social learning. Here classical conditioning, observational learning, and operant conditioning have all been implicated.

Much of the literature on childhood phobias relates specifically to school phobias. Although the term suggests a fear of school or school-related stimuli, many clinicians conceptualize this condition largely in terms of separation anxiety. Actually, it is likely that what has been referred to as school phobia can result from either fears related to school or separation anxiety. Careful assessment is

needed to determine the specific factors operative in any given case.

A variety of approaches have been employed in dealing with the phobic child. Systematic and in vivo desensitization, modeling, and operant conditioning approaches have all been found useful in specific cases. At least two cases also provide some evidence for the usefulness of implosive therapy, although this procedure has not been widely used. All things considered, it would appear that an approach involving modeling (of coping behavior in response to the feared stimulus), perhaps in conjunction with operant procedures (where the child is rewarded for progressively closer interactions with the phobic object) would have much to recommend it.

In conclusion, although much has been written concerning childhood phobias, we actually know very little. Many of the publications in the phobia literature are theoretical in nature, many more are simply of the case study variety, and most deal with school phobia. Much more well-designed research related to other types of childhood phobias is needed, including investigations of correlates of childhood phobias and of the relationship between phobias and variables such as social class and family characteristics. Also needed are studies of a controlled nature that compare the effectiveness of various treatment procedures in dealing with specific types of childhood phobias.

Obsessions and Compulsions

Description and Diagnosis

Obsessive-compulsive neurosis is a relatively rare condition of childhood (Milby et al., 1983), and relatively few papers have been written and little research conducted in this area. Nevertheless data from some descriptive studies are available that provide information concerning the way in which this condition is manifested in children.

The primary manifestation of obsessive-compulsive neurosis may be either obsessions, compulsions, or a combination of the two. Both obsessions and compulsions involve intrusive, repetitive, and stereotyped behaviors: Obsessions involve repetitive and unwanted thoughts or ideas, whereas compulsions involve stereotyped behaviors that the individual feels compelled to perform. The person may realize that such thoughts or behaviors are irrational and nonsensical but is nevertheless powerless to control them. Specific guidelines for a diagnosis of obsessive-compulsive disorder, as presented in DSM-III, are provided in Table 6.9. Although these diagnostic criteria are not specific to children, they would seem appropriate, because it has been suggested that the disorder takes a similar form in children and adults (Rapoport, 1985).

The way these symptoms may be displayed by children is illustrated in Figure 6.5.

Developmental Factors in Obsessive-Compulsive Behavior

Several writers have noted that normal children often display obsessive ideation and compulsive behavior at certain stages of their development. Kessler (1972) writes that these normal manifestations of compulsive behavior tend to peak around the age of 2 years, at age 7 to 8, and in early adolescence. Judd (1965), in his discussion of compulsive behavior, commented that

> It is not only seen in earlier development but the normal play of all children is replete with evidence of ritualistic and compulsive behavior. . . . Anyone who has observed a child meticulously stepping on sidewalk cracks, tapping a stick back and forth along a fence, touching street lights as they pass, etc., . . . cannot help but be impressed with the compulsive quality of this activity. (p. 138)

The presence of certain obsessive and compulsive behaviors may be considered quite normal, then, especially at certain stages of development, and would not be termed neurotic. Such childhood behaviors are considered maladaptive when they become severely disruptive and interfere with ability to function in the environment or result in a significant amount of distress on the part of the child (Kennedy, 1983).

TABLE 6.9. DSM-III CRITERIA FOR OBSESSIVE-COMPULSIVE DISORDER.

A. Either obsessions or compulsions:

Obsessions: recurrent, persistent ideas, thoughts, images, or impulses that are ego-dystonic, i.e., not experienced as voluntarily produced, but rather as thoughts that invade consciousness and are experienced as senseless or repugnant. Attempts are made to ignore and suppress them.

Compulsions: repetitive and seemingly purposeful behaviors that are performed according to certain rules or in a stereotyped fashion. The behavior is not an end in itself, but is designed to produce or prevent some future event or situation. However, either the activity is not connected in a realistic way with what it is designed to produce or prevent, or may be clearly excessive. The act is performed with a sense of subjective compulsion coupled with a desire to resist the compulsion (at least initially). The individual generally recognizes the senselessness of the behavior (this may not be true of children) and does not derive pleasure from carrying out the activity, although it provides a release from tension.

B. The obsessions or compulsions are a significant source of distress to the individual or interfere with social or role functioning.

C. Not due to another mental disorder, such as Tourette's disorder, schizophrenia, major depression, or organic mental disorder.

Source: American Psychiatric Association (1980). © 1980, American Psychiatric Association and reprinted with permission of the publisher.

FIGURE 6.5. The Case of Mina C.

This girl, whose tenth birthday occurred on the date of her second psychiatric interview, was fourth in a sibling group of five. Her father, age 49, has inherited considerable wealth and also worked as a biomedical scientist in research and teaching. Her mother, 43 years old, was depressed and had experienced long-term psychotherapy for neurotic and character problems. Mina herself had had a sudden onset, just as she was turning 8 years old, of rather exhausting (for her) and disquieting (for others) obsessions and compulsions.

Some of the things Mina reported were rather odd, but nobody considered her psychotic. She shook everything she encountered, large or small, to see if it was hollow or unstable — she hoped for solidity and stability, but even if she knew that a wall or table was unmovable she tried to shake it. She felt compelled to test her environment. She confessed minor wrongdoing endlessly, she said, and gave as examples of this her telling the maid (who toilet trained her) each time she set foot on the floor with only her socks on, or whenever she sat or lay on her father's bed. She was compelled to blow kisses to her toys to prevent their coming alive and either doing her harm or being killed by "someone." Moreover, she said, "If I don't kiss my toys goodnight I feel they'll resent my not giving them any love or attention." . . . She felt driven to lay dresses upside down across chair backs. She also had counting rituals, particularly with light switches; "I have to count two not to go over and flip the switch over my sister's bed. Sometimes I feel guilty anyway, so I count to five, then five and a half, and then one. I do it up to 25. I try hard to make it odd so I can stop sooner. If it's even I have to keep it up." Utilizing her verbal IQ of 131, she stated, "My brain says, do it or you'll have a guilty feeling."

Source: Adapted from Adams, 1973, p. 122, with permission, Brunner/Mazel Publishing Co.

Etiology: Theoretical Views

Both analytic and behavioral views of this disorder have been presented in the literature, although less precisely than in the case of phobic reactions. The psychodynamic point of view commonly assumes that the origin of obsessive-compulsive neurosis lies in the anal stage of psychosexual development, the stage during which toilet training takes place and conflict between parent and child may occur over issues of conformity and independence. It is thought that these conflicts can generate intense feelings of hostility, which may be inadequately resolved, resulting in fixation or partial fixation at this stage of development. It is further assumed that at later periods, when under stress, the individual may regress back to this earlier stage of development, leading to a revival of these unresolved conflicts and the behaviors and personality patterns characteristic of the anal stage. In this view, obsessive-compulsive symptoms represent outward attempts to deal with the threatening impulses resulting from these reactivated conflicts (Cameron, 1963). Nemiah (1967) succinctly stated the analytic position:

The psychoanalytic theory of the obsessive compulsive reaction ascribes the appearance of symptoms to a defensive regression of the psychic apparatus to the preoedipal anal-sadistic phase, with the consequent emergence of earlier modes of functioning of the ego, superego and id. These factors along with the employment of specific ego defenses (isolation, undoing, displacement) combine to produce the classical symptoms of obsessions, compulsions and compulsive acts. (p. 925)

Behavioral views of obsessive-compulsive behavior have likewise not been well delineated, but have often focused on the anxiety-reducing function of compulsive behaviors (see Emmelkamp, 1982). In support of this position, Carr (1970, 1974) conducted several studies with adults using psychophysiological measures of arousal, the results of which suggest that "compulsive behaviors occur at high levels of autonomic activity and serve to reduce these levels to those characteristic of the individual in the resting state." Observations in line with this have also been made by Rachman, DeSilva, and Roper (1976). Thus, while it is unclear exactly how compulsive behaviors develop, they may frequently be maintained as a result of the reinforcing properties of anxiety reduction. Although this position seems most relevant to overt compulsive behaviors, it may be that such a view can also be applied to obsessional thoughts as well, if it is assumed that obsessional ideation may serve to help the individual ward off other even more anxiety-arousing thoughts (Emmelkamp, 1982).

It should be noted that in addition to these perspectives, other factors have been implicated in the development of obsessive-compulsive behaviors. These include genetic factors, nonspecific neurological impairments, defects in serotonin metabolism, as well as problems in family relationships (Milby, Wendorf, & Meredith, 1983). At this point, however, none of these views are well supported by empirical research.

Prevalence

It is clear that the disorder is quite rare in both adults and children. Sturgis (1984), citing figures for adults indicating a rate of .05% in the general population, suggests that it is also second only to multiple personality in scarcity among neurotic populations. Regarding studies with children, Judd (1965) found a rate of 1.2% in his study with inpatient and outpatient children. Adams (1973) has suggested a figure of less than 2% of emotionally disturbed children. A more recent study by Hollingsworth, Tanguay, Grossman, and Pabst (1980) has found the disorder to occur at a rate of .2% in a clinic population. Although the figures suggested are not identical, they suggest a low rate of occurrence, even within a psychiatric population. Prevalence figures for the general population are less frequently found in the literature. However, one study by Rutter, Tizard, and Whitmore (1970) has suggested a figure of .003%.

Research: Correlates of Obsessive-Compulsive Disorder

In one early descriptive study, Judd (1965) examined the records of all children age 12 and below who were seen in a child psychiatric facility over a 5-year period. Those whose records indicated a diagnosis of obsessive-compulsive neurosis or the presence of compulsive symptoms were selected for further study. An attempt was made to select from among these cases patients who could legitimately receive a diagnosis of obsessive-compulsive neurosis, based on the following criteria: (a) the presence of well-defined obsessive-compulsive symptoms; (b) these symptoms had to be the most prominent evidence of psychopathology; and (c) these symptoms had to be severe enough to interfere with functioning. Additional information concerning children so diagnosed was obtained by inspection of patient records and consultation with the children's therapists.

A total of 405 children were seen over the 5-year span of the study. Of these, 34 had been diagnosed as obsessive-compulsive or showed the presence of compulsive characteristics. Only five of these children, however, met the criteria set for the diagnosis of obsessive-compulsive neurosis.

The focus of the study was to determine factors associated with this diagnosis, and Judd found a total of eight characteristics that appeared to be descriptive of all five of the children selected. Judd observed that in each case there was a sudden onset of obsessive-compulsive symptoms. All the children displayed above average intelligence. In each case obsessive and compulsive symptoms occurred together. In all five cases the symptoms the child displayed were disruptive to the environment (for example, were irritating or embarrassing to parents or others). All children appeared to show evidence of marked guilt feelings. Judd also noted that although all of these children displayed evidence of an active fantasy life, in no case was there evidence of psychosis.

Adams (1973) has provided similar data drawn from a larger sample of 49 obsessive-compulsive children age 15 and below seen at the University of Florida. Table 6.10 presents certain findings of Adam's survey and compares these figures with those obtained by Judd in the study outlined above.

It would seem that there is some agreement between the two studies. First of all, both reports support the notion that obsessive-compulsive neurosis does occur in children, although it appears to be rare. Both surveys found obsessive-compulsive children to be above average in intelligence, supporting the observations of many clinicians. Both suggest that obsessions and compulsions usually occur together, a finding that appears to support the view of some researchers (see Carr, 1974) that obsessions and compulsions are basically variants of the same disorder. Adams and Judd both indicate that most children receiving this diagnosis display a considerable amount of guilt and have an active fantasy life. Both studies suggest the presence of aggression directed toward the parents. In addition to the findings already cited, Adams also found that

TABLE 6.10. CHARACTERISTICS OF OBSESSIVE-COMPULSIVE CHILDREN IN TWO STUDIES.

Characteristic	Adams	Judd
Size of population studied	49	5
Age range	15 and under	12 and under
Mean age of onset	5.84 years	7.5 years
Range of onset age	1 to 13 years	6 years 4 months to 10 years 2 months
Gender	39 boys, 10 girls	3 boys, 2 girls
Onset	Sudden 34%	Sudden 100%
Intelligence	Normal 16%, above normal 84%	Above normal 100%
Obsessions and compulsions	Both, 78%	Both, 100%
Symptom disruptive	86% yes	100% yes
Guilt prominent	88% yes	100% yes
Moral code rigid	47% yes	100% yes
Fantasy life active	92% yes	100% yes
Psychosis possible	88% no	100% no
Bowel training punitive	41% yes, 37% no, 22% not by history	20% yes, 80% no
Precipitating event	45% yes	80% yes
Phobias present	53% yes	80% yes
Aggression to parents	98% yes	80% yes
Premorbid normality	73% yes	80% yes

Source: From Adams (1973). © 1973, Brunner/Mazel Publishing Co. and reprinted by permission.

in 71.4% of the cases there was evidence of obsessional behavior on the part of other family members. Judd found that in four of the five cases studied there was some evidence of psychopathology displayed by relatives and that this pathology often involved obsessive-compulsive features.

One point of interest concerns the relationship between obsessive-compulsive neurosis and childhood psychosis: Both Adams and Judd reported that the possibility of psychosis was considered to be present in only a very small percentage of cases (none in Judd's study). An obvious reason may have been that both authors attempted to select only those cases in which obsessive-compulsive features were the most prominent characteristic. In regard to the relationship between this disorder and psychosis, however, several writers (e.g., Kessler, 1972) have pointed out that schizophrenic patients as well as members of other diagnostic groups also display compulsive, stereotyped, and ritualistic behaviors, resulting in problems of differential diagnosis. Note that in Judd's survey 29 patients with reported obsessive-compulsive symptoms were eliminated as not meeting the criteria for the diagnosis of obsessive-compulsive neurosis and that 25 of these 29 subjects eliminated were judged to be schizophrenic, providing some evidence of a relationship between compulsive behavior and schizophrenia.

A somewhat more recent study (Hollingsworth et al., 1980) has replicated the findings of Judd and Adams regarding the low prevalence of the disorder. Also of interest is the fact that this study found 82% of the parents of obsessive-compulsive children to suffer from serious psychiatric or medical illness. In the families of 17 children considered in the study, seven mothers, four fathers, and one sister were also found to show evidence of obsessive-compulsive neurosis. Pointing to the high rates of psychological problems and of physical illness of parents and the relatively high frequency of physical illness in the children themselves (29%), the authors suggest that the obsessive-compulsive symptoms of these children served as a defense against anxiety generated by stressful life situations.

Rapoport et al. (1981) have also provided information on nine adolescents with obsessive-compulsive disorder. These investigators obtained psychological and family data as well as comparing these subjects with controls on several neurophysiological, electrophysiological, and biomedical measures. In terms of psychological test findings, the group was found to be somewhat above average in intelligence (Mean IQ = 111), to score approximately at grade level in terms of achievement (when not acutely disturbed), and to display no evidence of thought disorder as reflected on the TAT or Rorschach. Child Behavior Checklists (Achenbach & Edelbrock, 1983b) completed by the mothers suggested a group displaying problems of an "internalizing" rather than an "externalizing" nature. Of special interest is the finding that all of the obsessive-compulsive children were judged to have experienced suicidal thoughts and to have met the criteria for major depressive disorder subsequent to the development of obsessions and compulsions. Unlike the findings of Hollingsworth et al. (1980), family members of adolescents included in this study showed little evidence of major psychopathology or serious medical illness, raising the possibility that referral biases may have contributed to the differences between the studies.

Regarding the other measures, as a group there was no evidence of major physical problems or of neurological abnormalities as assessed by EEG and CT scan measurements. The sleep EEGs of the obsessive-compulsive group was, however, found to resemble young adults with primary depressive disorder. As compared to control subjects, obsessive-compulsive subjects showed no differences in terms of sustained attention, reaction time, nor in terms of autonomic arousal, responsivity, or habituation to stimulation. No differences were found in terms of biochemical measures.

Studies such as these fail to provide much in the way of definitive evidence concerning obsessive-compulsive disorders in children, because they are based on small samples, lack adequate controls in most instances, and have yielded conflicting findings on some points.

They do, however, suggest possible correlates deserving of further investigation and provide a basis for developing specific hypotheses to be evaluated in more well-controlled research.

Prognosis

Relatively little information is available regarding the long-term outcome of obsessive-compulsive disorder with children. However, some data have been provided by Hollingsworth et al. (1980), who were able to follow up 10 of 17 children with this diagnosis after a mean interval of 6.5 years (when subjects averaged approximately 20 years of age). Although the severity of the symptoms was found to be less, 7 of the 10 still reported obsessive-compulsive behavior. One subject had developed an acute schizophrenic reaction that had been resolved. One was found to have been hospitalized for depression and suicidal thoughts. Although a number of these subjects (30%) had displayed significant school-related problems at the time they were initially seen for treatment, all were performing adequately in school at the time of follow-up. Indeed, all of those who were of college age (7 of 10) were enrolled in college or had graduated. Regarding social relationships, it is noteworthy that none of those who were 20 or older (7 subjects) had married, and only 3 of the total 10 were even dating. These findings suggest that whereas treatment may result in positive changes, children with this disorder are likely to continue to display problems associated with their condition into adulthood.

Treatment of Obsessions and Compulsions

There are relatively few publications reporting on the treatment of obsessive-compulsive children. Several approaches to the treatment of this disorder in adults, however, have been reported. These have involved the use of drugs, especially the tricyclic antidepressants (imipramine, clomipramine) as well as behavioral approaches such as systematic desensitization, exposure, thought stopping, contingent shock, and response prevention. Although there is data (often from uncontrolled studies) to support the effectiveness of each of these approaches, none has been found to be totally effective. For an overview of behavioral treatments see Emmelkamp (1982). One procedure that has received increasing research support in recent years is response prevention, particularly when it involves exposure of the individual to the situation eliciting compulsive behavior (Sturgis, 1984). Most of the research related to the effectiveness of this procedure has also been conducted with adults, but one study has described its use with a child displaying compulsive behavior. This case will be described here to illustrate some of the essential elements of the response prevention procedure and its potential applicability for dealing with this problem in children.

In this study, Stanley (1980) reported the treatment of an 8-year-old girl whose ritualistic behavior and obsessional checking severely restricted her day-to-day activities. For example, she had to fluff her pillows 3 times before beginning to undress for the night. Bed covers had to be placed so that the fringes only just touched the floor all the way around. At night, after removing her slippers, she banged them on the floor upside down then right side up 3 times, and placed them in parallel under the bed. She went to the toilet 3 times before going to bed and often woke up at night to carry out the same ritual. All dressing was done 3 times (even after going to the toilet), and toys had to be checked and rechecked before leaving the room where they were kept. Before carrying out each of these rituals the girl had to sing a specific nursery rhyme.

In treatment, parents and other members of the family were encouraged to not reward any compulsive behavior by treating the girl differently because of her compulsions. Response prevention involved working with the girl and her parents and arranging for her to be prevented from engaging in any of the above behaviors more than once at a specific time. This was followed by developing a series of situations that tended to elicit compulsive behaviors and grading them in terms of their "upset" value for the girl. These situations were presented in order, beginning with the mildest situation first, and moving to situations where she might become very upset if she could not carry out her compulsions, while in each situation her parents prevented the carrying out of the compulsive behavior (hence response prevention).

The use of this procedure was found to be quite successful; symptoms disappeared after 2 weeks of treatment, and there had been no recurrence of the problem at 1-year follow-up. The specific factors related to the effectiveness of response prevention have not been clearly determined. However, extinction is probably primarily responsible for the decrease in compulsive behavior and the reduction of anxiety associated with this procedure (Foa, Steketee, & Milby, 1980).

As was mentioned before, a number of studies with adults have provided support for the effectiveness of response prevention procedures. Indeed, this is likely to be the preferred treatment procedure for individuals displaying problems of compulsive behavior. In spite of its apparent value in dealing with ritualistic behavior, response prevention seems to be less useful in dealing with obsessional ruminations occurring in the absence of accompanying rituals (Gelder, 1979). Proven procedures for dealing with obsessive thoughts in the absence of compulsive behavior have not been developed, although it has been suggested that procedures akin to negative practice, where the person is instructed to repeatedly engage in thinking the unwanted thought(s) for extended periods of time, may be of value (Rachman, 1976). A combination of exposure and thought stopping has also been found to be reasonably effective (Sturgis, 1984). Related to this issue, one child-study by Kellerman (1981) involved the treatment of "homicidal" obsessions in a 12-year-old by employing several procedures such as hypnosis, covert reinforcement, thought stopping, and a variant of negative practice. Although this combination of procedures was successful in reducing the child's symptoms, the specific role of factors such as thought stopping and negative practice is unclear.

More research related to the effectiveness of these approaches is needed. For a more detailed overview of treatments of child obsessive-compulsive disorder, see Dollinger (1983).

Obsessions and Compulsions in Childhood: Overview

Obsessive-compulsive disorder is reflected in either obsessions, compulsions, or a combination of the two. Obsessions are repetitive, undesirable thoughts or impulses that are intrusive and that the individual cannot rid from conscious awareness; compulsions involve repetitive stereotyped behaviors that the individual may view as nonsensical but nevertheless feels compelled to engage in. Although many children display obsessive ideation and compulsive behaviors at certain stages in their development, it is only when these behaviors begin to seriously interfere with the child's ability to function that the obsessive-compulsive label would be considered appropriate. In general, this condition seems somewhat rare, probably occurring in less than 2% of the child psychiatric population.

Theoretical views of obsessive-compulsive neurosis have not been well delineated, although both psychodynamic and behavioral views have been presented. Although we know little concerning the original development of obsessions and compulsions, compulsive behavior appears to be *maintained* as a result of the reinforcing properties of the anxiety reduction that accompanies such behavior.

The literature related to this condition consists almost entirely of descriptive studies, and therefore little definitive information is available about etiology. Some correlates of this disorder have been suggested: For example, such children tend to be of above average intelligence, display a rigid moral code accompanied by marked guilt feelings, and have an active fantasy life. In many instances these children seem to show other problems, such as phobias and the display of aggression toward parents, and there is some evidence that the disorder may be accompanied by depressive features. Some, but not all, investigators have found that children with this disorder display a high frequency of physical illness and that their parents show increased levels of psychological and physical problems. Further research is clearly needed to address these preliminary findings.

Aside from some case study data supporting the use of certain behavioral approaches, there is little information concerning optimal treatments of this condition.

SOMATOFORM DISORDERS

DSM-III lists several conditions under the heading of somatoform disorders. These include somatization disorder, conversion disorder, hypochondriasis, and psychogenic pain disorder. A feature common to each is that they present with symptoms that appear to be physical in nature, but for which no organic basis can be found. On this basis it is usually assumed that they are of psychogenic origin.

The first two of these disorders are most relevant to a discussion of childhood psychopathology, because they represent conditions sometimes found in childhood that have been traditionally grouped under the label childhood hysteria. Although our knowledge concerning these disorders is scant, in the sections to follow we will discuss the ways in which they are manifest in childhood and the factors believed to contribute to their development. Because much of the work in this area was done prior to the publication of DSM-III and has dealt with the broader area of "childhood hysteria" (rather than the more well-delineated conditions presented in DSM-III), our presentation will follow more traditional lines. However, we will comment on present day terminology and current diagnostic distinctions as is appropriate.

Traditional Views of Hysterical Neurosis

In considering the general topic of childhood hysteria it is necessary to first consider the ways in which the terms *hysteria* and *hysteri-*

cal neurosis have been used in the clinical and research literature. Historically, the category hysterical neurosis has been used to refer to two somewhat different conditions: conversion reactions and dissociative reactions. Conversion reactions were seen as disorders in which there were symptoms suggestive of physical disorder, such as blindness, deafness, numbness, or paralyses of various body parts, for which no organic bases could be found. A major assumption concerning these disorders was that they resulted from repressed anxiety being "converted" into bodily symptoms (hence the term *conversion reaction*). Dissociative reactions were seen as disorders characterized by an alteration in the individual's state of consciousness as in amnesia, sleepwalking, and multiple personality. It has generally been assumed that these disorders are functional (psychological) in nature.

In spite of the fact that hysterical neurosis has long been characterized in this manner (and that the bulk of the existing research has been conducted within this framework), the term *hysteria* has been largely eliminated from the DSM-III system. DSM-III now includes the category somatization disorder to refer to disorders that are characterized by

recurrent and multiple somatic complaints of several years duration for which medical attention has been sought but which are apparently not due to any physical disorder. Complaints are often presented in a dramatic, vague or exaggerated way or are part of a complicated medical history in which many physical diagnoses have been considered. (American Psychiatric Association, 1980, p. 241)

Conversion reactions are *now* included as a separate category, independent of hysteria (somatization disorder), under the broad heading of somatoform disorders, and dissociative reactions are now classified separately from the somatoform disorders.

Traditionally, it has been suggested that hysteria may also be reflected in a specific pattern of personality characteristics including self-centeredness, demandingness, suggestibility, impulsiveness, exhibitionism, lack of emotional control, emotional lability, seductiveness, immaturity, and dependency (Chodoff & Lyons, 1958). Indeed, it has often been assumed that persons with this type of "hysterical personality" are more likely to develop hysterical disorders. Although the precise relationship between the so-called hysterical personality and hysterical disorder is unclear, the consensus of opinion seems to be that, although there is some overlap, the two do not necessarily occur together (Turner, Jacob, & Morrison, 1984). This view is reflected in DSM-III by the inclusion of a separate category (histrionic personality disorder) for use in those instances where histrionic characteristics are prominent in the absence of somatization or conversion disorder symptoms.

Despite the fact that the term *hysteria* has, in the past, been used in a variety of ways, the bulk of the child literature deals primarily with conversion reactions, as dissociative reactions have seldom been found in young children (Kessler, 1972). It is these problems that we will primarily concern ourselves with here.

Childhood Conversion Reactions

Description and Diagnosis

Over the years several authors have provided guidelines for the diagnosis of childhood hysteria and/or conversion reactions. In an early paper Robins and O'Neal (1953) suggested that for a diagnosis to be made the child should be found to display a variety of symptoms lasting over an extended period of time. Among the symptoms considered as most diagnostic were "pseudoneurologic" or somatic complaints (e.g., loss of sensation, paralysis, abdominal complaints, nausea, and so on) and "nervousness" or the somatic manifestations of anxiety such as heart palpitations, breathing difficulty, paresthesias, dizziness, fatigue, and weakness. Referring specifically to conversion reactions (rather than to the more general category of hysteria), Rock (1971) suggested that a diagnosis requires the presence of at least one prominent somatic symptom, either motor (e.g., paralysis) or sensory (e.g., loss of vision). He noted that it must be determined that the symptom is without a physiological basis and of a psychogenic origin.

An additional feature often suggested as characteristic of conversion disorders has been referred to as *La belle indifference*, pointing to the fact that persons with conversion reactions are often considered quite comfortable with their symptoms and do not display evidence of anxiety regarding their condition (Kessler, 1972). Despite the popularity of the notion, Robins and O'Neal (1953) found that children diagnosed as hysteric often displayed evidence of both pseudoneurologic symptoms (conversion symptoms) *and* anxiety. Maloney (1980), in studying 105 children diagnosed as showing conversion reactions, found preadolescent children to frequently show great concern over their symptoms. Indeed, Goodyer (1981) has suggested that "*La belle indifference* is the exception rather than the rule and that when it does occur, it may be of a fluctuating nature" (p. 185). Other findings cited by Turner et al. (1984) also suggest that adults with conversion reactions often show heightened levels of anxiety, although the anxiety may not always be displayed overtly. Although it may be true that some individuals with conversion disorders are indifferent to their symptoms, it seems unlikely that this is characteristic of most persons with this disorder. Indeed, it seems likely that the often stated absence of anxiety in such individuals may be, in part, reflective of the psychoanalytic view that in conversion reactions anxiety is "converted" into somatic symptoms rather than being expressed overtly. (For an example of how conversion symptoms can be manifest clinically see Figure 6.6).

The DSM-III criteria for making a diagnosis of conversion disorder are presented in Table 6.11. As can be noted, these criteria require not only that the person display physical dysfunction that cannot be explained in terms of "a known physical disorder or pathophysiological mechanism," but that evidence be provided that psychological factors are contributors to the person's condition. This requirement seems desirable to prevent *diagno-*

FIGURE 6.6. Conversion Reaction

> A boy aged nine years, two months, with a past psychiatric history of conduct disorder, was referred . . . for investigation of partial loss of vision in both eyes. The symptom had come on suddenly when he had complained to his mother that "things seemed blurred." It lasted from five minutes to two hours at any one time and occurred at intervals during weekdays and weekends with no obvious pattern of frequency. After two weeks reassurance by parents, the symptoms had not altered and the G.P. was called. He could find no organic cause for the blurred vision and felt that psychological factors were involved.
>
> Physical investigation revealed no abnormalities in the child's neurological or ophthalmological state. Psychiatric assessment found the boy to be of low self-esteem, generally withdrawn, and preferring the individual attention of one adult.
>
> His mother had a past history of depression and his father drank excessively. It was noted that his symptoms occurred within hours of father leaving the house following marital discord. Management included increasing his self-esteem and peer group relationships and paying little attention to the "symptoms." The relationship between "symptoms" and marital discord was explored with the parents while the boy was in the hospital. The presenting complaint had disappeared by one month and on follow-up in out-patient and at 12 months, the patient remained symptom free, was functioning well at home and school and physically was in good health.

Source: Goodyer (1981). © 1981 Pergamon Press and reprinted by permission.

TABLE 6.11. DSM-III DIAGNOSTIC CRITERIA FOR CONVERSION DISORDER.

A. The predominant disturbance is a loss or alteration in physical functioning suggesting a physical disorder.

B. Psychological factors are judged to be etiologically involved in the symptom, as evidenced by one or more of the following:

   1) there is a temporal relationship between an environmental stimulus that is apparently related to a psychological conflict or need and the initiation or exacerbation of the symptom.

   2) the symptom enables the individual to avoid some activity that is noxious to him or her.

   3) the symptom enables the individual to get support from the environment that otherwise might not be forthcoming.

C. It has been determined that the symptom is *not* under voluntary control.

D. The symptom cannot, after appropriate investigation, be explained by a known physical disorder or pathophysiological mechanism.

E. The symptom is not limited to pain or to a disturbance in sexual functioning.

F. Not due to Somatization Disorder or Schizophrenia.

Source: American Psychiatric Association (1980). © 1980 American Psychiatric Association and reprinted with permission.

sis by exclusion, whereby one is thought to display a conversion reaction simply because a physical basis for the person's problem cannot be determined. That physical contributors be "ruled out" *and* psychological contributors be "ruled in" before a diagnosis is made is crucial, because research with adult patients has shown that a sizable number of persons with this diagnosis are subsequently found to have actual organic disease (Turner et al., 1984).

Etiology: Dynamic and Sociopsychological Formulations

From a psychodynamic point of view, conversion reactions, like other neuroses, are often thought to result from intrapsychic conflict between unacceptable thoughts, wishes, or impulses displayed by the individual and various aspects of the personality (id, ego, superego). It is assumed that these impulses are defended against by repressing both the conflict and the associated anxiety, with the anxiety being converted into physical symptoms that are both a partial expression and symbolic representation of the unconscious underlying conflict.

Ullmann and Krasner (1975) have proposed a sociopsychological formulation of hysteria (conversion reactions) that differs in a number of respects from the psychoanalytic position, although both views see symptoms as a way of avoiding anxiety-arousing situations. Ullmann and Krasner's position has been well summarized by Achenbach (1982), who has indicated

> rather than ascribing the symptoms to conversion of unconscious conflicts into somatic form, they [Ullmann and Krasner—brackets added] see parallels between hysterical symptoms and behavior in hypnosis, role playing, placebo treatments, and malingering. Although hysterics are not regarded as deliberately faking organic symptoms, their behavior can be understood as controlled by cues and reinforcers that provide stronger incentives to manifest such symptoms than to avoid them. This implies that hysterical

> symptoms can be removed by manipulating the relevant cues and reinforcers. (p. 356)

There is currently little data concerning the validity of either theoretical view. The formulation presented by Ullmann and Krasner, incorporating learning principles and based on research findings related to social influence techniques, would appear to be more amenable to experimental test and, on this basis, to have the greater utility.

Prevalence

Exact prevalence figures are difficult to determine, as estimates vary widely depending on factors such as age, the population sampled, and the diagnostic criteria employed. Estimates, however, have been presented by a number of workers in the area. Robins and O'Neal (1953), for example, found only 27 cases of hysteria among 51,311 child psychiatric cases seen at one facility over a 15½-year-period. Rae (1977), employing a strict definition of conversion reactions, has found prevalence rates ranging from 3 to 13% in three settings serving pediatric and child psychiatric patients. Goodyear (1981) has reported a figure of .5% in a facility serving pediatric inpatients. Finally, Maloney (1980) has reported a figure of 16.7% for pediatric inpatients referred for psychiatric consults. Although these findings vary for children seen in various clinical settings, it would seem that the disorder is relatively rare in the general child population. Accurate estimates here, however, are unavailable.

Correlates of Childhood Hysteria and Conversion Reactions

Although considerable attention has been given to the so-called hysterical disorders in adulthood, there are relatively few published articles pertaining to such disorders in children. The literature that does exist consists mostly of theoretical papers or simple descriptive investigations that provide only tentative findings regarding the variables that may contribute to this disorder.

The Role of Cultural Factors. One early study by Proctor (1958) reviewed the records of 191 consecutive child psychiatry referrals. Twenty-five of these patients (13%) were diagnosed as hysteric. Of these patients, 80% displayed conversion reactions. Fifty-six percent of the sample was male, and 33% of the sample was black. Proctor has pointed out that only 10% of the total patient population was black, making this an overrepresentation of blacks in the childhood hysteria group.

Noting that the prevalence figure obtained (13%) was considerably higher than that found in other studies at that time, Proctor suggested that cultural factors may have been responsible. He observed that the particular geographic area from which this sample was drawn was predominantly rural, of lower educational and socioeconomic status, and was characterized by superstition and what he termed "primitive and repressive attitudes." Proctor posited that this sort of culture is especially conducive to the development of such disorders, thus highlighting cultural factors as being of major etiological importance. Proctor also suggested that cultural factors may be of importance in determining the course of the disorder. For example, he observed that in an earlier study, Robins and O'Neal (1953) were unable to find adult males diagnosed as hysteric. In attempting to account for child-adult differences Proctor argues that

> this is probably in large part a cultural phenomena inasmuch as the . . . phenomena seen in hysteria are considered feminine traits in our society, but are traits which are at least partially acceptable throughout childhood. Hence, within the framework of social acceptance and approval, hysteric mechanisms could be readily used by the male in childhood, but not later in life. Such traits are more socially and culturally acceptable for women than men, and it would seem that hysteria would be more acceptable to women. (p. 405)

Correlates of Conversion Reactions. Rock (1971) has provided some information about the characteristics of children displaying frank conversion reactions. Of the 10 children included in his study, Rock observed that all but 1 were average to above average in intelligence; all but 1, however, were deficient in terms of academic performance. Most displayed poor peer relationships and most showed evidence of depression. All were judged to be overly dependent. Rock noted that in all cases the symptoms of these children were preceded by some sort of precipitating event.

Among the characteristics observed in the families of these children were overprotectiveness on the part of the mother, fathers who appeared ineffectual, and parents who generally displayed interpersonal problems. The parents also seemed to contribute to the development of the conversion reaction by serving as a model or by paying significant attention to the child's somatic complaints.

In what is probably the only partially controlled study in this area, Maloney (1980) reviewed the hospital records of 105 children with hysterical conversion reactions who were originally seen for psychiatric evaluation as pediatric inpatients. For comparison purposes these cases were matched with a similar number of children from the same population who showed no evidence of this disorder (although this group had also been seen for psychiatric evaluations). In terms of descriptive information, the average age of children with conversion reactions was 12.1 years, and there was an approximately equal number of males and females found to display this disorder. Despite the fairly equal sex ratio (which has not always been found; see Goodyer, 1981; Rae, 1977) there did seem to be significant sex differences in the type of conversion symptoms displayed. Maloney suggests that although males and females showed symptoms such as abdominal pain about equally, females more often presented with symptoms such as headache and syncope (fainting), while males more often displayed paralysis and pseudoseizures.

In terms of other characteristics, it was found that in some 97% of the cases conversion reactions had their onset following a significant family stress. Fifty-eight percent displayed unresolved grief reactions, and in 88%

of the cases communication problems within the family were noted. Significant differences between conversion reaction patients and the comparison group were found on each of these variables. Although not differing from controls, it is noteworthy that in 85% of the cases children with conversion reactions were also found to have a clinically depressed parent. Regarding these findings pertaining to family characteristics, it is relevant that Goodyer (1981) also found significant psychiatric disorders in the families of 73% of his 15 cases. Of special note is the fact that in 60% of these cases, at least one of the parents displayed a clinical anxiety disorder, and in one instance the parent had previously experienced a conversion reaction.

Although the studies presented here represent a rather scant literature and provide only very tentative findings, taken together they seem to suggest that further research into the role of cultural and family variables may be especially worthwhile.

Prognosis

There is little data on the long-term outcome of children with conversion reactions. Information that is available suggests that most children with this disorder have a favorable prognosis. Support for this view comes from a 1-year follow-up of 13 cases by Goodyer (1981). Of these, 10 children (66%) were found to be symptom free and functioning well in terms of psychological adjustment and school performance a year after discharge. One child was said to have been readmitted for the same presenting problem, one remained in psychiatric treatment (although there was no further evidence of conversion reactions), and an additional child was receiving educational help for underachievement.

Treatment

Consistent with the views of Ullmann and Krasner (1975) regarding the role of social variables in the development of conversion reactions, there have been several attempts to deal with childhood conversion reactions

through the use of behavioral methods. To illustrate, Alford, Blanchard, and Buckley (1972) report the treatment of a 17-year-old girl who displayed a 10-year history of vomiting after every meal, for which no physical cause could be found. As an assessment of the girl's behavior suggested that she was particularly sensitive to attention, an attempt was made to manipulate social contact to gain control over the problem behavior. Employing an extinction procedure, therapy consisted of having staff members and other patients avoid and ignore the patient on those occasions where she vomited or reported being nauseated. This resulted in a rapid reduction in vomiting, and a 7-month follow-up indicated that the patient had vomited only once since discharge.

Dealing with a different type of problem, Delamater, Rosenbloom, Conners, and Hertweck (1983) have described the treatment of a 10½-year-old boy with a hysterical paralysis of both legs. The treatment in this case involved withdrawal of reinforcement for symptomatic behavior and the use of positive reinforcement for successive approximations of walking behavior. These authors report that the boy regained full use of his legs within 2 weeks as well as becoming more interactive and less lethargic and dejected. These positive gains were maintained at a 6-month follow-up.

Case studies such as these seem to provide at least tentative support for the usefulness of behavioral approaches in the treatment of childhood conversion reactions. It may be noted that approaches such as the ones described here, which emphasize the role of social reinforcement, are not at all inconsistent with an emphasis on the role of family variables. Indeed, it may be within the family that illness behaviors are modeled and reinforced through attention and other social behaviors. Although there have been no published studies addressing this point, it may be that an optimal approach to treatment is one that emphasizes behavior change methods within the context of a broader family therapy approach.

Overview

The studies cited here are generally reflective of the published literature related to childhood hysteria and conversion reactions, in that they do not provide definitive information concerning the nature of the disorder, and none are of an experimental nature. Although such studies give little basis for generalization, they do provide some insights into the nature of this disorder that may be examined more systematically in future research.

Results of these clinical studies suggest that childhood hysteria and conversion reactions generally occur infrequently in the general population but may be found more frequently in cultures characterized by lower educational levels, lower socioeconomic status, and a general lack of sophistication concerning bodily functions. The disorder occurs in both male and female children but seems to be largely restricted to females in adulthood. Although often of average intelligence, children with conversion disorders appear to be underachievers and seem to display other problems, such as feelings of depression, anxiety, poor peer relationships, and an overdependence on others. The disorder seems most often to be preceded by some precipitating event and is often related to stress experienced within the family. Additionally, such children seem to come from homes where parents display interpersonal problems (often displaying psychiatric problems themselves) and in which somatic complaints may be modeled and reinforced. Although relatively little information is available concerning the most appropriate focus of treatment, it seems that behavioral procedures, perhaps employed within the context of family treatment, may be of value.

AFFECTIVE DISORDERS

Background

Affective disorders represent primary disturbances of emotion or mood. These disorders can involve extremes of depression or elation (or a combination of the two) and can range from conditions that are mildly to severely in-capacitating. Whereas a range of affective disorders are seen in adults (American Psychiatric Association, 1980) and have been the subject of much research (see Carson & Carson, 1984), the literature on affective disorders of childhood is much more limited. Thus, with the exception of a few isolated case reports (see, for example, Sylvester, Burke, McCauley, & Clark, 1984), there is almost no literature on manic disorders in childhood. Although the situation is somewhat more positive in the case of childhood depression (accounting for our emphasizing this disorder in the present chapter), our knowledge base with regard to depression in childhood is also quite limited.

Although the late 1970s and early 1980s have witnessed a burgeoning interest in the topic of childhood depression, prior to this time even the existence of this disorder was seldom acknowledged. The lack of attention paid to childhood depression seems to derive from the fact that many clinicians have questioned whether there is actually such a condition. Pearce (1977) noted that the term *depression* can refer to a normal lowering of mood, such as an emotional response to adversity (sadness, unhappiness), to an abnormality of mood that constitutes a specific syndrome or disorder, or to an illness characterized by depressed mood (that is qualitatively different from usual) and with a recognized etiology and prognosis. Although it would be acknowledged by most clinicians that children can and do display depressive affect (feelings), the existence of childhood depression as a specific disorder, separate from other conditions, has been contested. Evidence related to this issue has been reviewed by Cantwell (1982) and Lefkowitz and Burton (1978).

In spite of the controversy over the existence of childhood depression as a diagnostic entity, several descriptive studies suggest that some children do display a constellation of behaviors — persistent crying, negative self-evaluations, lowered activity level, behavioral withdrawal, verbal statements related to self-destruction — that could be legitimately subsumed under the heading of depression as the term is commonly used. Based on these clinical studies, it would also appear that in some instances these behaviors may persist over time and interfere with the child's ability to function. It would therefore appear that the topic of childhood depression deserves consideration. (For overviews of methodological and conceptual issues related to childhood depression see Cantwell, 1982; Petti, 1983.)

Depression in Infancy

Although the present discussion centers around depression as experienced in later childhood, a fair amount of attention has been directed toward the study of so-called anaclitic depression in infancy, focusing primarily on the effects of early separation on child behavior. It has been shown, for example, that prolonged separation of the infant from his mother can result in behaviors suggestive of depression (Bowlby, 1960; Spitz, 1946). In considering the nature of the behaviors associated with separation, Hetherington and Martin (1972) described the child's reaction as follows:

> First there is a period of "protest" during which the child cries a great deal, asks for parents if he can talk, shows restless hyperactivity, and is easily agitated. After about a week some children decrease their overt protests and manifest what has variously been called despair, depression or withdrawal. They become unresponsive and lose interest in the environment. The facial muscles sag and the face presents the generally accepted features of sadness and dejection. Loud wailing and crying may be replaced with low intensity whimpering or sobbing. Most children of this age are likely to recover after several weeks from this depression-withdrawal phase and return to normal interests and responsiveness in their environment. (p. 62)

As studies of separation in humans have often confounded separation with other variables, such as hospitalization and institutionalization (Harlow & Suomi, 1971), some investigators have chosen to examine the effects of separation in analogue studies employing non-

human primates. Harlow and Suomi report that a number of studies (Kaufman & Rosenblum, 1967; Seay & Harlow, 1965; Seay, Hansen, & Harlow, 1962) have shown that when young monkeys are separated from their mothers after initial attachment, they display reactions similar to those observed in human infants who have experienced separation. Animal analogues always pose problems of generalization, but these results suggest that separation in and of itself may play a prominent role in infant depression.

Description and Diagnosis

A variety of features have been associated with childhood depression and are presumed to be of importance in the diagnosis of this disorder. Cytryn, McKnew, and Bunny (1980), for example, list a number of prominent features that can be categorized under the heading of mood changes, such as dysphoria, sadness, hopelessness, loss of pleasure, decreased concentration, low self-esteem, and suicidal thoughts and gestures. They also suggest that somatic complaints, feelings of loneliness, separation anxiety, loss of interest in activities, and disturbances in social, school, and family relationships may be of significance. Several of these features are reflected in the case of Bobby described in Figure 6.7.

Depression in childhood is sometimes described as taking several forms. Cytryn and McKnew (1972), for example, suggested the existence of three types: acute depressive reactions, chronic depressive reactions, and masked depressive reactions.

Acute Depressive Reactions

In this category are children who display obvious manifestations of depression and whose depression is preceded by some identifiable precipitating event. These events may vary from case to case but often involve major object loss. Cytryn and McKnew (1972) say this may involve parental loss through separation or may take more subtle forms, such as withdrawal of interest or affection by some im-

FIGURE 6.7. Bobby: A Case of Childhood Depression

When seen for an interview, Bobby appeared as a rather dejected looking 10-year-old who seemed to be much more serious than one would expect for a child of his age. Bobby indicated that his parents had brought
him to the clinic because "they think I have emotional problems." When
asked to elaborate, Bobby said that he wasn't sure what emotional problems really were but that he thought they were upset because "I cry sometimes." In observing Bobby in the playroom it was obvious that his activity level was well below that expected for a child of 10. He showed a lack
of interest in the toys that were available to him, and the interviewer was
unable to get him interested in any play activity for more than a few minutes. In questioning him about home and school, Bobby indicated that he
didn't like school because he didn't have any friends, and he wasn't good
at playing games like baseball and soccer like the other kids were, stating
"I'm not really very good at anything." He stated that, at home, things were
"OK" except that "my parents work most of the time, and we never do anything together like other families." When asked what he would wish for
if he could have any three wishes granted he indicated; "I would wish that
I was the type of boy my mother and father want, I would wish that I could
have friends, and I would wish that I wouldn't feel sad so much."

In speaking with the parents, the mother reported that she and her husband had become increasingly concerned about their son during the past
year. She indicated that he always seemed to look sad and cried a lot for
no apparent reason and that he appeared to have lost interest in most of
the things that he used to enjoy doing. The mother confirmed Bobby's statements that he had no friends, indicating that he had become more and more
of a loner during the past 6 to 9 months. She stated that his schoolwork
had also suffered in that he is unable to concentrate on school assignments
and seems to have "just lost interest." The mother notes, however, that her
greatest concern is that he has recently spoken more and more frequently
about "killing himself," saying that the parents would be better off if he
wasn't around.

portant individual in the child's environment.
Children in this category are said to display
a relatively good premorbid history, with depression only becoming manifest in response
to precipitating events.

Chronic Depressive Reactions

This category classifies cases in which children display obvious depressive affect and
other characteristics associated with depression and have a poor premorbid history, with
depressive features becoming gradually apparent rather than suddenly observable, as in
the case of acute depressive reactions. In the
case of chronic depressive reactions, the back-

ground of such children is characterized by
a long history of frequent separations and loss
rather than a single major precipitating event.

Masked Depressive Reactions

This category was originally suggested as appropriate for cases in which the child's depression is "masked" or overshadowed by other
clinical features. The child may display hyperactive behavior, psychosomatic problems, or
delinquent behavior, which serve as the reason for referral, and which are often thought
of as being "depressive equivalents." Cytryn
and McKnew (1972) suggest that in such cases
the "underlying" depression, although not ob-

vious, may become apparent within the context of clinical interaction; for example, it may be displayed in response to projective tests and in the periodic expression of depressive affect.

DSM-III in the Diagnosis of Childhood Depression

Many clinicians and researchers have suggested characteristics thought to be of importance in making a diagnosis of childhood depression, and classification systems such as that just described have been proposed. Nevertheless, workers in the area have not been consistent in the criteria they have employed in making diagnostic judgments. Indeed, there are few specific, agreed upon guidelines that state how many characteristics are required and to what degree they must be present to warrant a diagnosis of childhood depression. Obviously such criteria are needed to facilitate communication and research.

Although the diagnostic criteria for affective disorders presented in DSM-III (American Psychiatric Association, 1980) were not designed primarily for use with children, there is reason to believe that they may prove to be useful with younger age groups. The appropriateness of these criteria for the diagnosis of childhood depression was first suggested by Cytryn, McKnew, and Bunny (1980), who indicated that the characteristics defining depressive disorders within the DSM-III system are quite similar to those most clinicians would associate with childhood depression. They also point out that the categories of acute and chronic depression that were a part of their earlier classification scheme (see Cytryn & McKnew, 1972) can both be subsumed under the DSM-III heading of major depressive disorder: Acute depression would be noted by indicating a single episode of depression with severe psychosocial stressors (Axis IV), chronic depression by indicating recurrent episodes of depression and a positive family history. Cytryn et al. (1980) add that although DSM-III does not provide for the classification of masked depression, this category has gen-

erally not been found to be as useful as the other two categories (acute and chronic) and is not judged to be essential. This position regarding the concept of masked depression (depressive equivalents) is also shared by others currently active in this area (see Cantwell, 1982; Poznanski, 1983 for critiques of this concept).

The DSM-III criteria's usefulness with children has also been suggested by the fact that these criteria have been found of value in several studies assessing the prevalence of child depression in the general and clinical child populations (Carlson & Cantwell, 1980; Kashani, Barbero, & Bolander, 1981; Kashani & Simonds, 1979) as well as in other studies of childhood depression (see Kovacks, Feinberg, Crouse-Novak, Paulauskas, & Finkelstein, 1984). These criteria are presented in Table 6.12.

Note that although the criteria presented here include delusions, hallucinations, and bizarre behavior, which may be manifest in some cases of severe depression in adults, such characteristics are not necessary for a diagnosis of depression when employing the DSM-III criteria. Indeed, in the case of depression, as it is most often seen in children, it would be assumed that such symptoms would be absent. So-called psychotic depression in children is extremely rare, and the discovery of such symptoms in children meeting the other criteria for a diagnosis of depression is extremely unlikely.

Etiology: Theories and Conceptual Models of Depression

Several conceptual models have been proposed to account for depressive reactions. Because these have typically been presented to account for adult depression, in most cases it is unclear to what extent they may be useful in understanding depression in childhood. There are, however, preliminary data to suggest that certain of these models may be of some relevance.

TABLE 6.12. DSM-III CRITERIA FOR DEPRESSIVE DISORDER.

A. *Dysphoric mood or loss of interest or pleasure* in all or almost all usual activities and pastimes. The dysphoric mood is characterized by symptoms such as the following: depressed, sad, blue, hopeless, low, down in the dumps, irritable. The mood disturbance must be prominent and relatively persistent, but not necessarily the most dominant symptom, and does not include momentary shifts from one dysphoric mood to another dysphoric mood, e.g., anxiety to depression to anger, such as are seen in states of acute psychotic turmoil. (For children under six, dysphoric mood may have to be inferred from a persistently sad facial expression.)

B. *At least four of the following symptoms* have been present nearly every day for a period of at least two weeks (in children under six, at least three of the first four):

   1) *Poor appetite or significant weight loss* (when not dieting) or *increased appetite or significant weight gain* (in children under six, consider failure to make expected weight gains)

   2) *Insomnia or hypersomnia*

   3) *Psychomotor agitation or retardation* (but not merely subjective feelings of restlessness or being slowed down) (in children under six, hypoactivity).

   4) *Loss of interest or pleasure in usual activities*, or decrease in sexual drive . . . (in children under six, signs of apathy)

   5) *Loss of energy; fatigue*

   6) *Feelings of worthlessness*, self-reproach, or excessive or inappropriate guilt (either may be delusional)

   7) *Complaints or evidence of diminished ability to think or concentrate*, such as slowed thinking or indecisiveness not associated with marked loosening of associations or incoherence

   8) *Recurrent thoughts of death*, suicidal ideation, wishes to be dead, or suicide attempt

C. *Neither of the following dominate the clinical picture* when an affective syndrome is absent (i.e., symptoms in criteria A and B above):

   1) *Preoccupation with a mood-incongruent delusion or hallucination*

   2) *Bizarre behavior*

D. *Not superimposed* on either schizophrenia, schizophreniform disorder, or a paranoid disorder

E. *Not due to any organic mental disorder or uncomplicated bereavement*

Source: American Psychiatric Association (1980). © 1980 American Psychiatric Association and reprinted by permission of the publisher.

Biological Views

Biological views of depression have typically focused on the role of genetic factors and the possible role of specific biochemical abnormalities, especially those involving neurotransmitters (chemicals that facilitate the transmission of nerve impulses). Regarding the hypothesized role of genetic factors, Kashani et al. (1981) have reviewed twin studies, which, when taken together, suggest concordance rates of 76% for affective disorders in monozygotic twins as compared to a rate of 19% for dizygotic twins. They note a concordance rate of 67% for monozygotic twins

reared apart. Although the specific mode of genetic transmission has not been determined, these studies appear to provide general support for the role of genetic factors, at least in adult patients. Although there is evidence from descriptive studies that depressed children often have depressed parents (Brumback, Dietz-Schmidt, & Weinberg, 1977; Poznanski & Zrull, 1970), the data regarding the role of genetic factors in children is less clear. Although there is some evidence from adult studies that biochemical factors may play a significant role in some (but probably not all) depressed patients (Kashani et al., 1981), only the most preliminary work in this area has been conducted with children, and definitive findings are not available.

The Life Stress Model

A number of studies have suggested that depression may result, in part, from the experiencing of major life changes, especially negative ones (e.g., separation, divorce, death in the family, job loss, etc.). Adult studies by Paykel and his associates (see Paykel, 1974) have documented that depressed psychiatric patients show higher levels of negative life changes than do control subjects. Paykel has also reported heightened levels of negative life changes in suicide attempters. Studies by Johnson and Sarason (1978) and Sarason, Johnson, and Siegel (1978) have also documented relationships between negative life change and measures of depression in nonclinic subjects.

Research with children and adolescents has also provided some support for the role of life stress in depression. For example, research by Johnson and McCutcheon (1980) and Siegel (1981) has documented relationships between cumulative negative life changes in children and indices of depression, and Cohen-Sandler, Berman, and King (1982) have provided data suggestive of a relationship between life stress and suicidal behavior in children. Even though it is unlikely that life stress is the sole cause of depression in either children or adults, these findings suggest that it may well be a significant contributor.

The Psychoanalytic Model

Psychoanalytic views tend to highlight the role of object loss in the development of depression. The loss may be real, as in the loss of a parent through death, divorce, or separation, or it may be more symbolic. According to this formulation, depression occurs as a result of an individual (who has suffered the loss) identifying with the lost love object. Because the individual is thought to have ambivalent feelings toward the lost object as a result of identification, he or she turns the feelings of hostility against the self and thus experiences depression. This type of reaction to loss is believed to occur primarily in persons who are fixated at the oral stage of psychosexual development, who are overly dependent, and who subsequently experience a significant loss.

Behavioral and Cognitive Models

Beck (1967, 1974; also see Kovacs & Beck, 1978) has focused on the role of cognitive factors in depression. Beck assumes that depression is related to the way individuals perceive events in their environment and that the depressed individual displays a disposition to interpret events in such a way as to contribute to feelings of self-blame, failure, and hopelessness, influencing his or her general mood and way of relating to the outside world.

Several behaviorally oriented views of depression have been proposed. Ferster (1974) and Lewinsohn (1974) theorize that the various manifestations of depression may result from a lack of sufficient positive reinforcers in the environment, which may be caused by factors ranging from a change in residence to a failure to display appropriate social and vocational skills that would result in reinforcement. Thus, from this position as well as from the analytic view, depression may be related to significant loss.

An additional theory of depression, which focuses on the role of learning, has been presented by Seligman (1974; also see Seligman, 1978), who describes depression in terms of learned helplessness. Although Seligman's reformulation of his original learned helplessness model is somewhat more complex than his original views, this model essentially suggests that depression results in individuals who, as a result of their learning history, perceive themselves as having little or no control over rewards and punishers in their environment. As Kashani et al. (1981) have noted, studies have not yet specifically focused on the relationship between helplessness and childhood depressive disorder, although some preliminary work with children has involved the learned helplessness paradigm.

Prevalence

Several prevalence studies have focused on frequency of occurrence within various clinical populations. For example, Weinberg, Rutman, Sullivan, Penick, and Deitz (1973) found that 57% of children ages 6 to 12 who were referred to an educational diagnostic clinic met their criteria for depressive disorder. Brumback, Jackoway, and Weinberg (1980) found 62 of 100 consecutive referrals to an educational and diagnostic center to show evidence of childhood depression. Pearce (1977) estimated that somewhere between 15 and 20% of children referred for psychiatric help can be expected to display a depressive disorder. Kashani, Barbero, and Bolander (1981) found that 7% of children age 7 to 12 admitted to a pediatric ward showed evidence of depression.

These findings seem to suggest that a fairly high frequency of childhood depression is found among children referred for educational and psychiatric problems and that a significant number of children in pediatric settings also show evidence of this problem. Not all investigators have obtained similar findings, however. Poznanski and Zrull (1970), for instance, found that only 14 of 1,758 child psychiatric patients met their criteria for childhood depressive disorder, although a total of 98 of those cases were judged to show evidence of at least moderate depression. Discrepant findings about the prevalence of childhood depression within clinic populations have also been noted by Kashani and Simonds (1979), who cite figures derived from other studies ranging from 2.3 to 59%. Most likely these differences reflect the fact that the studies cited did not employ similar criteria in determining the presence of depression. Studies that assess the prevalence of "depressive symptoms," "depressive mood," or that report the number of children scoring as depressed on a checklist for depression will yield very different findings from studies investigating childhood depression as a specific disorder.

A recent study of the relationship between diagnostic criteria and prevalence figures, conducted by Carlson and Cantwell (1980), selected a random sample of 210 children from a larger population of clinic cases seen at the UCLA Neuropsychiatric Institute. These children were assessed with regard to the presence of depressive symptoms at intake and for the presence of depression as indicated by elevated scores on the children's short form of the Beck Depression Inventory. Interviews were conducted with 102 of the children in order to provide data concerning the degree to which these children met DSM-III criteria for a diagnosis of depressive disorder. The study found that 60% of the children had depressive symptoms, 49% displayed evidence of depression on the depression inventory, but only 28% of the children who were assessed via diagnostic interview were judged to meet DSM-III criteria.

There have also been some studies of prevalence in the general population. Again, the figures obtained vary depending on the criteria employed. For example, Albert and Beck (1975), in a study of 63 seventh and eighth graders, found that 33% displayed evidence of moderate to severe depression, as indicated by scores on the Beck Depression Inventory. In a more ambitious study, however, Kashani and Simonds (1979) conducted interviews with the parents of 103 children, ages 7 to 11, randomly selected from the general population, to determine how many of these children met the DSM-III criteria for major depressive disorder. The diagnosis was determined to be applicable in only 1.9% of the cases, although approximately 18% showed evidence of depressive affect. When compared to the above figures, based only on questionnaire responses, these latter data probably provide a more accurate picture of the prevalence of depressive *disorder* in the general child population.

Although it is difficult to draw conclusions based on the results of studies presented here, the prevalence of depressive disorder seems to be relatively low in the general child population but more frequent among children seen in clinical facilities. Because of the careful nature of the study and the objectivity of the criteria employed, the figure provided by Carlson and Cantwell (1980) of 28% seems to be a reasonable estimate of overall prevalence in the clinical population, although the figure varies depending on whether inpatients or outpatients are considered (Carlson and Cantwell found rates of 16 and 36% for outpatients and inpatients, respectively). Further studies using specific criteria such as those provided by DSM-III are needed to assess the representativeness of these estimates.

Research: Correlates of Childhood Depression

Numerous authors have commented on the relationship between childhood depression and family variables. Cytryn and McKnew (1972), for example, suggested that different types of depression are associated with different family backgrounds. Here they noted that families of children with acute depression typically show no evidence of gross psychopathology and often display considerable strength and cohesion, whereas most children with chronic depression have a family history of depressive illness.

Other authors, although not employing the same classification system, have also found a history of depression in the families of depressed children. In a sample of 20 depressed children, Connell (1972) found evidence of a relative who was depressed in 12 of the cases; in 4 other cases there was evidence of some other types of psychopathology. Likewise, Poznanski and Zrull (1970) found that in almost 50% of their sample of depressed children at least one parent displayed depression. And Brumback et al. (1980) found a family history of psychiatric or behavioral disturbance in 71% of 62 cases of childhood depression, and in 42% of these cases there was a positive family history of depression. Although the frequency of parental depression in the families of depressed children appears to be fairly high, it is not clear whether it is higher than in families of children displaying other types of psychiatric problems. Nor is it clear whether a high rate of parental depression suggests hereditary factors, common environmental factors leading to depression in both parent and child, or depression resulting from the child's "identification" with a parent who is depressed, as has been suggested by Poznanski and Zrull.

Descriptive studies have also revealed other similarities between depressed children and their parents. Children diagnosed as depressed reportedly often display overt aggressive behaviors and poorly controlled emotional outbursts, whereas parents of these children are said to have serious problems handling aggression and hostility. Further it has been suggested that parents of depressed children are often rejecting and respond to their children in a detached, impersonal manner, if they are available to them at all (Poznanski & Zrull, 1970). These descriptions of the family environments of depressed children are quite consistent with Lewinsohn's (1974) position that depression may result from a lack of sufficient positive reinforcers. Such an environment might also be expected to result in feelings on the child's part of helplessness and that he or she has little or no control over his/her environment — feelings that, according to Seligman (1974), may be related to depression. It must be noted, however, that descriptions of families of depressed children have been based on observations of a limited number of cases and that more extensive and better controlled studies are necessary to determine if these parental and family characteristics are more generally associated with childhood depression. One example of the type of research needed has been provided by Puig-Antich (1982; cited in Cantwell, 1982). Here an attempt was made to study family interactions in a sample of depressed children via a family interview technique. Of special interest was the fact that markedly deficient mother-child relationships were found, but only during the time when the children were seriously depressed. Restricted peer relationships (as compared to normal and disturbed children) were found both during the active phase of the depression and after "recovery." Although more data are necessary, these findings tentatively suggest not only that social skills deficits and problems in peer relationships may be a significant problem for depressed children, but that perhaps certain types of parent-child interactions may be a result rather than a cause of childhood depression.

In a fairly recent study Leon, Kendall, and Garber (1980) have attempted to provide information regarding other correlates of childhood depression. In this study, data from 138 elementary school children and their parents was obtained in order to assess the presence of childhood depression and other characteristics that might relate to depressive features. From this group 21 children were selected who showed significantly elevated scores on the depression scale of the Personality Inventory for Children (PIC). Also selected were 21 children who displayed no evidence of depression on this measure. Other measures obtained on these children included the Conners Parent and Teacher Questionnaires (which tap a range of problem areas such as conduct problems, anxiety, learning problems, psychosomatic problems, etc.), the Kovacs and Beck Childhood Depression Inventory, The Peabody Picture Vocabulary Test, and the Cognitive Processes Inventory for Children (which is designed to assess attributions concerning the causes of events, expectations regarding the future, aspirations, etc.). A number of measures were found to be significantly related to childhood depression.

Children high in depression were found to display significantly more conduct problems, anxiety, impulsivity, hyperactivity, learning problems, psychosomatic problems, and tension than did nondepressed children. Teachers' reports suggested that depressed subjects showed more inattention and passivity than did comparison subjects. Also, depressed children were found to attribute positive events more often to external causes and negative events to internal causes than did nondepressed children. Although it is not certain

that children judged to be depressed, as a result of elevations on the PIC Depression Scale, are comparable to children meeting DSM-III criteria for depressive disorder, the results do suggest that depressive features may be related to a range of other problem behaviors that may cause difficulties for the child. It would also appear that the tendency for depressed children to make internal attributions for negative events and external attributions for positive events is quite consistent with the cognitive view of depression as proposed by Beck (1967), although further work in this area with children is warranted.

In one of the few investigations of biochemical correlates of childhood depression, Cytryn, McKnew, Logue, and Desai (1974) studied eight children age 6 to 12 diagnosed as cases of depression. The investigators assessed the level of norepinephrine (a neurotransmitter) and the levels of other urinary metabolites (vanillymandelic acid and 3-methyl-4-hydroxyphenylethyl glycol) and compared them with values obtained from 22 normal 10-year-old boys examined in an earlier study. The comparisons revealed lowered levels of norepinephrine and vanillymandelic acid in depressed subjects, suggesting the possibility of biochemical abnormality. Further, the deviations from normal values were more apparent in children with chronic depression than those displaying "masked" or acute depression. Although these results are suggestive, Cytryn and his colleagues note that the observed changes may simply reflect the lower activity level of hospitalized depressed children. Also the small sample employed makes it difficult to draw firm conclusions from the results of this particular study. Cantwell (1982) in reviewing this and the few other biochemical studies has summarized the present situation as follows:

> what little work has been done in the biology of major depressive disorder in childhood suggests that the clinical picture of a major depressive disorder in childhood analogous to that seen in adults selects a group of children who also differ in many of these biological parameters in the same way that

adults [with depression] differ from normals. (p. 74)

Further studies in this area, with controls for variables such as activity level, hospitalization, and larger samples are in order.

Prognosis

Given debate over the existence of childhood depression and the forms it may take, along with the fact that the disorder was largely ignored until recently, it is perhaps not surprising that little information is available regarding the long-term prognosis for depressed children. There is, however, some available data. For example, Poznanski, Krahenbuhl, and Zrull (1976) reevaluated 10 depressed children after an average time interval of 6½ years. The subjects in this study were among those originally described by Poznanski and Zrull (1970) in their study of overtly depressed children described earlier. At the time of reevaluation one-half of the children were still judged to be clinically depressed, and the authors reported that the behavior of these children closely resembled that of depressed adults. It was also observed that the aggressiveness originally seen in these children had decreased, but that most children had become more dependent in their behavior. Parental rejection and deprivation, which was found to be associated with depression in the earlier study, was also found to be correlated with continuing depression at the time of follow-up. An additional follow-up study of depressed children has been conducted by Kovacs et al. (1984). These investigators have found that for children diagnosed as having a major depressive disorder (using DSM-III criteria), the peak rate of remission is around 15 to 18 months after onset, with a maximal recovery rate being 92% a year and a half after diagnosis. They note that if the child does not recover by this time, recovery is not likely during the next year. Findings were also reported for children displaying adjustment disorder with depressive mood and dysthymic disorder (an additional category reflective of

depression that has not previously been used with children). Here it was noted that by 9 months after diagnosis 90% of children with adjustment disorders recovered, with the peak recovery interval being between 6 and 9 months. In contrast, the median time to recovery for those children with dysthymic disorder was more than 3½ years. It may be noted that the poor recovery rate for children meeting the criteria for dysthymic disorder is perhaps not surprising, as DSM-III criteria require evidence of symptoms for at least a year before a diagnosis can be made, almost guaranteeing a more chronic course. For both major depressive disorder and dysthymic disorder, early age of onset was predictive of a more protracted illness. Given these findings, further studies using DSM-III criteria for adjustment disorder (with depressed mood) and dysthymic disorder would seem warranted, as would additional studies designed to assess the prognosis for childhood depressive disorders.

Relationship to Suicidal Behavior

One especially troublesome aspect of child and adolescent depression is its relationship to suicidal behavior. Although suicide is thankfully relatively rare among prepubertal children, it does occur within this age group. At later ages it assumes more significant proportions. According to the National Center for Health Statistics (1977), successful suicide rates range from 1 per 100,000 persons for those 10 to 14 years of age to in excess of 7 per 100,000 in the 15- to 19-year age group. Indeed, at present, suicide is the third leading cause of death among adolescents (behind accidents and homicide), and it appears to be on the increase (Rosenn, 1982). Even though our knowledge of those variables that contribute to child and adolescent suicide is far from complete, and there are numerous misconceptions regarding suicide in childhood (see Table 6.13), it is indeed a significant problem.

That suicidal behavior is significantly re-

TABLE 6.13. TEN MISCONCEPTIONS ABOUT SUICIDAL BEHAVIOR IN CHILDHOOD.

1. Suicide under the age of six does not occur.
2. Suicidal behavior in latency is extremely rare.
3. Psychodynamically and developmentally, true depression is not possible in childhood.
4. Since children do not understand the irreversibility of death, they cannot actually be considered suicidal.
5. Suicide attempts in children are impulsive and are not the result of longstanding preoccupation.
6. Children are too cognitively and physically ineffective to implement a suicide plan successfully.
7. Most suicidal acts in childhood are merely manipulative and not dangerously destructive.
8. Since almost all children periodically make statements such as "If I don't get my way, I'll kill myself," almost all suicidal threats in youngsters need not be taken seriously.
9. Children don't have readily available means to kill themselves.
10. If a self-destructive effort is made by a child, it is almost always in response to a very recent, overwhelming precipitant.

Source: Rosenn (1982). © 1982 Plenum Press and reprinted by permission.

lated to depression is suggested by a number of studies. Carlson and Cantwell (1982), for example, have found children hospitalized for suicide attempts to obtain significantly higher scores on the Childhood Depression Inventory than children who had made attempts in the past. These investigators also documented a significant relationship between seriousness of suicidal ideation and depth of depression as rated by both clinician and child. Additionally, Crumley (1979) has found that for some 40 suicide attempters, the most common DSM-III psychiatric diagnosis was major affective disorder (in the absence of manic episodes). Such findings are quite consistent with the results of several earlier studies, reviewed by Pfeffer (1981), which have indicated a frequent history of depression during the months preceding childhood suicide attempts. Given that life stress has been implicated as a contributing factor in childhood depression, it is of interest to note that Cohen-Sandler, Berman, and King (1982) have found suicidal children to display increased levels of life stress, including disruptions in the family, losses, and separations.

Although there is evidence to link suicidal behaviors in childhood to depression, other factors have also been implicated as contributors. These include problematic family communication patterns, parental conflict, parental loss through divorce or separation, specific suicidal motivations (e.g., to make others feel guilty), the desire to avoid severe and unavoidable stress, and the presence of serious psychopathology, among others (Pfeffer, 1981).

A consideration of the treatment issues that must be dealt with in responding to a suicide attempt is beyond the scope of the present chapter (see Bassuk, Schoonover, & Gill, 1982, for an excellent coverage of such issues). However, it is clear that all such attempts should be considered seriously. Even though children sometimes appear to make attempts to elicit attention and to manipulate parents, our ability to accurately predict intent is often inadequate for distinguishing between the manipulative child and one who really wishes to die. Beyond this, there are cases where children may make what appear to be "manipulative" gestures that turn out successful because of the child underestimating the lethal nature of the attempt. Suicidal attempts and threats should always be taken seriously.

Suicidal children are generally felt to be in need of intensive therapy to deal with the crisis that surrounds the suicidal threat and to resolve the problems that have contributed to the situation. Approaches to treatment may include outpatient psychotherapy, drug treatments, and/or hospitalization if needed. That this treatment must include adequate follow-up is suggested by research findings that the maximum risk for successful suicide is some 2 years after an initial unsuccessful attempt (Pfeffer, 1981).

Treatment of Childhood Depression

At present there is little evidence regarding the most effective way to treat children and adolescents who display serious depression. Although some clinicians have suggested the value of individual, group, and family therapies, the effectiveness of these approaches with depressed children has not been studied, and the specific indications for such treatments have not been worked out (Pearce, 1977). Given that these approaches are used in the treatment of depressed children, research related to their effectiveness is essential.

There are some indications that drug therapies may be of value (Ambrosini and Puig-Antich, 1985). Here tricyclic antidepressants such as imipramine (Tofranil) and amitriptyline (Elavil) seem to produce the most positive results. Although most drug studies with depressed children are of an uncontrolled nature, there are findings to suggest that approximately 75% of children treated with these drugs respond favorably to treatment (Cantwell, 1982). Despite the potential usefulness of antidepressant medication, Kashani et al. (1981) note that there is a general consensus that when drugs are employed, they must be accompanied by attention to various aspects of the child's environment (e.g., family, school environment).

Regarding the potential usefulness of a multimethod approach, Cantwell (1982) has reported on a total of five studies with depressed adults that evaluated the combined effects of psychotherapy and tricyclic antidepressants. All of these showed a superiority of the combined approach over the use of either approach alone. Research designed to assess the additive effects of these approaches with children is clearly warranted.

Childhood Depression: Overview

In spite of considerable debate over the existence of childhood depression, there is increasing evidence that children can display mood disturbances and other behaviors commonly associated with a diagnosis of depression in adults. It has also been suggested by several workers in this area that the DSM-III diagnostic criteria for depressive disorder, although primarily intended for use with adults, may be quite adequate for diagnosing depression in children as well.

Although prevalence estimates vary widely as a result of investigators using differing criteria for diagnosing depression, it would appear that the disorder is somewhat rare in the general population (a figure of around 2% has been suggested). Figures for children displaying depressive *symptoms* are much higher. Available data from studies employing DSM-III criteria indicate that as many as 16% of child clinic outpatients and perhaps as many as 36% of clinic inpatients show evidence of depressive disorder.

The specific etiological factors related to childhood depression are unknown. Conceptual models of depression have suggested the importance of object loss, life stress, low rates of positive reinforcement, learned helplessness, maladaptive cognitive sets, and biological factors, but the applicability of these models to childhood depression is unclear. Descriptive studies with depressed children have implicated the role of family environment and have given rise to speculation on the role of genetic factors. There have also been studies that have provided data suggestive of a relationship between negative life changes and depression, as well as some findings suggesting the possible importance of maladaptive cognitions in childhood depression. Despite these preliminary findings, further investigation is needed before any conclusions are warranted.

There is not much information available about the most effective treatment for children displaying depression. The value of individual, group, and family treatment has been suggested, but there is little data on the effectiveness of these approaches. Depressed children may respond well to certain antidepressant medications, but data from additional, more well-controlled studies are needed to assess effectiveness and side effects associated with drug treatment.

SUMMARY

Over the years, several childhood behavior problems have been observed that appear less severe than pervasive developmental disorders and schizophrenia and do not seem related to organic impairment. These problems, currently grouped under the headings of anxiety, affective, and somatoform disorders within DSM-III, have traditionally been considered under the more general heading of neurotic disorders. Included here are childhood phobias, obsessions and compulsions, conversion reactions, and childhood depression, among others. There is some similarity among these disorders, because each is on the internalizing end of the internalizing-externalizing dimension of child psychopathology; in each case it is primarily the child rather than those in his or her environment that suffers most as a result of the condition. Although individuals of differing theoretical orientations might disagree as to the specific mechanisms involved, most clinicians concur that the child's family and social environment probably play an important role in the development of these disorders. Interacting with these variables may be constitutional factors such as dimensions of child temperament.

As the preceding sections of this chapter suggest, knowledge related to these disorders is sketchy. Most of the available literature is of the case study variety and is descriptive in nature; the absence of experimental studies and studies employing control groups is especially conspicuous. The reason for this lack of research is not entirely clear, but it is probably related to the fact that a majority of problems discussed in this chapter occur rather infrequently, or at least are infrequently observed by clinicians working in mental health settings. Moreover, the defining characteristics of these disorders are often not well delineated, making subject selection for research difficult.

It appears that the existing literature related to the conditions discussed here, while providing a basis for hypothesis generation, does not give sufficient grounds for many conclusions and generalizations. After surveying the available literature on phobias in childhood and examining the state of knowledge in this area Miller et al. (1974) chose to title their review "Phobias of Childhood in a Pre-Scientific Era." A look at the literature on childhood phobias appearing since that time suggests that a similar title would still be appropriate. The existing literature related to the other conditions discussed here suggests that they belong to that era as well.

SUGGESTED READINGS

Adams, P. L. (1973). *Obsessive children: A sociopsychiatric study*. New York: Brunner/Mazel. Extensive case histories and data concerning children diagnosed as obsessive compulsive.

Cantwell, D. P. (1982). Childhood depression: A review of current research. In B. Lahey & A. Kazdin (Eds.) *Advances in clinical child psychology* (Vol. 5). New York: Plenum. A detailed overview of current research in the area of childhood depression.

Hawton, K., & Osborn, M. (1984). Suicide and attempted suicide in children and adolescents. In B. Lahey & A. Kazdin (Eds.) *Advances in clinical child psychology* (Vol. 7). New York: Plenum. An excellent chapter that provides a detailed coverage of the literature related to childhood suicide.

Kessler, J. (1972). Neurosis in childhood. In B. Wolman (Ed.), *Manual of child psychopathology*. New York: McGraw-Hill. Good coverage of a psychodynamic view of childhood neurotic disorders.

Morris, R. J., & Kratochwill, T. R. (1983). *Treating children's fears and phobias: A behavioral approach*. New York: Pergamon Press. Probably the most comprehensive text dealing with childhood phobias to be published to date.

7 PSYCHOLOGICAL FACTORS AND PHYSICAL DISORDERS OF CHILDHOOD

The disorders to be considered in the present chapter differ from those discussed elsewhere in the text in that their symptoms are physical rather than psychological in nature. However, this does not imply that psychological factors are irrelevant to these conditions, as these factors may serve to maintain or worsen the symptoms of an existing illness or, under some circumstances, contribute to the development of the disorder. In other instances, psychological changes may *result from* rather than *contribute to* physical disorders, as in the case of certain chronic illnesses.

In the sections to follow we will focus on a range of physical problems of childhood (often considered under the headings of psychosomatic or psychophysiological disorders) by considering evidence regarding the contribution of psychosocial factors to the development, maintenance, and/or exacerbation of these conditions. This will be followed by a more general discussion of the impact of chronic illness on the child and family. First, however, it would seem necessary to consider the general concept of psychosomatic illness and the ways in which views of psychosomatic (psychophysiological) disorders have changed over the years in order to place our discussion of specific disorders in context.

PSYCHOLOGICAL FACTORS AFFECTING PHYSICAL CONDITION: A HISTORICAL PERSPECTIVE ON "PSYCHOSOMATIC DISORDERS"

Psychosomatic or psychophysiological disorders have traditionally been thought of as physical conditions in which psychological factors play a causal or at least contributory role. Unlike many conditions that are manifest in maladaptive behavior, and unlike conversion reactions, in which bodily functions are impaired in the absence of physical cause, psychophysiological disorders involve actual structural damage to the body or the existence of some pathophysiological process. The psychological factors presumed to play a role in the development of these disorders range from exposure to high levels of stress over prolonged periods of time (Selye, 1956, 1979), to unconscious conflicts (Alexander, 1950), to the experiencing of emotions, such as feelings of threat or hostility (Graham, Kabler, & Graham, 1962).

It has been proposed by some that the sort of psychological factors described here primarily affect individuals who are predisposed to develop physical problems of a specific nature. Historically, however, many clinicians have tended to focus primarily on the role of psychological variables, choosing to ignore the possible contributions of relevant biological factors. Indeed, many authors have treated these disorders as though they were strictly psychogenic in nature.

A variety of conditions have been characterized as psychosomatic disorders. Conditions frequently included under this heading are hypertension, peptic ulcers, ulcerative colitis, anorexia nervosa, and bronchial asthma. Also included by some writers (Siegel, 1983; Werry, 1979) are enuresis and encopresis, as these conditions present with physical symptoms that are sometimes assumed to result from psychological factors. To illustrate the range of disorders associated with this label, it can be noted that in DSM-II (American Psychiatric Association, 1968) psychophysiological skin disorder, muscular-skeletal disorder, respiratory disorder, cardiovascular disorder, hemic and lymphatic disorder, gastrointestinal disorder, genitourinary disorder, endocrine disorder, and psychophysiological disorders of the special senses were all included under the general heading of psychophysiological (psychosomatic) disorders. Some have even suggested that conditions such as cancer might be appropriately considered within this category, because there is at least some evidence that stress and other psychological factors may play a role in the development of malignant neoplasms (Greer & Morris, 1975; Jacobs & Charles, 1980), perhaps through the modification of immunological competence (Jemmott & Locke, 1984).

Despite the popularity of the concept of psychosomatic disorder and the range of conditions considered under this heading, there has been considerable debate as to which disorders should be considered within this category and indeed whether such a category is warranted at all.

As can be seen from the preceding discussion, the belief that there are physical disorders that are distinguishable from others on the basis of having a psychogenic etiology (or that are significantly influenced by psycho-

logical factors) has traditionally characterized the thinking of many clinicians. Nevertheless, views regarding the *concept* of psychosomatic disorders are changing in the direction of a more holistic perspective (Lipowski, 1984). This more recent conceptualization of the interrelationships between psychological and biological factors in health and illness is perhaps most clearly reflected in the following statements by Lipowski (1977) who has suggested

> The concept of psychogenesis of organic disease . . . is no longer tenable and has given way to the multicausality of all disease. . . . It is consonant with this doctrine to view social and psychological factors as co-determiners of health and illness and thus as elements having etiological and modifying significance in human morbidity. The relative contribution of these factors varies from disease to disease, from person to person, and from one episode of the same disease in the same person to another episode. . . . If the foregoing arguments are accepted then it becomes clear that to distinguish a class of disorders as "psychosomatic disorders" and to propound generalizations about "psychosomatic" patients is misleading and redundant. Concepts of single causes and of unilinear causal sequences, for example, from psyche to soma and vice versa are simplistic and obsolete. (p. 234)

Thus, Lipowski and those who would agree with him argue against considering *any* specific group of disorders as psychosomatic (or psychophysiological, or whatever else one might wish to call them to infer psychogenic causality). Further, they would argue against the dualistic approach often taken by investigators who consider psychological and physiological variables separately in the search for etiological factors related to specific disorders. They contend that all disorders, whether traditionally considered psychosomatic or not, involve the interplay of biological and psychosocial factors and that to focus on one to the exclusion of the other is to ignore information essential to an understanding of these conditions.

These views are generally reflected in the DSM-III classification system. DSM-III no longer includes psychophysiologic disorders as a diagnostic category but rather the category psychological factors affecting physical condition (see Table 7.1). This category is not for making a "diagnosis" per se but is intended as a more general category for use in those cases where there is evidence that some physical condition is initiated, maintained, or exacerbated by psychological factors (Looney, Lipp, & Spitzer, 1978). This approach is consistent with the position taken by Lipowski (1977, 1984), in that it is based on the assumption that the role of psychological factors is not limited to some restricted group of psychosomatic disorders but that such factors contribute in different ways to a broad range of physical conditions.

These more recent views notwithstanding, many clinicians and researchers have traditionally assumed that psychosocial factors are of greater significance in some disorders than in others. And, as a result, more attention has been focused on the possible role of psychological contributors to these specific disorders. In this chapter we will focus on several physical conditions of childhood that have sometimes been considered as psychosomatic in nature and presumed to be influenced, at least to some degree, by psychological and social variables. Included here are childhood asthma, anorexia nervosa, ulcerative colitis, enuresis, and encopresis. Although psychosocial variables have also been linked to certain other physical disorders of childhood, the conditions considered here seem to be the ones best represented in the clinical and research literature.

CHILDHOOD ASTHMA

Background

Asthma affects somewhere between 2 and 4% of the child population (Graham, Rutter, Yule, & Pless, 1967; Melamed & Johnson, 1981). Although asthma can occur among adults as well as children, approximately 60% of all asthmatics are below the age of 17 (Alexander, 1980), indicating that it is primarily a disorder of children and adolescents. Among this group it appears to occur more often among boys than girls, the sex ratio being approximately 2:1 (Jones, 1976).

The specific etiology of asthma is unknown. Clemow, King, and Brantly (1984) note that in excess of 300 etiological hypotheses have been proposed to account for the disorder. They suggest that currently the most popular view is that the development and subsequent manifestations of asthma result from a complex interaction of immunological, neurological, and psychological factors. The fact that asthma appears to run in families (Jones, 1976) has also implicated the role of genetic factors, causing some to suggest that asthma involves the inheritance of a respiratory system that may be overly responsive to a variety of stimuli, environmental and/or psychological (Purcell, Weiss, & Hahn, 1972; Ratner & Silberman, 1953). It should be pointed out that this is not at all inconsistent with views emphasizing immunological and neurological variables, as these may be influenced by genetic factors. Although such views are plausible, the specific etiological factors involved in the development of childhood asthma have yet to be documented.

Description

The disorder is characterized by severe difficulties in breathing, manifested in coughing, sneezing, and shortness of breath, which

TABLE 7.1. DIAGNOSTIC CRITERIA FOR PSYCHOLOGICAL FACTORS AFFECTING PHYSICAL CONDITION (DSM-III).

A. Psychologically meaningful environmental stimuli are temporally related to the initiation or exacerbation of a physical condition (recorded on Axis III).
B. The physical condition has either demonstrable organic pathology (e.g., rheumatoid arthritis) or a known pathophysiological process (e.g., migraine headache, vomiting).
C. The condition is not due to a somatoform disorder.

Source: American Psychiatric Association (1980). © 1980 American Psychiatric Association and reprinted by permission.

results from a narrowing of the air passages, usually due to increased mucus secretion or excessive swelling of the trachea and bronchi. These symptoms can occur intermittently or be of a more chronic nature. It is generally assumed that asthma *attacks* can result from a variety of factors including infection, exposure to allergens of various types (pollen, dust, animal hair), and psychological stress. Rees (1964), however, found that in many instances these factors interact to produce symptoms. In a study of precipitants of asthma attacks, Rees found that attacks resulted from allergens alone in only 5% of his sample of asthmatic children, from infection alone in 21%, from psychological factors alone in another 21%, but from a combination of these factors in an additional 53%. This suggests that in many cases asthma attacks result from a combination of factors rather than from either biological and psychological factors acting in isolation. For an excellent description of the nature of the problems faced by an asthmatic child and his parents see Figure 7.1.

Prognosis

The prognosis of asthma is generally favorable, in that symptoms often improve substantially during or after adolescence. In this regard Clemow, King, & Brantley (1984) cite findings indicating that as many as 75% of child cases tend to remit by the end of adolescence. The seriousness of the disorder in some cases, however, is suggested by the fatality

FIGURE 7.1. The Experience of Childhood Asthma

The early-onset asthma patient and his or her family face some very severe hardships. These youngsters tend to grow up watching the other children play from the livingroom side of the front window. Most have poor self-concepts. Often both academic and social development suffer greatly because of the amount of time lost from school and the restricted and specialized contacts with agemates. They face both peers and adults who are variously indulgent, or lacking in understanding their difficulties. Often these children react with shame and embarrassment, and/or demandingness to the extreme. At home their asthma may become the sole focus around which all family activities and concerns come to revolve. Their parents may feel responsible, guilty, and helpless; and at other times resentful and angry. Certainly, an asthma sufferer can learn to manipulate others with the disorder, or use it to avoid unpleasant activities or situations. It is also often difficult for the patient to sort out clearly what he or she really can do, from what is accomplished in the face of asthma. Many maladaptive and inappropriate behavior patterns can develop, as patient and family struggle with the ravages of this disorder. Such patterns can severely cripple family life and retard the social and psychological development of the child. Often, the undesirable behavior patterns affect the course of the disorder substantially. Asthma is, of course, potentially life threatening, and many patients have experienced bouts of *status asthmaticus*, which on occasion may have brought them close to death. Such experiences often generate enduring anxiety responses which can manifest themselves in fears of death, hospitals and treatment. Some patients develop conditioned fear responses, which can begin at even the first signs of wheezing. The frantic, worried behavior of parents and those treating the patient can exacerbate the young patient's fear.

Source: Alexander (1980). © 1980 Plenum Publishing Co. and reprinted with permission.

rate, which has been estimated at 1.5 per 1,000 cases per year (Purcell et al., 1972).

Research

Investigations of Asthmatic Subgroups

It has been observed that when asthmatic children are removed from their home for purposes of residential treatment some continue to display considerable difficulty, whereas others show a spontaneous remission of their symptoms. Observations of these differences have led some investigators to conclude that there are specific subgroups of asthmatic children and to hypothesize that different factors contribute to the development and/or maintenance of symptoms in these groups. A number of studies highlighting the differences between these groups have been conducted. It has been found, for example, that these groups differ in terms of the stimuli that tend to precipitate asthma attacks. In one study comparing children who did and did not show remission, Purcell (1963) found that attacks were precipitated more often by emotions (anger, depression, anxiety) in the rapidly remitting group and by infection and specific allergens in nonremitting children. Additionally, assessment of child-rearing attitudes has suggested that parents of children displaying symptom remission tended to be more authoritarian and to display more punitive attitudes than parents of nonremitting children (Purcell, Bernstein, & Bukantz, 1961; Purcell et al., 1972).

Some support for the subgroup hypothesis also comes from a study by Block, Jennings, Harvey, and Simpson (1964). An Allergic Potential Scale (APS) was used to separate asthmatic children into groups that did and did not display a somatic predisposition to allergic reactions; the severity of asthmatic symptoms was similar for the entire sample. It was reasoned that psychological factors may play a more prominent role in groups of children displaying asthmatic symptoms in the absence of a predisposition to allergic reactions than in children showing clear evidence of biolog-

ical predisposition (e.g., family history of allergic reactions, specific environmental allergens). This view was backed by the findings of Block et al. (1964) When the two groups were compared, low APS children tended to display more evidence of psychological problems, and the parents of these children tended to be more rejecting and depriving than were parents of children who showed more of a biological predisposition toward allergic reaction. Also, more negative interaction patterns were found to exist between mothers and fathers of the low APS children as compared to the high APS group.

Although the results of these studies suggest that there may be subgroups of asthmatic children who vary in the degree to which psychological factors contribute to their disorder, several comments are in order. First, any differences between subgroups are likely to be relative rather than absolute. That is, whereas psychological factors may play a more prominent role (than biological or environmental factors) in precipitating asthma attacks in selected children, asthma precipitated by psychosocial stimuli almost always coexists with asthma precipitated by physically defined stimuli and vice versa (Purcell, 1975). This position is quite consistent with the findings of Rees (1964), cited earlier, which indicated that although asthma attacks can result from environmental, biological, or psychological factors, they most often result from multiple causes. A second point is that if psychological factors are indeed of greater relevance in some asthmatic children, they most likely serve to influence the frequency, severity, and/or duration of symptoms rather than being related to the development of the disorder per se. Indeed, there is no evidence to suggest that psychological factors play a causal role in the initial development of the disorder (Alexander, 1980).

Taken together these findings suggest that psychosocial factors *can* play a prominant role in influencing asthmatic symptomology and that there may be some children who are influenced by these factors to a greater degree than others.

Family Variables in
Childhood Asthma

The fact that asthmatic children react differently to being removed from the home provides reason to hypothesize that psychological and family variables may play an important role in at least some cases of childhood asthma. This does not, however, prove that family variables are involved, as admission to residential treatment removes the child not only from potential family conflicts and perhaps other stressors, but also from the physical environment in which his or her asthmatic symptoms were displayed; thus the child is not only removed from the family environment but also from allergens and other possible nonpsychological precipitants of asthma attacks. To adequately examine the role of family variables it is necessary to separate the effects of the physical and the family environment. One way this may be accomplished is by allowing the asthmatic child to live at home while at the same time separating the child and his parents. Exactly this approach was taken by Purcell et al. (1969). Their investigation involved an extensive study of 25 chronically asthmatic children under several experimental conditions. Based on the results of interviews designed to determine the degree to which emotional responses served to precipitate asthma attacks, it was predicted that 13 of these children would improve (predicted positive group) when separated from their families but that 12 would not (predicted negative group). These predictions were based on the notion that in cases where emotional responses were reported to precipitate asthma attacks, psychological and family variables might play a more prominent role.

The study itself was divided into four phases, each lasting 2 weeks. During each segment a variety of dependent measures were obtained, including expiratory peak flow rate, amount of medication required, daily history of asthma, and the results of a daily clinical exam. The first phase of the study (qualification) simply involved a 2-week period in which the investigators interviewed the families of asthmatic children to determine whether they met the criteria for inclusion in the study. At this stage parents were simply told that the investigators were conducting a study of asthmatic children and that their help was requested in obtaining preliminary information; there was no mention of separation at this time. During the second (preseparation) phase, the possibility of separation was discussed and agreed upon in the 25 cases. Stage three involved a 2-week separation of the parents and child; the parents moved out of the home, and the child was cared for by a substitute parent. This allowed for maximum alteration of the child's family environment while holding essential elements of the physical environment constant. The final stage involved a reunion of the parents and child and an additional 2-week observation period during which dependent measures were obtained.

Comparisons were made between dependent measures obtained during the 2-week separation period and those obtained during other phases of the study when the children and parents were together. Data from the predicted positive group showed significant changes in the improved direction on all measures obtained during the period of separation (see Figure 7.2). Essentially no differences were observed as a result of separation in the predicted negative group where social and psychological factors were presumed to play a less important role in eliciting asthma attacks. Asthmatic children who improved during their families' absence were found to return to their initial level of severity upon reunion with their family.

These results strongly suggest that the occurrence of asthmatic symptoms in certain children is related to family variables. These results, however, provide little information regarding the precise nature of those family variables that contribute to the child's symptoms or the way in which they influence the manifestations of the disorder.

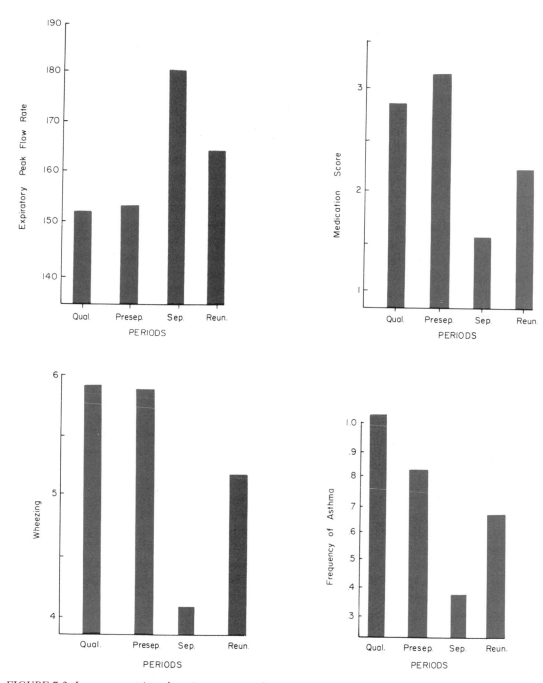

FIGURE 7.2. Improvement in asthmatic symptoms when children whose asthma was reportedly precipitated by emotional responses were separated from their parents. Source: Adapted from Purcell et al. (1969). © 1969 American Psychosomatic Society and reprinted by permission.

Emotional States and Childhood Asthma

It was noted earlier that children who display spontaneous remission of asthmatic symptoms upon admission to residential treatment often report that emotions are common precipitants of asthma attacks. In the just-cited study (Purcell et al., 1969) it was also found that the reporting of emotions as frequent elicitors of asthma attacks was predictive of children's response to separation from their families. These results, along with clinical observations, led Purcell (1975) to focus more specifically on the role of emotional states and their relationship to asthmatic symptoms.

In an attempt to relate the role of such emotional states to the findings obtained in earlier studies suggesting the importance of family variables, Purcell wrote that "these latter variables may be thought of as distal antecedents since it is certainly quite plausible that they affect the type, frequency, intensity, and duration of emotional states" (p. 121). Thus, family variables may influence the occurrence and severity of asthmatic symptoms because of their role in producing specific emotional states.

To examine the contribution of emotional states in greater detail, Purcell (1975) conducted a study designed specifically to investigate the relationship between asthmatic symptoms and emotional responses. This study recorded expiratory peak flow rates on asthmatic children at 20-minute intervals and also consistently monitored vocal behaviors during the 20 minutes prior to the obtaining of each measure by use of a miniature radio transmitter worn by the child. Output from the transmitter was recorded on tape at a recording station located some distance from the child. Vocal behaviors were rated with regard to categories of emotion (such as anger or excitement) as well as for type of vocal behavior (such as laughing or yelling). In this manner it was possible to determine whether symptoms, indexed by peak flow rates, were related to emotional responses and vocal behaviors.

Although the predicted relationship between peak flow rates and these categories of responding were not obtained on all subjects, the results did suggest that in some instances exacerbation of symptoms was related to emotional responses as well as to vocal behaviors. It might be noted that in this study it was not possible to adequately assess the relationship between specific emotions and peak flow rates as a function of subgroup. It is possible that specific emotional responses may play a greater role in eliciting symptoms in some groups of asthmatic children than in others, a notion certainly suggested by the results of the studies cited earlier, which indicated that asthmatic children could be distinguished based on the results of an interview designed to determine precipitants of asthma attacks. Further studies such as the one described here, for example, designed to determine the relationship between emotional states and symptom severity, conducted with groups of asthmatic children categorized into subgroups based on Allergic Potential Scale Scores (Block et al., 1964) would seem to be in order.

Further Studies of Psychological Factors in Childhood Asthma

Numerous other studies designed to relate psychological and social factors to childhood asthma have been conducted, but unfortunately many of them have been designed simply to investigate differences between asthmatic and nonasthmatic children or differences between parents of asthmatic and nonasthmatic children, without considering the possibility that subgroups of asthmatic children might exist. As might be expected, the results of these studies have been contradictory. For example, Neuhaus (1958) found significant differences between asthmatic children and normal controls on measures of neuroticism and other psychological variables assessed by means of projective tests. It was also found, however, that children with cardiac problems differed from normals and that there were no significant differences between children with asthma and those with cardiac disorders. These results provide little information concerning psychological variables specific to childhood asthma. In a large scale study that sampled all subjects in a given population, Graham, et al. (1967) found no differences between 76 asthmatic children and a group of normals in terms of frequency of psychopathology. On the other hand, Miller and Baruch (1950) found differences between children with allergic disorders (some of which were asthmatic) and normal controls on variables such as the expression of hostility. Other studies comparing heterogeneous groups of asthmatic children with controls have contributed to these inconclusive findings.

Although there is some evidence (such as that cited above) that family-related variables or other stressors that elicit emotional responses may influence asthmatic symptomatology, there is no evidence for any specific personality pattern that may contribute to childhood asthma. Nor is there evidence that the majority of asthmatic children display any form of major psychopathology. Indeed, when studies have found asthmatic children to differ from normals on adjustment-related variables, asthmatic children have generally not been found to differ from children with other chronic illnesses (when such children have also been studied). These findings seem to suggest that the adjustment problems displayed by some asthmatic children are the result of experiencing a chronic illness, rather than being related to either the development or manifestations of asthma (Alexander, 1980).

Panic-Fear and Childhood Asthma

Rather than trying to document the effects of psychological variables on asthma, one somewhat different line of research that has yielded interesting findings relates to the so-called panic-fear dimension in asthmatic patients. This research has examined the specific attitudes of asthmatics toward their symptoms and the relationship between these attitudes and the course of their illness.

The panic-fear dimension has to do with the degree to which asthmatics display subjective feelings of being scared, panicky, worried, or frightened in response to asthma attacks. Those high on this panic-fear dimension seem to be generally fearful, emotionally labile individuals who tend to feel helpless and give up easily in the face of difficulty (Dirks, Kinsman, Horton, Fross, & Jones, 1978; Dirks, Nelson, Jones, & Kinsman, 1977). Research has suggested a relationship between asthmatics' status on the panic-fear dimension and variables such as the degree to which they adhere to medication regimens, the degree to which they require medication for asthmatic symptoms, and length of hospitalization. Panic reactions experienced by those high on this dimensions can also interfere with cooperation in emergency treatment and cause unnecessary psychological discomfort (Alexander, 1980; Dahlem, Kinsman, & Horton, 1977). Dirks et al. (1977) also found panic-fear to be related to the amount of medication prescribed upon discharge from residential treatment. Although these studies tell us little about the role of psychological factors in the development of asthma or in eliciting asthma attacks, they suggest that the attitudes and coping strategy adopted by the asthmatic patient in response to his or her symptoms has an effect on the course of the illness.

Treatment

Treatment of childhood asthma is usually largely medical in nature, often involving the use of corticosteroid drugs, along with hospitalization in severe cases. A variety of psychotherapeutic approaches have also been employed, including psychoanalytically oriented psychotherapy, group therapy, family therapy, hypnosis, and behavior modification. Although it might be assumed that psychological approaches to treatment may be of value, there are few well-controlled studies to support this view. Preliminary data suggest that procedures such as systematic desensitization and relaxation training may have some effects (Lukeman, 1975). Unfortunately, while such procedures have often been found to bring about a *statistically significant* degree of improvement in pulmonary function, changes have often not been large enough to be *clinically* meaningful. It should be noted, however, that many of the studies investigating these treatment procedures have been conducted with severely ill asthmatic inpatients, and it may be that these treatment methods are capable of bringing about more meaningful changes in children showing less severe manifestations of the disorder (Alexander, 1980).

Although the effectiveness of behavioral treatments in bringing about clinically meaningful changes in lung function has been questioned (at least in severe cases of asthma), there are suggestions from clinical reports that behavioral procedures such as desensitization may be quite useful in dealing with the panic-fear responses displayed by many asthmatic children. Indeed, Alexander (1980) has suggested that deconditioning therapies would appear to be the treatment of choice for asthma panic responses. There is clearly a need for well-controlled research to document this assertion.

Based on the material reviewed earlier concerning the existence of subgroups of asthmatic children who vary in terms of the relative contributions of psychological factors, one might predict that psychological approaches to treatment would be more effective with certain asthmatic children. Studies of the effectiveness of psychotherapy and behavioral procedures with relevant subgroups of asthmatic children are clearly warranted. Giving the findings by Purcell et al. (1969) on the effects of manipulating family variables on asthmatic symptomatology, studies assessing the effectiveness of family-based treatments on subgroups of asthmatic children would also appear to be especially worthwhile.

ANOREXIA NERVOSA

Background

In 1694 Richard Morton published what was probably the first paper pertaining to anorexia nervosa. He described a girl of 18 and a boy of 16 who developed a condition he referred to as "nervous atrophy." These two cases were characterized primarily by excessive weight loss; the individuals were described as looking like "skeletons clad only in skin." (For an additional graphic account of the disorder see Figure 7.3.) Other early accounts of the disorder were authored by Gull (1868) and Lasegue (1874). Gull, who was the first to use the term *anorexia nervosa*, noted that the disorder occurred primarily in young women and was often accompanied by other symptoms in addition to weight loss, such as amenorrhea (cessation of menstruation), constipation, lowered pulse and respiration, and hyperactivity in the absence of organic disease. Both Gull and Lasegue believed the disorder to be of psychogenic origin. Since these early case studies much has been written concerning this disorder, although its etiology remains unknown, and no one method of treatment has been found to be uniformly effective (Bemis, 1978). In the sections to follow we will present information concerning the general nature of this disorder and review relevant research findings in this area.

Description and Diagnosis

Although clinicians differ in their views as to what characteristics must be present before a diagnosis of anorexia nervosa should be made, a number of features have been associated with the disorder. A major feature is an active refusal to eat, accompanied by severe weight loss. Lesser, Ashenden, Debuskey, and Eisenberg (1970) noted that this refusal to eat may occur in the context of a good appetite, with actual loss of appetite occurring only secondary to the resulting starvation. Therefore, the term *anorexia nervosa* (mean-

FIGURE 7.3. Anorexia Nervosa

At fifteen Alma had been healthy and well-developed, had menstruated at age twelve, was five feet six inches tall, and weighed one hundred twenty pounds. At that time her mother urged her to change to a school with higher academic standing, a change she resisted; her father suggested that she should watch her weight, an idea that she took up with great eagerness, and she began a rigid diet. She lost rapidly and her menses ceased. That she could be thin gave her a sense of pride, power, and accomplishment. She also began a frantic exercise program, would swim by the mile, play tennis for hours or do calisthenics to the point of exhaustion. Whatever low point her weight reached, Alma feared that she might become "too fat" if she regained as little as an ounce. There were many efforts to make her gain weight, which she would lose immediately, and she had been below seventy pounds most of the time. There was also a marked change in her character and behavior. Formerly sweet, obedient, and considerate, she became more and more demanding, obstinate, irritable, and arrogant. There was constant arguing, not only about what she should eat but about all other activities as well.

When she came for consultation she looked like a walking skeleton, scantily dressed in shorts and a halter, with her legs sticking out like broomsticks, every rib showing, and her shoulder blades standing up like little wings. Her mother mentioned, "When I put my arms around her I feel nothing but bones, like a frightened little bird." Alma's arms and legs were covered with soft hair, her complexion had a yellowish tint, and her dry hair hung down in strings. Most striking was the face — hollow like that of a shriveled-up old woman with a wasting disease, sunken eyes, a sharply pointed nose on which the juncture between bone and cartilage was visible. When she spoke or smiled — and she was quite cheerful — one could see every movement of the muscles around her mouth and eyes, like an animated anatomical representation of the skull. Alma insisted that she looked fine and that there was nothing wrong with her being so skinny. "I enjoy having this disease and I want it. I cannot convince myself that I am sick and that there is anything from which I have to recover."

Source: Bruch (1978). © Harvard University Press and reprinted by permission.

ing "nervous loss of appetite") may be somewhat of a misnomer (Halmi, 1985).

In addition to refusing food, anorexics have often been reported to induce vomiting or to consume large quantities of laxatives to rid the body of food that is consumed, thus further contributing to their emaciation. Sometimes individuals with this disorder also show evidence of bulimia (which can also occur apart from anorexia nervosa), where they engage in binge eating episodes, only to later purge themselves by using laxatives and/or vomiting. Individuals with anorexia nervosa frequently appear unconcerned about their weight loss and physical status. They often actively deny illness, appear to enjoy losing weight, and apparently have a desired body image of extreme thinness. Many if not most anorexics also display a severely distorted body image, which results in their perceiving themselves as overweight even while in a state of starvation.

Among girls who have begun to menstruate, amenorrhea may occur. This cessation of menstruation usually precedes or coincides with the onset of weight loss, although it sometimes follows it. It is generally agreed that the amenorrhea is not secondary to starvation, as was previously thought, but due to factors associated with the disorder itself.

In spite of their self-induced starvation, anorexics often show evidence of overactivity. Dally (1969) points out that starvation itself often brings about restlessness and overactive behavior. It has been suggested, however, that some anorexic individuals increase their activity level deliberately to encourage weight loss. Leon and Dinklage (1983) have noted that in very conscientious and compulsive individuals this exercise may take the form of complex rituals that represent rigorous attempts to burn up calories. These authors suggest that such exercises may also serve to distract the anorexic individual from the severe hunger pangs that may be experienced.

Anorexics may also display a variety of characteristics that result largely from their emaciation: hypotension, slow pulse rate, changes in skin, hair, nails, and teeth, swelling of the lower extremities, and so forth. Bodily resistance to disease may be lowered, and the patient may develop other complications, which not infrequently result in death.

While this disorder is thought by many to result from psychological factors, it must be distinguished from disorders of organic etiology, such as Simmond's disease, which may be characterized by some of the same symptoms. Factors to consider in the differential diagnosis of these two disorders were presented by Farquarson and Hyland (1983), and general reviews of the features of anorexia nervosa have been presented by Bemis (1978), Bruch (1973), Johnson, Thompson, and Schwartz (1984), and Leon and Dinklage (1983). Specific diagnostic criteria for anorexia nervosa as presented in DSM-III (American Psychiatric Association, 1980) are provided in Table 7.2.

Prevalence

As with other disorders, prevalence figures vary markedly depending on the criteria used in diagnosis. Thus, while Crisp, Palmer, and

TABLE 7.2. DSM-III DIAGNOSTIC CRITERIA
FOR ANOREXIA NERVOSA.

A. Intense fear of becoming obese, which does not diminish as weight loss progresses.
B. Disturbance of body image, e.g., claiming to "feel fat" even when emaciated.
C. Weight loss of at least 25% of original body weight or, if under 18 years of age, weight loss from original body weight plus projected weight gain expected from growth charts may be combined to make the 25%.
D. Refusal to maintain body weight over a minimal normal weight for age and height.
E. No known physical illness that would account for the weight loss.

Source: American Psychiatric Association (1980). © 1980 American Psychiatric Association and reprinted by permission.

Kalucy (1976) suggest that the disorder occurs to some degree in 1 out of every 200 girls of school age and about twice as often in girls between 16 and 18, Halmi (1974) estimates that the prevalence is only .24 to .61 cases per 100,000, thus making it quite rare in the general population. Regardless of specific prevalence figures, there seems to be a general consensus that the incidence of the disorder is on the rise (Bemis, 1978; Halmi, 1985; Maloney & Klykylo, 1983) and is increasing at a rate that is more rapid than can be explained by a simple increased awareness of symptoms of the disorder (Leon & Dinklage, 1983).

The disorder occurs in both males and females, although it is much less common in males; results of a number of surveys suggest that only about 5 to 15% of all cases are males (Bemis, 1978).

Age of Onset

Anorexia nervosa appears to be largely a disorder of adolescence and young adulthood, with most cases developing before age 25 (Halmi, 1974; 1985). Onset has often been observed to coincide with puberty, although it can continue into adulthood as a chronic disorder. Kay and Leigh (1954) noted that of 38 cases studied, 76% had become anorexic before age 26, with the onset in most cases being between 16 and 20. Halmi (1974), in a study of 94 patients, found 8% to have had an onset before 10 years, 31% between 10 and 15 years, 47% between 16 and 25 years, and only 13% after age 25. Although follow-up data will be considered later, it is of interest to note that prognosis seems especially poor when onset is prior to age 14 (Dally, 1969).

Etiological Factors

At present the etiology of anorexia nervosa is unknown, although there has been much theorizing about causal factors. Etiological views have implicated the role of psychodynamic factors, learning, and family variables, as well as genetic and other biological factors.

Psychodynamic Perspectives

An overview of various psychodynamic views of anorexia nervosa has been presented by Dally (1969). One early analytic theory proposed by Walker, Kaufman, and Deutch (1940) is focused on the symbolic meaning of eating. Dally, referring to this position as the "oral impregnation theory," explains that "in terms of this theory, the main symptoms of anorexia nervosa represent an elaboration and acting out in the somatic sphere of pregnancy fantasies." From this point of view anorexia nervosa represents "the wish to be impregnated through the mouth which results at times in compulsive eating, and at other times in guilt and consequent rejection of food." (p. 10) Dally adds that

> many writers have come to believe that food and eating are equated with unconscious pregnancy wishes, and that anorexia nervosa represents a rejection of these. Disgust and fear of eating, amenorrhea, and the bloated sensations following eating are seen as symbolic of pregnancy and its rejection. (p. 10)

Other dynamically oriented writers have focused on the reluctance of these patients to grow up, arguing that not eating is seen by anorexic patients as one way of avoiding adult responsibilities. Others, noting that onset is often associated with puberty, observe that a failure to eat may prevent the development of sexual characteristics, thus allowing the patient to avoid having to deal with threatening sexual conflicts created by the occurrence of puberty (Dally, 1969). Still other psychodynamically oriented workers such as Bruch (see Bruch 1973, 1978) have focused on the importance of ego deficits resulting from disturbed mother-child interactions, which contribute to a disturbed body image and a perceived lack of control over one's body that may lead to anorexic behavior under stressful conditions. Although such views have received a fair amount of attention from dynamically oriented clinicians, empirical support is generally lacking, and certain of these views (especially those involving such things as notions of "oral impregnation" fantasies) must be viewed as speculative at best.

Behavioral Perspectives

Leon (1979) has focused on cognitive-behavioral processes in the development of anorexia nervosa. Here she suggests that food aversions in such patients may develop through a conditioning process whereby eating is paired with excessively negative thoughts and images related to weight gain. As this relationship between negative thoughts and food consumption is strengthened over time the person is assumed to develop strong feelings of revulsion and disgust toward food and eating. Continued food avoidance is seen as being reinforced by the sense of control (and the reduction of anxiety) that the anorexic feels as a result of being able to control his or her life through food restriction. Some very preliminary support for this point of view has been provided by Leon, Bemis, and Lucas (cited in Leon & Dinklage, 1983), who have found anorexic patients to report that dieting and weight loss contributed to a greater sense of control over their lives and that previously enjoyable foods had become unpleasant to taste. Although this view seems quite plausible, much more research will be necessary before one can draw any firm conclusions regarding its adequacy as an explanation of the severe food avoidance seen in this disorder.

The role of environmental factors in anorexia nervosa has been emphasized by Ullmann and Krasner (1975). According to these authors, it is useful to conceptualize noneating (food avoidant) behavior as an operant response that is reinforced by environmental consequences. Here it is assumed that regardless of how the disorder originally develops, it is maintained at least in part by the reactions of other individuals to this behavior. However, although social reinforcers may be of importance in *maintaining* food refusal, this explanation does not account for the origins of the disorder. It also does not account for other characteristics of anorexia nervosa that are unlikely to be under the control of environmental factors, such as early amenorrhea. Nevertheless, this point of view does serve to highlight the importance of attending to the role of factors in the patient's environment that can contribute to this disorder.

Family Perspectives

The role of family variables in anorexia nervosa has been implicated by Minuchin, Rosman, and Baker (1978). These authors have taken a "systems"-oriented position in arguing that the symptoms of this disorder cannot be viewed apart from the role they play within the family. It is assumed that family variables contribute to the child's problem and that the child's problem in turn plays a significant role in maintaining family homeostasis. Based on their clinical experiences, Minuchin et al. have suggested that there are several family characteristics that contribute to "psychosomatic" disorders. These include (a) enmeshment (where family roles become blurred, and family members are so close that individuality is lost), (b) overprotectiveness (where the concern of the family over the safety of its members becomes so great that it interferes with the development of autonomy, activities, and interests outside the family), (c) rigidity (where there is a strong commitment

on the part of family members to maintain the status quo within the family), and (d) lack of conflict resolution (where family conflicts are denied or where attempts to deal with conflict are avoided). Minuchin and his colleagues also noted that psychosomatic families are frequently characterized by a high level of conflict between the parents, which cannot be resolved because of faulty patterns of interaction. The symptoms of the anorexic child are seen as playing a regulatory role in the family system by keeping parental conflict from getting out of control and threatening the stability of the family. To illustrate, Minuchin et al. (1978) note that the symptomatic child may play a role in a variety of ways:

> Parents unable to deal with each other directly unite in protective concern for their sick child, avoiding conflict by protective detouring. Or a marital conflict is transformed into a parental conflict over the patient and her management. In some families, the child is recruited to taking sides by the parents, or intrudes herself as a mediator or helper. The effectiveness of the symptom bearer in regulating the internal stability of the family reinforces both the continuation of the symptom and the peculiar aspects of the family organization in which it is emerged. (p. 32)

Although the validity of this family-oriented view has not been sufficiently tested, there are research findings quite consistent with this view (see Crisp, Harding, & McGuinness, 1974; Kalucy, Crisp, & Harding, 1977), suggesting that there is increased parental conflict in the families of anorexics and that increased weight gain on the part of the child may result in increased problems displayed by parents.

Biological Perspectives

As anorexia nervosa presents a severe threat to physical health, it is not surprising that attention has also been given to the possible role of biological factors in the development of this disorder. Although no physical cause of this disorder has been found, some tentative support for the role of genetic factors is suggested by the fact that monozygotic twins appear to show much higher concordance rates for the disorder than do dizygotic twins. In this regard, Garfinkel and Garner (1982), in an overview of reports presenting twin data, found a concordance rate slightly in excess of 50% for MZ twin pairs, as compared to a rate of only 11% for DZ twins. The total number of twin pairs upon which these findings were based ($n = 36$), however, make it necessary to view these findings with caution. In addition to genetic factors, other authors have suggested that anorexia nervosa may be associated with hypothalamic dysfunction (Gold, Pottash, Sweeny, Martin, & Davies, 1980; Lupton, Simon, Barry, & Klawans, 1976) and that abnormalities of neurotransmitter regulation may contribute to the disorder (Halmi, Owen, Lasley, & Stokes, 1983). Although it is often difficult to determine that biological indices obtained from anorexic patients are reflective of causal factors rather than simply the result of a changed physiological state due to starvation, research into the possible role of biological factors as contributors to this disorder is becoming increasingly popular.

The Role of Precipitating Factors

It is logically difficult to argue that events preceding the onset of a disorder play a causal role in the development of that disorder. It is nevertheless interesting that many authors have suggested that anorexia nervosa is often precipitated by certain events. Dally (1969), in his sample of 140 anorexics, found that events such as death or serious illness in the family, personal illness, failure at work or school, or events capable of provoking sexual conflicts frequently preceded onset. Kay and Leigh (1954) estimated that two-thirds of their patients experienced major changes in interpersonal relationships prior to onset. Other studies likewise record a high frequency of precipitating events (Halmi, 1974; Morgan

& Russell, 1975; Piazza, Piazza, & Rollins, 1980). These observations, although tentative, are consistent with a growing body of research that suggests that life stress (life changes) may contribute to the development of physical and psychological problems of various types (Holmes & Masuda, 1974; Johnson, 1982; Johnson & Sarason, 1985).

Other precipitating factors are also posited. Many writers note that the onset of anorexia nervosa is often preceded by a marked concern with being overweight and attempts at dieting. In some instances dieting and excessive concern over weight are reported to have resulted from derogatory statements made by others concerning the person's weight. Others are reported to have begun dieting because of the belief that food affected their complexion, and still others because they wished to prevent their breasts and hips from developing (Dally, 1969). Lesser et al. (1960) noted that in 40% of their sample, weight loss began with self-enforced diets initiated because of self-consciousness. Similarly, Kay and Leigh (1954) found that in 42% of their cases onset was preceded by voluntary dieting, often because the patients "abhorred fat people or the idea of becoming fat" (p. 412).

Anorexia Nervosa: Relationship to Bulimia

Bulimia refers to frequent episodes of uncontrolled binge eating during which the person may consume extremely large quantities of high-caloric foods within a short period of time. The person usually sees the binge eating as abnormal, yet may be unable to control it and may be fearful of not being able to stop eating once he or she begins. In such cases there may be an alternation between binge eating and the use of fasting, self-induced vomiting, and laxative use, all of which are designed to rid the body of the large amount of food eaten. This syndrome has been referred to by a number of labels including "bulimarexia," "bulimia nervosa," "dysorexia," "purge-vomiters," and the "abnormal weight control syndrome" (Maloney & Klykylo, 1983;

Schleisier-Stropp, 1984). Although this syndrome is thought to occur as a separate disorder (Schleisier-Stropp, 1984), bulimic eating is also often seen as part of anorexia nervosa. Casper, Eckert, Halmi, Goldberg, and Davis (1980), for example, found that of 105 patients hospitalized for anorexia nervosa, 47% showed evidence of bulimia. Garfinkel, Moldofsky and Garner (1980) have also found approximately the same percentage of anorexics to engage in a combination of binge eating and purge-vomiting.

A number of researchers have become interested in the similarities and dissimilarities between anorexic patients who attempt to lose weight through fasting (restricters) and those whose fasting alternates with bulimia, vomiting, or laxative use. In one study, designed to look at these differences, Casper et al. (1980) found that whereas restricters showed more introversion and little obvious distress, anorexics with bulimia displayed higher levels of anxiety, depression, guilt, and bodily complaints. These findings led the authors to conclude that patients with bulimia should be viewed as forming a distinct subgroup among individuals with anorexia nervosa. Data obtained by Strober (1981) has suggested that anorexics with bulimia tend to display more evidence of affective disturbance and alcohol use as well as childhood histories of behavior disorders. In Strober's study the parents of the patients with bulimia showed higher levels of marital discord, more psychiatric and physical health problems, and were rated as being more distant from their children than were parents of nonbulimic anorexics. Finally, anorexic patients with bulimia were found to report more stressful life changes prior to the onset of their illness than did nonbulimic patients. Additional data, provided by Strober (1984), has also provided support for the relationship between bulimic episodes and life stress. Here adolescents with bulimia showed significantly higher levels of life stress than restricters. Although the overall level of life stress was lower, restricters also showed higher levels of life stress in the year preceding the onset of their disorder than did normals.

Although additional work is needed to further delineate the differences between various subgroups of patients with anorexia nervosa, it would appear that the distinction between anorexics with and without bulimia is an important one. Particularly important is the fact that binge-vomiters often show high levels of depression and that suicide is reported to be the most common cause of death in this disorder (Crisp, 1982; Maloney & Klykylo, 1983).

Follow-Up Data

Although some individuals completely recover from anorexia nervosa, it often takes the form of a chronic disorder characterized by periodic remissions and relapses. The seriousness of the disorder is suggested by the fact that anywhere from 3 to 21% of anorexics die from the disorder or complications associated with it (Leon & Dinklage, 1983).

Findings concerning the long-term outlook for persons diagnosed as having anorexia nervosa have been somewhat variable. For example, Kay (1953) found that follow-up of 38 cases after 2 to 19 years showed that 45% displayed menstrual irregularities, 65% displayed disturbances of appetite, and 50% displayed low or fluctuating weight. In a later publication that summarized the results of their studies and others, Kay and Shapiro (1965) wrote

> The onset of anorexia nervosa augurs a considerable period of ill health. The illness itself seldom lasts for less than two or three years, and in about one quarter of the cases persists much longer; these patients remain more or less permanently undernourished, and eccentric in their attitudes toward food. Many others make a partial recovery but remain thin, or else fluctuate in weight. In the majority of cases seen by psychiatrists neurotic symptoms or personality defects are found at follow up and social and sexual adjustment are impaired. (p. 117)

Dally and Sargent (1966) indicated that after 3 to 5 years, 72% of their patients ($n = 30$) were considered *improved* in terms of weight gain and social adjustment. Morgan and Russell (1975), however, found that after a follow-up of approximately 4 years, only 40% of their sample had made what was judged to be a good recovery in terms of both physical and psychological adjustment. Garfinkel, Moldofsky, and Garner (1977), in a follow-up study of some 42 treated cases, found that after approximately 32 months, 50% were doing well, whereas 19% were judged to display a poor outcome. A history of bulimia and purge-vomiting was seen as a predictor of poorer prognosis. Despite these somewhat variable results, findings from follow-up, studies, taken together, suggest an overall *recovery* rate of somewhere between 40 and 60% (Crisp et al., 1977). Although some anorexics make a good recovery and others improve to varying degrees, these findings, considered along with the high mortality rate, suggest a relatively poor prognosis.

Treatment

Approaches to the treatment of anorexia nervosa have been reviewed by Bemis (1978), Van Buskirk (1977), and Maloney and Klykylo (1983). Some treatments focus exclusively on hospitalization, bed rest, and high-caloric diets, often combined with drug treatments of some sort (such as insulin, chlorpromazine, or antidepressant medications), and intubation (tube feeding) if necessary (Dally & Sargent, 1966; Williams, 1958). Maloney and Farrell (1980) have also developed a procedure whereby essential nutrients are infused intravenously to sustain anorexic patients who cannot eat.

Some have employed operant conditioning procedures (Agras & Werne, 1977; Garfinkel, Kline, & Stancer, 1973), making activities, privileges, and social reinforcers of various types contingent on eating or weight gain. Other clinicians, viewing some cases of ano-

rexia nervosa as resulting from weight phobia, have used systematic desensitization (Hallstein, 1965; Schnurer, Rubin, & Roy, 1973), and still others have affirmed the usefulness of other forms of individual, group, or family therapy (Barcai, 1971; Bruch, 1973, 1977; Minuchin, et al. 1978; Piazza et al., 1980; Piazza, Carni, Kelly, & Plante, 1983; Rosman, Minuchin, Baker, & Liebman, 1977).

Van Buskirk (1977) has cogently argued that treatment effectiveness must be viewed from a dual perspective: effectiveness in bringing about rapid weight gain, to remove the patient from immediate physiological danger, and effectiveness in maintaining the obtained changes over time. Although methodological difficulties inherent in many studies make it difficult to draw firm conclusions about the effectiveness of treatment, the approach that reportedly produces the largest weight gain per week is one that employs operant conditioning combined with drug treatment and a high-caloric diet. There is some reason to believe, however, that such a treatment in and of itself is not entirely adequate, in that gains tend not to be maintained unless some form of outpatient treatment is also employed. Actually this is quite predictible, because, one would not assume that being reinforced for eating in the hospital or being given drugs and high caloric foods would in any way modify those psychological or environmental factors that may have led to the development of anorexia in the first place. Van Buskirk (1977) observed that from the point of view of maintenance, family and supportive therapies appear to be the most useful, with the value of involving the patient's family in this outpatient treatment being especially apparent. Although more adequately controlled research is necessary to document effectiveness, preliminary reports by Minuchin et al. (1978) that their family-oriented approach with anorexic families is effective in as many as 86% of the cases suggests that family therapy may indeed by quite useful in the overall management of the anorexic patient. In sum, there appears to be at least general research support for a multimodal approach to the treatment of patients with this disorder.

CHILDHOOD ULCERATIVE COLITIS

Description

Ulcerative colitis is an often life-threatening disorder of the gastrointestinal system that occurs in both children and adults, with children and adolescents accounting for 10 to 40% of the cases (Kirsner, 1970; Werry, 1979b). The disorder is characterized by inflammation and ulceration of the colon and rectum; associated symptoms include diarrhea, passing of blood and mucus in the stools, loss of appetite, weight loss, and anemia. Abdominal pains, vomiting, and fecal incontinence are present in some cases. In older children, retardation of pubertal development can also occur (Daum, Boley, & Cohen, 1973).

In some instances ulcerative colitis develops gradually and takes a form of a chronic disorder, characterized by periodic mild attacks. In other cases it is more acute in nature, appearing suddenly and, in some cases, resulting in death in a matter of months unless surgical intervention occurs. It is manifested in this acute fulminating form in approximately 10% of the cases (Werry, 1979b). The overall mortality rate is in the range of .4 to .8 per 100,000 (Morowitz & Kirsner, 1969). Moreover, persons displaying this disorder also show a higher incidence of cancer of the bowel in later life. Karlin and Kirsner (1978) noted that in unselected cases about 5% later develop carcinoma. This is considerably more likely if the disorder has been present over 10 years and if the onset occurred during childhood.

Incidence

Bargen (1969) reported that the annual incidence for this disorder is somewhere between .45 and 2 per 100,000, although figures as high as 6.5 per 100,000 have been reported. The disorder is somewhat more common in females than in males, the sex ratio being about 1.5:1. American Jews are 4 to 5 times more likely to show this disorder than members of other racial groups, and caucasians are affected more often than are blacks (Daum et al., 1973).

Etiology

Views Emphasizing Biological Factors

Gastroenterologists and other nonpsychiatric physicians have generally tended to focus on physical causes of the disorder. Allergies, bacterial and viral infections, nutritional deficiencies, and immunological phenomena are among the factors that have been implicated in this regard (Daum et al., 1973). Werry (1979b) has noted that the discovery of anticolonic antibodies in individuals displaying ulcerative colitis has resulted in an increase in the popularity of immunological views, although the causal role of such antibodies has not yet been conclusively demonstrated.

Views Emphasizing Psychosocial Factors

Although often conceding that biological factors may be involved, many mental health professionals have argued that psychosocial variables are of primary importance in the development of this disorder. As a result, ulcerative colitis has often been considered as a classic example of a psychosomatic or psychophysiological disorder (Finch, 1980).

Support for the psychogenic view has come largely from purely descriptive studies, which have focused on characteristics of children with ulcerative colitis and their families. The results of these largely poorly controlled studies have led numerous investigators to draw a variety of conclusions regarding the dynamics involved in the disorder and the psychological and family variables related to it. For example, Chapman and Loeb (1955) suggested that "these are very depressed children who are struggling with anger and guilt toward very hostile and rejecting mothers," and go on to suggest that "the bloody diarrhea of these children serves both a physiologic and symbolic function in expressing the angry impulses which they feel, but with which they cannot deal consciously" (p. 22). Likewise, Finch and Hess (1962) reported that the following features were descriptive of family relationships in their sample of 17 ulcerative colitis cases:

> In all cases, the parental relationships revealed a passive, ineffectual father and an aggressive dominating mother. Superficially the fathers might initially appear effectual and the mothers occasionally feminine, but closer scrutiny proved otherwise. A striking observation by the social worker was the inability of all these parents to express overt hostility in an appropriate manner. The relationships between the fathers and sons seemed to show little emotional involvement, while on the contrary, that between the fathers and daughters was deep and best described as seductive. In all cases, the mothers appeared dominating and controlling toward the patient regardless of sex. The child was the object of hostility and rejection by the mother, but this was rarely overtly expressed. The mother reacted consciously in the opposite fashion, demonstrating extreme, though superficial, concern for the child and demanding complete submissiveness from him. These mothers also had a tendency toward seductiveness for their sons. (pp. 249–250)

As for the personality characteristics of the patients themselves, the authors had this to say:

> The personality characteristics of these children are strongly reminiscent of those ascribed to adult ulcerative colitis patients. The children exhibited obsessive-compulsive character traits and were constricted, defensive, guilty, and covertly hostile. All had problems including sexual identification. They tended to behave in a pseudomature fashion, but their inability to handle stress revealed the "brittle" nature of their personality structure. Under even minor stress the precarious defensive operations gave

way to infantile responses, and the child would be thrown back upon denial as the primary defense. Primative fantasies involving the patient's body (sexual and digestive organs) were common and there was repeated concern that the body was somehow faulty or defective. Perhaps related to this deeply ingrained self-concept was the constant need on the part of these children to achieve, and to think and behave "like a good child." (p. 253)

Although many authors, pointing to the findings of descriptive studies, have stressed the importance of psychological and family variables in cases of ulcerative colitis, the results of such studies must be viewed with caution, for most of them have been plagued with serious methodological difficulties. They have most often been retrospective in nature, have employed small samples, and have often been conducted without including control groups of normals or other children displaying problems of a physical nature (Feldman, Cantor, Soll, & Bachrach, 1967; Werry, 1979b). More well-controlled studies (of which there are few) have generally failed to provide data confirming the role of psychological factors. For example, Feldman et al. (1967), in a detailed study comparing 34 ulcerative colitis patients with normal controls and gastroenterology patients without colitis, found essentially no differences between ulcerative colitis patients and controls. In another study by Fishler and Fogel (1973) it was discovered that when patients with ulcerative colitis were compared with control children who had other chronic diseases, no differences were found, even though children with colitis did show above-average IQ and some deviations from a normative sample in terms of selected Rorschach variables. Clinical observations notwithstanding, better controlled studies fail to support a psychogenic explanation for the development of ulcerative colitis, and there is little evidence that psychological factors contribute significantly to the manifestations of the disorder once acquired (although few studies have provided data specifically related to this issue). Although more research in this area is needed, at this time it seems that there is little reason to view ulcerative colitis as a disorder primarily influenced by psychological factors. Based on the available literature, one wonders whether the psychodynamics sometimes attributed to children with ulcerative colitis are not more in the eye of the beholder than actually reflective of the children themselves.

Despite the generally unsupportive findings just described, it would seem that one potentially worthwhile area for future investigation would involve the long-term impact of this chronic illness on the child and, in particular, its influence on the personality and social development of children who are affected.

Treatment

Treatment of ulcerative colitis is largely medical in nature. In severe cases removal of the colon may be necessary. In other instances management of the disorder is accomplished by use of corticosteroid drugs, among others (Daum et al., 1973). Over 40% of all patients with this disorder will ultimately require surgery (Werry, 1979b).

No well-controlled studies have investigated the efficacy of psychotherapy with children displaying this disorder. Perhaps the most useful role of psychotherapeutic procedures may be in helping the child deal with this distressing and often embarrassing condition and in attempting to minimize any problematic psychological effects that may result from the condition itself.

ENURESIS

Description and Diagnosis

Although most children become toilet trained without any difficulty (see Chapter 3), the acquisition of bladder control is sometimes delayed. In these cases, children continue to wet their clothing or bed after an age where micturitional control is normally attained. The term *enuresis* is used to refer to such cases

of delayed control. Criteria used by DSM-III in making a diagnosis of enuresis are as follows:

A. Repeated involuntary voiding of urine by day or night.
B. At least two such events per month for children between the ages of 5 and 6, and at least one event per month for older children.
C. Not due to physical disorder, such as diabetes or a seizure disorder. (American Psychiatric Association, 1980, p. 80)

Thus, enuresis may be of the diurnal (day-wetting) or the nocturnal (bed-wetting) variety or may represent a combination of the two. Diurnal enuresis unaccompanied by bed-wetting is quite unusual (Berg, 1979), but approximately 30 percent of children with nocturnal enuresis also display diurnal wetting as well (Forsythe & Redmond, 1974). Nocturnal enuresis is the most common, and much of the published literature deals with this type. It has been suggested that enuresis can also be considered as either primary or secondary; primary referring to cases in which the child never developed control over urination, secondary to cases in which the problem developed after the child initially became continent for a period of time. A further distinction is that some children wet the bed continuously and others only intermittently (Lovibond & Coote, 1970).

Prevalence

The problem of enuresis appears to be a common one. Baller (1975) estimated that there are probably more than 3 million enuretics in the United States, if children between the ages of 3½ and 17 are considered. Christopherson and Rapoff (1983) suggest that as many as 20% of all 5-year-olds and as many as 10% of all 10-year-old children still wet the bed. Although enuresis appears to decline with increasing age, some individuals continue to display this problem into adulthood (Cushing & Baller, 1976). Thorne (1944), for example, found that of Army recruits examined during

World War II, approximately 2.5% had not achieved full bladder control. This figure is similar to the results of more recent investigations.

Etiology

Delayed control over micturition can result from a variety of factors, and several theoretical views regarding etiology have been proposed. These views can be grouped under two general headings: psychodynamic and physiological/behavioral (Lovibond & Coote, 1970). Psychodynamic theories are of several types, but all tend to view enuresis as merely symptomatic of some more basic emotional disturbance. Researchers have examined the relationship between enuresis and indices of child psychopathology to test the adequacy of such formulations. Considering the results of a number of these investigations, Werry (1972) concluded

> There is a significant but small and infrequent correlation between enuresis and psychopathology. This means that the majority of enuretics in the population (as opposed to those seen by physicians and especially those referred to psychiatrists) do not have any apparent emotional disturbance. Furthermore, in those that do, the causal relationship to the symptom of enuresis is unestablished and in some cases, at least, it may be coincidental or secondary to the enuresis. (p. 150)

In a more recent review of the findings related to enuresis and the presence of psychological problems, Schaefer (1979) also found the bulk of the evidence to suggest that the majority of enuretic children show no evidence of emotional disturbance. Such findings provide little support for a psychodynamic point of view.

Physiological/behavioral theories view enuresis as resulting from a failure to develop adequate cortical control over subcortical mechanisms and/or as a habit deficiency. Some stress primarily the role of learning, seeing enuresis as a failure to develop necessary conditioned reflexes. It is not too difficult to believe that both factors may be involved, because learning experiences may contribute to the development of cortical control. The precise relationship between these variables is unclear, however. Although a maturational explanation may be adequate to account for cases of primary enuresis where the child has never been dry (as are explanations that emphasize inadequate learning), it is a less compelling explanation for the behavior of children displaying secondary enuresis, for these children are assumed to have displayed evidence of bladder control before the onset of enuresis. The initial development of continence suggests that children with secondary enuresis have in fact matured sufficiently to have control over micturition and that learned control over reflexive voiding has occurred. How, then, might one account for secondary or acquired enuresis? In a consideration of this problem, Yates (1970), citing an explanation originally put forth by Young (1965), wrote

> If we regard achievement of continence as involving the acquisition of a complex skill, then it follows that high drive levels would interfere with the initial acquisition of the skill and further, where the skill had been achieved, but only tenuously, the subsequent introduction of high drive levels would tend to break down the skill. From this [it may be] deduced that coercive training on the part of the parents, with punishment or threats for wetting, would make it more difficult for the child to acquire control and would produce a reversion to wetting (the acquired enuresis cases) in children who had reached a stage of apparent control, but where over-learning was minimal. (p. 85)

This formulation accounts for both primary and secondary enuresis from a learning-maturational point of view, by assuming that high levels of stress can interfere with the development and maintenance of micturitional control. Although the plausibility of this explanation is in its favor, further research is needed to adequately assess its validity.

In addition to psychodynamic and behavioral views, a third type of explanation high-lights depth of sleep as an important factor in nocturnal enuresis. This view presumes that the bed-wetting child may be in such a deep state of sleep that he or she fails to respond to the sensations produced by a full bladder. Support for this argument has been provided by some EEG studies that indicate that bed-wetting often occurs during deep sleep, although it can occur during other stages as well. But other studies have failed to demonstrate that enuretics are less easily awakened than normals (Werry, 1979b). Still other experiments suggest that deep sleep may occur after, rather than during, the time in which wetting occurs (Faschingbauer, 1975). These contradictory findings call for further research.

Regarding etiology, some have also pointed to the possible role of hereditary factors in enuresis, noting that parents of enuretic children often report having had problems with incontinence during childhood themselves (Shaffer, 1985). For example, several studies report that around 40 to 50% of enuretic children have a family history of bed-wetting. According to Baller (1975), estimates range from as low as 17% to as high as 66%. The fact that a sizable proportion of relatives of enuretics are reported to have been enuretic is not necessarily evidence for the role of hereditary factors; this relationship could just as easily be explained in terms of environmental influences.

Treatment

Treatment of the enuretic child has taken many forms, some of them valuable, some ineffective, and others potentially harmful. Less effective approaches have included special diets, injections of various substances (sterile water, paraffin), bladder and rectal irrigations, making the child sleep on his or her back, on a hard mattress, not allowing the child to sleep on his or her back, and so forth (Yates, 1970).

More reasonable forms of treatment in use today involve certain drugs, conditioning ap-

proaches, and more traditional forms of psychotherapy. In a review of studies of the treatment of enuresis, Faschingbauer (1975) discovered that in excess of 500 drugs have been used in treatment. Studies of the effectiveness of these drugs have produced varying results. At present the most popular drug treatment involves the use of imipramine (Tofranil), a tricyclic antidepressant. Although negative results can be found in the literature (Blackman, Benton, & Cove, 1965), the results of several controlled studies support this drug's effectiveness in suppressing enuresis (Kardash, Hillman, & Werry, 1968; Miller, Champelli, & Dinello, 1968; Shaffer, Costello, & Hill, 1968), although relapse is common when the drug is discontinued (Doleys, 1983).

The most popular of the behavioral approaches to treatment is the bell and pad procedure, originally developed by Mowrer and Mowrer (1938). Briefly, this procedure involves having the child sleep on a urine-sensitive pad that is constructed so that when the child urinates a circuit is completed, activating a buzzer or bell that is loud enough to awaken the child. The child is then required to get up and urinate in the toilet. The rationale behind this treatment is that if the bell, which results in awakening, can be paired over a period of trials with the sensations associated with a distended bladder, the child (as a result of classical conditioning) will come to awaken and inhibit urination in response to these stimuli. Training with this procedure usually continues until the child is dry for at least 2 weeks. (Lovibond & Coote, 1970, Schaefer, 1979, and Yates, 1970, provide a more detailed discussion of this approach.)

This method has been found to be quite successful in the elimination of bed-wetting. Faschingbauer (1975) remarks that if one considers the large number of studies using the bell and pad, involving more than 1,300 children, the "cure" rate is in excess of 73%, with about 89% benefiting at least to some degree. One problem with this procedure has been the relapse rate, estimated in some cases to be as high as 30%. There is some evidence, however, that this can be reduced if, after initial training, children are gradually required to increase their fluid intake just prior to going to bed. O'Leary and Wilson (1975) suggested that this provides the child with an opportunity for overlearning and may also possibly result in an increase in bladder capacity. Whatever the specific factors involved, this does seem to bring about a significant reduction in relapse rate (Young & Morgan, 1972).

A different behavioral approach, Retention Control Training, has been used by Paschalis, Kimmell, and Kimmell (1972), who have dealt with enuresis by reinforcing children for inhibiting urination for longer and longer periods of time. Although there is research to suggest that this approach is less effective than the bell and pad with bed-wetting, it does seem to be useful with daytime enuresis (Doleys, 1983). Johnson and Thompson (1974) have also reported the successful use of modeling in the treatment enuresis. Finally, an additional behavioral approach, Dry Bed Training, has been developed by Azrin, Sneed, and Foxx (1974). This is a very intense training program that includes a number of elements such as nighttime awakening, positive practice in appropriate toileting behaviors (e.g., getting up from bed, going to the toilet, pulling pants down, sitting on toilet for several seconds, pulling pants up, and returning to bed), retention control training (as described above), positive reinforcement for appropriate toileting behaviors, and cleanliness training (e.g., removing wet sheets, cleaning mattress, making bed, showering after accidents, dressing self in fresh night clothes etc.). These behavioral procedures are combined in an intensive treatment package that is usually carried out in 1 evening, with follow-up and maintenance procedures being employed until the child has 14 dry nights. In a review of research regarding the effectiveness of this approach, Christopherson and Rapoff (1983) have cited studies suggesting that the approach is superior to both retention control training and the urine alarm.

Some data concerning the effectiveness of traditional psychotherapy with enuretic children has been provided by the results of a study conducted by DeLeon and Mandell (1966). In this study 5- to 14-year-old children were assigned to a bell and pad conditioning treatment, a psychotherapy condition, or a control condition. Percentage improvement figures for these three groups were 86.3, 18.2, and 11.1%, respectively; results that cast doubt on the value of psychotherapy and support the conditioning treatment. A thorough overview of behavioral treatments of enuresis has been provided by Doleys (1983).

ENCOPRESIS

Description and Diagnosis

The term *encopresis* usually refers to difficulty in controlling defecation after the age of 3 or 4 years. By this age approximately 70% of normal children have achieved bowel control, and it may be assumed that continued soiling after age 4 represents a deviation from a normal developmental sequence. The specific criteria for the diagnosis of encopresis presented in DSM-III (American Psychiatric Association, 1980) are

A. Repeated voluntary or involuntary passage of feces of normal or near-normal consistency into places not appropriate for that purpose in the individual's own sociocultural setting.
B. At least one such event a month after the age of 4.
C. Not due to a physical disorder such as aganglionic megacolon. (p. 82)

Anthony (1957) has described encopresis as being of two varieties: continuous or discontinuous. Continuous encopresis refers to cases where the child has never developed bowel control, discontinuous to cases where the child initially developed bowel control but subsequently became incontinent. (The reader will note the close similarity between these types and primary and secondary enuresis, which were discussed earlier.) Anthony hypothesized that the continuous type results from a lack of or very lax toilet training, whereas the discontinuous type, on the other hand, derives from very rigid and coercive training by the parent. Thus, toilet training that is either too rigid or too lax is thought to result in encopresis. Although it is commonly assumed that encopretic children of the continuous type simply require the appropriate training, it has been suggested that the child displaying encopresis of the discontinuous type is more seriously disturbed and more in need of prolonged intensive therapy (Young & Goldsmith, 1972). However, there currently seems to be little evidence that these two groups of children actually respond differently to specific treatments or differ in degree of psychopathology.

Prevalence

As encopresis seems to decline with age, prevalence figures vary depending on the age of the children considered in any particular study. In a review of a number of studies presenting prevalence data, however, Doleys (1983) has cited figures a high as 8.1% for 3-year-olds and as low as 1% for children in the 10- to 12-year range.

Physical Factors and Soiling

As the DSM-III guidelines emphasize, the term *encopresis* is used for cases where a specific organic etiology is not discernible. When assessing the case of a child who has not developed bowel control within the normal age range, it is important to rule out organic involvement; lack of bowel control can be related to a host of physical factors, such as defects of the spinal canal, inflammation of the spinal cord, and other injury or disease. One condition in particular that should be ruled out is Hirschsprungs disease, which is characterized by an absence of ganglionic cells in the rectum and large intestine (Wright, 1973), a disease that can be fatal if left untreated. Physical examination of the child without bowel control is also necessary for other reasons. In some instances encopretic

children display what has been referred to as psychogenic megacolon, in which the child's colon and rectum become impacted with large amounts of fecal material. Here, the child may adapt to the sensations associated with fullness in the rectum and lose normal bowel tone, becoming unaware of the need to defecate and soiling himself as feces are gradually forced out through the dilated anus. In such cases, dealing with the condition medically may be necessary prior to undertaking any other form of intervention procedure.

Etiology

Theoretical views regarding the etiology of encopresis have not been well formulated, although individuals from both psychoanalytic and more behavioral orientation have proposed explanations. Doley's (1983) overview of analytic views indicates that most theorists postulate encopresis to be a sign or symptom of underlying conflict. Doleys writes

> These underlying conflicts may be in a form of lack of parental love, guilt value of feces, separation anxiety, fear of loss of feces, pregnancy wishes, aggression against a hostile world, response to familial dysfunction, and dramatic separation from the mother between oral and anal stages of psychosexual development. (p. 212)

He notes that the struggle for power between the parent and child, which may result during the course of toilet training, has also been suggested to be of etiological significance. In general, there is relatively little research bearing on the relationship between unconscious conflicts and encopresis. Nor is there much data suggesting that encopretic children, taken together, display psychological difficulties to any greater degree that do nonencopretic children.

On the behavioral side, the focus is typically on lack of appropriate training in those cases where bowel control has never been attained and either on reinforcers in the environment that maintain soiling or avoidance learning (associated with painful defecation) leading to retention (and subsequently encopresis) in the case of encopretics who have previously shown evidence of bowel control (Doleys, 1983). It might also be noted that a learning-maturational point of view similar to that discussed earlier with regard to enuresis may also be of value in understanding the development of encopresis. That is, we may assume that the learning of appropriate eliminative behavior is a complex skill requiring a level of cortical maturation sufficient for the inhibition of powerful eliminative reflexes, as well as learning to use bodily sensations as cues to engage in activities leading to appropriate toileting. As has been suggested in the case of enuresis, an approach to toilet training that is stressful for the child might make it more difficult for the child to initially develop bowel control and make it more likely that loss of control will occur in periods of later stress. It may also be the case that some children are simply delayed in the development of cortical control sufficient to inhibit inappropriate defecation.

Treatment

Clinicians of a psychodynamic pursuasion, tending to view encopresis (particularly the discontinuous type) as symptomatic of underlying disorder, have often used individual psychotherapy in the treatment of this disorder. Although certain of these studies have reported good remission rates, it is not clear whether these improvement rates are significantly higher than those occurring in the absence of treatment (Doleys, 1983).

A number of case studies suggest that behavioral approaches can be effective in the treatment of encopresis. These approaches have usually involved the application of operant procedures, which either positively reinforce the child for sitting on the toilet and for appropriate defecation or provide mild punishment for soiling, with extinction being accomplished by removing reinforcers that typically follow soiling. Sometimes a combination of these procedures is employed. In some instances such procedures are supple-

mented by the use of suppositories to stimulate bowel movements that can then be rewarded. For a highly successful example of such an approach, see Wright (1975). It must be noted that although there are a range of reports that support the usefulness of operant procedures in the treatment of encopresis, the bulk of these have been of an uncontrolled nature. More systematic and well-controlled studies designed to investigate these approaches and determine the most essential elements for successful treatment are clearly needed. (For an excellent presentation of factors to consider in the clinical treatment of encopresis, see Christopherson and Rapoff, 1983.)

CHRONIC ILLNESS IN CHILDHOOD

In the preceding sections our discussion has been focused on the role of psychosocial factors as they impact on physical illness (i.e., the extent to which such factors are important in the original development or in the subsequent manifestations of various physical conditions). It is also likely that the stress associated with certain physical illnesses, especially chronic ones, can in some instances contribute significantly to the development of psychological and family problems. The stressors resulting from chronic medical conditions can be illustrated by a brief overview of three such disorders: juvenile diabetes, chronic renal disease, and childhood cancer.

Juvenile Diabetes

Juvenile diabetes is an endocrine disorder of childhood that occurs in approximately .1% of the child and adolescent population (Mattsson, 1972). This hereditary disorder is characterized by insufficient insulin production by the pancreas, making it impossible for the body to utilize glucose (sugar) necessary for maintaining essential bodily functions. The disorder usually presents with symptoms such as weight loss, excessive thirst, frequent urination, fatigue, and abnormal blood sugar levels. If left undiagnosed, the child may become comatose and require emergency medical care. As there is no "cure" for this disorder, it requires life-long medical management designed to maintain the appropriate insulin levels necessary to keep the disorder under control.

The sources of stress in juvenile diabetes are multiple. First, unlike the more common type of diabetes seen in adults (which can often be dealt with through dietary management), children with juvenile-onset diabetes must adhere to a strict medical regimen to maintain control over their illness. This usually involves injections of insulin at least once per day and sometimes more often. There are also dietary restrictions that make it necessary for the child to keep track of what is eaten and that preclude eating many foods the child may wish to eat. To make certain that their dosage of insulin matches their body's need (which may vary depending on many factors such as exercise, diet, overall physical health, and perhaps stress level), they must monitor glucose levels (and other variables) through testing their urine several times per day to avoid excessively high levels of blood sugar, due to too little insulin (hyperglycemia) or abnormally low levels of blood sugar (hypoglycemia) due to too much insulin. Thus, it is necessary for the child to be constantly vigilant to his or her medical needs so as to avoid unpredictable, and sometimes embarrassing, hypoglycemic states or insulin reactions. In some case, often referred to as "brittle" diabetics, control over diabetic symptoms may be especially difficult even with careful medical management. As the child gets older the realization that the disorder is incurable and that this constant monitoring of the illness will be necessary for the duration of his or her life can also be a significant source of stress. An additional issue relates to the fact that juvenile-onset diabetes can result in a range of significant complications. Although these may not be experienced until many years after the onset of the disease, they are significant in that they may result in blindness, kidney failure, cardiac problems, and serious circulatory difficulties, among other problems. As a result of such complications, life span may be shortened and/or the quality of later life seriously impaired. Even though these complications may not occur in childhood, the prospects of experiencing them may become a significant source of concern as the child or adolescent begins to develop an awareness of the realities of the disease.

It must be noted that it is not only the child who is stressed by juvenile diabetes. In the very young child, it is the parent who must take primary responsibility for the medical management of the illness, who must deal with distress experienced by the child when insulin injections are given, and who must deal with the child's questions and emotional reactions as he or she learns of the problems that will have to be faced. Further, parents who were aware of the possibility of having a diabetic child prior to conception may display significant levels of guilt over having a child who must experience such an illness. Indeed, the disorder represents a significant source of stress that must be dealt with by the entire family.

Johnson (1980), in providing a comprehensive review of the literature regarding psychosocial variables and juvenile diabetes, has noted that most studies have focused on the role of psychological variables in the development or later manifestations of diabetes. In this regard the condition could have just as well been considered in the preceding section, as there is *some* evidence that variables such as stress may contribute to diabetic instability (the contribution of such variables to the etiology of the disorder is much less clear, however). Finding few studies designed to investigate the impact of this disorder, Johnson concluded that we know relatively little about how children and families actually adjust to diabetes, the nature of those variables that relate to successful coping, or effective ways for families to deal with the illness at differing points in the child's development. Given the undeniable sources of strain associated with this chronic illness, studies of this type seem essential.

End-Stage Renal Disease

There are a wide range of etiological factors, both acquired and congenital, that can lead to an inability of the kidneys to perform their usual functions of filtering waste materials from the blood. In some instances the loss of kidney function is only partial, and the problem can be dealt with through dietary and pharmacological approaches. In other instances kidney function deteriorates to the point that artificial means are necessary to support life. When decreased kidney function reaches this point and is irreversible the condition is referred to as end-stage renal disease. This condition is relatively rare in childhood and adolescence, with the annual incidence being somewhere between 1.5 and 3.5 per million (Ettenger, Korsch, Main, & Fine, 1979).

Given the presence of end-stage renal disease, treatment is likely to involve two stages, each accompanied by unique stressors. Although the ultimate goal is likely to be transplantation, dialysis is usually necessary to sustain life prior to transplant surgery.

Hemodialysis

Dialysis involves reliance on an artificial kidney machine that is used to filter waste materials and toxins from the patient's blood. Often the child will be required to undergo dialysis up to 3 times per week for periods of 3 to 4 hours at a time. While undergoing dialysis, it is common for the child to be placed on a restricted diet that limits such things as fluids, sodium, and potassium. Dialysis is necessary until such time as an appropriate donor can be found and the child can be transplanted (this may range from months to years). If transplantation is not possible (because of an inability to find a suitable donor or because of some physical condition that would compromise the transplanted kidney), dialysis will be necessary throughout life.

There are other potential stressors associated with the disorder and the need for dialysis. For example, most children undergoing dialysis for long periods of time fail to grow at a normal rate and thus fall behind their peers in stature and many fail to show normal levels of sexual development upon reaching adolescence. Along with these factors are a range of potentially serious complications associated with dialysis. Included here are anemia, hypertension, and the development of seizures, among others. The ultimate complication, death, is also a possibility. Although children who cannot be transplanted are often maintained on dialysis for relatively long periods of time, survival rates after 5 years of dialysis are reported to vary from around 90 % for children receiving home dialysis to 65 to 70 % for children receiving hospital dialysis (Ettenger et al., 1979). Clearly such a possibility represents a significant source of stress.

Transplantation

For most children with end-stage renal disease transplantation is the goal. Although receiving a new kidney will help avoid the pain of having needles inserted at the time of dialysis, avoid the child's reliance on an artificial kidney, and to some extent reduce dietary restrictions, transplantation brings with it an additional set of stressors and issues that must be confronted. First, a compatible donor must be found. In some instances this is not too difficult, as the child may have a relative who is a close blood and tissue match and wishes to be a donor. Even in this situation, however, the child may have concerns over receiving a kidney from another family member and the implications that this "gift" may have for later interactions with the donor, especially if this is a sibling. In those instances where a live donor is unavailable, it may be necessary to resort to a cadaver donor, if a close match can be found. In this case receiving a kidney from someone who has already died may arouse a significant degree of anxiety in the child. In either event, locating a suitable donor requires that the child (and perhaps another family member) confront the stress of still an additional hospitalization and major surgery and all that involves (Siegel, 1983).

Although the child (and his or her parents) may often see transplantation as a solution to the health problems, this is not entirely the case. After transplantation the child must continually take immunosuppressive drugs in order to prevent the body from rejecting the kidney. Unfortunately, these drugs have significant side effects. From a physical standpoint, a major side effect is that the drugs serve to lower the body's immune system so as to make the child more susceptible to infection and the development of other illnesses. From a psychological perspective, other side effects are of perhaps greater significance. These include acne, growth suppression, and obesity. As a result of these side effects, it is not uncommon for the transplanted child to appear as a short, overweight child with puffy cheeks who looks much younger than his or her years. Although this may not be problematic for the very young child, such side effects can be quite troublesome for adolescents, in some cases to the extent that they fail to comply with the drug treatment and thus run the risk of rejection. Even if the child is totally compliant, the fact that the kidney might be rejected at any time is a constant source of concern; even in cases where transplantation seems successful, this does not mean that the kidney will last a lifetime. In one follow-up study of 69 children who had received transplants, Fine et al. (1978) found that 5 years after transplantation 73% of those who had received a kidney from a live related donor had a functioning graft, whereas the figure was only around 40% for those transplanted the first time with a kidney from a cadaver donor. It might be noted that despite rejection, it is not uncommon for children to receive more than one transplant as long as there are no major contraindications for transplantation.

What is the impact of the illness, dialysis, and transplantation on the child and family? Unfortunately, as in the case of diabetes, there is little good information. In reviewing the relatively sparce literature regarding the long-term effects of dialysis on children Clemow et al. (1984) cites the results of some studies

that have suggested that children undergoing dialysis tend to experience problems such as irritability, depression, poor peer relationships, increased dependency, and problems in relating to siblings. Regarding the effects of transplantation (which cannot really be separated from the effects of dialysis and the disease itself), Fine et al. (1978) have provided some personality test data on 41 children obtained 1 year after transplantation. The measures employed included the California Test of Personality, which was used to index overall level of adjustment, and the Piers-Harris Scale to assess level of self-esteem. Thse investigators found no differences between transplant patients and scores obtained by the normative group on the California Test for Personality, except for scores reflecting social adaptation. Here transplant patients were found to display lowered levels of adaptation, which is not surprising given the restricted range of socialization experiences these children often have as a result of time spent in dialysis, in the hospital, and the like. Transplanted patients were also found to display lower levels of self-esteem, which these investigators attributed to the physical side effects of the immunosuppressant drugs. Although the authors did not specify the methods of data collection, they also commented on the impact of illness and transplantation on the family. They note that the effects appeared to be relatively nonspecific and that unless there were major medical complications following transplant surgery, the families usually returned to their previous level of functioning within a year following transplantation. They note, however, that the likelihood of problems was highly related to level of family functioning prior to the child's illness, with the stress of the illness significantly exaggerating any existing family related difficulties, sometimes to a pathological degree. Clemow et al. (1984) have cited other studies of child transplant patients that have yielded mixed findings; some suggesting poor levels of adjustment and others indicating a favorable outcome during the posttransplant period. In attempting to integrate these findings, they have suggested that the available data indicates that the frequency of adjustment problems is significantly lower following transplantation than while undergoing dialysis. Intuitively this would seem likely, because, despite the fears of rejection and concerns over the side effects of drug treatment, transplantation moves the child and family in the direction of a more normal life style. It must be emphasized, however, that there are few really good studies in this area and that the studies that have been conducted have not sufficiently assessed the range of child and family variables that may be influenced by this illness and its treatment.

Childhood Cancer

Of the chronic illnesses of childhood, cancer is perhaps the most stressful. This is in part because of the intrusive nature of the treatments involved, in part because it has commonly been associated with a fatal outcome, and partially because of the unpredictable nature of the disease(s).

A diagnosis of childhood cancer is likely to involve treatment with either surgery, radiation therapy, chemotherapy, or some combination of these. All of these treatments can be stressful in terms of their effects. For instance, in the case of certain malignancies (e.g., bone cancer), amputation may be deemed necessary to stop the spread of the disease. In the case of malignant brain tumors, surgery designed to remove the malignant growth may result in irreversible neurological impairment. Radiation therapy involving the central nervous system may also have long-term effects on levels of intellectual functioning. The chemotherapy that is employed with certain types of cancers may result in extreme nausea and vomiting and the development of conditioned food aversions, which make it difficult for the child to eat enough to receive the proper nutrients. Chemotherapy may also result in the child's hair falling out, a side effect that is severely distressing to many children and adolescents. As can be seen, not only does the disease pose a threat to the well-being of the

child, but the treatments necessary to halt the disease can be damaging and quite stress-inducing in and of themselves.

Clearly the greatest source of stress is the potentially terminal nature of the disease. In terminal cases, parents have to confront the fact of their child dying and deal with how to respond to the child's communications regarding the nature and seriousness of his or her illness. The child must deal with limitations imposed by the disease and the treatments involved and, in terminal cases, must come to grips with the likelihood of his or her own death. Regarding this issue, Koocher (1983) has cited research indicating that even children as young as 5 or 6 appear to develop an awareness of the seriousness of their illness. Koocher cites a number of studies suggesting that in cases with a potentially fatal outcome, the child is at significant risk for the development of emotional problems. Here he cites as common symptoms increased anxiety, loss of appetite, insomnia, social isolation, emotional withdrawal, depression, apathy, and ambivalence toward parents or others who care for the child. Such reactions are also not uncommon in the other family members who anticipate the death of a child. (For an excellent discussion of how to facilitate adaptive family communications when dealing with terminal illness, see Spinetta, 1982.)

Although confronting the possibility of death is a part of living with childhood cancer, it is gratifying to note that the prognosis for this group of diseases is now much more favorable than it was 15 or 20 years ago. Due to improved methods of treatment and adjunctive medical care, it is not uncommon for children who would have died within a matter of months a decade or so ago to now live for 5 years or more. Indeed, Koocher and O'Malley (1981) cite statistics suggesting that with diseases such as acute lymphoblastic leukemia, children today have a 50 : 50 chance of surviving 5 years or more in the disease-free state, and an increasing number of children are being considered cured. As Spinetta (1982) has noted, this trend has resulted in a changed perspective in dealing with childhood cancer from an emphasis on "preparing for death to one of preparing for life." Even the fact of increased survival, however, brings with it a set of stressors. Commenting on the nature of these stressors, Koocher (1983) has noted

> Not the least of these is the matter of long term uncertainty and the stresses of chronic helplessness this induces. . . . What of the families of such patients? Should they attempt to anticipate the child's death and accommodate to the loss, or should they attempt to deny and repress their anxieties about parental loss while hoping for the best? Either course may lead to long term psychological sequelae. (p. 1276)

As a result of work by several very prolific workers in the area (such as Gerry Koocher at Children's Hospital in Boston and John Spinetta at San Diego), we are beginning to develop an appreciation of the impact of childhood cancer on both the child and his or her family and to develop ways of helping such families cope with the stress of the cancer experience. Despite these efforts, more work is clearly needed.

Coping With Chronic Illness: An Overview

From these brief descriptions it should be obvious that chronic illness brings with it many stressors that impact on both the child and family. Stressors similar to the ones described here also occur in other chronic conditions such as asthma and ulcerative colitis, discussed earlier, as well as in diseases such as hemophilia, cystic fibrosis, sickle-cell disease, and a range of others. In all of these diseases children have to cope with distressing physical symptoms, restrictions in their normal activities, hospitalization that separates them from their parents, medical procedures and treatments that can be painful or accompanied by troublesome side effects, and in some instances, the prospect of death. For parents who care for their children, all of these factors affect them as well. In addition to the emotional stress that results from having a

seriously ill child, parents also must deal with many practical issues related to the illness, such as how to pay the high costs of medical care and how to obtain the necessary medical care in some instances.

Some of the very real practical problems families can encounter in dealing with a chronic illness are illustrated by a family seen by one of the authors in which their 9-year-old girl had suddenly developed end-stage renal disease. This family lived in a small town that was approximately 4 hours driving time from the nearest major medical center. An evaluation by medical center nephrologists suggested that, although the girl should ultimately be considered for transplantation, dialysis would be necessary for a period of at least several months. Because there were no facilities close to the girl's home that could provide for this type of treatment, it was determined that the girl would have be be dialyzed at the medical center's dialysis unit. Treatment required the girl being on the kidney machine 3 days per week (Monday, Wednesday, and Friday) for 3 to 4 hours each day. As living at home would have required the child's mother to drive a total of 8 hours per day 3 days per week simply to get to and from the medical center, it was decided that she and child would rent a room for the two of them to stay in during the 5 days of the week it was necessary to be in town for treatment. The father remained at home to work at his job to support the family. Such an arrangement not only resulted in a serious financial hardship on the family, but also resulted in a separation of the mother and child from the father just at the time when the support of all family members was needed to help the child and family cope with the illness and its treatment. A range of issues such as these often combine with the stress resulting from the child's illness to further tax the families' coping abilities.

Although space does not permit a detailed review of the literature regarding those factors that influence adaptation to chronic illness, an excellent overview of such factors has been provided by Clemow et al. (1984). These authors note that despite the stressors associated with chronic illness, chronically ill children, as a group, do not invariably display major psychological problems. Instead, there is marked variability in the ways the children and their families react to illness-related stressors. Clemow et al. note that variables such as age of onset, degree of chronicity, the child's cognitive style, and family stability all appear to be important in determining how the child will respond. Additionally, it may be recalled that Koocher (1983), in discussing the impact of childhood cancer on the family, has noted that dealing with the stress of illness is likely to enhance any preexisting psychological or family problems that may have been present prior to disease onset. Although not minimizing the degree of distress experienced, it would seem that there is reason to believe that previously well-adjusted children and families are more likely to adequately cope with illness than are those with preexisting difficulties.

Helping families cope with the stress of chronic illness would seem to be an important part of the child's total treatment. Although a great deal of skill, along with a high level of empathy on the part of the clinician, is necessary to successfully intervene in such cases, psychologists trained to work in this area can have a significant impact in mobilizing support systems and opening channels of family communication necessary to help the family cope with the stress they are experiencing. For excellent overviews of factors to consider in dealing with families of chronically ill children, see Drotar (1981) and Spinetta (1982).

THE EMERGING AREA OF PEDIATRIC PSYCHOLOGY

As must be obvious from the material presented in this chapter, the interests of child-oriented psychologists are not limited to dealing with traditional mental health issues and the so-called psychological disorders of childhood. Today, more and more psychologists are being employed in diverse settings where they work with children displaying a variety of physical health problems. This may

be as a psychologist in a university medical center who works in a department of pediatrics as a consultant or as a full-time faculty member. It may be as a psychologist associated with a group of pediatricians in private practice. In other cases it may be as a faculty member, employed in a traditional clinical psychology program, who happens to have a strong interest in pediatric problems and has established relationships with some health care facility in order to facilitate research or clinical activities. There are other settings where one might find psychologists involved in health-related endeavors as well.

This increasing involvement of psychologists in child health care reflects an increased awareness that problems associated with a range of physical disorders can be dealt with through the application of psychological principles and that psychosocial variables are importantly related to health and disease states. This awareness has resulted in the recent development of new areas of specialization, often referred to by labels such as behavioral medicine, medical psychology, health psychology, or clinical health psychology (Melamed & Siegel, 1980; Millon, Green, & Meagher, 1982). Regardless of the specific label employed, all focus on the interrelationships between psychological and social variables and health or on the use of behavioral principles in dealing with problems of physical health. When working in the child area, the term *pediatric psychology* is often used to refer to the involvement in health-related areas.

Although an agreed-upon definition of pediatric psychology would be difficult, Roberts, Maddux, Wurtele, and Wright (1982) have listed a number of characteristics of this area (and those working in the area) that, when taken together delineate the nature of this area of specialization and provide a general definitional framework.

1. Pediatric psychology is closely allied with clinical child psychology. The American Psychological Association recognizes the Society for Pediatric Psychology as affiliated with the specialty Section on Clini-

cal Child Psychology under the larger Division of Clinical Psychology.

2. Pediatric psychology is a field within medical or health care psychology. As such, pediatric psychology is concerned with physical health and illness and the relationship between psychological factors and physical health, illness, and disease. Health is seen as a global concept with less importance placed on physical-mental distinctions. . . .

3. The pediatric psychologist typically works in a medical or primary health care setting. These locations may include hospitals, clinics, pediatric practices, developmental centers, and health maintenance organizations. This medical setting is basically nonpsychiatric. The implications of this include the following characteristics: (a) the psychologist is at the point of initial patient presentation rather than at the end of a series of referrals; (b) presenting problems are seen in their earlier stages of development, usually before they become moderately or seriously debilitating; (c) problems include a higher proportion of medically related disorders; (d) diagnostic evaluations and therapeutic interventions are primarily psychologically formulated rather than oriented to psychiatric modalities; (e) the pediatric psychologist sees more patients and spends less contact time with each one.

4. The pediatric psychologist may serve in multiple roles. One may, at different times and often at the same time, function as consultant, diagnostician, therapist, researcher, information resource, and innovator. (p. 196)

In considering these characteristics of the pediatric psychologist and the general area of pediatric psychology one can see that the topics covered in this chapter, regarding the impact of psychological factors on physical illness and the impact of illness on child and family, clearly fall within this area.

SUMMARY

In this chapter we have considered a range of physical conditions of childhood and the degree to which they are related to psychosocial variables. Although DSM-III no longer includes the diagnostic category of psychophysiological disorders, a number of the disorders discussed here have often been considered under this heading.

Historically, psychophysiological or psychosomatic disorders have been thought of as physical conditions in which psychological factors play a major role. Many have assumed such factors to play a direct *causal* role in the development of these conditions; others have tended to view psychosomatic disorders simply as conditions in which psychosocial factors play a contributory role, perhaps in combination with other variables.

A major question is whether there are, in fact, disorders that fit either of the definitions given above. First, are there indeed physical disorders that are psychogenic in nature? One would have to conclude that this has still to be demonstrated. After considering the research findings reported here concerning asthma, anorexia nervosa, ulcerative colitis, enuresis, and encopresis in children, it must be said that no evidence exists to support a causal relationship between psychological variables and the *original development* of these disorders. In his review of the available evidence concerning the role of psychogenesis in both adult and child "psychosomatic disorders," Weiss (1974) concluded that there was, at that time, little evidence for the psychogenic proposition. Research during the intervening decade has yielded few findings that would cause one to modify this conclusion.

Regarding the second use of the concept, one might ask whether there are disorders, such as those considered here that are affected by psychological and social variables regardless of etiology. Here a qualified answer in the affirmative is in order. There is evidence that psychological factors can influence the *manifestations* of somatic illness. In the case of asthma, it has been documented that psychological and family variables can influence the course of the illness, at least in some asthmatic children (Purcell, 1975). It is likely that stress or other psychological or family variables also influence the ultimate manifestations of certain other childhood disorders (e.g., anorexia nervosa, enuresis, encopresis, juvenile diabetes) to some extent. Weiss (1974) in his critique of the psychosomatic disorder concept, however, has argued that the use of such a term (psychosomatic) to designate a specific group of disorders may be meaningless, because it is not clear that the influence of psychosocial variables can be limited to only the disorders commonly placed under this heading. Indeed, as Lipowski (1977) suggested, it may be that *most* disorders result from a combination of physical and psychological factors, rather than from either acting in isolation. It would therefore seem reasonable to conclude that although a variety of disorders have traditionally been considered as psychosomatic and psychological factors appear to play a contributing role in some, if not many, physical conditions, it is inappropriate to consider these apart from other disorders. In this regard, it was noted that DSM-III now provides a general category, psychological factors affecting physical condition, for use in those cases where psychological variables are assumed to contribute to the development, maintenance, and/or exacerbation of *any* physical disorder (not just those previously thought of as psychosomatic).

In addition to discussing the contribution of psychosocial variables to childhood physical illness, the present chapter also dealt with the impact of chronic illness on children and their families. It was pointed out that chronic illness brings with it a range of stressors (e.g., dealing with physical limitations, painful medical procedures and treatments, the threat of death, financial and practical problems in obtaining treatment) that can severely tax the coping abilities of the child and family. The nature of these stressors was illustrated by briefly considering three chronic illnesses: juvenile-onset diabetes, end-stage renal disease, and childhood cancer. Although there is a lack of controlled research designed to study the impact of such illnesses on various areas of child and family functioning (and such studies are needed), it would seem that illness-related stressors can result in psychological and family difficulties that may necessitate intervention to facilitate coping.

The health-related issues covered in this chapter, although different from those usually dealt with by the traditional child mental health professional, are commonly dealt with by those who identify with the rapidly developing area of pediatric psychology.

SUGGESTED READINGS

Garfinkel, P. E., & Garner, D. M. (1982). *Anorexia nervosa: A multidimensional perspective.* New York: Brunner/Mazel. An in-depth coverage of the topic of anorexia nervosa, which presents both clinical issues and research findings.

Lipowski, Z. J. (1977). Psychosomatic medicine in the seventies: An overview. *American Journal of Psychiatry, 134,* 233–244. An excellent paper that presents contemporary views of psychosomatic disorders and the area of psychosomatic medicine.

Sperling, M. *Psychosomatic disorders in childhood.* (1978). New York: Jason Aronson. Considers a variety of "psychosomatic" disorders from a psychoanalytic perspective.

Tuma, J. M. (1982). *Handbook for the practice of pediatric psychology.* New York: John Wiley & Sons. An excellent collection of chapters, authored by experts in the field, which deals with the area of pediatric psychology.

Moos, R. (1984). *Coping with physical illness.* New York: Plenum. An excellent edited text that contains chapters dealing with a range of chronic childhood illnesses.

8 INTELLECTUAL AND COGNITIVE DISORDERS: MENTAL RETARDATION AND LEARNING DISABILITIES

The last 25 years have witnessed a revolution in both professional and social attitudes toward mental retardation. Formerly the responsibility of physicians, today's mentally retarded children are cared for largely by educators and psychologists. Hospitals for the mentally retarded have been replaced by community-based programs and, probably the most fundamental change of all, early pessimistic attitudes about the educability of the mentally retarded have given way to a new optimism. Training methods developed during the course of clinical research have played an important role in changing attitudes and practices. The literature has grown at such an explosive rate over the past two decades that a comprehensive review is not possible in the space limitations of one chapter. Instead, this chapter will concentrate on the interplay between research and practice, highlighting important advances in applied clinical research.

In addition to mental retardation, the present chapter also reviews recent research and theory in the area of learning disabilities. Placing mental retardation and learning dis-abilities in the same chapter does not mean that we believe the two disorders to be closely related. On the contrary, we feel they should be carefully distinguished and that this can best be done by comparing them on various dimensions — a process facilitated by describing both in the same chapter. Thus, although both mental retardation and learning disabilities are clearly intellectual disorders, they will be shown to be quite different problems.

The chapter begins with the delineation of mental retardation and proceeds to a discussion of its etiology. Recent research and theories are reviewed next, followed by a discussion of remedial and therapeutic programs. Learning disabilities are covered next, and their background, diagnosis, etiology, and remediation are contrasted with mental retardation. Future directions for research and treatment are also described. The chapter concludes with a discussion of the special problems faced by the exceptionally gifted child. Although great intellectual prowess is clearly not a disorder, a fair amount of attention has been devoted to gifted children. This work is described in the last section of this chapter.

BACKGROUND: THE CONCEPT OF MENTAL RETARDATION

The professions of medicine, psychology, education, and law are all to some degree involved in deciding who is mentally retarded. Because these professions often have conflicting aims, they have adopted somewhat different definitions of mental retardation. The predictable result is a bewildering array of labels and enormous confusion both in research and practice. It is necessary, therefore, to begin our discussion by filling in some of the background behind the term *mental retardation* and of the population to which the term refers.

Although some children have always had trouble "keeping up" with others, it was not until the present century that educators and psychologists came to dominate the field of mental retardation. Before this, mental retardation was largely regarded as a medical problem, with lawyers called in when involuntary commitment became necessary. Physicians determined whether a child was mentally retarded on the basis of a physical exam and clinical observations; if a child was found mentally retarded, it was the physician who decided what treatment was required. Unfortunately, this purely "clinical diagnostic" procedure was vague and open to biasing influences. Because each evaluation was subjective, factors other than a child's ability (social class, for instance) could affect the outcome. For this reason, when intelligence tests were introduced they were hailed as providing objective (unbiased) data and thereby bringing rigor and precision to the diagnosis of mental retardation. Although today intelligence tests are under attack for their *alleged* bias, at the turn of the century they were seen as a way of making intellectual assessments *more* rather than *less* democratic. (See Cronbach, 1975, for a lively discussion of the vicissitudes of mental tests since the turn of the century.)

Intelligence Tests and Mental Retardation

In Chapter 1, we described how Galton's false start at constructing an intelligence test was followed by the successful development of an overall index of intellectual functioning by Binet & Simon (see Binet & Simon, 1966). This test, published in 1905, consisted of 30 items reflecting children's ability to understand and reason using objects and problems common to their environment. In a later revision, Binet introduced the notion of "mental age," the highest age level at which a child can perform adequately. Several other methods for summarizing the results of intelligence tests were introduced in the years following Binet's scale, including the intelligence quotient or IQ. Today, of course, all intelligence tests yield an IQ score. (Several popular intelligence tests were introduced in Chapter 2.) Because intelligence tests have been found successful in predicting academic success (at least for large groups), it is not surprising that they were quickly adopted as objective methods for identifying the mentally retarded. IQ criteria for classifying children as mentally retarded—usually an IQ score below 70— were established by law in many states, and test scores became the major diagnostic criterion of mental retardation, especially in America.

This extreme reliance on IQ scores was never justified and would have surprised Binet and Simon, who saw the tests as merely one source of diagnostic data (Kite, 1976). In fact, Binet and Simon recommended a three-part evaluation of the academic potential of children including a medical exam, an educational assessment, and an intelligence test. These three sources of data, they suggested, should be combined "clinically" to produce a composite picture of the child's social adequacy. Although Binet's views prevailed in England where the Mental Deficiency Act of 1913 required that "social adequacy" as well as IQ be taken into account in diagnosing mental retardation, this practice did not become common in America until almost 1950, and even today, IQ tests play a dominant role in determining who will be labeled mentally retarded. Yet IQ tests have severe limitations that make their use for diagnostic purposes problematic.

Problems in the Use of
Intelligence Tests to
Define Mental Retardation

Intelligence Tests are Culturally Biased. Although introduced as a remedy for biased clinical judgment, intelligence tests are, themselves, "culturally" biased—indeed there is no way to construct a useful test that is unbiased. Schools, after all, reflect the values of the dominant culture. Because intelligence tests seek to predict school performance, which is a function of cultural factors, the tests must also be affected by cultural values. Although it is certainly possible to develop tests that do not discriminate against those who are not members of the dominant culture (Dubois, 1939; Williams, 1972), these tests are in no sense "culture-free," and unless the schools themselves change, these tests are not likely to be very good predictors of school performance. Needless to say, if tests are culturally biased, any score chosen as an indicator of mental retardation is likely to include a disproportionate number of children who are not members of the dominant culture. Calling such children mentally retarded does violence to our implicit notions of intelligence because it makes mental retardation at least partially a societal phenomenon. Recent attempts to measure intelligence using EEGs and event-related brain potentials (ERPs) (see Chapter 5) have been reported, but these measures have not yet come into common use (Hendrickson & Hendrickson, 1980).

Intelligence Test Scores are Atheoretical. The scores generally derived from intelligence tests (that is, IQ scores) are not typical of the measures one expects to find in scientific endeavors. IQ scores, unlike measures of physical characteristics such as height or weight, are not direct measures of traits but, rather, indicants of the rank order or relative standing of an individual in a given population. If a similar approach were taken to the measurement of height, a value of 100 would be assigned to the population's average height, regardless of whether the population consisted of giants or pygmies. This *relativistic* approach to measurement is sometimes justified by appeals to operationalism such as "Intelligence is defined as what the intelligence test measures" or, put less crudely, "If an intelligence test's scores bear systematic relationships to other data agreed to reflect intelligence, then the test can be considered meaningful." This approach to measuring intelligence may provide sufficient information for predictive purposes, but operationalism alone is no substitute for understanding the underlying theoretical nature of intelligence. Just as a relative measure of height does not tell us how tall a person is in any absolute sense, IQ test scores do not tell us how intelligently someone behaves. In a culture with many geniuses, those with average performance would be considered mentally retarded. In another culture, the same performance may be considered quite adequate or even superior. For this reason, IQ test scores, by themselves, have few implications for treatment or amelioration.

The Distribution of IQ Scores Is Largely Arbitrary. Psychology textbooks routinely use a normal, bell-shaped curve with a mean of 100 and a standard deviation of 15 to represent the distribution of intelligence test scores in the population. What is often left unsaid in these presentations is that the normal distribution of intelligence—as opposed to IQ test scores—is a hypothesis, not a proven fact. Moreover, it is impossible to validate this hypothesis by demonstrating that intelligence test scores are normally distributed, because intelligence tests are deliberately constructed to yield a normal distribution of scores with a mean of 100 and a standard deviation of 15. Thus, not only are IQ scores relative measures, the form of their distribution is set out in advance rather than determined empirically from the data, as is typical in science. The normal distribution produced by IQ tests ensures that only a small percentage of the population falls 2 standard deviations or more below the mean (below 70). If an IQ cutoff of 70 is used to diagnose mental retardation, we should expect to find over 5 million mentally retarded Americans, all ages considered. In fact, this is many times the number of identified mentally retarded in the country. Clearly, as we shall show, the diagnosis of mental retardation is not based solely on IQ scores!

Intelligence Test Scores, Behavior, and Mental Retardation

As we have shown, IQ test scores are inadequate criteria (at least by themselves) on which to base the diagnosis of mental retardation. The most important problem in using IQ tests for this purpose is that they are not clearly related to behavior. In studies conducted some time ago but still relevant today, O'Connor and Tizard (1956) demonstrated that many residents of an institution for the mentally retarded had IQ scores above 100 and that the mean for all individuals admitted during the course of the study was higher than the usual criterion of 70. It seems that many individuals with IQs below 70 are managing to live their lives without being labeled mentally retarded, whereas others with IQ scores well above 70 are having difficulties severe enough for them to be institutionalized. Because IQ test scores are mainly designed to predict school performance, it would seem that some way of measuring the ability to function in society (social competence) is absolutely necessary in order to determine whether an individual is adequately meeting society's intellectual and social demands. In the next section, we shall show how social competence and intelligence both determine whether a child will be diagnosed mentally retarded.

DIAGNOSIS: WHO ARE THE MENTALLY RETARDED?

The exclusive reliance on IQ scores as the criteria for mental retardation in America began to change largely due to the efforts of E. A. Doll, director of the Vineland (NJ) Training School for many years. Doll developed the standardized, age-graded, Vineland Social Maturity Scale (1965), which yields a social quotient intended for use along with intelligence tests in diagnosing mental retardation. This widely used measure has recently been extensively revised by Sparrow, Balla, and Chicchetti (1984). Today, the practice of including a measure of social maturity in any evaluation for mental retardation has become just as important as intelligence testing. In fact, Figure 8.1 illustrates how it is possible to recognize mental retardation by a failure in social development even *without* the administration of IQ tests.

Although the Vineland scale was an advance over previous diagnostic methods, it is still a relatively simple instrument. The need for more elaborate and sophisticated approaches to the assessment of mentally retarded children eventually resulted in the landmark publication by the American Association on Mental Deficiency (AAMD) of the *Manual of Terminology and Classification in Mental Retardation* (Heber, 1959), which has been revised several times. The manual defines mental retardation as follows: "Mental retardation refers to significantly subaverage general intellectual functioning existing concurrently with deficits in adaptive behavior, and manifested during the developmental period" (Grossman, 1977, p. 11).

This definition, as can be seen, explicitly includes both intellectual and social competence as necessary criteria for the diagnosis of mental retardation, although it is recognized elsewhere in the manual that both intelligence and social competence can be measured in various ways. The relationship between adaptive behavior, intellectual functioning, and

FIGURE 8.1. A Mentally Retarded Child

Nathan, a 14-year-old boy, was brought in by his mother because of trouble in his special classroom, including restlessness, fidgeting, and being difficult to understand. He had been adopted from a Latin American country, and little was known of his early history, except that he had suffered from malnutrition. His mother provided a detailed history for the boy since the time of his adoption, noting that he sat at age 19 months, stood at age 40 months, walked at age 4 years, 2 months, and said "bye-bye," his first word, at age 30 months. Extensive medical workup, including an electroencephalogram, pneumoencephalogram, and chromosome studies, provided no clues as to the etiology of the boy's delayed development.

Nathan's teacher described him as "meaning well, but causing a lot of problems." His mother reported that he was "very aware of relationships and vibes," but unable to deal with the abstract. She stated that he had very limited speech, daydreamed, became easily frustrated, and was difficult to take to stores because he liked to run up to people and touch them, often frightening them.

During examination, the boy stared at the examiner, grabbed his hand, and tried to pull him to the toy chest. The boy made a few sounds — "da," "ah," and "wa" — but none could be considered real words. However, he used gestures to indicate his understanding of words such as "telephone," "car," "cookie," and "spoon." He was able to follow four-step commands, but did not seem to comprehend questions such as "How are you feeling?" His play was what might be expected from a much younger child.

Source: Spitzer, Skodol, Gibbon, & Williams, 1981. © American Psychiatric Association, reprinted with permission.

the diagnosis of mental retardation is illustrated in Figure 8.2. The DSM-III diagnostic criteria for mental retardation appear in Table 8.1. As may be seen, the criteria follow the AAMD definition very closely.

The DSM-III, again following the AAMD, distinguishes several levels of subnormal intelligence. Significantly subaverage intelligence is defined as a score 2 or more standard deviations below the mean of the intelligence test scores. (Actually, the DSM-III, acknowledging that no measure is perfect, refers to "zones" of IQ scores rather than absolute cutoff points.) Within this subaverage range, four levels of subnormality are defined — mild, moderate, severe, and profound mental retardation — corresponding to successively lower IQ score cutoffs. The subclasses of mental retardation are described in Table 8.2. On the whole, the number of children in a category decreases down the range from mild to

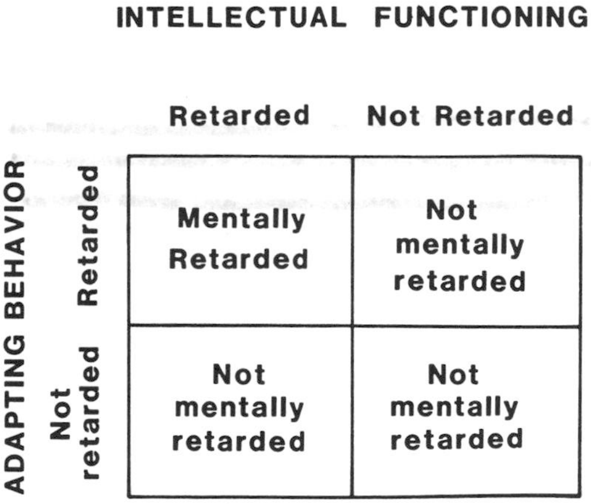

INTELLECTUAL FUNCTIONING

FIGURE 8.2. The relationship between adaptive behavior and intellectual function. As may be seen, of the four possibilities, only one is justifiably called mental retardation. Source: Grossman (1983). © American Association for Mental Deficiency and reprinted with permission.

TABLE 8.1. DSM-III DIAGNOSTIC CRITERIA
FOR MENTAL RETARDATION.

A. Significantly subaverage general intellectual
functioning: an IQ of 70 or below on an individually administered IQ test (for infants, since
available intelligence tests do not yield numerical values, a clinical judgment of significant
subaverage intellectual functioning).
B. Concurrent deficits or impairments in adaptive
behavior, taking the person's age into consideration.
C. Onset before the age of 18.

Source: American Psychiatric Association (1980). © American
Psychiatric Association and reprinted with permission.

profoundly mentally retarded, although the
actual number of children found in the lowest range exceeds that expected on the basis
of the normal distribution of IQ scores (Dingman & Tarjan, 1960). This distortion of the
normal curve by an excess of cases at the
lower end is usually taken to be the result of
special environmental factors (injury or disease, for example) that can cause mental retardation in individuals who would otherwise
have been distributed throughout the IQ
range. We will have more to say about these
children later in this chapter.

Diagnosis and the Measurement of Adaptive Behavior

The DSM-III (criterion B) requires that impairments in adaptive behavior be considered
relative to a child's age when diagnosing men-

TABLE 8.2. DSM-III SUBCATEGORIES
OF MENTAL RETARDATION.

Subtype	IQ Level
Mild	50–70
Moderate	35–49
Severe	20–34
Profound	Below 20

Source: American Psychiatric Association (1980). ©
American Psychiatric Association, 1980, and reprinted with permission.

tal retardation. In other words, children at
different developmental stages are expected
to perform different adaptive behaviors. Very
young children, for example, are expected to
perform significantly fewer adaptive behaviors than more developmentally advanced
children. As we go up the chronological scale,
the ability to live autonomously and to manage one's own affairs becomes increasingly
important. The changing criteria of social
competence with developmental stage is illustrated by some examples taken from the
AAMD manual and presented in Table 8.3.
An interesting aspect of the relationship between chronological age and society's demands
is that the individual who has difficulty as a
student may adjust adequately as an adult
when social competence is judged by different
criteria. As we shall see, the incidence of mental retardation does indeed change with age,
increasing during the school years and decreasing during adulthood.

The development of adaptive behavior
scales has lagged behind the development of
intelligence tests. The most commonly used
measure is still the Vineland Social Maturity
Scale, originally developed by Doll (1965).
The revised edition (Sparrow et al. 1984),
which involves conducting a semistructured
interview with a parent, teacher, or other
caregiver (rather than actual behavioral observation), consists of a wide range of items
that provide data regarding adaptive skills in
such areas as communication, daily living,
socialization, and motor behavior, as well as
the assessment of maladaptive behaviors. The
scale covers the ages from birth to 18 years 11
months and is also suitable for low-function-
ing adults.

Other attempts to develop objective scales
to assess adaptive behavior have met with
varying degrees of success (see Mittler & de
Jong, 1981, for several reports). The largest
and most promising effort, the Adaptive Behavior Scale (Nihira, Foster, Shellhaas, &
Leland, 1974), has two parts. Part I consists
of items chosen from other scales on the basis
of item analyses and validity studies. Part II
focuses on environmental demands, assessing

TABLE 8.3. EXAMPLES OF ADAPTIVE BEHAVIOR NORMS.

Age	Self-Help	Motor	Language
1	Opens mouth for feeding	Sits alone	Imitates sounds
1–2	Finger feeds	Stands alone	One or two words
2–3	Uses cup	Walks alone	Several words
3–4	Partially dresses self	Balances on one foot	Two-word phrases
5–6	Ties shoes	Dresses self	Normal sentences

Source: Adapted from Grossman (1973).

behaviors considered unacceptable by those responsible for the care of the individual (violent behavior, for example). Factor analytic studies of the Adaptive Behavior Scale are reviewed by Nihira (1978). In general, these studies yield three factors for Part I (personal self-sufficiency, community self-sufficiency, and personal-social responsibility) and two factors for Part II (acting-out aggression and withdrawal). These factors represent adaptive dimensions that develop at different rates. For example, 90% of the development of personal self-sufficiency occurs before 12 years among the mildly mentally retarded; the same level of development among the severely mentally retarded can take 18 years or more.

Validity studies of the Adaptive Behavior Scale (Nihira & Shellhaas, 1970) have shown that the scale can be used to determine a child's placement in an educational program as well as to measure the effectiveness of interventions. Examples of the tasks and behaviors measured by the Adaptive Behavior Scale appear in Table 8.4.

An approach to assessment that combines aspects of intelligence testing, adaptive behavior assessment, and behavioral assessment is described by Kiernan and Jones (1980). They call their approach the Behavior Assessment Battery (BAB) and note that it was designed not only to determine an individual child's level of functioning, but also to permit each child to be placed in an appropriate level in a treatment program. An important aspect of the BAB is its objective specification of criterion behaviors for each skill measured.

For example, the ability to track moving objects is assessed by nine different, carefully specified tasks. For example

Criterion behavior. The child's eyes initially follow an object that moves rapidly along an irregular trajectory. Because of its speed and eccentric motion the eyes lose their fixation upon it. The child looks for the object and locates it.

Presentation. The object is presented at the center of the visual field at a distance of 40 cm. When the child is looking the object should be moved in a series of curves and angular movements, with equal distribution of movements in vertical and horizontal planes stopping at a point on the edge of the visual field.

The reliability of the BAB has been found high enough to warrant its use in practical situations, and it represents one of the latest attempts to develop useful measures for assessing mental retardation.

Epidemiology and Prevalence of Mental Retardation

No matter what assessment approach is taken, it should be clear that diagnosing mental retardation requires consideration of both intellectual functioning and social adaptation. To some extent, who is called mentally retarded depends on what measures are used and the cut-off criteria adopted for these measures. For this reason, it is difficult to be too explicit about the prevalence of mental retardation. The usual estimate of 3% of the

TABLE 8.4. AAMD DIMENSIONS OF ADAPTIVE BEHAVIOR.

PART 1:

A. *Independent Functioning.* Taps skills related to eating, toilet use, maintaining cleanliness, care of clothing, dressing and undressing, locomotion, and other indices of independent functioning.

B. *Physical Development.* Assesses behaviors reflective of sensory and motor development.

C. *Economic Activity.* Assesses ability to handle money and to shop for items with and without supervision.

D. *Language Development.* Assesses the use of language in speaking and writing, the comprehension of written and spoken language, and the use of language in social situations.

E. *Numbers and Time.* Taps the ability to use numbers in performing simple tasks and the ability to use the concept of time.

F. *Domestic Activities.* Assesses the degree to which the individual engages in a variety of behaviors around the home, such as room cleaning, laundry, table setting, and food preparation.

G. *Vocational Activities.* Items relate to the individual's ability to perform jobs of varying complexity and the use of good work habits.

H. *Self Direction.* Assesses initiative, perseverance, and use of leisure time.

I. *Responsibility.* Items tap the degree to which person shows responsibility for personal belongings and general conscientiousness.

J. *Socialization.* Assesses characteristics such as cooperation, consideration of others, participation in group activities, and social maturity.

PART 2:

A. *Violent-Destructive Behavior.* Taps the degree to which individuals threaten or use physical violence, damage personal property, damage the property of others, and display severe temper problems.

B. *Antisocial Behavior.* Items reflect the degree to which person teases or bosses others, disrupts the activities of others, and shows disrespect for others.

C. *Rebellious Behavior.* Items relate to behavior such as the ignoring of instructions and regulations, rebellious attitude toward authority, and misbehavior in group settings.

D. *Untrustworthy Behavior.* Items deal with lying, cheating, and taking the property of others without permission.

E. *Withdrawal.* Reflects tendencies toward inactivity and shyness.

F. *Stereotyped Behavior.* Assesses the frequency of stereotyped repetitive behavior and the displaying of odd mannerisms.

G. *Inappropriate Interpersonal Manners.* Items reflect the degree to which person shows socially inappropriate behavior in interpersonal situations.

H. *Unacceptable Vocal Habits.* Reflects disturbing vocal characteristics such as talking too loud and making unpleasant noises, among others.

I. *Eccentric Habits.* Items tap behaviors such as removing clothing, eating inedibles, drooling, wearing unusual articles, and so forth.

J. *Self-Abusive Behavior.* Deals with behavior that results in physical injury to self.

K. *Hyperactivity.* Items reflect above average levels of activity.

L. *Sexually Aberrant Behavior.* Items deal with inappropriate masturbation, and socially unacceptable sexual behavior.

M. *Psychological Disturbance.* Items deal with excessive demands for attention or praise, hypochondriacal tendencies, poor reaction to frustration, overestimation of abilities, lack of emotional control, etc.

N. *Use of Medications.* Items provide information regarding the use of prescribed medications such as tranquilizers, stimulants, or anticonvulsants.

Source: Adapted from Nihira, K., Foster, R., Shellhaas, M., & Leland, H., (1974).

population is probably a close approximation, but the rate varies with age, population characteristics, and the definition of mental retardation (Macmillan, 1977). For example, prevalence rates differ for urban and rural populations and are also related to socioeconomic class (Lemkau & Imre, 1969; Tarjan, Wright, Eyman & Keeran, 1973). Moreover, there are some differences across national groups as well (Helgason, 1964; Wald, 1969; see also the chapters on epidemiology in Mittler & de Jong, 1981).

Two large-scale epidemiological studies of the prevalence of mental retardation were conducted in upstate New York (New York State Department of Mental Health, 1955) and Aberdeen, Scotland (Birch, Richardson, Baird, Horobin, & Illsley, 1970), respectively.

The first study consisted of a census of all suspected mentally retarded children in the Syracuse, NY metropolitan area. In this study, the prevalence of mental retardation was found to vary with age. Below the age of 5, the prevalence was found to be .45%. In contrast, almost 4% of children between the ages of 5 and 9 were identified as mentally retarded. Almost 8% of children between 10 and 14 and 4.5% of those between 15 and 19 were similarly classified. In another study, Lemkau and Imre (1969) also found that mental retardation is quite rare among small children, rises in frequency to a peak during the secondary school years, and then drops again in early adulthood. Prevalence changes with age because the demands made upon individuals change with age. The latter study also found that social class influenced diagnostic practices. Poorer children were more likely to be classified mentally retarded, as were rural children.

It seems there is no clear-cut answer to the question of who is mentally retarded. We have seen that the mentally retarded are not merely individuals who score below a certain level on intelligence tests but also those who show deficits in social adaptability. Although intellectual performance and social behavior are correlated (particularly at low IQ levels), this correlation is not perfect. Moreover, decisions about who is mentally retarded will depend on the measures used and the criteria adopted for diagnosis. The prevalence of mental retardation also fluctuates with age. As children grow older, the demands made upon them by society change; the same child can therefore succeed at one stage but not at another. Prevalence also fluctuates with sex, race, and socioeconomic status, indicating once again that mental retardation is not a characteristic of a child like height or eye color, but the complex result of a child's interaction with the environment.

ETIOLOGY OF MENTAL RETARDATION

Because there are many different causes of mental retardation (biological, social, and psychological), writers have found it useful to group etiological factors into categories. The most common categorical distinction is between *endogenous* causes that originate within the child (inherited disabilities, for example) and *exogenous* causes, such as disease or accidents. Exogenous causes may also be psychological (emotional trauma, inadequate parenting). Furthermore, in many cases, endogenous and exogenous causes may interact. The present discussion distinguishes between three types of etiologies: those that are primarily biological (and, therefore, endogenous), those that are primarily psychological or social, and those that represent the interaction of biological and social variables. In practice, purely psychological etiologies are rare—most cases of mental retardation represent the interaction of biological and psychological variables.

Biological Factors in Mental Retardation

Genetic factors play at least some role in many forms of mental retardation. In fact, nearly 80% of the causes of mental retardation have a genetic component (Begab, 1981). Genetic factors are also at least partly responsible for the transmission of intelligence in general. We will first discuss several types of mental retardation known to result from genetic abnormalities, leaving aside for the present the more difficult problem of the inheritance of intelligence.

Genetic Abnormalities

Metabolic Defects. Genetically transmitted defects in intelligence are almost always accompanied by mental retardation. These defects may take the form of an inability to metabolize certain food constituents. Galactosemia, an inability to metabolize lactose (milk sugar), for example, may result in mental retardation unless lactose is eliminated from the child's diet. Over 50 such metabolic defects have been described (Neisworth & Smith, 1978), and new ones are being uncovered all the time (Mendelson et al. 1981). Despite the large number of conditions, each is individually rare, and as a group they contribute only slightly to the overall incidence of mental retardation (Hutt & Gibby, 1979). The best known of the metabolic defects is *phenylketonuria.*

Phenylketonuria (PKU) is a genetically transmitted recessive trait. This means that an affected child must have inherited a recessive gene from each parent, neither of whom need be affected themselves. The defect is an inability to metabolize the amino acid phenylalanine and it is easily diagnosed by the excessive phenylalanine in the body. Although PKU's association with mental retardation has been known for over 40 years, it is still not entirely clear why this metabolic defect affects intelligence. In any case, early urinanalysis of infants makes diagnosis easy. The 1 in every 10,000 children evidencing PKU (Carter, 1970) is placed on a low phenylalanine diet, which serves to prevent the symptoms of PKU (epilepsy, eczema, deformities of the skull, and mental retardation) from developing. The average IQ of untreated children is 25 (Dobson, 1976), but treated children do much better. The outcome of treatment depends on how early the child is placed on the special diet, as shown in Table 8.5. Successfully treated children can grow to become well-functioning adults, who may, of course, have children themselves. All of these children will be carriers of PKU and may produce PKU children if they mate with another carrier. Clearly, PKU individuals need and deserve genetic counseling, particularly because carriers can be identified biochemically (Stern, 1981). New developments in enzyme replacement therapy (providing patients with enzymes necessary to metabolize certain foods) have been successful in treating other metabolic diseases and may hold hope for the future treatment of PKU; there is also the possibility that research into recombinant DNA techniques will one day permit us to prevent

TABLE 8.5. AGE OF INITIATION OF LOW-PHENYLALANINE DIET AND IQ IN PKU CHILDREN.

Age Diet Started (in weeks)	Mean IQ
Before 13	89
14–26	74
27–156	50
After 156	26

Source: Adapted from Baumeister (1967).

genetic disorders in the first place (Begab, 1981).

There are other metabolic disorders that can also result in mental retardation. Tay-Sachs disease, Nieman-Pick disease, and Hurler's disease are the ones reported most frequently in the literature. All three are examples of the lipidoses, diseases characterized by degeneration of neural tissue accompanied by the accumulation of lipids (derivatives of the fatty acids found in neural tissues). Tay-Sachs disease, the first to be recognized, is marked by listlessness, progressive atrophy of neurons, mental retardation, blindness, convulsions, and paralysis. Children with the disease rarely live beyond 2 years. Those who begin to show the disease later in childhood (when it may be called amaurotic family idiocy or Batten's disease) deteriorate slowly over a number of years. Tay-Sachs is most likely a lysosome storage disease (Kolodny, 1981). Lysosomes are small organs present in all mammalian cells. Because of an inability to break down certain natural substances, the lysosomes continually expand and interfere with cell functioning. Tay-Sachs is supposed to be more common among Jews of eastern European descent (Volk, 1964), but there is some controversy over this point (Crome & Stern, 1967), and it certainly occurs among other groups (Rao, Subhash, & Narayanan, 1981). Hurler's disease, or gargoylism, is the most common of the lipidoses. These children are typically short and have coarse hair, thick lips, low-set ears, claw-like hands, and heart defects. Nieman-Pick disease children may be blind and epileptic with enlarged livers and spleens. Both Hurler's and Nieman-Pick disease also result in mental retardation.

Dominant Traits. Unlike most metabolic defects that are the result of recessive genetic traits, some types of mental retardation are the result of dominant traits. These can turn up in children when just one parent is affected. An example of such a trait is tuberous sclerosis. This illness takes its name from the multiple nodules found in the brains of affected individuals. These nodules contain atypical cells of varying size and large amounts of calcium. In addition to mental retardation, many somatic anomalies are known to accompany tuberous sclerosis, including skin, heart, and kidney defects. The incidence of tuberous sclerosis is estimated at only 1 in every 300,000 people, mostly females (Dawson, 1954; Dupont, 1981). At least a dozen other genetically dominant disorders are known to produce mental retardation (Van Den Berghe, Fryns, Parloir, Deroover, & Keulemans, 1981). All such genetically dominant diseases are rare. A far greater number of cases of mental retardation are caused by "genetic accidents" such as Down's syndrome.

Down's Syndrome (Mongolism). The condition known as Down's syndrome (after the first person to write about it — Langdon Down) is not inherited in the same way as PKU or tuberous sclerosis. In about 95% of cases, Down's syndrome is the result of a genetic abnormality that occurs because one pair of maternal chromosomes fails to separate during meiosis. Instead of the usual 46 chromosomes (23 pairs), affected children have 47. Ordinarily the extra chromosome is attached to pair number 21 (for this reason, the condition is sometimes referred to as trisomy 21), but other forms have been described (Robinson & Robinson, 1976). [Translocation (1 chromosome becomes attached to another) and deletion (part of one chromosome's genetic material is missing) may also cause Down's syndrome in a small number of children.]

The parents of Down's syndrome children are usually genetically normal. However, when the occasional Down's syndrome female reproduces, the available statistics indicate that half the offspring are similarly affected (Crome & Stern, 1967).

The physical characteristics of Down's syndrome children are readily recognized even in the newborn (Cleland, 1978). The children have small heads and ears. Their heads have flat backs, their tongues are fissured, and their eyes have a slight oriental cast (hence "mongolism"). The children's hands are spadelike with short fingers. Their muscles lack proper tone, and they are likely to have numerous health defects. Many Down's syndrome children die early in childhood (Vaughn & McKay, 1975), but those who survive until 5 or so have an almost normal life expectancy (Forsmann & Akesson, 1970). For this reason, as well as because of its relatively high frequency of 1 in every 600 U.S. births (President's Committee, 1976), Down's syndrome accounts for between 5 and 10% of the institutionalized mentally retarded in America. A Down's syndrome child is described in Figure 8.3.

The likelihood of having a child with Down's syndrome is closely related to maternal age. For mothers younger than 29, the risk is 1 in 3,000; for those over 34, the probability of having an afflicted child increases to 1 in 1,000. The probability climbs to 32 in 1,000 for mothers over 45.

Mental retardation is apparent in Down's syndrome during the first year (Neisworth & Smith, 1978). Although the average intelligence test scores obtained by affected children are low, a fair amount of variability is possible, with some children scoring as high as the borderline mentally retarded range (Hayden & Haring, 1977). There is also great variability in personality among the children. Although many Down's syndrome children are placid and friendly, others may be difficult and aggressive (Gibson, 1978).

Longitudinal studies of Down's syndrome children (Carr, 1975, for example) have found their cognitive and social development

FIGURE 8.3. Down's Syndrome

A 15-year-old boy was brought to the emergency room by his mother, who, clutching the on-call resident's arm, pleaded, "You've got to admit him; I just can't take it anymore." The patient had been taken home from a special school by his mother 6 months previously. The mother showed the resident papers from the school that indicated that the patient's IQ was 45. He had had several placements, beginning at age 8. After a year or so away, the patient would be brought home by his mother, who had always been racked with guilt over his mental retardation and her inability to manage him in the home. The patient was an only child whose parents had been divorced for the past 4 years. The father had moved to another city.

During the past 6 months at home, the patient had increasingly become a behavior problem. He was about 5'9" and weighed close to 200 pounds. He had become destructive of property at home — breaking dishes and a chair during angry tantrums — and then, more recently, physically assaultive. He had hit his mother on the arm and shoulder during a recent scuffle that began after she tried to get him to stop banging a broom on the apartment floor. The mother showed her bruises to the resident and threatened to call the mayor's office if the hospital refused to admit her son.

On examination the boy had the typical signs of Down's syndrome, including thick facial features, slightly protruding tongue, epicanthal fold of the eyelids, and Simian crease of the palms of the hands. With indistinct and slurred speech, the boy insisted that he "didn't mean to hurt anybody."

Source: Spitzer, Skodol, Gibbon, & Williams (1981). © American Psychiatric Association, 1981, and reprinted with their permission.

to be qualitatively similar to that of normal children although slower and less even (the Down's syndrome children were subject to developmental spurts). The Down's syndrome children tended to lose ground to the normal children as they got older, but their future was not so pessimistic as was once thought. Indeed, fewer Down's syndrome children are being institutionalized today than formerly (Hutt & Gibby, 1979). Intervention programs designed to help stimulate intellectual development in Down's syndrome and other mentally retarded children are described later in this chapter.

The prevention of Down's syndrome is currently an important research topic (see chapters on prevention in Mittler & De Jong, 1981b, for instance). This work has taken several paths. One approach is to identify those factors (like maternal age) that appear correlated with Down's syndrome. A second approach is to reveal exactly how the genetic anomaly affects intelligence. For example, trisomy 21 may affect pituitary functioning,

which, in turn, affects brain function (Murdoch, 1981). A third approach to prevention is concerned with genetic counseling and amniocentesis. By identifying Down's syndrome children before birth (easily done by the technique of amniocentesis or even by blood tests that can be done at the very beginning of pregnancy; Robinson, 1982), some parents have made the decision to prevent the pregnancy from continuing. The common use of early detection techniques has led to a 50% decrease in the number of Down's syndrome children born to women over 35 in New York City between 1965 and 1975 (Hansen & Jahiel, 1981). In fact, early detection in women over 35 has led to a change in the relationship between maternal age and Down's syndrome. In many parts of the world, mothers younger than 35 have become the principle source of Down's syndrome patients (Koulischer & Gillerot, 1981).

Other Chromosomal Abnormalities. Klinefelter's syndrome, like Down's syndrome, is also associated with an extra chromosome. In this case, however, the problem is an extra female chromosome (X chromosome) in males. It is also possible to find males with three or even more X chromosomes. Such children occur in about 1 of every 400 births (Moore, 1959). Affected boys are tall and thin, their testes are small, and they do not mature sexually. Mild mental retardation is found in about one third of Klinefelter's syndrome boys (Valentine, 1966).

Turner's syndrome occurs in females who have only one rather than two X chromosomes. These girls have only rudimentary ovaries and may be mildly mentally retarded (Crome & Stern, 1967). Lejeuene's or "cri du chat" (cat's cry) syndrome is the result of one partially missing chromosome (part of one of the number 5 pair). Affected children are mentally retarded and have a weak, meowing cry. Interestingly, these children have eyes that slant in the opposite direction to Down's syndrome children.

Genetics and Mental Retardation: Overview

The syndromes discussed thus far are all examples of how genetically transmitted traits (dominant and recessive) and genetic accidents can result in mental retardation. Although these causes are responsible for a great many mentally retarded children, there are some mentally retarded children who have no demonstrable genetic defect nor any inherited specific genetic disability. This does not mean that genetics plays no part in these children's mental retardation. Many researchers feel that intelligence is a trait determined by the cumulative effects of many gene pairs working together. That is, they believe that intelligence is determined polygenically. Height is a polygenic trait, determined by several gene pairs working in an interactive fashion. If intelligence is also polygenic, then it, like height, could be expected to be distributed normally in the population. Most people fall somewhere in the middle of the distribution, but some can be expected to fall in the low end merely due to the random shuffling of

genes. Although plausible, a problem for the polygenic view is that intelligence (as measured by intelligence tests) varies with social class and culture. It is not immediately clear why an inherited trait should be subject to social class influences. We shall return to the inheritance of intelligence later in this discussion. First, however, we will continue our discussion of biological factors in mental retardation by looking at prenatal and postnatal factors.

Prenatal Risks

Mental retardation can result from physical, chemical, or biological agents acting on the developing embryo or fetus. Because some of these agents may affect the developing child without overtly disturbing the mother or interfering with the pregnancy, they are often difficult to identify with any precision. Nevertheless, a literature has developed that allows us to focus on several important risks. It should be kept in mind that prenatal etiological factors have different effects at different stages of pregnancy. During the embryonic stage (the first 2 to 3 months) serious physical malformations may be caused by agents that have little or no effect later in pregnancy.

Maternal Diet. As noted in Chapter 1, animals born to starved mothers display many malformations, particularly in their central nervous systems (Winick, 1976). In humans, the relationship between a mother's diet and the subsequent mental development of her offspring is still a controversial area. For one thing, we need to consider why a pregnant woman is malnourished in the first place. Usually maternal malnutrition severe enough to affect the child is associated with other factors such as extreme poverty or maternal mental retardation, which, in themselves, may contribute to mental retardation in the child.

Of course, extreme dietary deficiencies during pregnancy, such as lack of iodine, may result in mental retardation in the child. The diets found in most developed countries are not generally poor enough to be a significant factor in mental retardation. In fact, even severe dietary restrictions have not been found to produce intellectual retardation in unborn children. One large study of service-eligible males born in Holland during or immediately following the German blockade-produced famine of Word War II found no evidence that the reduced maternal caloric intake during pregnancy had affected the intellectual functioning of the boys at age 19 (Stein, Susser, Saenger, & Marolla, 1972). Although the study had several methodological flaws (boys severely affected by maternal malnutrition during pregnancy may not have lived to age 19 or may have been ineligible for conscription), it does imply that within a fairly large range of caloric intake, maternal nutrition may not strongly affect a child's intellectual functioning. Reviewing studies of maternal nutrition, including those experiments in which mothers with presumed poor nutrition (poor, urban black mothers) had their diets supplemented with vitamins and proteins, Susser and Stein (1981) concluded that maternal diets, within the range commonly found in developed countries, has little effect on the cognitive functions of children later in life, provided the children receive an adequate diet after birth.

Teratogenic Agents. Drugs used during pregnancy and, to a lesser extent, x-ray radiation may produce fetal malformations. Events such as the atomic bombing of Japan and the thalidomide disaster of the 1960s, in which a medication given to pregnant women led to the birth of hundreds of deformed children, illustrate the teratogenic (development-affecting) power of such agents on the developing child (Robson, Sullivan, & Smith, 1965). No one really knows the number of mentally retarded children whose condition is the result of teratogenic agents during pregnancy. It seems clear, however, that any drug, x-ray, or other potentially harmful agent should be avoided by pregnant women unless overwhelmingly indicated. This advice applies not only to prescription drugs, but also to commonly available nonprescription drugs as well. As noted in Chapter 1, mothers ad-

dicted to heroin produce children who must undergo narcotic withdrawal during the first few days of life, and mothers who use alcohol heavily produce children with various facial deformities, stunted growth, and mental retardation (Streissguth, 1976). Even heavy cigarette smoking may damage the unborn child (Kline, Stein, Susser, & Warburton, 1981).

Prenatal Infection. Prenatal infections are only a small factor in the causation of mental retardation (Baroff, 1974). Nevertheless, illnesses such as rubella (German measles), if contracted during the embryonic stage of pregnancy, can have profound effects on the developing child (Wright, 1971). The commonly available rubella vaccine should reduce the number of birth defects attributable to this disease in the future. Other infections such as syphilis and a variety of viruses may also result in mentally retarded children, but cases are rare in developed countries.

Rh Incompatibility. Rh blood factors are inherited; an individual may be either positive (the Rh factor is present) or negative for the trait. When the mother is negative and the father Rh positive, some (or all) of their children may be Rh positive. In such cases, mothers produce antibodies against the "foreign" substance in their fetus's blood. The outcome may be a number of fetal defects including mental retardation. Rh incompatibility rarely affects a first-born child, because it takes several pregnancies for the antibody level to build up. For later pregnancies, blood transfusions at birth or in utero are the most common treatments.

Prematurity. Premature birth, because of maternal illness, poor health, or other factors, results in children with low birth weights. A percentage of these children will be mentally retarded (Kiely, Paneth, & Susser, 1981). Prematurity is related to socioeconomic status, race, and other social variables as well as biological factors, and it is often difficult to identify which factor is responsible for slow cognitive development. Nevertheless, it is safe to state that low birth-weight infants are at considerable risk. Drillen (1964) found an average developmental quotient of 80.2 (mean = 100) among 4-year-olds with birth weights under 1,600 grams (3 pounds, 7 ounces) compared to the average developmental quotients for children of higher birth weights but from the same developmental background. The largest study of prenatal and environmental influences on cognitive development to date is the cooperative prenatal study reported by Broman, Nichols, and Kennedy (1975). This study of 53,043 American women and their children has produced a mountain of data. Figure 8.4 illustrates the relationship between IQ at age 4 and birth weight for white children as obtained from Broman et al.'s data. The relationship is curvilinear. Low birth weight is related to low IQ scores. As birth weight increases so does IQ — up to a point. When birth weight exceeds 4,000 grams (about 9 pounds), IQ scores begin to

drop again. This drop reflects the adverse effect of factors associated with high birth weight such as maternal diabetes and some birth injuries. Recent surveys have shown that today's high quality neonatal units have drastically reduced the likelihood of mental retardation among low birth-weight children (Kiely et al., 1981).

Postnatal Risks and Birth Injury

Cerebral Palsy. As noted in Chapter 5, even with today's carefully monitored delivery rooms, some children are still injured during the birth process. The long-term effect of pressure, anoxia (lack of oxygen), and other birth traumas may be, among other things, mental retardation. Early brain damage may also result in a number of motor disorders that are sometimes found in conjunction with mentally retarded intelligence. As a group, these disorders are known as cerebral palsy.

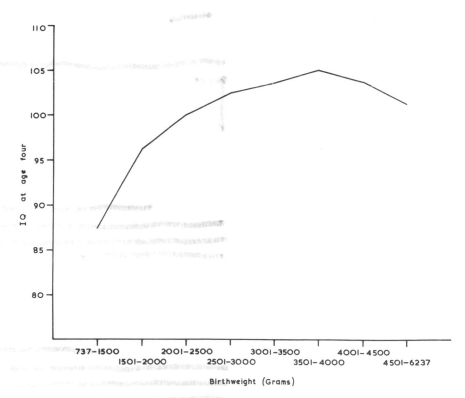

FIGURE 8.4. Relationship between birth weight and IQ at age 4 years. Source: Broman et al. (1975). © by Lawrence Erlbaum Associates and reprinted with permission.

Because cerebral palsy can result from several different types of brain damage, it should be no surprise that the degree of mental retardation among affected children varies widely. Although it is difficult to measure intellectual functioning in these children because their ability to respond is restricted by their motor handicap, it appears from those that can be tested that only about 45 to 60% are mentally retarded, with the rest showing average or above average intelligence. The incidence of cerebral palsy as caused by delivery-related accidents appears to be decreasing as high quality neonatal units become available in more places in the world (Kiely et al., 1981).

Infections and Poisons. Diseases such as meningitis and encephalitis, chemical insults such as lead poisoning, and extremely poor nutrition can all result in mental retardation. To some extent, just about any poison, trauma, or disease can affect intellectual functioning, either biologically or indirectly, by interacting with social-psychological variables. Public health campaigns to eliminate the residential use of lead-based paint, for example, have served to reduce the number of children whose problems are the result of lead poisoning (see Fein, Schwartz, Jacobson, & Jacobson, 1983, for a review of the literature on environmental toxins and development).

Biology and Mental Retardation. The biological and genetic etiologies of mental retardation discussed so far do not individually account for large numbers of mentally retarded children. Even taken together, biological causes account for only about one third of those diagnosed mentally retarded. Despite their relatively low statistical frequency, they are in some ways easier to understand and certainly easier to prevent than the complex psychobiological etiologies we turn to next.

Psychosocial Factors in Mental Retardation

For several centuries, the literature on intellectual development has contained descriptions of children brought up in unusual environments. Children raised by wolves or locked in attics rarely develop normally, and their mental retardation is no surprise. These reports, however, rarely provide the data necessary for scientific evaluation. For hard data, we must turn to more mundane sources. For example, earlier in this century, Skeels and Dye (1939) reported dramatic IQ increases among children transferred from orphanages to other institutions where they received a great deal of stimulation and intense mothering. Other studies (Goldfarb, 1955; Spitz, 1945, 1947) have also purported to demonstrate the detrimental effects of early orphanage upbringing, particularly when the institutional environment offered few opportunities for intellectual stimulation. Although these findings were the subject of considerable controversy (see particularly, Pinneau, 1961), there seems little doubt that early psychosocial experiences may profoundly influence intellectual and even physical development (Cleland, 1978).

Broman et al.'s 1975 study of 50,000 women and their offspring provides a great deal of information about the relationship between IQ at age 4 and various psychosocial variables. Among these are the child's birth order (they claim that first-borns tend to score higher than later-born children), socioeconomic status, and maternal education. We have already alluded to some of the difficulties involved in relating birth order to intelligence (the confluence model) in Chapter 1. Even putting these data aside, however, the fact remains that Broman et al. found social characteristics to be better predictors of a child's IQ score at age 4 than a combination of over 100 biological variables! Clearly, there is little question that psychosocial factors present early in life affect later intellectual functioning.

Cultural-familial Retardation

The diagnostic label cultural-familial retardation refers to those mentally retarded individuals who have no demonstrable biological cause for their mental retardation and who have at least one mentally retarded parent or sibling. These children generally score above

50 on intelligence tests, thus placing them in the mildly mentally retarded range. Two thirds of mentally retarded individuals fall into this category (Hutt & Gibby, 1979).

The etiology of cultural-familial mental retardation is unclear. Mentally retarded children who grow up in families with one or more mentally retarded members may be exhibiting the effects of genetics, responding to their subnormal environment, or both. Over the years, the relative emphasis placed on heredity or environment as determining causes has run in cycles: Genetic theories give way to environmental theories that are then replaced by new genetic theories. To a large extent, these are changes in emphasis rather than absolute changes (all theorists admit the importance of both genetic and environmental influences), and many times the reason for change has more to do with politics than with new scientific discoveries (Cronbach, 1975). Today, the controversy continues to rage, and it is unlikely to be settled in the near future.

Before we examine the nature-nurture question more closely, we should reemphasize a point that we have already made. No one doubts that psychosocial variables have an effect on intellectual development. The problem facing researchers is not whether psychosocial factors are important, but just how large a role they play. Unfortunately, the relative importance of genetic and environmental variables is difficult to establish because they interact. Thus, individuals who inherit, say, only a modest intellectual endowment may still excel if they develop in specially enriched environments. A great deal of effort has been devoted to explicating the role of genetics and environment in the transmission of intelligence, but many points remain unsettled and controversial for reasons that will become clear in the following discussion.

Genetics and Cultural-familial Retardation. As noted, it is commonly believed that mildly mentally retarded individuals who meet the criteria for cultural-familial retardation are those who were unlucky enough to fall at the low end of the normal distribution of intelligence. This hypothesis is derived from a number of assumptions; IQ scores are measures of intelligence, intelligence is inherited polygenically, and intelligence is normally distributed in the population. Although it is true that traits determined by the interaction of many genes are usually distributed normally, there are skill measures that produce other distributions. Bowling and golf scores, for example, have highly skewed distributions, with a few very high scores and many average to low scores. Although most psychologists assume that IQ scores are distributed normally, other distributions are possible.

The normal distribution of intelligence is a critical assumption of polygenic models of inheritance. The typical assumption is that 5 to 12 gene pairs (depending on who is writing) contribute to the development of intelligence. Cultural-familial retardation is the unfortunate result of inheriting "low intelligence" genes, whereas geniuses inherit "high intelligence" genes, and everyone else has some mixture of both. The polygenic model of cultural-familial retardation is applied mostly to children with IQ scores between 50 and 70. Scores below 50 reflect the influence of accidents and disease, hence their somewhat greater occurrence than would be expected from the normal distribution.

In order to get a smoothly continuous distribution of IQ scores, polygenic models incorporate the concept of "reaction range." The notion is that any particular genetic disposition may produce a range of IQ scores, or reaction range, depending on the environment in which the individual develops. This is just another way of saying that a single genotype can produce many different phenotypes. Although this is a common premise among geneticists, we must be careful not to use the reaction range concept in a self-serving manner. For example, those who believe the environment is more important than genetics attribute similar IQ scores among siblings raised in the same home to environmental influences, whereas those who emphasize genetics explain different IQ scores obtained for individuals raised together as the result of different genetic endowments. Clearly, evidence for genetic or environmental determinants of intelligence needs to be gathered in ways that avoid this circularity. In the next section we will review some of this evidence, but before doing so, let us make explicit exactly what the researchers are trying to demonstrate.

In order to argue that cultural-familial retardation is to some extent genetically determined, researchers must demonstrate that genetic dispositions operate either independently or by interacting with specific environments. In some types of genetic research (botany, for example), genetic contributions to specific traits are demonstrated by selectively breeding different plants. In human research, other methods must be used. These research procedures are themselves the subject of controversy and often yield results that are difficult to interpret. To state that the heritability of intelligence among American school children is .80 means that 80% of the variation in intelligence test scores is the result of genetic factors, and 20% is due to other factors. Heritability estimates always refer to a particular population, and heritability estimated for one population will not necessarily be applicable to other populations. A good example of the limits of heritability estimates in making between-population comparisons is given by Bee (1978):

> In small villages in the rural areas of Mexico the people are quite a bit shorter than the people in the larger cities, such as Mexico City. Height . . . is a heritable trait: this is as true in the Mexican villages—where the tallest children are born to the tallest parents —as in the city. So there is high heritability within each group. But what about the difference between the groups? Is that difference the result of hereditary differences between the village and city people? The city families do not have more "tall" genes. The group difference is apparently largely the result of diet. When the diet of the village people is improved, they grow as tall as the city people. (p. 245)

Although the entire enterprise of calculating heritability estimates for intelligence has

been questioned (Layzer, 1972, 1974), heritability estimates occupy a central position in the intelligence literature. In fact, it has been reported several times that the heritability of IQ (in America and England) is about .80 (Jensen, 1969). This figure is based on several types of data, with the two most important sources being studies of identical twins and studies of adopted children.

Identical or monozygotic (MZ) twins are genetically identical. Therefore, the greater the influence of genetic factors on IQ, the closer MZ twins should resemble one another. Indeed, studies of MZ twins have found correlations of .80 to .95 between their IQs. These correlations substantially exceed the .40 to .70 correlations reported between the IQs of ordinary siblings and DZ twins (Vandenberg, 1971). It is not possible to conclude from these data that intelligence is inherited, because MZ twins are also likely to share more similar environments than siblings or DZ twins who may not even be of the same sex. Stronger evidence comes from studies of twins, who for one reason or another were separated early in life and raised apart.

Pairs of separated twins are hard to find, but several studies have been published (Burt, 1955, 1966; Juel-Nielson, 1965; Newman, Freeman, & Holzinger, 1937; Shields, 1967). Of these investigations, the largest and the one reporting the highest correlations for MZ twins raised apart was Burt's. Unfortunately, a great deal of criticism and controversy has surrounded Burt's work (see Dorfman, 1978; Kamin, 1974), and his data are sufficiently suspect to make them inappropriate for use in deriving heritability estimates. The correlations obtained from several other studies appear in Table 8.6.

As can be seen, these correlations are lower than those obtained for identical twins raised together, probably reflecting the influence of environmental factors. Moreover, even these correlations are likely to be inflated because some of the separated twins were raised in similar environments (such as relatives' homes). Unfortunately, most twin studies do not provide information on the similarity of environments.

TABLE 8.6. INTELLIGENCE TEST SCORE CORRELATIONS
FOR MZ TWINS REARED SEPARATELY.

Author	Number of Twin Pairs	Correlation
Newman et al. (1937)	19	.67
Shields (1962)	38	.78
Juel-Nielson (1965)	12	.68

Studies of adopted children have provided the second major source of evidence for the heritability of intelligence. Burks (1928) and Leahy (1935), for example, both compared the IQ score resemblance of foster children to their foster parents with the correlations between natural children and their parents. The correlation between foster children's IQs and the mean of their foster parents' IQs was .20 and .18 in Burks's and Leahy's studies, respectively. In natural families, these correlations were .52 and .61. This difference is presumably due to the natural families' shared genes.

In another study, Skodak and Skeels (1949) found the IQs of adopted children to correlate .32 with the educational level of their biological mothers (with whom they did not live) but only .02 with the educational levels of their foster mothers who had raised them from infancy. This difference is presumably a reflection of the shared genes between mother and child. The interpretation is difficult, however, because adoption agencies try to place children in "good" foster homes. The mothers in these homes tend to be very similar, making for little variability in their educational levels and necessarily low correlations with their foster children's IQ scores. (If the mothers' educational levels do not vary, they will not change with changes in the child's IQ, and the two sets of scores will fail to correlate.)

In a study by Horn, Loehlin, and Willerman (reported by Munsinger, 1975) a correlation of .32 was found between the IQ scores of biological mothers and their children given up for adoption. The correlation between foster mother's IQ and their foster child's IQ was only .15. The correlation between foster mothers' and natural mothers' IQs was .18. This result suggests that children are not necessarily being placed in homes identical to those they were born into and strengthens the conclusion that intelligence is at least partly inherited.

We could go on reviewing similar studies, but the overall situation would not change. There are several reviews of the literature the interested reader may consult (see Brody & Brody, 1976, for a particularly objective review). However, several conclusions can be drawn from the discussion thus far. First, good data are sparse concerning the heritability of intelligence. Moreover, the claim that 80% of the variation in IQ scores in America is due to genetic factors (Jensen, 1969) is almost certainly too high. Careful researchers (e.g., Jencks, 1972) have suggested much lower heritabilities. The data available are probably not reliable enough to permit us to judge which estimates are correct. Nevertheless, it seems clear that genetics play *some* part in the transmission of intellectual functioning.

Most of the research on the heritability of intelligence has been concerned with IQ scores. We pointed out earlier that more than just low IQ is required for an individual to be called mentally retarded, and so this research, based as it is on IQ scores, is only indirectly related to mental retardation.

The conclusion that intelligence may be partly inherited in no way diminishes findings regarding environmental effects on the development of intelligence. Even if we were to find that intellectual functioning is largely inherited, it would not rule out the role of environmental effects. One can inherit a genetic disposition to grow very tall, but a poor diet or early disease may result in only average height. Similarly, intellectual functioning will always depend on environmental influences for its expression. The significance of this fact is often overlooked in examining genetic research because the results are reported as correlations, which are statistics that depend on rank order rather than absolute values. Thus, one might find a high correlation between a biological mother's intelligence test score and her adopted child's score, even though the child scored much higher than the mother (this is in fact the finding obtained by Skodak & Skeels, 1949). As long as high-scoring mothers have high-scoring children, the correlations will remain quite high, even though the absolute IQ scores are quite different. In fact, studies have found that improving early environments can have a beneficial effect on children's IQ scores. A study by Schiff et al. (1978) found marked improvements in school and test performance of lower class children adopted early in life into middle class families. Indeed, these children performed at the level expected in their adopted homes and were indistinguishable from other children reared in similar environments.

Insofar as cultural-familial retardation is concerned, then, it seems reasonable to conclude that individuals may inherit some genetic disposition that makes intellectual functioning difficult but that the environment in which they are raised plays an important role in determining the level of functioning they actually achieve.

Etiologies of Mental Retardation: Conclusions

We have seen that mental retardation may result from many factors, some largely biological and others largely psychosocial. In the majority of individuals called mentally retarded, no physical abnormality is present. In the case of cultural-familial retardation, some combination of heredity and environment is responsible for the low intellectual functioning. Psychosocial interventions (adoption, for example) can produce significant changes in intellectual functioning. In the next section we look more closely at current research and theory in mental retardation.

RESEARCH AND THEORY IN MENTAL RETARDATION

Psychological investigations into the nature of mental retardation have taken many forms. In some experiments mentally retarded children and adults are put into controlled situations in order to study selected aspects of learning and conditioning. Other researchers have focused on the cognitive manipulations that the mentally retarded use to solve problems and process information. Explosive growth in the number of publications on mental retardation in the past decade or two makes a complete literature review impossible in this chapter. We shall confine ourselves instead to a description of the types of research conducted with mentally retarded children and, to the extent possible, a prediction of future trends. We shall not be dealing to any great extent with advances in psychometrics or with factor analytic studies, but rather with theoretically guided research designed to clarify the nature of cognitive deficits.

Before turning to our discussion of the research, there are several methodological issues in studying mentally retarded children that deserve careful scrutiny.

Methodological Issues in Research with the Mentally Retarded

To make this discussion of methodology concrete, let us first create a hypothetical hypothesis. Let us suppose that an experimenter is interested in testing the hypothesis that the mentally retarded prefer to memorize verbal material by rote, relying less on the semantic aspects of words to help organize their memories than do normal children.

An experimenter, operating in a straightforward fashion, gathers together a group of mentally retarded children (defined by both intellectual and social competence criteria) of similar age and a group of normal children of the same mean age but of normal intelligence. All of these children participate in an experiment in which they are asked to memorize lists of words that may be organized semantically or by rote. If the normal children use semantic organization to a greater extent than the mentally retarded children do, the experimenter (after applying the usual statistical tests) will conclude that his hypothesis has been supported and that mentally retarded individuals do not organize memory semantically. Although this conclusion seems warranted given the outcome, some possible problems make the conclusion somewhat less clear-cut. First, mentally retarded children may perform more poorly than normally intelligent children on many or all laboratory tasks because they have difficulty in understanding the instructions or just because of their overall intellectual deficit. Finding a difference between normal and mentally retarded children on any single measure does not permit the conclusion that mentally retarded children have a specific deficit. In order to search for specific deficits, researchers generally must use two tasks and look for a group-by-task interaction; that is, where the mentally retarded children differ from the normal children on the one test but not on the other.

If the experimenter adopts this more complicated approach he must select two tasks, one on which the normal children are expected to excel and a second on which the mentally retarded children are expected to do as well as the normals. In our present example this second task might involve a list that can only be organized by rote. The selection of these tasks is by no means simple, particularly since each task must be equally reliable and equal in its ability to discriminate between groups. If these conditions are not met, then spurious findings may result. Even in situations where these conditions are satisfied, the tasks must not be so easy that all normal children can easily do them (the so-called ceiling effect) or the experimental results will be difficult to interpret.

To the problems described thus far must be added an interpretive dilemma. Even if the experimenter meets the conditions for an adequate test and obtains the predicted group-by-task interaction, some writers have argued that he will still be unable to tell whether the defect is developmental — common to individuals at a certain developmental stage — or an actual deficit found only among the mentally retarded. To do this, they argue, one must use a control group composed of normal children of the same *mental* age as the mentally retarded children. Differences between these groups would evidence an actual deficit rather than a "developmental lag."

The careful reader will see that this argument puts too heavy a burden on intelligence tests. These measures may yield a score called mental age, but it is hardly an index of a stable developmental stage. A single mental age score may reflect several patterns of test scores, and it takes no account of the different fund of experience an older mentally retarded child may have accumulated. The logic of comparing mentally retarded children with children of similar mental age in IQ is faulty in other respects as well. It ignores the role of social maturity and produces the following reductio ad absurdum: If two groups of children actually do have the same mental age, and if this is a measure of their cognitive development, they should *never* differ in their performance on cognitive tasks in the laboratory. To the extent that they do differ, the tests have not adequately matched the two groups.

What should the erstwhile experimenter do then? Ultimately the answer comes down to the role of theory in research. No amount of methodological or statistical sophistication will compensate for the lack of adequate theory. An experimenter who sets out to test theoretically based hypotheses can, hopefully, predict how mentally retarded children will behave in a variety of experimental conditions and will then seek to assess the accuracy of these predictions. These experiments may very well study the mentally retarded as a population in their own right. In cases where comparisons with normal children are necessary, predictions verified in different ways by different experimenters will serve to validate the theories upon which they are based. Clearly no single experiment or single task will actually make all the difference: It is the pattern of research results that is most important. This doesn't mean that researchers should ignore the problems discussed; they are real and important. It does mean, however, that even when experiments are conducted flawlessly, there is still no substitute for a verifiable theory supported by results replicated in different settings. These theories need not be complex. As we shall see, even direct applications of learning theories originally developed in the animal behavior laboratory may be of great use in understanding the nature of cognitive deficits. Theories must, however, be testable and verifiable in a variety of situations.

Conditioning and the Assessment of Mental Retardation

Intellectual assessment by the use of psychometric instruments such as intelligence tests or scales of social maturity give only a global picture of a child's functioning. For purposes of rehabilitation it is necessary to have more specific knowledge of a child's precise learning problems. Some researchers have used conditioning techniques for this purpose.

Imagine a simple operant conditioning apparatus consisting of two light bulbs situated side by side on a wooden board. Beneath each light bulb is a lever. The board, lights, and levers sit on a table, with the levers in easy reach of a seated child. Alongside the board is a candy dispenser and cup, which is also in easy reach of the child. This simple apparatus has been used by operant conditioners to learn a great deal about individual mentally retarded children (Barrett & Lindsley, 1962).

To take but one example, conditions can be arranged so that pressing the left lever when the left light is on is reinforced by giving the child a candy for pressing the lever. No reward follows pressing the left lever when the right light is on, or pressing the right lever regardless of which light is on. Such a task allows one to assess variables such as motivation (defined as the total number of responses made in a session), ability to discriminate between stimuli, speed of learning, and so forth.

Mentally retarded children assessed in this sort of operant conditioning situation have been found to display a variety of strengths and weaknesses. Moreover, patterns of learning have been found to be highly variable. Thus, some children learn faster or slower than others; some children display problems with response differentiation, others with stimulus generalization, and so forth. The psychometric finding that the mentally retarded are below average in intelligence may thus be seen as a gross simplification. Rather, each child has individual problems and difficulties that are best treated by developing individualized training programs.

The conditioning paradigm may be used to assess complex skills such as concept formation as well as simple conditioned responses. Denny (1966) described the use of a conditioning instrument that allows the assessment of a child's understanding of color, time, and other higher-order mediating concepts. In work with skills such as discrimination learning, researchers have demonstrated that careful structuring of the conditioning environment can allow the mentally retarded to learn skills they were previously unable to learn. Sidman and Stoddard (1967), for example, reported great success in teaching the mentally retarded to make visual discriminations by carefully programmed successive approximations to the desired discrimination. The use of conditioning techniques to assess and train the mentally retarded has resulted in numerous ingenious contributions. (Lambert, 1980, reviews this work). Although there is no doubt that this research will continue to bring new insights into mental retardation, conditioning research has not provided the only theoretical framework for conceptualizing intellectual functioning. As a result of the increasing interest in cognition in experimental psychology, a number of researchers have attempted to apply the methods used by cognitive psychologists to the study of the mentally retarded. Cognitive theories may be capable of explicating further the nature of the cognitive deficit.

Cognitive Psychology and Mental Retardation

Cognitive psychologists working in the field of intelligence have tried to replace the traditional variables with constructs drawn from information-processing models of cognition (see Goldberg, Schwartz, & Stewart, 1977; Hunt, Lunneborg, & Lewis, 1975; Schwartz & Wiedel, 1978; and Wiedel & Schwartz, 1983). There are many different information-processing models of cognition. Each has its unique features, but all share many characteristics as well. For example, these models are usually presented as a series of "stores" (e.g., Broadbent, 1971). Environmental information is first held in a sensory specific store (visual, auditory, etc.). These are some-

times referred to as "buffer" stores because they have large capacities, but the information within them decays rapidly unless it is "attended" to. The result of paying attention is that information is passed on to a limited capacity *short-term memory store* where it is either "rehearsed" or replaced by new information. Rehearsal results in the transfer of information to a more-or-less permanent *long-term memory store.* The physical reality of the various stores is highly doubtful; they are meant to be descriptive of cognitive processes, not neuroanatomy.

The outline of a general information-processing model of cognition appears in Figure 8.5. The model is simplified, showing information going in one direction only. In actuality, higher processing levels "feed back" information to lower levels. For example, one of the reasons we sometimes make mistakes about what we hear or see — as in visual illusions — is because our expectancies (which are stored in long-term memory) lead us to perceive highly probable stimuli even when they are not present.

Each of the information-processing stages in Figure 8.5 can be further subdivided into more specific cognitive processes. For example, Figure 8.6 describes the processing stages

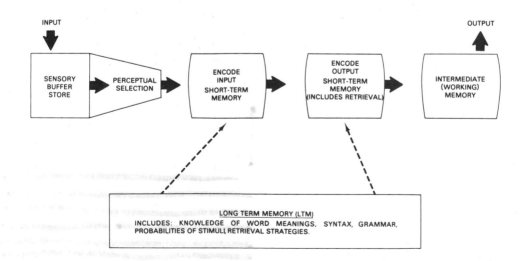

FIGURE 8.5. A general information-processing model. Information is input from the environment and passes through a number of stores. The information is analyzed in the light of knowledge already present in long-term memory.

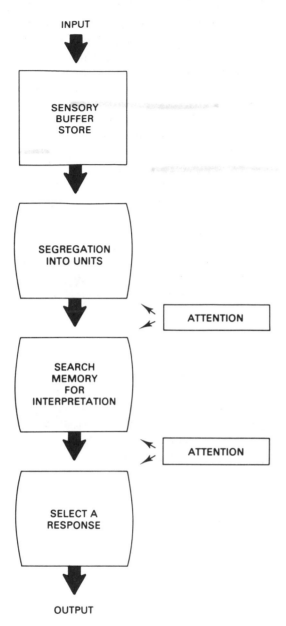

INPUT

SENSORY
BUFFER
STORE

SEGREGATION
INTO UNITS

ATTENTION

SEARCH
MEMORY
FOR
INTERPRETATION

ATTENTION

SELECT A
RESPONSE

OUTPUT

FIGURE 8.6. A simplified model of information processing in perception

involved in selective attention and perception. As can be seen, stimuli pass first into a
sensory buffer store. This information is then
segregated into units according to the physical characteristics of the stimuli and the laws
of Gestalt psychology. The salient features of
these units are used to search long-term mem-

ory. The search continues until an interpretation of the stimuli is found and a response
is made.

Clearly, if mentally retarded children differ from others in the quality or duration of
stimuli in their sensory stores, the entire chain
of information processing would necessarily
be influenced. For this reason, attention and
perception in mentally retarded children have
been studied in some detail. Much of this research is reviewed by Ross and Ward (1978),
who conclude that, for visual information
processing at least, mentally retarded and
normal children have qualitatively similar
short-term memory stores. This conclusion
may not apply to the auditory store, however, where findings have been more variable
(Gerjudy, Winters, Puilen, & Spitz, 1969).

An important difficulty in performing perceptual research with mentally retarded children is the possibility that differential familiarity with the experimental stimulus materials
may affect the results. For example, many
studies use letters of the alphabet as stimulus
materials. Because mentally retarded children are less likely to know the letters of the
alphabet than normal children, they will be
at a disadvantage and will show cognitive
deficits that they may not show if the stimuli
were equally familiar to both groups. An example of how familiarity can affect experimental results is provided by Das (1971). He
required mentally retarded and nonmentally retarded children to search a visual array
for a "target" stimulus. When the targets
were equally familiar to both groups, their
performance was also equal. However, when
stimuli more familiar to the nonmentally
retarded than the mentally retarded children
were used, performance was better among
the nonmentally retarded children.

Several experimenters have found that
mentally retarded children are slower perceptual information processors than nonmentally retarded children. However, this difference in speed is not found when mentally
retarded children are compared with nonmentally retarded children of the same mental age (Stanovich, 1978). This finding is an

important reminder that normal children of the same chronological age as mentally retarded children have a much higher "mental age." For this reason, the appropriate control group for experiments with mentally retarded children will often be a group of younger, normal children of the same "mental age." When such comparisons have been done, mentally retarded children have been found to process perceptual information similarly to younger children. In other words, mentally retarded children have not been found to be qualitatively different from others; rather they seem to process perceptual information in a manner appropriate to much younger children. We turn next to studies of higher-level information processing in mentally retarded children, including those processes involved in language and memory.

Language and Memory

Language ability influences memory and thinking in several ways. One of the most important is its role in organizing information. For example, in Chapter 4 we noted that autistic children tend to rely on the physical aspects of stimuli, ignoring "deeper" codes; consequently they were at a disadvantage in certain memory tasks when compared with children who did use deeper, semantic codes to organize their recall. Mentally retarded children have sometimes been found to behave similarly to autistic children, but the experimental results have been inconsistent. A research program reported by Herriot, Green, and McConkey (1973) that was developed to study memory organization in the mentally retarded has provided considerable insight into the role of language and memory in cognitive processing among the mentally retarded.

In a series of free recall experiments in which children had to remember word lists, Herriot et al. found that mentally retarded children tend to make minimal use of semantic cues to organize their recall. That is, they are unlikely to group items from a single semantic category together in recall. In this

respect they resemble autistics. The investigators went beyond this finding to see whether they could manipulate clustering and thereby the amount recalled. They found that clustering can be increased by providing the mentally retarded subjects with the category names either when the verbal stimuli were first presented or during recall. The opportunity to sort list items into categories, or even merely instruction to the subjects to "organize" their recall, improved both clustering and the amount recalled. Because each type of experimental manipulation improved performance (except among the severely mentally retarded) it seems justified to conclude that the processes necessary for semantically organizing memory are available in the repertoire of at least the moderately mentally retarded and may be aided in many different ways. The effect of general instructions to organize is most important in this regard, as these instructions do not directly prime any cognitive strategy but still result in improved performance. This suggests that with some mentally retarded individuals an indication that the use of organizational strategies is appropriate in a situation will be sufficient to ensure their use. Herriot et al. also provided evidence that some mentally retarded individuals can be taught to use organizational processes.

Severely mentally retarded individuals did not respond as well to the experimental manipulations as the moderately mentally retarded. It is not possible to say whether the more severely mentally retarded subjects actually lacked the ability to semantically cluster verbal materials; they may have the ability but require different sorts of cues or training before using it. The problem of differential familiarity also enters into the situation, because the severely mentally retarded may be less familiar with the semantic relationships among words than the moderately mentally retarded children are.

Additional research in short-term memory and problem solving has been reviewed in the various issues of the *International Review of Research in Mental Retardation*. This research may be summarized as indicating no reliable differences between the cognitive structures used by mentally retarded subjects and those used by normal subjects to accomplish cognitive tasks. In terms of information-processing theory, the structure of memory appears to be the same in the mentally retarded and in normals (Belmont, 1966). To a large degree, cognitive processes appear to be similar as well. Where differences have been found they appear to primarily be attributable to difficulties in knowing when to employ rehearsal or other cognitive strategies, or an inability to use strategies where time pressure is important (Ellis, 1970). Unlike the case of autistic children, no clear-cut cognitive deficit has been developed out of the work on information processing with the mentally retarded. This is to be expected, however, given the heterogeneous nature of mental retardation. It seems clear that the problems the mentally retarded have in the processing of information are more a matter of degree than of kind and that careful specification of how to do a task may often lead to improvement. Training the mentally retarded in where to use certain cognitive strategies and how to apply these in various situations would seem to be an obvious way to improve their performance. Various approaches to cognitive remediation are described in the papers of Mittler and de Jong (1981a).

REMEDIATION AND PREVENTION OF MENTAL RETARDATION

Institutional Training

Early efforts to help the mentally retarded in America mainly took the form of state facilities for the handicapped. Large institutions were built that by today's standards are anachronistic, dehumanizing, and often horrifying (Blatt & Kaplan, 1966). Such institutions have been the focus of professional scrutiny for years and are giving way to smaller, community-based facilities. Large institutions continue to exist in most states,

but they have changed. The institutionalized population has tended to become increasingly made up of the severely and profoundly mentally retarded. Although there is still rather more "custodial care" than one would like, the therapeutic role of these institutions is more pronounced today than in the past. To a large extent this progress is due to the widespread dissemination of behavior modification procedures.

Behavior modification in institutions is usually aimed at helping the severely and profoundly mentally retarded learn the self-help skills necessary for everyday living. Several such procedures are described in detail in Chapter 10. For example, by making access to food contingent on desirable table behaviors and by preventing access to food when undesirable habits are evidenced, "eating behavior" (table manners) has been shown to be highly sensitive to modification (Baroff, 1974). Similarly, the severely mentally retarded have been toilet trained through the use of carefully constructed behavior modification programs (Yates, 1970). Perhaps most noticeable has been the use of behavior modification to control undesirable ward behavior. For example, Wiesen and Watson (1967) were able to eliminate the constant attention-seeking behavior of a young child, who was interfering with the attendant's ability to interact with other children, by using "time-out" (social isolation) in response to the child's interference with adults and positive reinforcement for social interaction with other children. Troublesome behaviors of all sorts (aggression, self-injury, etc.) have all improved via behavior modification (Murphy & Wilson, 1981).

There is no doubt that institutions have welcomed and benefited greatly from the introduction of behavior modification methods. Nevertheless the institutions remain, on the whole, poorly staffed havens for the most profoundly mentally retarded. Children who have learned the necessary self-help skills are today more likely to be placed in foster group homes in which house parents, usually nonprofessionals but guided by professionals, care for mentally retarded children in a home environment, or to actually be adopted into foster homes where practicable (Eyman & Begab, 1981, see also Matson & Mulick, 1983, on the training of community living skills — telephoning, shopping — for those about to go to half-way houses).

Education and Treatment in the Schools

Today the overwhelming majority of moderately and mildly mentally retarded children are being cared for in public or private day schools. Most states require that all such children be assigned to some form of special education; unfortunately, precisely what is involved in such classes is not universally clear. Jurisdictions differ in their requirements for teachers, in the size of their classes, and in their teaching methods. This lack of uniformity makes research aimed at assessing the worth of special education extremely difficult to conduct. An added problem in evaluating educational programs is the different goals for different children. Moderately mentally retarded children (mostly those with IQ scores below 50) are usually taught self-help skills. Mildly mentally retarded children (those with IQ scores between 50 and 75), on the other hand, are often subjected to intense educative efforts designed to teach ordinary academic subjects. Behavior modification as well as instructional programs based on information-processing models of cognition have been applied to the mildly mentally retarded (Chipman, 1981; Kiernan, 1981). Even computer-assisted instruction has been adapted to the special education needs of the higher functioning mentally retarded child (Brebner, Hallworth, & Brown, 1981; Lally, 1981).

Special education programs have been designed either to teach a specific skill such as reading or to improve the cognitive strategies (memory, attention, abstract thinking) thought to underlie information-processing in general (see Butterfield, 1981, for an example of the latter approach). Specific skill training and the teaching of cognitive strate-

gies each have their adherents; in practice, both types of education are usually necessary.

Because of its heterogeneous nature, overall assessments of special education are notoriously difficult to conduct (Baroff, 1974). Nevertheless, specific factors in the special educational environment have been found to be particularly important in determining the success of an educational program. The first and most important factor determining the success of an educational program is the students' initial ability. Brighter students routinely perform better in any remedial educational program (Bryan & Bryan, 1975). Second, classroom atmosphere has been found to exert an important influence over how well children learn. Together, these two factors (student's initial ability and classroom atmosphere) account for over 50% of the variance in school achievement (Bryan & Bryan, 1975), leaving only about half the variance to be accounted for by specific instructional methods. In other words, the success of a special education program is as much determined by the type of students in the program and the teacher's style as it is by what educational approach the teacher follows.

An important issue in the special education field is whether mentally retarded (and other handicapped) children should be taught in separate classes or integrated (mainstreamed) into normal classes. At one time, there were few special classes for mentally retarded children, who were either made to struggle along in the normal class or who were excluded from school entirely. Community pressure soon saw special classes established just about everywhere, but soon these were seen as discriminatory because they removed children (many of whom were black) from the normal classroom. Opinion polarized, as it often does in educational matters, with some advocating mainstreaming for just about every child, and others defending the need for special classes. Occasionally research studies are conducted, but for the reasons already stated (special education does not always mean the same thing), these studies are usually inconclusive (Macmillan & Semmel, 1977).

Not everyone sees the question in purely dichotomous terms. Deno (1970), for example, views special education as a continuum in which children are integrated into normal classrooms where possible and supplemented with special education where necessary. Deno's position seems justified by the research data available (Robinson & Robinson, 1976), but decisions have not been made solely on the basis of research data. Politics has entered into the debate. There are 200 or more U.S. laws and numerous court decisions concerning educating the handicapped (Chinn, Drew, & Logan, 1979). It is difficult indeed for the individual clinician to maintain a focus on the best interests of the individual child in the face of all this controversy and political debate, but this is, in fact, what the clinician must do. Some children need special classes where their self-esteem can be developed without constant comparisons with the more talented children found in normal classes; others need the stimulation and role models provided by children in normal classrooms. Politics and slogans are not replacements for careful clinical judgment.

Prevention

We have already touched on several preventive measures in our discussion of the etiology of mental retardation. Immunization programs, genetic counseling, and early identification of physical handicaps have already begun to have an effect on the prevalence of mental retardation (see the papers on prevention in Mittler & de Jong, 1981). In addition, for Down's syndrome children, cosmetic surgery can remove the most obvious physical manifestations of the syndrome.

For those children whose mental retardation can be uncovered early in life, special infant intervention programs have been instituted in order to prevent — as far as possible — educational failure as the children grow older. These early stimulation programs are described in some detail later in this book in the chapter concerned with prevention. For

this reason, the present discussion is limited to just a brief overview of early intervention programs aimed specifically at mentally retarded children.

Early intervention programs for mentally retarded children (and those "at-risk" to develop mental retardation) were developed in the 1960s and 1970s in response to the obvious need for such programs and the supportive social climate. Today, in the 1980s, early intervention programs have become less popular. There are several reasons for this change: poor standards of research, methodological problems, and a reduction in the money available for such projects. The demise of many early intervention programs before they could be adequately tested means that, to a large extent, we are still unsure of their value. Although recent research reviews (Brickner, Siebert, & Casuso, 1980; Simeonsson, Cooper, & Scheiner, 1982) are mildly optimistic, the truth is that we still do not know much about the effectiveness of early intervention programs.

Part of the problem is that *early intervention* is a term that embraces many different activities. Whether or not early intervention is found effective depends on what the intervention involves, who receives it, and how success is measured. Although there are similarities among programs (most involve some combination of occupational, physical, and speech therapy along with educational and psychological interventions), there are important differences as well. For example, sometimes parents are recruited to help in the intervention process; sometimes they are ignored. The subjects of intervention programs are sometimes specified (e.g., Down's syndrome children), but more often they are described generally as "mentally retarded." Finally, outcome measures of success range from developmental scales to intelligence tests to clinical evaluations or parental reports.

Although many studies of the effectiveness of early intervention programs have been conducted, there are few that are not seriously methodologically flawed. Many studies have no control groups, and few of those that do have control groups assign children randomly to the treatment or control condition. Sample sizes are often too small for statistical analyses, and data are not always clearly presented. All reviewers of this area emphasize the need for more careful research.

Early intervention programs are expensive and may have important effects on the lives of the children involved. As psychologists, we owe it to these children to make sure that the programs they are involved in are the best that can be designed. Placing children in ineffective programs not only wastes resources, it also means that these children may be taken away from more beneficial activities. In order to judge the effectiveness of early intervention programs, psychologists must be careful to evaluate all of the data in a critical manner. Unfortunately this is not always done.

For example, a survey of textbooks in the developmental and abnormal psychology areas revealed that many of them referred to an early intervention project begun in Milwaukee in the 1960s (Sommer & Sommer, 1983). This program, which provided an enriched environment, nutrition, and health care for "at-risk" children, was said to have produced average improvements of 24 IQ points when the children were compared with controls who did not participate. These are impressive gains indeed. Unfortunately, these data were never published in a refereed journal, where they could be reviewed by the scientific community, nor have they been made available to other researchers. For this and other reasons, many researchers have begun to suspect the reliability, validity, and even the very existence of the Milwaukee project's data (Sommer & Sommer, 1983). Nevertheless, it is not uncommon for the findings of this project to be cited approvingly. The lesson is clear: Psychologists owe it to children to carefully consider research findings and to maintain a healthy skepticism about such programs. (This does not, however, mean that early intervention programs are without value; see Slaughter, 1983.)

Mental Retardation and Other Cognitive Disorders

This chapter has so far concentrated on the problems of the mentally retarded. We have discussed the history of the concept of mental retardation, definitions of mental retardation, etiology, research, treatment, and prevention. But mental retardation is not the only intellectual problem affecting children. Some children can have near normal intelligence and adequate adaptive functioning and still be unable to keep up at school. These children are often referred to as learning disabled, and they are discussed next.

LEARNING DISABILITIES: BACKGROUND

Since World War II, nearly everyone's life has become tied up in one way or another with new technology. Requirements for jobs have become increasingly strict, leading to a doubling in the number of Americans with college degrees. The increasing importance of education has resulted in more concern about those who fail to learn in school. This concern, coupled with advances in medicine, psychology, and education has produced an entirely new field of specialization—learning disabilities.

The term *learning disability* was apparently first used by the pioneer special educator Samuel Kirk in the early 1960s (see Kirk, 1972), but problems similar to those described by Kirk have been known to physicians and educators for over 100 years. The field of learning disabilities has a beginning of sorts with the famous 19th century neurologist, Paul Broca, who along with others noted that the language disorder known as expressive aphasia (see Chapter 5) most often occurs in patients with damage to the left cerebral hemisphere (Broca, 1861). Broca was one of the first to report a separation of function between the two cerebral hemispheres as well as a connection between anatomy and function. (The phrenologists had been looking for such a connection for years without success.) Shortly after Broca's discovery, Carl Wernicke (1874) described several other brain sites involved in language functioning.

Following these reports, it was only a short time before researchers began to look for a relationship between specific brain lesions and learning disabilities, particularly reading problems. Déjerine (1892) described several "alexias" (reading disabilities due to brain damage), and other reports soon followed. The notion that brain damage can produce reading disorders soon became well established; so well established, in fact, that brain damage became an explanation for reading problems even when the only evidence for such damage was the reading problem itself.

For example, Morgan (1896) published the case study of a boy who, despite obvious academic talent in other areas, seemed unable to learn to read. Generalizing from cases of acquired alexia, Morgan thought that the parts of the brain found damaged in cases of alexia (mostly the left angular gyrus) were "underdeveloped" in this boy. This circular reasoning (brain damage is inferred from the reading disability and also used to explain the same disability) was also adopted by Hinshelwood (1917), who summarized the growing field of "dyslexia" (which originally meant reading disability due to brain damage) in his book *Congenital Word Blindness*. In this book, Hinshelwood made it clear that reading problems are due to *word blindness*, an inherited brain disability that makes it impossible for some people to associate meaning with words. As there was no evidence for actual tissue damage in the brain's of dyslexics, word blindness soon came to mean "neurological immaturity" (a failure of the brain to develop) rather than actual anatomical damage.

The notion of neurological immaturity or "developmental delay" also figured importantly in the early 20th century writings of Samuel Orton (reprinted, 1966). Orton, who worked in an Iowa clinic, claimed that reading disabled children frequently reversed letters when reading and writing and were more often left-handed or ambidextrous than normal readers. Orton theorized that reading disability was the result of a failure to develop cerebral dominance. He claimed that visual inputs are registered simultaneously in both cerebral hemispheres, but in the nondominant hemisphere (usually the right), the visual percept is reversed! According to Orton, the dominant hemisphere normally suppresses this reversed image but, in people with incomplete dominance, competition between the hemispheres leads to reading problems. Orton called this problem "strephosymbolia" or "twisted symbols." Orton never had any evidence for his theory; in fact, it is completely nonsensical. It implies that there are two visual images projected like movies onto viewing screens on the back of the head, one correct and the other backwards. In reading disordered children, some homunculus sits in the middle of the head looking at these two pictures and gets confused. This view has little to do with how the visual system actually works (there are no viewing screens in the head), and it is not even clear that reading disabled children really do reverse letters more often than other children (Critchly & Critchly, 1978). Nevertheless, Orton's notions were very popular in the early part of this century, and many people (although rejecting Orton's perceptual theory) continue to believe that reading disorders are related to problems in cerebral dominance.

Beginning in the late 1960s and continuing to the present day, learning disabilities have been loosening their connection with neurology. As educators and psychologists became more involved in the field, the emphasis shifted from physiological theorizing to behavioral models and interventions. However, there is still some confusion about the role of brain damage in learning disabilities.

The close relationship between learning disabilities and brain dysfunction was encouraged for many years by research in the area of attention deficit disorders and hyperactivity. As noted in Chapter 5, most, if not all, children with attention deficit disorder have problems keeping up in school. As much of the theorizing concerning attention deficit disorder involves brain dysfunction, learning disabilities, hyperactivity, and attention deficit disorder are continually lumped together in a confusing manner. Even today, when great efforts have been made to keep these disorders separate, many researchers and textbook writers continue to confuse the various categories. In the next section, we shall attempt to define learning disabilities and show how they can be differentiated from other, similar, disorders.

DIAGNOSING LEARNING DISABILITIES

There are several currently used definitions of learning disabilities. The most commonly cited definition, however, is the one developed by the National Advisory Committee on Handicapped Children and incorporated into the Children with Specific Learning Disabilities Act (1969). (This definition has been reworded slightly in newer legislation but the general thrust remains unchanged.) This definition reads as follows:

> Children with specific learning disabilities exhibit a disorder in one or more of the basic psychological processes involved in understanding or in using spoken or written language. These may be manifested in disorders of listening, thinking, talking, reading, writing, spelling or arithmetic. They include conditions which have been referred to as perceptual handicaps, brain injury, minimal brain dysfunction, dyslexia, developmental aphasia, etc. They do not include learning problems which are due primarily to visual, hearing or motor handicaps, to mental retardation, emotional disturbance or environmental disadvantage [Public Law 91-230, Children with Specific Learning Disabilities Act].

This definition implicitly embodies three important points of view. First, it relies a great deal on the idea that learning problems can be exhibited independent of sensory dysfunction or motor handicaps. Second, the definition focuses on the *basic* learning processes — those information-processing mechanisms that underlie learning and cognitive performance. The third important aspect of the definition is its implicit reliance on "disparity"; that is, the definition implies by the exclusion of retardation as a cause, that a learning disabled child achieves at an *unexpectedly* low level given his or her potential. The definition excludes those whose learning disabilities are *primarily* due to mental retardation, cultural deprivation, and sensory defects. Excluding these children is somewhat arbitrary, because disadvantaged children, for example, may also be learning disabled, and serves mainly the administrative function of reducing the number of children for whom particular services will be provided.

The definition of learning disabilities given above, although a useful guide, presents several theoretical and practical problems. Some of these problems are due to our ignorance about important factors in learning. For example, the definition states that learning disabilities stem from a "disorder in one or more of the basic psychological processes involved in" learning. At present, however, these processes are largely unknown, and this part of the definition has no definite referent. Another problem is the insistence that learning disabilities not be secondary to sensory dysfunction, mental retardation, or cultural deprivation. As these conditions are often present in children with difficulties in learning, the definition suggests that it is possible to determine whether, for a particular child, a learning disability is related to, independent of, or interacting with another particular defect. In practice, however, the tools do not at present exist to tell us, for example, whether a child's reading problem is independent of his or her cultural deprivation or caused by it, or whether the two interact in some complex fashion. Myers and Hammill (1976) suggest that if we adhere strictly to the definition embodied in the act, only a "well behaved child with a high IQ from a middle class home who has a severe reading problem. . . is a clearcut case of learning disability" (p. 9 & 10). Although this view may seem overly critical, it does appear that in actual practice the "official" definition is frequently ignored, and children with difficulties in learning, whatever their background, are considered to be learning disabled (Smith, 1982; Tomlinson, 1981).

Learning Disabilities in the DSM-III

The DSM-III includes several learning disorders in the category of specific developmental disorders. We have already encountered this category in our discussion of developmental language disorders in Chapter 5. As noted in the earlier discussion, a primary diagnosis of specific developmental disorder is given only when other disorders are not present. For example, an autistic child with delayed language development is diagnosed autistic rather than developmental language disordered. Similarly, a child with delays in all areas of cognitive development is diagnosed mentally retarded rather than listing all of the specific delays.

In practice, this means that children who receive the specific developmental disorder diagnosis will also meet the requirements of the definition of learning disabilities given above—they will have normal development in areas other than the one in question. This does not mean, however, that children with

specific developmental disorders may not also have conduct disorders or attention deficit disorders. Because specific developmental disorders are coded on DSM-III Axis II (see Chapter 2) and most others are coded on Axis I, it is possible for a child to be diagnosed as both attention deficit disorder and specific developmental disorder.

Two of the specific developmental disorders are problems generally considered to be learning disabilities: developmental reading disorder and developmental arithmetic disorder. The DSM-III diagnostic criteria for these disorders is given in Table 8.7.

As can be seen, these criteria follow from the definition of learning disabilities given above, and they suffer from the same problems. Nevertheless, it is possible to apply these definitions in clinical settings once certain assumptions are made. The most important of these assumptions is that intelligence tests really tap intellectual capacity, and the second is that all children receive adequate instruction in reading and arithmetic in the normal school curriculum. Figure 8.7 describes the cases of two children who were diagnosed using the DSM-III criteria. Note how their cases depend crucially on these two assumptions. The two cases also illustrate many of the important characteristics of learning-disabled children; these are described in more detail in the next section.

TABLE 8.7. DSM-III CRITERIA FOR DEVELOPMENTAL READING DISORDER AND DEVELOPMENTAL ARITHMETIC DISORDER.

Developmental Reading Disorder:
    Performance on standardized, individually administered tests of reading skill is significantly below the expected level, given the individual's schooling, chronological age, and mental age (as determined by an individually administered IQ test). In addition, in school, the child's performance on tasks requiring reading skills is significantly below his or her intellectual capacity.

Developmental Arithmetic Disorder:
    Performance on standardized, individually administered tests of arithmetic achievement is significantly below expected level, given the individual's schooling, chronological age, and mental age (as determined by an individually administered IQ test). In addition, in school, the child's performance on tasks requiring arithmetic skills is significantly below his or her intellectual capacity.

Source: American Psychiatric Association (1980). © 1980 American Psychiatric Association and reprinted by permission.

FIGURE 8.7. Specific Developmental Disorders

Maryanne (Developmental Reading Disorder)

Maryanne is 11 years old and in the fifth grade. Although she sometimes seems to try very hard, her school work is very poor, particularly in the area of reading. Standardized educational tests estimate her reading to be at the second-grade level. Her spelling is also poor, and her handwriting often illegible. Maryanne's classroom behavior is beginning to annoy her teacher as well. She seems easily frustrated and prone to shouting out, even when warned to keep silent. She has recently begun to refuse to even try to do her homework. Her mother, who also had difficulty learning to read, believes that Maryanne is so constantly frustrated by her inability to do the work that she has just "given up."

Psychological tests revealed that Maryanne has an IQ of 105, well in the average range. She showed no signs of organic brain dysfunction nor did she appear particularly unhappy. There were signs, however, of a negative self-concept particularly with regard to academic ability. A school conference between Maryanne's mother, teacher, and the psychologist resulted in her being transferred to a special education class.

Sean (Developmental Arithmetic Disorder)

Sean, a 13-year-old boy, was referred for psychological testing because of what his teacher described as his mental block about arithmetic. Despite extra remedial sessions and even some private tutoring, Sean just doesn't seem to be able to deal with anything more than basic addition and subtraction. Psychological testing found him to have an IQ of 101, and educational testing revealed no problems in any subject other than mathematics. He was reading at a level appropriate to his grade and seemed to understand written directions.

Further assessment indicated that Sean was a sociable, happy boy with many friends. He was good at sports and basically cooperative at school. He feared, however, that his problems learning mathematics would prevent him from pursuing higher education.

Characteristics of the Learning Disabled

The medical model already encountered in this book is, not surprisingly, a popular one in the field of learning disabilities. Early demonstrations of the relationship between brain damage and difficulties in learning have led to what must be considered a crude form of tautological reasoning. That is, because some brain-damaged individuals have learning disabilities, the converse has also been assumed to be true. Hence diagnoses of minimal brain damage are made on the basis of perceptual, cognitive, and learning disabilities. Alternative models of learning disabilities are certainly possible, however. For example, some learning disabilities may be considered to be the result of inadequate reinforcement histories, whereas others may be the outcome of poor information-processing strategies.

A number of classification systems have been developed to describe and classify groups of learning-disabled children. By and large these systems are atheoretical listings of various objective (and some not-so-objective) characteristics of children's behavior as dictated by a particular model of learning disability. Thus those who adhere to a medical model are most likely to describe and classify children on the basis of behavioral signs that presumably represent underlying defects. Hyperactivity, for instance, may be taken as a sign of underlying minimal brain dysfunction. Those who subscribe to an operant learning point of view usually opt for descriptions of learning histories, reinforcement contingencies, and the like, ignoring underlying defects. Interestingly, there is more overlap between different models than their various authors would have us believe. Some similar behaviors continue to be reported time and again, whether writers adhere to a medical or behavioral model (see Table 8.8). There are many theories extant to explain each of these behaviors and, for now at least, these are listed without comment. The reader should keep in mind, however, that the characteristics listed in Table 8.8 are only a small portion of those that appear in the literature and that their relationship to some difficulty in learning how to read, do arithmetic, or

whatever is, in most cases, presumed rather than proven. In the following discussion, we describe some of the more important characteristics of learning-disordered children in greater detail.

Hyperactivity and Attentional Deficits

Hyperactivity was discussed in some detail in connection with attention deficit disorder in Chapter 5. It is a frequently reported behavioral symptom and is often present to some degree in children with learning disabilities. Having said all this, we must emphasize that there is no necessary connection between hyperactivity and learning disabilities; it is quite possible for a child to have difficulties learning to read, for example, without any attentional deficit or hyperactivity. Even among children with both learning disabilities and attention deficit disorders, the two problems are better kept separate. For one thing, they do not both respond to the same treatments. As described in Chapter 5, drugs appear to

TABLE 8.8. CHARACTERISTICS OF LEARNING-DISABLED CHILDREN.

Characteristic	Description
1. Hyperactivity	Excessive mobility and restlessness often resulting in inattentiveness and distractibility
2. Perceptual-motor difficulties	Poor coordination, as for example in copying visually presented materials
3. Disorders of emotionality	Can range from high-strung nervousness to unprovoked temper outbursts
4. Incoordination	Physical awkwardness
5. Attentional problems	Distractibility; continuous repetition of a once-appropriate response in a new situation
6. Impulsivity	Inability to inhibit responses
7. Memory deficits	Either short- or long-term deficits
8. Language difficulties	Can range from an inability to use or understand language to poor vocabulary or syntax
9. "Soft" neurological signs	Suggestive but not conclusive indications of brain damage
10. Specific learning disability	Inability or difficulty in learning to read, do arithmetic, etc.

Source: Adapted from Bryan & Bryan (1975).

help some attention deficit disordered children deal with their hyperactivity without improving scholastic performance.

Perceptual-Motor Difficulties

Because perceptual problems are often found among brain-injured patients (see Chapter 5), it is not surprising — given its origins — that the field of learning disabilities has always included a strong emphasis on the importance of perceptual-motor difficulties (see Cruickshank, 1977, for instance). Although all of the senses have been investigated, by far the greatest emphasis has been placed on visual perception. No one doubts that children who cannot see properly or who have trouble interpreting what they see will have problems in school. The difficulty comes in arguing in the other direction; that is, children who have trouble learning must have problems in visual perception. To make such an argument, it is necessary to have some measure of visual perception independent of the particular learning situation. That is, demonstrating that a child has difficulty discriminating among the letters of the alphabet is not sufficient proof that the child has a perceptual problem. After all, there are other reasons why a child may be unable to make such discriminations (the child may not understand the task or may be unmotivated, for example). To show that visual perception deficits are responsible for learning disabilities, researchers must show that learning-disabled children perform poorly on an independent test of visual perception and that performance on this test is correlated with school performance.

Reid and Hresko (1981) review attempts by several theorists and researchers to demonstrate the importance of visual perceptual deficits in learning disabilities. On the whole, the literature does tend to show some relationship between defects in visual perception and learning disabilities, but these relationships are not very strong. Furthermore, these correlations do not necessarily imply that visual perception deficits cause learning disorders. Indeed, just the opposite relationship is equally possible. For example, some learning-disabled children have trouble labeling alphabetic characters. Although this difficulty could be the result of a perceptual deficit, it is just as likely to result from the learning disability itself (the children may not have learned letter names). Thus, it is possible to argue that some perceptual deficits are the *result* rather than the *cause* of learning disabilities.

The evidence for the role of other perceptual deficits (hearing, touch, etc.) in learning disabilities is even thinner than that for visual perception. Thus, it is not surprising that practice and drill in perceptual training programs (about which we will have more to say later in this chapter) do not necessarily result in academic gains (Reid & Hresko, 1981).

Memory and Language Deficits

Memory deficits have been postulated to be responsible for at least some of the difficulties encountered by learning-disabled children, although the evidence is not really consistent (Swanson, 1979). A potentially important finding in this area was reported by Dumaresq (1976) who discovered that learning-disabled children fail to cluster related items together in memory unless they are given specific categorization cues. This finding suggests that at least some learning-disabled children have cognitive capacities greater than those they ordinarily demonstrate. However, even this finding must be qualified, as some researchers have found differences in performance depending on whether the items to be remembered are presented visually or auditorally (Suiter & Potter, 1978).

Characteristics of Learning Disabled Children: A Point to Remember

Although we have used the term *learning disabled* in the preceding discussion as if it referred to a specific population, it should be clear that the term really refers to a general category of children who may or may not be alike in various ways. About the only characteristic the children are certain to share is poor performance in some subject at school. As we shall show, in the next section, the heterogeneous nature of learning-disabled children is complemented by the number of different etiologies that may be responsible for children having trouble in one or more school subjects.

Prevalence

It has been estimated that 28% of American elementary school children have some sort of learning disability, and some writers have suggested that the prevalence may even be higher (Rubin & Balow, 1971). Needless to say, estimates of the prevalence of learning disorders are made difficult by the varying criteria used by diagnosticians and epidemiologists. For example, some epidemiological studies distinguish between specific learning disabilities and general backwardness, whereas others do not. Prevalence estimates also vary with the source of the data — official statistics, total population studies, or clinic samples. To complicate matters even further, prevalence varies with age, sex, and socioeconomic class (Farnham-Diggory, 1978).

Tansley and Panckhurst (1981) review several dozen prevalence studies conducted in countries throughout the world. They note that prevalence estimates tend to cluster around three levels. The highest estimates (20% or more) are obtained by studies that use a very general criterion of learning disability such as "reading behind grade level." The middle level estimates (10 to 15%) are produced by studies that require children to have specific problems in a school subject (e.g., 2 years behind grade level on reading test). The lowest estimates (2 to 5%) are obtained in those studies that use a very strict criterion of learning disability (e.g., normal intelligence, 2 years or more behind in reading, and failure to respond to normal instruction). This last group represents the "core" learning-disabled population. Beyond this core, definitions tend to get fuzzy, including

as they often do underachievers, the poorly motivated, and so forth.

Even the lowest estimate of 2 to 5% represents a significant number of children and an important problem for school authorities. Surveys reviewed by Tansley and Panckhurst (1981) indicate that the schools are having difficulty coping. In some districts, one third to one half the children needing special educational services are not receiving them.

RESEARCH AND THEORY IN LEARNING DISABILITIES

In the past 20 years, there has been far more theorizing about learning disabilities than research. This is beginning to change, however, and today, learning disability is an active research field. This research can be divided into two categories: etiological studies that attempt to shed light on the causes of learning disabilities and descriptive research designed to identify the strengths and weaknesses of learning-disabled children. Both research categories are discussed in the present section. Research concerned with remediation will be reviewed in a later section of this chapter.

Etiological Theories and Research

Obviously, there is no single cause of learning disabilities. The distinction between organically based and psychological-environmentally based hypotheses made in several other places in this book is equally applicable here. In most instances (as we have also noted previously) organic and nonorganic causes are extremely difficult to separate.

Organic Hypotheses

MBD. In some children sensory or central nervous system defects may leave general intelligence intact while adversely affecting the ability to learn specific academic subjects. As noted earlier, these cases are rare. The usual procedure is to rule out of our definition of learning disabilities those children whose problems can be clearly traced to either a sensory or nervous system defect. This means that if one is to hold an organic hypothesis for the origin of learning disabilities, then one must develop that hypothesis around an organic deficit rather different from those discussed earlier in this chapter as contributors to the etiology of mental retardation. The usual choice for those who postulate an organic cause for specific learning disabilities is a syndrome referred to as minimal brain dysfunction (MBD).

The term *MBD* has been supplanted in the DSM-III by the new category of attention deficit disorder described in Chapter 5. Although the same children are being described, the new name does not imply an organic etiology, whereas the old one does.

MBD, sometimes referred to as minimal cerebral dysfunction, has been hypothesized to underlie many common learning disorders (Wender, 1971). Whether this term refers to actual anatomical or physiological lesions in the brain or to deficits in the way the brain goes about processing information (programming) is not at all clear. As we shall shortly, structural malformations and programming deficits have different implications for understanding and treating learning disorders. There is often an unfortunate tendency to infer the presence of MBD from the fact that a child has a learning disability, then to explain the same disability by reference to the child's MBD. This sort of circular reasoning can only be avoided by employing indices of MBD independent of the learning disabilities themselves. At present no generally agreed-upon indices exist, and therefore, MBD has not proven to be a useful concept in either the understanding or treatment of learning disabilities (Gomez, 1967). This does not mean that organic factors play no role in the etiology of learning disorders. Empirical relationships between events known to cause brain damage, such as anoxia during birth and later learning problems (Crome & Stern, 1967) strongly suggest that a relationship between brain dysfunction and learning disabilities does exist. Unfortunately there are few direct signs of what these brain dysfunctions might be and how they are to be diagnosed.

Not only have learning disabilities been attributed to MBD, but there have also been attempts to show that MBD (and, therefore, learning disabilities) are inherited (Hermann, 1959). Although these studies have found that learning disabilities do appear more common in close relatives, none have adequately controlled for environmental similarities. As we shall show, environmental factors can exert a strong influence on learning.

Cerebral Laterality. As noted earlier, hypotheses about faulty cerebral dominance date back at least to Orton's writings in the first part of this century and probably even earlier. Although Orton's perceptual theory has few adherents today, there are still many who believe that "laterality" problems are responsible for learning disabilities, particularly reading disability. The notion behind the laterality hypothesis is that learning disabilities are related to cerebral organization, specifically faulty cerebral dominance.

An enormous number of laterality studies have appeared in the literature in recent years (see Tansley & Panckhurst, 1981, for a review). The basic logic behind these experiments is as follows:

1. Distinct learning-disabled and nondisabled groups may be identified;
2. The groups perform differently on some laterality task;
3. The experimental task reflects differences in brain lateralization;
4. Therefore, the groups differ in laterality.

For this logic to work, several conditions must be met. First, the learning-disabled and nondisabled groups must be clearly identifiable. Otherwise, different definitions of learning disability across studies will give rise to different findings. Second, the laterality task must be reliable, or high within-group variance will make between-group comparisons impossible. Finally, the laterality task must be a valid indicator of cerebral organization.

Unfortunately, research on the role of laterality in learning disabilities has failed to meet any of these requirements.

As we saw in the discussion of prevalence studies, learning disabilities have no universally agreed upon definition. Thus, the failure to find laterality differences between groups in some studies may be because the differences do not exist in the first place or because of using the "wrong" definition of learning disorder. By the same token, when differences are found, it is not clear what group characteristics are responsible for them.

Even when groups are clearly specified, researchers still have the problem of ensuring that their laterality measures are reliable and valid. The measures typically used in such research (hand preference, dichotic listening, visual perception in each visual field, preference for music and speech, ear and face temperature, and performance on verbal and performance tests) are not reliable enough to distinguish between different groups (see Schwartz & Kirsner, 1984, for a review). For example, even the seemingly objective measure of handedness produces different results depending on whether it is hand preference or skill that is measured. The reliability of dichotic listening has been found to vary between .21 and .74 (the correlations between two administrations of a dichotic listening test according to Blumstein, Goodglass, & Tratter, 1975). With such low reliability, it is not surprising that the validity of many laterality measures has also been found to be fairly poor (see Schwartz & Kirsner, 1982, 1984 and Schwartz, 1984, for reviews of this work).

Given these methodological problems, it seems necessary to agree with the various reviewers (Naylor, 1980; Tansley & Panckhurst, 1981; Young & Ellis, 1981) that the research so far does not indicate that cerebral laterality problems underlie most learning disabilities.

There are of course some people, who because of brain injury (stroke patients, for example) lose the ability to read. Sometimes, these individuals can compensate for their injuries by having the right hemisphere take over some of the cognitive skills involved in reading (Coltheart, 1980). For the majority of reading-disabled children, however, the hemispheric lateralization hypothesis, despite its popularity, has not proven to be of much value.

Visual Defects. The emphasis on perceptual dysfunction among learning-disabled children mentioned earlier has its parallel in etiological theories based on visual defects. The notion is that children with reading problems may have visual problems. Now it seems clear that because print must be seen to be read, children with uncorrected visual handicaps will have difficulty learning to read. This, of course, does not imply that the reverse is true—children who have difficulty learning to read must have a visual defect. Not only is such an assumption untenable on purely logical grounds, it also lacks any research support.

Many different visual defects have been reported among reading-disabled children by optometrists and, sometimes, opthalmologists. These are generally discovered by screening a large population of reading-disabled children for visual defects, isolating those that have them, and then assuming that the visual defects are the cause of their reading disorders. The next step is usually to offer a "cure" for reading disability based on correcting the visual problem. Cures include exercises to increase eye-hand coordination, walking a wooden beam while staring at a target, following a swinging target with both eyes, patching one eye, and many similar interventions (see Dunlop & Dunlop, 1981; Frostig, 1972; Spache, 1981).

Reviews of these programs have been published (see Schwartz, 1984). Although research in the area is generally poor (few studies use control groups, for instance), it seems clear that a small number of children may be helped. The vast majority of reading-disabled children, however, have no visual defect in the first place and are therefore not helped by these programs. This conclusion was also reached by James Hinshelwood almost a century ago:

> The optical aspect of vision has long been studied with great attention. The anatomy, physiology, pathology and physics of the eye have been investigated with the greatest care. The cerebral or mental aspect of vision, however, has not received the same attention. Yet the brain contributes quite as much to each visual act as the eye. . . . We are apt to forget that we see with our brains as well as with our eyes. (cited in Pirozollo, 1979, p. viii)

Psychologists have made a start at unravelling the psychological factors involved in learning disabilities. We shall discuss some of this work later in this chapter. First, however, we should mention some of the alternatives to organic hypotheses — the psychoenvironmental hypotheses.

Psychoenvironmental Hypotheses

As we have seen in our earlier discussion of environmental influences on mental functioning (and in the discussion of attention deficit disorder in Chapter 5), a variety of childhood factors can influence general mental functioning later in life. This is especially true for learning disabilities. Early deprivation (emotional, cultural, or even sensory), emotional problems, or even growing up in a poor family can all play a role in later learning disabilities (Myers & Hammill, 1976; Tansley & Panckhurst, 1981). Motivation, which is often a function of parental interest, also determines whether children will display learning problems (Ackerman, 1979). Once a child enters school, variables such as teacher expectations, poor teaching, and teaching methods can exert a strong influence (Tansley & Panckhurst, 1981).

A problem for any research that attempts to link environmental variables with learning disorders is the fact that even in poor environments, only a minority of children actually develop learning disorders. It would seem necessary to postulate some special weakness in such children that makes them especially sensitive to environmental variables. Exactly how much of a child's learning disability results from individual weaknesses and how much is due to environmental influences is impossible to determine at present.

Descriptive Theory and Research

As in so many of the areas discussed in this book, learning disabilities have been conceptualized rather differently by those who focus on the role of learning (e.g., Hewett, 1970) and those whose orientation is cognitive. The former are concerned with the environmental conditions (reinforcement contingencies, primarily) that influence the acquisition of a response, whereas the latter tend to focus on how information is transformed and used by the individual to solve intellectual problems. The type of research conducted, the models employed to guide research, and even the attempts at amelioration made by psychologists will be strongly influenced by whether they adopt a learning-conditioning theoretical framework or an information-processing one. We shall illustrate the important differences between the two points of view by examining their respective approaches to reading disabilities. Although similar, differences also exist in their respective approaches to other learning problems.

Reading and Conditioning

In his book on learning disabilities, Ross (1976) gives the following account of the relationship between reading and reinforcement:

> When a child looks at a printed word on a page and says the word aloud, it is easy to view this sequence as the presentation of a stimulus and the emission of a verbal response. If, following the correct response, the teacher said "good" . . . the next time the child is presented with that word, the

child will again emit the correct reading response. (p. 159)

Ross, therefore, puts reading on the same
footing as any other operant response. It follows, then, that if the reading situation is
carefully analyzed and reinforcement contingencies applied in a sensitive and individualized manner, most if not all children can be
taught to read.

Working within this framework, Ryback
and Staats (1970), using reading-disabled children's parents as therapists, sought to demonstrate the efficacy of behavior modification
in a program they called the Staats Motiva-
tion-Activating Reading Technique (SMART).
In this program, the child first learns a list of
words (with prompting, if necessary), then
learns to read aloud a story made up of these
words; he then reads the story silently and is
tested for comprehension. At all stages in the
training process the child is reinforced with
tokens that can be traded for money. The
reinforcements are graded and administered
by parents. Only four children were included in this study, and each was tested with a
multidimensional reading scale both before
and after training. The children were also
tested for their ability to read the words used
in the program both initially and at the end
of training.

Predictably, all four children learned most
of the words used in the program; these, after
all, were the words being taught, reinforced,
and practiced. The children also improved
their scores on the reading scale. The average
improvement for the four children was just
under two grade levels. This program's results are impressive indeed, although the lack
of a control group and the complex nature of
the training makes it difficult to determine
which aspects of the training (the reinforcement contingencies, parents' attention, etc.)
were responsible for the gains. Although Ryback and Staats did not report data on comprehension, their program did not permit
progression until questions designed to test
comprehension were answered correctly. The

implication, then, is that their subjects not
only learned to recognize the words that they
saw, but that they also learned to comprehend what the words meant. This, after
all, is the essence of reading. It is not clear
from their study, however, how such comprehension developed. Clearly the children
must have already had the ability to attach
meaning to words, for they were never trained
to do so in the program. But where did this
ability come from? It is possible, for example, to teach children to "read" a foreign
language aloud, even one in a foreign alphabet, without comprehending what they are
saying—opera singers do this all the time.
Conditioning theories have had little to say
about comprehension, which has been left
almost entirely to the cognitive theorists.

Reading and
Information Processing

In terms of the information-processing model of cognition referred to earlier, reading
is a complicated perceptual and memory process. A skilled reader makes use of sensory,
semantic, lexical, and other types of knowledge to accomplish his or her task. Moreover,
these various sources of information interact
in complex ways. An information-processing
analysis of reading presents several problems
for the operant conditioning point of view.

First, from the conditioning view, sequential (left to right, in English) scanning of the
printed page is a necessary part of learning
to read (Ross, 1976). This, of course, follows
from the notion of each word or phrase as a
stimulus for a reading response. In fact,
however, fixations on the written page are
not sequential and have been found to be
quite variable. The reader sometimes goes
left to right but may even scan right to left
(Kolers, 1970). Reading is also context-de-
pendent (Nash-Weber, 1975).

The reading and interpretation of a word
depend as much on the words that follow it
as on the words that precede it. Similarly, the
perception of words depends on the seman-

tic and syntactic environments in which they are encountered. The meaning of a written or spoken word depends on the context in which it appears, where "context" refers to events that precede and follow. For example, consider the sentences (taken from Rumelhart, 1977) (a) They are eating apples; (b) The children are eating apples; (c) The juicy red ones are eating apples. These are all readily understandable, even though, in the last sentence, for example, the first noun phrase refers to the class of "eating apples" rather than to an "apple eater," as in the first two sentences. Cognitive psychologists have given a great deal of attention to reading in recent years (see Schwartz, 1984, for example), and a number of information-processing models of the reading process have been developed and have begun to be applied to the study of the reading disabled. An example of this approach is the research conducted by Morrison, Giordani, and Nagy (1977), who addressed themselves to the problem of experimentally separating the various processes involved in processing printed information. As noted earlier, large amounts of information are initially perceived by the visual system, but this information is lost unless attended to, encoded, and transferred to short-term memory. Morrison et al. used a partial report technique in order to determine whether the locus of reading disability was in the perceptual or memory processes involved in reading. Reading-disabled and average children briefly viewed sets of eight visual forms (alphabetic letters, geometric, or abstract forms). After the stimuli were removed, an indicator appeared directly beneath the place where one of the forms had been displayed. The delay between stimulus offset and the appearance of the indicator was varied from 0 to 2 seconds. The children had to decide which form the indicator pointed to by picking it out of a card that contained all of the forms in the original display. By noting accuracy at various delays, the researchers could estimate whether information was initially perceived, how long it took to decay, and whether it was

transferred to permanent storage. Morrison et al. found poor and normal readers to be equally accurate when delays lasted up to 300 milliseconds. As this has been estimated as the amount of time visual stimuli reside in the precategorical sensory store, it seems that this store is not the locus of reading disability. Normal readers were much better than poor readers at recognizing letters or forms with delays of 500 to 2,000 milliseconds, which were thought to reflect the encoding stage of memory. Thus, it appears that encoding and organizational deficits are responsible for the poor readers' problems. Moreover, these deficits are not solely verbal, as they applied to abstract forms as well as letters. An example of an information-processing model of reading appears in Figure 8.8

Reading Disability and Language

The relationship between reading disability and language ability is not entirely clear. According to Sticht (1979), for example, reading is one of two ways to gain meaning from language; the other is through listening (or *auding* in Sticht's terminology). In early childhood, auding is superior to reading, but as children become more proficient readers, the two skills usually converge. Sticht and Beck (1976) published a test, the *Literacy Assessment Battery* (LAB), which measures the ability to understand oral and written language in adults. Similar scales are available for children (Spache, 1972). The logic behind this approach is inherently appealing. If a person shows poor performance in both auding and reading, then he or she does not have a reading problem per se but rather has a general language comprehension problem. Only when there is a discrepancy between auding and reading can a specific reading disability be inferred. Because most educational tests do not assess reading and auding separately, it is usually impossible to tell whether the child who does poorly has a general language comprehension problem or a specific reading disorder.

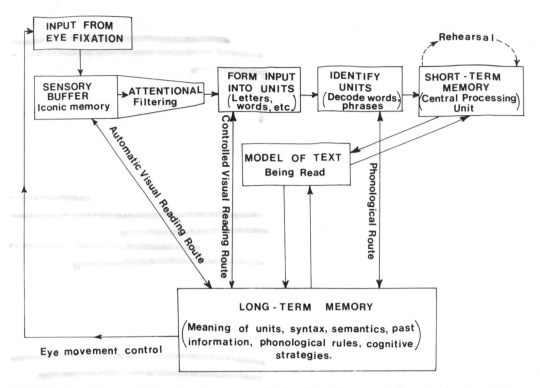

FIGURE 8.8. Outline of an information-processing model of reading. The arrows indicate the direction of information flow. Visual information is stored briefly in a sensory specific store. Highly familiar visual units in this sensory store can access meanings in long-term memory directly. Normally, however, attentional processes filter extraneous information out of the sensory store while transferring the remainder to short-term memory. This information is used to form reading units that can access meaning in long-term memory. Meaningful units are kept in short-term memory in their proper order until a meaningful interpretation can be made. This interpretation is incorporated into a model of the text being read. At every stage in the process, information residing in long-term memory can feed forward to interact with decoding processes. Source: Schwartz (1984). © 1984 Plenum Publishing Company and reprinted with permission.

EDUCATING THE LEARNING-DISABLED CHILD

Many remedial approaches have been applied to the learning disabled. Thus some children with attention deficit disorders receive stimulant medication whereas others receive behavior modification or special education and many receive a combination of all three.

We have already seen that stimulant medication, by itself, is not likely to have a major impact on academic performance and that it must often be supplemented with additional remedial techniques. For many children, this means participation in some sort of behavior

modification program. One such program has already been described in the previous section on approaches to reading disorders. Other behavioral intervention techniques for the learning-disabled are discussed by Hallahan & Kauffman (1976).

Perhaps the best known attempt to manage a classroom purely by behavior modification was the Santa Monica Madison School Plan (Hewett, 1968). The plan used the concept of an engineered classroom in which children were permitted to learn at individual rates, and a "check-mark" system was used to provide reinforcement (each time a goal was achieved, the child received a check mark that could be traded for more tangible rewards). In addition to scholastic goals, the children were also rewarded for social interaction and for behaviors that would facilitate their return to normal classrooms. Although the program was reported as successful for helping learning-disabled children return to the classroom, there is some question about whether the improvements lasted once the reinforcements were removed and how well the behaviors learned in the engineered classroom generalized to normal classrooms (Reid & Hresko, 1981). More recently, attention has been focused on cognitive behavior modification as a way of teaching children self-monitoring strategies (see Meichenbaum & Goodman, 1971, for example). Children are taught to ask themselves questions as they work ("Am I doing this correctly?" or "How am I doing?"). They may also be taught to repeat task instructions to themselves. Although success has been reported using these techniques to help learning-disabled children, many studies have failed to find evidence that self-monitoring techniques generalize to the normal classroom (see Reid & Hresko, 1981, for a review). Moreover, the verbal skills necessary for cognitive behavior modification may not be present in many learning-disabled children. Thus, although behavior modification techniques have been widely applied and found successful in helping children while the program is in progress, the evidence for their ability to improve academic performance in the normal classroom (their generalizability) is still fairly weak (Backman & Firestone, 1979; Reid & Hresko, 1981; Wulbert & Dries, 1979).

Although special education is by far the most common intervention for learning-disabled children, there is, as we have already pointed out, no specific set of procedures common to all special education programs. Nevertheless, there are similarities. Perhaps the most popular approach is perceptual-motor skills training. Programs such as the one developed by Frostig and Horne (1964) are based on the hypothesis that training in perceptual-motor skills will facilitate the learning of "higher" skills, such as reading (which pre-sumably rely on these more basic skills). In Frostig's program, children practice tasks designed to improve eye-hand coordination, the ability to create geometric designs, and the ability to separate figure from ground. Frostig and Horne reported that their training program contributed to improved reading achievement, but this result has been notoriously difficult to replicate (Hammill, 1972). Thus, although perceptual-motor training may sometimes be of help to children, there is at present no clear-cut demonstration of its value in helping the learning disabled to achieve academic success.

Starting from the observation that learning-disabled children are often awkward, Delecato (1966) developed a series of "patterning" exercises that are claimed to help the brain develop appropriate patterns of functioning. The therapy consists of a series of exercises such as creeping or crawling that are repeated many times. This approach has attracted numerous adherents over the years but has no experimental support (Bryan & Bryan, 1975).

Specific special educational programs have been designed to help children who have learning disabilities (see Reid & Hresko, 1981, for a description of several techniques). These programs vary from those that use typical teaching strategies (those used in the normal classroom) but proceed more slowly and with more repetition to those that use special teaching strategies. The latter category includes such things as multisensory learning (in which the same material is taught visually, auditorally, and even through touch), hyperlearning (in which children are given much feedback and praise), and many others. Although good results have been reported for all programs at one time or another by teachers, there is little experimental evidence supporting their value. Some writers believe that all educational programs succeed to the extent that they give the learning-disabled child extra practice (Schwartz, 1984).

A good example of an instructional approach that can be applied to remedial (or normal) reading instruction is the *DISTAR* program (Engelmann & Bruner, 1974). The *DISTAR* reading program is divided into levels; it begins with simple skills and moves up to comprehension. At the lowest level, children are taught to identify letters and letter sounds; they then move on to word and sentence skills and finally to understanding passages and stories. The program is self-paced, and children can proceed to new tasks as soon as they have mastered the old ones. Slower children receive extra practice. *DISTAR* has been found to help children reach higher levels of reading ability than would otherwise be expected (Abt Associates, 1976).

The issue of mainstreaming, which we encountered in regard to the mentally retarded, is even more relevant to the learning disabled. In this field, too, opinions tend to be polarized, with some advocating that the children be segregated into special classes and others calling for integration. Once again, the best arrangement appears to be a flexible one in which children receive special, segregated treatment where necessary and are integrated into normal classrooms where possible. Deno (1970) produced a "cascade" model of special education services that clearly shows how children can be placed in the "least restrictive environment" suitable to their needs. Her model appears in Figure 8.9.

Regardless of which approach to remediation is adopted, there are some general principles that are applicable to all: Remediation should be started as early as possible, should be tailored to the individual child, should be as motivating as possible, and should involve a great deal of practice.

SPECIAL PROBLEMS OF THE GIFTED CHILD

It may seem something of a surprise to see gifted children included in a chapter devoted to intellectual and cognitive disorders. After all, gifted children are, by definition, superior in intellectual skills. Unfortunately, this does not mean that they are without problems. Although gifted children certainly do not require remediation, they do require special attention if certain problems are to be avoided (Gallagher, 1979; Webb & Mecksworth, 1982).

Interest in the especially gifted child is not a new phenomenon. Baumgarten (1930) described several gifted children who could perform amazing feats at very young ages. One child, the great chess master Reshevsky, could play 20 opponents simultaneously when he was 8 years old. According to Baumgarten, such children often developed emotional problems because of their special abilities. These made them different from other children (which they are, again, by definition) and interfered with their normal social development. The early precocity of Baumgarten's children was an important cue to their special talents. But not all gifted children are precocious. Einstein, for example, didn't talk until he was 4 or read until he was 7, and Thomas Edison was considered mentally retarded by both his parents and teachers (Holden, 1980). Thus, it seems that some gifted individuals are easier to identify early in life than others.

The only really large-scale attempt to study the development of gifted individuals remains Terman's study of high-IQ California children (see Oden, 1968; Terman, 1925–1959; Sears, 1977). The study began in the 1920s and continues to the present day. What Terman did was to identify 1,528 California school children with IQ scores over 135. These children were interviewed and tested at the time and periodically reinterviewed and tested over the years. As a group, Terman's children fared very well indeed. Many became professionals, most made more money than the national average, and they were even healthier than their less talented contemporaries. Clearly, nothing in this study suggests that gifted children are at a greater risk to develop emotional problems than average children. In fact, Terman's subjects were healthier and better adjusted (according to their own reports) than the average population. Moreover, most of Terman's gifted children attended normal classes in typical schools.

However, there were few "super-geniuses" in Terman's group. Although one member

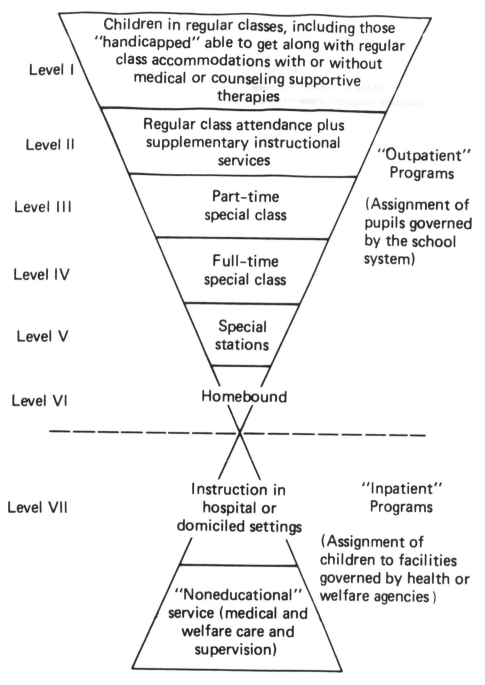

FIGURE 8.9. Cascade model of special educational services. Note the many possible levels of segregation. The proper level depends on the best interests of a particular child. Source: Adapted from Deno (1970). © 1970 The Council for Exceptional Children and reprinted with permission.

was a motion picture director who won several Oscars and several were well-known scientists, there were no Einsteins nor any great artists or musicians (no Beethovens). Perhaps it is these truly exceptional children who are most different who are also most "at-risk." Currently no one really knows. However, research on the special aptitudes and problems of the gifted is presently being conducted in several centers, and the U.S. Department of Education's Office of Gifted and Talented is encouraging additional research and practical training throughout the country.

SUMMARY

The mentally retarded, long the subject of social concern, are finally getting a fair measure of professional attention. Confusion about the definition of mental retardation still exists, but the problems inherent in relying on intelligence test scores as the sole diagnostic criterion are now widely recognized. A definition based on both intelligence test performance and social competence is theoretically justified but difficult to practice because the development of social competence measures has lagged behind the psychometric sophistication of intelligence tests. The prevalence of mental retardation is rather difficult to determine with any precision because of varying definitions and diagnostic procedures. Although an estimate of about 3% is widely accepted, the prevalence changes for different age groups, and is a function of the varying demands made by society on the individual at different ages. The prevalence of mental retardation is greatest during the school years.

Genetics, biochemical factors, accidents, and disease all play some role in the etiology of mental retardation. The majority of mentally retarded children, however, fall into the cultural-familial retardation category, in which the contributions of heredity and environment have still not been completely sorted out. Both operant conditioning studies and cognitive information-processing experiments have begun to shed light on the nature of the deficits responsible for mental retardation, although the questions asked by the two types of researchers are quite different.

Learning-disabled children, who by definition are of normal potential, have been the object of much attention in recent years. The incidence of learning disabilities has been estimated to be quite high, and no clear cause or causes for the various disabilities has yet been discovered. Although both behavioral and cognitive models have proven useful in conceptualizing learning disabilities, behavioral models, particularly those based on operant conditioning, have formed the basis for most treatment programs. Treatment for the mentally retarded can take many other forms. Severely and profoundly mentally retarded children are still likely to be found in large institutions, although the trend is definitely away from such institutions and toward smaller, community-based facilities. Moderately mentally retarded children and the learning disabled are usually not institutionalized but, rather, cared for in public or private day schools. A number of special programs have been developed to help the mildly mentally retarded and learning-disabled child, but on the whole the evidence for the value of any particular program is mixed. Training programs based on behavioral principles seem, at present, to be the most efficacious, but their generalizability and usefulness for "higher" skills is still under investigation. We shall discuss behavior modification procedures in more detail in Chapter 10.

The special problems faced by very gifted children are also being recognized. At present, research into the identification and training of the intellectually gifted child has become a lively area of psychological inquiry.

SUGGESTED READINGS

Mittler, P., & de Jong, J. M. (1981). *Frontiers of knowledge in mental retardation.* Baltimore, MD: University Park Press. A collection of papers covering virtually every aspect of social and biological research into mental retardation.

Reid, D. K., & Hresko, W. P. (1981). A

cognitive approach to learning disabilities. New York: McGraw-Hill. A review of the diagnosis and treatment of learning disabilities with an emphasis on cognitive theories and research.

Matson, J. L., & Mulick, J. A. (Eds.). (1983). *Handbook of mental retardation.* New York: Pergamon. Contains reviews of most areas of mental retardation research and treatment.

Vitello, S. J., & Soskin, R. M. (1985). *Mental retardation: Its social and legal context.* Englewood Cliffs, NJ: Prentice-Hall. An excellent small book that examines mental retardation within a social context.

9 JUVENILE DELINQUENCY

Carl is a 15-year-old who has been a resident of a state training school for 6 months. His current offense involved breaking into the apartment of an elderly woman in order to get money to buy drugs. While in the apartment, he was surprised by the woman who returned home earlier than expected. When the woman attempted to summon help, Carl hit her with a vase, resulting in a subsequent hospitalization for head injuries. He was stopped by two neighbors as he was leaving the apartment with the woman's radio and some jewelery. When later asked how he felt about the woman being hurt, he simply stated "she shouldn't have come home while I was there." A review of Carl's police record indicates that he has been arrested on three earlier occasions, twice for breaking and entering, and once for assault.

Mark, age 17, has been in court 3 times during the past 2 years. This time he is charged, along with three other adolescents, with auto theft. His two prior arrests were for stealing a car stereo and for participating in the break-in of a local liquor store. Mark and his friends, all members of "The Diablos" (a local adolescent gang), are reportedly well-known to the police because of several fights they have had with other gangs and because they are suspected of a number of other break-ins during the past several years.

Joey, age 13, and his brother, age 11, come from a family where they have frequently been the victims of abuse. Recently, after becoming angry with the younger boy and hitting him several times, the mother ordered him out of the house, telling him not to return until he "could learn to behave." Scared and angered by yet another abusive episode, Joey convinced his brother that they should leave home. Finding that they had no place to stay, the two of them decided to spend the first night in an abandoned school several blocks from their home. Having no food and still afraid to return home, they broke into a neighborhood grocery store and stole a loaf of bread, several packages of luncheon meat, potato chips, and several soft drinks. They were immediately apprehended by the police, charged with a break-in, and, after an investigation of the family situation, committed to the state. At that point they were sent to the state Diagnostic and Reception Center, a receiving facility for juvenile offenders.

Although the cases presented here differ in several respects (and we will comment further on this variability in later sections), they all involve illegal acts, committed by youngsters under the age of 18. As such they fall within the *legal* category of juvenile delinquency.

The problem of juvenile crime would appear to be a serious one. For example, statistics provided by the Federal Bureau of Investigation suggest that in 1981 there were some 9,668 persons arrested for various charges, ranging from less serious offenses (e.g., vagrancy, disorderly conduct, drunkenness) to more serious crimes such as murder, forcible rape, robbery, aggravated assault, burglary, larceny-theft, arson, and motor vehicle theft. Juveniles under the age of 18 were responsible for some 20% of these arrests. Of special interest is the fact that, of the more serious crimes listed above, juveniles below the age of 18 accounted for over 33% of the cases (U.S. Department of Commerce, 1983).

Further data are provided by juvenile court statistics. Figure 9.1 provides information concerning the number of cases per 1,000 children (age 10 to 17) seen in juvenile court

between the years 1960 and 1979. As can be seen, the proportion of juvenile court cases has steadily increased over the years. In 1979 almost 5% of the juvenile population was seen in juvenile court, as compared to approximately 2% in 1960 (Statistical Abstracts of the United States, 1982–1983). Although these statistics are of interest, it must be noted that they are somewhat difficult to interpret. Arrest rates, for example, may be influenced to some unknown degree by the fact that many offenders are never detected and apprehended. And many who are apprehended may never be seen in juvenile court for vari-

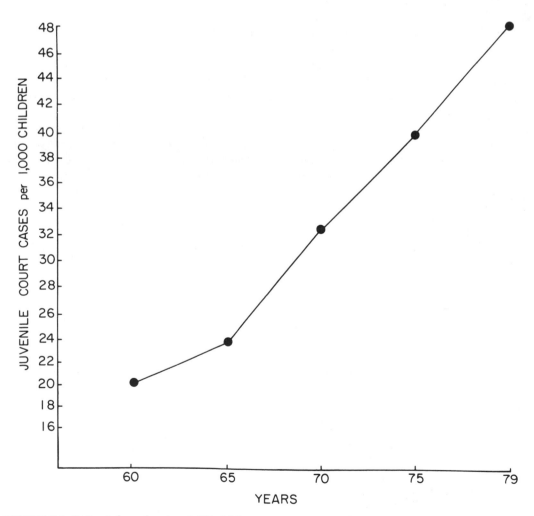

FIGURE 9.1. Estimated number (per 1,000 children ages 10 to 17) of delinquency cases seen by juvenile courts 1960–1979. Source: Adapted from U.S. Department of Commerce, (1983).

ous reasons (e.g., inability of parents to get a good lawyer). Further, both arrest rates and juvenile court statistics may relate to prevailing law enforcement practices, which may vary with political climate and other factors, as well as to the frequency of actual juvenile offenses. Despite these limitations, however, the available statistics do seem to indicate that the juvenile crime is a serious social problem and one that is on the increase.

It is of interest to note that while delinquency has traditionally been considered a male problem, female arrest rates have increased dramatically in recent years. For example, between 1968 and 1977 the increase in female arrests was 3 times greater than the increase in male arrests (FBI, 1978). Covering a slightly different time span, Knopf (1984) has cited figures suggesting that between 1965 and 1981, delinquent offenses involving females increased by 78% as opposed to an increase of only 44% for males. Female delinquency appears to be an increasingly serious problem.

When one considers the cost resulting from increased rates of delinquency in terms of money necessary to support juvenile courts and centers for the rehabilitation of juvenile offenders, plus the costs, both financial and personal, to the victims of delinquent acts, the magnitude of the problem becomes apparent. It is not surprising that much attention has been given this problem by sociologists, psychologists, and other professionals.

In this chapter we will consider views about the causes of delinquency, research into the correlates of delinquent behavior, the relationship between delinquency and other child/adolescent problems, as well as a range of treatment approaches designed to deal with this problem. We will then turn our attention to the problem of adolescent drug abuse.

Delinquency: A Problem of Definition

The term *delinquent* may have a personal meaning for many of us, conjuring up images of an adolescent who skips school, hangs out at the pool hall, steals, snatches purses from elderly ladies, runs with a gang, uses drugs, is aggressive, or is unmanageable by his parents. These subjective meanings, however, do not clearly specify which individuals ought to be grouped within this very general category.

It is good to keep in mind that the term *delinquency* is a legal one, used to refer to a juvenile (usually under the age of 18) who has committed an act that would be considered illegal for an adult. Delinquency laws in most states also have what are called omnibus provisions, which give juvenile courts jurisdiction over juveniles who display a variety of other behaviors (status offenses) not forbidden by criminal laws (Gibbons, 1981; Lewis, 1985). These provisions may make it illegal for juveniles to be truant from school, associate with "immoral" persons, stay out after curfew, be incorrigible, or engage in certain other behaviors that would not be illegal for an adult. In the legal sense, then, a juvenile may be considered delinquent either as a result of breaking some state, federal, or local law or for engaging in some other behavior considered specifically illegal for juveniles.

For purposes of research, investigators have employed a variety of different operational definitions (that is, statements of how individuals will be classified as delinquent). Some workers in the area have considered juveniles who have been arrested, regardless of later disposition. For others the term has been used to refer specifically to those who have been seen in juvenile court. Still others have considered as delinquent those juveniles who report having committed illegal acts, even though they may have never come to the attention of law enforcement personnel. Finally, some researchers have chosen to focus mainly on juveniles who have been incarcerated for the commission of illegal acts. Delinquency can be defined in any of these ways for purposes of a given research study, but it is important to note that the way one defines delinquency has implications for the nature of the research findings that will be obtained.

This can readily be seen by addressing the question of incidence and prevalence. If one considers as delinquent only those who have been committed to a juvenile institution, the magnitude of the problem will not appear as great as if one considers the number seen in juvenile court (most juveniles seen in court do not end up in institutions), or the number arrested by police (most juveniles who are arrested do not appear in juvenile court). All of these figures would be quite low in comparison to those obtained by considering individuals who admit to delinquent behavior even though not caught. For instance, it was mentioned earlier that approximately 5% of the juvenile population was seen in juvenile court in 1979. But studies of "normal" individuals, responding to anonymous questionnaires, suggest that perhaps as many as 80 to 90% may actually engage in "illegal" behaviors (Moore & Arthur, 1983). The extent of "hidden delinquency" appears to be much greater than the extent of delinquency defined in terms of arrest records, juvenile court appearances, or incarceration rates.

It might be argued that there is no one way of defining delinquency that is more adequate than others in all instances: Different research questions may demand that delinquency be defined in different ways. However, it is important to keep in mind that research findings will be influenced by the definition employed. By the same token, any figures related to the incidence of juvenile delinquency should be interpreted with caution, for we have no good way of assessing the actual frequency of illegal acts committed by juvenile offenders. Statistics based on arrest records, juvenile court appearances, and incarceration rates may well be influenced, to some unknown degree, by variables such as race, socioeconomic status, and prevailing law enforcement practices.

DIMENSIONS OF DELINQUENCY

In addition to the problems of definition, there has also been an unfortunate tendency on the part of workers in the area to consider delinquency as a unitary construct. Thus, many researchers have attempted to deter-

mine "antecedents of delinquency," "correlates of delinquency," and methods appropriate to the treatment of "delinquents," without considering the marked variability within this legally defined group. Whether delinquents are defined as juveniles who have been arrested, those who have been incarcerated, or those who have simply admitted illegal acts, these individuals are probably much more different than alike (consider, for example, the three cases presented at the beginning of the chapter). In light of this variability, it is not surprising that studies that fail to consider differences between delinquents often yield inconsistent results and few generalizable findings.

As a result of the observed variability within this population, a number of studies have been directed toward investigating the possibility that subtypes or meaningful dimensions of delinquency may exist. Illustrative of such studies is a classic investigation by Quay (1964). In this study Quay obtained ratings on a total of 24 behavioral traits (based on case history data) using 115 institutionalized male delinquents as subjects. These data were subsequently factor analyzed. These analyses yielded a total of four relatively independent factors (clusters of interrelated behavioral characteristics) that seemed to represent meaningful dimensions of delinquent behavior. These factors were labeled socialized-subcultural delinquency, unsocialized-psychopathic delinquency, disturbed-neurotic delinquency, and inadequate-immature delinquency.

Socialized-Subcultural Delinquency

Delinquents scoring high on this dimension were defined in terms of characteristics such as has bad companions, stays out late at night, is accepted by a delinquent subgroup, and has strong allegiance to selected peers. They were also found to be rated low on characteristics such as shyness and seclusiveness.

The results of other studies indicate that, as a group, persons high on this dimension show little evidence of psychopathology and tend to be of lower socioeconomic status. Together the findings suggest that the socialized-subcultural delinquent may best be thought of as a relatively normal individual whose delinquent modes of behavior relate to interaction with a delinquent subgroup.

Unsocialized-Psychopathic Delinquency

Unlike the socialized-subcultural delinquent, juveniles scoring high on this dimension seem to show little tendency to have "bad companions," participate in gang activities, or be accepted by a delinquent subgroup. This person would be described as a solitary rather than a group-oriented delinquent. Other behaviors found by Quay to be descriptive of unsocialized-psychopathic delinquency include defiance of authority, assaultiveness, quarrelsomeness, irritability, impudence, verbal aggressiveness, feelings of persecution, and inability to profit from praise or punishment. Other studies describe such individuals as distrustful of others, displaying inadequate guilt feelings, and seeking out rather than attempting to avoid trouble (Quay, 1979b).

Although many professionals would hesitate to apply a diagnostic label of psychopathic personality to an adolescent, the use of the term *unsocialized-psychopathic delinquency* emphasizes the perceived similarity between such individuals and characteristics often associated with adults who are considered sociopathic, psychopathic, or diagnosed as antisocial personality (DSM-III, American Psychiatric Association, 1980).

Disturbed-Neurotic Delinquency

In contrast to the subgroups already considered, the disturbed-neurotic delinquent appears to be a generally unhappy, timid, shy, and withdrawn individual who is prone to worry and displays guilt and anxiety over his or her behavior. Physical complaints may also be prominent. Quay (1972) noted that

delinquents of this type are less aggressive, are accepting of authority, more amenable to change, and less likely to repeat their delinquent behavior than other types of delinquents. It would seem reasonable to characterize this type of delinquent as one whose major problems are psychological in nature and whose delinquent behavior is secondary to these emotional problems.

Inadequate-Immature Delinquency

A fourth, less prominent dimension also found by Quay was labeled inadequate-immature delinquency. Those scoring high on this dimension tend to be easily frustrated, picked on by others, passive and preoccupied, and usually not accepted by delinquent peers (Quay, 1964, 1972). Rather than having major psychological problems, these juveniles simply appeared to have a poorly developed behavioral repertoire, to be relatively inadequate in their functioning, and unable to cope with the demands of their environment (Quay, 1979).

Dimensions of Delinquency: An Overview

At this point it would seem important to comment on the relationship between these empirically derived dimensions and DSM-III categories for classifying antisocial behavior. Within DSM-III, antisocial behaviors of children and adolescents are considered under the general heading of conduct disorders. According to the developers of this system, these disorders involve "a repetitive and persistent pattern of conduct in which either the basic rights of others or major age-appropriate societal norms or rules are violated" (American Psychiatric Association, 1980, p. 45). Four major subtypes of conduct disorder are described, with the specific diagnosis depending on the degree to which the person does or does not show adequate social relationships and the presence (or absence) of aggressive-antisocial behavior. Specific diagnostic categories include undersocialized aggressive, undersocialized nonaggressive, socialized aggressive, and socialized nonaggressive types. Tables 9.1 and 9.2 illustrate this approach by providing diagnostic criteria for the undersocialized-aggressive and socialized-nonaggressive categories.

Although there is overlap between these categories of conduct disorder and the dimensions described above (especially as regards the socialized and undersocialized dimension), there seems to be little reason to employ these categories instead of the more well-substantiated ones just described. In this regard it may be noted that the four dimensions first described by Quay (1964) have been replicated in a number of other studies of delinquent behavior. Dimensions similar to these have also been defined in studies of nondelinquent behavior-disordered children (see Chapter 2). They have been found in analyses of data provided by males and females and in analyses of data other than case history material, such as from behavior checklists and personality measures. Although all of the

dimensions have not been found in every study, each has been found with surprising regularity, suggesting that they are very reliable dimensions.

In reviewing correlates of these dimensions, Quay (1979b) has emphasized the importance of distinguishing among these specific delinquent subgroups. He has noted, for example, that several studies comparing delinquents and nondelinquents in terms of level of moral development have produced inconclusive results, but that later investigations comparing unsocialized-psychopathic delinquents, disturbed-neurotic delinquents, and socialized-subcultural delinquents have suggested clear differences. These studies have suggested that psychopathic delinquents are significantly lower in moral development than the other two groups and that this group differs significantly from nondelinquents, whereas neurotic and subcultural delinquents do not (Jurkovic & Prentice, 1977). These findings serve to emphasize again that delinquents cannot be considered a homogeneous group, and that failure to take this heterogeneity into

TABLE 9.1. DSM-III CRITERIA FOR CONDUCT DISORDER, UNDERSOCIALIZED AGGRESSIVE TYPE.

A. A repetitive and persistent pattern of aggressive conduct in which the basic rights of others are violated, as manifested by either of the following:

1) Physical violence against persons or property (not to defend someone else or oneself), e.g., vandalism, rape, breaking and entering, fire setting, mugging, assault.

2) Thefts outside the home involving confrontation with the victim (e.g., extortion, purse-snatching, armed robbery).

B. Failure to establish a normal degree of affection, empathy, or bond with others as evidenced by no more than one of the following indications of social attachment:

1) has one or more peer-group friendships that have lasted over six months.

2) extends himself or herself for others even when no immediate advantage is likely.

3) apparently feels guilt or remorse when such a reaction is appropriate (not just when caught or in difficulty).

4) avoids blaming or informing on companions.

5) shares concern for the welfare of friends or companions.

C. Duration of pattern of aggressive conduct of at least six months.

D. If 18 or older, does not meet the criteria for Antisocial Personality Disorder.

Source: American Psychiatric Association (1980). © 1980 American Psychiatric Association and reprinted with permission.

TABLE 9.2. DSM-III CRITERIA FOR CONDUCT DISORDER, SOCIALIZED NONAGGRESSIVE TYPE.

A. A repetitive and persistent pattern of nonaggressive conduct in which either the basic rights of others or major age-appropriate societal norms or rules are violated, as manifested by any of the following:

    1) chronic violations of a variety of important rules (that are reasonable and age appropriate for the child) at home or at school (e.g., persistent truancy, substance abuse).

    2) repeated running away from home overnight.

    3) persistent serious lying in and out of the home.

    4) stealing not involving confrontation with a victim.

B. Evidence of social attachment to others as indicated by at least two of the following behavior patterns:

    1) has one or more peer-group friendships that have lasted over six months.

    2) extends himself or herself for others even when no immediate advantage is likely.

    3) apparently feels guilt or remorse when such a reaction is appropriate (not just when caught or in difficulty).

    4) avoids blaming or informing on companions.

    5) shows concern for the welfare of friends or companions.

C. Duration of pattern of nonaggressive conduct of at least six months.

D. If 18 or older does not meet the criteria for Antisocial Personality Disorder.

Source: American Psychiatric Association (1980). © 1980 American Psychiatric Association and reprinted with permission.

account can obscure important information about variables related to delinquent behavior.

Other studies also suggest important correlates of these dimensions. Clear differences have been found between psychopathic delinquents and those characterized as neurotic and subcultural in responding to boring tasks requiring sustained attention (Orris, 1969). Skrzypek (1969), in a study of stimulus preferences that compared psychopathic and neurotic delinquents, found psychopathic delinquents prefer complex, novel, and arousing stimuli over the more mundane stimuli preferred by neurotic delinquents. Additionally, the neurotic group was found to have anxiety scores more than double those of the psychopathic group.

Research by Hetherington, Stouwie, and Ridberg (1971) suggested that these dimensions are related in important ways to family interaction patterns. There is some evidence that position on these dimensions is related to degree of social dysfunction in later life,

with unsocialized-psychopathic and immature types having a greater likelihood of serious problems than the disturbed-neurotic or socialized-subcultural delinquent (Quay, 1979b). There is also some suggestion that unsocialized-psychopathic delinquents are more likely to display repeat offenses after being incarcerated than are socialized delinquents (Henn, Bardwell, & Jenkins, 1980). Finally, recent research by Ellis (1982) focusing on the relationship between delinquency and empathy has found delinquents, as a group, to show lower levels of empathy than nondelinquents. Further analyses that assessed subgroup differences in empathy found disturbed-neurotic delinquents to be the least empathic, followed by unsocialized-psychopathic delinquents, and socialized-subcultural delinquents (who did not differ from nondelinquents). Each of these three delinquent groups were found to differ significantly from one another, again suggesting the importance of making distinctions among delinquents.

Given the evidence that these dimensions

of delinquency are differentially related to meaningful variables, it behooves researchers to take these dimensions into account in conducting delinquency research. By considering the fact that delinquents differ from one another in important ways, it may be possible to determine antecedents and correlates of various "types" of delinquency and to develop treatment approaches tailored to fit various delinquent subgroups.

ETIOLOGICAL VIEWS OF DELINQUENCY

Over the years a variety of theoretical points of view have evolved to account for delinquent behavior, ranging from fairly well-formulated theoretical statements to loose collections of hypotheses. Some of these theories have been presented to account for delinquency per se, whereas others have focused on particular types of antisocial behavior. These views have varied in the amount of attention given to sociological, psychological, and biological variables.

Theories of delinquency have been considered in detail by several current authors (Gibbons, 1981; Rutter & Giller, 1983; Trojanowicz & Morash, 1983), so only a brief overview of some of these views will be presented here.

Sociological Views

Numerous writers have emphasized the role of social factors in the development of delinquency. Two of the major sociological views focus on the consequences of an individual's inability to reach socially valued goals (material goods, status) through legitimate means. Merton (1957), for example, pointed to the fact that individuals reared in lower socioeconomic-status families have goals and desires similar to those of the middle class. He suggested that when they find themselves unable to achieve these goals through legal means, because of social constraints, they resort to delinquent behavior to reach them. Similarly, Cloward and Ohlin's (1969) "op-portunity structure theory" postulates that juveniles from lower social classes become alienated, blaming society for their limited opportunity to achieve important goals and for failing to meet their needs; as a result such individuals tend to affiliate with a delinquent subculture within which they can achieve status, realize certain goals, and cope with their feelings of alienation. Other sociological theories have also been proposed to account for the cultural transmission of delinquency (Shaw & McKay, 1969), group delinquency (Thrasher, 1963), and middle-class delinquency (Vaz, 1967).

Psychodynamic Views

Although sociologists have understandably tended to focus on the role of social factors, many psychologists, particularly those with a psychodynamic orientation, emphasize the role of intrapsychic factors. Here the general view is that antisocial behavior is reflective of some form of psychopathology. As Wirt and Briggs (1965) have noted

> The fundamental intrapsychic pathology is often attributed to faulty interpersonal relationships especially between parents and children in the early years (or months) of life. Disturbances of these relationships produce neurotic, psychotic, or character disordered behaviors, some of which are antisocial. It becomes antisocial through one of several routes. In some cases the individual, because of neurotic guilt, seeks to be punished; in some cases the individual, because of displaced hostility, seeks revenge on society or symbolic persons or objects; in some cases the individual, because of panic arising from displaced anxiety, thinks that he is protecting his endangered psyche or physical being by attacking others or destroying property he erroneously believes is intent on harming him. (pp. 14–15)

Although there are several psychodynamic views of delinquency causation, this characterization by Wirt and Briggs is fairly representative of those emphasizing the importance of intrapsychic factors.

Delinquency as Learned Behavior

Others have focused on the role of learning in an attempt to explain delinquent behavior. Most notable in this respect are Sutherland's "differential association theory" (Sutherland & Cressy, 1978) and the social learning theory of Bandura and Walters (1963). Both place much importance on the individual's interaction with others who display antisocial behavior and on the rewards that often result from such behavior. Much aggressive and delinquent behavior is explained as being learned as a result of exposure to parents, peers, and others who model aggressive and criminal behavior. This vicarious learning may be combined with a lack of exposure to models who exhibit prosocial behaviors and with reinforcement of delinquent behavior in the natural environment.

The focus on the role of learning in the development of delinquency has led many to implement behavioral programs for treating juvenile offenders, which will be considered in a later portion of this chapter.

Delinquency as Stimulation Seeking

Farley (1973) has proposed an arousal/sensation-seeking model of delinquency. From this point of view, delinquents are characterized as individuals with physiological (inherited) arousal deficits, who, because they are underaroused (that is, have a less than optimal level of arousal), display a tendency to seek out novel, exciting activities in order to increase their arousal level and attain some optimal level of stimulation. It is assumed that given an environment lacking sufficient socially acceptable opportunites for stimulation, these high sensation seekers may tend to engage in behaviors that are unacceptable but produce high levels of stimulation.

In a similar vein, Quay (1965) characterized psychopathic individuals as pathological stimulation seekers, suggesting that because of their lower reactivity or tendency to adapt

more readily than normals to new stimuli, they may show characteristics of sensory deprivation, including the tendency to seek out stimulating activities, some of which may be antisocial. Research bearing on the relationship between delinquency and sensation seeking is considered further in a later section.

CORRELATES OF DELINQUENCY AND ANTISOCIAL BEHAVIOR

Hereditary Factors in Delinquency

Many investigators interested in the causes of antisocial behavior have spotlighted the possible contribution of genetic factors. The role of heredity is suggested by the fact that parents and other relatives of delinquents and adult lawbreakers are often found to display antisocial and criminal behavior, an observation that must be tempered by the recognition that the tendency for antisocial behavior to run in families may result from either environmental or genetic factors.

Support for the view that genetic factors may be involved has, however, been found in the results of twin studies. Rosenthal (1975), in a review of nine studies examining the concordance rates for psychopathy and criminal behavior in monozygotic (MZ) and same-sex dizygotic (DZ) twins, discovered that across studies the concordance rates for MZ twins was roughly $2\frac{1}{2}$ times that of DZ twin pairs. Crow (1974) and Cadonet (1978) have also found that adoptees separated at birth from their parents, who displayed antisocial behavior, had higher rates of antisocial behavior than control subjects whose parents were not judged antisocial. These findings provide further support for the role of genetic factors.

In spite of these findings, available evidence would seem to suggest that environmental factors probably play a more prominent role in the development of antisocial behavior than do genetic factors (Rosenthal, 1975). For example, Rutter (1972b) has suggested that delinquent behavior is not inherited as such, but that inherited temperamental differences, in association with family discord and disruption, may contribute to the development of antisocial modes of responding. Heredity does not destine one to become psychopathic or to engage in antisocial behavior, although it may be one of the contributing factors.

Chromosomal Abnormalities and Antisocial Behavior

It has also been surmised that chromosomal abnormalities may contribute to antisocial behavior. In 1961 it was determined that some males display what has been referred to as the XYY syndrome, having one more than the usual compliment of Y chromosomes (Sandberg, Koepf, Ishihara, & Hauschka, 1961). Individuals with this syndrome often display a variety of characteristics that distinguish them from the general population, including below-average IQ, greater-than-average height, and tendencies toward social withdrawal and behavioral problems. Other physical anomalies may also be present. This syndrome has been shown to occur in approximately 1 of every 1,000 male births (Hook, 1973). Of particular interest is the fact that XYY males seem to be overly represented in mental and penal institutions. In a survey of the literature on the XYY syndrome, Owen (1972) cited findings that the rate of the XYY syndrome in such settings is 4 to 5 times the presumed general population rate, findings that have led many to speculate that this syndrome may genetically predispose individuals to antisocial behavior. Although the bulk of the literature relates to adults rather than children, case reports by Ratcliff and Field (1982) have suggested a possible relationship between XYY characteristics and childhood emotional problems, which in some instances may present with symptoms of conduct disorder.

At present the relationship between the XYY chromosomal make-up and antisocial behavior is unclear. Most persons displaying antisocial behavior do not display this syndrome, and not all persons with the syndrome display antisocial behavior. So whereas some relationship may exist, this particular chromosomal abnormality does not account for the vast majority of delinquent or criminal behavior. It might be pointed out that even if one accepts the view that XYY individuals show a tendency toward antisocial behavior, this does not necessarily imply that the behavior is genetically based. As Rosenthal (1975) has pointed out, individuals with chromosomal abnormalities may simply be more likely to show antisocial behavior as a result of the psychological distress resulting from the physical anomalies associated with the syndrome.

Social Class and Delinquency

Much attention has been given to the relationship between social class and delinquency. It has been assumed by many, and indeed taken for granted, that the bulk of delinquent behavior is committed by juveniles from lower social classes and that juveniles from middle and upper classes contribute insignificantly to the overall delinquency problem. This is reflected in several theories of delinquency that deal with variables operative within the lower-class social structures that might contribute to delinquent behavior. What is the relationship, if any, between social class and delinquency?

Research findings suggest that, at least with urban youth, there is an inverse relationship between socioeconomic class and arrests and prosecutions for a juvenile offense (Davids, 1973; West & Farrington, 1973). Official delinquency rates, then, appear to be higher among youth from lower social classes. (These findings have not always been replicated when youths from rural areas and small communities have been considered.) An important question is whether these findings, based on official delinquency rates, reflect the actual degree of law-breaking behavior engaged in by youths from various socioeconomic groups or whether they relate more to prevailing law enforcement practices (which may be biased in favor of those from higher social classes).

As was discussed earlier, a number of studies have attempted to assess law-violating behavior by obtaining anonymous self-reports of delinquent behavior. These studies have found that the vast majority of youth report engaging in behavior that could be classified as illegal. Several studies have used this self-report approach in attempting to assess the relationship between social class and delinquency. In general, these studies have found little in the way of a relationship between reports of delinquency and socioeconomic status (Empey, 1978; Gold & Petronio, 1980).

Although the results of these self-report studies seem to suggest that delinquent behavior is unrelated to social class, this interpretation has been questioned by recent studies that have assessed both the rate and severity of delinquent offenses in addition to their occurrence. Reviews of this literature (Elliot & Ageton, 1980; Hindelang, Hirschi, & Weis, 1979; Rutter & Giller, 1983) have suggested that whereas self-report studies *have* found the majority of youths from various social classes to report "delinquent" behavior, many of the offenses reported are not serious ones. Thus, self-reported offenses frequently reflect behaviors that may be "illegal" but that would not be likely to get the child into the juvenile justice system, even if caught. Elliot and Ageton (1980) have also found, even with self-report studies, that when both the *rate* and *severity* of self-reported offenses are considered, social class is found to be inversely related to indices of "severe" delinquency. These findings would seem to imply that although juveniles from the upper social classes (as a group) may engage in "delinquent" activites, these "illegal" acts are *on the whole* less severe and less frequent that those displayed by lower class youth (as a group). Commenting on the results of these and other studies Rutter and Giller (1983) have concluded

> The evidence suggests that there is a modest (but not strong) association between low social status and delinquency, but that this association applies mainly at the extremes of the social scale, that it is due in part to social class differentials in detection and prosecution, and that, in so far as it applies to real differences in delinquent activities, the association is largely confined to the more serious delinquencies. Moreover, even that association is more strongly evident with measures of parental unemployment or reliance on welfare than with indices of parental occupation or education. (pp. 136–137)

It would appear that an argument can be made for some degree of relationship between more serious forms of delinquent behavior and social class (whether delinquency is indexed in terms of official statistics *or* self-report). This should not, however, be taken to mean that serious delinquency is restricted to only the lower social class. Although lower social class youth may be overly represented among more serious offenders, youth from all socioeconomic groups contribute to the existing delinquency problem.

Family Variables and Delinquency

It is generally assumed that family variables play a crucial role in the development of delinquent behavior. This is not surprising, because it is reasonable to expect that children of parents who model antisocial behavior might behave in a similar fashion, that parents who are lax in discipline might have children who have little regard for social rules, and that a family environment characterized by marital discord, hostility, and tension might result in aggressive behavior on the part of juveniles exposed to such an environment. In fact, a variety of research studies have implicated family variables in delinquency causation.

The Glueck Studies of Delinquency

One of the early studies in this area was conducted by Sheldon and Eleanor Glueck (Glueck & Glueck, 1950). It involved a comparison of 500 delinquent and 500 nondelinquent boys from highly delinquent neighborhoods. The subjects were matched for age, race, ethnic background, and IQ. Of particular interest was which factors would discriminate between these two groups of adolescents, all of whom had been exposed to a presumably unfavorable environment. A number of family variables proved to be of significance.

As a group, parents of delinquents were found to more often display serious physical problems as well as emotional, intellectual, and behavioral disturbances. There was also more evidence of alcoholism, criminal behavior, and "immorality" than in parents of nondelinquents. The relationships between parents of delinquents were characterized by more conflict and incompatability than were the families of nondelinquents, and, as one might expect, families of delinquents were more often characterized by separation, divorce, and prolonged absence of a parent from the home.

As for parent-child attitudes, parents of delinquents were found to be much less likely to show warmth, sympathy, and affection toward their children. Mothers of delinquents were found to be far more permissive than mothers of nondelinquents. Fathers of delinquents tended to be stricter in their discipline than were fathers of nondelinquents and more often resorted to the use of physical punishments. Also, inconsistent discipline was more than twice as prominent among fathers of delinquent boys.

Even though all of the families in this study might be characterized as of lower social class, families of delinquents were more apt to be dependent on welfare agencies for financial aid, the main reason being an unwillingness of the breadwinner to assume responsibility for supporting the family.

> Families of delinquents were far more inclined than those of nondelinquents to live from hand to mouth and from day to day, borrowing without thought of their ability to reimburse and showing little comprehension of the need to limit expenditures to conform to their meager incomes (Glueck & Glueck, 1968, p. 7).

Families of delinquents were also found to display less regularity in general family routine and a higher degree of disorganization than families of nondelinquents.

Other Studies of Family Variables

A variety of other investigations have explored the relationship between family variables and delinquency. Because much of this research has been described in detail elsewhere (Hetherington & Martin, 1979; Moore & Arthur, 1983; Trojanowicz & Morash, 1983), it will be discussed only briefly here.

In general, studies have found parents of delinquents to display lower levels of moral judgment, to be more exteme in terms of discipline (permissiveness-restrictiveness), to be more hostile and rejecting, to be more likely to use physical punishment, to be more erratic and inconsistent in discipline, to show higher levels of parental conflict, and to display higher rates of antisocial behavior (Hetherington & Martin, 1979; Moore & Arthur, 1983). It may be noted that these findings are in line with the earlier results of the Glueck and Glueck study.

Two points need to be made concerning this literature. First, the fact that a number of studies have found differences between families of delinquents and nondelinquents does not necessarily mean that such variables are causally related to delinquent behavior, for the data are correlational in nature. This does not mean that such variables do not exert a causal influence, simply that most studies do not allow us to conclude that this is so. A second point is that most studies in the area have treated delinquents as a homogeneous group and have not considered that various "types" of delinquency (disturbed neurotic, unsocialized psychopathic, socialized subcultural, inadequate immature) may be differentially related to family variables. As Hetherington and Martin (1979) remark, such distinctions are probably quite important. Citing the results of early studies by Hewitt and Jenkins (1946) and Lewis (1954), they note that disturbed-neurotic delinquency seems related to an overcontrolling approach to discipline, whereas unsocialized-psychopathic delinquency is related to parental rejection, and socialized-subcultural delinquency to permissiveness, neglect, and exposure to delinquent norms. Research by Hetherington, Stouwie, and Ridberg (1971) also suggests that these dimensions of delinquency are related to different patterns of family interaction. Studies of this type are few in number, but they show that researchers conducting future studies in this area would be well advised to take these dimensions into account. Family variables may play a more important and perhaps different role in some types of delinquency than in others.

Psychological Factors in Delinquency

Numerous studies have sought to assess the presence of psychological problems in delinquents and nondelinquents, but their findings have not been totally clear. In many cases the assessment of psychopathology has been subjective in nature, and sometimes the assessment has been made by individuals who were aware of the subjects' group membership, thus introducing the possibility of bias. In most instances no distinction between subgroups of delinquents has been made.

Gibbons (1981), in a review of studies comparing rates of psychopathology in delinquents and nondelinquents, has concluded that "most juvenile offenders are relatively normal youths in terms of personality structure in that they do not exhibit aberrant motives, deep-seated psychological tensions, or other marks of psychological disturbances" (p. 123). This statement should not be interpreted as suggesting that there are not delinquents who have serious psychological problems but simply that most legally defined delinquents do not display evidence of major psychological disorders. As studies have not typically distinguished between "subtypes" of delinquents, we cannot be certain that some delinquents do not show higher rates of psychopathology than others. Indeed, one study (Genshaft, 1980), which obtained MMPI data from delinquents classified as disturbed-neurotic, unsocialized-psychopathic, and socialized-subcultural types, suggested that the disturbed-neurotic group did in fact display a greater degree of psychopathology than did the other types. Additional studies of this type are needed.

It could be argued that in some cases delinquency itself, even in the absence of other evidence of maladjustment, may be equated with psychopathology. Regarding this issue, Moore and Arthur (1983) have cited studies suggesting that even though delinquent offenses are relatively common, most delinquents (perhaps as many as 45 to 55%) commit only one offense prior to adulthood. There are, however, other more chronic offenders. These are children who usually begin their delinquent activities at an early age and show a continued pattern of more serious delinquent offenses as they become older. Moore and Arthur note that although these recidivist delinquents represent a minority of the total delinquent population, they account for a majority of the total number of delinquent acts committed. As these chronic offenders frequently display a seriously maladaptive pattern of antisocial behavior, which is likely to continue into adulthood, it is suggested that this delinquency is psychopathological in its own right (Moore & Arthur, 1983).

Despite studies investigating personality correlates of delinquency, it can be said with some confidence that there is no evidence for a "delinquent personality"; there seem to be no particular personality characteristics that are descriptive of most delinquents. A major problem in studies of personality correlates is, again, the tendency of researchers to consider delinquents as a homogeneous group. If there are indeed several types or dimensions of delinquency that may be related to different etiologies, it is not surprising that studies that have failed to consider these differences have typically yielded negative or inconsistent findings.

Although few psychological variables have been found to be consistently related to delinquency, one that has received increasing attention in recent years is sensation seeking. Interest in this variable seems to have been stimulated by the theoretical notions of Farley (1973) and Quay (1965), cited earlier.

As was indicated earlier in the chapter, sensation seeking is reflected in behaviors that might be presumed to increase arousal level. Sensation seekers tend to prefer the novel to the familiar and often engage in thrilling and frequently risky behaviors. It has been suggested that tendencies toward sensation seeking result from having a (perhaps biologically determined) arousal deficit, which results in the individual displaying a less than optimal state of arousal. Seeking stimulation is thus seen as an attempt to increase the level of stimulation and arousal to some more optimal level. Indices of these variables can be obtained through the use of questionnaires (Zukerman, 1974) or by employing experimental tasks that assess preferences for stimulating versus nonstimulating stimuli.

A number of studies have suggested a correlation between paper-and-pencil measures of sensation seeking and aspects of delinquent behavior. For example, Farley and Sewell (1976) found that adjudicated delinquents scored significantly higher on a measure of sensation seeking than did nondelinquents matched for age, sex, and socioeconomic status. Among incarcerated female delinquents, Farley and Farley (1972) found high sensation seekers to make more escape attempts, to be punished more often for disobeying supervisors, and to engage in more aggressive behaviors than low sensation seekers. Similar results have also been found for male delinquents. Sensation seeking has also been shown to be significantly related to increased drug usage and extent and variety of sexual behavior (Zuckerman, 1974).

It is unclear whether delinquents as a group can be characterized as high sensation seekers. This was suggested by Farley (1973), but

Quay (1965) has tended to equate stimulation seeking with psychopathy. Indeed, the experimental studies considered earlier, comparing delinquents scoring high on various dimensions of delinquency, indicated that unsocialized-psychopathic delinquents tended to show the highest levels of stimulation-seeking behavior. Moreover, this group has been found to differ from other delinquents (e.g., disturbed-neurotic delinquents) on this variable (Quay, 1979b). Although more data is needed, it would seem that the unsocialized-psychopathic dimension is most highly correlated with tendencies toward sensation seeking.

DELINQUENCY AND OTHER PROBLEMS OF CHILDHOOD

Learning Disabilities

As indicated in the preceding chapter, the term *learning disabilities* generally refers to a disability in understanding and/or using spoken or written language. Included here are disorders of listening, talking, reading, writing, or spelling that are not primarily due to specific visual, auditory, or motor handicaps (Hobbs, 1975).

Noting that many juvenile delinquents perform poorly in school and that there is a high correlation between dropping out of school and delinquent behavior, a number of authors have suggested that the experiencing of learning disabilities may be an etiological factor in the development of delinquent behavior. One account of this hypothesized relationship has been presented by Berman & Siegal (1976):

The cycle begins with early problems at home. The child was showing perceptual and attention problems even prior to school, but the behavior was written off as "ornery" or "uncooperative" personality. The child enters the early grades of school already accustomed to the fact that he won't be able to do things as well as expected of him, that he will fail and be humiliated continually. This prophecy is fulfilled in school as teachers, considering the child "a behavior problem," punish and ridicule him for failures or for behaviors that he cannot control. The child begins to think of himself as a loser, as someone who can never hope to live up to what people expect of him.

Rather than face the embarrassment of continual failure in front of friends and teachers, the behavioral signs become even more pronounced. Clowning around and general disruptiveness become the ways which best insulate this youngster from having to face continual and repeated failure. He becomes much more successful as a clown or troublemaker than he ever could as a student.

Teachers now are completely diverted away from any learning problems and concentrate solely on how to deal with the child's behavior. He gets further and further behind and becomes more and more of a problem. Eventually, he's suspended, drops out, or is thrown out of school to roam the streets, and the inevitable road to delinquency is well under way. (pp. 45–46)

Athough many professionals who work with delinquents report a fairly high frequency of learning disabilities, the findings from research studies have yet to document a *causal* link between childhood learning problems and later delinquency (Lane, 1980; Murray, 1976). This state of affairs should not be taken to mean that there is no association between these variables; existing research has simply not been adequate to demonstrate the validity or invalidity of a causal hypothesis.

The fact that this may indeed by an area worthy of further investigation is suggested by the results of a fairly well-controlled study by Berman and Siegal (1976). In this study a group of 45 delinquent males ages 15 to 18 were compared with a control group of 45 nondelinquent adolescents, matched for age, race, sex, and, to some extent, socioeconomic status. The delinquent group was made up of adolescents incarcerated for the first time at a Rhode Island juvenile correctional facility. All subjects were administered the Halstead-Reitan Neuropsychological Test Battery and several other measures of neuropsychological

status that provided indices of neuropsychological abilities and deficits that could be associated with specific forms of learning disability. It was found that delinquents performed more poorly on nearly all of these measures than did controls. Delinquents, although scoring in the normal range, were found to be significantly lower in IQ (particularly verbal intelligence) and significantly impaired in terms of perceptual organization and ability to comprehend and utilize conceptual material of a verbal nature. Berman and Siegal draw attention to the fact that the deficits found to characterize delinquents in this study are not different from those found in children with early school learning problems. Based on individual data from the study, the authors note that approximately 56% of the delinquents in this sample could be characterized as having some form of specific learning disability. In a larger group ($n = 122$) of institutionalized delinquents, selected without regard to race, sex, or age, the authors report 70% could be considered as having some specific disability. These findings may be compared with a rate of 23% found in a control group of nondelinquents drawn from similar socioeconomic backgrounds.

Wolff, Waber, Bauermeister, Cohen, and Ferber (1982) have likewise compared incarcerated delinquents (from lower middle-class backgrounds) with children from two matched (age, sex, race) control groups. Subjects in one control group were similar to the delinquent group in socioeconomic background, whereas those in the second control group came from upper middle-class families. Here delinquents were found to differ from subjects in both control groups in terms of displaying minor neurological signs and in showing selective impairments in language functions, which are commonly associated with learning disabilities or reading retardation. These findings led the authors to conclude that many of these delinquents displayed problems consistent with a diagnosis of severe and specific learning disabilities.

It may be noted that subjects in both of these groups were incarcerated delinquents, making it unclear to what extent similar findings would be obtained if noninstitutionalized delinquents were examined. The results of one less well-controlled study of nonincarcerated delinquents, however, would seem to suggest that neurological impairment and learning difficulties may be characteristic of many noninstitutionalized delinquents as well (Robbins, Beck, Pries, Jacobs, & Smith, 1983).

The results of these studies, along with those of other less well-controlled investigations (see Lane, 1980, for a review), appear to provide support for a relationship between learning disabilities and delinquent behavior. Having said this, it is important to emphasize that this does not necessarily mean that these disabilities play a causal role in the development of delinquency; antisocial behavior may result in learning problems, or both antisocial behavior and learning problems might result from adverse family backgrounds (Schonhaut & Satz, 1983). Nevertheless, the results of studies such as those cited here suggest that further work in this area is in order.

Hyperactivity

There seems good reason to believe that there is a relationship between childhood hyperactivity and later antisocial behavior. Much of this evidence has been reviewed by Cantwell (1978) and Satterfield (1978).

Evidence for such a relationship comes from investigations of the childhood histories of adults who display antisocial behavior patterns and from follow-up studies of children diagnosed as hyperactive. Numerous studies have found that a significant percentage of adults displaying antisocial behavior were considered hyperactive in childhood. Follow-up studies have also suggested that a sizable minority of hyperactive children later display antisocial behavior and are not infrequently considered to be sociopathic in adulthood. For example, one follow-up study by Mendelson et al. (1971) of teenagers who had previously been diagnosed as hyperactive revealed that approximately 60% of these children had some contact with the police.

Similarly, Huessy, Metayer, and Townsend (1974), reporting on 84 hyperactive children followed up after 8 to 10 years, found that such children were 20 times more likely to be incarcerated in a delinquent institution than persons from the general population.

Both Cantwell and Satterfield note another indirect bit of evidence linking hyperactivity and antisocial behavior — the fact that both seem to respond to stimulant medication. It has been shown that a sizable proportion (about three-quarters) of hyperactive children respond to stimulant drugs such as Ritalin and Dexadrine. Findings from other studies indicate that positive changes in the behavior of delinquents (Eisenberg et al., 1963; Maletzky, 1974) and psychopathic adults (Hill, 1947) also result from treatment with similar drugs. And it has been suggested that delinquents who respond best to stimulant drugs are those who were considered hyperactive earlier in childhood (Maletzky, 1974).

In regard to this apparent link between hyperactivity and delinquency, it should be noted that studies by Satterfield, Cantwell, and Satterfield (1974) suggested that there may be a subgroup of hyperactive children who are characterized by lowered central nervous system arousal, as indicated by EEGs and lowered galvanic skin responses. It is this group that seems to respond best to stimulant medication, which seems to bring about an increase in arousal level. Satterfield et al. (1974) theorized that activity level may be reduced because stimulant drugs increase cortical inhibition. But there are those (Zentall, 1975) who see the hyperactive child as underaroused (or underarousable) and experiencing a less than optimal level of stimulation; here hyperactive behavior is seen as one way to increase arousal level. From this point of view the use of stimulant medication may result in a more optimal level of arousal, thus reducing the child's need to seek out stimulation. If one adopts this position, then at least some hyperactive children may be viewed as stimulation seekers. Cantwell (1978) noted that there is a significant body of data indicating that many individuals displaying antisocial personality disorders also display autonomic response patterns similar to hyperactive children (that is, seem underaroused). These findings fit with Quay's notions that psychopathic individuals may be viewed as pathological sensation seekers. The similarity between this subgroup of individuals displaying antisocial behavior and the previously described group of hyperactive children who seem underaroused is obvious. Cantwell (1978) has written

> Speculating somewhat, one might suggest that it is this subgroup of hyperkinetic children with low CNS arousal who become antisocial personalities in later life. And it is this subgroup of antisocial personalities and hyperkinetic children who respond positively to stimulant medication. This would suggest that in some children the mechanism of association between hyperkinesis and antisocial behavior is the persistence of some physiological abnormality. (p. 258)

Although a relationship between hyperactivity and delinquent and antisocial behavior may exist, many hyperactive children do not become delinquent, and many delinquents do not have histories of hyperactivity, making it apparent that all delinquency cannot be accounted for by this explanation. One might speculate that it is the unsocialized-psychopathic delinquent who is most likely to be characterized by a history of hyperactivity (and presumably lowered arousal level) and that other factors must be sought to account for other dimensions of delinquency.

DELINQUENCY AND LATER BEHAVIOR

An issue of considerable significance concerns what happens to youth judged to be delinquent as they grow older. Do they "outgrow" their antisocial modes of behavior or continue to engage in illegal activities?

One of the most ambitious studies dealing with this issue was conducted by Glueck and Glueck (1968). These two investigators carried out a massive follow-up evaluation of 500 delinquent and 500 nondelinquent boys

seen in their 1950 study, which was described earlier (Glueck & Glueck, 1950). At the time of the original study the boys ranged in age from 9 to 17 years (Mean age = 14.5). In the follow-up study, 438 of the delinquent and 442 of the nondelinquent boys were evaluated at age 25 and at age 31.

The overall findings were that on almost all dimensions, former delinquents had a less favorable outcome than nondelinquents. Delinquents were found to show a higher incidence of psychological problems and were more often characterized as psychopathic. Compared to nondelinquents, delinquents at follow-up were found to show higher rates of marital instability, were more likely to be on welfare, had more friends who were criminals or "disreputable," and were less likely to have learned any sort of trade or skill. The vast majority of nondelinquent boys continued to be law abidding, but at age 31, 84.4 % of the former delinquents had been convicted at least once as a result of a court appearance during the previous 6 years. The authors note that more serious forms of criminal behavior tended to decline with age, although this decline was accompanied by an increased frequency of offenses such as drunkenness, vagrancy, simple assault, and family-related offenses such as desertion.

These findings are consistent with those obtained by Robins (1966), who found increased rates of criminal behavior (as indexed by arrests and incarcerations) and serious problems in adult adjustment (as indexed by conduct problems in the military, excessive drinking, financial dependency, marital friction, promiscuity, gambling, etc.) in adults who had delinquent records as children. It is of interest to note that in this study, being sent to a juvenile correction center was a better predictor of outcome in adulthood than were measures of family stability, socioeconomic status, or any other child behavior. Almost one half of all those incarcerated in childhood were diagnosable as antisocial personality in adulthood (Robins, 1979).

These follow-up studies suggest a generally unfavorable outlook for juveniles who become known to legal authorities for antisocial behavior. Whether this is characteristic of adjudicated delinquents as a group or whether the prognosis for some subgroups of delinquents is better than for others is an important question. Generally, the prognosis would seem to be the poorest for those juveniles who engage in seriously delinquent acts of a varied nature and whose antisocial behaviors began as preadolescents (Moore & Arthur, 1983).

TREATMENT OF DELINQUENCY

Institutionalization and Institutionally Based Programs

One traditional approach to dealing with delinquents, particularly those with extensive histories of lawbreaking, is institutionalization. Most states have one or more institutions for the treatment of juvenile offenders, facilities usually referred to as training schools, reform schools, or detention centers. The nature of these institutions varies considerably, ranging from those with active therapeutic and rehabilitative programs to those that are more custodial in nature. Unfortunately, two features common to most state-run institutions are overcrowding and understaffing, making optimal treatment exceedingly difficult.

Because institutions vary in size, staff-resident ratio, commitment to treatment, treatment orientation, and other dimensions, it is difficult to make general statements about their effectiveness. The prevailing view, however, seems to be that institutionalization per se does little to prevent future antisocial behavior. It has even been suggested that the delinquent culture operative within such institutions may teach and reinforce delinquent modes of behavior. Recidivism rates for various institutions have suggested that perhaps as many as 70 to 80% of boys who are incarcerated in state institutions are likely to be rearrested within a year or so after their release (Cohen & Filipczak, 1971; Gibbons, 1976). It is therefore not surprising that a variety of experimental treatment programs, designed for use within the institution, have been developed during recent years, in an effort to reduce the recidivism rate. Two well-known programs, the CASE program and the Cascadia project, are described below.

CASE (Contingencies Applicable to Special Education)

Cohen and Filipczak (1971) have examined the effectiveness of a token economy (see Chapter 10) in the modification of delinquent behavior. In this program, the CASE (Contingencies Applicable to Special Education) project, conducted at a federal government training school in Washington, DC, the major focus was on academic behaviors. The rationale for this emphasis was that residents included in the program were sufficiently deficient academically to preclude their finding any sort of meaningful employment and that this would increase the likelihood of future delinquent behavior. Developing academic skills that might increase residents' later employability was seen as one way to decrease recidivism.

Residents were rewarded with points for engaging in desirable academic behaviors and for increases in academic achievement. Points could be cashed in for a wide range of back-up reinforcers, including special meals, noninstitutional clothing, a private room, and better room furnishings.

Evaluation of the program suggested that residents showed improvement in terms of both academic and social behaviors. Follow-up studies also indicated that, at least during the first 2 years after release, residents had a recidivism rate substantially below that of boys who were institutionalized but not part of the CASE program. Unfortunately, 3 years after treatment recidivism rates for these groups did not differ, suggesting the need for a program designed to maintain changes resulting from the earlier treatment.

The Cascadia Project

In a series of publications Sarason (1968, 1978) and Sarason and Ganzer (1971) have described an intervention program based on the use of modeling principles. This program, conducted at the Cascadia Juvenile Reception-Diagnostic Center in Tacoma, WA, had residents (convicted offenders) observe models who depicted a variety of situations that they might face in the future. Modeled scenes included depictions of how to apply for a job, how to resist temptation by peers, how to delay gratification, and so forth. Following the models' enactment of various scenes, observers were asked to summarize and explain the content of the scenes and were requested to take turns role-playing the situations that had been modeled. After this, attention was turned to how behaviors displayed by the models might be applied to a variety of day-to-day situations. The program lasted a total of 16 sessions. The assumption underlying this approach to intervention was that juvenile offenders lack the requisite skills for behaving in a socially acceptable manner, and that those skills can be effectively transmitted via modeling and role-playing.

In order to evaluate the effectiveness of the program, residents receiving modeling were compared with residents who participated in a discussion-treatment group and residents who participated in neither of these two conditions. Dependent measures included self-reports, staff ratings of various behaviors, follow-up interview data, and recidivism rates.

Significant effects were found on most of these measures for both modeling and discussion groups (participants in the discussion group dealt with the same topics as did the modeling group but did not observe or engage in role-playing), suggesting that both procedures were of some value. Sarason (1978) commented that characteristics of delinquents seemed to be related to positive treatment effects: "Neurotic personalities, as well as the more passive dependent and less socially adequate boys who required greater structure, responded most favorably to modeling procedures. On the other hand, subject characterized as being more aggressive or sociopathic responded positively to discussion groups" (p. 308). It was also noted that highly anxious individuals benefited more from modeling than did low-anxious boys.

Of particular interest are the data regarding recidivism, obtained at 33 months after treatment, after 4 years, and after 5 years. Most impressive is the fact that after 5 years residents who had participated in the modeling and discussion groups had recidivism rates less than half that found for controls who had received standard institutional treatment (Sarason, 1978). The length of follow-up makes these results particularly impressive and suggests that procedures employed in both the modeling and discussion groups were effective, but perhaps with different "types" of delinquents. The potential value of such a skills-oriented approach to delinquency is supported by recent findings suggesting that youths classified as delinquent frequently display multiple deficits in academic, interpersonal, and work-related skills (Dishion, Loeber, Stouthamer-Loeber, & Patterson, 1984) and by the results of other studies (see Ollendick & Hersen, 1979) that highlight the value of social skills training with incarcerated delinquents. Further work related to treatment approaches of this type is clearly needed.

Community-Based Approaches

In addition to institutionally based treatments, a range of other programs have sought to deal with delinquent offenders within the community. This move toward community-based treatment has been partly due to the fact that such treatments are usually less costly than treatment within an institution. It has also frequently been assumed that changes brought about within the context of a community-based program are more likely to generalize to the youths' home environment than are those occurring within an institutional setting and that there is no need for institutional treatment in cases where the offender is not considered dangerous. Finally, since the mid-1970s, the push toward deinstitutionalization has been spurred on by the passage of the Juvenile Justice and Delinquency Act, which prohibits the institutionalization of status offenders who have not committed illegal acts.

Because an overview of community-based programs is beyond the scope of the present chapter (see Trojanowicz & Morash, 1983 for a more detailed coverage), we have chosen to focus on two of the better known programs that will serve to illustrate the diverse nature of this approach to intervention.

Highfields

The Highfields project, begun in 1950 in New Jersey, involved an early attempt to move away from traditional institutionally based treatment programs. Approximately 20 male juvenile offenders who had not been previously incarcerated were treated within the context of a small residential treatment center, which, unlike most larger institutions, consisted of a large house with minimal attention to security precautions. During their stay at Highfields, which usually lasted about 4 months, boys were involved in supervised work programs, performed various tasks at the center, were given recreational opportunities, and were involved in an intensive group therapy program. This group therapy program, which has been referred to as a Guided Group Interaction, was the major focus of the total program. Group sessions were designed to change attitudes that contributed to delinquent behavior, modify self-concept, and cut through those defenses employed by juvenile offenders that tended to stand in the way of rehabilitation. (For a more detailed overview of this program see McCorkle, 1958.)

Studies of the effectiveness of this project have compared recidivism rates for Highfields residents with rates of recidivism for boys who were similar to Highfields residents but committed to state training schools. Although it is not possible to be certain that these two groups were comparable, initial comparisons suggested that recidivism rates for those treated at Highfields were significantly lower than for those institutionalized in a traditional reformatory (Weeks, 1958). These findings, plus the fact that this treatment program involved relatively little staff, that it was more economical than institutional treatment, and that the length of treatment was less than the typical state institution, suggested that the program was at least moderately successful. It should be noted, however, that along with these seemingly positive findings, one must consider that a significant number (around 18%) of Highfields residents did not complete treatment, being returned to court because of their unsuitability for the program. Gibbons (1981) noted that a reanalysis of the data has suggested that if these delinquents had been considered program failures (rather than not considerd in the initial analyses), the success rates for the Highfields and training school programs would have been quite similar. Although this would suggest that the Highfields program may have been less effective than originally thought, it is noteworthy that the Guided Group Interaction procedures, developed at Highfields, have been widely used in a variety of settings, both in and out of institutions.

Achievement Place

Achievement Place is a home-style residential treatment program established in 1967 in Lawrence, Kansas. This program was developed in large part by faculty and students from the Department of Human Development at the University of Kansas and is one of the most sophisticated applications of behavioral procedures to the treatment of juvenile offenders (see Fixsen, Phillips, & Wolf, 1978; Fixsen, Wolf, & Phillips, 1973; Phillips, 1968).

Achievement Place consists of a home run by two trained houseparents that is capable of housing up to eight boys. Boys in the program are required to attend school regularly during their stay and have regular work responsibilities. Central to the program is a token economy program (somewhat similar to that used in the CASE project), in which the boys earn points for engaging in appropriate behaviors and can lose points for displaying unacceptable behavior. Points earned can be exchanged for a variety of back-up reinforcers, such as allowance money or permission to watch TV, go to town by themselves, or stay up later than usual.

Controlled studies conducted within the context of the Achievement Place program suggest that this token program is indeed effective in modifying a wide range of desirable and undesirable behaviors. Further, Phillips, Fixsen, and Wolf (1973) have compared recidivism rates of boys treated at Achievement Place with those of boys from the Kansas Boys' School and boys released on probation. Whereas over 50% of the boys from the two other groups were found to have committed some delinquent act within a year after release, only 19% of the former Achievement Place residents were found to have engaged in further delinquent behavior. Increases in school achivement for the latter group were also found. For more detailed reviews and critiques of the Achievement Place literature, see Gross and Brigham (1980) and Hoefler and Bornstein (1975).

Miscellaneous Approaches to Treatment

Many other treatment approaches have been used with delinquents. Redner, Snellman, and Davidson (1983) have, for example, reviewed a range of additional behaviorally oriented programs that are somewhat similar to those described here. Traditional individual and group psychotherapies have been employed (Trojanowicz & Morash, 1983), as

has family therapy (Klein, Alexander, & Parsons, 1977) and less traditional psychotherapeutic approaches such as Reality Therapy (Glasser, 1965) and Transactional Analysis (Berne, 1961; Jesness, 1975).

Taking more of a preventative approach, O'Donnell, Lydgate, and Fo (1979) have employed a "buddy system" in which volunteers were trained to work with problem youth in developing positive relationships, in pinpointing problem behaviors, and attempting to modify them through the use of behavioral contingencies. This approach was found to be effective in changing a variety of behaviors such as school attendance, fighting, returning home after hours, and so forth. Although the program did not focus specifically on modifying "delinquent" behavior, information regarding its effectiveness in preventing future arrests was obtained by comparing participants in the program with a control group who had not been assigned to a buddy. When subjects with a history of delinquency were considered, participants were found to have a significantly lower arrest rate at follow-up than did controls. However, participating in the buddy system appeared to result in an increased probability of arrest among those with no prior history of delinquency. The authors suggest that this iatrogenic effect may have resulted from participants with a nondelinquent background being exposed to youth who may have served as models for delinquent behavior.

Still other, less orthodox methods for dealing with delinquency have been proposed. Take, for example, programs such as that depicted in the television program, "Scared Straight," which was originally aired in 1979. In the New Jersey-based program, delinquents were presented with the horrors of prison life by being exposed to a prison environment where inmates portrayed, in graphic terms, what these youths could expect if they continued to break the law (e.g., being beaten and raped). This program was reported to be effective with from 80 to 90% of the several thousand youth who had gone through it and resulted in many prominent public figures advocating the development of additional similar programs (Gibbons, 1981). That programs that appear too successful to believe usually are is suggested by Gibbons who has indicated

> The "Scared Straight" episode is an example of an altogether too common phenomenon in the United States, in which a panacea for crime and delinquency is enthusiastically accepted, followed later by disillusioning evidence showing that the supposed miracle cure for lawbreaking is worthless. . . . In our view, there are compelling arguments against adoption of correctional endeavors such as the "Scared Straight" program illustrated, even if they produce the results claimed for them. There are serious moral questions that need to be raised about activities that expose juveniles to the harsh verbal abuse and other experiences that are involved in correctional programs of this kind. However, the evidence indicates that this is another in a long list of panaceas that have come and gone from the correctional scene. A follow-up study showed that about 57% of the youngsters who had been through the program had not been charged with new offenses in the 6 months following their participation, but 78% of a control group of youths who had not been in the program had remained free from delinquency during the same period! These results suggest that the program not only failed to achieve the results proclaimed for it, it may even have been harmful to a sizable number of youthful offenders. (pp. 333–334)

These statements not only serve to comment on the effectiveness of this particular program, but also underline a point emphasized throughout the book: Clinical procedures should be based on research findings rather than intuition and personal belief.

THE PROBLEM OF DRUG ABUSE

Any discussion of delinquency would be incomplete without considering the problem of drug abuse. The problem is of relevance, because using alcohol and other drugs is itself illegal. As we will see later, the use of drugs is also correlated with other types of delinquent behavior such as that described in the preceding sections. In this section we will consider the nature of several commonly used drugs, the extent to which drugs are used by children and adolescents, and factors that appear to contribute to drug usage, as well as briefly comment on approaches to treatment.

The Use and Abuse of Drugs

Drug use by children and adolescents can be at various levels. Many if not most adolescents experiment with drugs such as tobacco, alcohol, or marijuana but never use any of them to a significant degree. A smaller number of individuals become social users. They may drink or use some other drug such as marijuana at parties or other social gatherings but are not heavily into drug use apart from these occasions. A still smaller number of youth engage in more serious drug abuse. Here, the seriousness of the problem may be reflected in using a particular drug more frequently or in using a broader range of drugs.

Some, but not all, drugs have properties that can lead to a physical dependence on the drug (addiction). Two terms, *tolerance* and *withdrawal* are usually associated with the development of physical dependence. Thus, with some drugs, like alcohol for example, the individual comes to tolerate larger and larger amounts of the drug and finds it necessary to ingest larger doses in order to experience the same drug effects. Physical dependence is also reflected in the occurrence of withdrawal effects, which are experienced if the person stops taking the drug too quickly. The symptoms of drug withdrawal range from those that are simply uncomfortable to those that are fatal. Although more difficult to quantify, it appears that individuals can also develop a psychological dependence on certain drugs, where they come to rely on the effects of these drugs to help them function on a daily basis, even though they may not display physical addiction.

Even though drug usage of any type is potentially problematic, because even experimenting with drugs such as alcohol or marijuana can result in serious accidents should the person try to drive or engage in certain other activities while intoxicated, heavy drug use and addictive behavior represent a truly significant problem because of the interfering effects they can have on the lives of the youth involved.

Frequently Abused Drugs

As a number of current texts have provided detailed descriptions of commonly abused drugs and their physical and psychological effects, the present coverage will be limited to a brief overview of these. Our discussion draws on several recent sources (Bassuk, Schoonover, & Gelenberg, 1983; Hofmann, 1983; Schuckit, 1984), which are recommended for those desiring more detailed information concerning specific drug effects.

Central Nervous System Depressants

In this category are a group of substances that are similar, in that they have a calming or sedative effect at low doses and sleep-inducing or hypnotic effects at higher doses. Perhaps the single most popular drug in this category is alcohol. Indeed, recent surveys indicate that over 90% of all high school seniors have tried alcohol, and as many as 6% may use it on a daily basis (Kandel, 1982). This popularity is undoubtedly related to the fact that alcohol is a legal drug for older individuals, thus making it easily available for youngsters who wish to try it. The effects of alcohol are quite familiar to most. It should be noted, however, that whereas alcohol may lead to a variety of pleasurable effects (e.g., a sense of well-being, an enhanced sense of competence, euphoria) at lower levels, its overall effects are to depress central nervous system activity. At higher levels these effects are seen in the familiar problems of coordination, speech difficulties, the disinhibition of behav-

ior, and problems in judgment that charcterize drunkenness.

Other depressant drugs include a range of sedatives and anti-anxiety medications, which fall under the headings of barbiturates and benzodiazepines, as well as certain other drugs that have sedative-hypnotic properties. Among the barbiturates are sedatives such as Amytal, Nembutal, and Seconal, as well as phenobarbital (Luminal), which is primarily used in treating seizure disorders, but which also has sedative-hypnotic effects. The benzodiazepines are anti-anxiety drugs ("minor" tranquilizers), which have largely replaced the barbiturates in the medical treatment of anxiety. Librium and Valium, perhaps the most popular of these drugs, are widely used by the general population. One other sedative-hypnotic that should be mentioned is methaqualone (Quaalude). This drug has been popularized, not only because of the feelings of intoxication that are generally associated with drugs of this type, but also because of its supposed (but not demonstrated) aphrodisiac properties.

All of these drugs can result in physical dependence (e.g., are addicting) when taken regularly. Certain of these drugs, (e.g., the barbiturates) are not infrequently associated with deaths due to overdoses. A potentially lethal mixture is the use of drugs such as those just described with alcohol, as the synergistic effects of their combined use may increase the likelihood of drug overdose.

Psychedelics or Hallucinogens

The two most well-known examples of this category are marijuana and LSD. Marijuana, which is derived from the Indian hemp plant, grows wild in many parts of the world and has become a most popular drug among adolescents and adults. The psychoactive ingredient in marijuana is tetrahydrocannabinol (THC), which when smoked produces a heightened awareness of sounds and colors, an altered time sense, disinhibition of behavior, relaxation, euphoria, and a sense of well-being. It may also result in sleepiness, increased levels of sexual arousal, and, in some cases, problems with short-term memory. In some instances individuals experience suspiciousness or paranoid ideation. At high dose levels hallucinations can also occur.

Although marijuana does not typically result in serious physical dependence, there are a variety of issues associated with its use. As the drug produces a state of intoxication it poses the same hazards as alcohol should one attempt to drive or engage in certain other activities while "under the influence." As Krug (1983) has noted, the effects of marijuana on mental functioning may also create serious problems in learning for those youth who use it frequently. Also noted are the apparent effects of the drug on suppressing testosterone production (which may affect the development of secondary sex characteristics in pubescent males who use the drug), as well as the fact that, like cigarettes, marijuana contains a significant load of carcinogens.

Although there are a number of other psychedelic drugs (e.g., Mescaline, Psilocybin), the best known is probably LSD (D-lysergic acid diethylamide). LSD is a synthetic hallucinogen that became quite popular in the late 1960s because of its assumed mind-expanding properties. Although the use of LSD has declined since that time, it is still used with some frequency.

Although not addicting, when taken orally, even at relatively low doses, LSD has rather potent effects that may last for several hours. These include "an increased awareness of sensory input; a subjective feeling of enhanced mental activity; a perception of usual environmental stimuli as novel events; altered body images; a turning of thoughts inward; and a decreased ability to tell the difference between one's self and one's surroundings" (Schuckit, 1984, p. 138). The person may also experience strong emotional states, which can range from euphoric (a "good trip") to nightmarish (a "bad trip"), as well as visual hallucinations and delusional thoughts. It may be noted that fatalities have reportedly occurred because of persons apparently believing they can fly, jump off of buildings, or

engage in similarly dangerous feats while under the influence of the drug.

In some cases individuals have "flashbacks" weeks or months after taking LSD, during which they experience sensations and feelings that bear some similarity to the original drug effects (e.g., euphoria, feelings of detachment, visual illusions) and that may last anywhere from minutes to hours. Although these flashbacks may not actually impede the persons' ability to function, they may be quite frightening if they are perceived as signs of a developing mental illness or as an indication of permanent damage resulting from the use of the drug. Krug (1983) has noted that these flashback experiences usually are self-limiting and cease within 2 years if the person ceases to use marijuana and other hallucinogenic substances.

In addition to the possibility of inadvertently harming one's self while under the influence of the drug, it appears that LSD can result in drug-induced psychotic episodes in persons with prior psychiatric problems, and there is some suggestion that the use of the drug may result in chromosomal damage and possible birth defects if taken during pregnancy (Schuckit, 1984).

Stimulants

Stimulants, as the name suggests, serve to increase the activity of the central nervous system. Although most of us consume stimulants on a daily basis in drinking coffee, tea, and certain soft drinks (which contain caffeine) or in smoking cigarettes (which contain nicotine), the most commonly abused stimulants are the amphetamines and methamphetamine (often referred to as "speed"). Included here are a variety of drugs that are often prescribed for weight control, for the treatment of hyperactive children, or to decrease fatigue in persons who must stay awake for long periods of time (e.g., college students at exam time, truck drivers). Examples include methylphenidate (Ritalin), dextroamphetamine (Dexedrine), and methamphetamine (Desoxyn). Although such drugs are most often taken orally, they are sometimes taken intravenously to get a quicker and more pronounced effect.

Stimulant drugs typically result in increased mental alertness and ability to concentrate, euphoria and an increased sense of competence, along with a decreased need for sleep, decreased appetite, and sometimes increased sexual arousal.

An additional, currently popular stimulant drug is cocaine, which has been medically used as a local anesthetic. The drug typically comes in the form of a white powder that is either taken intervenously or inhaled (snorted), although it can also be mixed with tobacco and smoked. Its intoxicating effects are similar to those of the other stimulants.

Stimulant drug usage can result in both physical and psychological dependence. Although these drugs elicit certain pleasant experiences at low to moderate doses, at higher levels the person may become restless, anxious, confused, and irritable. At still higher doses the user may experience a drug-induced psychosis that resembles paranoid schizophrenia.

Narcotics

Narcotics represent a group of drugs that are often used medically as pain killers. They are highly addicting and can result in both physical and psychological dependence within a relatively short period of time if taken on a regular basis. These drugs include opium, codine, morphine, and heroin, which are derived either directly or indirectly from the opium poppy, as well as a variety of synthetic opiates (e.g., Darvon, Demerol), which are also used as pain killers.

The immediate effects of taking a narcotic drug are likely to be euphoria, followed by a sense of deep relaxation and tranquility, during which the person may become drowsy and perhaps drift into a light sleep. Some drugs, like heroin, have other pleasurable effects as well. For example, when taken intravenously, heroin may result in what has been described as an "orgasm-like" experience

that is primarily centered in the abdominal area. This experience, often referred to as a "rush," "kick," or "flash," may last anywhere from 30 to 60 seconds and may combine with the other drug effects to increase the desirability of the drug.

Problems with using narcotics relate to their highly addictive nature and the withdrawal symptoms experienced if the drug is not taken regularly. In order to avoid withdrawal the drug may have to be taken as often as every 4 to 8 hours. This may make it necessary for the person to spend a great deal of time simply making sure that enough of the drug is available to meet his or her needs for the next dose. As these drugs are both illegal and expensive to obtain, it often becomes necessary for the person to find some way of financing the addiction. This frequently results in involvement in some sort of illegal activity to support the drug habit. In the case of the intravenous drug user, contacting diseases such as hepatitis is a possibility due to using needles that are not sterile. It has also been determined that intravenous drug users are "at risk" for the development of Acquired Immune Deficiency Syndrome (AIDS), a newly recognized disease that decreases the individuals immunity to disease and leads to the development of often fatal infections and rare types of cancer. Further, the potential for a fatal overdose of these drugs is probably higher than for any of the other drugs that we have considered, with the possible exception of the CNS depressants.

Other Abused Drugs

In addition to those just described, there are still other substances that are used and abused by children and adolescents. One of the most commonly used, probably because of its easy availability and the presence of numerous role models, is tobacco. When it is considered that cigarettes, which contain the stimulant nicotine, are addicting (Krug, 1983) and that 70% of high school seniors report having tried them and 20% use them on a

daily basis (Kandel, 1982), there would seem
to be cause for concern. This concern appears well founded given the relationship
between cigarette smoking and problems
such as cancer and heart disease and the possibility of a relationship between smoking
during pregnancy and decreased birth weight
(Naeye, 1981).

Finally, it is not uncommon to hear of
children and adolescents who attempt to "get
high" on a variety of other readily available
substances to which they have easy access.
Among these are glue, nail polish remover,
various cleaning solutions, gasoline, lighter
fluid, and aerosols. The effects are described
below:

> The usual "high" begins within minutes and
> lasts a quarter to three-quarters of an hour,
> during which the individual feels giddy and
> light-headed. Most users report a decrease
> in inhibitions along with a floating sensa-
> tion, misperceptions or illusions, clouding of
> thoughts and drowsiness, and occasionally
> amnesia during the height of the inhalation
> episode. (Schuckit, 1984, p. 162)

Although the effects of these inhalants, in
small amounts, may be somewhat transient,
their long-term use can result in a variety of
serious problems such as the possibility of permanent brian damage as well as impairments
in kidney and liver function, and there is
always the possibility of a fatal overdose.

Prevalence of Drug Usage Among Children and Adolescents

Statistics suggests that juvenile drug usage is
quite common. Johnston, Bachman, and
O'Malley (1981), for example, have provided
data on the percentage of high school seniors
who report ever having used various drugs as
well as the percentage who report using these
drugs on a daily basis. These data are presented in Table 9.3.

Here it can be seen that more than 90%
of high school seniors report having used
alcohol at some time in their life. Over 70%
report having smoked cigarettes, and 60%

TABLE 9.3. PREVALENCE OF ADOLESCENT
DRUG USE.

Drug Type	Ever Used	Daily User
Alcohol	93%	6.0%
Cigarettes	71%	20.3%
Marijuana	60%	7.0%
Stimulants	32%	1.2%
Inhalants	17%	.2%
Cocaine	17%	.3%
Sedatives	16%	.2%
Hallucinogens	16%	.2%
Tranquilizers	15%	.1%
Other Opiates	10%	.1%
Heroin	1.1%	0%

Source: Adapted from Johnston et al. (1981).

had tried marijuana. Although a fair number
of adolescents reported using stimulants, inhalants, sedatives, and narcotics, these drugs
appear to have been experimented with by
a smaller number of students. These figures,
along with those reflecting daily usage, suggest that a sizable number of youth experiment with drugs and that certain of these
drugs are seriously abused by some adolescents who use them on a daily basis. Given
that it is quite possible to abuse drugs by using them less frequently than this, it would
seem likely that the actual degree of drug
abuse is somewhat higher than that suggested
by the figures presented here. Indeed Singer
and Isralowitz (1983) cite statistics suggesting
that as many as 20 to 40% of all high school
students use alcohol or other drugs excessively.

Trends in Drug Use

Figure 9.2 provides information regarding
trends in juvenile drug use between 1975 and
1980 for a number of substances. Although
experimentation with some substances (e.g.,
tobacco) appears to have declined somewhat,
and the use of others (e.g., heroin) has remained relatively stable, there has been an
apparent increase in the use of certain other
drugs. Especially noteworthy is the increased
use of both marijuana and cocaine.

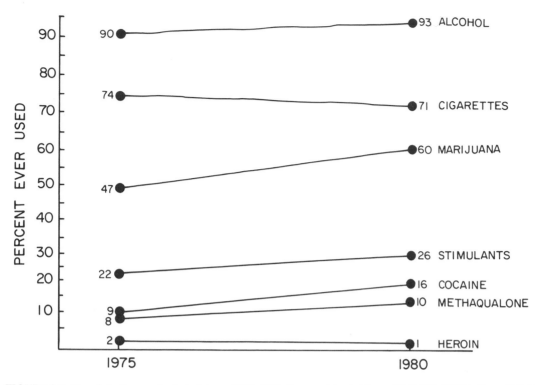

FIGURE 9.2. Trends in the use of selected drugs 1975–1980. Source: Adapted from ADAMHA (1981); Krug (1983).

Stages of Drug Usage

Research has suggested that individual drugs are seldom used in isolation but that the use of one drug is likely to be associated with the use of others. Additionally, both longitudinal and cross-sectional research (Kandel, 1975; Kandel & Faust, 1975; Huba, Wingard, & Bentler, 1981) has suggested a developmental progression in adolescent drug usage, whereby individuals move in a stepwise fashion, through various levels, toward more and more serious drug involvement.

According to Kandel (1982) the most common sequence is one where the use of legal (for adults) drugs sets the stage for using illicit substances, with almost no one beginning his/her drug involvement with "hard" drugs. Here the adolescent is likely to begin by using beer and wine, move on to using hard liquor and/or cigarettes (the use of hard liquor being more typical), then on to marijuana, and finally to the use of other illicit

drugs. Kandel also notes that there are some data, provided by Jessor, Donovan, and Widmer (1980), to suggest a fifth stage characterized by problem drinking, which may occur after experimentation with marijuana and before involvement with other illegal drugs.

Although these stages represent usual patterns of progression, this does not mean that adolescents invariably pass through each stage in exactly this way. Kandel has also emphasized that an individual's position in this sequence does not necessarily mean that they will move on to the next level, as this typically occurs with only a subset of the individuals at each stage. Although other variables may be involved, progression to a more advanced stage of drug use is highly related to the seriousness of drug usage at the stage the individual has already attained (Kandel & Faust, 1975). For example, an adolescent who has only experimented with marijuana is much less likely to move on to hard drugs than is the adolescent who has used marijuana extensively. Those individuals who begin their drug involvement at an earlier age (e.g., eighth grade or below) also appear to show more frequent drug usage and an increased likelihood of involvement with all drugs (Kandel, 1982). Finally, it should be pointed out that not all individuals who progress through these various stages become continuous users (Fishburne, Abelson, & Cisin, 1980). However, as many as a fourth of the total youth population are estimated to proceed through all four of these stages by their mid-20s, and by this age as many as two thirds pass through the first three: beer or wine; cigarettes or hard liquor; marijuana (Kandel, 1982).

Drug Use and Delinquency

A question of special relevance to the present chapter has to do with the relationship between drug use and delinquent behavior. At the most general level a relationship is assured, because taking drugs such as the ones discussed here is illegal and itself represents law-breaking behavior. But what of the relationship between drug use and other forms of delinquency?

One study that has provided information regarding these questions has been conducted by Johnston, O'Malley, and Eveland (1978). These investigators surveyed a stratified random sample of over 2,000 high school students from across the United States and obtained information regarding both drug use and delinquent activities. This data was obtained when participants were in the tenth grade and at four additional follow-up periods, covering an 8-year time span.

Drug involvement was indexed by grouping subjects into five categories reflecting increased levels of drug use: (a) subjects with no drug history, (b) those who had only used marijuana, (c) those who had experimented with one, two, or three pills (defined as amphetamines, barbiturates, hallucinogens, cocaine, or methaqualone), (d) those who had engaged in more than experimental use of one or two pills, and (e) those who had en-

gaged in more than experimental use of three pills or any use of heroin. Because subjects who used hard drugs (e.g., "pills," heroin) also tended to use marijuana, this 5-point classification system provided a general index of degree of drug involvement. Reports of delinquent behavior were combined to yield two separate indices: interpersonal aggression and theft/vandalism.

When these variables were assessed at the same point in time, a significant relationship was found between drug use and both measures of delinquency, such that students reporting greater involvement with drugs showed more evidence of delinquent behavior. Although drug use was correlated with both types of delinquency, the relationship to theft/vandalism was considerably stronger than with interpersonal aggression. Thus, drug use seems to bear a stronger relationship to crimes against property than crimes against people. A general relationship between drug use and delinquent behavior has also been found by other investigators (see, for example, Hundleby, Carpenter, Ross, & Mercer, 1982; Jessor & Jessor, 1977).

As the Johnston et al. (1978) study was longitudinal in nature, the researchers were able to also assess the relationship between delinquent behavior and drug use across time. Here it was possible to obtain information as to whether drug use was more likely to precede delinquency or whether delinquency was more likely to precede drug abuse. In conducting sophisticated cross-lag analyses, Johnston et al. found strongest support for a relationship between drug use and delinquency in which delinquency increases the likelihood of drug use. Johnston et al. have suggested

What we . . . conclude from these explorations is that nonaddictive use of illicit drugs does not seem to play much of a role in leading users to become the more delinquent people we know them to be on the average. The reverse kind of causation seems considerably more plausible, that is, that delinquency leads to drug abuse. For example, we think it quite possible that delinquents who, because of their delinquency, become part of a deviant peer group are more likely to become drug users because drug use is likely to be an approved behavior in such a peer group. . . . Both delinquency and drug use are deviant behaviors, and therefore both are more likely to be adopted by individuals who are deviance prone. (pp. 155–156)

Other longitudinal studies (see Kandel, 1982) have also provided data in support of this proposition.

Taken together it would appear that, except for a probable relationship between alcohol abuse and aggressive behavior (Tinklenberg, 1975), drug use probably does not, in and of itself, play a causal role in the development of delinquent behavior. Rather, drug use and delinquency are more likely to both be manifestations of a more general pattern of unconventional attitudes and deviant behavior that is displayed by some children and adolescents (Kandel, 1982; Trojanowicz & Morash, 1983).

Contributors to Drug Abuse

Many studies have sought to determine those variables that contribute to adolescent drug abuse. Although space limitations preclude a detailed review of this literature (see Braucht, Brakarsh, Follingstad, & Berry, 1973; Kandel, 1982; Trojanowicz & Morash, 1983, for overviews), a range of variables have been suggested as correlates of drug use. Problem drinkers have been described as lacking in personal controls, aggressive and impulsive, and as displaying various neurotic features such as anxiety, depression, and low self-esteem. Marijuana users have been described as being more vulnerable to frustration and more group-dependent, open to experience, socially perceptive, self-confident, rebellious, narcissistic, pleasure seeking, irresponsible, and nonconforming, and less self-controlled than nonusers. Amphetamine users have been characterized as anxious, introverted, lacking in self-confidence, and intropunitive (self-critical, guilty). Narcotic users have been found to be immature, insecure, irresponsi-

ble, egocentric, and to freqeuntly show evidence of personality disorders (Braucht et al., 1973).

In considering correlates such as these it must be noted that many studies in this area have been plagued by methodological problems, making it difficult to draw firm conclusions regarding the significance of their findings. Many investigations have employed small or unrepresentative samples, have been retrospective in nature, or have otherwise lacked appropriate controls (Braucht et al., 1973). An additional problem is that in many instances, where personality variables have been found to be significantly correlated with drug use, it has been impossible to determine whether these variables play a causal role in the development of drug abuse or are simply correlates of drug-taking behavior.

There are, however, certain variables that are worthy of special comment, because they have repeatedly been found to relate to drug use and have been shown to be predictive of differing *levels* of drug abuse in well-designed longitudinal studies. Most relevant in this regard is the role of peer and family influences. The importance of these variables has been summarized by Kandel (1982):

At the earliest levels of drug involvement, that of involvement in a legal drug such as alcohol, adolescents who have engaged in a number of minor delinquent activities, who enjoy high levels of sociability with their peers, and who are exposed to peers and parents who drink, start to drink. . . . The use of marijuana is preceded by acceptance of a cluster of beliefs and values that are favorable to marijuana use and in opposition to many standards upheld by adults, by involvement in a peer environment in which marijuana is used, and by participation in the same minor forms of deviant behaviors which precede the use of hard liquor. By comparison, the use of illicit drugs other than marijuana is preceded by poor relationships with parents; by exposure to parents and peers who themselves use a variety of legal, medical, and illegal drugs; by psychological distress; by heavy involvement in marijuana; and by a series of per-

sonality characteristics somewhat more deviant than those which characterize the
novice marijuana or hard liquor user. (pp.
338–339)

These findings strongly support a social
learning explanation of drug use, in which
initial drug-taking behavior is encouraged
by exposure to various models (e.g., friends
and parents) who engage in drug use themselves and who, in the case of peers, may reinforce such behaviors. This peer reinforcement, when combined with reinforcing drug
effects (euphoria, increased confidence, decreased psychological distress, novel experiences, etc.) may serve to maintain drug-taking
behavior. In the case of addicting drugs, their
subsequent use may be maintained through
negative reinforcement that derives from
avoiding the symptoms of psychological and
physical withdrawal. It would appear that
the likelihood of drug use is further increased
in those instances where there are minimal
negative sanctions against drug use, as in the
case of families that promote unconventional
ways of thinking and behaving and have only
loose religious affiliations (Braucht et al.,
1973). Given the relationship between delinquency and drug use (cited earlier), one may
assume that many of the variables that contribute to delinquency play a role in drug
abuse as well.

Treatment of Drug Abuse

There are few established programs or treatments designed specifically for use with the
adolescent substance abuser. For those who
display drug addictions, treatments similar to
those used with adults may be utilized. Here
an attempt is usually made to help the person decrease his or her physical dependence
on the addicting drug, while at the same time
developing attitudes and a life style that minimize the likelihood of future drug involvement. Decreasing physical dependence may
involve strict drug withdrawal or detoxification, which is done under medical supervision
so as to minimize problems related to physical
withdrawal. In other instances, as in the case
of heroin addiction, treatment may involve

the use of still other drugs. For example, the
heroin addict may be treated with methadone
maintenance, where he or she is given the
synthetic narcotic methadone as part of therapy. Methadone, when taken orally, does not
result in the same "rush" as is experienced
with heroin; it is assumed to decrease the
persons craving for heroin, and it avoids the
problem of heroin withdrawal (Schuckit,
1984). Typically, methadone maintenance
is only one part of a rehabilitation program
designed to decrease the person's reliance
on drugs. After a period of maintenance, attempts are usually made to decrease reliance
on the drug by gradually decreasing the dosage. Although this approach is used with adolescents, it is not a common treatment because methadone is highly regulated in its use
(especially with those below 16) and because
there are not large numbers of youthful heroin addicts.

Other approaches to treating addictive behavior have involved the use of therapeutic
communities. Perhaps the best known of these
is the Synanon program, developed in the late
1950s in Santa Monica, CA, by an ex-alcoholic.
This privately funded program involves treating narcotic addicts within a very structured
and somewhat authoritarian program run by
ex-addicts. The program reflects the belief
that addiction results from personal weaknesses and that these must be dealt with in
order to decrease a reliance on drugs. To deal
with these weaknesses, individuals entering
the program are typically assigned rather
low-level responsibilities (e.g., janitorial or
kitchen work) and minimal privileges and are
required to work their way up in order to obtain more privileges and greater responsibility
within the program. The focus of the program is on developing positive life styles and
vocational skills and supporting drug abstinence while, at the same time, cutting through
the defensiveness and manipulativeness seen
as being characteristic of the drug addict.
This is done through involvement in the overall treatment milieu (of which the individual
is a part 24 hours a day), as well as through
intense group therapy interactions. Although

the Synanon program was developed primarily for the treatment of adults, this program and others modeled after it have also been used in the treatment of adolescents.

Because most adolescent drug abusers do not display narcotic addictions and are often not willing to become involved in residential treatment, outpatient counseling programs are widely used as a method of treatment. Here drug abusers are provided with support in developing and maintaining a drug-free life style, in developing vocational skills, and in dealing with personal problems through individual or group therapy.

In addition to the treatment approaches just described, other methods for dealing with drug abuse have included preventative approaches that have focused on helping drug users develop alternatives to drug-related activities as well as those emphasizing drug education.

Unfortunately there appears to be little good research related to the effectiveness of various treatments. Some very general findings, however, have been provided by Sells and Simpson (1980). These investigators conducted a large scale outcome study of some 3,131 persons (selected from over 40,000 cases) who had been treated in 52 different drug programs that offered various types of treatments: outpatient detoxification, methadone maintenance, therapeutic communities, and drug-free counseling. Defining success in terms of drug abstinence, along with other criteria (e.g., absence of criminal behavior, necessity for further treatment), it was found that after 3 years these treatments showed varying success rates. Outpatient detoxification, for example, resulted in a success rate of approximately 20%, methadone maintenance a rate of 30%, therapeutic communities a rate of 37%, and outpatient programs approximately 34%. These rates can be compared with a success rate of 21% for individuals seen for drug-related intake evaluations but not treated. With the exception of detoxification, each form of treatment was found to be associated with a significantly better outcome than no treatment. It might be noted, however, that

methadone maintenance and therapeutic communities were only effective with individuals having heroin or other opiate addictions and the drug-free counseling programs with individuals who were nonaddicted drug users.

Although this study would not meet stringent criteria for well-controlled research on a number of counts (e.g., nonrandom assignment to treatments, heavy reliance on self-report data), it does provide tentative data suggesting that several widely used forms of treatment may be of some value, as compared to not receiving treatment. However, it is noteworthy that the overall success rates of the best of these treatments is quite low (e.g., 37%). This would suggest that there is still much to learn regarding effective treatments of drug abuse. Regarding other variables that might contribute to treatment effectiveness, Trojanowicz and Morash (1983) have suggested that, given the literature documenting the importance of family variables as contributors to drug abuse, approaches emphasizing family-based treatments would seem to have much to offer.

SUMMARY

Juvenile crime is a serious social problem whose apparent increase is most dramatically reflected in an increased frequency of more serious offenses by juveniles and an increasing rate of offenses committed by females.

Although workers in the area have often treated delinquency as a unitary construct, it should be emphasized that juveniles legally designated as delinquent are an extremely heterogeneous group. Indeed, it has been demonstrated that there are several dimensions of delinquent behavior.

The most prominent dimensions of delinquency defined in the literature seem to be socialized-subcultural delinquency, unsocialized-psychopathic delinquency, disturbed-neurotic delinquency, and inadequate-immature delinquency. In brief, the socialized-subcultural delinquent seems to be a relatively normal individual whose delinquent behavior may relate to interaction with a delinquent subgroup. The unsocialized-psychopathic delinquent, on the other hand, seems to be a solitary delinquent who typically shows no allegiance to delinquent peers, displays little anxiety, shows inadequate guilt feelings, and seems not to profit from usual forms of praise or punishment. Similarity to the adult psychopathic individual has been noted. The disturbed-neurotic delinquent is described as generally unhappy, shy, and anxious, and likely to display marked degrees of guilt over his or her behavior. Some would suggest that illegal behaviors displayed by such individuals are the result of acting out neurotic conflicts. Finally, the inadequate-immature delinquent appears to be a generally inadequate individual who has a poorly developed behavioral repertoire and is generally unable to cope with the demands of the environment. It is likely that each of these dimensions of delinquent behavior may be related to different etiological factors and have different correlates and that individuals rated high on these different dimensions may respond differently to treatment programs.

Major theoretical views of delinquency causation range from those that emphasize social factors, to psychodynamic views, to those stressing the role of learning. The contribution of genetic factors has also been considered.

Numerous studies have considered the relationship between delinquency and social class, family variables, psychological variables, and other problems of childhood and adolescence. Although some interesting correlates of delinquency have been suggested, much of the research in these areas has been characterized by contradictory and unreplicated findings. It is likely that this has resulted in part from the failure of most researchers to take into account the heterogeneous nature of the delinquent population or the variables related to dimensions of delinquency.

Treatments of delinquency include traditional institutional treatments, which have been characterized by extremely high recidivism rates, community-based programs, and programs based on behavioral principles. At present behavioral programs designed to provide juveniles with skills necessary to cope with the demands of the natural environment appear to hold the most promise.

Also considered in this chapter was the problem of drug use. Although few youth become serious abusers of drugs, a large proportion of adolescents experience drugs such as tobacco, alcohol, and marijuana by the end of their high school years. A smaller number try other drugs such as stimulants, CNS depressants, and narcotics.

In considering the relationship between drug use and other types of delinquency, such as that discussed in the present chapter, it was suggested that research generally fails to support the notion that drug use leads to delinquent behavior. Rather, delinquency and drug use both seem to be associated with unconventional attitudes and ways of behaving. If anything, delinquency appears to precede drug use in most cases.

Although contributors to adolescent drug use are likely to be multiple and diverse, the role of peers and parents seems to be especially important. Having parents who encourage or are tolerant of liberal views and who themselves model drug use, along with friends who use drugs and reinforce drug-taking behavior, appears to increase the probability of usage.

Although there are a variety of treatment approaches that have been used in dealing with adolescent drug abusers, it would appear that most of these are ineffective with the majority of those treated. Further work in developing effective treatments is sorely needed.

SUGGESTED READINGS

Rutter, M., & Giller, H. (1984). *Juvenile delinquency: Trends and perspectives*. New York: Guilford. Probably the most up-to-date and comprehensive text on delinquency presently available.

Keith, C. R. (1984). *The aggressive adolescent: Clinical perspectives*. New York: The Free Press. This edited volume contains a broad range of chapters dealing with both psychological and biological factors that relate to aggressive behavior as well as treatment.

Hofmann, F. G. (1983). *A handbook on drug and alcohol use* (2nd ed.). New York: Oxford University Press. This book provides a detailed review of the biomedical and psychological effects of alcohol and drug use.

10 PSYCHOLOGICAL APPROACHES TO CHILD TREATMENT

This chapter deals with a range of approaches that have been used in the treatment of child psychopathology. As will be seen, these approaches do not fit neatly under any one heading but encompass a heterogeneous group of intervention procedures based on different principles and theoretical formulations.

We will outline here some of the more widely accepted approaches to child treatment and provide information regarding the relationship between these approaches and theory and research. The question of effectiveness of psychotherapy in general, and of various treatment approaches in particular, will be addressed by considering relevant research. This chapter, however, should by no means be considered an exhaustive survey of the literature, but rather an attempt to provide the reader with a "feel" for the present status of practice and research in the area of child and family treatment and an awareness of important issues in the field. Several well-written and extensive reviews of various aspects of child treatment are to be found in the published literature and will be referred to throughout this chapter.

MODELS OF PSYCHOPATHOLOGY AND APPROACHES TO CHILD TREATMENT

As was noted in Chapter 1, various models of psychopathology or general ways of conceptualizing abnormal behavior have evolved over the years. As the treatment approaches to be discussed are all derived from differing theoretical frameworks, the essential features of several of these models will be briefly summarized here.

Until recently, variations on the medical model were the theoretical views best represented in writings on childhood psychopathology. Although the earliest version of this model was based on the assumption that abnormal behavior results from some underlying physical disorder, there are other examples of the model that are medical models by analogy. Perhaps the best example is the psychodynamic perspective. Here abnormal behavior is viewed as analogous to the symptoms of physical disease; just as physical symptoms often result from some underlying physical condition, so abnormal behavior is thought to be symptomatic of underlying pathology. These underlying difficulties, however, are presumed to be of a psychological nature and to take the form of fixations, unresolved complexes, intrapsychic conflicts, and so forth. Given this focus on the underlying causes of abnormal behavior, it is assumed that in order for therapy to be effective, one must determine and deal with the basic underlying problem, rather than simply attempting to modify the abnormal behavior itself.

Adoption of this psychodynamic/medical model has had a tremendous impact on the fields of clinical psychology and psychiatry and until recently provided the most widely accepted framework for understanding deviant behavior. Virtually all psychodynamically oriented approaches to psychotherapy with adults and children are based on this model and are designed to deal with underlying causes of abnormal behavior, whether through talking, as in the case of adults, or through play when working with children.

A second model, which came into prominence in the late 1940s and early 1950s is the client-centered model. This model reflects the very positive view that individuals have within themselves the capacity for personal growth and will behave in ways that are "self-enhancing," in the absence of outside interference. Abnormal behavior is thought to result from experiencing adverse conditions that impede personal growth within the person's social environment. In treatment, attempts are made to provide a therapeutic atmosphere that counteracts these detrimental influences and facilitates personal growth, self-actualization, and the development of more adaptive ways of relating. As will be seen later, this perspective is best represented in Virginia Axline's nondirective approach to play therapy.

A third, somewhat different conceptualization of abnormal behavior, the behavioral model, sees maladaptive behavior as largely the result of learning and environmental factors. (However, this view in no way dismisses the contribution of biological factors to certain types of deviant behavior.) From the behavioral perspective, the focus is on external (environmental) rather than internal (intrapsychic) determinants of behavior and on those aspects of the environment that elicit and/or maintain maladaptive behavior. Consistent with this emphasis, treatment is directed toward modifying maladaptive behaviors — those behaviors that have led the child to be labeled deviant or referred for treatment — instead of attempting to treat underlying causes of an intrapsychic nature. This position also prefers to apply learning principles (and/or other empirically based psychological principles) in attempting to deal with deviant behavior over the more indirect methods often espoused by more psychodynamically oriented therapists. In recent years the number of psychologists and psychiatrists adopting this view of abnormal behavior has increased, and so has the tendency on the part of practitioners to employ behavioral methods in the treatment of childhood problems.

An additional position that has not been well delineated as a model but nevertheless seems to qualify as such might be referred to as the family model of psychopathology. This view tends to focus on disturbances within the family rather than disturbances within individuals in attempting to account for pathological behavior, a point of view well characterized by Achenbach (1974):

> It is based on the assumption that the family is a social system and that each member's behavior is a function of pressures existing within the system. The symptoms of a child brought to treatment are thus not regarded primarily as manifestations of the child's pathology but as manifestations of the family's pathology. Moreover, the child's symptoms are regarded as having a definite function in the family so that their disappearance without other changes in the family can produce new symptoms in other family members or a dissolution of the family system. Consequently, the child is referred to as the "identified patient," i.e., the one identified as a patient by the other family members — but the family is viewed as the appropriate unit of treatment. (p. 610)

The family model is in some respects similar to the general medical model described earlier. In this case, however, the underlying cause is assumed to reside within the family rather than the individual, and the focus of treatment is on dealing with family variables rather than intrapsychic factors.

One final point is in order regarding the models of psychopathology presented here. Even though we have tried to capture the essence of these ways of conceptualizing deviant behavior in order to illustrate some of the assumptions underlying various approaches to child treatment, they have been presented in a very general manner. In considering these models, it should be kept in mind that in actuality there is no such thing as "*the* medical model," "*the* behavioral model," or "*the* family model" of psychopathology. As we have seen, medical models vary from those that presume a physiological basis for many abnormal behaviors to those that presume some underlying cause for abnormal behavior but assume the cause to be of a psychological nature. Behavioral conceptualizations of maladaptive behavior range from those that focus exclusively on overt behaviors, dismiss the importance of cognitions as mediators of behavior, and attempt to account for behavior largely in terms of stimulus-response relationships, to those that see cognitions (self-instructions, self-statements, etc.) as importantly related to deviant response patterns. There are obviously large numbers of behaviorally oriented clinicians who would fall somewhere between these two positions. Likewise, not all client-centered clinicians would view psychopathology in exactly the same way, and family-oriented clinicians may vary considerably in the precise way they see family variables as contributing to maladaptive child behavior.

In fact, it might be said that every clinician has his or her own personalized model of psychopathology that serves as a general framework for thinking about deviant behavior seen in the clinical setting. These personalized models of psychopathology may closely resemble those considered here or may differ in certain respects. Whatever the specific assumptions of these models, they are likely to have a significant influence on the approach to treatment that one takes in working with children.

APPROACHES TO CHILD TREATMENT: AN OVERVIEW

The most widely employed psychological approaches* to child treatment are play therapy (individual psychotherapy with older children), family therapy, and behavior modification. Like the models on which they are based, these approaches show a great deal of variability within themselves. For example, there are several approaches to play therapy, most notably client-centered and analytically oriented approaches (which may be conducted either individually or in groups). Likewise, there are a variety of behavioral approaches, including operant conditioning, modeling, desensitization, cognitive behavior modification, and others. There are also several approaches to family therapy, reflecting different views of the exact role of the family in the development of psychopathology and how best to modify family-based problems.

In addition, various forms of therapy used with adults (analytic, client-centered, etc.) have also been employed in the treatment of adolescents. Still other approaches, based on different models, emphasize the use of parents as therapists for their own children.

Not only are there numerous approaches to treatment, but in actual practice different approaches are often combined. Thus, a child

*In this chapter we have chosen to focus on "psychological" approaches to treatment and have therefore not considered more biologically based treatment approaches such as drug treatments of various childhood disorders employed by medically trained practitioners. Although not covered in this chapter, such approaches *are* discussed in earlier chapters dealing with specific disorders. Thus, Chapter 4 has considered drug treatments of children with pervasive developmental disorders. Chapter 5 has discussed the use of stimulant drugs in treating hyperactive children. Chapter 6 has described the use of antidepressant drugs in treating depressed children. And Chapter 7 has considered the usefulness of drugs in treating childhood enuresis. For a more general overview of pharmacological approaches to treatment see Campbell, Green, Perry, and Anderson (1983) or Greenhill (1985).

in play therapy may also be involved in family therapy or in a behavioral program designed to deal with a specific problem behavior. A child seen in family therapy might also receive medication to control undesirable behavior, or the parents of a child in individual therapy may receive counseling to improve parent-child relations.

From this brief overview it should be obvious that child treatment often involves the application of a diverse array of intervention procedures. In the sections to follow we will discuss a range of these approaches, beginning with more traditional methods that are usually associated with the term *child psychotherapy*. This will be followed by a consideration of behavioral and family therapies and discussions of parent training and residential treatment.

ON THE EFFECTIVENESS OF PSYCHOTHERAPY

Over the years clinical psychologists and other practitioners have often tended to assume that procedures employed in treatment were so obviously of value that no evaluation of their effectiveness was necessary. Others, however, have concerned themselves with the question of whether various forms of psychotherapy really work—and if they do, why. One early attempt to provide information on this score involved investigation of the effectiveness of psychotherapy with adults. Before considering this data, however, it is appropriate to consider some minimal requirements for studies investigating the effectiveness of treatment, against which the results of studies to be discussed in later sections can then be judged.

Some Minimal Requirements for Psychotherapy Outcome Studies

The simplest design that allows conclusions concerning treatment effectiveness is the treatment-control group design, in which at least one group of individuals receives some form of psychotherapy, while individuals in the control group receive no treatment. Usually members of both groups are assessed on variables thought likely to change as a function of treatment both before and after to determine if those in the treatment group display greater change than do subjects in the control group. The control group in this design is included to control for the possibility that individuals may change over time in the absence of any form of treatment, due to maturation, changed environment, or whatever. An adequate control group, however, must be comparable to the group receiving treatment. Its members should display problem behaviors similar to those of the treatment group, should be evaluated by similar procedures, and should be similar with regard to their (or perhaps their parents') motivation for treatment. In practice, obtaining a comparison group that is comparable to the treatment group in all respects is often difficult due to ethical considerations and practical problems. But similarity between these groups is necessary if meaningful conclusions are to be drawn. If the two groups are comparable in all respects and are evaluated before and after treatment on relevant variables, and if the group receiving treatment is observed to change to a significantly greater degree than do subjects in the control group, there is then some basis for assuming that the treatment being evaluated is effective.

Variations on this basic experimental-control group design can involve the inclusion of additional groups to control for attentional factors and expectancy effects. Similar designs can also involve the comparison of more than one form of treatment with relevant control groups (see Heimberg & Becker, 1984).

It should be noted that although the experimental-control group design represents the minimal requirements for an adequate psychotherapy outcome study, it is still less than optimal for answering many questions about the effectiveness of psychotherapy. Its limitations will be discussed in a later section.

Effectiveness of
Adult Psychotherapy

In a now classic publication, Eysenck (1952) sought to determine whether the percentage of patients who improved with psychotherapy was greater than the percentage who improved due to spontaneous remission (the disappearance of symptoms without any form of specific treatment). Based on the results of two studies that had assessed the percentage of improvement found in patients who had not received systematic psychotherapy, Eysenck concluded that one could expect improvement to occur spontaneously in approximately two-thirds of neurotic patients without any form of treatment. Eysenck acknowledged the difficulties inherent in the use of a post hoc control group, but argued that no better controls were available. Based on the spontaneous remission rate derived from these two studies, he concluded that for psychotherapy to be considered effective, it would be necessary to show that considerably more than two-thirds of the patients seen in psychotherapy improved after treatment; that is, that changes due to treatment occur to a greater degree than changes due to spontaneous remission. In evaluating the results of 19 psychotherapy studies reported in the literature, he found that only about 64 to 66% of the patients who received treatment had improved. Eysenck concluded that the results of this survey provided little evidence for the effectiveness of adult psychotherapy.

Although this study has often been cited in support of the charge that psychotherapy is ineffective, numerous criticisms of Eysenck's paper have attempted to highlight methodological inadequacies (e.g., Bergin & Lambert, 1978). These criticisms have centered on the failure to demonstrate that patients seen in psychotherapy and patients in the studies' control groups were comparable. It has also been suggested that patients in control groups may have in fact received some sort of therapy, although not as systematically as that of the treatment groups and not labeled as such.

Another argument is that it is not certain that the criteria for improvement in the psychotherapy and control groups were similar. It has also been pointed out that other studies have failed to demonstrate that the spontaneous remission rate is as high as the two-thirds figure given by Eysenck.

For example, Lambert (1976), in a review of research data regarding spontaneous remission rates, concluded that a better estimate of the spontaneous remission rate is approximately 43% for "untreated" individuals and about 53% for persons receiving "minimal" treatment.

Although the Eysenck paper certainly does not provide support for the notion that psychotherapy is of value, its methodological inadequacies make its negative findings difficult to interpret. Probably the paper's greatest contribution is that it has stimulated a great deal of thought and research in the area of psychotherapy and has led investigators to think in terms of more precise questions about psychotherapy and more methodologically adequate ways to answer them.

Effectiveness of
Child Psychotherapy

In a study similar in many ways to Eysenck's, Levitt (1957) attempted to obtain a measure of the effectiveness of psychotherapy as typically practiced with children by reviewing a number of psychotherapy studies that reported information related to outcome. The ages covered by these studies ranged from preschool to 21 years, but with very few cases over 18 (median age 10 years). Most of the patients included in the studies were classified as neurotic. Levitt reported that across all studies, 67% of the patients were improved at the close of therapy, although a somewhat higher percentage was found to be improved at follow-up, suggesting that it may require some time after the end of therapy for the effects of therapy to be realized (Wright, Moelis, & Pollack, 1976). The reader will notice that this figure is quite similar to the improvement figure reported by Eysenck (1952) for adult psychotherapy. Levitt noted a great deal of variability from study to study, however. For example, in the study reporting the poorest outcome, only 43.1% were found to have improved. In the study reporting the best outcome, 85.7% of the patients were reported improved. This implies that there is a significant degree of variability in the effectiveness of child psychotherapy, with the 67% figure representing the average rate of improvement.

Like Eysenck, Levitt attempted to obtain a control group in order to assess improvement occurring in the absence of psychotherapy. For comparison he chose to use follow-up data on clinic defectors: children who had been brought to the clinic for help and who were accepted for treatment, but who did not follow through. Levitt reasoned that such persons should serve as adequate controls, inasmuch as they had gone through the same procedures in all respects as therapy patients had but had not received treatment. Two studies that provided follow-up data and improvement figures on such children were found, and it was determined that the overall rate of improvement in these two groups was 72.5%, which Levitt suggested could be used as a baseline figure for evaluating the effectiveness of child psychotherapy. On the basis of the 67% improvement figure for treated children and the 72.5% figure for those not treated, it would seem that treated children at the close of the treatment are no better off than are control children who have received no treatment whatsoever. Based on these comparisons, Levitt (1957) wrote; "It now appears that Eysenck's conclusions concerning the data for adult psychotherapy are applicable to children as well: The results do not support the hypothesis that neurotic disorder is facilitated by psychotherapy" (p. 193). Subsequently, Levitt (1963, 1971) published additional data suggesting a similar conclusion. Table 10.1 reports the combined outcome data for patients in these treatment studies.

In his original paper, Levitt (1957) provided some information about the kind of psy-

TABLE 10.1. REPORTS OF OUTCOME OF PSYCHOTHERAPY WITH CHILDREN.

Diagnostic Group	n	% Improved
Neurotic at close	4,539	67.4
Psychotic at close	252	65.1
Acting out at close	349	55.0
Total at close	5,140	66.4
Neurotic at follow-up*	4,219	78.2

*Estimated median interval of 4.8 years after close.
Source: Levitt (1971). © 1971 John Wiley and Sons and reprinted by permission of the publisher.

chotherapy that children in the treatment groups received that is important in the interpretation of the results of his survey.

> There are a number of different kinds of therapists that have been used in the studies reported here. The therapists have been psychiatrists, social workers, and teams of clinicians operating at different points in the patients' milieu. Therapeutic approaches included counseling, guidance, placement, recommendations to schools and parents, as well as deeper level therapies. In some instances the patient alone was the focus of attention. In others, parents and siblings were also treated. The studies obviously encompassed a variety of theoretical viewpoints although these are not usually specified (p. 194)

This points to the ambiguity of the term *psychotherapy* as it is often used. This study, along with Eysenck's (1952), suggests that to the extent that it is appropriate to ignore important variables such as the characteristics of the therapists and their orientation, the nature of the patient's problems, and the specific nature of the intervention procedures employed, psychotherapy may be judged on the average to be ineffective. As a prelude to later discussion, one might ponder whether the general question, "Is psychotherapy effective?" is an appropriate one.

In addition to the problems inherent in the nature of the question it asked, Levitt's study, again like Eysenck's, has been criticized on methodological grounds. For example, the use of clinic defectors as a control group has been questioned. This group may not be at all appropriate for comparison with treatment groups, it has been suggested, because children who fail to enter treatment may differ on many dimensions from those who follow through with treatment offered them. To the extent that groups were not initially equated on important variables, comparisons between the two groups are largely meaningless.

An additional study of the effects of treatment with children that employed controls selected in a somewhat different manner was conducted by Shepherd, Oppenheim, and Mitchell (1966, 1971). This investigation compared a group of 50 child guidance clinic patients and a group of matched children who had never received treatment. Children in the clinic group ranged in age from 5 to 15 years. Children deemed psychotic, brain damaged, or epileptic were not included in the study. Clinic patients were matched on the basis of age, sex, and behavior with subjects who had never been involved in treatment but who, in a survey, were found to display behaviors comparable to those found in the treatment group. Independent ratings of severity of disturbance made at the time of matching indicated that the children in the clinic and nonclinic groups did not differ on this variable to a significant degree, although there was a nonsignificant "trend" toward more severe ratings in the clinic children.

After two years, 65% of the treated group were judged to have improved, 18% to have remained unchanged, and 16% to have deteriorated. Of the matched children, 61% were rated as improved, 30% had remained unchanged, and 9% had become worse. These results suggest that, on the average, treatment had little effect. It is interesting to note, however, that there seems to have been a greater degree of variability with regard to change in the treatment group. Not only did a slightly larger percentage of patients in this group improve, but a greater percentage of clinic patients also became worse than in the nontreatment group. Although the difference in

variability between the two groups may or may not have been significant, the trend is of interest because it is consistent with the observations of other researchers that psychotherapy can make people better or can make them worse. This issue and its implications for understanding the results of certain psychotherapy studies will be taken up in a later section.

Although it employed different controls, the study by Shepherd et al. yielded findings consistent with the results obtained by Levitt, in that they suggest many children with neurotic disorders improve with the passage of time without any specific form of treatment and that the percentage improving with treatment (defined in various ways) may not be significantly greater. Taken together, these studies provide little support for the general effectiveness of child psychotherapy.

As was said earlier, however, not only have these and similar studies been faulted on methodological grounds but it has been questioned whether attempting to assess the effectiveness of child psychotherapy, or for that matter adult psychotherapy, by simple treatment-control group comparisons (particularly when the studies are based on already published reports) is a worthwhile endeavor, because such studies do not take into account important patient and therapist variables (Barrett, Hampe, & Miller, 1978).

A RESTATEMENT OF THE PSYCHOTHERAPY EFFECTIVENESS QUESTION

Many investigators are coming to view the general question of the effectiveness of psychotherapy addressed in these early studies as one of limited value. This is in part because the term *psychotherapy* refers to a wide variety of procedures, and in part because there is a great deal of variability within both patient and therapist populations. Kiesler (1966), in a very influential paper, pointed to a number of myths that pervade the adult psychotherapy literature and are apparent in the child therapy literature as well. These have been referred to as "uniformity assumption myths." The first of these, the "patient uniformity myth," is the myth that "patients at the start of treatment are more alike than they are different" (p. 110). Kiesler showed that this assumption has resulted in the grouping together of patients for research purposes regardless of the nature of their problems, a procedure that is likely to make the results of research meaningless. He noted that even though patients may be similar in that they have become involved in therapy, they are probably much more different than alike. Grouping such individuals together and failing to take into account individual differences leaves an investigator in a poor position to say with whom therapy is effective or ineffective. A given approach to therapy may be very effective for some but quite ineffective for others, but the net result of a standard treatment-control group comparison might be a finding of no differences between treatment and control groups, implying no effectivenes of treatment.

A second myth Kiesler cites is the "therapist uniformity myth": "Perhaps an even more devastating practice in psychotherapy research has been the selection of various therapists for a research design on the assumption that these therapists are more alike than different and that whatever they do with their patients may be called 'psychotherapy'" (p. 112). Kiesler suggests that there may be marked individual variations among therapists, as well as variability in the effectiveness of various types of therapy, and that failing to take such differences into account can also obscure important information. To see how failing to take therapists' differences into account can cloud important issues, one need only consider a point first alluded to by Bergin (1966).

After surveying research in the area of psychotherapy, Bergin arrived at a conclusion that was widely viewed as having important implications for the practice of psychotherapy and seemed to be supported by findings in the literature: that "psychotherapy may cause people to become better or worse adjusted than comparable people who do not receive such treatment" (p. 244). Bergin noted that in many studies, although no differences between treatment and nontreatment groups were found, there tended to be a significant difference in within-group variability.

> The criterion, or change scores for treatment groups attain a much wider dispersion than do those of control groups even though the mean change in both groups is quite similar. Typically, control subjects (Ss) improve somewhat, with the varying amounts of change clustering about the mean. On the other hand, experimental Ss are typically dispersed all the way from marked improvement to marked deterioration. (p. 235)

The discovery that therapy can make some patients worse, referred to as the deterioration effect, clashed with the traditionally held view that therapy can only help. More recent reviews continue to document the existence of such deterioration effects (see Lambert, Bergin, & Collins, 1977). Research findings, although often controversial, have suggested that improvement or deterioration in therapy may be related to a number of variables. For example, patients who perceive therapists as showing high levels of genuineness, nonpossessive warmth, and empathy tend to improve, according to some results, whereas patients who perceive their therapists as displaying low levels of these conditions tend to deteriorate (Mitchell, Bozarth, & Krauft, 1977; Truax & Mitchell, 1971). Other research has likewise suggested a relationship between various patient characteristics and improvement-deterioration (Lambert & Asay, 1984).

These findings have obvious implications for understanding the results of early studies, such as those of Eysenck with adults and Levitt with children, that found no differences on average between treated and untreated groups. If it is true that some patients are improved whereas others are made worse by treatment, then one might expect to find few differences between treatment and control subjects in general. The question then becomes who is helped, who is made worse, and what variables related to therapist characteristics or treatment techniques are correlated with change. Based on findings such as those just cited, it has been suggested that the appropriate question to ask about the effectiveness of psychotherapy is, What type of treatment is effective with what type of patient when administered by what type of therapist under what conditions? A similar conclusion was reached by Heinieke and Strassman (1976) after they reviewed available research concerning the effectiveness of child psychotherapy. Answers to these types of questions necessarily involve the use of more complex experimental designs of a factorial nature rather than simple treatment-control group comparisons. For an overview of factors to consider when conducting this type of psychotherapy research, the reader is referred to Kiesler (1971) and Gottman and Markman (1978).

Unfortunately, although research involving adult psychotherapy has begun to advance in complexity and is beginning to obtain answers to questions such as those posed here (see Garfield & Bergin, 1978; Hersen, Michelson, & Bellack, 1984), to date few investigations of traditional child psychotherapy have gone beyond simple treatment-control group designs to address the more complex issues raised here. Indeed, it has been suggested that the field of child psychotherapy has progressed very little since the early 1960s (Barrett et al., 1978).

TRADITIONAL APPROACHES TO CHILD TREATMENT

In the preceding sections we have considered research findings related to the effectiveness of traditional child psychotherapy, with therapy being broadly defined. These research findings, however, provide little information regarding the nature and effectiveness of specific treatment approaches. We will now consider in more detail the nature of several approaches to child psychotherapy as well as findings related to effectiveness.

The Nature of Child Psychotherapy

Although adults most often express themselves, their conflicts, their needs, and their wishes through the medium of language, the child is thought to express himself or herself most clearly through play. For this reason various approaches to play therapy (e.g., analytic, client-centered) have become accepted methods for treating the child who is too young to benefit from the verbal interchanges that characterize psychotherapy with older children. Indeed, one recent survey (Tuma & Pratt, 1982) has suggested that play therapy is the predominant treatment modality used with preadolescent school-aged children, with over 50% of child clinicians using this approach.

Play therapy typically involves the interaction of a child and a therapist in a playroom equipped with a variety of play materials. The specific play materials may vary with the therapist and orientation, but often include puppets or dolls of varying colors, sizes, apparent ages and sex, drawing materials, balls, and modeling clay. Games such as checkers and dominoes are often used with somewhat older children for whom other play materials may be inappropriate. Play therapists differ in theoretical orientation and in terms of the specific procedures they employ, but there seems to be one basic assumption shared by all: that the child expresses important aspects of his or her personality through play (as well as through verbalizations) and that insight into the nature of a child's problems can be gained by observing play activities.

Even though many child clinicians are proponents of play therapy, there are differences of opinion concerning the role of play in the treatment process. Some feel that the therapeutic effects of play are secondary to the value of the relationship between the child and the therapist, which may be facilitated by play activities. Others, although not denying the importance of relationship factors, argue that play itself has a decided cathartic value for the child. At present there seems to be little data concerning this issue.

Although many forms of treatment have been used with children, the most well-known approaches to play therapy are those derived from the psychodynamic and client-centered models of psychopathology, which were discussed earlier. Similar approaches to treatment have also used in working with adolescents who, as a result of their age, are less suitable for play therapy. Although the basic *principles* of analytic or client-centered therapy are similar whether one is working with children or adolescents, the approach taken with adolescents is more like that employed with adults, in that the emphasis is placed on verbal interactions rather than play behaviors.

Whether working with children in play therapy or adolescents in more verbally oriented psychotherapy, the goals of therapy are likely to be the same. These usually include attempts to resolve the specific problems that brought the child to therapy as well as attempting to foster constructive personality change so as to minimize the likelihood of experiencing further problems in the future.

Analytically Oriented Play Therapies

Psychoanalytic approaches to play therapy are best represented in the work of Klein (1932) and Anna Freud (1946). From Klein's perspective, primary importance is to be placed on the symbolic meaning of the child's play, which is thought to reflect the child's unconscious conflicts and fantasies. Thus, free play is treated in much the same way as free association in adult analysis, and the nature of the unconscious conflicts suggested by the child's play is interpreted directly to the child. As Klein has written, "a precondition for the psychoanalysis of a child is to understand and interpret the fantasies, feelings, anxieties, and experiences expressed by play or, if play activities are inhibited, the cause of this inhibition" (p. 228). An assumption basic to this approach is that the development of insight and the reexperiencing of early emotions and fantasies are both necessary in order to bring about personality change. A case example,

taken from Klein (1955) is presented in Figure 10.1 to illustrate this basic approach.

Despite the early popularity of Klein's approach in both the United States and England, other analytically oriented therapists have approached treatment somewhat differently. Although adhering to the basic tenets of analytic theory and affirming the usefulness of play as a therapeutic medium, Anna Freud, for example, has advocated an approach that differs from Klein's on several counts. Her approach is much more oriented toward the present than the past, focuses on conscious as well as unconscious material, and places much less importance on the symbolic interpretation of play behaviors. Rather than assuming play to invariably reflect intrapsychic conflict, Freud also takes into account that play activities may relate to current environmental influences that impact on the child. This more moderate position is most reflective of contemporary psychoanalytic thought.

Nondirective Play Therapy

Axline (1947) has developed a client-centered approach to play therapy based on the notion that the seeds for personality change reside within the individual rather than within the therapist. Here it is assumed that the child has a drive toward self-actualization and more adaptive behavior and that given therapeutic conditions favorable for change, the child is capable of dealing effectively with his or her own problems. The approach has been described by Axline as follows:

> Nondirective play therapy . . . may be described as an opportunity that is offered to the child to experience growth under the most favorable conditions. Since play is the natural medium for self expression, the child is given the opportunity to play out his accumulated feelings of tensions, frustrations, insecurity, aggression, fear, bewilderment, and confusion.
>
> By playing out these feelings, he brings them to the surface, gets them out in the open, faces them, learns to control them, or abandons them. . . . When he has achieved

emotional relaxation, he begins to realize the power within himself, to make his own decisions, to become psychologically more mature, and, by so doing, realize selfhood. (p. 16)

Whereas these comments illustrate the nature of therapy in the abstract, the specific nature of this approach is illustrated in the following principles provided by Axline (1947) as guidelines for conducting nondirective therapy:

1) The therapist must develop a warm friendly relationship with the child, in which rapport is established as soon as possible.
2) The therapist accepts the child exactly as he is.
3) The therapist establishes a feeling of permissiveness in the relationship so that the child feels free to express his feelings completely.
4) The therapist is alert to recognize the *feelings* the child is expressing and reflects those feelings back to him in such a manner that he gains insight into his behavior.
5) The therapist maintains a deep respect for the child's ability to solve his own problems if given the opportunity to do so. The responsibility to make choices and to institute change is the child's.
6) The therapist does not attempt to direct the child's actions or conversation in any manner. The child leads the way; the therapist follows.
7) The therapist does not attempt to hurry the therapy along. It is a gradual process and is recognized as such by the therapist.
8) The therapist establishes only those limitations that are necessary to anchor the therapy to the world of reality and to make the child aware of his responsibility in the relationship. (p. 75)

As can be seen from these principles, the primary emphasis is not on the use of "therapy techniques," but in providing an atmosphere conducive to constructive personality change. Major importance is placed on the nature of the relationship between therapist and child. Here it is considered important that the therapist display a nonjudgmental and permissive attitude toward the play of the child and that the child be accepted completely as an individual. Little attention is paid to past experiences and unconscious processes, and little or no use is made of interpretations such as those employed by more analytically oriented therapists. Instead, techniques such as "reflection of feeling" (therapist statements that mirror the feelings expressed by the child) are often used to help the child clarify and understand his or her feelings and thus develop insight into the nature of his or her difficulties. These reflections of feeling are also thought to communicate to the child the information that the therapist is a person who is empathic and understanding of the child's feelings and thereby further enhance the therapeutic relationship. An illustration of how this approach is reflected in therapy is presented in Figure 10.2.

Even though the analytic and nondirective approaches to play therapy have received the most attention in the literature and have attracted the most adherents, it should be noted that other approaches to play therapy have also been developed. For an up-to-date discussion of these approaches the interested reader should consult Schaefer and O'Connor (1983).

Again it should be noted that even though we have chosen to focus our discussion on play therapies, because of their particular relevance to child treatment, both analytically oriented and nondirective approaches have also been employed with adolescents in a manner similar to that used with adults.

Play Therapy Research

Little systematic research has been undertaken into the process and outcome of play therapy. Lebo (1953), in an early review article on the status of nondirective play therapy, found several studies at that time had tried to assess what actually takes place during client-centered play therapy sessions. In general Lebo interpreted these studies as indicating that attitude changes do occur as a result of therapy and that such changes can be quantified for purposes of research: For example, one study by Landisberg and Snyder (1946) found an increase in physical activity and expression

FIGURE 10.1. The Case of Peter

In the selections to follow Klein describes her initial contacts with a young boy, Peter, who is described as displaying a neurotic disorder. The nature of his problems are described as follows: To mention some of his difficulties: he seemed unable to play, could not tolerate any frustration, was timid, plaintive, and unboyish, yet at times aggressive and overbearing, very ambivalent toward his family, and strongly fixated on his mother. She told me that Peter had greatly changed for the worse after a summer holiday, during which, at the age of 18 months, he shared the parents' bedroom and had the opportunity to observe their sexual intercourse. On that holiday he had become very difficult to manage, slept badly, and relapsed into soiling his bed at night, which he had not done for some months. He had been playing freely until then, but from that summer onward he stopped playing and became very destructive toward his toys; he could do nothing with them but break them. Soon afterward his brother was born, and this increased all his difficulties.

In the first session Peter started to play; he soon made two horses bump into each other and repeated the same action with different toys. He also mentioned that he had a little brother. I interpreted to him that the horses and the other things bumping together represented people — an interpretation which he first rejected and then accepted. He again bumped the horses together, saying that they were going to sleep, covered them up with bricks, and added, "Now they're quite dead; I've buried them." He put the motorcars front to rear in a row, which, as became clear later in the analysis, symbolized his father's penis, and made them run along, then suddenly lost his temper and threw them about the room, saying, "We always smash our Christmas presents straight away; we don't want any." Smashing his toys thus stood in his unconscious for smashing his father's genitals; in fact, during this first hour he broke several toys.

In the second session Peter repeated some of the material of the first hour, in particular the bumping together of cars, horses, etc., speaking again of his little brother, whereupon I interpreted that he was showing me how his mummy and daddy bumped their genitals together (using of course his word for genitals) and that he thought that their doing so caused his brother

of negative feelings as therapy progressed. Unfortunately, however, this conclusion was based solely on an analysis of the therapy records of four cases, and no controls were employed for purposes of comparison; thus it is not certain that such changes would not also have occurred in the absence of any form of therapy.

Lebo also cited a number of other studies that had investigated play therapy as a treatment in cases involving allergies, personality disorders, mental deficiency, and the handling of racial conflicts. For the most part these early outcome studies provided little in-

formation about the effectiveness of nondirective play therapy, because the majority of them simply attempted to assess (sometimes not too carefully) changes in small groups of children undergoing treatment, without the benefit of comparison with controls who did not receive treatment. Because of such problems, little can be said about the effectiveness of play therapy based on these early studies.

Later investigations, although not devoid of methodological difficulties, have, however, tended to provide more information. Cox (1953), for instance, investigated the effectiveness of client-centered play therapy in

FIGURE 10.1. (*continued*)

to be born. This interpretation produced more material, throwing light on his very ambivalent relation toward his little brother and toward his father. He laid a toy man on a brick which he called a "bed," threw him down, and said he was "dead and done for." He then re-enacted the same thing with two toy men, choosing figures he had already damaged. I interpreted that the first toy man stood for his father whom he wanted to throw out of his mother's bed and kill and that one of the two toy men was again the father and the other himself to whom his father would do the same. The reason he had chosen two damaged figures was that he felt that both his father and himself would be damaged if he attacked his father.

This material illustrates a number of points of which I shall mention only one or two. Because witnessing the sexual intercourse of his parents had made a great impact on his mind and roused strong emotions such as jealousy, aggressiveness, and anxiety, this was almost the first thing which Peter expressed in his play. There is no doubt that he no longer had any conscious knowledge of this experience, that it was repressed, and that only the symbolical expression of it was possible for him. I have reasons to believe that if I had not interpreted that the toys bumping together were people, he might not have produced the material which came up in the second hour. Furthermore, had I not, in the second hour, been able to show him some of the reasons for his inhibition in play by interpreting the damage done to the toys, he would very likely — as he did in ordinary life — have stopped playing after breaking the toys.

There are children who at the beginning of the treatment may not . . . play in the way Peter did . . . But it is very rare for a child completely to ignore the toys laid out on the table. Even if he turns away from them he often gives the analyst some insight into his motives for not wishing to play. In other ways, too, the child analyst can gather material for interpretations. Any activity, such as using paper to scribble on or to cut out, every detail of behavior, such as changes in posture or in facial expression, can give a clue to what is going on in the child's mind.

Source: Klein (1955). © 1955 American Orthopsychiatric Association and reprinted with permission.

a study employing two groups of nine children matched with regard to age, sex, residential placement, and level of adjustment. Pre- and posttreatment measures were obtained on TAT measures and a sociometric measure of adjustment. At week 12 significant differences on both measures of adjustment were found between the play therapy treatment group and the matched no-treatment control group. Significant differences were also found at week 27, when adjustment measures were again obtained. Dorfman (1958) also showed therapeutic gains in play therapy that were greater than those found in control subjects.

It might be pointed out that these findings have relevance mainly for client-centered approaches to play therapy. There have been few, if any, studies evaluating the effectiveness of psychoanalytically oriented play therapy; most studies of this approach are of the case study variety and provide little reliable information concerning the value of such treatment.

Several studies have been designed to compare the effectiveness of play therapy with other approaches to child treatment or to assess the relative effectiveness of various forms of play therapy. Clement and Milne (1967),

FIGURE 10.2. The Case of Tom

Tom was 12 years old, above average in intelligence, nice-looking, but seriously maladjusted both at home and at school. He was referred for play therapy because he was antisocial, aggressive, and insisted that everyone blamed him unfairly for the trouble in which he usually found himself. Tom had a stepfather, also a half-sister who was much younger than he, and who was the darling of the family.

Tom had spent most of his life with his grandmother, but 2 years previous to the time when he was referred for therapy, his mother had taken him back to live with her and the step-father and the half-sister. Tom did not get along at all well with them. Nor did he get along with the children in school, for he had never been permitted to play with other children until he started to school and had difficulty in adjusting to other personalities.

In this case the reader will note how quickly and graphically Tom played out his problem, mainly through the use of puppets. It is interesting to notice how the same puppets were used for different characters that were alike in their relationship to him. The father and school principal represented dictatorial authority to Tom. His ambivalent feeling toward his father seemed to be shown by the two parts the puppets played, first beating up the father and then defending him. The boy's play certainly seemed to be definitely correlated with his feelings and attitudes and problems.

First Contact

Tom came into the room, wearing his hat and coat, and sat down at the table. He had a little tin whistle in his hand and twisted the mouthpiece off and on as he sat there. His expression was very serious. He avoided the therapist's eyes.

Tom: Well, here I am. I just came because . . . out of curiosity, you know. I couldn't understand what Mother was talking about. She said that you would help me with my problems, but I don't have any problems.

Therapist: You don't think you have any problems, but your curiosity made you look into this.

Tom: Oh yeah! I'm curious. Always stickin' my nose in everything. Thought I'd come and see.

Therapist: You would like to see what counseling is like.

Tom: Counseling. That's the word I couldn't remember. Yeah. Only I haven't any problems. (*Pause.*) Except that . . . well . . . a . . . my dad

for example, investigated the effectiveness of different forms of group play therapy, employing 11 third-grade children referred by teachers for being shy and withdrawn. These children were randomly assigned to one of three groups: a token reinforcement group, a verbal group, and a control group. The token group was seen in group play therapy once a week for 50-minute sessions and also received tangible reinforcers for social approach behaviors. The verbal group was given the same group play therapy treatment as the token group, including verbal reinforcements usually given by therapists, but without tangible reinforcers. The authors note that this group was quite similar to the typical play therapy group found in many child guidance centers. Control subjects met in a play thera-

FIGURE 10.2. (*continued*)

... *step*-dad, really ... I can't stand him and he can't stand me, and when he's home and when I'm home there's trouble, trouble, trouble. I make too much noise. I'm in the way. I put my feet up on things. We can't stand each other. The only time I can bear to be around the house is when he is gone.

Therapist: You and your father don't get along well together.

Tom: My *step*-father.

Therapist: Your *step*-father.

Tom: But I don't have any problems.

Therapist: Even though you and your step-father don't get along, you don't feel that that is any problem.

Tom: Nope. And all the kids pick on me. They don't like me. (*Pause.*) I can't think of anything to say. Mother said I was to talk about my problems, but I don't have any problems.

Therapist: Let's forget what your mother said to talk about. Just talk about anything you want to bring up. Or don't talk at all, if you'd rather not.

Tom: Like that flag episode last week? You want to hear about that? They all ganged up on me. 'Cause I said "I spit on the flag." And I said, "Heil Hitler!" They all ganged up on me. But I really didn't spit on the flag. I just did it to get their goats. Believe me, I did, too.

Therapist: You wanted to get their goats and you certainly did. To say something shocking like that got their attention right away.

Tom: I don't know why I did it, though. I really wouldn't spit on the flag. I'm a good American. I have too much respect for the flag to spit on it. But that's what I did. They ganged up on me and beat me up. I was outnumbered.

Therapist: You can't understand why you sometimes do things like that.

Tom: Not because I got beat up, either. I just ——— But I haven't got any problems.

Therapist: You don't like to admit that you have problems.

Tom (laughing): That's about the size of it. I really have more than my share of problems. My step-dad. And our substitute teacher. Gosh, she's mean. And nobody likes me. I don't know why. I don't think there is a person alive who doesn't have problems.

Therapist: You really believe that everybody has problems then, and that you are really no different from anyone else.

(*continued*)

py room but interacted together in the absence of a therapist. Each group received a total of 14 therapy sessions. Several dependent measures were obtained, including grades, Children's Manifest Anxiety Scale scores, measures of social adjustment, measures on a behavior problem checklist, and a Q-sort measure of general psychological adjustment.

None of the groups were found to have changed in terms of grades or measures of anxiety, possibly because all groups were close to the norm at the outset. Nor were differences found on the general adjustment measures. The control group failed to display any changes in terms of objective measures. The token group, however, displayed an increase in social approach behavior and a decrease in problem behavior as assessed by the Behavior

FIGURE 10.2. (*continued*)

Tom: Only I'll admit that I've got problems. Some people won't admit it.

Therapist: You're ready to start by admitting that you've got problems.

Tom: My life is no picnic.

Therapist: You're not very happy.

Tom: Would anybody ever know what I say? My mother or anybody? Are you writing what I say down?

Therapist: I'm making some notes; but no one will ever be told what you say during this time.

Tom (with deep sigh): You know this is a mighty peculiar situation. Are you writing this down?

Therapist: Some of it. Just for my own information.

Tom: Yeah. (*Long pause.*)

Tom: Teachers don't care what happens. No one cares what happens to a guy, and here it is after school and you're not even my teacher and I don't bother you. I don't get in your hair. And yet ——— (*shrugs shoulders*).

Therapist: You didn't think other people cared enough about what happens to a guy and yet . . .

Tom: I was *curious*.

Therapist: You were *curious*.

Tom: Of course! I ——— Well, there isn't anything that really bothers me. Not really, I mean. I don't let it.

Therapist: You think you have things pretty well under control.

Tom: Well, yeah. Only I ——— Well, I can't think of anything to say. I haven't got anything to say.

Therapist: If you haven't anything to say, you haven't anything to say. (*Pause.*) If you care to come back next Thursday, I'll be here. If you don't care to, I would appreciate it if you would let me know by three o'clock next Thursday.

Tom: Yeah. I sure would.

Therapist: If you care to go now, you may. Or if you care to stay longer, you may. Use this time as you see fit.

Problem Checklist. The verbal play therapy group was also found to increase in terms of social approach behavior. Although both token and verbal play therapy groups exhibited greater change than that found in the control group, the group that received play therapy plus token reinforcement displayed the greatest change. Although this study provides support for the hypothesis that group play therapy is superior to no treatment, at least on certain variables, it suggests that a more valuable approach is one that uses operant conditioning procedures in the play therapy context. Further studies along these lines have been conducted by Clement, Fazzone, and Goldstein (1970) and Clement, Roberts, and Lantz (1970).

In a study by Miller et al. (1972), 67 phobic children ages 6 to 15 were assigned at random to one of three groups: systematic desensitization, play therapy (individual psychotherapy with older children), or a "waiting list" control group. Treatment involved three sessions per week for a total of 8 weeks. The dependent variables included ratings of an independent clinical judge as well as parental ratings. No differences were found between groups when judges' ratings were considered. Analysis of parental ratings, however, suggested that both desensitization and play therapy

FIGURE 10.2. (*continued*)

Tom: Yeah. (*He removes his hat and coat.*) I'm in no hurry.

Therapist: Think you might like to stay a little longer.

Tom: Yeah. I like to look around in here. You don't care, do you?

Therapist: Look around if you like.

Tom (looking at everything in the room): I bet the kids like to paint.

Therapist: You think they do?

Tom: I do, too. Only in my room at school . . . Say. If I ever got a problem it's that sub. She could furnish all the crab meat in the world. Only you'd probably get indigestion and die.

Therapist: You don't like the sub.

Tom: You catch on. (*He examines the clay.*) This would be fun, too. (*Picks up the puppet.*) I could make up plenty of funny plays about the fixes I get in. Just my autobiography would bring tears to their eyes.

Therapist: You think your life is sad.

Tom: Well. I mean it is certainly full of something. I'm always in trouble. (*Tom puts puppet on his hand.*) Now see here. I'll *murder* you if you don't do as I say. See? (*Voice is completely changed — low, deep, threatening.*)

Therapist: He feels like murdering someone.

Tom: I do, too, sometimes. Only of course (*laughs*) I don't. Respect for the law and all that, you know. But tell you what. Next time I come I'll put on a play. Episode One. My life and troubles.

Therapist: All right. Next time you come you present your life and troubles.

Tom (playing with the different puppets): I'm sure I could make some of these.

Therapist: Think you might even be able to make some puppets. (*He continues to play with them.*) Your time is up for today, Tom.

Tom: Well, so long. I'll see you tomorrow.

Source: Axline (1947). © V. Axline and reprinted by permission of the author.

had a significant effect on the specific phobia as well as on fears in general when compared with control children. Desensitization and play therapy did not differ significantly in terms of effectiveness. Young phobic children were also found to benefit from treatment to a greater extent than did older phobics, regardless of the treatment approach. A follow-up to this investigation (Hampe, Noble, Miller, & Barrett, 1973) suggested that 1 to 2 years later the original effects of play therapy and desensitization were no longer related to outcome, with 80% of all children either symptom-free or significantly improved. Follow-up findings, however, were muddled by the fact that a number of children who had not improved in the original study (including controls) had received further treatment between the time of termination and follow-up.

Ney, Palvesky, and Markley (1971) used a somewhat different experimental design to examine the relative effectiveness of operant conditioning and play therapy in the treatment of schizophrenic children. One group of 10 patients received 50 sessions of play therapy followed by 50 sessions of operant conditioning treatment (reinforcement for imitating adults, communicating, etc.) A second group, matched on relevant variables, received 50 sessions of operant training followed by 50 sessions of play therapy. This design allows for the assessment of differences between the groups receiving the two forms of treatment both after the first 50 sessions and later after the second 50 sessions. In general, the children receiving operant conditioning treatment were found to differ in terms of outcome measures from patients treated with play therapy. The differences associated with operant conditioning were only significant, however, after the second 50 sessions of therapy (when the children had already been given 50 sessions of play therapy). An as yet unanswered question is whether play therapy in fact enhances the effectiveness of operant procedures with patients such as those employed in this study.

In general, findings related to the effectiveness of play therapy suggest that in certain cases such treatment results in changes greater than those observed in nontreated subjects. Too few studies, however, have been conducted to allow meaningful conclusions to be drawn about the effectiveness of specific play therapy approaches, although there is some suggestion that play therapy may be more effective if operant procedures are also employed.

Group Approaches to Psychotherapy*

Although child psychotherapy is most often conducted on an individual basis, many clinicians have advocated treating children in groups. One obvious advantage of this approach is that, all things being equal, it may represent a more efficient use of professional time, because several children can be seen in the same amount of time that would usually be spent in treating an individual child. Additionally, there are those who would argue that group therapy is the most effective form of treatment for certain types of childhood problems. For example, many children re-

*This section draws heavily on a presentation of group treatment approaches provided by Johnson, Rasbury, and Siegel (in press).

ferred for treatment have major problems in relating to others in a satisfying manner. Some are shy, socially withdrawn, and seriously deficient in important social skills. Others have just the opposite problem of being overly aggressive. Group therapy provides an excellent context within which such children can learn more adaptive ways of relating. Thus, the child who is withdrawn may learn that it is safe to be more assertive and outgoing with others and may develop the skills necessary to behave in this manner. Likewise, the group may have a socializing influence on the overly aggressive child, who may come to adopt more desirable ways of interacting. Because changes in group therapy result from actual interactions with other children, rather than from simply talking about relationship issues (as in individual therapy), there should also be greater generalization of behavioral changes to the child's natural environment than in individual therapy.

Additional advantages of group treatment derive from the fact that the child may gain a better understanding of how his or her behavior is seen by others and through learning first hand that the problems he or she displays are not unique, but may have also been experienced by other group members. In many instances effective ways of dealing with problems can be found by learning how others in the group have successfully dealt with similar problems in the past. These factors would suggest that group treatments may have much to offer, especially in those cases where problems in the area of peer relationships are of special concern.

A range of group approaches have evolved over the years. The diversity of these treatment methods has been illustrated by Wenar (1982), who has noted:

> They involve . . . diverse ages (from preschoolers to adolescents), psychopathologies (the entire gamut has been treated on a group basis), special interest groups (father-absent boys, teenage pregnant girls), techniques (structured tasks, games, discussions ranging from dreams to current happenings, fantasy play, role playing, dance, body

movement, and art), goals (release of inhibitions, relief of anxiety and guilt, increased control and coping skills, modification of the self concept, insight), conceptual models (psychoanalytic, nondirective, behavioral, gestalt, and transactional analysis) and they are performed in . . . a variety of settings (child guidance clinics, private practice, schools, hospitals, detention homes) with the therapist's role varying from passive observer to active director. (p. 398)

As space limitations preclude considering the entire range of group approaches (for overviews see Kraft, 1980; Schiffer, 1984), we will limit our discussion to two approaches that serve to illustrate the essence of the group method as applied to children.

Activity Group Therapy

This approach, developed by Slavson (1943), laid the groundwork for most later group therapies with children and adolescents (Kraft, 1980). Activity Group Therapy was originally developed for use with children in the 8- to 12-year age range who displayed less severe forms of psychopathology (e.g., children who were shy, withdrawn, dependent, or who displayed general conduct or behavior problems) and who were seen as likely to benefit from socialization experiences. In this approach the setting for therapy is a large room equipped with a variety of materials, such as art supplies, model boats or planes, wood, metal, leather, and plastic, as well as tools for working with these materials. The therapy room also typically contains a bathroom and a kitchen area for snack time, which is part of each therapy session. As might be obvious, the term *Activity Group Therapy* is derived from the fact that the setting for therapy is one in which children can engage in a range of activities instead of simply talking with one another. This focus on activities is thought to provide an initial avenue for the expression of conflict and a basic framework for the interaction among group members. As therapy progresses, however, it is assumed that involvement in activities becomes secondary to the interaction among group members and

that the therapeutic change occurs primarily through such interactions.

Treatment, which typically consists of weekly meetings (for 2-hour sessions), takes place in groups of from four to eight children, with the groups being balanced in terms of group membership. For example, an attempt would be made to have a mix of aggressive and shy and withdrawn children rather than a group composed of those with similar behavioral styles. This attention to group balance is seen as essential in order to stimulate appropriate group interactions and to inhibit inappropriate acting out.

Although analytically oriented, Slavson has argued that the activity group therapist should be empathic, supporting, and helpful but essentially nondirective. While attempting to model appropriate behaviors and to convey a sense of responsibility (through the proper use of tools and supplies, for example), the therapist relies on the group members to provide the necessary structure for the group. Thus, it is primarily the group that must deal with acting-out behaviors and the expression of inner conflicts as these are reflected in inappropriate behaviors directed toward group members (or the therapist). As nondirectiveness on the part of the therapist forces the children to handle tasks on their own and requires that they, rather than the therapist, work toward the resolution of conflicts with other group members, therapy is assumed to increase their self-confidence as well as facilitate the development of more adaptive social behaviors. (For a more detailed discussion of this approach, see Schiffer, 1977; and Slavson & Schiffer, 1975).

Activity-Interview Group Psychotherapy

This approach, which was also pioneered by Slavson and his colleagues (see Slavson, 1943; Slavson & Schiffer, 1975), was developed for children in the 8- to 12-year age range who show more serious types of psychopathology than can be dealt with in Activity Group Therapy. Slavson and Schiffer (1975) have also described a variation on this approach (Play Group Therapy) for somewhat younger children. These approaches differ from Activity Group Therapy in that therapy sessions typically consist of both a discussion (interview) phase (where various issues are dealt with verbally by the group) and an activity phase (where children can engage in various types of play activities). The types of play materials employed in this approach are also different from those used in Activity Group Therapy. Here, the materials are more similar to those used in analytically oriented play therapy, being specifically selected to elicit play behaviors reflective of the child's inner conflicts and current concerns.

As this approach is used with children who may show significant psychological disturbances, the therapist provides more structure and guidance and is much more active than in Activity Group Therapy. The therapist may ask questions, comment on the behaviors of group members, and become an active participant in group discussions. The therapist also provides appropriate interpretations of group dynamics as well as interpretations of the play behaviors and verbalizations of individual group members in order to facilitate the development of insight into the nature of personal conflicts and promote constructive personality change. In this respect, Activity-Interview Therapy and Play Group Therapy are quite similar to individual analytically oriented play therapy.

In addition to interaction with the therapist, group members may also benefit from interpretations and comments provided by other children during group discussions and play activities, as well as from the group process per se. One example of how the interaction among group members can benefit more than one child at a time is suggested by the following example, provided by Schiffer (1977):

> Robert places a small infant doll headfirst into a toy toilet bowl, angrily hitting it on the buttocks. He then examines its desperate state, feet sticking up in the air. Catching the eye of the observing therapist, he ap-

pears guilty. Sandy spots this play and says laughingly, "Look at that!" Robert, as if his "secret" has been exposed, is silent. *Therapist*: "He's upside down." Robert nods. Sandy says, almost hopefully, "Maybe he'll drown." No response from Robert. *Therapist*: "Maybe he did something to make you angry." *Robert*: "Yeah". Then Sandy adds, "Babies are no good." The therapist affirms that, "Babies do get a lot of attention." This was all the encouragement Robert needed. He began to speak angrily of his feelings about his infant sibling and his sense of rejection. He and Sandy spoke quite openly, now encouraged by the discovery that they shared a common source of irritation: younger siblings. The therapist listened, occasionally nodding. Toward the end he offered: "It's not easy getting used to new babies after you've been the only one. Mother and father get so busy with them that they kind of forget you're around. I can see why you sometimes wish babies would go away. (pp. 383–384)

This example at once illustrates how children can learn from the group that they are not unique in their feelings, how issues that arise within the group often are of relevance to more than one child, and how dealing with such issues can be facilitated by the therapist. This brief excerpt also serves to illustrate the type of topics and interactions that are frequently dealt with within the context of traditional group therapy.

Miscellaneous Approaches to Group Therapy

Without considering them in any detail, it should be noted that there are a range of other methods that have been used for treating children in groups. These approaches have varied along a number of dimensions. Some (especially those used with young children) have included play or other activities as an essential part of therapy, whereas others (e.g., those employed with adolescents) have usually relied almost totally on verbal interactions among group members. Even among those approaches that include play activities, there are differences in the degree to which play behaviors versus verbalizations stimulated by play activities are emphasized. Approaches have also varied considerably in terms of theoretical orientation. For example, both Redl (1944) and Ginott (1961) have developed analytically oriented approaches that are similar in some respects to Activity Group therapy, while Axline (1947) has applied the same principles as used in nondirective play therapy to group work with children. Finally, approaches to group treatment have also been derived from the behavioral model (see Graziano, 1972; Rose, 1972). Although there is considerable variability among these behaviorally oriented approaches, all focus on effecting actual behavior change rather than dealing with intrapsychic conflicts or attempting to bring about global personality change. And each relies on the use of social learning principles such as modeling, positive reinforcement, and the like (to be discussed later) to bring about such changes.

Effectiveness of Group Therapies

Even though there are many testimonials to the effectiveness of group therapy and a variety of studies that have sought to assess its effectiveness with children, the situation here is much the same as with research on individual psychotherapy. Many studies have been methodologically flawed and have been plagued by the same uniformity assumption myths (which are equally problematic in this area) as was the case with research on individual psychotherapy, discussed earlier. It is therefore not surprising that a review of the child group therapy literature by Abramowitz (1976) failed to yield evidence in support of the group approach. Indeed, this review found that about a third of the studies had positive outcomes, about a third had mixed outcomes, and about a third showed no evidence of change. Although there was some suggestion that behavioral approaches may be somewhat more effective, the evidence for none of the group approaches was impressive. Clearly, more adequate studies along the lines

suggested for individual psychotherapy are needed.

FAMILY THERAPY IN THE TREATMENT OF CHILDHOOD DISORDERS

In recent years increasing emphasis has been placed on treating the child within the context of the family. This family-oriented approach to treatment is based on the assumption that the locus of pathology is not just within the individual who is designated as the "identified patient," but is often found to be within the context of family relationships (although theorists vary in the degree to which they emphasize individual vs. family variables). The family therapist often sees individual treatment as futile, because child behavior may not be modifiable in the absence of significant changes with in the family. Further, many family therapists assume that a certain degree of homeostasis exists within the family unit, so that changes in the behavior of one individual also affect other family members. Deviant behavior displayed by a child is often viewed as symptomatic of a more general family disturbance, and it is thought that an alleviation of problem behaviors in the child without dealing with the underlying family problem may result in the "family pathology" being expressed by other family members — a sort of symptom substitution at the family level.

Based on these assumptions, a general goal of family therapy is usually an improvement in the nature of family relationships. It is assumed that if family relationships and interaction patterns can be changed, in a nonpathological direction, this will result in a reduction of the problem behaviors displayed by family members. As the actual goals of therapy may differ, depending on the particular orientation of the therapist, Table 10.2 provides a general listing of goals endorsed by some 290 family therapists. Also listed is the proportion of therapists who endorsed specific goals as being of major importance.

Therapy itself usually involves the entire

TABLE 10.2. PRIMARY GOALS OF THERAPISTS
WITH FAMILIES IN TREATMENT.

Improved Communication	85%
Improved Autonomy and Individuation	56%
Improved Empathy	56%
More Flexible Leadership	34%
Improved Role Agreement	32%
Reduced Conflict	23%
Individual Symptomatic Improvement	23%
Improved Individual Task Performance	12%

Note. Percentages represent the proportion of therapists who indicated that these were primary goals with all families.
Source: Adapted from Group for the Advancement of Psychiatry (1970).

family: the child, parents, siblings, and perhaps members of the extended family. Working with them is a therapist and perhaps also a cotherapist. In some cases both a therapist and cotherapist are used because the two therapists working together can often serve to model appropriate modes of interaction and can check on each other to make sure neither therapist sides with specific family members. The presence of a cotherapist is also of value because family therapy frequently involves a much more active interchange of ideas, feelings, and behavior than is usually seen in individual treatment; two therapists are often necessary to capture the richness of these interchanges and therapeutically respond to them. Within this setting the therapist(s) and family interact, focusing on problems within the family, with emphasis on relationships and maladaptive interaction and communication patterns among family members.

Approaches to Family Therapy

Up to this point we have been speaking of family therapy in general terms, as though there was one approach to treating the family. In reality there are a wide variety of approaches. Indeed, Levant (1984) has cited some 22 varieties of family therapy that he has suggested can be grouped under one of three basic models. Following this approach to classification, the basic features of each of

these models will be briefly noted to illustrate the diversity of family treatment approaches.

The Historical Model

Under this heading are several approaches to family therapy that are derived from, or at least compatible with, psychodynamic theory as applied to the family. Examples of therapies included under this heading are the psychodynamic approaches of Ackerman (1958) and Framo (1982), the multigenerational approach of Bowen (1978), and the intergenerational-contextual approach of Boszormenyi-Nagy (Boszormenyi-Nagy & Ulrich, 1981). The essential nature of these approaches is described in the following:

> The approach to therapy in these schools involves freeing individuals from their excessive attachments to the previous generation. This occurs through a process of uncovering these attachments, gaining insight into their inappropriateness, and gradually giving them up. The therapist's role involves facilitation of this process, either through the interpretation of the relationship between past attachments and present behavior, or through "coaching" . . . clients as they attempt to form more appropriate, present-oriented, adult relationships with members of their family of origin. (Levant, 1984, p. 81)

These statements clearly illustrate that although each of the approaches associated with this model involve working within the context of the family, considerable emphasis is placed on the role of individual psychodynamics, because these influence the relationship between family members and contribute to the problems the family is experiencing. It may be noted that in some respects these approaches are not unlike group methods such as Activity-Interview Group Therapy (discussed in the preceding section) in which considerable attention is given to the treatment of individual psychopathology within the context of group therapy.

The Structure/Process Model

Rather than emphasizing intrapsychic factors as contributors to family problems, these approaches see family problems as contributors to individual psychopathology. Included within this category are communication approaches, such as that developed by Jackson (Jackson & Weakland, 1961), problem-solving approaches (Haley, 1976), Structural Family Therapy (Minuchin, 1974), and behavioral approaches to family treatment (Patterson, Ray, & Shaw, 1968; Werry, 1979a).

> These approaches are concerned with the current patterns of interaction of the family, and with the relationship of these patterns to the symptoms or presenting problem of the identified patient. Some variation exists among these schools in whether the interactional patterns are viewed from a structural or process perspective, whether the primary aim is broad (that is, to change the structure) or more narrow (that is, to remove the symptom), and whether the orientation is drawn from systems theory or learning theory. But as a group, they differ sharply from the historical approaches in dismissing history taking, uncovering, interpretation, and insight as irrelevant to the treatment process, and in focusing at the system level, giving little or no consideration to the psychology of the individual. They also contrast sharply with the experiential therapists in playing down the importance of feelings or affect in the treatment process. (Levant, 1984, p. 83)

Although approaches within this category vary, with some focusing on improving communications and family interactions, others on restructuring the family organization, and still others on changing reinforcement contingencies that contribute to problem behavior, all deal with current variables that are operative at the family (rather than the individual) level.

The Experiential Model

Representative of this model are client-centered (Levant, 1978), humanistic-communication (Satir, 1967), and Gestalt (see Kempler, 1981) approaches, among others. These approaches, which are based on existential-phenomenological theoretical orientations, differ from those just discussed in that they focus more on helping family members become self-actualized and experience a better quality of life than on modifying family structure or alleviating the specific problem behaviors of family members. Within this framework the therapist attempts to be a facilitator who observes and reflects on the process of family interactions and encourages "intensified affective experiences" in family members so as to foster personal growth and self-actualization. Here it is assumed that such changes are facilitated by the therapist actively joining in the family process and interrelating with the family in a genuine and nondefensive manner (Levant, 1984).

Other Approaches to Family Intervention

There are still other approaches to family treatment that differ from the ones just described. For example, MacGregor, Ritchie, Serrano, and Schuster (1964) described a form of treatment called multiple impact therapy (MIT). This approach, developed at the University of Texas Medical Center at Galveston, involves an entire team of therapists working intensively with a family for a period of 2 days or more. Treatment entails interaction of therapists with the entire family, with family members as individuals, and with various family subgroups. The MIT approach has been most widely used with families of adolescents who are experiencing a crisis situation of some sort, the goals being resolution of the crisis and development of more adaptive relationship patterns that will enable families to deal with subsequent problems.

Speck and Attneave (1971) described another rather unique procedure that they refer to as social-network therapy. This approach, which also entails intervention by a team of therapists, involves entire kinship systems. Here the family, friends, neighbors, and other persons significant to the family may be assembled for meetings in the home of the nuclear family, involving up to 30 or 40 people. The goals of this approach are to open new channels of communication, strengthen bonds among individuals, deal with pathological relationships, and generally maximize the collective potential of this network for providing social support and working out family-related difficulties.

Family Therapy Research

Presently there are few firm conclusions that can be reached regarding the effectiveness of family therapy. Even though the quality of research in this area has improved in recent years (Jones, 1980), many studies have involved a relatively small number of families, have failed to obtain adequate pretherapy measures against which outcome measures might be compared, or have failed to employ adequate control groups. Even the most basic elements of a controlled study have been neglected in many instances. Thus, with some notable exceptions, studies have often simply reported the application of a particular family therapy approach to a small number of families without adequately measuring change or presenting evidence that any changes observed could not have been accounted for in terms of the passage of time or other extraneous variables. (For an overview of specific issues to consider in evaluating family therapy see Frude, 1980.)

The status of this area can be illustrated by considering the findings of DeWitt (1978), who has provided an in-depth review of the outcome literature. This reviewer was able to find 31 studies that reported on at least two or more family therapy cases and that clearly specified the nature of therapy outcome. Of these studies, 23 failed to employ any sort of control group and were judged to lack other elements of good experimental design. Results of these studies suggested a general success rate of 72%, when cases judged to be "slightly improved" were considered, and a success rate of 64% when such cases were deleted and a more stringent criterion for improvement maintained. Of the eight studies that did employ a control group, five compared family therapy with groups receiving minimal or no treatment. Even though the results of these five studies tend to favor family therapy, they tell us little about the effects of family therapy per se, because positive findings could

have resulted from nonspecific factors (attention, expectancy effects, etc.) rather than from the active ingredients of family therapy itself. The remaining three studies employed adequate control groups and compared family therapy with other types of treatment. Only one of them provided strong support for the effects of family therapy. Although there is some reason to believe that family therapy works, these results suggest that strong evidence concerning its effectiveness appears to be lacking. (For additional reviews of this literature see Gurman & Kniskern, 1978; Wells & Dezen, 1978.)

Many of the points raised earlier in our discussion of the effectiveness of individual psychotherapy would seem to be equally applicable to family therapy outcome research, for here too few studies have attempted to investigate the relationship between patient (family) variables, therapist variables, and outcome (DeWitt, 1978). With over 20 different "schools" of family therapy (Levant, 1984), statements regarding the effectiveness of family therapy per se are meaningless. Some approaches may turn out to be quite effective, whereas others may be worthless or even harmful. What is needed are not only more well-controlled studies of family therapy effectiveness, but also studies of a more complex nature, capable of providing information about which types of family therapy are effective with which type of family difficulties when offered by therapists differing in terms of various characteristics. It is unfortunate that questions of this type are only beginning to be asked (Levant, 1984).

BEHAVIORAL APPROACHES TO CHILD TREATMENT

Behavioral approaches to child treatment have taken many forms. Some approaches have involved the application of operant learning principles. Others have employed what could be considered classical conditioning procedures. Others have tended to emphasize the role of observational learning. Still others, rather than focusing on overt behaviors, have been designed to modify maladaptive cognitions presumed to be related to inappropriate modes of responding. Thus, there is presently a wide range of approaches termed *behavioral* in use in child treatment, including systematic desensitization, in vivo desensitization, modeling, implosive therapy, overcorrection procedures, bell and pad procedures, emotive imagery, cognitive behavior modification, and a host of approaches based on operant principles—token economies, contingency contracting, and time-out procedures, among others.

Thus, child behavior therapy cannot be thought of or defined in terms of a specific group of techniques or approaches—nor should it. It would be more appropriate to define behavior therapy, child or otherwise, as a general orientation that involves the application of empirically derived principles, especially learning principles, to the modification of maladaptive behavior. Within this orientation, behavior is defined broadly, in terms of cognitive, overt-behavior, or physiological responses. Major emphasis is placed on the relationship between such behaviors and environmental factors that elicit and/or maintain these behaviors, and on the ways that these environment-behavior relationships can be altered to bring about constructive behavior change.

Existing behavioral treatment approaches have been used to deal with a wide range of childhood problems on both a group and individual basis. In the following sections we will look at several of these approaches to behavior modification with children.

Systematic Desensitization

Systematic desensitization is a treatment procedure that has been widely used with adults to deal with maladaptive anxiety and avoidance responses. The procedure, as originally proposed by Wolpe (1958), involves three basic aspects. One is training in progressive relaxation (see Table 10.3). The second is the construction of an anxiety hierarchy composed of items that can be presented in imagery and are graded from low to high according to the amount of anxiety they elicit when imagined (see Table 10.4). The third aspect of the desensitization package involves a graded presentation of the hierarchy items while the patient is in a deeply relaxed state. The process of gradually working through items in the hierarchy while relaxed is purported to bring about a reduction in anxiety responses. The basic rationale underlying this approach is that one cannot be both fearful and relaxed at the same time. It is assumed that if one can be helped to relax (or engage in some other behavior incompatible with anxiety) in the presence of anxiety-producing stimuli, one's anxiety responses to these stimuli will be weakened.

Not only can desensitization be conducted with hierarchy items presented in imagery (systematic desensitization), but in vivo desensitization is also possible. This involves graded exposure of the patient to an actual (rather than imagined) feared or anxiety-eliciting situation or object while he or she is at the same time engaging in some other response thought to be incompatible with anxiety. The classic study illustrating this approach is by Jones (1924), who was able to successfully eliminate a fear of rabbits in a young child by feeding the child while gradually moving a cage containing a rabbit closer and closer over a period of several treatment sessions. In vivo desensitization may be quite useful when a child has serious problems with imagery or does not respond with anxiety to imagined hierarchy items related to the feared situation. This approach might also be used when a child is unable to relax in response to relaxation instructions, because it allows anxiety-inhibiting responses other than relaxation to be employed, as eating was used by Jones in the case mentioned. On the other hand, certain fears that would be difficult to deal with in vivo appear more suitable for systematic desensitization. For instance, it is possible to construct anxiety hierarchies related to fears of storms, war, and death and other, more abstract fears, but it would be difficult if

TABLE 10.3. AN INTRODUCTION TO THE RELAXATION TRAINING STEPS
OF SYSTEMATIC DESENSITIZATION.

Steps in Relaxation

1. Take a deep breath and hold it (for about 10 seconds). Hold it. Okay, let it out.
2. Raise both of your hands about half way above the couch (or arms of the chair) and breathe normally. Now, drop your hands to the couch (or down).
3. Now hold your arms out and make a tight fist. Really tight. Feel the tension in your hands. I am going to count to three and when I say "three" I want you to drop your hands. One . . . Two . . . Three.
4. Raise your arms again, and bend your fingers back the other way (toward your body). Now drop your hands and relax.
5. Raise your arms. Now drop them and relax.
6. Now raise your arms again, but this time "flap" your hands around. Okay, relax again.
7. Raise your arms again. Now relax.
8. Raise your arms above the couch (chair) again and tense your biceps. Breathe normally, and keep your hands loose. Relax your hands. (Notice how you have a warm feeling of relaxation.)
9. Now hold your arms out to your side and tense your triceps. Make sure that you breathe normally. Relax your arms.
10. Now arch your shoulders back. Hold it. Make sure that your arms are relaxed. Now relax.
11. Hunch your shoulders forward. Hold it, and make sure that you breathe normally and keep your arms relaxed. Okay, relax. (Notice the feeling of relief from tensing and relaxing your muscles.)
12. Now turn your head to the right and tense your neck. Relax and bring your head back again to its natural position.
13. Turn your head to the left and tense your neck. Relax and bring your head back again to its natural position.
14. Now bend your head back slightly toward the chair. Hold it. Okay, now bring your head back slowly to its natural position.*
15. This time bring your head down almost to your chest. Hold it. Now relax and let your head come back to its natural resting position.
16. Now, open your mouth as much as possible. A little wider, okay, relax. (Mouth should be partly open afterwards.)
17. Now tense your lips by closing your mouth. Okay, relax.
18. Put your tongue at the roof of your mouth. Press hard. (Pause) Relax and allow your tongue to come to a comfortable position in your mouth.
19. Now put your tongue at the bottom of your mouth. Press down hard. Relax and let your tongue come to a comfortable position in your mouth.
20. Now just lie (sit) there and relax. Try not to think of anything.
21. To control self-verbalizations, I want you to go through the motions of singing a high note—not aloud! Okay, start singing to yourself. Hold that note. Okay, relax. (You are becoming more and more relaxed.)
22. Now sing a medium tone and make your vocal cords tense again. Relax.
23. Now sing a low note and make your vocal cords tense again. Relax (Your vocal apparatus should be relaxed now. Relax your mouth.)
24. Now close your eyes. Squeeze them tight and breathe naturally. Notice the tension. Now relax. (Notice how the pain goes away when you relax.)
25. Now let your eyes relax and keep your mouth open slightly.
26. Open your eyes as much as possible. Hold it. Now relax your eyes.
27. Now wrinkle your forehead as much as possible. Hold it. Okay, relax.
28. Now take a deep breath and hold it. Relax.
29. Now exhale. Breathe all the air out . . . all of it out. Relax. (Notice the wondrous feeling of breathing again.)
30. Imagine that there are weights pulling on all your muscles making them flaccid and relaxed . . . pulling your arms and body down into the couch.
31. Pull your stomach muscles together. Tighter. Okay, relax.
32. Now extend your muscles as if you were a prizefighter. Make your stomach hard. Relax. (You are becoming more and more relaxed.)
33. Now tense your buttocks. Tighter. Hold it. Now relax.
34. Now search the upper part of your body and relax any part that is tense. First the facial muscles. (Pause 3 to 5 sec.) Then the vocal muscles. (Pause 3 to 5 sec.) The neck region. (Pause 3 to 5 sec.) Your shoulders . . . relax any part that is tense. (Pause) Now the arms and fingers. Relax these. Becoming very relaxed.

(continued)

TABLE 10.3. AN INTRODUCTION TO THE RELAXATION TRAINING STEPS
OF SYSTEMATIC DESENSITIZATION (*continued*).

35. Maintaining this relaxation, raise both of your legs (about a 45° angle). Now relax. (Notice that this further relaxes you.)
36. Now bend your feet back so that your toes point toward your face. Relax your mouth. Bend them hard. Relax.
37. Bend your feet the other way . . . away from your body. Not far. Notice the tension. Okay, relax.
38. Relax. (Pause) Now curl your toes together as hard as you can. Tighter. Okay, relax. (Quiet . . . silence for about 30 seconds.)
39. This completes the formal relaxation procedure. Now explore your body from your feet up. Make sure that every muscle is relaxed. (Say slowly) — first your toes, your feet, your legs, buttocks, stomach, shoulders, neck, eyes, and finally your forehead — all should be relaxed now. (Quiet — silence for about ten seconds). Just lie there and feel very relaxed, noticing the warmness of the relaxation. (Pause) I would like you to stay this way for about one more minute, and then I am going to count to five. When I reach five, I want you to open your eyes feeling very calm and refreshed. (Quiet — silence for about one minute.) Okay, when I count to five I want you to open your eyes feeling very calm and refreshed. One . . . feeling very calm; two . . . very calm, very refreshed; three . . . very refreshed; four . . . and five.

Note: Adapted in part from Jacobson (1938), Rimm (1967, personal communication), and Wolpe and Lazarus (1966).
Source: Morris & Kratochwill (1983). © 1983 Pergamon Press and reprinted with permission.
*The child should not be encouraged to bend his/her neck either all the way back or forward.

not impossible to present these situations concretely.

During recent years much research has been done regarding the effectiveness of systematic desensitization procedures with adult fears and phobias, and in fact the effectiveness of the desensitization package with this age group is well documented (Emmelkamp, 1982). The effectiveness of these procedures in child treatment is less clear, however, because desensitization procedures have been less frequently applied to children, and the majority of studies involving children have been of the case study variety. Nevertheless, there is reason to believe that both systematic and in vivo desensitization may be useful in dealing with fear and anxiety in younger age groups.

The application of desensitization procedures to childhood problems was illustrated by Tasto (1969), who reported the treatment of a 4-year-old boy with a severe phobia for loud and sudden noises. Because there were problems in obtaining desired results with imagery presentations, treatment involved muscle relaxation paired with in vivo presentation of fear-related stimuli. After six sessions the fear was eliminated, with no recurrence at follow-up. Montenegro (1968) treated two children who displayed pathological degrees of separation anxiety. These children were successfully treated in 15 and 16 ses-

TABLE 10.4. EXAMPLE OF DESENSITIZATION HIERARCHY FOR TEST-TAKING ANXIETY.

- You wake up in the morning and think of the test that you have to take next week.
- You go to school and your teacher reminds the class to study because it is only 5 days before your exam.
- It's 2 days before your test and your friend, Bob, asks you if you're about ready for the test.
- You're sitting in your room the night before the exam going over the material that is to be covered on the test.
- You're on the school bus going to school on the day of the test and you overhear someone in your class saying that she has heard that the test will be a hard one.
- You're sitting in your seat waiting for the exams to be passed out.
- You get your test and read the first question and can't seem to think of the answer.

sions, respectively, through the use of in vivo procedures. The children were separated from their mothers for progressively longer and longer periods of time and by increasing distance, and feeding responses were used to produce a physiological state antagonistic to anxiety.

Kondas (1967) has conducted one of the few studies designed to examine the role of the various components of the total systematic desensitization package in bringing about fear reduction in children. This study employed 23 children ages 11 to 13 who displayed serious examination anxiety. These children were assigned to one of four groups: systematic desensitization, relaxation training only, hierarchy visualization without relaxation, and no treatment control. Treatment was conducted in groups. The results suggested that the total systematic desensitization package was effective in bringing about significant fear reduction when compared with results for the children not receiving treatment. Relaxation training was also found to bring about transient fear reduction, but visualization of hierarchy items in the absence of relaxation failed to bring about any significant change. In a group study of test-anxious sixth graders Deffenbacher and Kemper (1974) likewise found systematic desensitization to be superior to no treatment. As for other applications of systematic desensitization: Hallstein (1965) reported the successful treatment of anorexia nervosa in a 12-year-old girl as has Ollendick (1979); fears of water (Bentler, 1962), dogs (Lazarus, 1959), school (Garvey & Hegreves, 1966), and ambulances and hospitals (Lazarus & Rachman, 1957) have likewise been dealt with successfully; so have reading anxiety (Word & Rozynko, 1974) and dream-induced anxiety (Cavior & Deutsch, 1975). For more detailed coverage of this literature see Morris & Kratochwill, 1983.

Taken together, all these studies suggest that desensitization is a viable treatment approach for dealing with certain childhood fears and anxieties. Additional well-controlled group studies are badly needed, however, to assess the relative effectiveness of systematic desensitization and in vivo desensitization in dealing with various types of anxiety-based childhood problems and to compare desensitization procedures with other approaches designed to reduce childhood fear. Finally, although group studies such as those cited (along with several others) have suggested that children treated with systematic desensitization show greater decreases in anxiety than children not receiving treatment, further investigations utilizing appropriate controls are needed to determine whether these effects are indeed the result of desensitization procedures or merely of nonspecific factors.

One particularly interesting variation on systematic desensitization is Emotive Imagery. This procedure was originally developed by Lazarus and Abramovitz (1962) for treating child fears in those cases where children had difficulties with progressive relaxation. The approach is similar to desensitization in that a hierarchy of fear-eliciting themes is developed. However, rather than training the child in relaxation, the clinician attempts to determine the child's hero (e.g., Batman, Spiderman) and the kinds of thoughts and feelings the child has concerning this person. Treatment consists of having the child close his or her eyes and imagine a sequence of events made into a story about the hero. Gradually, as the child shows evidence of positive feelings that result from imagining this story, anxiety-arousing scenes from the hierarchy are introduced. In a manner similar to relaxation, positive feelings, associated with the imagined activities of the child and his or her hero, are assumed sufficient to inhibit anxiety elicited by the presentation of fear-related scenes. As with desensitization, fear-inducing scenes are presented gradually and movement up the hierarchy is determined by the child's ability to imagine earlier scenes without experiencing anxiety. For example, the following scene was used in treating a school-phobic child with emotive imagery:

> Imagine that Batman and Robin have asked you to assist them in catching a criminal. They lend you a special wrist radio so that they can contact you whenever necessary.

Nobody must know the secret, that you are actually helping Batman and Robin to solve a crime right in your own school. Batman says to you "Peter, I have placed a secret message in your school locker. When you go to school tomorrow morning, go to your locker as soon as possible and read the message. Then destroy it!" Of course you don't want to tell Batman and Robin about your fears, so you go to school the next morning and head straight for your locker. Picture yourself going to school. As you ride toward the school in the bus, you are wondering what the message will say. You get into the school yard, get out of the bus, and you walk slowly to your locker. You don't want to rush there because you don't want to make anyone suspicious. (Lazarus, 1977, p. 101)

Although there has been no controlled research on this technique, the results of a number of case studies suggest that it may well be useful in the treatment of childhood fears. Lazarus and Abramovitz (1962) and Lazarus (1977) have reported on the successful use of this procedure with children displaying a variety of fears and phobias. Indeed, Lazarus and Abramovitz have suggested that, on the average, treatment only took three to four sessions to complete. In addition to these case studies, several other authors have reported on the use of this technique in treating fears of school (Boyd, 1980) and the dark (Jackson & King, 1981). Clearly, research is needed to assess the efficacy of this approach in a more well-controlled manner.

Implosive Therapy

Stampfl and Levis (1967, 1968) have described an approach to therapy, labeled implosive therapy, that is also designed for dealing with maladaptive anxiety-based behaviors. Described as a "learning-theory-based psychodynamic behavioral therapy," the procedure is grounded in the assumption that anxiety responses can be eliminated through the process termed *extinction* if stimuli evoking strong anxiety or fear responses are presented in the absence of primary reinforcement. The implosive therapy procedure involves a symbolic presentation, in imagery, of cues that are thought to serve as conditioned stimuli for anxiety. These hypothesized cues are presented in scenes, in the most vivid manner possible, in order to elicit a maximal anxiety response. Here is how it was originally described by Stampfl and Levis:

> At each stage of the process an attempt is made by the therapist to obtain a maximal level of anxiety evocation from the patient. When a high level of anxiety is achieved, the patient is held on this level until some sign of spontaneous reduction in the anxiety-inducing value of the cues appear (extinction). The process is repeated, and again, at the first sign of spontaneous reduction of fear, new variations are introduced to elicit an intense anxiety response. This procedure is continued until a significant diminution in anxiety has resulted. (p. 500)

A number of implosive therapy studies with adults have been published that provide evidence of the effectiveness of this procedure in dealing with fear and avoidance behavior. These studies have involved "normal" adults with fears as well as psychiatric patients (Boudewyns & Shipley, 1983). Even though there have been no experimental investigations of implosive therapy with children, case studies have reported positive results. Smith and Sharpe (1970) report a case in which implosive therapy was used to treat a 13-year-old boy who displayed a school phobia that was primarily related to fear of being called on in class, of making mistakes, and of being laughed at by teachers and peers. Treatment involved a total of six implosive therapy sessions and the elimination of reinforcers at home for not attending school. After the fourth session, return to school was accomplished with a report of only minimal anxiety. After session six treatment was terminated, as no school related anxiety was apparent. At a 13-week follow-up, regular school attendance without anxiety was reported, as was increased academic performance.

A second case study by Ollendick and Gruen (1972) involved the treatment of an 8-year-old boy who displayed a bodily injury phobia that was mainly reflected in a fear of bleeding to death. Treatment consisted of two implosive therapy sessions designed to elicit maximal anxiety responses by presenting scenes in imagery related to bodily injury. The scenes presented below are those employed in treatment. They were presented in such a way as to result in "a smooth flowing sequence of imagery," in the authors' words.

1. You are alone walking through a forest going to a lake to fish and you hear weird noises and see strange things.
2. The wind begins blowing very hard, and you trip and hit your head on a rock.
3. When you get up, blood trickles down your forehead into your eyes, nose and mouth.
4. You feel dizzy and lost. You cry but no one is there to help you. You feel all alone and the blood continues to trickle.
5. You fall down again and when you open your eyes you see brown, hairy rats all around you. There are hundreds of them, and they are coming after you . . . to eat you.
6. They begin nibbling at your feet, biting your toes, and pulling them off. They are scratching and showing their teeth. It's getting very dark now, and it's raining.
7. Now they are over your whole body, running across it and biting you all over. Blood runs from all parts of your body, and you hear the thunder and there is lightning.
8. They pierce your neck. You wish someone would come, even an ambulance, but it doesn't. You scream and a big, hairy rat jumps in your mouth. You feel him biting your tongue and scratching you.
9. Finally, the rats that feed on your blood grow and become man-size. They tear off your arms and just keep on attacking you. They tear out your eyes and you can't get away from them. (Ollendick & Gruen, 1972, p. 391)

The authors note that after both sessions the boy was given relaxation training and reassured that he was all right. Although the therapy was found to not only elicit extreme anxiety in the therapy room, but initially at home as well, it was effective in the elimination of the child's fear.

The results of these two case studies suggest that in some cases implosive therapy may be effective in reducing childhood fears. However, whether the approach is superior to other, less nerve-racking approaches is open to question. Studies comparing implosive therapy with other procedures, such as desensitization, modeling, and using children as subjects, are needed to resolve this issue.

Modeling and the Modification of Childhood Behavior

It has become obvious that many behaviors are acquired vicariously, through the observation of others. In fact, Bandura (1971) has suggested that "virtually all learning phenomena that result from direct experience can occur vicariously, as a function of observing other people's behavior and its consequences for them" (p. 655). Research findings are accumulating in support of this view. It is also becoming increasingly apparent that giving individuals who display problem behaviors an opportunity to view role models engaging in appropriate adaptive behaviors can be of therapeutic value. For general reviews of the modeling literature, see Perry and Furukawa (1980) and Rosenthal and Bandura (1978). A general overview of the clinical applications of modeling procedures as employed with children has been presented by Kirkland and Thelen (1977). Morris and Kratochwill (1983) have likewise provided an overview of modeling procedures in the treatment of childhood fears and phobias.

A number of published studies suggest the usefulness of modeling procedures in the treatment of childhood problem behavior. Probably the most extensive research in this area has been conducted by Bandura and his colleagues at Stanford University. For example, in an early study Bandura, Grusec, and Menlove (1967) examined the effectiveness of modeling with dog-phobic children ages 3 to 5 years. Twenty-four children were assigned to one of four conditions. In the first group, children observed a fearless model who displayed increasingly greater approach responses toward a live dog in a highly positive context. Group 2 children viewed the same approach behaviors on the part of the model, but in a neutral context. In group 3, children observed a dog in a positive context, whereas in group 4, children observed neither the dog nor the model but did participate in the positive (party) activities. Observation of the model interacting in a progressively more fearless manner with the dog was found to result in a significant reduction in avoidance behavior, as compared with change observed in control groups. The context had no reliable effect on behavior.

In a second study in this series, Ritter (1968) employed group modeling procedures with children displaying fears of snakes. Treatment involved two sessions lasting 35 minutes each. In one condition the children observed models (other children) interacting in a progressively more fearless manner with a live snake. In a second condition the therapist and children modeled positive approach responses toward the snake, and the children were also encouraged to participate in approach-behaviors with the models. In general the participant modeling procedure resulted in the greatest degree of fear reduction, but both participant modeling and vicarious modeling procedures resulted in a greater reduction of avoidance behavior than that found in controls.

A third study by Bandura and his associates (Bandura, Blanchard, & Ritter, 1969) compared the effectiveness of symbolic (filmed) modeling, guided participant modeling, and systematic desensitization in treating snake-phobic adolescents and adults. All three approaches resulted in significant fear reduction, with the approach involving live modeling plus guided participation the most effective. This approach was found to eliminate fears in 92% of those receiving treatment. In addition to these studies, modeling procedures have also been used to reduce anxiety in children about to undergo surgery (Melamed & Siegel, 1975) and to deal with dental fears (Melamed, 1979).

Modeling, it appears, is a very powerful procedure for dealing with childhood fears, especially when the opportunity to observe a live model is combined with guided participation. These findings further suggest that in some cases this approach may be more effective than systematic desensitization. Certainly modeling would seem to be a good alternate form of treatment for the young child who may be a poor candidate for desensitization because of difficulties with relaxation or imagery.

The use of modeling has not been restricted to the treatment of fears. Sarason (1978), for example, has described the use of modeling procedures with incarcerated delinquents. Treatment was based on the notion that these children had difficulty functioning in an acceptable manner due in part to a lack of adaptive behaviors in their repertoire. The children participated in modeling sessions centering around specific problem areas. For instance, they observed models who displayed appropriate job interview behaviors, modeled ways of coping with peer pressure, and modeled how to deal adaptively with authority figures such as policemen. Observation of modeling scenes was followed by role-playing sessions. At 3-year follow-up the children in the modeling groups were found to have a recidivism rate approximately half that of the control group, which did not receive modeling or role-playing experiences. Moreover, at the end of treatment the modeling group was also found to differ from control children in terms of counselor ratings of behavior. Self-reports suggested that those who received treatment had learned a great deal about socially appropriate behavior in general. At a 5-year follow-up differences in recidivism rates between subjects in the modeling and control groups were still evident (Sarason, 1978), indicating that modeling procedures can also be used to teach or facilitate new adaptive behaviors in individuals showing few such behaviors. As noted in Chapter 3, it has also been demonstrated that it is possible to reduce aggressive child behaviors by exposing observers to nonaggressive models or by having them observe models whose aggressive behavior is disapproved of or punished (Bandura, 1973; Kirkland & Thelen, 1977).

In other areas, Azrin and Foxx (1974) have

used modeling procedures combined with re-inforcement in the toilet training of normal preschool children. Johnson and Thompson (1974) have reported the successful treatment of a 5-year-old enuretic child by the use of modeling procedures. In this instance the enuretic child's young sibling was used as a model and was reinforced for appropriate toileting behavior in the presence of the enuretic child. Modeling procedures, com-bined with reinforcement, have also been employed to facilitate the development of language and other skills in seriously im-paired and mute autistic children (Lovaas, 1977) and to increase interactive behavior in socially withdrawn children (see Strain & Kerr, 1981). Indeed, modeling, combined with reinforcement for appropriate behavior and other behavioral procedures, has been widely used in teaching adaptive social skills to children. (For overviews of the rapidly growing area of social skills training, see Cartledge & Milburn, 1980; Michelson et al., 1983; Van Hasselt, Hersen, Whitehill, & Bellack, 1979.)

A somewhat different approach to model-ing has been described by Creer and Miklich (1970), who used self-modeling in the treat-ment of a 10-year-old asthmatic boy who dis-played immature nonassertive behaviors as well as other minor problems, such as over-sleeping and failing to keep his room tidy. As part of the procedure the patient was first asked to role-play both appropriate and in-appropriate behaviors and was recorded on videotape while doing so. Appropriate be-haviors that were role-played and filmed con-sisted of scenes of the child getting out of bed promptly and making the bed, initiating con-tact with other children, and initiating ap-propriate interactions with adults; inappro-priate behaviors he typically engaged in were also filmed. The role-playing involved in making the videotapes was not in itself found to result in behavioral change. The filmed scenes of the child engaging in appropriate and inappropriate behaviors were then used as modeling stimuli, and it was found that the appropriateness of behavior varied as a function of the type of modeling scenes ob-served. That is, when the child observed modeling scenes depicting appropriate be-haviors, this resulted in an increase in de-sirable behavior, but observing scenes of in-appropriate behaviors resulted in increases in those behaviors. Treatment ended with the use of modeling scenes depicting appropriate behaviors. This resulted in an increase in appropriate behaviors, which was found to have been maintained at a 6-month follow-up. Additional findings related to the effec-tiveness of self-modeling have been provided by Miklich, Creer, Alexander, and Nichols (1972) and by Dowrick and Dove (1980), who successfully used this approach to im-prove the swimming performance of children displaying serious physical handicaps related to spina bifida. Research comparing self-mod-eling with modeling procedures that employ other persons as models seem to be in order.

Although numerous studies suggest that modeling procedures are of therapeutic value in dealing with varied childhood problems, there have been surprisingly few reports of modeling treatments being employed in ac-tual clinical practice. The reason may be the administrative and practical problems in-volved in finding appropriate models and preparing them to fill that role in therapy ses-sions. But the research evidence to date sug-gests that the potential value of modeling in changing behavior makes overcoming these obstacles quite worthwhile.

Operant Approaches to Child Behavior Modification

Of all the approaches to child behavior mod-ification, the operant approach has clearly been the most popular (Phillips & Ray, 1980). It has been found to be of value in increasing desirable behaviors in children displaying be-havioral deficits as well as in decreasing mal-adaptive behaviors in children displaying be-havioral excesses. It has proved effective both with individuals and with children in groups, and programs using this approach have ranged from those carried out by professionals to those administered by parents trained in behavior management techniques.

A discussion of the principles of operant learning is beyond the scope of this chapter and will not be presented here; the interested reader seeking more background on operant methods should consult sources such as Reynolds (1975) or Honig and Staddon (1977) for a thorough presentation of operant concepts and procedures. In a general way, however, it can be said that the operant approach to behavior modification is based largely on the premise that behavior is controlled by its consequences. Thus, behavior can be increased by arranging contingencies so that the behavior of interest is followed by either positive reinforcement (reward) or negative reinforcement (the removal of an aversive stimulus). Likewise, behavior may be weakened or eliminated through punishment (an aversive stimulus is made contingent on the behavior) or extinction (a reinforcer that typically follows the behavior is removed). In essence the operant approach involves careful assessment of target behaviors (behaviors that have led the child to be labeled deviant and that are regarded as desirable to change), assessment of the contingencies in the environment that reinforce and maintain these behaviors, and rearrangement of environmental contingencies so that more adaptive behaviors are increased, maladaptive behaviors are decreased, and/or behaviors are brought under appropriate stimulus control. The focus is on response-consequence relationships and on the stimulus context in which reinforced (or punished) responses occur.

An overview of several approaches to the operant modification of child behavior is presented in the following sections to illustrate the applicability of this approach. Kazdin (1980), Ollendick and Cerny (1981), and Ross (1981) provide in-depth reviews of the literature in this area.

Positive Reinforcement Procedures

Positive reinforcement procedures are based on the principle that it is possible to increase the probable occurrence of a behavior by following the behavior with reinforcement (re-

ward). These procedures have been widely used to increase the frequency of adaptive and prosocial behaviors in children showing behavioral deficits of various types and have also been employed to eliminate undesirable behavior by increasing incompatible responses. It should be noted that in practice behaviorists often combine positive reinforcement procedures with other approaches — extinction, punishment and so on — so that in most cases published reports do not report the effects of reinforcement alone but of the total treatment program. The following examples, however, illustrate the usefulness of reinforcement procedures with childhood behavior problems.

Neal (1963) employed positive reinforcement procedures in the successful treatment of encopresis, reinforcing children for appropriate defecation. Pedrini and Pedrini (1971) and Plachetta (1976) likewise employed positive reinforcement procedures in controlling encopresis, whereas Tomlinson (1970) used this approach to increase voluntary elimination in a child displaying bowel retention.

Kimmel and Kimmel (1970) and Paschalis et al. (1972) used instrumental conditioning procedures with positive reinforcement in the treatment of noctural enuresis. In the latter study, subjects were 35 children, ranging in age from 4 to 13 years old, who reportedly never had a dry night. Treatment involved reinforcing subjects for inhibiting urination after a report of a need to urinate. The withholding time was gradually increased 2 to 3 minutes a day until a criterion of waiting 45 minutes was achieved. At 3-month follow-up 15 of the 35 children were nonenuretic, and 8 additional children displayed considerable improvement. These results suggest that positive reinforcement contingent on the inhibition of micturition during the day is of value in modifying nocturnal enuresis. Foxx and Azrin (1973) and Azrin and Foxx (1974) also described a program that relied heavily on positive reinforcement procedures and was shown to be successful in the rapid toilet training of normal youngsters.

Positive reinforcement procedures have not only been employed in dealing with eliminative disturbances. Azerrad and Stafford (1969) used reinforcement procedures to increase eating behaviors in a 13-year-old girl with anorexia nervosa. Treatment involved giving points, which could be redeemed for a variety of back-up reinforcers, contingent on the amount of food eaten. Findings that reinforcement can increase eating rate have also been obtained by Barlow, Agras, and Leitenberg (1967). Brooks and Snow (1972) brought about increased academic performance in a 9-year-old boy who displayed serious academic difficulties using this approach: Free time with a female teacher's aide and the opportunity for recreational reading were both made contingent on academic output and used as reinforcers.

Hyperactive behavior has also been dealt with in terms of positive reinforcement. Patterson, Jones, Whittier, and Wright (1965), in an early behavioral study, reinforced a hyperactive child (diagnosed as "brain-damaged") within the classroom for each time interval during which he did not display evidence of hyperactive behavior. Treatment lasted for 3 months, during which the child displayed a significant reduction in nonattending behavior. No changes were noted in a control subject who received no treatment. These treatment gains were maintained at 4-week follow-up. Taking a somewhat different approach, Ayllon and Rosenbaum (1977) report several studies in which hyperactivity and classroom disruptions were reduced by increasing academic behaviors within the classroom through positive reinforcement procedures. This approach seems to have much to recommend it, because it is not only directed toward modifying disruptions, but also toward increasing academic performance. It is also an excellent example of how undesirable behavior can be modified indirectly, by reinforcing behaviors that are incompatible with undesirable modes of response.

In addition positive reinforcement procedures have been used to increase "sex-appropriate" behaviors in gender-disturbed males (Rekers, 1977), in the treatment of elective mutism (Williamson, Sewell, Sanders, Haney,

& White, 1977), and in the modification of noncompliant child behavior (Forehand & Peed, 1979; also see Forehand & McMahon, 1981). And as the chapter on autism noted, shaping procedures combining positive reinforcement and modeling have been employed in the development of speech and other social and self-help behaviors, such as personal hygiene and elementary interpersonal skills, in autistic children. More detailed reviews of these procedures as applied to autistic children have been presented by Lovaas, Young, and Newsom (1978), Lovaas (1977), and Schreibman, Charlop, and Britten (1983).

The studies cited here, which are representative of those reported in the literature, suggest that procedures involving positive reinforcement (often combined with other approaches) are of value in dealing with many of the behavioral problems commonly encountered in clinical work with children.

Negative Reinforcement Procedures

As we have seen, following a behavior by a reward increases the frequency of that behavior. When a behavior is followed by the escape from or avoidance of an aversive stimulus, that behavior is also increased. The latter is the basic principle behind negative reinforcement.

Athough there are numerous examples in everyday life of behaviors that are maintained by this process, negative reinforcement has been employed less often than positive reinforcement in behavior modification. Kazdin (1975) has suggested two reasons for this state of affairs. First of all, positive procedures are quite effective in increasing behavior, he observes, and do not involve aversive elements, as negative reinforcement procedures do. Second, he notes that the continued application of aversive events to be escaped from or avoided may itself have a variety of undesirable side effects. For these reasons negative reinforcement procedures have typically been used only when positive procedures have not been found to be effective, and there are few examples of these procedures having been applied with children.

One classic example, however, is provided by Lovaas, Schaeffer, and Simmons (1965), who employed negative reinforcement procedures in dealing with autistic children. In their study baseline measures were first obtained on the autistic subjects' approach behaviors toward adults following a verbal request: It was noted that the subjects displayed little or no approach behavior. After these baseline measures were obtained, the subjects were placed in an experimental room, on a grid through which an electric current could be passed. Trials consisted of having the children stand barefoot on the grid and turning on the current, with termination of the shock made contingent on appropriate approach behavior toward the adult experimenters. In one phase of the study, the children could avoid shock completely by approaching the trainer within 5 seconds after being requested to do so. Escape and avoidance of shock resulted in increased approach behavior on the part of the autistic subjects. Effects were found to be fairly durable, and "increases in affectionate and other social behaviors toward adults increased after adults had been associated with shock reduction" (p. 99). Whaley and Tough (1968) have also applied negative reinforcement procedures to eliminating self-destructive behavior in a severely mentally retarded subject. Several publications involving the application of negative reinforcement with adults have also reported positive results.

Extinction Procedures

Extinction in this context means the removal of a reinforcer that formerly typically followed a response, a procedure that decreases the probability of that response. Extinction procedures in behavior modification are employed to weaken or eliminate undesirable behavior and are often combined with reinforcement procedures in behavioral programs where the purpose is not only to weaken undesirable behavior, but also to increase behaviors that are more appropriate.

An early example of extinction as a behavior modification procedure was presented in the study by Williams (1959) that was briefly described in Chapter 3. Williams reported on the treatment of a 21-month-old child who displayed severe tantrum behaviors upon being left by the parents after being put to bed. The parents often had to spend up to 2 hours in the room until the child fell asleep. Based on the assumption that parental attention was the reinforcer maintaining the tantrum behavior, treatment involved extinction through removal of such attention. Parents were instructed to put the child to bed in a relaxed fashion, leave the room, and not reenter the room, regardless of the child's tantrum behavior. At the beginning of treatment the duration of crying after being put to bed was 50 minutes. The duration dropped to less than 15 minutes by the second night, and by the tenth night tantrum behavior had disappeared completely. Accidental reinforcement of tantrum behavior by an aunt resulted in the return of this behavior to the original level, but it was extinguished quickly a second time. The extinction curves are presented in Figure 10.3. No further tantrums were reported to have occurred at a 2-year follow-up.

Alford et al. (1972) employed an extinction procedure to modify what they termed "hysterical vomiting" in a 17-year-old female. This patient had a history of vomiting after every meal since the age of 7. She had been referred to numerous physicians, who had found no physical basis for her condition. When it was determined during assessment that the girl was particularly sensitive to attention, a decision was made to gain control over her vomiting by the manipulation of social contact. Treatment involved the withdrawal of attention by staff and patients whenever she vomited or reported feeling nauseated. This procedure resulted in the elimination of vomiting, and a 7-month follow-up indicated that she had vomited only once after being discharged from the hospital.

It was noted earlier that extinction procedures are often combined with reinforcement. An example of this approach is provided in

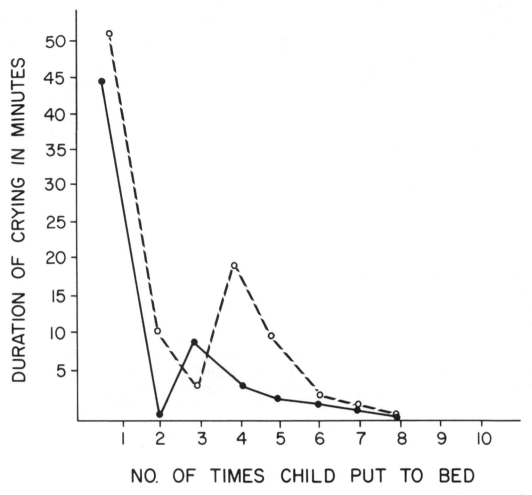

FIGURE 10.3. Length of crying in two extinction series, as a function of successive occasions of being put to bed. Source: Williams (1959). © American Psychological Association and reprinted with permission.

a study by Hart, Allen, Buell, Harris and Wolf (1964), who successfully eliminated crying in two preschool children. Intervention involved extinction by withholding teacher attention when the children cried, while at the same time making attention contingent on appropriate behaviors displayed at the times crying usually occurred. Extinction plus reinforcement was also employed by Hall et al. (1971) to reduce arguing and increase classroom productivity in a 15-year-old mentally retarded male. The usefulness of peer involvement in the modification of

behavior was suggested by Pierce (1971), who employed extinction procedures to modify bizarre classroom behavior displayed by a 12-year-old female. This was accomplished by requesting the children in the girl's class not to attend to such behaviors and to reinforce more appropriate behaviors. These manipulations were found to bring about the desired behavioral changes.

In addition to these studies a number of investigations employing extinction procedures with adults have also produced findings that support their effectiveness.

Punishment Procedures

Punishment typically involves the application of an aversive stimulus contingent upon a response and results in a decreased probability of responding. Several examples of punishment procedures are to be found in the child behavior modification literature, although punishment has been less frequently used than positive procedures.

Lang and Melamed (1969) treated a 9-month-old male whose life was endangered by persistent vomiting, which had resulted in severe weight loss. Treatment involved electric shock made contingent on vomiting, and application of these contingencies resulted in decreased vomiting and subsequent weight gain. Additional findings, such as those of Kohlenberg (1970), also suggest that contingent shock may be of value in the treatment of persistent vomiting in adults, but that booster treatments may be needed if the vomiting is not completely suppressed.

Several studies have suggested that punishment procedures may be effective in dealing with certain behaviors of autistic children. For example, studies by Lovaas et al. (1965) found shock to be effective in eliminating self-stimulatory and tantrum behaviors. Butcher and Lovaas (1968) have reported the successful supression of head banging by employing contingent shock. Lovaas and Simmons (1969) found shock to be effective in bringing about an immediate suppression of self-destructive behavior. It is noteworthy that in the latter study, it was also possible to reduce self-destructive behavior through nonreinforcement (extinction), but that this procedure was much slower to show results than was the application of shock contingent on these behaviors. The effects of shock, however, appeared to be limited to the situation in which the shock had been received; in other words; the children seemed to be able to accurately discriminate between shock-contingent and noncontingent situations. Shock has also been employed in the treatment of persistent sneezing (Kushner, 1968) and in the modification of dangerous climbing behaviors in an autistic child (Risley, 1968). For a more detailed review of studies employing shock as a punisher in reducing severely disruptive and dangerous behaviors in psychotic and mentally retarded patients, the reader should consult Harris and Ersner-Hershfield (1978).

Although shock was used as a punisher in a number of studies in the 1960s and early 1970s, primarily in the reduction of self-destructive behavior, its use has declined in recent years. Harris and Ersner-Hershfield (1978) comment that this is due to lay and professional resistance to the use of such procedures, and to the fact that often the behavior-modifying effects of shock do not generalize to nontreated situations and are not maintained. In addition, several authors have pointed to a number of unlooked-for side effects that are often associated with punishment procedures and may be especially prominent in the use of shock. These side effects include undesirable emotional reactions that may interfere with new learning, the possibility that the punishing agent (the therapist) may come to be regarded as an aversive stimulus to be avoided, and the fact that punishment of a given behavior serves to model aversive control procedures. Finally, the use of punishment by therapists may be reinforced by the fact that it leads to a reduction of undesirable behavior, so that the subsequent use of aversive control procedures may be increased through negative reinforcement (Kazdin, 1975). It is obvious that a consideration of alternative approaches should be seriously undertaken prior to using punishment procedures with children, although in some cases, severely self-destructive behaviors, for example, these procedures may be the treatment of choice if other means have failed to reduce these behaviors.

The use of shock is not the only punishment procedure that has been used to reduce undesirable behaviors. For example, as noted in Chapter 3, time-out procedures (considered a type of punishment by some) have been widely used to deal with a variety of child behavior problems, such as tantrums and aggressive behaviors. For an overview of this approach see Gelfand and Hartman (1984). An additional approach that has received widespread attention by clinicians in recent years is overcorrection. This procedure, developed by Foxx and Azrin (1972), is seen as having several advantages over the punishment procedures described above, for it not only serves to reduce inappropriate behavior, but also, educates the person about the effects of his or her behavior on the environment and teaches more appropriate behaviors.

Foxx and Azrin described two types of overcorrection. In the first, restitutional overcorrection, the child is required to restore the disturbed environment to the state it was in prior to his or her inappropriate behavior and to subsequently improve the environment over its original condition. As an example, the child who throws food and drink on the floor might be required to first clean up the mess and then perhaps mop the entire floor and replace the food and drink. The rationale here is that the offender must assume responsibility for the disruption caused by his or her behavior by being required to restore the environment to a greatly improved state. Central to this approach is the identification of the effects of the child's inappropriate behavior on the environment, the implementation of procedures that rectify the situation, and beyond this, teaching the child appropriate rather than inappropriate behaviors.

The second type of overcorrection is positive practice overcorrection, designed for use in situations where behaviors may have little effect on the environment and the restitutional approach would be inappropriate. An example of the sort of behavior that might be dealt with using this approach to overcorrection is the self-stimulatory behavior often seen in autistic children. The child is simply required to practice engaging in more appropriate behaviors in those situations where inappropriate behavior is displayed. Thus, a child who constantly engages in repetitive rocking may be required to practice sitting for extended periods of time without rocking. Or the autistic child who engages in stereo-

typed hand movements may be required to engage in behaviors involving more appropriate use of the hands.

In the case of both types of overcorrection, compliance with the required activities is encouraged through verbal instructions if possible or with the degree of physical assistance necessary to bring about compliance if verbal instruction is not sufficient. It should be noted that in overcorrection the behaviors required of the child are to be practiced for an extended period of time, with no reinforcement being given by the therapist. This, combined with the fact that the child may be physically assisted in the performance of these behaviors, contributes to the aversiveness of the procedure.

Whereas overcorrection procedures have been most widely used with institutionalized adults, they have also been employed in reducing maladaptive child behavior. Foxx and Azrin described the successful use of positive practice overcorrection in modifying head weaving, and Harris and Romanczyk (1976) used this approach to modify head and chin banging. Straus, Rubinoff, and Atkeson (1983) have likewise used a combination of positive practice and restitutional overcorrection, along with reinforcement for abstaining from head banging to reduce nocturnal head banging. Foxx and Azrin (1973) also applied the overcorrection method to the toilet training of young nonhandicapped children. Here the overcorrection procedure involved having children change their clothing following every toilet accident and practice correct toileting procedures for a total of ten trials: This technique yielded a 97% reduction in accidents. Several studies have also used overcorrection to modify classroom management problems (Azrin, Azrin, & Armstrong, 1977; Azrin & Powers, 1975; Bornstein, Hamilton, & Quevillon, 1977). Finally, it was noted previously that overcorrection has been widely used with mentally retarded adults and has been demonstrated to be effective in reducing a variety of inappropriate behaviors such as hitting, biting, and throwing objects. More detailed reviews of studies employing overcorrection procedures may be found in Foxx and Bechtel (1982) and Ollendick and Matson (1978).

There still remain a number of questions regarding this approach, having to do with the effectiveness of overcorrection as compared to other procedures designed to reduce behaviors, the degree to which discrete aspects of the total overcorrection package contribute to behavior change, and the extent to which overcorrection procedures may have negative side effects similar to those linked to other types of punishment (Axelrod, Brantner, & Meddock, 1978).

It seems clear that punishment procedures such as those considered in this section may be useful in reducing inappropriate behaviors in certain instances, although the degree to which these changes generalize and are maintained has sometimes been questioned. Assuming the effectiveness of these procedures, there are still a number of issues that must be considered prior to any decision to employ them. First, are there procedures other than punishment — such as extinction, reinforcement of incompatible behaviors, and so on — that can effectively deal with the behavior(s) in question? It is our belief that the majority of disruptive child behaviors seen in clinical practice can be effectively dealt with without resorting to the use of punishment. Second, the possibility of negative side effects as described by Kazdin (1975) and discussed earlier should be taken into account. If the use of punishment is considered essential, it is our opinion that the use of procedures such as time-out techniques (see Chapter 3) and possibly overcorrection should be considered carefully before resorting to more extreme procedures, such as contingent shock. It could be argued that the use of shock as a punisher would be ethical only in the most extreme case, where other procedures are not effective and where the potential harm experienced by the child as a result of the inappropriate behaviors is greater than the harm inflicted through the use of such punishment procedures. A case in point might be the autistic child who engages in severe self-destructive behaviors such as head banging, finger biting, and so on, if other procedures for reducing these behaviors do not work. Finally, behavioral programs should do more than teach what behaviors should not be engaged in. They should also focus on teaching the child what behaviors are appropriate in a given situation. In this regard we agree with Rimm and Masters (1979), who suggest that any use of punishment be combined with positive reinforcement for appropriate behavior. (For an excellent and detailed discussion of the use of punishment in behavior modification see Matson and DiLorenzo, 1984.)

Token Programs

The use of operant principles in child behavior modification has not been limited strictly to individual applications, but has been extended to work with groups as well. In brief, these programs usually involve the specification of certain target behaviors for modification and the subsequent reinforcement of these behaviors with tokens that can later be redeemed for a variety of back-up reinforcers. Tokens, which come in a variety of forms, serve to reinforce and maintain behavior because they come to function as conditioned reinforcers as a result of their pairing with back-up reinforcers. Token programs have been successfully employed in modifying the behaviors of both adults and children. A thorough overview of token reinforcement programs, illustrating their use on both an individual and group level, has been presented by Kazdin (1977).

The potential advantages of token over tangible reinforcers were listed by Kazdin and Bootzin (1972), who wrote that they

1. Bridge the delay between the target response and back-up reinforcement. 2. Permit the reinforcement of a response at any time. 3. May be used to maintain performance over extended periods of time when the back-up reinforcer cannot be parcelled out. 4. Allow sequences of responses to be reinforced without interruption. 5. Maintain their reinforcing properties because of their relative independence of deprivation states.

6. Are less subject to satiation effects. 7. Provide the same reinforcement for individuals who have different preferences in back-up reinforcers. 8. May take on greater incentive value than a single primary reinforcer since according to Ferster and DeMyer (1962) the effects resulting from association with each primary reinforcer may summate . . . (p. 343)

In sum, tokens may in many cases have definite advantages over other types of reinforcers, especially when operant procedures are employed with groups, thus necessitating the frequent dispensing of reinforcers to different individuals for a variety of behaviors at different times.

Kazdin and Bootzin (1972) and Kazdin (1977) have also delineated the basic procedures involved in setting up a token program. A first step is to determine behaviors that will be targets for modification. Second, decisions must be made concerning the nature of back-up reinforcers. These may take the form of activities that can be made available to individuals in exchange for tokens or "canteen items" that can be purchased with tokens. The third stage in the development of the program is the establishment of tokens as conditioned reinforcers. Kazdin and Bootzin note that this may simply involve explaining to individuals in the program that when they earn tokens they can be exchanged for reinforcers, but that in other cases it may be necessary to establish the reinforcing value of the tokens directly, by giving out a limited number of tokens and allowing the subjects to spend them to establish their value. Finally, the rules of the program must be determined: how many tokens will be given for specific behaviors, the cost of back-up reinforcers, and whether there will be fines for inappropriate behaviors. And of course other factors, such as those related to staff training, must also be considered.

Token economies have been employed to modify behaviors in a wide variety of settings. Here we will illustrate but a few of these applications. Phillips (1968) set up such a program in a home-style, community-based residential treatment center for predelinquent boys known as Achievement Place. This project was already mentioned in our earlier discussion of the treatment of juvenile delinquency. Here we will describe in more detail its token economy program. Targets consisted of behaviors such as housecleaning, punctuality, proper grammar, and doing homework. Performance of these behaviors was reinforced by points, which could be cashed in for a variety of back-up reinforcers available in the natural environment, such as the use of a bicycle, payment of allowance, permission to watch TV or eat snacks, permission to go downtown, and permission to stay up past bedtime. These reinforcers were made available to boys in the center on a weekly basis and could be obtained if a sufficient number of points had been earned. Other special reinforcers could be bought at an auction by the person bidding the highest number of points. The program also involved negative contingencies, in that points could be lost by engaging in inappropriate behaviors such as receiving failing grades, disobeying rules, and stealing. Application of these contingencies was found to be successful in effectively modifying the various target behaviors. Additional findings concerning the effectiveness of Achievement Place have been reported by Fixsen et al. (1973) and Phillips, Phillips, Fixsen, and Wolf (1971). Liberman, Ferris, Salgado, and Salgado (1975) have successfully employed a similar program in the treatment of juvenile offenders.

Aitchison and Green (1974), noting that some token programs, such as those just considered, have been conducted in situations where few subjects were involved and where staff were professionals with MA and PhD degrees, attempted to assess the effectiveness of a token economy in a state hospital psychiatric setting. A total of 60 male and female residents from an adolescent unit were involved in the program, and staff consisted of five nonprofessional psychiatric aides with no previous training in operant procedures. In this program, two classes of behavior were selected for modification: room maintenance and ward maintenance. Contingencies were arranged so that target behaviors were reinforced by points (heart-shaped paper punches), which were redeemable for back-up reinforcers in the hospital environment. Results indicated that specific behaviors related to both room and ward maintenance could be modified by these procedures. The study also showed that contingent reinforcement was more effective than verbal demands in altering behavior and, further, demonstrated a functional relationship between reinforcement contingencies and behavioral change. Results of this study were interpreted as supporting the notion that token programs are feasible even with relatively large groups of residents and on units staffed by nonprofessionals.

The classroom has also been a popular context for the application of token programs. In an early study O'Leary and Becker (1967) established a token program in a classroom of 17 nine-year-old children termed "emotionally disturbed." These children displayed numerous undesirable behaviors—temper tantrums, crying, and fighting, among others. Behaviors selected for modification were pushing, answering without raising hand, chewing gum, eating in class, name-calling, making disruptive noises, and talking. The program was applied to all the children, but eight subjects were selected for the most intensive study. After the collection of initial baseline data regarding the percentage of observational intervals during which deviant behavior occurred, the intervention program was introduced. Appropriate performance (nonoccurrence of deviant behavior) was reinforced by ratings of 1 to 10 placed in a small booklet on the child's desk. Ratings were designed to reflect the extent to which children displayed appropriate behaviors. Points were exchangeable for prizes ranging in value from 1¢ to 29¢ (candy, a pennant, comics). Early in the program points were immediately redeemable for back-up reinforcers; then the delay between behaviors and reinforcers was gradually increased up to a maximum of 4 days. The purpose of the delay was to grad-

ually transfer control from token reinforcers to such teacher behaviors as attention and praise. To facilitate this transfer the teacher paired praise and attention with the administration of token reinforcers (points). Group display of deviant behaviors during baseline and intervention phases of the program are presented in Figure 10.4. As the figure shows, the percentage of deviant behaviors was reduced from a level of about 65 to 91% during baseline to about 3 to 6% by the end of the token program. Similar results were also found for other children in the class. These changes from the baseline to the token phase were regarded as highly significant.

Classroom-based token programs have also been successfully used by others to modify inattentiveness and disruptive behavior and increase academic performance (Kazdin, 1977).

Token Programs: The Issue of Generalization. Reviews of the literature strongly sug-

FIGURE 10.4. Average percentages of deviant behaviors during baseline and token periods

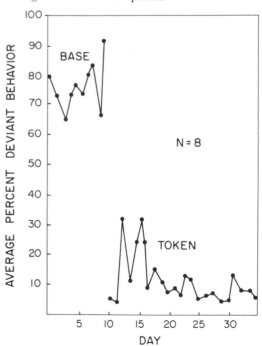

N = 8

Source: O'Leary and Becker (1967). © 1967 by the Council for Exceptional Children and reprinted by permission.

gest that token economies are often effective in modifying various behaviors in individuals with various sorts of problems in various settings. Although bringing about behavioral changes in psychiatric hospitals, delinquent treatment centers, and classrooms must be considered an accomplishment, the extent to which behavioral changes generalize to the natural environment is still in question. That is, to what extent are changes maintained when the person leaves the context in which the token program has been operative and the treatment contingencies are no longer in effect? Relatively few studies have investigated extent of generalization to the nontreatment environment, but those that have done so have yielded mixed results. In reviewing the literature related to response maintenance within token economy programs, Kazdin (1977) concluded that behaviors brought under control through the use of token programs often revert back to baseline upon termination of the program although there are exceptions. Even though more recent studies have, in some cases, provided somewhat stronger support for the generalization effects of token programs (especially when the token economy represents only one component of the total intervention effort), generalization to extra-treatment settings is still rather unpredictable (Kazdin, 1982). This suggests that generalization cannot be expected to occur automatically and must be programmed. To consider treatment complete, it appears that one must introduce appropriate contingencies during the treatment program and also alter contingencies in the individuals' natural environment to ensure that changes are maintained. The same would hold for operant procedures applied at the individual level (Phillips & Ray, 1980). A detailed review of procedures designed to enhance generalization in operant behavior modification programs has been provided by Wehman, Abramson, and Norman (1977).

Overview of the
Operant Approach

In the preceding sections we have cited numerous examples of the application of oper-

ant procedures in the modification of childhood behavior. A few additional statements about the operant literature seem to be in order, however.

With the exception of publications having to do with token programs, reports in the operant literature are most often of the $n = 1$ variety. Although one can have some faith in the findings of controlled studies using single subject designs, such as those considered in Chapter 2, many studies in this area have gone no further than collecting pretreatment baseline data and monitoring changes occurring after the introduction of treatment contingencies. Although positive changes are often reported in these studies, there can be no assurance that the observed changes were due to the treatment procedures employed rather than to extraneous variables. In spite of the frequency of uncontrolled case reports, however, there are a sufficient number of well-controlled studies to strongly support the usefulness of an operant approach to the modification of deviant child behavior. This is not to imply that an operant approach ought to be considered preferable to other behavioral approaches in dealing with all types of child behavior. We simply suggest that in those situations where a careful assessment has determined maladaptive behavior to be controlled largely by the consequences of this behavior, the use of operant procedures alone or in combination with other procedures should be considered.

Cognitive Behavior Modification

Although most behavioral approaches have tended to focus on overt observable behaviors, recent attempts have been made to apply behavioral principles in the modification of cognitive processes (Kendall, 1981, 1984; Meichenbaum, 1977, 1979a, b). An assumption basic to this approach is that the self-statements and self-instructions (or the absence of them, in some instances) emitted by the individual are importantly related to maladaptive behaviors and that maladaptive cognitions can be modified directly in order to bring about behavioral change.

Illustrative of this approach is an early study by Meichenbaum and Goodman (1971) assessing the effectiveness of a cognitive training program developed for use with hyperactive impulsive elementary school children. Here children were assigned either to a cognitive training group or one of two control conditions. In the cognitive training group, subjects were given a variety of tasks to perform, some visual-motor and others more cognitive in nature. The experimenter initially served as a model, talking aloud as he performed the task. The subject next performed the task while being instructed by the experimenter, then while self-instructing out loud. Finally children performed the task while emitting covert (subvocal) self-instructions.

The purpose of the procedure was to teach appropriate self-instructions that would facilitate nonimpulsive task performance. Here is an example of the types of modeled verbalizations displayed by the experimenter and later employed by the subject:

> Okay, what is it I have to do? You want me to copy the picture with the different lines. I have to go slow and be careful. Okay, draw the line down, down, good; then to the right, that's it; now down some more and to the left. Good, I'm doing fine so far. Remember, go slow. Now, back up again. No, I was supposed to go down. That's okay, just erase the line carefully . . . Good, even if I make an error I can go slowly and carefully. Okay, I have to go down now. Finished, I did it. (p. 117)

It will be noted that these verbalizations involved evaluation of the nature of the task, self-guidance instructions, and self-reinforcement for appropriate performance. (For an outline of the general procedures employed in the cognitive-behavioral approach see Table 10.5.)

Pre- and posttreatment measures were obtained on several variables, including the Porteus Maze test, Kagan's MFF test of impulsivity-reflectivity, and three performance subjects of the WISC (picture arrangement, block design, and coding). Results indicated that this cognitive self-instructional training program brought about significantly greater changes in impulsive children than were found in attentional controls (subjects who interacted with the therapist but did not receive treatment) or no-treatment control subjects, with regard to the Porteus Maze test, a prorated performance IQ on the WISC, and the measure of cognitive impulsivity. These changes were found to be maintained at 1-month follow-up.

Similarly, Camp, Blom, Hebert, and van Doorninck (1977) have developed a "Think Aloud" program for teaching self-instructional and problem-solving skills to hyperaggressive children. Here children are taught, through modeling and behavioral rehearsal, to ask and generate answers to a variety of questions (e.g., What is my problem? What is my plan? Am I using my plan? How did I do?) while dealing with a range of impersonal (e.g., coloring a picture while staying within the lines) and interpersonal (e.g., getting another child to play a game) training tasks. In an initial evaluation of this program with 6- to 8-year olds, Camp et al. found children who participated in the program to show significant improvements (relative to controls) in prosocial behavior and on several cognitive measures. The program, however, seemed to have little impact on reducing aggressive behavior (as assessed by teacher ratings).

Other studies (Bornstein & Quevillon, 1976; Kanfer, Karoly, & Newman, 1975; Kendall & Finch, 1978) have also suggested the usefulness of these sorts of cognitive-behavioral procedures in modifying impulsive, hyperactive, aggressive, and fearful behaviors in children.

Although the results of such studies suggest that it is possible to use behavioral procedures to modify cognitive processes and that such modifications may be related to positive behavioral change, the clinical utility of cognitive-behavioral approaches with children remains to be demonstrated (Hobbs, Moguin, Tyroler, & Lahey, 1980). In this regard, Hobbs et al. note that despite positive findings, many studies in this area are flawed methodologically and that there is insufficient data to demonstrate that behavioral change is durable and generalizes to the nontreatment environment. Nevertheless, the

TABLE 10.5. CONTENT AND SEQUENCE OF SELF-INSTRUCTIONAL
PROCEDURES WITH IMPULSIVE CHILDREN.

Content of self-instructions

Problem definition	"Let's see, what am I supposed to do?"
Problem approach	"I have to look at all the possibilities."
Focusing of attention	"I better concentrate and *focus in*, and think only of what I'm doing right now."
Choosing an answer	"I think it's this one . . . "
Self-reinforcement	"Hey, not bad. I really did a good job."
or	
Coping statement	"Oh, I made a mistake. Next time I'll try and go slower and concentrate more and maybe I'll get the right answer."

Sequence of self-instructions

- The therapist models task performance and talks out loud while the child observes;
- The child performs the task, instructing himself or herself out loud;
- The therapist models the task performance while whispering the self-instructions; followed by
- The child performing the task, whispering to himself or herself;
- The therapist performs the task using covert self-instructions with pauses and behavioral signs of thinking (e.g., stroking beard or chin),
- The child performs the task using covert self-instructions.

Source: Kendell (1981), as adapted from Kendell (1977), Kendell and Finch (1978); Meichenbaum (1975); Meichenbaum and Goodman (1971). © 1981 Plenum Publishing Co. and reprinted by permission.

positive findings that have emerged thus far suggest that further efforts to develop cognitive-behavioral approaches and to empirically assess their effectiveness are likely to be worthwhile.

PARENTS AS THERAPISTS

During recent years various theoretical points of view have evinced more and more interest in training parents, usually mothers, to serve as therapists for their own children. This approach would seem to make a great deal of sense intuitively, because if parents could be taught to interact with their children in a more therapeutic manner within the context of therapy, then any resulting changes should be more durable due to the extension of therapy into the home after formal treatment has ceased. Moreover, it is possible that parents trained to interact in more appropriate and therapeutic ways with the identified patient may also come to interact in perhaps a more appropriate manner with other children in the family, so training parents as therapists may thereby result in a saving of professional time in some cases.

The exact nature of the parent's role in child treatment has varied considerably depending on the theoretical orientation of the individual therapist. Procedures have ranged from client-centered approaches aiming to train parents to be more empathic, to behavioral approaches designed to train parents to become more effective in contingency management. (See Reisinger, Ora, & Frangia, 1976, for a review of these approaches.)

Filial Therapy

Guerney (1964) has developed a therapeutic approach that he has labeled filial therapy, and that has parents serve as therapists for their children in a play therapy context. Initially parents are given group training in client-centered play therapy. These group sessions (involving a number of parents) focus not only on the development of play therapy techniques, but also on parents' feelings and reactions. After this initial training parents are given the opportunity to observe demonstration play therapy sessions by the therapist. They are also given the opportunity to conduct play therapy sessions with their own child or the child of another group member and to receive corrective feedback from the primary therapist and other group members.

When both parent and therapist feel that play therapy techniques have been mastered, parents are instructed to undertake play therapy sessions with their child or children in the home. Usually therapy sessions are conducted once or twice a week. As therapy progresses parents continue to meet on a weekly basis with the therapist to deal with any problems arising from therapy and with parental attitudes and feelings in a nondirective manner.

The goals of filial therapy are similar to the goals of client-centered play therapy in general: the development of a helping, empathic, and nonjudgmental relationship between the child and the therapist that will enable the child to achieve maximum self-growth. While little controlled research has been conducted concerning the effectiveness of filial therapy, some tentative evidence for its effectiveness has been provided by Stover and Guerney (1967), Stover, Guerney, and O'Connell (1971), and Guerney (1979).

Parents as Behavior Modifiers

Other attempts to use parents as therapists have been more behavioral in their orientation. For example, Krapfl, Bry, and Nawas (1968) have presented a technique with which parents are trained to use operant conditioning procedures with their children. This approach has many of the same features as filial therapy but differs in specific procedures involved and in theoretical orientation. Training involves instructing parents in the principles of operant conditioning and later having the parent interact with the child in a play situation with the primary therapist observing through a one-way mirror. Instructions designed to aid the parent in responding appropriately to the child's behaviors are presented by means of the "bug-in-the-ear" device, a small battery-operated hearing-aid-like receiver through which instructions can be transmitted from a microphone on the other side of the mirror. By employing these pro-

cedures, maladaptive parental reactions to child behavior can be observed and parent behavior modified so that it no longer maintains deviant child behavior. Through such training it is possible to provide the parent with more effective behavior management skills for use in the home.

Numerous other reports describing the use of parents as behavior therapists have also been published. They have often involved training parents in the application of behavioral procedures designed to deal with specific types of child behavior problems, including autistic self-destructive behavior, aggressive behavior, noncompliance, enuresis, and conduct disorders, among others. The growing influence of parent training from a behavioral perspective is indicated by the fact that in his 1974 review O'Dell was able to find a total of 70 studies that had employed parents as therapists and corroborated the effectiveness of this procedure. Many more studies have been published since that time. The work by Patterson and his colleagues at the Oregon Research Institute (see Patterson, 1974; Patterson et al., 1973; Patterson & Fleischman, 1979) represents some of the most careful work in the area.

The use of parents as behavioral change agents is clearly a rather popular approach, and one that, as was mentioned earlier, may have certain advantages over individual treatment conducted by professionals. There may be some difficulties in implementing this approach, however. First, a major problem in employing parents as therapists is the dropout rate. It is not uncommon to find parents who expect others to take primary responsibility for dealing with their child's deviant behavior and who seem to be relatively unmotivated to become involved in a program that demands they play a primarily therapeutic role. Indeed, Phillips and Ray (1980) note that in studies of parent training drop-out rates run as high as 75%. Here it is appropriate to recall that parental behaviors are subject to environmental contingencies just as child behaviors are. And just as attention can be given to finding ways of effectively reinforcing appropriate child behavior, clinicians may also need to consider ways of rewarding parental behaviors involved in carrying out behavior change programs, to ensure parents' compliance with the program and continued involvement. A second problem is that marital conflict within the home can reduce the likelihood of success, because a lack of agreement between parents about appropriate ways of dealing with the child's behavior may result in inconsistent application of the program. In such instances it may be necessary to deal with the marital conflict before attempting to implement a parent-as-therapist program. Finally, a major problem with many parent training programs is that they have relied on mothers as change agents, presumably because of difficulties in getting fathers to come in for training sessions. This may well create problems, for parents may find themselves working at cross purposes and being inconsistent in their responses to the child if both are not involved in the program and do not agree how problem behavior should be dealt with. In view of the important role played by fathers within the family, the involvement of both parents in parent training programs appears to be important. (For an excellent collection of chapters dealing with various behavioral approaches to parent training see Dangel & Polster, 1984.)

RESIDENTIAL TREATMENT

Although many children can be treated successfully on an outpatient basis using procedures such as those described in earlier sections, certain children display problems that require inpatient treatment. For this reason residential treatment units for children and adolescents have been established as part of numerous psychiatric facilities. These facilities vary greatly in terms of treatment, ranging from those offering essentially a 24-hour treatment milieu to those providing little more than custodial care for residents. Specific approaches to treatment also vary depending on the prevailing theoretical orientation of professional staff.

Typically, residential treatment programs consist of a unit where children can reside on a 24-hour-per-day basis. The programs usually include the opportunity to attend school on a regular basis and to engage in a variety of therapeutic ward activities. Recreational activities are usually provided, and in some cases residents have the opportunity to engage in additional activities, such as occupational therapy geared to the specific age level of the child. In some programs privileges and activities are automatically available to all residents; in others, the program is designed so that privileges are contingent on appropriate behavior. Children in residential treatment are often seen in ongoing individual therapy by a psychologist, psychiatrist, or social worker, and in some cases the entire family is involved in treatment as well.

Although this may not be descriptive of all inpatient child treatment programs, it illustrates the elements that are included in most of them to greater or lesser degree. More detailed descriptions of residential treatment programs for children displaying various types of psychopathology have been provided by Barker (1974), Quay (1979a), Romanczyk, Kistner, and Crimmins (1980), and Wilson and Lyman (1983).

Research on Residential Treatment

A review of the earlier literature related to inpatient treatment of adolescents was published by Beskind (1962). In this review Beskind cited several follow-up studies that assessed the status of adolescent patients at various intervals after termination of treatment, noting that a variety of such studies have found that 68 to 75% of residents display "symptomatic improvement" at the time of discharge and that this outcome is unrelated to diagnosis and treatment approach. None of these studies, however, employed control groups, and therefore the results provide little information to show that the same symptomatic improvement would not have occurred in the absence of treatment. This failure to employ control groups in evaluating the effectiveness of child and adolescent residential treatment programs has been a major shortcoming not only of the studies cited by Beskind, but of most later publications as well. Most studies of outcome have simply described the nature of the particular treatment program under consideration and then proceeded to give data related to success rate at discharge and at follow-up. There have, however, been exceptions. For instance, Beckett, Lennox, and Grisell (1968) conducted a study designed to compare two forms of residential treatment. One approach involved a general milieu-oriented approach on an open ward. Emphasis was put on school and the program was staffed by nurses, teachers, therapists, and others who were involved in setting limits on disturbed behavior. Severe disturbances were dealt with either by use of a "quiet room" or, in the some cases, by transfer to an adult unit. Patients were involved in psychotherapy, and in some cases work with the parents was also undertaken.

The second approach consisted of a treatment program that attempted to associate "the patients' responsibility for their behavior with enjoyment of personal privileges." Thus, ward privileges were made contingent upon certain behaviors and could be restricted if inappropriate behaviors were displayed. Decisions concerning the granting or restriction of privileges were made by a patient government committee composed of residents. Patients in this program were also involved in individual therapy, school, and family therapy.

Subjects consisted of approximately 40 males (mean age 15 years) who received one of the two forms of treatment. Patients in the two groups were equated as closely as possible on a total of 39 clinically relevant variables. At 3-year follow-up no differences were found between the two groups of patients in terms of academic achievement, general functioning, or overall level of adjustment. Approximately 75% of both groups were rated as functioning effectively, and 40% of both groups were considered recovered. The group in which privileges and restrictions were contingent on behavior, however, displayed sig-

nificantly less aggressive and antisocial behavior than did patients in the more traditional treatment program. Results of an earlier study conducted by Beckett and his colleagues (Beckett, Pearson, & Rubin, 1962) also suggested the superiority of an adolescent treatment unit, with an emphasis on school and the "diffusion of therapists," over treatment of adolescents on an adult psychiatric unit.

Other studies with children diagnosed as childhood schizophrenic (Goldfarb, Goldfarb, & Pollack, 1966) and autistic (Werner, Ruttenberg, Dratman, & Wolf, 1967) have investigated the effectiveness of various forms of residential treatment with such patients. Goldfarb et al. (1966), in a comparison study, found residential treatment to be more effective than a day-care program for nonorganic-schizophrenic children, but found no differences between the two types of treatment when schizophrenic children who displayed organic problems were considered. These findings held only for the less severely disturbed children; neither type of treatment was helpful for children who were the most severely impaired.

Werner et al. (1967) evaluated the effectiveness of three types of programs in the treatment of autistic children. One of the groups was in a large state hospital providing mainly custodial care. The second was treated in a modern state institution with school and therapy programs and a variety of planned activities. However, it was noted by the authors that this program was executed with indifference and that staff attitudes and staff turnover resulted in much inconsistency and a nontherapeutic atmosphere. The third group received treatment in a day-care center offering psychoanalytically oriented treatment focusing on establishing relationships between children and staff.

Change was assessed by means of a behavior checklist for autistic children. The third (analytically oriented day-care) program was found to be the most effective in bringing about changes in terms of interpersonal relationships, psychosexual development, and environmental mastery, as assessed by the checklist. None of the programs produced changes in vocalization or communication. Results of this study suggest that treatment programs characterized by intense staff involvement are the most effective in dealing with such children. Whether the particular approach to treatment or simply the close involvement of staff with children produced change is open to question.

Other residential facilities have employed token economies on a unit level rather than more traditional approaches. Evidence related to the effectiveness of such programs was considered earlier (also see Kazdin, 1977).

It would appear that we know relatively little about the effects of residential treatment. Although some studies developed to deal with specific problems such as delinquency (see Chapter 9) have been shown to yield positive outcomes, these studies tell us little about residential treatment approaches that are more commonly used with disturbed children. The evidence to date, such as it is, suggests that even if positive changes do result from treatment they often are not maintained after the child is discharged from the treatment program (Wilson & Lyman, 1983). Even though it seems likely that some approaches to residential treatment are more effective than others with some types of children who display certain types of problems, the available data provides little information at this level of specificity.

SUMMARY

In the present chapter we have considered a variety of psychological approaches to child treatment that are based on different principles and associated with different models of psychopathology. These range from traditional psychoanalytic and client-centered approaches, to individual and group psychotherapy, and to somewhat more recent methods of intervention such as family therapy and behavior modification.

Many clinicians who use these procedures assume that they are so obviously of value that no formal evaluation of their effectiveness is necessary. Others, however, have been more concerned with documenting treatment effectiveness and providing an empirical basis for the usefulness of these methods in the clinical setting. Early studies of treatment effectiveness were simply designed to determine whether patients who received psychotherapy (regardless of kind) improved more than those not receiving treatment. These studies, however, provided little information concerning psychotherapy effectiveness, due to methodological weaknesses and in particular the failure to take into account relevant patient, therapist, and treatment variables. It has been suggested that instead of asking "Is psychotherapy effective?" it is more useful to ask, "What type of therapy is most effective with what type of patient when provided by what kind of therapist under what conditions?" Research designed to answer such questions is likely to involve the use of factorial designs rather than simple treatment-control comparisons. Few studies employing such designs are to be found in the child treatment literature.

In addition to these more general studies of therapy effectiveness, there has been research on the effectiveness of the various play therapies, group therapies, and family therapies that have been described here. Unfortunately, there are still relatively few conclusions that can be reached regarding the efficacy of these approaches, as many of these studies have lacked appropriate controls or have been otherwise methodologically flawed. Although there is some reason to believe that certain of these approaches may be of value in treatment effectiveness, for the most part, remains to be demonstrated.

The therapeutic approach that has received the most research attention in recent years is the behavioral approach. Although many uncontrolled case studies are to be found in the literature, a number of reasonably well-controlled investigations suggest that procedures such as desensitization, modeling, and various operant conditioning approaches are effective in treating a variety of childhood problems. There is also some evidence to suggest that training parents in behavior management techniques may be useful in terms of helping parents deal more effectively with a wide range of problem behaviors and in increasing the likelihood that behavior changes resulting from treatment generalize to the natural environment.

Some research related to residential treatment of disturbed children and adolescents has also appeared in the literature, although research in this area has been less frequent than studies of nonresidential treatments. Much of the research that does exist, however, is plagued by methodological problems similar to those seen in other types of treatment studies. Few conclusions can be drawn regarding the effectiveness of such treatments.

As the above statements suggest, an overview of the child treatment literature indicates a lack of truly well-controlled and methodologically sound studies in many areas. As these approaches to treatment are widely used with children in clinical settings, investigations designed to determine those approaches to treatment that are most beneficial to children displaying different types of problems are greatly needed if we are to offer our child clients the most effective ways of resolving their difficulties.

SUGGESTED READINGS

Hersen, M., Michelson, L., & Bellack, A. S. (1984). *Issues in psychotherapy research.* New York: Plenum. An edited text dealing with various conceptual and methodological issues related to research on psychotherapy.

Reisman, J. M. (1973). *Principles of psychotherapy with children.* New York: John Wiley & Sons. A somewhat older, but still excellent presentation of general principles of child psychotherapy from a traditional point of view.

Schaefer, C. E., & O'Connor, K. J. (1983). *Handbook of play therapy.* New York: John Wiley & Sons. An edited text that contains chapters dealing with a wide range of approaches to play therapy. Probably the most detailed introduction to play therapy techniques available.

Levant, R. F. (1984). *Family therapy: A comprehensive overview.* Englewood Cliffs, NJ: Prentice-Hall. An excellent coverage of various approaches to family therapy.

Gelfand, D. M., & Hartman, D. (1984). *Child behavior analysis and therapy* (2nd ed.). New York: Pergamon. This is an excellent book that provides the student with the knowledge necessary for implementing effective behavior change programs with children.

Kendall, P. C. & Braswell, L. (1985). *Cognitive-behavioral therapy for impulsive children.* New York: Guilford. Provides an excellent overview of how cognitive-behavioral procedures are used with problem children.

Dangel, R. F., & Polster, R. A. (1984). *Parent training.* New York: Guilford. An excellent collection of chapters that focus on training parents to deal with problem child behaviors.

11 PREVENTION OF CHILDHOOD PSYCHOPATHOLOGY

The preceding chapters have been concerned with the etiology and treatment of childhood psychopathology. Now we turn our attention to the problem of preventing psychopathology from developing in the first place. In terms of alleviating unnecessary suffering and reducing the enormous financial burden of psychopathology, prevention is probably the most important research area in clinical psychology. Unfortunately, it is also one of the most neglected.

Following a general review of the background of prevention activities, several types of prevention will be discussed. The chapter concludes with some reflections on current problems and future trends in treatment and prevention.

BACKGROUND, DEFINITIONS, AND PROBLEMS

The modern approach to the prevention of psychopathology has its roots in two related historical traditions. The first, the mental hygiene movement, brought about public recognition of the importance of mental health and prevention of mental illness. The second tradition, public health medicine, has provided the foundation for many currently popular preventive techniques. Both traditions have proved important to attempts to prevent psy-

chopathology, but neither has yet produced a methodology that can be applied specifically to the psychological problems of childhood.

The Mental Hygiene Movement

The publication of *A Mind That Found Itself* by Clifford Beers in 1908 began a social movement that, in somewhat altered form, remains alive today. Beers's description of his dehumanizing experiences in three Connecticut mental institutions won public sympathy and sparked the formation of the National Committee on Mental Hygiene in 1913. At first the committee's goal was to reform the practices of mental hospitals, but its aims quickly expanded to include the prevention of psychological problems as well. Because the early childhood years were viewed as crucial in the later development of psychopathology, child guidance clinics were established to provide early therapeutic intervention. The clinics were first established in conjunction with juvenile courts (see Chapter 1), but after a while achieved independent status. In the process of becoming independent, however, child guidance clinics moved away from their original goal of prevention toward more traditional psychotherapeutic activities, and instead of attempting to prevent psychopathology in the community began to provide services for a small population of children already diagnosed as "disturbed." In line with the prevalent psychoanalytic views of the time, these clinics specialized in one-to-one, long-term psychotherapy of an "uncovering" and interpretive variety. Under these circumstances the number of children that could be treated was clearly quite small, and preventive activities became a relatively insignificant part of the clinics' functioning.

Although traditional psychotherapeutic forms of intervention, in which one or several patients and a therapist are in ongoing contact, were and still are the dominant mode of intervention in child psychopathology, the mental hygiene movement did encourage professionals and the general public to view the problems of psychopathology in a broader perspective. Psychopathology came to be seen as at least partially a sociocultural phenomenon, and by the late 1950s it had become quite common to consider psychopathology and its prevention within a sociological framework (Hollingshead & Redlich, 1958). Although the exact changes in society required to prevent psychopathology were not known — and are still largely unknown — by the 1960s both the professional community and the public were ready for change. It was out of this desire for social change that the community mental health center movement was born.

Spurred on by notable changes in society's attitude toward mental illness and by the report of the Joint Commission on Mental Illness and Health, *Action for Mental Health* (1961), the U.S. Congress passed the Community Mental Health Centers Act of 1963. In this legislation, community mental health centers funded jointly by federal and local sources were envisioned as providing "comprehensive" mental health services to "catchment areas" of 75,000 to 200,000 people. Although thought of as communities, in rural areas of sparse population, catchment areas could be as large as half of a state, and were often not communities in the traditional sense.

Each community mental health center was to provide some mixture of inpatient and outpatient care, emergency services, partial hospitalization, consultation, and community education programs. Particular emphasis was placed on three "basic" functions: training, education, and prevention. Consultation and education programs serving the courts, schools, and other social agencies as well as early identification and treatment programs were the major techniques of prevention available to these centers. Some of them have made significant progress in implementing these preventive functions (see Cowen, Gardner, & Zax, 1967; Erikson, 1976; Gelfand & Hartmann, 1977); many, however, have never moved beyond offering the same sort of traditional psychotherapy services provided by private clinics (Segal, 1975).

Financial problems brought on by the general economic recession of the 1970s and 1980s and by changes in political views have severely reduced the financial resources available to community mental health centers. Moreover, their role as treatment providers to adults (a role emphasized in the *Action for Mental Health* report) has greatly overshadowed their role in prevention. So although community mental health centers remain important potential resources for prevention, it is a potential that remains largely untapped.

The mental hygiene movement and its successor, the community mental health center movement, have not eradicated psychopathology in adults or children. Both, however, made important contributions. Together they brought to public consciousness the social nature of many types of psychological problems. Thanks to their efforts, attempts to deal with the causes of psychopathology are now widely recognized to require intervention programs more complicated than any tried thus far. And in the last decade or so, methodologies developed in the field of public health have begun to be adapted to the task of preventing psychopathology (Lamb & Zusman, 1979; Murphy & Frank, 1979).

Public Health and the Prevention of Psychopathology

The treatment of psychopathology discussed in Chapter 10 involves the interaction of a therapist on the one hand and a child or family on the other. Prevention requires a much broader focus, in which a community or, perhaps, a society at large becomes the "patient." In order to see how a whole society can function as a patient, it is instructive to examine the approach of medical authorities to problems of public health.

The goals of any public health program are the control, and, if possible, the total elimination, of a disease. This is most easily achieved when two conditions are met: (a) the etiological factors giving rise to a disease are known; and (b) a method of prevention is available. The best examples of successful public health campaigns are the mass immunization programs that have virtually eliminated such once-common diseases as smallpox.

Although prevention is most successful when precise etiologies are well known, public health campaigns can also be effective when etiologies are unclear. In these latter instances, a correlated factor may be discovered that, when controlled, prevents a disease from spreading. The incidence of cholera, for example, was greatly reduced by restricting access to contaminated water supplies, even before the actual connection between cholera and water purity was understood. Quarantines instituted to prevent the spread of disease may also be effective, even when the exact nature of a disease's transmission is unknown.

For some types of psychopathology — primarily those that are organically based — public health measures have been effective in reducing morbidity (the number of individuals suffering from a condition). Certain types of pathology have been prevented entirely. Changes in diet, for instance, have virtually eliminated pellagra and its attendant psychopathology. Similarly, the removal of lead from interior house paints has reduced the number of cases of lead poisoning in children and consequent brain damage. We have also noted several times in this book how genetic counseling can be used to prevent certain pathologies. Unfortunately, however, most psychological disorders have not been amenable to large scale public health measures because their etiology is unknown and no effective

methods of prevention are available. Despite these difficulties, attempts to prevent psychopathology have been mounted. The remainder of this chapter is devoted to an examination of some of them, both successful and unsuccessful.

Types of Prevention

Three types of prevention will be reviewed in this chapter: primary, secondary, and tertiary.

Primary Prevention. Eliminating the cause of a problem, and thus preventing its occurrence, is the goal of primary prevention. This is the aim of mass immunization programs. It is most successful when clear-cut etiological factors are identified and effective means of combating these factors are available. Primary prevention is what most laymen mean when they talk about "preventing" a disease.

Secondary Prevention. The goal of secondary prevention is the early identification and amelioration of problems, thereby preventing more serious disorders from developing. For example, psychological screening early in life may uncover problems just beginning to develop. School health programs that include vision testing, for example, hope to bring about early intervention where needed and thereby prevent later reading problems. Secondary prevention activities may sometimes be difficult to distinguish from those used in primary prevention, but the two types can be differentiated by the temporal focus of their activities. Primary prevention takes place before problems arise; the focus is on the etiological antecedents of psychopathology. Secondary prevention takes place at an early stage in a problem's emergence, before more serious difficulties develop.

Tertiary Prevention. Tertiary prevention involves limiting the after-effects of psychopathology and is therefore closely related to the concept of rehabilitation. This type of prevention is not generally amenable to large-scale intervention programs; rather, tertiary prevention, like treatment in general, usually focuses on the individual.

Each type of prevention will be discussed in this chapter. Although attempts will be made to keep each separate, in practice various combinations of preventive approaches are applied to a particular problem. We shall begin with a look at some attempts to prevent psychopathology from developing, that is, primary prevention.

PRIMARY PREVENTION

Because the focus of primary prevention is on the antecedents of psychopathology, it is no surprise that attempts at primary prevention programs have been greatly hindered by the lack of consensus about what exactly is to be prevented. In other words, the failure to adequately define the concept of mental health has made it exceedingly difficult to evaluate primary prevention programs (Albee & Joffe, 1977). But these difficulties have not kept psychologists and others from developing programs aimed at the primary prevention of psychopathology. There is no doubt that the programs to be described in this section can be improved, but it appears that such improvements will only follow new discoveries about the causes of psychopathology and improved, generally accepted, definitions of psychological health.

In this section we shall not deal with all attempts to prevent psychopathology, but will instead discuss some promising general research areas in which it appears that progress has been made. Needless to say, our primary concern is with attempts to prevent psychopathology in children, and programs mainly aimed at adults will not be covered here unless they also affect children. Four areas of preventive activity will be covered: educational programs, the prevention of schizophrenia, the prevention of delinquency, and the primary prevention of mental retardation.

Educational Programs

Programs designed to promote "positive mental health" through education about psychopathology and its causes have been promoted by governmental, charitable, and religious organizations and have taken forms ranging from an educational curriculum for school children (Forgays, 1978; Roen, 1967) to large-scale media campaigns. These efforts all share the belief that the information conveyed by these programs will change attitudes and thereby prevent the development of psychopathology. The programs most directly related to children have been set in the schools and emphasize either the quality of the school environment or specific additions to the school curriculum.

School Atmosphere

Biber (1961) and her colleagues (Biber & Franklin, 1967) emphasized the importance of the total school atmosphere in "infusing mental health principles in every school process" (Biber, 1961, p. 348). They proposed teaching methods that, they asserted, promote cooperation between children and staff. Flexible curricula and a generally informal school atmosphere are also part of their program. Because this approach does not try to prevent specific problems but rather to improve psychological health in general, evaluation is quite difficult, for there are no standard measures or definitions of mental health. The evaluations performed by Biber and her colleagues (Minuchin, Biber, Shapiro, & Zimiles, 1969) were plagued by methodological inadequacies. Although their findings seem to indicate differences between children attending schools of different "atmospheres" (traditional vs. modern is the usual dichotomy, although the definitions of both types make the dichotomy seem more like strict versus lax), these differences have not been related to psychopathology. An interesting finding reported by Minuchin et al. (1969) is that sex differences were important in determining how a child responded to a particular school "atmosphere," raising the possibility that boys and girls may differentially profit from school atmospheres, one being best for girls and another best for boys. This hypothesis, of course, conflicts with Biber's notion that one type of school atmosphere is best for emotional development generally.

School Curriculum

Roen (1967) described a behavioral sciences curriculum aimed at children in the primary school grades. The purpose for including this subject in the primary grades is not merely instructional; Roen also expected to prevent emotional disorders by increasing the children's ability to cope with life. Moreover, Roen argued, knowledge of the behavioral sciences will make school more comfortable and will also allow children to spread their knowledge to the community, encouraging psychologically healthy attitudes in others. Any program in the behavioral sciences that could accomplish all of this would be valuable indeed. Roen's proposed curriculum involves teaching children about such things as heredity, Erickson's stages of development, learning (mostly conditioning, in his program), thinking, testing, and so forth. Although knowledge in these areas is probably valuable, we can see no particular reason why it would prevent psychological problems. In fact, an evaluation of this program by Spano (1965) failed to find any differences in measures of "mental health" or personal adjustment for children exposed to the behavioral sciences curriculum, as compared to those who did not participate in the program. Spano did find that children in the program showed more "democratic" behavior than those who were not involved. The program may therefore have some effects, but for the present the prevention of psychopathology by the teaching of psychology has not been demonstrated. Similar programs suggested by others (see Ojemann, 1967, for example) have also not been shown to have an effect on children's psychological adjustment.

Some writers have placed specific importance on sex education as a means of preventing various problems (not all psychological) later in adolescence and adulthood (Gordon, 1974; McCary, 1973). Many school districts have incorporated sex education into their curriculum, but no one really knows whether sex education, as usually taught, serves a primary prevention function. Because it is known that some adolescents are less likely to use contraception than others even though they do not wish to become parents (Litt, Cuskey, & Rudd, 1980), it may be possible to develop educational programs aimed specifically at this "high risk" group.

There have also been school-based and media-based educational programs designed to convince children not to take up health-threatening habits such as smoking, drinking, and drugs (Evans, 1978, for example). Unfortunately, evaluations of these programs have found them to be less successful than we might have hoped (Berberian, Gross, Lovejoy, & Paparella, 1976). One study (Stuart, 1974) actually found that students who participated in a school-based drug education program *increased* their use of drugs after the program!

In his review of 60 studies, Davis (1965) concluded that, on the whole, educational programs aimed at improving mental health in general had not proven particularly worthwhile. As noted earlier, mental health has no generally accepted definition, making nonspecific programs difficult to evaluate. Moreover, educational programs have typically made little use of psychological findings. One type of educational program that has become extremely popular in the last 10 years and that does try to use psychological research findings, seeks to improve children's behavior by teaching parents methods of child rearing.

Parent Training

Although there has never been any lack of child-rearing advice (Benjamin Spock's book *Baby and Child Care* has sold over 25 million copies), recent trends have been toward formal training in psychological principles. Books such as Becker's *Parents Are Teachers* (1979) and Patterson and Guillon's *Living With Children* (1968) that try to teach parents how to apply behavioral principles to child rearing have become very popular. Similarly, programs such as *Parent Effectiveness Training* (Gordon, 1977) and *Systematic Training for Effective Parenting* (Dinkmeyer & McKay, 1976), which use group settings and seminars to teach parents how to apply psychological principles to the problems of rearing children, have also become immensely popular (and profitable).

A recent survey of the field found 26 commercially available training manuals purporting to advise parents on how best to use psychological principles in raising their children (Bernal & North, 1978). There are probably an equal number of training programs. Most of these programs teach parents how to control reinforcements and punishments in child rearing. The assumption underlying the teaching of psychological skills to parents is that these skills will be useful not only in coping with children in the short term, but also in preventing the development of future serious problems. A review of more than 70 studies concerning parent training in behavior modification by O'Dell (1974) was generally favorable, although O'Dell noted the need for additional research comparing the effectiveness of the various training techniques. More recent research substantiates the effectiveness of these programs (see Wells, Forehand, & Griest, 1980, for instance) in generalizing improved behavior to areas not actually covered in the programs.

Although parent training programs appear to help some parents cope with their children, there are parents who do not seem to benefit. These latter parents tend to be less educated, from lower social classes, and under greater social and psychological stress than the middle-class parents for whom the programs are designed (Wahler, Leske, & Rogers, 1979). What this means is that the families with the greatest likelihood of producing children with behavior problems are the least likely to benefit from parent training. It is also unclear whether parent training exerts any long-lasting effect on children as they grow up. It would be worthwhile to know whether parent training results in the prevention of specific psychological problems in adolescents. At present, this information is unavailable.

Programs for Children "At-Risk" to Develop Psychopathology

Because primary prevention requires intervening before problems develop, it is important to know which children are most likely to develop psychological problems. The programs described so far are applied indiscriminately to all children or parents. If they could be targeted toward those children most "at-risk," they would be less expensive and, perhaps, more likely to work.

An example of a program directed toward children at-risk to develop psychological problems is the brief therapy offered to parents who are about to divorce and their children. As noted in Chapter 1, children of divorced parents have an increased probability of developing psychological problems (although such problems are not inevitable; see Bernard, 1981). Offering therapy and other counseling to families in the midst of divorce may prevent these problems from occurring (Felner, Farber, & Primavera, 1980; Hetherington, Cox, & Cox, 1978; Scheiner, Musetto, & Cordier, 1982; Wallerstein & Kelly, 1977). School-based programs for such children have also been described (Crossman & Adams, 1980; Drake, 1979).

Attempts to prevent child abuse (again, see Chapter 1 for a description of the size of the problem) by identifying those children most likely to be the victims of abuse and neglect have also been described in the literature (Fanaroff, Kennell, & Klaus, 1972; Garbarino, 1980; Leiderman, 1974). As it turns out, abusive parents are not easy to identify (Steele & Pollock, 1974). Child abuse appears to be the result of a complicated interaction of parental and child characteristics (see Friedrich & Boriskin, 1978, for example), exacerbated during times of acute family stress. Although it seems logical to provide parent training and other interventions to parents likely to abuse their children, there is presently no strong evidence that such procedures actually result in the prevention of child abuse.

Specialized primary prevention programs have been developed to prevent psychological problems from developing in a variety of situations. For example, preschool children from low-income families have received psychological interventions designed to help them overcome their fear of visiting the dentist (Siegel & Peterson, 1981). Similar programs have been developed to help children who must undergo surgery deal with their inevitable fears (Peterson & Shigetomi, 1981). Other similar interventions are described by Green (1982).

A program with a difference is described by Pfohl (cited in Garmezy & Rutter, 1983). The program, called the Children's Anxiety Management Program (CAMP), is designed to teach children ways of coping with stress. The idea is that children who understand and can deal with stress will be much less vulnerable to stress-induced disorders. The program is administered by the teacher or school psychologist and includes training in behavioral techniques such as relaxation, modeling, and assertiveness. Exposure to stressors and rehearsal are also part of the program.

One specific disorder that has received a great deal of attention is schizophrenia, the subject of the next section.

Primary Prevention of Schizophrenia

Schizophrenia is the most prevalent severe psychological problem in adults. Although schizophrenia is not common in childhood, it is generally agreed that preventive activities have to begin quite early in life if they are to be successful. Unfortunately, despite a huge mass of research data, we still have no clear idea of schizophrenia's cause and no methods for preventing its development. Nevertheless, potentially important advances have been made in areas related to prevention, and there is hope that new preventive measures will develop out of recent research. Some promising research programs will be described in this section.

Research on schizophrenia is very difficult. There is no equivalent in schizophrenia research of studying the spread of a virus (or other disease-causing agent) by injecting laboratory animals with the pathogen and observing the course of the disease: As far as we know laboratory animals are not susceptible to schizophrenia. Moreover, we cannot introduce conditions thought to produce schizophrenia into the lives of average children in order to determine if the hypothesized condi-

tions really are related to schizophrenia, because if we are correct, we would have caused otherwise normal children to be schizophrenic. Because of these ethical and practical problems, much of the research in schizophrenia has involved the study of adult schizophrenics. Studying the already schizophrenic adult is a doubtful enterprise, however, as any peculiarities discovered could just as well be the result of being schizophrenic as a cause of schizophrenia. The only ethical and scientifically meaningful course open to investigators is to study the development of children and attempt to prevent schizophrenia from developing. The success of a particular preventive technique does not necessarily establish that a particular factor *causes* schizophrenia, but to the extent that preventive efforts are successful we have at least isolated likely causes for further study. Because only a small number of children actually become schizophrenic, it would be an impossibly inefficient strategy to apply preventive methods to an unselected sample of children. Therefore some method of identifying those children most vulnerable to schizophrenia is necessary. One possibility is to study the children of schizophrenic parents, who are much more likely to develop schizophrenia than children from normal families (Kallman, 1946). One such research project was begun in 1962 by Mednick and his coworkers (Mednick, Schulsinger, Higgins, & Bell, 1974). Its goal is the identification of etiological factors related to schizophrenia that have implications for the development of preventive programs.

Mednick and his colleagues identified 207 high-risk children in the population of Copenhagen, Denmark; each child had a chronically schizophrenic mother. A group of 104 control children were selected for comparison purposes. These children came from normal families that had had no hospitalizations for mental illness for three generations. Denmark is an excellent location for this type of research, because there is very little emigration and the government keeps accurate records of current addresses, making long-term follow-up easier than in most other nations. The Danish government also keeps accurate records of psychiatric hospitalizations. The study began in 1962 and is still in progress, and it is expected that the children will continue to be followed.

The design of the Denmark study is based on estimates of the incidence of schizophrenia in normal and high-risk populations. Research by Kallman (1946), for example, indicates that approximately 50% of high-risk children will develop some sort of psychopathology and that of these about 30% will be schizophrenic. These children, then, can be compared with the remaining high-risk children who develop problems other than schizophrenia, the high-risk children who do not develop problems, and the low-risk children in order to determine variables related to schizophrenia. This research design is depicted in Figure 11.1.

Although the study of high-risk children solves many of the problems associated with alternative methods of studying schizophrenia, it is not entirely free of difficulties. For example, the effects of genetics and early upbringing are likely to be confounded in the high-risk sample, because schizophrenic mothers may employ atypical child-rearing practices. Although at least some of this problem can be solved by comparing adopted high-risk children with those raised by their natural mothers, other problems remain. For example, the high-risk approach is heavily dependent on the diagnostic criteria used to define schizophrenia. Different diagnostic criteria will lead to the inclusion of different individuals in the experimental sample and will have a direct influence on the validation of any etiological factors (Gottesman, Carey, & Hanson, 1983).

The advent of the DSM-III has, indeed, led to a reassessment of earlier findings. Erlenmeyer-Kimling et al. (1983), for example, found that many of the children followed in their longitudinal study of early indicators of schizophrenia were no longer the children of schizophrenics when newer diagnostic criteria were applied. Fortunately, they found that their main indicators were still predictive of those who later became schizophrenic.

In any event, there are no adequate alternatives to the longitudinal study of high-risk children that do not create more problems than they solve. In addition to the Copen-

FIGURE 11.1. Design and rationale of a study of children at high-risk for schizophrenia

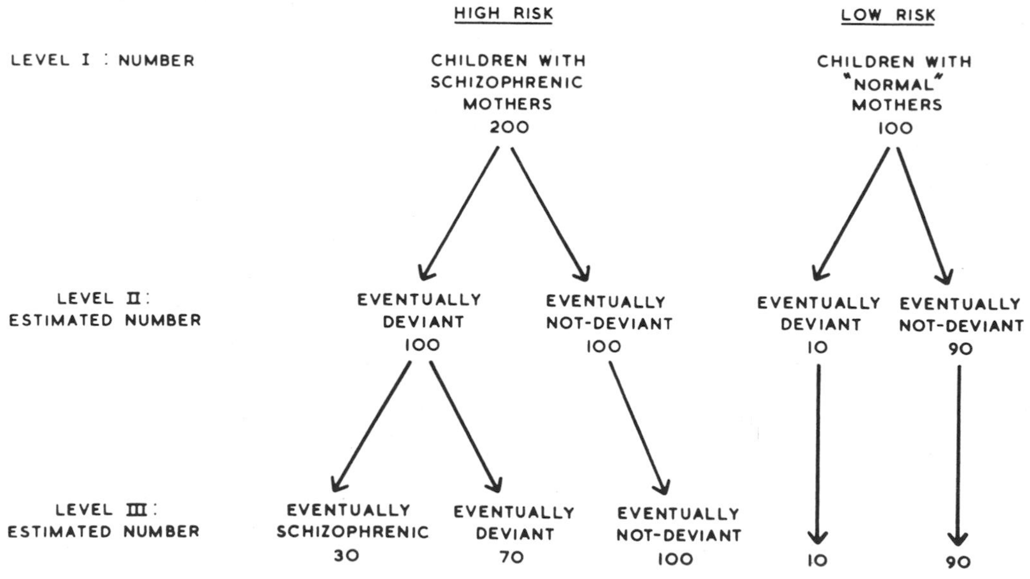

Source: Mednick et al. (1975). © 1975 by Academic Press and reprinted with permission.

hagen project, a number of other high-risk studies are currently in progress (see Erlen-meyer-Kimling et al., 1983; Wynne, Crom-well, & Matthysse, 1978).

Mednick and his coworkers (Mednick et al., 1975; Mednick & Witkin-Lanoil, 1977) have initiated a project aimed at applying preliminary data gathered during the course of the Copenhagen study. This prevention project is being conducted on Mauritius, an island formerly under British rule that lies in the Indian Ocean several hundred miles off the coast of South Africa, which is a racially and ethnically complex country rather different from Denmark. The study began with the collection of data on a large number of variables for a sample of over 1,800 children. Two hundred children have been selected to participate in the study on the basis of initial testing, and about half of these children have a type of autonomic functioning, hyperresponsivity,* which was found to be characteristic of children who developed schizophrenia in the Copenhagen study (Mednick & Schulsinger, 1968) and which is supposedly characteristic of adult schizophrenics (Gruzelier & Venables, 1972). Fifty of the hyperresponsive children and 50 of the normal children have been enrolled in special nursery schools where several preventive interventions have been initiated. Behavior modification programs, parent substitutes for those children without parents, fostering of interpersonal relationships, and other similar interventions have shown initial success in preventing early pathology (Mednick & Witkin-Lanoil, 1977).

The children will be followed for a number of years in order to determine whether these early preventive interventions are successful in preventing the later development of schizophrenia. Success will be determined by comparing the children in the nursery schools with those not enrolled. It seems safe to predict that a great deal of attention will be given to the results of this and similar studies (e.g., Rolf, 1976) as they become available.

Currently, the etiology of schizophrenia is unknown, and by its very nature it is a difficult topic for research. Nevertheless, it would appear that promising first steps have been made and that the future will see progress in our understanding of schizophrenia and our ability to prevent it from developing. Next we turn our attention to a different sort of problem: antisocial behavior and juvenile delinquency.

Primary Prevention of Antisocial Behavior and Delinquency

Cultural standards and sociopolitical atmosphere color our attitudes toward crime and delinquency. Depending on the time and the place, it has been customary to consider juvenile delinquents as products of deprived environments, morally inferior, genetically scarred, or some combination of all three. Although a distinction is often made between *dysocial* delinquents (members of a deviant subculture, such as a juvenile gang) and *asocial* delinquents (lone criminals acting outside the bounds of any cultural standards), in actual practice many delinquents cannot be so neatly classified. (These two categories are similar to the socialized-subcultural and unsocialized-psychopathic categories discussed in Chapter 9.) From the point of view of prevention, the distinction between dysocial and asocial delinquents is potentially useful if it can be shown that the two types of delinquency respond to different methods of prevention. Dysocial delinquency, for example, may be construed as the result of poverty, peer pressure, conformity to group norms, and the lack of proper role models (see Chapter 9). Preventive activities for this type of delinquency have taken the form of "wars on poverty," parent training, the provision of role models, and similar social interventions. Asocial delinquency, on the other hand, may be the result of a deviant environment interacting with a peculiar genetic disposition

---

*More recently, emphasis has been placed on distractibility and the inability to sustain attention (Harvey, Winters, Weintraub, & Neale, 1981).

(Schulsinger, 1974). The prevention of dysocial delinquency would seem to require information that can only be gained from studies
of children "at risk," designed along the lines
described earlier for schizophrenia. In fact,
studies of the development of children at high
risk for delinquency that are currently underway (Mednick, 1978; Offord & Jones, 1983)
are unfortunately hampered by the lack of a
good predictor of future criminal behavior,
making it more difficult to identify children
at risk for delinquency than for schizophrenia.
Nevertheless, developmental studies modeled
after the schizophrenia studies seem a prerequisite for future progress in the area of
delinquency.

Preventive activities aimed at dysocial delinquency, such as improved welfare, social
work contact with the families of children in
high crime areas, upgrading of schools, and
similar programs, may be justified on many
grounds, but there is little evidence that they
prevent antisocial behavior. Moreover, it is
quite doubtful that such evidence could even
be produced because of the lack of suitable
control groups. After all, no one is deliberately going to keep a group of randomly selected
children impoverished just to judge the effects
of poverty on later criminal behavior!

As usual, programs aimed at target populations using specific intervention techniques
are much easier to evaluate than are broad-
based social welfare programs. Here the study
most often cited is named after the Boston
suburbs where it was conducted, Cambridge
and Sommerville (McCord & McCord, 1969).
The Cambridge-Sommerville project attempted to prevent the development of delinquent
behavior in several hundred boys by providing social work services to their families and
counseling for the boys and by making available recreational activities not readily available in these suburbs. When compared with
boys given no special services, boys participating in the program committed the same
number of (equally serious) offenses. Although
this experiment in prevention must be classified a failure, it is not clear why the project
failed. The problem may have been with sub-

ject selection. That is, both dysocial and asocial type delinquents may have been included
in the sample, and the interventions used are
not likely to have much effect on asocial delinquents. Alternatively, the problem may
have been due to the use of ineffective preventive measures. Some idea of the sort of interventions that are needed can best be gained
from the high risk studies described earlier.
Although such studies have not yet been completed for delinquent youths, at least one large
research project attempted to do part of the
work by trying to predict which boys would
become delinquent. Based on a retrospective
examination of the records of 500 delinquent
boys, Glueck and Glueck (1970) developed a
scale for identifying potential delinquents, in
which the most important dimensions were
the degree of affection and supervision received from parents. Although this scale has
been referred to many times, careful cross-
validational studies have not demonstrated its
utility. Its use in prevention, as an indicator
of children at risk, is not indicated until such
evidence is presented.

Primary Prevention of Mental Retardation

The issues involved in the prevention of mental retardation are covered in some detail in
Chapter 8. From that discussion, it should be
clear that primary prevention cannot be applied to all forms of mental retardation. Some
types — particularly those resulting from cultural deprivation — respond only to secondary
and tertiary preventive efforts. Nevertheless,
it is true that many cases of mental retardation can be avoided.

Lab tests for metabolic diseases such as
phenylketonuria and galactosemia and subsequent dietary management can prevent afflicted children from becoming mentally retarded. Tests for Rh compatibility and early
(or even intrauterine) blood transfusions can
also prevent mental retardation from occurring. Genetic counseling coupled with lab
tests of chromosomal materials can also often
lead to the prevention of mental retardation.

Many of the details of these preventive procedures may be found in Chapter 8. For even greater detail see the review by Koch (1979). Secondary and tertiary prevention efforts will be discussed later in this chapter.

Primary Prevention: Current Status

As was already noted several times, the evaluation of prevention programs is quite difficult when programmers do not specify a particular criterion for success. Improved mental health is too broad and too vague a criterion to be useful for evaluative purposes. It is far easier to judge the success of preventive programs that specify the particular problem they hope to prevent.

The primary prevention of childhood psychopathology remains a largely unfulfilled hope. Nonspecific educational programs for children and for their parents, although seemingly worthwhile, have not been related to the prevention of any form of childhood psychopathology. Schizophrenia and the other psychoses of childhood are not well enough understood to be prevented, although the various high risk research programs hold some hope for the future. Delinquency, a costly and important social problem, has been the focus of a great deal of effort that has led to little noticeable change in its incidence. It would seem that high-risk studies may be of use in clarifying some of the potentially modifiable causes of delinquency as well.

It is fair to state that advances in the primary prevention of childhood psychopathology will await advances in our knowledge in many of the areas covered in this book. Primary prevention depends, as we have noted, on knowing what causes problems and knowing what interventions will prevent problems from developing. At present we are woefully ignorant in both areas.

In the next section, we turn to an examination of some attempts to identify incipient problems at an early stage in their development and prevent them from becoming worse.

SECONDARY PREVENTION

Secondary prevention refers to the early identification and treatment of psychological problems. To be most effective, secondary preventive activities must be aimed at rather large populations. A successful example of secondary prevention is the routine screening of babies for the presence of PKU (see Chapter 8) and the institution of a special diet for those with positive results. Unfortunately, there are no easy-to-administer, highly valid mass screening tests available for most psychological problems, nor are there therapeutic methods of known effectiveness for many serious problems of childhood (see Chapter 10). Research in the area of early detection is presently being carried out by many investigators and is one of the most important areas of research in clinical child psychology.

There are two assumptions underlying secondary prevention: (a) a problem is treated more easily if treatment begins early; and (b) the treatment is less harmful than the psychological disorder itself. As Zusman (1975) points out, these assumptions are almost invariably appropriate for physical disease but cannot be assumed to be true for many psychological problems. For instance, in the days when the only available treatment for schizophrenia was hospitalization in a state institution, early treatment may have actually been worse than the illness: the early identification of schizophrenics only meant that they would spend more of their life incarcerated. Even today the negative effects of labeling children psychologically disturbed may still outweigh the positive benefits of many currently available treatments. Workers in the field of secondary prevention need to carefully examine their intervention strategies and demonstrate not only their effectiveness in ameliorating a problem or preventing a more serious one from developing, but also their superiority over doing nothing at all. One of the first rules of medicine is equally applicable to the field of clinical psychology: "First do no harm!"

In reviewing the literature on secondary

prevention, it quickly becomes obvious that although most researchers acknowledge the need to evaluate their programs, few actually carry out more than a cursory examination of their results. The importance of secondary prevention programs to the child's future makes this cavalier attitude toward evaluation intolerable. In this section, where we will be discussing efforts aimed at the early identification and prevention of problems in the areas of school performance, antisocial behavior, several types of psychopathology, and crisis intervention, we will try to limit our coverage to programs that have been carefully evaluated.

School Failure

Disadvantaged children, those who live in impoverished circumstances and who are usually members of minority groups, generally do poorly in school (Coleman, 1966). In the past 20 years quite a large number of projects have been developed with the aim of changing this state of affairs, and much of this work has taken the form of early interventions designed to "compensate" for growing up in disadvantaged circumstances. These programs try to provide intellectually stimulating environments and in some cases train parents to change their home atmospheres in ways thought compatible with intellectual growth. Some of the early intervention programs have been national in scope, such as Project Head Start, whereas others have been local projects aimed at training specific skills.

Early intervention projects all share the aim of improving the school performance of the culturally disadvantaged child, but they go about achieving this aim in different ways. Even within a project, different methods may be used in different locations. Some Project Head Start centers, for instance, put their efforts into training specific skills such as reading or arithmetic, while others emphasize enriched cultural experiences and community action projects. Evaluating projects with such a diversity of methods and aims is obviously difficult, but is made somewhat easier if we

set out in advance generally applicable standards by which projects may be judged. Bronfenbrenner (1975) has suggested asking the following questions:

1. Do children continue to gain in intellectual development throughout the program?
2. Do children continue to improve or at least hold their gains after completing the program?
3. Is improvement related to the age at which a program begins?
4. What types of projects are most effective in the long run?
5. Which children in which circumstances are most likely to benefit from a particular project?

In order to answer these questions, early intervention programs must be planned with subsequent evaluation in mind. At the very least, follow-up data, carefully chosen control groups, and comparable assessment measures for determining educational achievement must be available. Many early intervention studies are not planned with subsequent evaluation in mind, and as a consequence the necessary information cannot be gathered. Of the numerous studies of early intervention in the literature, Bronfenbrenner (1975) found only seven that provided sufficient information to answer his five questions. These studies all involved preschool or primary school settings. Although these seven studies provided more information than most, it is still difficult to make comparisons among them because they used different selection methods and different experimental designs, and because a potentially important factor in the program's success, parental motivation, varied from study to study. Bronfenbrenner found that all seven programs produced gains in IQ scores and other standardized test scores during their first year. Programs that stressed tutoring in skills were slightly better than play-oriented programs in producing test score gains. Interestingly, as far as could be determined, neither early entry into the program (as early as age 1) nor longer enrollment (up to 5 years) resulted in greater or more enduring gains. A disappointing finding in virtually all studies is that after the early intervention program concluded, performance on cognitive tests declined. One or two years following a program's completion the children lost all of their gains and were back to the below-average level of functioning from which they had begun. The few apparent exceptions to this trend were the result of uncontrolled variables such as differences in the level of parental motivation. The sharpest decline in performance following a program took place at the time of entry into school and was particularly evident in extremely deprived children. Bronfenbrenner noted that the most important determinant of a child's performance in the program (and later in school) was the quality of his or her home environment. Indeed, the importance of home environment as a predictor of academic success far outweighed any individual differences in the type of program. Moreover, the most important period of the year for consolidating intellectual gains or for posting losses was found not to be during the school year, but in the summer vacation when children spend most of their time at home. Bronfenbrenner's study, although sobering, was not the last word on the matter of the effectiveness of broad-based social programs such as Project Head Start. Reanalyses of the data by several authors indicated that such programs are more successful than Bronfenbrenner concluded (see Magidson, 1978, for example). But these new findings have also been challenged (Bentler & Woodward, 1978). The picture has also been clouded by reports that question the veracity of some of the research data on early stimulation programs (see Sommer & Sommer, 1983, for example).

Despite this controversy, there do seem to be some data indicating that certain early educational and stimulation programs have some value.

For example, in a study by McKay, Sinisterra, McKay, Gomes, and Lloreda (1978), groups of chronically deprived children from Colombian families of very low economic status participated in an early intervention program that included nutritional guidance, improved health care, and educational enrichment. Before the program, the children were very poorly off; many were suffering from malnutrition, and the prognosis for future school success was quite poor. By school age, after the children had been in the program for a year or more, the gap between the children in the program and privileged children (from high-economic-bracket families) was appreciably narrowed. These gains were still evident after 1 year of primary school (1 year after the program ended).

Although the children did not actually reach the level of the privileged youth, their gains were nevertheless remarkable. It should be noted that the Colombian program involved an intense experience, 6 hours or more per day, that often included family members as well. It may be that this involvement of the child and his or her family was the crucial ingredient in the program's success. There is substantial evidence that preschool enrichment programs may, by themselves, be insufficient. Consider the results of an unusual study reported by Firkowska et al. (1978).

The city of Warsaw, Poland, was destroyed during World War II and rebuilt under a socialist government dedicated to allocating housing accommodation, schools, and cultural and health facilities without regard to social class. The six authors sought to determine whether the allocation scheme was successful and, if so, whether equal access to cultural and social facilities changed the relationship between family variables and school performance. The Raven's Progressive Matrices IQ test as well as tests of mathematical ability were administered to 14,000 school-aged children born in Warsaw in 1963. Data was also gathered on the children's families and on various characteristics of city and school districts. The authors were able to confirm that the goal of evenly distributing school and neighborhood attributes (number of libraries, number of theaters, access to post offices, type of housing, and so forth) was largely achieved. Yet despite the egalitarian distribution of social and cultural resources,

Firkowska et al. found that IQ scores and achievement test scores were still strongly related to such family factors as parental occupation and education. The authors concluded that egalitarian social policies had failed to override the strong association of family characteristics with school performance and cognitive development traditionally found in industrial societies.

Recognizing the overwhelming importance of family variables in intellectual growth, several early intervention studies have focused on improving early parent-child interactions (e.g., Levenstein, 1972). These projects attempt to improve school performance and intellectual abilities in general by improving mother-child interactions. Bronfenbrenner's review of this type of program is considerably more favorable than his review of preschool-based programs. Programs focusing on parent-child interactions result in substantial gains in IQ that are still evident several years after the formal program is terminated. Interestingly, in this sort of program, unlike school-based programs, the gains were cumulative, increasing for each year that the child spent in the program, and the greatest gains were noted for those children who began the program early in life. Positive changes were even noted for their younger siblings. The key element in the success of these programs appears to be the involvement of the parents in verbal interactions with their children on the topic of cognitive tasks. Some parents, usually those from the very lowest end of the socioeconomic ladder, found it difficult or impossible to adopt the techniques taught in the parent-child programs. As a result, at the very lowest end of the economic distribution, parent-child interaction programs fare little better than do school-based programs. Perhaps specially designed programs are necessary for intervening with this group of parents. The importance of early parent-child (and peer) interactions in determining the prognosis for high-risk children is demonstrated in the research studies described in Field et al. (1980).

It would seem reasonable to conclude, on the basis of the previous research, that some types of early intervention programs are effective in improving the intellectual performance of culturally deprived children. The gains made in an early intervention program are most likely to be maintained if the program involves the child's family and if it starts early in life. For the most severely impoverished and chronically deprived, however, intervention programs have been largely unsuccessful in boosting later school performance.

Although intellectual failure as measured by school performance and standardized tests may, in some cases, be prevented by early intervention, IQ test scores and achievement test scores reflect only part of a child's psychological functioning. We turn next to a consideration of the prevention of psychological problems that are rather different from intellectual failure.

Antisocial Behavior and Delinquency

As we have already noted, the primary prevention of delinquency is not yet possible, and we will have to know a great deal more about causes and possible therapeutic interventions before it will be. It is likely that the high risk research strategy employed with schizophrenics could be advantageously applied to the problems of antisocial behavior.

Secondary prevention does not rely on the ability to predict who will become delinquent, because intervention strategies are applied after the antisocial behavior has already been manifested. Several types of secondary prevention programs have reported promising results. One type that has many adherents involves the establishment of therapeutic residential communities in which youths learn to conform to more socially acceptable behavior norms.

Goldenberg (1968), for example, describes the Residential Youth Center project he ran in an inner-city area. In the center boys live in a home-like atmosphere in which they are required to take responsibility for the operation and governance of the center. Boys participating in the program were found to show a dramatic increase in gainful employment and a decrease in the number of "legal" contacts (brushes with the law) compared to a control group that did not participate in the program.

Another type of program that has reported success in the secondary prevention of delinquency is neighborhood-based but not residential. One such program was run by Schwitzgebel (1964), who employed delinquent boys for what they were told was a research study: The boys were paid to tape record their thoughts on the causes of delinquency and to engage in such behavior modification exercises as charting their own positive and negative behaviors. Schwitzgebel also had the boys recruit their friends for the project. The program, which was designed to help foster self-awareness among the boys, was reported successful, although its long-term effects are unclear.

There are many other residential and non-residential programs (see Chapter 9), some specializing in drug problems and others focusing on delinquent behavior. Although all report some degree of success, most are difficult to evaluate because they do not employ standard assessments, nor do they recruit comparable control groups. Still it seems fair to conclude that these projects have been at least partially effective. It would be worthwhile to pursue research aimed to isolate the potent ingredients of such preventive projects. Because traditional psychotherapy has not been shown to be effective with delinquents (Meeks, 1975), it is probable that the effectiveness of community-based and residential projects lies in their "social" nature.

Childhood Psychological Disorders

Because almost everything covered in this book can be referred to as an example of childhood psychopathology, it may seem odd that programs have been established to prevent this heterogeneous assortment of problems.

Such programs have been established, however, and they are doubtlessly effective — at least for some types of problems. Obviously no secondary prevention program will be appropriate for all types of psychopathology.

One project that has been carefully conducted and exhaustively researched is the Rochester Primary Mental Health Project under the general direction of Emory Cowen and his associates (Cowen et al., 1975). It operates from the principle that the school, which after the family is the most important social institution influencing children, is the ideal place to conduct early intervention projects. Moreover, all children attend school, thus making mass screenings possible, and the school environment provides the child with a number of intellectual and social challenges that allow observers to assess his or her coping ability.

In the Rochester project, a psychologist and a social worker are assigned to the primary school grades. All first-grade children are screened early in the school year, and all mothers have an interview with the social workers. Data from the social work interviews, psychological screenings, and teacher observations are combined and a prognosis made for each child. About one in three children is usually identified as potentially having problems ahead in adjusting to school and its demands. These children are given a variety of services (extra tutoring, after-school activities) using nonprofessionals, usually students, with the school mental health personnel serving as consultants. When these specially treated children were compared with controls, they were found superior on several indices of adjustment (Cowen, Gesten, & Wilson, 1979). Similar programs with equally good outcomes have been described by others. Sandler, Duricko, and Grande (1975) note, however, that these school-based programs have not been shown to produce better academic performance among the children.

Programs such as the Rochester project not only demonstrate the usefulness of early intervention for the children involved, but have secondary benefits as well. Teachers involved in such programs become better equipped to deal with the emotional problems of children, and all children, not just those at risk, benefit from the teacher's increased sensitivity. A possible negative aspect of programs like the Rochester project is the early labeling of potential problem children. To the extent that early screenings are fallible, some children may be incorrectly labeled as high risk. The possible self-fulfilling nature of such predictions is an important area of research and a consideration for all early intervention programs. Studies of the relative risks and benefits of early intervention programs are largely unavailable, but are necessary before widespread adoption of early intervention strategies.

Not all of life's surprises can be anticipated, and problems caused by unexpected events may be quite severe. These crises may have disastrous consequences unless attended to immediately. Attempts at crisis intervention are reviewed next.

Crisis Intervention

There are two types of changes that are of psychological significance in a child's life. One is the normal sort of change that comes with development. The other is a sudden, traumatic change, such as a death in the family. The latter may greatly stress a child's ability to cope. *Crisis intervention* is the general term for a broad range of techniques that can be introduced to help families deal with sudden change. Crisis intervention may take place in many settings: in drop-in centers, on hot lines, through pastoral counseling, even in the form of family interventions by specially trained policemen. All of these approaches share a common set of characteristics. They are brief, immediate (there are no waiting lists for crisis intervention services), focused on a specific problem, and often are offered by nonprofessional therapists. Caplan (1964), an authority on prevention, believes that crisis intervention is a form of primary prevention. Because those who receive help in crisis intervention settings define themselves as already having a problem, it makes more

sense, in our present scheme, to consider crisis intervention a form of secondary prevention. There are many different types of crisis intervention, and it occurs in various settings. We shall illustrate how it works with a specific example. The problems, the solutions, and the unanswered questions in the field of crisis intervention as a whole are suitably illustrated in the example of adolescent suicide.

Although suicide is generally taken to be a problem of middle and old age, statistics indicate that it is a very real problem in childhood as well. Suicide is 1 of the top 10 causes of death among children below 16 years of age (Haim, 1970), and in the United States, 11 of every 1,000 deaths in the adolescent age group is by suicide. When it is considered that accurate statistics for death by suicide are difficult to obtain, making the figures cited here low, we can see the magnitude of the problem. And the prevention of suicide depends on our ability to predict it.

Schneidman (1975), an active worker in the field of suicide prevention, makes a distinction between "lethality" and "perturbation" in the prediction of suicide. Perturbed individuals (those in a state of psychological crisis) may or may not be suicidal, and suicidal patients need not appear perturbed. In order to prevent suicide, therefore, it is necessary to concentrate on the characteristics associated with lethality rather than with emotional disturbance. Suicidal children have often undergone some stressful life event, usually a family crisis. Often (and this is still the best predictor) the child may have made a suicide attempt in the past. Abrupt changes in habits and suicidal statements are also important prognostic signs.

The management of suicidal individuals often takes place in a "crisis management" framework. There are hot lines presently operating in many cities that a suicidal individual can call for immediate counseling. Crisis intervention can also occur in an office or hospital or even at home. In any case, the goal is always the same. Attempts are made to support the individual emotionally until the crisis is past and more elaborate treatment can be instituted. In those sad cases where the suicide is successful, the survivors (the parents in the case of childhood suicide) may need crisis intervention as well to cope with the potentially serious burden of guilt and recrimination that may result.

It is impossible to gather data on the effectiveness of crisis intervention in the prevention of suicide, as one can certainly not form untreated control groups. The same problem arises in evaluating crisis intervention for other problems. At present, crisis intervention is aimed largely at adults, and childhood suicide is generally ignored. The importance of developing and assessing programs for children cannot be overstated.

Secondary Prevention: Current Status

Early identification and intervention have been shown, with varying degrees of evidence, to reduce intellectual deficits in disadvantaged children, modify delinquent behavior, lower the incidence of some types of psychopathology in school children, and perhaps defuse crises before they develop into more important problems. Although progress seems apparent, the difficulties involved in assessing the relative usefulness of many secondary prevention programs makes it very difficult to answer the question of whether secondary prevention programs are more beneficial than nothing at all. For the activities described in this section, the tentative answer seems to be yes, but more evidence is needed.

Further research is necessary in order to establish the cost effectiveness of secondary prevention programs, the long-term effectiveness of these programs, and the best way to develop such programs. Support for prevention programs is not likely to last forever without such evidence of their usefulness.

TERTIARY PREVENTION, CHILD ADVOCACY, AND FUTURE TRENDS

Tertiary prevention is aimed at rehabilitating children who have already developed some form of psychopathology. Its success depends

directly on the adequacy of treatment methods, as described in Chapter 10. It should be clear to the reader of this book that work in the area of tertiary prevention is well advanced and that rehabilitation is already a reality, at least for some behavioral problems. Although treatment methods are intensely studied, there are several hindrances to applying even proven effective treatments to achieve the goals of tertiary prevention. Some of these are discussed next.

Current Problems in Tertiary Prevention

Distribution of Services

Despite the growth of community mental health centers and training programs for mental health workers supported by the governments of several countries, the fact remains that most children in need of psychotherapeutic services are still not receiving them. The use of paraprofessionals and the development of outreach programs (e.g., Reichler & Schopler, 1976) have alleviated the problem somewhat, but there is a long way to go before psychological services will be available to all children who require them. One important difficulty is the multiple nature of service systems. Children with psychological problems may be "treated" by educators, physicians, social workers, or even the courts. Often children will not even be evaluated by mental health personnel until one of these other service providers has seen them first. None of these alternative sources of help are capable or knowledgeable enough to treat children in a psychologically appropriate developmental context. Moreover, none of these other sources of help is well equipped to do research or implement research findings. If the distribution of services is ever to be improved, it would seem imperative that closer cooperation between the various service providers be fostered. In the long run, it will be of little practical use to do costly research on the psychological problems of childhood if this research fails to be implemented because of the lack of cooperation and communication between competing social welfare systems.

Adequate Follow-ups

The longitudinal study of high-risk children, discussed in the earlier section on the primary prevention of schizophrenia, is a research approach that should be generalized to other areas of childhood psychopathology. Delinquency, neuroses, and many other problems of childhood will not be understood or prevented until the etiological factors are isolated. For the methodological reasons described earlier, etiological factors are most likely to be isolated in long-term longitudinal studies. In addition, follow-ups of children lasting at least a year and preferably two are of great importance in determining the adequacy of treatments. As we have seen in the case of early educational interventions, even dramatic gains may disappear after the cessation of treatment.

Research Design and Sophistication

Achenbach (1978) points out several impediments to research into the treatment and prevention of psychopathology that must be overcome before substantial further progress can be expected. Perhaps one of the most important problems is the lack of standardized, valid, and reliable measures of normal and abnormal behavior. Researchers tend to use ad hoc measures of dubious validity in their studies, making comparisons across (and even within) research projects impossible. In addition to their failure to develop generally accepted measures, researchers in the field of child psychopathology have used research designs that are rather primitive by today's standards. The need to consider individual variation in such things as IQ, social class, and even sex differences in evaluating treatment methods has often been ignored. Because these and other variables have often been shown to be related to the outcome of psychological treatment, research designs should take such individual differences into

account, as treatments suitable for some types of children may turn out to be unsuitable for others. Finally, in addition to standard measures and sophisticated research designs, research in child psychopathology needs to become more programmatic; one-shot studies using idiosyncratic measures must give way to coordinated research programs if cumulative progress is ever to result.

Child Advocacy

As we have seen throughout this book, children have some basic human needs that are necessary for them to develop both physically and psychologically, but they are virtually powerless to obtain these needs for themselves. For this reason, recent years have seen the development of child advocacy — attempts to guarantee that children's rights and needs are understood and respected.

Children's rights were recognized by the United Nations, who adopted a declaration of human rights for the world's children in 1973. These rights included adequate antenatal care, nutrition, housing, medical care, and recreational opportunities. The declaration went further to state that children have the right to be reared in an atmosphere of affection and emotional security, ideally in their parent's home. Children should be protected from exploitation and commercial gain as well as from discrimination on the basis of race, religion, or any other grounds.

Although virtually everyone would agree with the sentiments embodied in the United Nations declaration, it should be obvious that the resolution has only moral, not legal, force. In order to ensure that the ideals expressed in the declaration of children's rights are realized, some countries have passed laws guaranteeing children's rights. In the United States, it is not only state legislatures (and Congress) that have helped ensure these rights, but also court decisions.

For example, prior to the late 1960s, juvenile offenders in most U.S. courts had no right to legal counsel or even to due process of law. Court decisions changed this situation for young criminal offenders, who must now be given access to legal counsel and proven guilty by the same standards applied to adult offenders. However, many juveniles placed in detention facilities are there not because of criminal behavior, but because their behavior displeases their parents or social authorities (truancy, promiscuity, disobedience). These children are detained in institutions (along with criminal offenders) for behaviors that would not be considered criminal if they were older.

The rationale for detaining such children is that the courts are acting to prevent immature persons from coming to harm while at the same time maintaining family strength and unity (Teitelbaum & Ellis, 1978). Some states have begun to permit teenagers to be treated as adults in certain circumstances (Keniston, 1977). This makes them less vulnerable to protective detention for misbehaviors such as truancy. But it also means that such children are responsible for their own welfare and will be treated as adults for any criminal offences they may commit.

In the United States, court decisions have affected children's rights in many areas. Court decisions involving custody in divorce cases often ignore the wishes of the child (Siegel & Hurley, 1977), and courts have ruled that children can be committed to mental hospitals and other institutions without benefit of independent legal counsel or the right of appeal.

Some laws and decisions have particularly important effects because they guarantee children the opportunity to specific treatment or interventions. Laws guaranteeing public education for every child no matter how handicapped fall into this category. There is no equivalent law regarding children's rights to psychological treatment, but the need to provide such services is widely recognized. Moreover, the need to ensure that children who participate in psychotherapeutic programs have their rights respected has also been noted. Koocher (1976) has even drawn up a "Bill of Rights" for children in psychotherapy (see Table 11.1). Unlike the U.N. resolution, which concentrates on physical

well-being, Koocher's is concerned with children's dignity.

Although we have come a long way in implementing the ideals contained in the United Nations declaration, we still have far to go. Social, community, and individual initiatives (see Edelman, 1981) will have to be mounted in order to change prevailing attitudes. In addition, it will be important *not* to enact laws that drive parents and children unnecessarily apart (Shore, 1979). Finally, it will be necessary, particularly for those in affluent nations, to note that simply obtaining sufficient food and medical care is a never-ending problem for most of the world's children. While American lawyers argue fine points of law before courts, children in Africa, Asia, India, and elsewhere lack the most basic of all human rights — the right to live. Who speaks for them?

Future Trends

This book has covered many topics in a diverse field. Although we have recognized progress in a number of research areas, it is clear that much remains unknown. Attention to the problems noted throughout the book will do much to ensure future progress, but progress is not entirely a function of improved research techniques. As we have noted several times, the field of psychopathology in general and childhood psychopathology in particular does not exist in a cultural vacuum. Changes in the political climate, in the predominant values of society, and in the economic picture exert important effects on the field.

Although the outlook for the future is, as always, unclear, there is reason to suspect that the western world is entering a prolonged and possibly painful period of economic stagnation and even decline. Continued economic prosperity, once taken for granted in industrialized nations, is now no longer a certainty. These economic considerations have forced governments to cut back spending, and costly social welfare programs providing services to children have been particularly hard hit. Although it is difficult and probably foolhardy

TABLE 11.1. A "BILL OF RIGHTS" FOR CHILDREN IN PSYCHOTHERAPY.

1. *The Right to Be Told the Truth.* Children should be informed of events that affect them and should never be lied to by the therapist.

2. *The Right to Be Treated as a Person.* This implies that the child's right to privacy and confidentiality should be respected and the therapist should not divulge information shared by the child in treatment sessions nor should sessions be recorded or observed without the child's knowledge or permission.

3. *The Right to Be Taken Seriously.* The therapist, in particular, should listen carefully to the child and neither dismiss nor make light of the child's observations, opinions, or feelings.

4. *The Right to Participate in Decision Making.* Like adults, children should be allowed to express their opinions in matters involving their lives, and their opinions should carry some weight. Too often adults make the important decisions involving children and only later inform the children. Therapists surely should not behave in this cavalier fashion toward children.

Source: Koocher (1976). © Wiley and reprinted with permission.

to try to predict the future, it seems unlikely that we will again see the ambitious and expensive social engineering programs of the 1960s. Unfortunately, there is no guarantee that only the ineffective programs will be cut back. In a field that is just beginning to develop adequate research methods and to establish a base of knowledge, cutbacks of any kind are almost certain to retard important advances.

One response to the problem of resource allocation is the concept of *networking* (Sarason & Lorentz, 1979). The notion behind networking is that duplication of services and just plain lack of money will prevent all communities from developing the facilities required to cope with the psychological problems of children. However, by sharing resources, communities can eliminate expensive duplication and still provide services to those in need. In certain areas (rural communities, for instance), resource sharing and networking is probably the only way to provide services to children in need.

Even if the economic picture were not a consideration, there are other forces at work that make the launching of large-scale social programs unlikely. Sociocultural explanations for psychological problems have been popular at least since World War II. Recent advances in such fields as behavioral genetics and biochemistry have begun to change the prevailing point of view. Today few researchers hold

the view that psychopathology is entirely a cultural phenomenon; few hold biology solely responsible either. Rather the trend is toward a biopsychological view. Indeed, it can be said that the biopsychological view is now becoming an increasingly prominent model of psychopathology and of medicine in general (Engel, 1977). Recognition of the biopsychological nature of all behavior will eliminate some long-standing quarrels of psychology. It will no longer be necessary to determine whether a problem is biological or psychological, if it is agreed that all are both. Treatment methods will also reflect the contribution of biology and psychology. The general acceptance of such "holistic" approaches to medicine illustrates the new view. It may be that in the years to come books dealing separately with psychopathology and medicine may be largely replaced by books on holistic health.

Before holistic, biopsychological theories become the norm a great deal of additional research is needed on the interface between biology and psychology. Exploration of this interface will likely be the main trend of the future.

SUMMARY

Prevention, although generally acknowledged to be important, has not received as much attention as have other areas of child psychopathology. Large-scale social programs such as the mental hygiene movement and the community mental health center movement have not lived up to their early promise. The adoption of public health approaches to the prevention of psychopathology has been hindered by our dearth of knowledge about the etiology and treatment of most psychopathological problems. Attempts at primary prevention in such areas as education and antisocial behavior have not been notably successful. In some cases — early identification of schizophrenia, for example — a beginning has been made. Secondary prevention has been a more active area than primary prevention because it does not require the ability to predict in advance who will develop psychological problems. Secondary prevention, through early identification and treatment has been attempted with varying degrees of success in the areas of intellectual deficits, disadvantaged children, delinquency, schizophrenia, and crisis intervention. In each area, a great deal remains to be done. Tertiary prevention, or treatment, was discussed at length in Chapter 10. Although tertiary intervention has advanced beyond the other types, problems remain in the uneven distribution of services, the lack of adequate follow-ups, and poor research design. The future is unclear, but it seems clear that large-scale, expensive social programs are things of the past. Small but coordinated projects, the adoption of "holistic" views of functioning, and increasingly sophisticated research are the predominant trends of the future. Increasing militancy among those concerned with children's rights has led to major changes in the way children are treated by the legal, educational, and medical systems. So far, these changes brought about by child advocates have primarily affected American and some other relatively well-off children in western countries. For most of the world's children, simply guaranteeing sufficient food to eat would be a major breakthrough.

SUGGESTED READINGS

Albee, G. W., & Joffe, J. M. (Eds.). (1977). *Primary prevention of psychopathology. Vol. 1. The issues.* Hanover, NH: University Press of New England.

Cowen, E. H., Trost, M. A., Lorion, R. P., Door, D., Izzo, L. D., & Isaacson, R. U. (1975). *New ways in school mental health: Early detection and prevention of school maladaptation.* New York: Human Sciences Press. This book is a detailed description of the Rochester secondary prevention project, a model for other workers and probably the best-documented attempt at secondary prevention in the schools.

Edelman, M. W. (1981). Who is for children? *American Psychologist, 36,* 109–116. This article discusses what is being done and what should be done to safeguard children's rights.

Roberts, M. C. & Peterson, L. (1984). *Prevention of problems in childhood.* New York: Wiley. An excellent edited text which contains chapters by many authorities in the field dealing with the prevention of various forms of childhood problems.

REFERENCES

Abelson, H. I., Fishburne, P. M., & Cisin, I. (1977). *National survey on drug abuse* (Vol. I). Washington, DC: U.S. Government Printing Office.

Abidin, R. (1983). *Parenting stress index: Manual.* Charlottesville, VA: Pediatric Psychology Associates.

Abramowitz, C. V. (1976). The effectiveness of group psychotherapy with children. *Archives of General Psychiatry, 33,* 320–326.

Abt Associates (1976). *Education as experimentation: A planned variation model* (Vol. 3). Boston: Author.

Achenbach, T. M. (1966). The classification of children's psychiatric symptoms: A factor analytic study. *Psychological Monographs, 80,* Whole No. 615.

Achenbach, T. M. (1974). *Developmental psychopathology.* New York: Ronald Press.

Achenbach, T. M. (1978). Developmental aspects of psychopathology in children and adolescents. In M. E. Lamb (Ed.), *Social and personality development.* New York: Holt, Rinehart & Winston.

Achenbach, T. M. (1980). DSM III in light of empirical research on the classification of child psychopathology. *Journal of the American Academy of Child Psychiatry, 19,* 395–412.

Achenbach, T. M. (1981). A junior MMPI? *Journal of Personality Assessment, 45,* 332–333.

Achenbach, T. M. (1982). *Developmental psychopathology* (2nd ed.). New York: Wiley.

Achenbach, T. M., & Edelbrock, C. (1983a). *Manual for the Child Behavior Checklist.* Burlington, VT: Author.

Achenbach, T. M., & Edelbrock, C. S. (1983b). Taxonomic issues in child psychology. In T. Ollendick & M. Hersen (Eds.), *Handbook of child psychopathology.* New York: Plenum.

Ackerman, N. W. (1958). *The psychodynamics of family life.* New York: Basic Books.

Ackerman, A. (1979). *The importance of motivation.* London: Helen Arkell Dyslexia Centre.

Adams, H. E., & Sutker, P. B. (1984). *Comprehensive handbook of psychopathology.* New York: Plenum.

Adams, P. L. (1973). *Obsessive children.* New York: Brunner/Mazel.

Agras, S., & Werne, J. (1977). Behavior modification in anorexia nervosa: Research foundations. In R. A. Vigersky (Ed.), *Anorexia nervosa,* New York: Raven Press.

Aitchison, R. A., & Green, D. R. (1974). A token reinforcement system for large wards of institutionalized adolescents. *Behavior Research and Therapy, 12,* 181–190.

Albee, G. W., & Joffe, J. M. (Eds.). (1977). *Primary prevention of psychopathology* (Vol. 1). Hanover, NH: University Press of New England.

Albert, N., & Beck, A. T. (1975). Incidence of depression in early adolescence: A preliminary study. *Journal of Youth and Adolescence, 4,* 301–307.

Alexander, A. B. (1980). The treatment of psychosomatic disorders: Bronchial asthma in children. In B. Lahey & A. Kazdin (Eds.), *Advances in clinical child psychology.* New York: Plenum.

Alexander, F. (1950). *Psychosomatic medicine.* New York: Norton.

Alford, G. S., Blanchard, E. B., & Buckley, T. M. (1972). Treatment of hysterical vomiting by modification of social contingencies: A case study. *Journal of Behavior Therapy and Experimental Psychiatry, 3,* 209–212.

Allen, K., Hart, B., Buell, S., Harris, R., & Wolf, M. (1964). Effects of social reinforcement on isolate behavior in a nursery school child. *Child Development, 35,* 511–518.

Ambrosini, P. J., & Puig-Antich, J. (1985). Major depression in children and adolescents. In D. Shaffer, A. A. Ehrhardt, & L. Greenhill (Eds.),

The clinical guide to child psychiatry. New York: The Free Press.

American Psychiatric Association (1968). *Diagnostic and statistical manual of mental disorders* (2nd ed.). Washington, DC: Author.

American Psychiatric Association. (1980). *Diagnostic and statistical manual of mental disorders* (3rd ed.). Washington, DC: Author.

American Psychological Association. (1981). Ethical principles of psychologists (revised). *American Psychologist, 36,* 633–638.

Anastasi, A. (1967). Psychology, psychologists, and psychological testing. *American Psychologist, 22,* 297–306.

Ando, H., & Tsuda, K. (1975). Intrafamilial incidence of autism, cerebral palsy and mongolism. *Journal of Autism and Childhood Schizophrenia, 5,* 267–274.

Anonymous. (1977). On being diagnosed schizophrenic. *Schizophrenic Bulletin, 3,* 4.

Anthony, E. J. (1957). An experimental approach to the psychopathology of childhood: Encopresis. *British Journal of Medical Psychology, 30,* 146–175.

Aries, P. (1962). *Centuries of childhood: A social history of family life* (R. Baldick, Trans.). New York: Vintage Books.

Arnold, G., & Schwartz, S. (1983). Hemispheric lateralization of language in autistic and aphasic children. *Journal of Autism and Developmental Disorders, 13,* 129–139.

August, G. J., Stewart, M. A., & Tsai, L. (1981). The incidence of cognitive disabilities in the siblings of autistic children. *British Journal of Psychiatry, 138,* 416–422.

Axelrod, S., Brantner, J. P., & Meddock, T. D. (1978). Overcorrection: A review and critical analysis. *Journal of Special Education, 12,* 367–392.

Axline, V. M. (1947). *Play therapy.* Boston: Houghton Mifflin.

Ayllon, T., & Rosenbaum, M. S. (1977). The behavioral treatment of disruption and hyperactivity in school settings. In B. Lahey & A. Kazdin (Eds.), *Advances in clinical child psychology* (Vol. 1). New York: Plenum.

Ayllon, T., Smith, D., & Rogers, M. (1970). Behavioral management of school phobia. *Journal of Behavior Therapy and Experimental Psychiatry, 1,* 125–128.

Azerrad, J., & Stafford, R. L. (1969). Restoration of eating behavior in anorexia nervosa through operant conditioning and environmental manipulation. *Behavior Research and Therapy, 7,* 165–171.

Azrin, N. H., & Foxx, R. M. (1974). *Toilet training in less than a day.* New York: Simon & Schuster.

Azrin, N. H., & Nunn, R. G. (1974). A rapid method of eliminating stuttering by a regulated breathing approach. *Behavior Research and Therapy, 12,* 279–286.

Azrin, N. H., & Powers, M. A. (1975). Eliminating classroom disturbances of emotionally disturbed children by positive practice procedures. *Behavior Therapy, 6,* 525–534.

Azrin, N. H., Sneed, T. J., & Foxx, R. M. (1974). Dry bed training: Rapid elimination of childhood enuresis. *Behavior Research and Therapy, 12,* 147–156.

Azrin, V. B., Azrin, N. H., & Armstrong, P. M. (1977). The student-oriented classroom: A method of improving student conduct and satisfaction. *Behavior Therapy, 8,* 193–204.

Backman, J., & Firestone, P. (1979). A review of psychopharmacological and behavioral approaches to the treatment of hyperactive children. *American Journal of Orthopsychiatry, 49,* 500–504.

Baer, D. M. (1962). Laboratory control of thumbsucking by withdrawal and representation of reinforcement. *Journal of Experimental Analysis of Behavior, 5,* 528–535.

Baer, D. M., Wolf, M. M., & Risley, T. M. (1968). Some current dimensions of applied behavior analysis. *Journal of Applied Behavior Analysis, 1,* 91–97.

Baker, A. F. (1983). Psychological assessment of autistic children. *Clinical Psychology Review, 3,* 41–49.

Bakwin, H., & Bakwin, R. M. (1972). *Behavior disorders of children* (4th ed.). Philadelphia: Saunders.

Baller, W. R. (1975). *Bedwetting: Origins and treatment.* New York: Pergamon.

Bandura, A. (1971). Psychotherapy based on modeling principles. In A. E. Bergin & S. L. Garfield (Eds.), *Handbook of psychotherapy and behavior change.* New York: Wiley.

Bandura, A. (1973). *Aggression: A social learning approach.* Englewood Cliffs, NJ: Prentice-Hall.

Bandura, A. (1977). *Social learning theory.* Englewood Cliffs, NJ: Prentice-Hall.

Bandura, A. (1981). Self-referent thought: The development of self-efficacy. In J. Flavell & L. Ross (Eds.), *Social cognitive development.* New York: Cambridge University Press.

Bandura, A., Blanchard, E. B., & Ritter, E. (1969). Relative efficacy of desensitization and modeling approaches for inducing behavioral, affective, and attitudinal changes. *Journal of Personality and Social Psychology, 13,* 173–199.

Bandura, A., Grusec, J. E., & Menlove, F. L. (1967). Vicarious extinction of avoidance behavior. *Journal of Personality and Social Psychology, 5,* 16–23.

Bandura, A., & Rosenthal, T. L. (1966). Vicarious classical conditioning as a function of arousal level. *Journal of Personality and Social Psychology, 3*, 54–62.

Bandura, A., & Walters, R. H. (1959). *Adolescent aggression*. New York: Ronald Press.

Bandura, A., & Walters, R. (1963). *Social learning and personality development*. New York: Holt, Rinehart, & Winston.

Barcai, A. (1971). Family therapy in the treatment of anorexia nervosa. *American Journal of Psychiatry, 128*, 286–290.

Bargen, J. A. (1969). *Chronic ulcerative colitis*. Springfield, IL: Charles C Thomas.

Barker, P. (1974). *The residential psychiatric treatment of children*. New York: Wiley.

Barkley, R. A. (1981). *Hyperactive children: A handbook for diagnosis and treatment*. New York: Guilford.

Barlow, D. H., Agras, W. S., & Leitenberg, E. (1967, September). *Control of classical neurotic "symptoms" through reinforcement and nonreinforcement*. Paper presented at the annual meeting of the Association for the Advancement of Behavior Therapy, Washington, DC.

Barlow, D. H., & Hersen, D. H. (1984). *Single case experimental designs*. New York: Pergamon.

Baroff, G. S. (1974). *Mental retardation: Nature, cause and management*. Washington, DC: Hemisphere Publishing.

Barrett, B. H., & Lindsley, O. R. (1962). Deficits in acquisition of operant discrimination and differentiation shown by institutionalized retarded children. *American Journal of Mental Deficiency, 67*, 424–436.

Barrett, C. L., Hampe, E., & Miller, L. C. (1978). Research on psychotherapy with children. In S. L. Garfield & A. E. Bergin (Eds.), *Handbook of psychotherapy and behavior change* (2nd ed.). New York: Wiley.

Bartak, L., Rutter, M., & Cox, A. (1975). A comparative study of infantile autism and specific developmental language disorder. I. The children. *British Journal of Psychiatry, 126*, 127–145.

Barton, E. J., & Ascione, F. R. (1984). Direct observation. In T. Ollendick & M. Hersen (Eds.), *Child behavioral assessment*. New York: Pergamon.

Bassuk, E. L., Schoonover, S. C., & Gelenberg, A. J. (1983). *The practitioner's guide to psychoactive drugs*. New York: Plenum.

Bassuk, E. L., Schoonover, S. C., & Gill, A. D. (1982). *Lifelines: Clinical perspectives on suicide*. New York: Plenum.

Bateson, G., Jackson, D. D., Haley, J., & Weakland, J. H. (1956). Toward a theory of schizophrenia. *Behavioral Science, 1*, 251–264.

Bauer, D. H. (1976). An exploratory study of developmental changes in children's fears. *Journal of Child Psychology and Psychiatry, 17*, 69–74.

Baumeister, A. A. (1967). The effects of dietary control on intelligence in phenylketoneuria. *American Journal of Mental Deficiency, 71*, 840–847.

Baumgarten, F. (1930). *Wunderkinder, psychologishe untersuchungen*. Leipzig: Johann Ambrosius.

Baxter, J. D., Martial, J. A., & Hallwell, R. A. (1979). Human growth hormone: Complementary DNA cloning and expression in bacteria. *Science, 205*, 602–607.

Bayley, N. (1969). *Bayley Scales of Infant Development*. New York: The Psychological Corporation.

Beck, A. T. (1967). *Depression: Clinical, experimental, and theoretical aspects*. New York: Harper & Row.

Beck, A. T. (1974). The development of depression: A cognitive model. In R. J. Friedman & M. M. Katz (Eds.), *The psychology of depression*. Washington, DC: Winston.

Beck, A. T., Ward, C. H., Mendelson, M., Molk, J. E., & Erbaugh, J. K. (1962). Reliability of psychiatric diagnoses 2: A study of consistency of clinical judgements and ratings. *American Journal of Psychiatry, 119*, 351–357.

Beck, S. J., Beck, A. G., Levitt, E. E., & Molish, H. B. (1961). *Rorschach's test, I basic processes* (3rd ed.). New York: Grune & Stratton.

Becker, W. (1971). *Parents are teachers*. Champaign, IL: Research Press.

Beckett, P. G. S., Lennox, K., & Grisell, J. L. (1968). Responsibility and reward in treatment. *Journal of Nervous and Mental Disease, 146*, 257–264.

Beckett, P. G. S., Pearson, C. E., & Rubin, E. (1962). A follow-up study comparing two approaches to the inpatient treatment of adolescent boys. *Journal of Nervous and Mental Disease, 134*, 330–338.

Bee, H. (1978). The effects of poverty. In H. Bee (Ed.), *Social issues in developmental psychology* (2nd ed.). New York: Harper & Row.

Beers, C. (1908). *A mind that found itself*. New York: Longmans, Green.

Begab, M. J. (1981). Frontiers of knowledge in mental retardation. In P. J. Mittler, & J. M. deJong (Eds.), *Frontiers of knowledge in mental retardation: Vol. II. Biomedical aspects*. Baltimore: University Park Press.

Bell, R. Q., & Waldrop, M. F. (1982). Temperament and minor physical anomalies. In Ciba Foundation Symposium Number 89, *Temperamental differences in infants and young children*. London: Pitman Books Ltd.

Bellack, L. (1975). *The TAT and CAT in clinical use* (3rd ed.). New York: Grune & Stratton.

Belmont, J. M. (1966). Long-term memory in mental retardation. In N. R. Ellis (Ed.), *International review of research in mental retardation* (Vol. 1). New York: Academic Press.

Belsky, J. (1980). Child maltreatment: An ecological integration. *American Psychologist, 35,* 320–335.

Bemis, K. M. (1978). Current approaches to the etiology and treatment of anorexia nervosa. *Psychological Bulletin, 85,* 593–617.

Bender, L. (1938). A visual motor Gestalt test and its clinical use. *American Orthopsychiatric Association Research Monograph,* No. 3.

Bentler, P. M. (1962). An infant phobia treated with reciprocal inhibition therapy. *Journal of Child Psychology and Psychiatry, 3,* 185–189.

Bentler, P. M., & Woodward, J. A. (1978). A Head Start re-evaluation: Positive effects are not yet demonstrable. *Evaluation Quarterly, 2,* 493–510.

Berberian, R. M., Gross, C., Lovejoy, J., & Paparella, S. (1976). The effectiveness of drug education programs: A critical review. *Health Education Monographs, 4,* 377–392.

Berecz, J. M. (1968). Phobias of childhood: Etiology and treatment. *Psychological Bulletin, 70,* 694–720.

Berg, I. (1979). Day wetting in children. *Journal of Child Psychology and Psychiatry, 20,* 167–172.

Berger, M. J., & Goldstein, D. P. (1980). Impaired reproductive performance in DES exposed women. *Obstetrics and Gynecology, 55,* 25–27.

Bergin, A. E. (1966). Some implications of psychotherapy research for therapeutic practice. *Journal of Abnormal Psychology, 71,* 235–246.

Bergin, A. E., & Lambert, M. J. (1978). The evaluation of therapeutic outcomes. In S. L. Garfield & A. E. Bergin (Eds.), *Handbook of psychotherapy and behavior change* (2nd ed.). New York: Wiley.

Berman, A., & Siegal, A. A. (1976). A neuropsychological approach to the etiology, prevention and treatment of juvenile delinquency. In A. Davids (Ed.), *Child personality and psychopathology.* New York: Wiley.

Bernal, M. E., & North, J. A. (1978). A survey of parent training manuals. *Journal of Applied Behavior Analysis, 11,* 533–544.

Bernard, J. M. (1981). The divorce myth. *Personnel and Guidance Journal, 60,* 67–71.

Berne, E. (1961). *Transactional analysis in psychotherapy.* New York: Grove Press.

Beskind, H. (1962). Psychiatric inpatient treatment of adolescents: A review of the clinical experience. *Comprehensive Psychiatry, 3,* 354–369.

Bettleheim, B. (1967). *The empty fortress.* New York: Free Press.

Biber, B. (1961). Integration of mental health principles in a school setting. In G. Kaplan (Ed.), *Prevention of mental disorders in children.* New York: Basic Books.

Biber, B., & Franklin, M. (1967). The relevance of developmental and psychodynamic concepts to the education of the preschool child. *Journal of Child Psychiatry, 6,* 5–24.

Binet, A., & Simon, H. (1966). The development of intelligence in children. In J. Rosenblith & W. Allinsmith (Eds.), *The causes of behavior: Readings in child development and educational psychology* (2nd ed.). Boston: Allyn & Bacon.

Birch, H. G., Richardson, S. A., Baird, D., Horobin, G., & Illsley, R. (1970). *Mental subnormality in the community. A clinical and epidemiological study.* Baltimore: Williams & Wilkins.

Blackman, S., Benton, A., & Cove, L. (1965). The effect of imipramine on enuresis. *American Journal of Psychiatry, 120,* 1194.

Blackstock, E. G. (1978). Cerebral asymmetry and the development of early infantile autism. *Journal of Autism and Childhood Schizophrenia, 8,* 339–353.

Blatt, B., & Kaplan, F. (1966). *Christmas in purgatory: A photographic essay in mental retardation.* Boston: Allyn & Bacon.

Bleuler, E. (1950). *Dementia praecox or the group of schizophrenias.* New York: International Universities Press. (Original work published 1911).

Block, J., Jennings, P. H., Harvey, E., & Simpson, E. (1964). Interaction between allergic potential and psychopathology in childhood asthma. *Psychosomatic Medicine, 26,* 307–320.

Blum, G. S. (1960). The Blacky pictures with children. In A. I. Rabin & M. R. Haworth (Eds.), *Projective techniques with children.* New York: Grune & Stratton.

Blumstein, S., Goodglass, H., & Tratter, V. (1975). The reliability of ear advantage in dichotic listening. *Brain and Language, 2,* 226–236.

Boll, T. J. (1973). Effect of age of onset of brain damage on adaptive abilities in children. *Proceedings of the 81st Annual Convention of the American Psychological Association, 8,* 511–512.

Boll, T. J. (1978). Diagnosing brain impairment. In B. Wolman (Ed.), *Clinical diagnosis of mental disorders.* New York: Plenum Press.

Bonvillian, J. D., Nelson, K. E., & Rhyne, J. M. (1981). Sign language and autism. *Journal of Autism and Developmental Disorders, 11,* 125–137.

Bories, J. (Ed.) (1978). *Diagnostic limitations of*

computerized axial tomography. Berlin: Springer-Verlag.

Borison, R. L., Ang, L., Chang, S., Dysken, M., Comaty, J. E., & Davis, J. M. (1982). New pharmacological approaches in the treatment of Tourette's syndrome. In A. J. Friedhoff & T. N. Chase (Eds.), *Gilles de la Tourette syndrome*. New York: Raven.

Borland, B. L., & Heckman, H. K. (1976). Hyperactive boys and their brothers: A 25 year follow-up study. *Archives of General Psychiatry, 33*, 669–675.

Bornstein, B. (1949). Analysis of a phobic child. *Psychoanalytic Study of the Child, 3–4*, 181–226.

Bornstein, P. H., Hamilton, S. B., & Quevillon, R. (1977). Behavior modification by long distance: Demonstration of functional control over disruptive behavior in a rural classroom setting. *Behavior Modification, 1*, 369–389.

Bornstein, P. H., & Quevillon, R. (1976). The effects of a self-instructional package on overactive preschool boys. *Journal of Applied Behavior Analysis, 9*, 178–188.

Boszormenyi-Nagy, I., & Ulrich, D. M. (1981). Contextual family therapy. In A. S. Gurman & D. P. Kniskern (Eds.), *Handbook of family therapy*. New York: Brunner/Mazel.

Boudewyns, P. A., & Shipley, R. H. (1983). *Flooding and implosive therapy*. New York: Plenum.

Boullin, D. J., Coleman, M., O'Brien, R. A., & Rimland, B. (1971). Laboratory predictions of infantile autism based on 5-hydroxitryptamine efflux from blood platelets and their correlation with the Rimland E-2 score. *Journal of Autism and Childhood Schizophrenia, 1*, 63–71.

Bowen, M. (1978). *Family therapy in clinical practice*. New York: Jacob Aronson.

Bowlby, J. (1960). Grief and mourning in early infancy and early childhood. *Psychoanalytic Study of the Child, 15*, 1–32.

Boyd, L. T. (1980). Emotive imagery in the behavioral management of adolescent school phobia: A case approach. *School Psychology Digest, 9*, 186–189.

Bradshaw, J. L., & Nettleton, N. C. (1983). *Human cerebral asymmetry*. Englewood Cliffs, NJ: Prentice-Hall.

Braucht, G. N., Brakarsh, D., Follingstad, D., & Berry, K. L. (1973). Deviant drug use in adolescence: A review of psychosocial correlates. *Psychological Bulletin, 79*, 92–106.

Brazelton, T. B. (1956). Sucking in infancy. *Pediatrics, 17*, 400–404.

Brazier, M. (1964). Stimulation of the hippocampus in man using implanted electrodes. In M. Brazier (Ed.), *Brain function* (Vol. 2). Los Angeles: University of California Press.

Brebner, A., Hallworth, H. J., & Brown, R. I. (1981). *Computer-assisted learning and the handicapped*. In P. J. Mittler & J. M. deJong (Eds.), *Frontiers of knowledge in mental retardation. Vol. I. Social, educational and behavioral aspects*. Baltimore: University Park Press.

Brickner, D., Siebert, J. M., & Casuso, V. (1980). Early intervention. In J. Hogg & P. J. Mittler (Eds.), *Advances in mental handicap research* (Vol. 1). New York: Wiley.

Broadbent, D. E. (1971). *Decision and stress*. London: Academic Press.

Broadhurst, D. D., Edmunds, M., & MacDicken, R. A. (1979). *Early childhood programs and the prevention and treatment of child abuse and neglect* (Report OHDS 79-30198). Washington, DC: National Center on Child Abuse and Neglect.

Broca, P. (1861). Perte de la parole. Ramollissement chronique et destruction partielle du lobe anterieur gauche du cervau. *Bulletin de la Societe d'Anthropologie, 2*, 235–238.

Brody, E. B., & Brody, N. (1976). *Intelligence: Nature, determinants and consequences*. New York: Academic Press.

Broman, S. H., Nichols, P. L., & Kennedy, W. A. (1975). *Preschool IQ: Prenatal and early developmental correlates*. Hillsdale, NJ: Erlbaum.

Bronfenbrenner, U. (1975). Is early intervention effective? In M. Guttentag & E. I. Streuning (Eds.), *Handbook of evaluation research* (Vol. 2). Beverly Hills, CA: Sage.

Brooks, R. B., & Snow, D. L. (1972). Two case illustrations of the use of behavior modification techniques in the school setting. *Behavior Therapy, 3*, 100–103.

Brown, G. W., Birley, J. L., & Wing, J. K. (1972). Influence of family life on the course of schizophrenic disorders: A replication. *British Journal of Psychiatry, 121*, 241–258.

Brown, L., Sherbenow, R. J., & Dollar, S. J. (1982). *Test of Nonverbal Intelligence, A language-free measure of cognitive ability*. Austin, TX: Pro-Ed.

Brown, P., & Elliot, R. (1965). Control of aggression in a nursery school class. *Journal of Experimental Child Psychology, 2*, 103–107.

Bruch, H. (1973). *Eating disorders: Obesity, anorexia nervosa, and the person within*. New York: Basic Books.

Bruch, H. (1977). Psychological antecedents of anorexia nervosa. In R. A. Vigersky (Ed.), *Anorexia nervosa*. New York: Raven.

Bruch, H. (1978). *The golden cage: The enigma of anorexia nervosa*. Cambridge: Harvard University Press.

Brumback, R. A., Dietz-Schmidt, S. G., & Weinberg, W. A. (1977). Depression in children referred to an educational diagnostic center: Diagnosis and treatment and analysis of criteria and literature review. *Diseases of the Nervous System, 38,* 529–535.

Brumback, R. A., Jackoway, M. K., & Weinberg, W. (1980). Relation of intelligence to childhood depression in children referred to an educational diagnostic center. *Perceptual and Motor Skills, 50,* 11–17.

Brumback, R. A., & Weinberg, W. A. (1977). Childhood depression: An explanation of a behavior disorder in children. *Perceptual and Motor Skills, 44,* 911–916.

Bryan, T. H., & Bryan, J. H. (1975). *Understanding learning disabilities.* New York: Alfred Publishing.

Buchsbaum, M. S., & Haier, R. J. (1982). Psychopathology: Biological approaches. *Annual Review of Psychology, 34,* 401–430.

Buchsbaum, M. S., Rigal, F., Coppola, R., Cappelletti, J., King, C., & Johnson, J. (1981). A new system for gray-level surface distribution maps of electrical activity. *Electroencephalography and Clinical Neurophysiology, 53,* 237–242.

Buck, J. N. (1948). The H-T-P test. *Journal of Clinical Psychology, 4,* 151–157.

Burgermeister, B. B., Blum, L. H., & Lorge, I. (1972). *Columbia Mental Maturity Scale* (3rd ed.). New York: Harcourt Brace Jovanovich.

Burks, B. S. (1928). The relative influence of nature and nurture upon mental development: A comparative study of foster parent—foster child resemblance and true parent/true child resemblance. *27th yearbook of the National Society for the Study of Education* (Part I). Bloomington, IL: Public School Publishing.

Burns, R. C., & Kaufman, S. H. (1970). *Kinetic family drawings.* New York: Brunner/Mazel.

Burt, C. (1955). The meaning and assessment of intelligence. *Eugenics Review, 47,* 81–91.

Burt, C. (1966). The genetic determination of differences in intelligence: A study of monozygotic twins reared together and apart. *British Journal of Psychology, 57,* 137–153.

Butcher, B., & Lovaas, O. I. (1968). Use of aversive stimulation in behavior modification. In M. Jones (Ed.), *Miami symposium on the prediction of behavior: Aversive stimulation.* Coral Gables, FL: University of Miami Press.

Butler, N. R., Goldstein, H., & Ross, E. M. (1972). Cigarette smoking in pregnancy: Its influence on birthweight and perinatal mortality. *British Medical Journal, 28,* 127–130.

Butterfield, E. C. (1981). Instructional techniques that produce generalized improvements in cognition. In P. J. Mittler & J. M. deJong (Eds.),

Frontiers of knowledge in mental retardation. Vol. I. Social, educational and behavioral aspects. Baltimore: University Park Press.

Cadonet, R. J. (1978). Psychopathology in adopted away offspring of biologic parents with antisocial behavior. *Archives of General Psychiatry, 35,* 176–184.

Cameron, J. R. (1977). Parental treatment, children's temperament, and risk of childhood behavior problems. *American Journal of Orthopsychiatry, 48,* 140–147.

Cameron, N. (1963). *Personality development and psychopathology.* Boston: Houghton Mifflin.

Camp, B. W., Blom, G. E., Hebert, F., & van Doorninck, W. J. (1977). "Think aloud": A program for developing self-control in young aggressive boys. *Journal of Abnormal Child Psychology, 5,* 157–169.

Campbell, M., Anderson, L. T., Small, A. M., Perry, R., Green, W. H., & Caplan, R. (1982). The effects of haloperidol on learning and behavior in autistic children. *Journal of Autism and Developmental Disorders, 12,* 167–175.

Campbell, M., Green, W. H., Perry, R., & Anderson, L. T. (1983). Pharmacotherapy. In E. Walker & M. Roberts (Eds.), *Handbook of clinical child psychology.* New York: Wiley.

Campbell, S. B. (1976). Hyperactivity: Course and treatment. In A. Davids (Ed.), *Child personality and psychopathology* (Vol. 3). New York: Wiley.

Campbell, S. B. (1983). Developmental perspectives in child psychopathology. In T. Ollendick & M. Hersen (Eds.), *Handbook of child psychopathology.* New York: Plenum.

Cantwell, D. P. (1972). Psychiatric illness in the families of hyperactive children. *Archives of General Psychiatry, 27,* 414–417.

Cantwell, D. P. (1975). Genetic studies of hyperactive children. In R. R. Fieve, D. Rosenthal, & H. Brill (Eds.), *Genetic research in psychiatry.* Baltimore: Johns Hopkins University Press.

Cantwell, D. P. (1976). Genetic factors in the hyperactive syndrome. *Journal of the American Academy of Child Psychiatry, 15,* 214–223.

Cantwell, D. P. (1978). Hyperactivity and antisocial behavior. *Journal of the American Academy of Child Psychiatry, 17,* 252–262.

Cantwell, D. P. (1982). Childhood depression: A review of current research. In B. Lahey & A. Kazdin (Eds.), *Advances in clinical child psychology* (Vol. 5). New York: Plenum.

Cantwell, D. P. (1985). Organization and use of DSM III. In D. Shaffer, A. A. Erhardt & L. L. Greenhill (Eds.), *The clinical guide to child psychiatry.* New York: The Free Press.

Cantwell, D. P., Mattison, R., Russell, A. T., & Will, L. (1979). A comparison of DSM II and

DSM III in the diagnosis of childhood psychiatric disorders: Difficulties in use, global comparisons and conclusions. *Archives of General Psychiatry, 36*, 1227–1228.

Caplan, D., & Chomsky, N. (1980). Linguistic perspectives on language development. In D. Caplan (Ed.), *Biological studies of mental processes*. Cambridge, MA: MIT Press.

Caplan, G. (1964). *Principles of preventive psychiatry*. New York: Basic Books.

Carlson, G. A., & Cantwell, D. P. (1980). A survey of depressive symptoms, syndrome and disorder in a child psychiatric population. *Journal of Child Psychology and Psychiatry, 21*, 19–25.

Carlson, G. A., & Cantwell, D. P. (1982). Suicidal behavior and depression in children and adolescents. *Journal of the American Academy of Child Psychiatry, 21*, 361–368.

Carr, A. T. (1970). *A psychophysiological study of ritual behavior and decision processes in compulsive neurosis*. Unpublished doctoral dissertation, University of Birmingham, England.

Carr, A. T. (1974). Compulsive neurosis: A review of the literature. *Psychological Bulletin, 81*, 311–318.

Carr, J. (1975). *Young children with Down's syndrome. Their development, upbringing and effect on their families*. London: Butterworth.

Carson, T. P., & Carson, R. C. (1984). The affective disorders. In H. E. Adams & P. B. Sutker (Eds.), *Comprehensive handbook of psychopathology*. New York: Plenum.

Carter, C. H. (1970). *Handbook of mental retardation syndromes*. Springfield, IL: Charles C Thomas.

Cartledge, G., & Milburn, J. F. (1980). *Teaching social skills to children*. New York: Pergamon.

Casper, R. C., Eckert, E. D., Halmi, K. A., Goldberg, S. C., & Davis, J. M. (1980). Bulimia: Its incidence and clinical importance in patients with anorexia nervosa. *Archives of General Psychiatry, 37*, 1030–1035.

Casteneda, A., McCandless, B. R., & Palermo, D. S. (1956). The children's form of the Manifest Anxiety Scale. *Child Development, 27*, 317–326.

Cavior, N., & Deutsch, A. M. (1975). Systematic desensitization to reduce dream induced anxiety. *Journal of Nervous and Mental Disease, 161*, 433–435.

Cavior, N., & Dockecki, P. R. (1973). Physical attractiveness, perceived attitude similarity and academic achievement as contributors to interpersonal attractiveness among adolescents. *Developmental Psychology, 9*, 44–54.

Chapman, A. H., & Loeb, D. G. (1955). Psychosomatic gastrointestinal problems. *Journal of Diseases in Children, 92*, 717–724.

Chess, S. (1971). Autism in children with congenital rubella. *Journal of Autism and Childhood Schizophrenia, 1*, 33–47.

Chiarenza, G. A., & Papakostopoulous, D. (1982). *Clinical application of cerebral evoked potentials in pediatric medicine*. Amsterdam: Excerpta Medica.

Chinn, P. C., Drew, C. J., & Logan, D. R. (1979). *Mental retardation: A life cycle approach* (2nd ed.). St. Louis: Mosby.

Chipman, H. H. (1981). Understanding language retardation: A developmental perspective. In P. J. Mittler, & J. M. deJong (Eds.), *Frontiers of knowledge in mental retardation. Vol. I. Social, educational and behavioral aspects*. Baltimore: University Park Press.

Chodoff, P., & Lyons, H. (1958). Hysteria, the hysterical personality and "hysterical" conversion. *American Journal of Psychiatry, 114*, 734–740.

Chomsky, N. (1965). *Aspects of the theory of syntax*. Cambridge, MA: MIT Press.

Christopherson, E. R., & Rapoff, M. A. (1983). Toileting problems in children. In E. Walker & M. Roberts (Eds.), *Handbook of clinical child psychology*. New York: Wiley.

Cicchetti, D., Taraldson, B. J., & Egeland, B. (1978). Perspectives in the treatment and understanding of child abuse. In A. P. Goldstein (Ed.), *Perscriptions for child mental health and education*. New York: Pergamon.

Clarizio, H. F., & McCoy, G. F. (1983). *Behavior disorders in children* (3rd ed.). New York: Crowell.

Cleland, C. C. (1978). *Mental retardation: A developmental approach*. Englewood Cliffs, NJ: Prentice-Hall.

Clement, P. W., Fazzone, R. A., & Goldstein, B. (1970). Tangible reinforcers and child group therapy. *Journal of the American Academy of Child Psychiatry, 9*, 409–427.

Clement, P. W., & Milne, D. C. (1967). Group play therapy and tangible reinforcers used to modify the behavior of 8-year-old boys. *Behavior Research and Therapy, 5*, 301–312.

Clement, P. W., Roberts, P. V., & Lantz, C. E. (1970). Social models and token reinforcement in the treatment of shy, withdrawn boys. *Proceeding of the 78th Annual Convention of the American Psychological Association*. Washington, DC: American Psychological Association.

Clemow, L. P., King, A. R., & Brantley, P. H. (1984). Psychological factors in childhood illness. In H. Adams & P. Sutker (Eds.), *Comprehensive handbook of psychopathology*. New York: Plenum.

Clifford, M. M. (1975). Physical attractiveness and academic performance. *Child Study Journal, 5*, 201–209.

Cloward, R., & Ohlin, L. (1969). *Delinquency and opportunity*. Glencoe, IL: Free Press.

Clowes-Hollins, & King, N. (1982). Parents and siblings as behavior modifiers in the control of a common developmental problem (thumbsucking). *Journal of Clinical Child Psychology, 11*, 231–233.

Cohen, H. J., & Filipczak, J. (1971). *A new learning environment*. San Francisco: Jossey-Bass.

Cohen, H., & Weil, G. R. (1971). *Tasks of emotional development*. Lexington, MA: Heath.

Cohen, R., Montey, H., & Williams, D. (1980). Management of thumbsucking using self-recording with parent as observer and experimenter. *Perceptual and Motor Skills, 50*, 136.

Cohen-Sandler, R., Berman, A. L., & King, R. A. (1982). Life stress and symptomatology: Determinants of suicidal behavior in children. *Journal of the American Academy of Child Psychiatry, 21*, 178–186.

Cole, S. (1975). Hyperkinetic children: The use of stimulant drugs evaluated. *American Journal of Orthopsychiatry, 45*, 28–36.

Coleman, J., Butcher, J., & Carson, R. C. (1984). *Abnormal psychology and modern life* (7th ed.). Glenview, IL: Scott Foresman.

Coleman, J. S. (1966). *Equality of educational opportunity*. Washington, DC: U.S. Office of Education.

Coleman, M. (1976). *The autistic syndromes*. Amsterdam: North Holland.

Coltheart, M. (1980). Deep dyslexia: A right hemisphere hypothesis. In M. Coltheart, K. Patterson, & J. C. Marshall (Eds.), *Deep dyslexia*. London: Routledge & Kegan Paul.

Combs, M. L., & Slaby, D. A. (1977). Social skills training with children. In B. Lahey & A. Kazdin (Eds.), *Advances in clinical child psychology* (Vol. 1). New York: Plenum.

Commons, M. L., Richards, F. A., & Armon, C. (Eds). (1983). *Beyond formal operations: Late adolescent and adult cognitive development*. New York: Praeger.

Connell, H. M. (1972). Depression in childhood. *Child Psychiatry and Human Development, 4*, 71–85.

Conners, C. K. (1980). *Food additives and hyperactive children*. New York: Plenum.

Corbett, J., Harris, R., Taylor, E., & Trimble, M. (1977). Progressive disintegrative psychosis of childhood. *Journal of Child Psychology and Psychiatry, 18*, 211–220.

Cotman, C., & Nieto-Sampedro, M. (1982). Brain function, synapse renewal and plasticity. *Annual Review of Psychology, 33*, 371–402.

Cowen, E. L., Gardner, E. A., & Zax, M. (1967). *Emergent approaches to mental health problems*. New York: Appleton-Century-Crofts.

Cowen, E. L., Gesten, E., & Wilson, A. B. (1979). The Primary Mental Health Project (PMHP): Evaluation of current program effectiveness. *American Journal of Community Psychology, 7*, 293–303.

Cowen, E. L., Trost, M. A., Lorion, R. P., Door, D., Izzo, L. D., & Issacson, R. U. (1975). *New ways in school mental health: Early detection and prevention of school maladaptation*. New York: Human Sciences Press.

Cox, A., Rutter, M., Newman, S., & Bartak, L. (1975). A comparative study of infantile autism and specific developmental language disorder: II. Parental characteristics. *British Journal of Psychiatry, 126*, 146–159.

Cox, F. N. (1953). Socioeconomic status and individual adjustment before and after play therapy. *Journal of Abnormal and Social Psychology, 44*, 354–356.

Creer, T. L., & Miklich, D. R. (1970). The application of a self-modeling procedure to modify inappropriate behavior: A preliminary report. *Behavior Research and Therapy, 8*, 91–92.

Crisp, A. H. (1982). Anorexia nervosa at normal body weight: The abnormal-normal weight control syndrome. *International Journal of Psychiatry in Medicine, 11*, 203–233.

Crisp, A. H., Harding, B., & McGuinness, B. (1974). Anorexia nervosa: Psychoneurotic characteristics of parents: Relationship to prognosis. *Journal of Psychosomatic Research, 18*, 167–173.

Crisp, A. H., Kalucy, R. S., Lacey, J. H., & Harding, B. (1977). The long-term prognosis in anorexia nervosa: Some factors predictive of outcome. In R. A. Vigersky (Ed.), *Anorexia nervosa*. New York: Raven Press.

Crisp, A. H., Palmer, R. L., & Kalucy, R. S. (1976). How common is anorexia nervosa? A prevalence study. *British Journal of Psychiatry, 128*, 549–554.

Critchley, M., & Critchley, E. A. (1978). *Dyslexia defined*. Springfield, IL: Charles C Thomas.

Croghan, L., & Musante, G. (1975). The elimination of a boy's high-building phobia by in vivo desensitization and game playing. *Journal of Behavior Therapy and Experimental Psychiatry, 6*, 87–88.

Crome, L., & Stern, J. (1967). *The pathology of mental retardation*. London: Churchill.

Cronbach, L. J. (1975). Five decades of public controversy over mental testing. *American Psychologist, 80*, 1–14.

Crossman, S. M., & Adams, G. R. (1980). Divorce, single parenting and child development. *Journal of Psychology, 106*, 205–217.

Crow, R. R. (1974). An adoption study of antisocial personality. *Archives of General Psychiatry, 37*, 785–791.

Crowther, J. H., Bond, L. A., & Rolf, J. E. (1981). The incidence, prevalence, and severity of behavior disorders among preschool-age children in day care. *Journal of Abnormal Child Psychology, 9,* 23–42.

Cruickshank, W. M. (1977). Myths and realities of learning disabilities. *Journal of Learning Disabilities, 10,* 51–58.

Cruickshank, W. M., Bentzen, F. A., Ratzeburg, F. H., & Tannhauser, M. T. (1961). *A teaching method for brain injured and hyperactive children.* Syracuse, NY: Syracuse University Press.

Crumley, F. E. (1979). Adolescent suicide attempts. *Journal of the American Medical Association, 241,* 2504–2407.

Cushing, F. C., & Baller, W. R. (1976). The problem of nocturnal enuresis in adults: Special reference to managers and managerial aspirants. *Journal of Psychology, 89,* 203–213.

Cytryn, L., & McKnew, D. H. (1972). Proposed classification of childhood depression. *American Journal of Psychiatry, 129,* 63–68.

Cytryn, L., McKnew, D. H., & Bunny, W. E. (1980). Diagnosis of depression in children: A reassessment. *American Journal of Psychiatry, 137,* 22–25.

Cytryn, L., McKnew, D. H., Logue, M., & Desai, R. B. (1974). Biochemical correlates of affective disorders in children. *Archives of General Psychiatry, 31,* 659–661.

Dahlem, N. W., Kinsman, R. A., & Horton, D. J. (1977). Requests for as-needed (PRN) medications by asthmatic patients. *Journal of Allergy and Clinical Immunology, 60,* 295–300.

Dahlstrom, W. G., Welsh, G. W., & Dahlstrom, L. E. (1975a). *An MMPI handbook. Vol. 1. Clinical interpretation* (rev. ed.). Minneapolis: University of Minnesota Press.

Dahlstrom, W. G., Welsh, G. W., & Dahlstrom, L. E. (1975b). *An MMPI handbook. Vol. 2. Research developments and applications.* Minneapolis: University of Minnesota Press.

Dally, P. J. (1969). *Anorexia nervosa.* New York: Grune & Stratton.

Dally, P. J., & Sargent, W. (1966). Treatment and outcome of anorexia nervosa. *British Medical Journal, 2,* 793–795.

Dangel, R. F., & Polster, R. A. (1984). *Parent training.* New York: Guilford.

Darby, J. K. (1976). Neuropsychological aspects of psychosis in children. *Journal of Autism and Childhood Schizophrenia, 6,* 339–352.

Das, J. P. (1971). Visual search, stimulus interval and subnormal intelligence. *American Journal of Mental Deficiency, 16,* 357–361.

Daum, F., Boley, S. J., & Cohen, M. I. (1973). Inflammatory bowel disease in the adolescent patient. *Pediatric Clinics of North America, 20,* 933–944.

David, O. J. (1974). Association between lower level lead concentrations and hyperactivity in children. *Environmental Health Perspectives, 7,* 17–25.

David, O. J., Hoffman, S. P., Sverd, J., & Clark, J. (1977). Lead and hyperactivity: Lead levels among hyperactive children. *Journal of Abnormal Child Psychology, 5,* 405–410.

David, O. J., Hoffman, S. P., Sverd, J., Clark, J., & Voeller, K. (1976). Lead and hyperactivity. Behavioral response to chelation: A pilot study. *American Journal of Psychiatry, 133,* 1155–1158.

Davids, A. (1973). *Issues in abnormal child psychology.* Monterey, CA: Brooks/Cole.

Davidson, P. O. (1970). Thumbsucking. In C. G. Costello (Ed.), *Symptoms of psychopathology.* New York: Wiley.

Davis, J. A. (1965). *Education for positive mental health: A review of existing research and recommendations for future studies.* Chicago: Aldine.

Davison, G. C., & Neal, J. M. (1974). *Abnormal psychology.* New York: Wiley.

Dawson, J. (1954). Pulmonary tuberous sclerosis: Relationship to other forms of disease. *Quarterly Journal of Medicine, 23,* 113–145.

Deffenbacher, J., & Kemper, C. (1974). Counseling test-anxious sixth-graders. *Elementary School Guidance and Counseling, 9,* 22–29.

Déjerine, J. (1892). Des differentes varieties de cecite verbale. *Memoires de la Societe de Biologie, 27* Feb., 1–30.

Delamater, A. M., Rosenbloom, N., Connors, C. K., & Hertweck, L. (1983). The behavioral treatment of hysterical paralysis in a ten-year-old boy: A case study. *Journal of the American Academy of Child Psychiatry, 22,* 73–79.

Delecato, C. H. (1966). *Neurological organization and reading.* Springfield, IL: Charles C Thomas.

DeLeon, G., & Mandell, W. (1966). A comparison of conditioning and psychotherapy in the treatment of enuresis. *Journal of Clinical Psychology, 22,* 326–330.

DeMyer, M. K., Barton, S., DeMyer, W. E., Norton, J. A., Allen, J., & Steele, R. (1973). Prognosis in autism: A follow-up study. *Journal of Autism and Childhood Schizophrenia, 3,* 199–246.

DeMyer, M. K., Hingtgen, J. N., & Jackson, R. K. (1981). Infantile autism reviewed: A decade of research. *Schizophrenia Bulletin, 7,* 388–351.

Denny, M. R. (1966). A theoretical analysis and its application to training the mentally retarded. In N. Ellis (Ed.), *International review of research in mental retardation* (Vol. 2). New York: Academic Press.

Deno, E. (1970). Special education as developmental capital. *Exceptional Children, 37,* 229–237.

Department of Health, Education and Welfare. (1978). *Protection of human subjects: Research involving children* (Regulations 31786-31794). Washington, DC: Federal Register (Vol. 43, No. 141).

DeSanctis, S. (1908). Dementia precocissima. *Folio Neuro-biologica, 2,* 9–23.

DesLauriers, A. M., & Carlson, C. F. (1969). *Your child is asleep: Early infantile autism.* Homewood, IL: Dorsey Press.

DeWitt, K. N. (1978). The effectiveness of family therapy. *Archives of General Psychiatry, 35,* 549–561.

Deykin, E. Y., & MacMahon, B. (1980). Pregnancy, delivery and neonatal complications among autistic children. *American Journal of Diseases of Children, 134,* 860–864.

Diener, E., & Crandall, R. (1978). *Ethics in social and behavioral research.* Chicago: University of Chicago Press.

Dingman, H. F., & Tarjan, G. (1960). Mental retardation and the normal distribution curve. *American Journal of Mental Deficiency, 64,* 991–994.

Dinkmeyer, D., & McKay, G. D. (1976). *Systematic training for effective parenting.* Circle Pines, MN: American Guidance Service.

Dirks, J. F., Kinsman, R. A., Horton, R. J., Fross, K. H., & Jones, N. F. (1978). Panic-fear in asthma: Rehospitalization following intensive long-term treatment. *Psychosomatic Medicine, 40,* 5–13.

Dirks, J. F., Nelson, M. D., Jones, N., & Kinsman, R. A. (1977). Panic-fear: A personality dimension related to intractability in asthma. *Psychosomatic Medicine, 39,* 123–125.

Dishion, T. J., Loeber, R., Stouthamer-Loeber, M., & Patterson, G. R. (1984). Skills deficits and male adolescent delinquency. *Journal of Abnormal Child Psychology, 12,* 37–54.

Dobson, J. C. (1976). Intellectual performance of 36 phenylketonuria patients and their non-affected siblings. *Pediatrics, 58,* 53–58.

Doleys, D. M. (1983). Enuresis and encopresis. In T. H. Ollendick & M. Hersen (Eds.), *Handbook of child psychopathology.* New York: Plenum.

Doll, E. (1965). *Vineland Social Maturity Scale: Manual of directions* (rev. ed.). Minneapolis: Educational Test Bureau.

Dollard, J., Doob, L. W., Miller, N. E., Mower, O. H., & Sears, R. R. (1939). *Frustration and aggression.* New Haven: Yale University Press.

Dollard, J., & Miller, N. (1950). *Personality and psychotherapy.* New York: McGraw-Hill.

Dollinger, S. J. (1983). Childhood neuroses. In E. Walker & M. Roberts (Eds.) *Handbook of clinical child psychology.* New York: Wiley.

Dorfman, D. D. (1978). The Cyril Burt question. *Science, 210,* 1177–1185.

Dorfman, E. (1958). Personality outcomes of client-centered child therapy. *Psychological Monographs, 72,* No. 456.

Douglas, V. I., Parry, P., Marton, P., & Garson, L. (1976). Assessment of a cognitive training program for hyperactive children. *Journal of Abnormal Child Psychology, 4,* 389–411.

Douglas, V. I., & Peters, K. G. (1979). Toward a clearer definition of the attentional deficit of hyperactive children. In G. A. Hale & M. Lewis (Eds.), *Attention and the development of cognitive skills.* New York: Plenum.

Dowrick, P. W., & Dove, C. (1980). The use of self-modeling to improve the swimming performance of spina bifida children. *Journal of Applied Behavior Analysis, 13,* 51–56.

Drake, E. A. (1979). Helping the school cope with the children of divorce. *Journal of Divorce, 3,* 69–75.

Drillen, C. M. (1964). *The growth and development of the prematurely born infant.* Baltimore: William & Wilkins.

Drotar, D. (1981). Psychological perspectives in chronic childhood illness. *Journal of Pediatric Psychology, 6,* 211–227.

Drummond, C. (1983, June 1). A family in the shadow of an autistic child. *The Australian,* p. 7.

Dubey, D. T. (1976). Organic factors in hyperkinesis: A critical evaluation. *American Journal of Orthopsychiatry, 46,* 353–366.

Dubois, P. W. (1939). A test standardized on Pueblo Indian children. *Psychological Bulletin, 36,* 523.

Duckworth, J. (1979). *MMPI interpretation manual for counselors and clinicians.* Muncie, IN: Accelerated Development.

Dumaresq, M. (1976). *The relationship of stimulus organization, response cueing and practice to free recall performance of learning disabled children.* Unpublished doctoral dissertation, University of Oregon, Eugene.

Dunlop, D. B., & Dunlop, P. (1981). Orthoptic assessment of children with learning disabilities. *Australian Journal of Opthalmology,* 113–116.

Dunn, L. M., & Dunn, L. M. (1981). *Peabody Picture Vocabulary Test-Revised.* Circle Pines, MN: American Guidance Service.

Dunn, L. M., & Markwardt, F. C., Jr. (1970). *The Peabody Individual Achievement Test.* Circle Pines, MN: American Guidance Service.

Dupont, A. (1981). Medical results from registration of Danish mentally retarded children. In P. J. Mittler & J. M. deJong (Eds.), *Frontiers of knowledge in mental retardation: Vol. II. Biomedical aspects.* Baltimore: University Park Press.

Earls, F. (1981). Temperament characteristics and behavior problems in three-year-old children. *The Journal of Nervous and Mental Disease, 169,* 367–374.

Edelman, M. W. (1981). Who is for children? *American Psychologist, 36,* 109–116.

Edelson, S. R. (1966). A dynamic formulation of childhood schizophrenia. *Diseases of the Nervous System, 27,* 610–615.

Edwards, J. L., Shigley, R. H., & Edwards, R. P. (1976). A case report of an autistic boy: Selective responding to components of bidimensional visual and auditory stimuli. *Journal of Autism and Childhood Schizophrenia, 6,* 139–146.

Eisenberg, L. (1958). School phobia: A study in the communication of anxiety. *American Journal of Psychiatry, 114,* 712–718.

Eisenberg, L., Lachman, R., Molling, P., Lockner, A., Mizelle, J., & Conners, C. A. (1963). A psychopharmacologic experiment in a training school for delinquent boys. *American Journal of Orthopsychiatry, 33,* 431–447.

Elliot, D. S., & Ageton, S. S. (1980). Reconciling race and class differences in self-reported and official estimates of delinquency. *American Sociological Review, 45,* 45–110.

Ellis, N. R. (1970). Mental processes in retardates and normals. In N. R. Ellis (Ed.), *International review of research in mental retardation* (Vol. 4). New York: Academic Press.

Ellis, P. L. (1982). Empathy: A factor in antisocial behavior. *Journal of Abnormal Child Psychology, 10,* 123–134.

Eme, R., & Schmidt, D. (1978). The stability of children's fears. *Child Development, 49,* 1277–1279.

Emmelkamp, P. M. (1982). *Phobic and obsessive compulsive disorders.* New York: Plenum.

Empey, L. T. (1978). *American delinquency: Its meaning and construction.* Homewood, IL: Dorsey.

Engel, G. L. (1977). The need for a new medical model: A challenge for biomedicine. *Science, 196,* 129–136.

Englemann, S. E., & Bruner, E. C. (1974). *DISTAR reading level 1.* Chicago: Science Research Associates.

Erickson, M. T. (1978). *Child psychopathology.* Englewood Cliffs, NJ: Prentice-Hall.

Erikson, J. M. (1976). *Activity, recovery and growth.* New York: Norton.

Erlenmyer-Kimling, L., Cornblatt, B., & Golden, R. R. (1983). Early indicators of vulnerability to schizophrenia in children at high genetic risk. In S. B. Guze, F. J. Earls, & J. E. Barrett (Eds.), *Childhood psychopathology and development.* New York: Raven.

Ernst, A. R., Routh, D. K., & Harper, D. C. (1984). Abdominal pain in children and symptoms of somatization disorder. *Journal of Pediatric Psychology, 9,* 77–86.

Ernst, C., & Angst, J. (1983). *Birth order: Its influence on personality.* New York: Springer-Verlag.

Eron, L. D., & Huesmann, L. R. (1984). Television violence and aggressive behavior. In B. Lahey & A. Kazdin (Eds.), *Advances in clinical child psychology* (Vol. 7). New York: Plenum.

Ettenger, R. B., Korsch, B. M., Main, M. E., & Fine, R. N. (1979). Renal rehabilitation of children and adolescents with end-stage renal disease. In S. B. Chyatte (Ed.), *Rehabilitation in chronic renal failure.* Baltimore: Williams & Wilkins.

Evans, R. I. (1978). Deterring the onset of smoking in children: Knowledge of immediate physiological effects and coping with peer pressure, media pressure and parental modeling. *Journal of Applied Psychology, 8,* 126–135.

Exner, J. (1974–1978). *The Rorschach: A comprehensive system.* 2 vols. New York: Wiley.

Exner, J. E., & Weiner, I. (1982). *The Rorschach: A comprehensive system* (Vol. 3). New York: Wiley.

Eyberg, S., & Ross, A. W. (1978). Assessment of child behavior problems: The validation of a new inventory. *Journal of Clinical Child Psychology, 7,* 113–116.

Eyman, P. K., & Begab, M. J. (1981). Relationship between foster home environments and resident changes in adaptive behavior. In P. J. Mittler & J. M. deJong (Eds.), *Frontiers of knowledge in mental retardation. Vol. I. Social, educational and behavioral aspects.* Baltimore: University Park Press.

Eysenck, H. J. (1947). *Dimensions of personality.* London: Routledge & Kegan Paul.

Eysenck, H. J. (1952). The effects of psychotherapy: An evaluation. *Journal of Consulting Psychology, 16,* 319–324.

Eysenck, H. J. (1956). The inheritance of extraversion-introversion. *Acta Psychologica, 12,* 95–110.

Eysenck, H. J. (1960). *Handbook of abnormal psychology.* London: Pittman.

Eysenck, H. J., & Prell, D. B. (1951). The inheritance of neuroticism: An experimental study. *Journal of Mental Science, 97,* 441–465.

Eysenck, H. J., & Rachman, S. T. (1971). The application of learning theory to child psychiatry. In T. C. Howells (Ed.), *Modern perspectives in child psychiatry.* New York: Brunner/Mazel, 1971.

Fanaroff, A., Kennell, J., & Klaus, M. (1972). Follow-up of low birth weight infants: The predictive value of maternal visiting patterns. *Pediatrics, 49,* 287–290.

Farley, F. A. (1973). *A theory of delinquency*. Paper presented at the American Psychological Association annual convention, Montreal.

Farley, F. A., & Farley, S. V. (1972). Stimulus seeking motivation and delinquent behavior among institutionalized delinquent girls. *Journal of Consulting and Clinical Psychology, 39*, 94–97.

Farley, F. A., & Sewell, T. (1976). Test of an arousal theory of delinquency: Stimulation seeking in delinquent and nondelinquent black adolescents. *Criminal Justice and Behavior, 3*, 315–320.

Farley, F. A., Steinberger, H., Cohen, A., & Barr, H. L. (1979). Test of a theory of delinquency: Delinquent behaviors among institutionalized drug addicts as a function of arousal and the sensation seeking motive. *Criminal Justice and Behavior, 6*, 41–48.

Farnahm-Diggory, S. (1978). *Learning disabilities*. London: Fontana/Open Books.

Farquharson, R. F., & Hyland, H. H. (1964). Anorexia nervosa: A metabolic disorder of psychological origin. In M. R. Kaufman & M. Heiman (Eds.), *Evolution of psychosomatic concepts*. New York: International Universities Press.

Faschingbauer, T. F. (1975). Enuresis: Its nature, etiology, and treatment. *JSAS: Catalog of Selected Documents in Psychology, 5*, 194.

Federal Bureau of Investigation (1978). *Uniform crime reports*. Washington, DC: U.S. Department of Justice.

Fein, D., Humes, M., Kaplan, E., Lucci, D., & Waterhouse, L. (1984). The question of left hemisphere dysfunction in infantile autism. *Psychological Bulletin, 95*, 258–281.

Fein, G. G., Schwartz, S., Jacobson, S. W., & Jacobson, J. L. (1983). Environmental toxins and behavioral development. *American Psychologist, 38*, 1188–1197.

Feingold, B. F. (1975). *Why your child is hyperactive*. New York: Random House.

Feldman, F., Cantor, D., Soll, S., & Bachrach, W. (1967). Psychiatric study of a consecutive series of 34 patients with ulcerative colitis. *British Medical Journal, 3*, 14–17.

Felner, R. D., Farber, S. S., & Primavera, J. (1980). Children of divorce, stressful life events and transitions. In R. H. Price, R. H. Ketterer, B. C. Bader, & J. Monahan (Eds.), *Prevention in mental health*. Beverly Hills, CA: Sage.

Fenichel, O. (1946). *The psychoanalytic theory of neuroses*. London: Routledge & Kegan Paul.

Ferster, C. B. (1961). Positive reinforcement and behavioral deficits of autistic children. *Child Development, 32*, 437–456.

Ferster, C. B. (1974). Behavioral approaches to depression. In R. J. Friedman & M. M. Katz (Eds.), *The psychology of depression: Contemporary theory and research*. Washington, DC: Winston.

Feuerstein, M., Ward, M. M., & Le Baron, S. W. (1979). Neuropsychological and neurophysiological assessment of children with learning and behavior problems. In B. Lahey & A. Kazdin (Eds.), *Advances in clinical child psychology*. (Vol. 2). New York: Plenum.

Field, T. M., Goldberg, S., Stern, D., & Sostek, A. M. (Eds.). (1980). *High risk infants and children*. New York: Academic Press.

Finch, A. J., & Rogers, T. R. (1984). Self report instruments. In T. Ollendick & M. Hersen (Eds.), *Child behavioral assessment*. New York: Pergamon.

Finch, S. M. (1980). Psychological factors affecting physical condition (psychosomatic disorders). In H. I. Kaplan, A. M. Freedman, & B. J. Sadock (Eds.), *Comprehensive textbook of psychiatry III*. Baltimore: Williams & Wilkins.

Finch, S. M., & Hess, J. H. (1962). Ulcerative colitis in children. *American Journal of Psychiatry, 118*, 819–826.

Fine, R. N., Malekzadeh, M. H., Pennisi, A., Ettenger, R., Uittenbogaart, C. H., Negrete, V. F., & Korsch, B. M. (1978). Long term results of renal transplantation in children. *Pediatrics, 61*, 641–650.

Firestone, P. (1976). The effects and side effects of time-out on an aggressive nursery school child. *Journal of Behavior Therapy and Experimental Psychiatry, 6*, 79–81.

Firestone, P., & Prabhu, A. N. (1983). Minor physical anomalies and obstetrical complications: Their relationship to hyperactive and normal children and their families. *Journal of Abnormal Child Psychology, 11*, 207–216.

Firkowska, A., Ostrowska, A., Sokolowska, M., Stein, F., Susser, M., & Wald, I. (1978). Cognitive development and social policy. *Science, 2002*, 1357–1362.

Fishburne, P., Abelson, H., & Cisin, L. (1980). *The national survey on drug abuse: Main findings 1979*. Washington, DC: U.S. Government Printing Office.

Fishler, K., & Fogel, B. (1973). *Psychological correlates in children with ulcerative colitis*. Paper presented at the annual meeting of the American Psychological Association, Montreal.

Fixsen, D. L., Phillips, E. L., & Wolf, M. M. (1973). Achievement Place: Experiments in self-government with pre-delinquents. *Journal of Applied Behavior Analysis, 6*, 31–48.

Fixsen, D. L., Phillips, E. L., & Wolf, M. M. (1978). The teaching-family model: An example of mission-oriented research. In A. C. Catania & T. A. Brigham (Eds.), *Handbook of applied behavior analysis: Social and instruc-*

tional processes. New York: Irvington Press.

Fixsen, D. L., Wolf, M. M., & Phillips, E. L. (1973). Achievement Place: A teaching-family model of community based group homes for youth in trouble. In L. Hammerlynck, L. Handy, & E. Mash (Eds.), *Behavior change: Methodology, concepts, and practice.* Champaign, IL: Research Press.

Foa, E. B., Steketee, G., & Milby, J. B. (1980). Differential effects of exposure and response prevention in obsessive compulsive washers. *Journal of Consulting and Clinical Psychology, 48,* 71–79.

Folstein, S., & Rutter, M. (1978). A twin study of individuals with infantile autism. In M. Rutter & E. Schopler (Eds.), *Autism: A reappraisal of concepts and treatment.* New York: Plenum.

Forehand, R., & McMahon, R. J. (1981). *Helping the noncompliant child.* New York: Guilford.

Forehand, R., & Peed, S. (1979). Training parents to modify the non-compliant behavior of their children. In A. J. Finch & P. C. Kendall (Eds.), *Clinical treatment and research in child psychopathology.* New York: Spectrum.

Forehand, R., & Scarboro, M. E. (1975). An analysis of children's oppositional behavior. *Journal of Abnormal Child Psychology, 3,* 27–31.

Forer, B. R. (1950). A structured sentence completion test. *Journal of Projective Techniques, 14,* 15–29.

Forgays, D. G. (Ed.) (1978). *Primary prevention of psychopathology. Vol. 2. Environmental influences.* Hanover, NH: University Press of New England.

Forsmann, H., & Akesson, H. O. (1970). Mortality of the mentally deficient: A study of 12,903 institutionalized subjects. *Journal of Mental Deficiency Research, 14,* 276–294.

Forsythe, W. I., & Redmond, A. (1974). Enuresis and spontaneous cure rate. *Archives of Disease of Childhood, 49,* 259.

Foxx, R. M., & Azrin, N. H. (1972). Restitution: A method of eliminating aggressive-disruptive behavior of retarded and brain damaged patients. *Behavior Research and Therapy, 10,* 15–27.

Foxx, R. M., & Azrin, N. H. (1973). Dry pants: A rapid method for toilet training children. *Behavior Research and Therapy, 11,* 435–442.

Foxx, R. M., & Bechtel, D. R. (1982). Overcorrection. In M. Hersen, R. Eisler, & P. Miller (Eds.), *Progress in behavior modification* (Volume 13). New York: Academic Press.

Framo, J. L. (1982). *Explorations in marital and family therapy.* New York: Springer.

Francis-Williams, J. (1968). *Rorschach with children.* New York: Pergamon.

Frank, G. H. (1965). The role of the family in the development of psychopathology. *Psychologi-cal Bulletin, 94,* 191–205.

Frank, L. K. (1939). Projective methods for the study of personality. *Journal of Psychology, 8,* 389–413.

Frankenburg, W. K., Dodd, J. B., & Fandel, A. W. (1973). *Denver Developmental Screening Test.* Denver: Ladora Project & Publishing Co.

Freedman, A. M., Kaplan, H. I., & Sadock, B. J. (1976). *Modern synopsis of psychiatry* (2nd ed.). Baltimore: Williams & Wilkins.

Freeman, B. J., Ritvo, E. R., Guthrie, D., Schroth, P., & Ball, J. (1978). The behavior observation scale for autism. *Journal of the American Academy of Child Psychiatry, 17,* 576–588.

Freeman, B. J., Ritvo, E. R., & Schroth, P. C. (1984). Behavioral assessment of the syndrome of autism: Behavioral Observation System. *Journal of the American Academy of Child Psychiatry, 23,* 588–594.

Freeman, M. (1971). A reliability study of psychiatric diagnosis in childhood and adolescence. *Journal of Child Psychology and Psychiatry, 12,* 43–54.

French, J., Graves, P. A., & Levitt, E. E. (1983). Objective and projective testing of children. In E. Walker & M. Roberts (Eds.), *Handbook of clinical child psychology.* New York: Wiley.

Freud, A. (1928). *Introduction to the technique of child analysis.* New York: Nervous and Mental Disease Publishing Co.

Freud, A. (1946). *The psychoanalytic treatment of children.* London: Imago.

Freud, S. (1933). *Collected papers.* London: Hogarth.

Freud, S. (1955a). Analysis of a phobia in a five-year-old boy (1909). In *The complete works of Sigmund Freud* (Vol. 10). London: Hogarth Press.

Freud, S. (1955b). *Analysis of a phobia in a five-year-old boy.* London: Hogarth. (Original work published 1905)

Friedhoff, A. J., & Chase, T. N. (1982). *Gilles de la Tourette syndrome.* New York: Raven.

Friedman, D., Erlenmeyer-Kimling, L., & Vaughn, H. G., Jr. (1982). Cognitive brain potentials in children at high risk for schizophrenia: Progress, problems and prospects. In A. Rothenberger (Ed.), *Event related potentials in children.* New York: Elsevier.

Friedrich, W. N., & Boriskin, J. A. (1976). The role of the child in abuse: A review of the literature. *American Journal of Orthopsychiatry, 46,* 580–590.

Friedrich, W. N., & Boriskin, J. A. (1978). Primary prevention of child abuse: Focus on the special child. *Hospital and Community Psychiatry, 29,* 248–251.

Froebel, F. (1903). *The education of man.* New York: Appleton.

Frostig, M. (1972). Visual perception, integrative functions and academic learning. *Journal of Learning Disabilities, 5,* 1–15.

Frostig, M., & Horne, D. (1964). *The Frostig program for the development of visual perception.* Chicago: Follett.

Frude, N. (1980). Methodological problems in the evaluation of family therapy. *Journal of Family Therapy, 2,* 29–44.

Gaillard, A. W. K., & Ritter, W. (1983). *Tutorials in event related potential research: Endogenous components.* New York: North Holland.

Gallagher, J. J. (Ed.). (1979). *Gifted children: Reaching their potential.* New York: Trillium Press.

Galton, F. (1962). *Hereditary genius: An inquiry into its laws and consequences.* New York: Meridian Books. (Original work published 1862)

Garbarino, J. (1977). The human ecology of child maltreatment: A conceptual model for research. *Journal of Marriage and the Family, 39,* 721–735.

Garbarino, J. (1980). Preventing child maltreatment. In R. H. Price, R. F. Ketterer, B. C. Bader, & J. Monahan (Eds.), *Prevention in mental health.* Beverly Hills, CA: Sage.

Gardner, G. E. (1976). History of child psychiatry. In A. M. Freedman, H. I. Kaplan, & B. J. Sadock (Eds.), *Comprehensive textbook of psychiatry* (Vol. 2). Baltimore: Williams & Wilkins.

Gardner, R. A. (1985). *Separation anxiety disorder: Psychodynamics and psychotherapy.* Cresskill, NJ: Creative Therapeutics.

Garfield, S. L. (1974). *Clinical psychology.* Chicago: Aldine.

Garfield, S. L., & Bergin, A. E. (1978). *Handbook of psychotherapy and behavior change* (2nd ed.). New York: Wiley.

Garfinkel, P. E., & Garner, D. M. (1982). *Anorexia nervosa: A multidimensional perspective.* New York: Brunner/Mazel.

Garfinkel, P. E., Kline, S. H., & Stancer, H. C. (1973). Treatment of anorexia nervosa using operant conditioning techniques. *Journal of Nervous and Mental Disease, 157,* 428–433.

Garfinkel, P. E., Moldofsky, H., & Garner, D. M. (1977). The outcome of anorexia nervosa: Significance of clinical features, body image, and behavior modification. In R. A. Vigersky (Ed.), *Anorexia nervosa.* New York: Raven.

Garfinkel, P. E., Moldofsky, H., & Garner, D. M. (1980). The heterogeneity of anorexia nervosa: Bulimia as a distinct subgroup. *Archives of General Psychiatry, 37,* 1036–1040.

Garmezy, N. (1978). DSM III: Never mind the psychologists—is it good for our children? *Clinical Psychologist, 31,* 4–6.

Garmezy, N., & Rutter, M. (Eds.) (1983). *Stress, coping and development in children.* New York: McGraw-Hill.

Garvey, W. P., & Hegreves, J. R. (1966). Desensitization techniques in the treatment of school phobia. *American Journal of Orthopsychiatry, 36,* 147–152.

Gelder, M. (1979). Behavior therapy for neurotic disorders. *Behavior Modification, 3,* 469–495.

Gelfand, D. M. (1978). Social withdrawal and negative emotional states: Behavior therapy. In B. B. Wolman, J. Egan, & A. O. Ross (Eds.), *Handbook of treatment of mental disorders in childhood and adolescence.* Englewood Cliffs, NJ: Prentice-Hall.

Gelfand, D. M., & Hartmann, D. P. (1975). *Child behavior analysis and therapy.* New York: Pergamon.

Gelfand, D. M., & Hartmann, D. P. (1977). The prevention of childhood behavior disorders. In B. Lahey & A. Kazdin (Eds.), *Advances in clinical child psychology* (Vol. 1). New York: Plenum.

Gelfand, D. M., & Hartmann, D. P. (1984). *Child behavior analysis and therapy* (2nd ed.). New York: Pergamon.

Geller, E., Ritvo, E. R., Freeman, B. J., & Yuwiler, A. (1982). Preliminary observations on the effect of fenfluramine on blood serotonin and symptoms in three autistic boys. *New England Journal of Medicine, 307,* 165–169.

Gelles, R. J. (1978). Violence toward children in the United States. *American Journal of Orthopsychiatry, 48,* 580–592.

Genshaft, J. L. (1980). Personality characteristics of delinquent subtypes. *Journal of Abnormal Child Psychology, 8,* 279–283.

Gerjudy, I. R., Winters, J. J., Puilen, M. M., & Spitz, H. H. (1969). Subjective organization by retardates and normals during free recall of visual stimuli. *American Journal of Mental Deficiency, 73,* 791–797.

Gesell, A. L., & Thompson, H. (1938). *Patterns of early growth.* New York: Macmillan.

Gibbons, D. C. (1976). *Delinquent behavior* (2nd ed.). Englewood Cliffs, NJ: Prentice-Hall.

Gibbons, D. C. (1981). *Delinquent behavior* (3rd ed.). Englewood Cliffs, NJ: Prentice-Hall.

Gibson, D. (1978). *Down's syndrome. The psychology of mongolism.* Cambridge: Cambridge University Press.

Gillberg, C., Carlstrom, G., & Rasmussen, P. (1983). Hyperkinetic disorders in seven year old children with perceptual, motor and attentional deficits. *Journal of Child Psychology and Psychiatry, 24,* 233–246.

Gillberg, C., & Schaumann, H. (1982). Social class and infantile autism. *Journal of Autism and Developmental Disorders, 12,* 223–228.

Gillberg, C., & Svendsen, P. (1983). Childhood

psychoses and computed tomographic brain scan findings. *Journal of Autism and Developmental Disorders, 13,* 19–32.

Gillespie, W. H. (1971). Aggression and instinct theory. *International Journal of Psychoanalysis, 52,* 155–160.

Ginott, H. (1961). *Group psychotherapies with children.* New York: McGraw-Hill.

Gittelman, R. (1980). The role of psychological tests for differential diagnosis in child psychiatry. *Journal of the American Academy of Child Psychiatry, 19,* 413–438.

Gittelman, R., Abikoff, H., Pollack, E., Klein, D. F., Katz, S., & Mattes, J. (1980). A controlled trial of behavior modification and methylphenidate in hyperactive children. In C. K. Whalen & B. Henker (Eds.), *Hyperactive children, the social ecology of identification and treatment.* New York: Academic Press.

Gittelman-Klein (1978). Validity of projective tests for psychodiagnosis in children. In R. L. Spitzer & D. F. Klein (Eds.), *Critical issues in psychiatric diagnosis.* New York: Raven.

Glasser, A. J., & Zimmerman, I. L. (1967). *Clinical interpretation of the Wechsler Intelligence Scale for Children.* New York: Grune & Stratton.

Glasser, W. (1965). *Reality therapy: A new approach to psychiatry.* New York: Harper & Row.

Glennon, B., & Weisz, J. R. (1978). An observational approach to the assessment of anxiety in young children. *Journal of Consulting and Clinical Psychology, 46,* 1246–1257.

Glick, P. C., & Norton, A. J. (1977). Marrying, divorcing and living together in the U.S. today. *Population Bulletin, 32*(5).

Glueck, S., & Glueck, E. (1950). *Unraveling juvenile delinquency.* New York: Commonwealth Fund.

Glueck, S., & Glueck, E. (1968). *Delinquents and nondelinquents in perspective.* Cambridge: Harvard University Press.

Glueck, S., & Glueck, E. T. (1970) *Toward a typology of juvenile offenders.* New York: Grune & Stratton.

Goetting, A. (1981). Divorce outcome research: Issues and perspectives. *Journal of Family Issues, 2,* 350–378.

Goetz, C. G., & Klawans, H. L. (1982). Gilles de la Tourette on Tourette's syndrome. In A. J. Friedhoff & T. N. Chase (Eds.), *Gilles de la Tourette syndrome.* New York: Raven.

Gold, M., & Petronio, R. J. (1980). Delinquent behavior in adolescence. In J. Adelson (Ed.), *Handbook of adolescent psychology.* New York: Wiley.

Gold, M. S., Pottash, A. L., Sweeney, A. R., Martin, D. M., & Davies, R. V. (1980). Further evidence of hypothalamic-pituitary dysfunction in anorexia nervosa. *American Journal of Psychiatry, 137,* 101–102.

Goldberg, R. A., Schwartz, S., & Stewart, M. (1977). Individual differences in cognitive processes. *Journal of Educational Psychology, 693,* 9–14.

Goldenberg, I. S. (1968). The residential youth center: The creation of an assumption-questioning rehabilitative setting. In *Criminal corrections in Connecticut: Perspectives and progress.* West Hartford, CT: Planning Committee on General Administration.

Goldfarb, W. (1955). Emotional and intellectual consequences of psychological deprivation in infancy. In P. Hoch & J. Zubin (Eds.), *Psychopathology of childhood.* New York: Grune & Stratton.

Goldfarb, W., Goldfarb, N., & Pollack, R. C. (1966). Treatment of childhood schizophrenia: A three-year comparison of day and residential treatment. *Archives of General Psychiatry, 14,* 119–128.

Goldfried, M. R., & Kent, R. N. (1972). Tradiional versus behavioral assessment: A comparison of methodological and theoretical assumptions. *Psychological Bulletin, 77,* 409–420.

Goldman, J., Stein, C. L., & Guerry, S. (1983). *Psychological methods of child assessment.* New York: Brunner/Mazel.

Gomez, M. R. (1967). Minimum cerebral dysfunction (maximum neurological confusion). *Clinical Pediatrics, 6,* 589–591.

Goodyer, I. (1981). Hysterical conversion reactions in childhood. *Journal of Child Psychology and Psychiatry, 22,* 179–188.

Gordon, S. (1974). Second thoughts about sex education in the schools. In G. J. Williams & S. Gordon (Eds.), *Clinical child psychology: Current practices and future perspectives.* New York: Behavioral Publications.

Gordon, T. (1977). Parent effectiveness training: A preventive program and its delivery system. In G. W. Albee & J. M. Joffe (Eds.), *Primary prevention of psychopathology, Vol. 1. The issues.* Hanover, NH: University Press of New England.

Gottesman, I. I., Carey, G., & Hanson, D. R. (1983). Pearls and perils in epigenetic psychopathology. In S. B. Guze, F. J. Earls, & J. E. Barrett (Eds.), *Childhood psychopathology and development.* New York: Raven.

Gottman, J. M., & Markman, H. J. (1978). Experimental designs in psychotherapy research. In S. Garfield & A. Bergin (Eds.), *Handbook of psychotherapy and behavior change* (2nd ed.). New York: Wiley.

Goyette, C. H., Conners, C. K., & Ulrich, R. F. (1978). Normative data on revised Conners parent and teacher rating scales. *Journal of Abnormal Psychology, 6*, 221–236.

Graham, D. T., Kabler, J. D., & Graham, F. K. (1962). Physiological response to the suggestion of attitudes specific for hives and hypertension. *Psychosomatic Medicine, 24*, 159–169.

Graham, J. R. (1977). *The MMPI: A practical guide*. New York: Oxford University Press.

Graham, P., & Rutter, M. (1968). The reliability and validity of the psychiatric assessment of the child. II. Interview with the parent. *British Journal of Psychiatry, 114*, 581–592.

Graham, P., Rutter, M., & George, S. (1973). Temperament characteristics as predictors of behavior disorders in children. *American Journal of Orthopsychiatry, 43*, 328–339.

Graham, P., Rutter, M., Yule, W., & Pless, I. (1967). Childhood asthma: A psychosomatic disorder? Some epidemiological considerations. *British Journal of Preventive and Social Medicine, 21*, 78–85.

Graziano, A. M. (1972). *Group behavior modification with children*. New York: Pergamon.

Graziano, A. M., DeGiovanny, I., & Garcia, K. (1979). Behavioral treatment of child fears. *Psychological Bulletin, 56*, 804–830.

Green, A H. (1982). Child abuse. In J. R. Lachenmeyer & M. S. Gibbs (Eds.), *Psychopathology in childhood*. New York: Gardner Press.

Greenhill, L. L. (1985). Pediatric psychopharmacology. In D. S. Shaffer, A. A. Erhardt & L. L. Greenhill (Eds.), *The clinical guide to child psychiatry*. New York: the Free Press.

Greenspan, S., & Lourie, R. S. (1982). Developmental structuralist approach to the classification of adaptive and pathologic personality organizations: Infancy and early childhood. In S. Chess & A. Thomas (Eds.), *Annual progress in child psychiatry and child development*. New York: Brunner/Mazel.

Greer, S., & Morris, T. (1975). Psychological attributes of women who develop breast cancer: A controlled study. *Journal of Psychosomatic Research, 19*, 147–153.

Gross, A. M. (1984). Behavioral interviewing. In T. Ollendick & M. Hersen (Eds.), *Child behavioral assessment*. New York: Pergamon.

Gross, A. M., & Brigham, T. A. (1980). Behavior modification and the treatment of juvenile delinquency: A review and proposal for future research. *Corrective and Social Psychiatry, 26*, 98–106.

Grossman, H. J. (1977). *Manual on terminology and classification in mental retardation* (rev. ed.). Washington, DC: American Association on Mental Deficiency.

Group for the Advancement of Psychiatry (1966). *Psychopathological disorders in childhood: Theoretical considerations and a proposed classification*. Washington, DC: GAP.

Gruzelier, J. H., & Venables, P. H. (1972). Skin conductance orienting activity in a heterogeneous sample of schizophrenics: Possible evidence of limbic dysfunction. *Journal of Nervous and Mental Disease, 155*, 277–287.

Gualtieri, C. T., Hicks, R. E., & Mayo, J. P. (1983). Hyperactivity and homeostasis. *Journal of the American Academy of Child Psychiatry, 22*, 382–384.

Guerney, B. (1964). Filial therapy: Description and rationale. *Journal of Consulting Psychology, 28*, 304–310.

Guerney, L. F. (1979). Play therapy with learning disabled children. *Journal of Clinical Child Psychology, 8*, 242–244.

Gull, W. W. (1964). The address in medicine (1868). Reprinted in M. R. Kaufman & M. Heiman (Eds.), *Evolution of psychosomatic concepts*. New York: International Universities Press.

Gurman, A. S., & Kniskern, D. P. (1978). Research on marital and family therapy: Progress, perspectives, and prospect. In S. Garfield & A. Bergin (Eds.), *Handbook of psychotherapy and behavior change* (2nd ed.). New York: Wiley.

Hailman, J. (1969). How an instinct is learned. *Scientific American, 221*, 98–106.

Haim, A. (1970). *Adolescent suicide* (A. M. Sheridan-Smith, Trans.). London: Tavistock.

Haley, J. (1976). *Problem solving therapy*. San Francisco: Jossey-Bass.

Hall, R. U., Fox, R., Willard, D., Goldsmith, L., Emerson, M., Owen, M., David, F., & Porcia, E. (1971). The teacher as observer and experimenter in the modification of disrupting and talking-out behaviors. *Journal of Applied Behavior Analysis, 4*, 141–149.

Hallahan, D. P., & Kaufman, J. M. (1976). *Introduction to learning disabilities: A psychobehavioral approach*. Englewood Cliffs, NJ: Prentice-Hall.

Hallstein, E. A. (1965). Adolescent anorexia treated by desensitization. *Behavior Research and Therapy, 3*, 87–91.

Halmi, K. A. (1974). Anorexia nervosa: Demographic and clinical features of 94 cases. *Psychosomatic Medicine, 36*, 18–25.

Halmi, K. A. (1985). The diagnosis and treatment of anorexia nervosa. In D. Shaffer, A. A. Erhardt, & L. Greenhill (Eds.), *The clinical guide to child psychiatry*. New York: The Free Press.

Halmi, K. A., Owen, W. P., Lasley, E., & Stokes, P. (1983). Dopaminergic regulation in anorexia nervosa. *International Journal of Eating Disorders, 2*, 120–124.

Halpern, F. (1960). The Rorschach test with children. In A. I. Rabin & M. R. Haworth (Eds.), *Projective techniques with children*. New York: Grune & Stratton.

Hammill, D. (1972). Training visual perceptual processes. *Journal of Hearing Disabilities, 5,* 522–529.

Hampe, E., Noble, B., Miller, L. C., & Barrett, C. L. (1973). Phobic children one and two years post-treatment. *Journal of Abnormal Psychology, 82,* 446–453.

Hansen, H., & Jahiel, R. (1981). A population-based survey of amniocentesis in older pregnant women. In P. J. Mittler & J. M. deJong (Eds.), *Frontiers of knowledge in mental retardation: Vol. II. Biomedical aspects.* Baltimore: University Park Press.

Hanson, D. R., & Gottesman, I. I. (1976). The genetics, if any, of infantile autism and childhood schizophrenia. *Journal of Autism and Childhood Schizophrenia, 6,* 209–234.

Harlow, H. F., & Suomi, S. J. (1971). Production of depressive behaviors in young monkeys. *Journal of Autism and Childhood Schizophrenia, 1,* 246–255.

Harper, J., & Williams, S. (1974). Early infantile stress and infantile autism. *The Medical Journal of Australia, 1,* 341–346.

Harris, B. (1979). Whatever happened to Little Albert? *American Psychologist, 34,* 151–160.

Harris, S. L. (1979). DSM III — its implications for children. *Child Behavior Therapy, 1,* 37–46.

Harris, S. L., & Ersner-Hershfield, R. (1978). Behavioral suppression of seriously disruptive behavior in psychotic and retarded patients: A review of punishment and its alternatives. *Psychological Bulletin, 85,* 1352–1375.

Harris, S., & Powers, M. D. (1984). Diagnostic issues. In T. Ollendick and M. Hersen (Eds.), *Child behavioral assessment.* New York: Pergamon.

Harris, S. L., & Romanczyk, R. (1976). Treating self-injurious behavior of a mentally retarded child by overcorrection. *Behavior Therapy, 7,* 235–239.

Hart, B. M., Allen, K. E., Buell, J. S., Harris, F. R., & Wolf, M. M. (1964). Effects of social reinforcement on operant crying. *Journal of Experimental Child Psychology, 1,* 145–153.

Hartmann, E. R. (1980). Sleep disorders. In H. Kaplan, A. Freedman, & B. Sadock (Eds.), *Comprehensive textbook of psychiatry.* Baltimore: Williams & Wilkins.

Harvey, P., Winters, K., Weintraub, S., & Neale, M. (1981). Distractibility in children vulnerable to psychopathology. *Journal of Abnormal Psychology, 90,* 298–304.

Haryett, R. D., Hansen, F. C., & Davidson, P. O. (1967). Chronic thumbsucking: The psychological effects and the relative effectiveness of various methods of treatment. *American Journal of Orthodontics, 53,* 569–585.

Hastings, J. E., & Barkley, R. A. (1978). A review of psychophysiological research with hyperkinetic children. *Journal of Abnormal Child Psychology, 6,* 413–447.

Hathaway, S. R., & McKinley, J. (1943). *Manual for the MMPI.* New York: Psychological Corp.

Hauser, S., Delong, G., & Rosman, N. (1975). Pneumographic findings in the infantile autism syndrome. A correlation with temporal lobe disease. *Brain, 98,* 667–668.

Hayden, A. H., & Haring, W. G. (1977). The acceleration and maintenance of developmental gains in Down's syndrome school age children. In P. Mittler (Ed.), *Research to practice in mental retardation. Vol. 1. Care and intervention.* Baltimore: University Park Press.

Heber, R. (1959). A manual of terminology and classification in mental retardation. *American Journal of Mental Deficiency Monograph, 64,* 1–111.

Heimberg, R. G., & Becker, R. E. (1984). Comparative outcome research. In M. Hersen, L. Michelson, & A. Bellack (Eds.), *Issues in psychotherapy research.* New York: Plenum.

Heinieke, C. M., & Strassmann, L. H. (1976). Toward more effective research on child psychotherapy. *Journal of the American Academy of Child Psychiatry, 15,* 561–576.

Helgason, T. (1964). Epidemiology of mental disorders in Iceland. *Acta Psychiatrica Scandinavia Monograph,* Monograph No. 173.

Heller, T. (1930). Uber dementia infantalis. *Archiv für Kinderheilkunde, 37,* 661–667.

Hendrickson, D. E., & Hendrickson, A. E. (1980). Biological basis of individual differences in intelligence. *Personality and Individual Differences, 1,* 2–33.

Henn, F. A., Bardwell, R., & Jenkins, R. L. (1980). Juvenile delinquents revisited: Adult criminal activity. *Archives of General Psychiatry, 37,* 1160–1163.

Herbart, J. F. (1901). *Outlines of educational doctrine.* New York: Macmillan.

Herjanic, B., Herjanic, M., Brown, F., & Wheatt, J. (1975). Are children reliable reporters? *Journal of Abnormal Child Psychology, 3,* 41–48.

Herman, B. P., & Whitman, S. (1984). Behavioral and personality correlates of epilepsy: A review, methodological critique and conceptual model. *Psychological Bulletin, 95,* 451–497.

Hermann, K. (1959). *Reading disability: A medical study of word blindness and related handicaps.* Springfield, IL: Charles C Thomas.

Hermelin, B., & O'Connor, N. (1965). Visual imperception in psychotic children. *British Journal of Psychology, 56,* 455–460.

Hermelin, B., & O'Connor, N. (1970). *Psychological experiments with autistic children.* Oxford: Pergamon.

Herriot, P., Green, J. M., & McConkey, R. (1973). *Organization and memory: A review of a project in subnormality*. London: Methuen.

Hersen, M., Michelson, L., & Bellack, A. S. (1984). *Issues in psychotherapy research*. New York: Plenum.

Hetherington, E. M., Cox, M., & Cox, R. (1978). The aftermath of divorce. In J. H. Stevens, Jr. & M. Mathews (Eds.), *Mother/child father/child relationships*. Washington, DC: National Association for the Education of Young Children.

Hetherington, E. M., & Martin, B. (1972). Family interaction. In H. C. Quay & J. S. Werry (Eds.), *Psychopathological disorders of childhood*. New York: Wiley.

Hetherington, E. M., & Martin, B. (1979). Family interaction. In H. C. Quay & J. S. Werry (Eds.), *Psychopathological disorders of childhood* (2nd ed.). New York: Wiley.

Hetherington, E. M., Stouwie, R., & Ridberg, E. H. (1971). Patterns of family interaction and child rearing attitudes related to three dimensions of juvenile delinquency. *Journal of Abnormal Psychology, 77*, 160–176.

Hewett, F. (1965). Teaching speech to an autistic child through operant conditioning. *American Journal of Orthopsychiatry, 35*, 927–936.

Hewett, F. (1968). *The emotionally disturbed child in the classroom*. Boston: Allyn & Bacon.

Hewitt, L. E., & Jenkins, R. L. (1946). *Fundamental patterns of maladjustment: The dynamics of their origin*. Springfield, IL: State of Illinois.

Hill, D. (1947). Amphetamine in psychopathic states. *British Journal of Addictions, 44*, 50–54.

Hindelang, M. J., Hirschi, T., & Weis, J. G. (1979). Correlates of delinquency: The illusion of discrepancy between self-report and official measures. *American Sociological Review, 44*, 995–1014.

Hingtgen, J. N., & Bryson, C. Q. (1972). Recent developments in the study of early childhood psychoses: Infantile autism, childhood schizophrenia and related disorders. *Schizophrenia Bulletin, 5*, 8–54.

Hinshelwood, J. (1917). *Congenital word blindness*. London: Lewis.

Hirsch, S. R., & Leff, J. O. (1971). Parental abnormalities of verbal communication in the transmission of schizophrenia. *Psychological Medicine, 1*, 118–127.

Hobbs, N. (1975). *Issues in the classification of children*. San Francisco: Jossey-Bass.

Hobbs, S., Moguin, L., Tyroler, M., & Lahey, B. (1980). Cognitive behavior therapy with children: Has clinical utility been demonstrated? *Psychological Bulletin, 87*, 147–165.

Hodges, K., Kline, J., Fitch, P., McKnew, D., &

Cytryn, L. (1981). The Child Assessment Schedule: A diagnostic interview for research and clinical use. *Catalog of Selected Documents in Psychology, 11*, 56.

Hodges, K., Kline, J., Stern, L. Cytryn, L., & McKnew, D. (1982a). The development of a child assessment interview for research and clinical use. *Journal of Abnormal Child Psychology, 10*, 173–189.

Hodges, K., McKnew, D., Cytryn, L., Stern, L., & Kline, J. (1982b). The Child Assessment Schedule (CAS) diagnostic interview: A report on reliability and validity. *Journal of the American Academy of Child Psychiatry, 21*, 468–473.

Hoefler, S. A., & Bornstein, P. H. (1975). Achievement Place: An evaluative review. *Criminal Justice and Behavior, 2*, 146–167.

Hofmann, F. G. (1983). *A handbook on drug and alcohol use* (2nd ed.). New York: Oxford University Press.

Holden, C. (1980). A new visibility for gifted children. *Science, 210*, 879–882.

Hollingshead, A. B., & Redlich, F. C. (1958). *Social class and mental illness: A community study*. New York: Wiley.

Hollingsworth, C. E., Tanguay, P. E., Grossman, L., & Pabst, P. (1980). Long term outcome of obsessive-compulsive disorder in children. *Journal of the American Academy of Child Psychiatry, 19*, 134–144.

Holmes, T. H., & Masuda, M. (1974). Life change and illness susceptibility. In B. S. Dohrenwend & B. P. Dohrenwend (Eds.), *Stressful life events: Their nature and effects*. New York: Wiley.

Holsopple, J. Q., & Miale, F. F. (1964). *Sentence completion: A projective method for the study of personality*. Springfield, IL: Charles C Thomas.

Honig, W. K., & Staddon, J. E. (1977). *Handbook of operant behavior*. Englewood Cliffs, NJ: Prentice-Hall.

Hook, E. B. (1973). Behavioral implications of the human XYY genotype. *Science, 179*, 139–150.

Howlin, P. (1981). The effectiveness of operant language training with autistic children. *Journal of Autism and Development Disorders, 11*, 89–105.

Hoy, E., Weiss, G., Minde, K., & Cohen, N. (1978). The hyperactive child at adolescence: Cognitive, emotional and social functioning. *Journal of Abnormal Child Psychology, 6*, 311–324.

Huba, G. J., Wingard, J. A., & Bentler, P. M. (1981). A comparison of two latent variable causal models for adolescent drug use. *Journal of Personality and Social Psychology, 40*, 180–193.

Huessy, H., & Cohen, A. (1976). Hyperkinetic behaviors and learning disabilities followed over seven years. *Pediatrics*, 57, 4–10.

Huessy, H., Metayer, M., & Townsend, M. (1974). 8 to 10 year follow-up of 84 children treated for behavioral disorders in rural Vermont. *Acta Paedopsychiatry*, 10, 230–235.

Hull, C. L. (1943). *Principles of behavior*. New York: Appleton-Century-Crofts.

Hundleby, J. D., Carpenter, R. A., Ross, R. A., & Mercer, G. W. (1982). Adolescent drug use and other behaviors. *Journal of Child Psychology and Psychiatry*, 23, 61–68.

Hunt, E., Lunneborg, C., & Lewis, J. (1975). What does it mean to be high verbal? *Cognitive Psychology*, 7, 194–227.

Hutt, C., & Hutt, S. J. (1970). Stereotypes and their relationship to arousal: A study of autistic children. In C. Hutt & S. J. Hutt (Eds.), *Behavior studies in psychiatry*, Oxford: Pergamon.

Hutt, C., Hutt, S. J., Lee, D., & Ounstead, C. (1964). Arousal and childhood autism. *Nature*, 204, 908–909.

Hutt, M. L. (1977). *The Hutt adaptation of the Bender Gestalt Test* (rev. ed.). New York: Grune & Stratton.

Hutt, M. L., & Gibby, R. G. (1979). *The mentally retarded child*. (4th ed.). Boston: Allyn & Bacon.

Ireton, H., & Thwing, E. (1974). *Manual for the Minnesota Child Development Inventory*. Minneapolis: Behavior Science Systems.

Itard, J. (1932). *The wild boy of Aveyron*. (G. & M. Murphy, Trans.). New York: Appleton-Century-Crofts.

Jackson, D. D., & Weakland, J. H. (1961). Conjoint family therapy: Some considerations on theory, technique, and results. *Psychiatry*, 24, 30–45.

Jackson, H. J., & King, N. J. (1981). The emotive imagery treatment of a child's trauma induced phobia. *Journal of Behavior Therapy and Experimental Psychiatry*, 12, 325–328.

Jacob, T. (1975). Family interaction in disturbed and normal families: A methodological and substantive review. *Psychological Bulletin*, 82, 22–65.

Jacobs, T. J., & Charles, E. (1980). Life events and the occurrence of cancer in children. *Psychosomatic Medicine*, 42, 11–24.

Jastak, F. J., & Jastak, S. (1978). *Wide Range Achievement Test*. (4th ed.). Wilmington, DE: Jastak Associates.

Jemmott, J. B., & Locke, S. E. (1984). Psychosocial factors, immuniological mediation and human susceptibility to infectious disease: How much do we know? *Psychological Bulletin*, 95, 78–108.

Jencks, C. (1972). *Inequality: A reassessment of the effect of family and schooling in America*. New York: Basic Books.

Jensen, A. R. (1969). How much can we boost IQ and scholastic achievement? *Harvard Educational Review*, 39, 1–123.

Jersild, A. T., & Holmes, F. B. (1935). Methods of overcoming children's fears. *Journal of Psychology*, 1, 75–104.

Jesness, C. (1975). Comparative effectiveness of behavior modification and transactional analysis programs for delinquents. *Journal of Consulting and Clinical Psychology*, 43, 758–779.

Jessor, R., Donovan, J. E., & Widmer, K. (1980). *Psychosocial factors in adolescent alcohol and drug use: The 1978 national sample study and the 1974–1978 panel study: Final Report*. Boulder, CO: University of Colorado Institute of Behavioral Sciences.

Jessor, R., & Jessor, S. L. (1977). *Problem behavior and psychosocial development: A longitudinal study of youth*. New York: Academic Press.

Johnson, A. M. (1957). Discussion on school phobia. *American Journal of Orthopsychiatry*, 27, 307–309.

Johnson, C., Thompson, M., & Schwartz, D. (1984). Anorexia nervosa and bulimia: An overview. In W. Burnes & J. Lavigne (Eds.), *Progress in pediatric psychology*. Orlando, FL: Grune & Stratton.

Johnson, J. H. (1982). Life events as stressors in childhood and adolescence. In B. Lahey & A. Kazdin (Eds.), *Advances in clinical child psychology* (Vol. 5). New York: Plenum.

Johnson, J. H., Basham, R., & Gordon, B. N. (1984). *Temperament and indices of psychological adjustment in preschool-age children*. Unpublished manuscript, University of Florida.

Johnson, J. H., & McCutcheon, S. (1980). Assessing life stress in older children and adolescents: Preliminary findings with the Life Events Checklist. In I. G. Sarason & C. D. Spielberger (Eds.), *Stress and anxiety* (Vol. 7). Washington, DC: Hemisphere.

Johnson, J. H., Rasbury, W., & Siegel, L. (in press). *Approaches to child treatment: Theory, technique and research*. New York: Pergamon.

Johnson, J. H., & Sarason, I. G. (1978). Life stress, depression and anxiety: Internal-external control as a moderator variable. *Journal of Psychosomatic Research*, 22, 205–208.

Johnson, J. H., & Sarason, I. G. (1985). Life stress, health and adjustment: A consideration of research findings, methodological issues and methods of coping. In L. Siegel & C. Twentyman (Eds.), *Assessment and treatment in behavioral medicine*. New York: Springer.

Johnson, J. H., & Thompson, D. J. (1974). Modeling in the treatment of enuresis: A case study. *Journal of Behavior Therapy and Experimental Psychiatry*, 5, 93–94.

Johnson, S. B. (1980). Psychosocial factors in juvenile diabetes: A review. *Journal of Behavioral Medicine, 3,* 95–114.

Johnson, S. B. (1985). Situational fears and object phobias. In D. Shaffer, A. A. Ehrhardt, & L. L. Greenhill (Eds.), *The clinical guide to child psychiatry.* New York: The Free Press.

Johnson, S. B., & Melamed, B. G. (1979). The assessment and treatment of children's fears. In B. Lahey & A. Kazdin (Eds.), *Advances in clinical child psychology* (Vol. 2). New York: Plenum.

Johnston, L., Bachman, J. G., & O'Malley, P. (1981). *Highlights from student drug use in America 1975–1981.* Rockville, MD: National Institute on Drug Abuse.

Johnston, L., O'Malley, P., & Eveland, L. (1978). Drugs and delinquency: A search for causal connections. In D. Kandel (Ed.), *Longitudinal research on drug use: Empirical findings and methodological issues.* Washington, DC: Hemisphere.

Joint Commission on Mental Illness and Health. (1961). *Action for mental health.* New York: Basic Books.

Jones, H. G. (1960). Behavioral treatment of enuresis nocturna. In H. J. Eysenck (Ed.), *Behavior therapy and the neuroses.* Oxford: Pergamon.

Jones, M. C. (1924). A laboratory study of fear: The case of Peter. *Journal of Genetic Psychology, 31,* 308–315.

Jones, R. S. (1976). *Asthma in children.* Acton, MA: Publishing Sciences Group.

Jones, S. L. (1980). *Family therapy: A comparison of approaches.* Bowie, MD: Robert J. Brady Co.

Judd, L. L. (1965). Obsessive-compulsive neurosis in children. *Archives of General Psychiatry, 12,* 136–143.

Juel-Nielson, N. (1965). Individual and environment: A psychiatric-psychological investigation of monozygotic twins reared apart. *Acta Psychiatrica et Neurologica Scandinavica Monograph,* Monograph No. *113.*

Jurkovic, G. J., & Prentice, N. M. (1977). Relation of moral and cognitive development to dimensions of juvenile delinquency. *Journal of Abnormal Psychology, 86,* 414–420.

Kallman, F. J. (1946). The genetic theory of schizophrenia. *American Journal of Psychiatry, 103,* 309–322.

Kalucy, R. S., Crisp, A. H., & Harding, B. (1977). A study of 56 families with anorexia nervosa. *British Journal of Medical Psychology, 50,* 381–395.

Kamin, L. J. (1974). *The science and politics of IQ.* Hillsdale, NJ: Erlbaum.

Kandel, D. (1975). Stages in adolescent involvement in drug use. *Science, 190,* 912–914.

Kandel, D., & Faust, R. (1975). Sequences and stages in patterns of adolescent drug use. *Archives of General Psychiatry, 32,* 923–932.

Kandel, D. B. (1982). Epidemiological and psychosocial perspectives on adolescent drug abuse. *Journal of the American Academy of Child Psychiatry, 21,* 328–347.

Kanfer, F., Karoly, P., & Newman, A. (1975). Reduction of children's fear of the dark by competence related and situational threat related verbal cues. *Journal of Consulting and Clinical Psychology, 43,* 251–259.

Kanfer, F. H., & Saslow, G. (1969). Behavioral diagnosis. In C. M. Franks (Ed.), *Behavior therapy: Appraisal and status.* New York: McGraw-Hill.

Kanfer, R., Eyberg, S. M., & Krahn, G. L. (1983). Interviewing strategies in child assessment. In E. Walker & M. Roberts (Eds.), *Handbook of clinical child psychology.* New York: Wiley.

Kanner, L. (1943). Autistic disturbances of affective contact. *Nervous Child, 2,* 217–250.

Kanner, L. (1951). The conception of wholes and parts in infantile autism. *American Journal of Psychiatry, 108,* 23–26.

Kanner, L. (1965). Infantile autism and the schizophrenias. *Behavioral Science, 10,* 412–420.

Kanner, L. (1971). Follow-up study of eleven autistic children originally reported in 1945. *Journal of Autism and Childhood Schizophrenia, 1,* 119–145.

Kanner, L. (1972). *Child Psychiatry.* Springfield, IL: Charles C Thomas.

Kardash, S., Hillman, E., & Werry, J. (1968). Efficacy of imipramine in childhood enuresis: A double-blind control study with placebo. *Canadian Medical Association Journal, 99,* 263–266.

Karlin, D. A., & Kirsner, J. B. (1978). Premalignant disease of the colon and rectum. In W. E. Enker (Ed.), *Carcinoma of the colon and rectum.* Chicago: Year Book Medical Publishers.

Kashani, J., & Simonds, J. F. (1979). The incidence of depression in children. *American Journal of Psychiatry, 136,* 1203–1204.

Kashani, J. H., Barbero, G. J., & Bolander, F. D. (1981). Depression in hospitalized pediatric patients. *Journal of the American Academy of Child Psychiatry, 20,* 123–134.

Kashani, J. H., Husain, A., Shekim, W., Hodges, K., Cytryn, L. & McKnew, D. (1981). Current perspectives on childhood depression: An overview. *American Journal of Psychiatry, 138,* 143–153.

Kauffman, J. M., & Hallahan, D. (1979). Learning disability and hyperactivity (with comments on minimal brain dysfunction). In B. Lahey & A. Kazdin (Eds.), *Advances in clinical child psychology* (Vol. 2). New York: Plenum.

Kaufman, A. S. (1979). *Intelligent testing with the WISC-R*. New York: Wiley.

Kaufman, A. S., & Kaufman, N. L. (1983). *Kaufman Assessment Battery for Children: Interpretive manual*. Circle Pines, MN: American Guidance Services.

Kaufman, I. C., & Rosenblum, L. A. (1967). The reaction to separation in infant monkeys: Anaclitic depression and conservation-withdrawal. *Psychosomatic Medicine, 29*, 648–675.

Kay, D. W. K. (1953). Anorexia nervosa: A study of prognosis. *Proceedings of the Royal Society of Medicine, 46*, 669–674.

Kay, D. W. K., & Leigh, D. (1954). The natural history, treatment and prognosis of anorexia nervosa based on a study of 38 patients. *British Journal of Psychiatry, 100*, 411–431.

Kay, D. W. K., & Shapiro, K. (1965, April). The prognosis of anorexia nervosa. In J. E. Meyer & G. Feldman (Eds.), *Anorexia nervosa: Symposium AM 24/25*, Stuttgart, Germany: Georg Thieme Verlag.

Kazdin, A. E. (1975). *Behavior modification in applied settings*. Homewood, IL: Dorsey.

Kazdin, A. E. (1977). *The token economy: A review and evaluation*. New York: Plenum.

Kazdin, A. E. (1980). *Behavior modification in applied settings* (2nd ed.). Homewood, IL: Dorsey.

Kazdin, A. E. (1982a). The token economy: A decade later. *Journal of Applied Behavior Analysis, 15*, 431–445.

Kazdin, A. E. (1982b). *Single case experimental designs: Methods for clinical and applied settings*. New York: Oxford University Press.

Kazdin, A. E. (1983). Single case research designs in clinical child psychiatry. *Journal of the American Academy of Child Psychiatry, 22*, 423–432.

Kazdin, A. E., & Bootzin, R. R. (1972). The token economy: An evaluative review. *Journal of Applied Behavior Analysis, 5*, 343–372.

Kellam, S. G., Brown, C. H., Rubin, B. R., & Ensminger, M. E. (1983). Paths leading to teenage psychiatric symptoms and substance use: Developmental epidemiological studies in Woodlawn. In S. B. Guze, F. J. Earls & J. E. Barrett (Eds.), *Childhood psychopathology and development*. New York: Raven.

Kellerman, J. (1981). Hypnosis as an adjunct to thought-stopping and covert reinforcement in the treatment of homicidal obsessions in a twelve-year-old boy. *International Journal of Clinical and Experimental Hypnosis, 29*, 128–135.

Kelly, E. W. (1973). School phobia: Review of theory and treatment. *Psychology in the Schools, 10*, 33–41.

Kempler, W. (1981). *Experiential psychotherapy with families*. New York: Brunner/Mazel.

Kendall, P. C. (1981). Cognitive behavioral interventions with children. In B. Lahey & A. Kazdin (Eds.), *Advances in clinical child psychology* (Vol. 4). New York: Plenum.

Kendall, P. C. (1984). Cognitive behavioural self-control therapy for children. *Journal of Child Psychology and Psychiatry, 25*, 173–179.

Kendall, P. C., & Finch, A. J. (1976). A cognitive-behavioral treatment for impulse control: A case study. *Journal of Consulting and Clinical Psychology, 44*, 852–857.

Kendall, P., & Finch, A. J. (1978). A cognitive behavioral treatment for impulsivity: A group comparison study. *Journal of Consulting and Clinical Psychology, 46*, 110–118.

Kendall, P. C., & Finch, A. J., Jr. (1979). Strategies for research in child psychopathology. In A. J. Finch, Jr. & P. C. Kendall (Eds.), *Clinical treatment and research in child psychopathology*. New York: SP Medical and Scientific Books.

Kendler, K. S. (1983). A current perspective on twin studies of schizophrenia. *American Journal of Psychiatry, 140*, 1413–1421.

Keniston, K. (1977). *All our children: The American family under pressure*. New York: Harcourt Brace Jovanovich.

Kennedy, W. A. (1965). School phobia: Rapid treatment of fifty cases. *Journal of Abnormal Psychology, 70*, 285–289.

Kennedy, W. A. (1983). Obsessive-compulsive and phobic reactions. In T. Ollendick & M. Hersen (Eds.), *Handbook of child psychopathology*. New York: Plenum.

Kessel, F. S., & Siegel, A. W. (1983). *The child and other cultural inventions*. New York: Praeger.

Kessen, W. (1965). *The child*. New York: Wiley.

Kessler, J. W. (1966). *Psychopathology of childhood*. Englewood Cliffs, NJ: Prentice-Hall.

Kessler, J. W. (1972). Neurosis in childhood. In B. B. Wolman (Ed.), *Manual of child psychopathology*. New York: McGraw-Hill.

Kety, S. S. (1979). Disorders of the human brain, *Scientific American, 241*, 172–180.

Kiely, J. L., Paneth, N., & Susser, M. (1981). Low birth weight, neonatal care and cerebral palsy: An epidemiological review. In P. J. Mittler & J. M. deJong (Eds.), *Frontiers of knowledge in mental retardation: Vol. II. Biomedical aspects*. Baltimore: University Park Press.

Kiernan, C. (1981). Behavior modification and the development of communication. In P. J. Mittler & J. M. deJong (Eds.), *Frontiers of knowledge in mental retardation. Vol. I. Social, educational and behavioral aspects*. Baltimore: University Park Press.

Kiernan, C. C., & Jones, M. (1980). The Behavior Assessment Battery for use with the profoundly retarded. In J. Hogg & P. J. Mittler (Eds.), *Ad-

vances in mental handicap research (Vol. 1). New York: Wiley.

Kiesler, D. J. (1966). Some myths of psychotherapy research and the search for a paradigm. *Psychological Bulletin, 65,* 110–136.

Kiesler, D. J. (1971). Experimental designs in psychotherapy research. In A. E. Bergin & S. L. Garfield (Eds.), *Handbook of psychotherapy and behavior change.* New York: Wiley.

Kimmel, H. D., & Kimmel, E. (1970). An instrumental conditioning method for the treatment of enuresis. *Journal of Behavior Therapy and Experimental Psychiatry, 6,* 121–123.

Kirk, S. A. (1972). *Educating exceptional children* (2nd ed.). Boston: Houghton Mifflin.

Kirk, S. A., McCarthy, J. J., & Kirk, W. D. (1968). *Examiner's manual for the Illinois Test of Psycholinguistic Abilities.* Urbana, IL: University of Illinois Press.

Kirkland, K. D., & Thelen, M. (1977). Uses of modeling in child treatment. In B. Lahey & A. Kazdin (Eds.), *Advances in clinical child psychology* (Vol. 1). New York: Plenum.

Kirsner, J. B. (1970). Ulcerative colitis. 1970 — recent developments. *Scandinavian Journal of Gastroenterology, 6,* 63–91.

Klein, M. (1932). *Psychoanalysis of children.* New York: Norton.

Klein, M. (1955). The psychoanalytic play technique. *American Journal of Orthopsychiatry, 25,* 223–237.

Klein, N. C., Alexander, J. F., & Parsons, B. V. (1977). Impact of family systems intervention on recidivism and sibling delinquency: A model of primary prevention and program evaluation. *Journal of Consulting and Clinical Psychology, 45,* 469–474.

Kline, J., Stein, Z. A., Susser, M., & Warburton, D. (1981). New insights into the epidemiology of chromosomal disorders: Their relevance to the prevention of Down's syndrome. In P. J. Mittler & J. M. deJong (Eds.), *Frontiers of knowledge in mental retardation: Vol. II. Biomedical aspects.* Baltimore: University Park Press.

Klopfer, B., Ainsworth, M. D., Klopfer, W. G., & Holt, R. R. (1954). *Developments in the Rorschach technique. Vol. 1.* New York: Harcourt, Brace, & World.

Klopfer, W. G., & Taulbee, E. S. (1976). Projective tests. In M. R. Rosenzweig and L. W. Porter (Eds.), *Annual Review of Psychology.* Palo Alto, CA: Annual Reviews.

Knopf, I. J. (1984). *Childhood psychopathology* (2nd ed.). Englewood Cliffs, NJ: Prentice-Hall.

Koch, J. (1979). *International summit on prevention of mental retardation from biomedical causes.* (Doc. HE 23.102:D62). Washington, DC: U.S. Government Printing Office.

Koegel, R. L. Schreibman, L., O'Neill, R. E. & Burke, J. C. (1983). The personality and family interaction characteristics of parents of autistic children. *Journal of Consulting and Clinical Psychology, 51,* 683–692.

Koegel, R. L., & Wilhelm, H. (1973). Selective responding to the components of multiple visual cues by autistic children. *Journal of Experimental Child Psychology, 15,* 442–453.

Kohlberg, L. (1976). Moral stages and moralization: The cognitive-developmental approach. In T. Lickona (Ed.), *Moral development and behavior: Theory research and social issues.* New York: Holt, Rinehart, & Winston.

Kohlenberg, R. B. (1970). The punishment of persistent vomiting: A case study. *Journal of Applied Behavior Analysis, 3,* 241–245.

Kolers, P. A. (1970). Three stages of reading. In H. Levin & J. P. Williams (Eds.), *Basic studies in reading.* New York: Basic Books.

Kolodny, E. H. (1981). Diagnostic experience of a lysosomal storage diseases laboratory in 500 cases with mental retardation and nervous system degeneration. In P. J. Mittler & J. M. deJong (Eds.), *Frontiers of knowledge in mental retardation: Vol. II. Biomedical aspects.* Baltimore: University Park Press.

Kolvin, I. (1971). Psychoses in childhood — a comparative study. In M. Rutter (Ed.), *Infantile autism: Concepts, characteristics and treatment.* London: Churchill.

Kondas, O. (1967). Reduction in examination anxiety and stage fright by group desensitization and relaxation. *Behavior Research and Therapy, 5,* 275–281.

Koocher, G. P. (1976). A 'Bill of Rights' for children in psychotherapy. In G. P. Koocher (Ed.), *Children's rights and the mental health professions.* New York: Wiley.

Koocher, G. P. (1983). Grief and loss in childhood. In E. Walker & M. Roberts (Eds.), *Handbook of clinical child psychology.* New York: Wiley.

Koocher, G. P., & O'Malley, J. E. (1981). *The Damocles syndrome: Psychosocial consequences of surviving childhood cancer.* New York: McGraw-Hill.

Koocher, G. P., & Pedulla, B. M. (1977). Current practices in child psychotherapy. *Professional Psychology, 8,* 275–286.

Koppitz, E. M. (1964, 1975). *The Bender Gestalt Test for Young Children* (Vols. 1 & 2). New York: Grune & Stratton.

Koppitz, E. M. (1969). *Psychological evaluations of children's human figure drawings.* New York: Grune & Stratton.

Koulischer, L., & Gillerot, Y. (1981). Age of mothers at birth of Down's syndrome patients in Wallonia (South Belgium). In P. J. Mittler &

J. M. deJong (Eds.), *Frontiers of knowledge in mental retardation: Vol. II. Biomedical aspects.* Baltimore: University Park Press.

Kovacs, M. (1981). Rating scales to assess depression in school-aged children. *Acta Paedopsychiatrica, 46,* 305–315.

Kovacs, M., & Beck, A. T. (1978). Maladaptive cognitive structures in depression. *American Journal of Psychiatry, 135,* 525–533.

Kovacs, M., Feinberg, T. L., Crouse-Novak, M. A., Paulauskas, S., & Finkelstein, R. (1984). Depressive disorders in childhood: A longitudinal prospective study of characteristics and recovery. *American Journal of Psychiatry, 41,* 229–237.

Kraft, I. A. (1980). Group therapy with children. In A. M. Freedman, H. I. Kaplan, & B. J. Sadock (Eds.), *Comprehensive textbook of psychiatry* (3rd ed.). Baltimore: Williams & Wilkins.

Krapfl, J. E., Bry, P., & Nawas, M. M. (1968). Uses of bug-in-the-ear in the modification of parents' behavior. *Proceedings of the Association for the Advancement of Behavior Therapy.* New York: Academic Press.

Krug, D. A., Arick, J. T., & Almond, P. J. (1982). *Autism screening instrument for educational planning.* Portland, OR: ASIEP Education Co.

Krug, R. S. (1983). Substance abuse. In E. Walker & M. Roberts (Eds.), *Handbook of clinical child psychology.* New York: Wiley.

Kubicek, L. F. (1980). Organization in two mother-infant interactions involving a normal infant and his fraternal twin brother who was later diagnosed as autistic. In T. M. Field, S. Golaber, D. Stern, & A. M. Sostek (Eds.), *High risk infants and children: Adult and peer interactions.* New York: Academic Press.

Kuhn, T. S. (1962). *The structure of scientific revolutions.* Chicago: University of Chicago Press.

Kuhn, T. S. (1974). Second thoughts on paradigms. In F. S. Suppe (Ed.), *The structure of scientific theories.* Champaign, IL: University of Illinois Press.

Kushner, M. (1968). The operant control of intractable sneezing. In C. D. Spielberger, R. Fox, & B. Masterson (Eds.), *Contributions to general psychology.* New York: Ronald Press.

Kydd, R. R., & Werry, J. S. (1982). Schizophrenia in children under 16 years. *Journal of Autism and Developmental Disorders, 12,* 343–357.

Labbé, E. E., & Williamson, D. A. (1984). Behavioral treatment of elective mutism: A review of the literature. *Clinical Psychology Review, 4,* 273–292.

Lachar, D., & Gdowski, C. L. (1979). *Actuarial assessment of child and adolescent personality.* Los Angeles: Western Psychological Services.

Lachar, D., Gdowski, C., & Snyder, D. K. (1984). External validation of the Personality Inventory for Children (PIC) profile and factor scales: Parent, teacher and child ratings. *Journal of Consulting and Clinical Psychology, 52,* 155–164.

LaGreca, A. (1983). Interviewing and behavioral observation. In E. Walker & M. Roberts (Eds.), *Handbook of clinical child psychology.* New York: Wiley.

Lakatos, I., & Musgrave, A. (1970). *Criticism and the growth of knowledge.* Cambridge: Cambridge University Press.

Lally, M. (1981). Computer-assisted teaching of sight word recognition for mentally retarded children. *American Journal of Mental Deficiency, 85,* 383–388.

Lamb, H. T., & Zusman, J. (1979). Primary prevention in perspective. *American Journal of Psychiatry, 136,* 12–17.

Lambert, J. L. (1980). Stimulus fading procedures and discrimination learning by retarded children. In J. Hogg & P. J. Mittler (Eds.), *Advances in mental handicap research* (Vol. 1). New York: Wiley.

Lambert, M. J. (1976). Spontaneous remission in adult neurotic disorders: A revision and summary. *Psychological Bulletin, 83,* 107–119.

Lambert, M. J., & Asay, T. P. (1984). Patient characteristics and their relationship to psychotherapy outcome. In M. Hersen, L. Michelson, & A. Bellack (Eds.), *Issues in psychotherapy research.* New York: Plenum.

Lambert, M. J., Bergin, A. E., & Collins, J. L. (1977). Therapist-induced deterioration in psychotherapy. In A. S. Gurman & A. M. Razin (Eds.), *Effective psychotherapy: A handbook of research.* New York: Pergamon.

Lambert, N. M., Sandoval, J., & Sassone, D. (1978). Prevalence of hyperactivity in elementary school children as a function of social system definers. *American Journal of Orthopsychiatry, 48,* 446–463.

Lambert, N. M., Windmiller, M., Sandoval, J., & Moore, B. (1976). Hyperactive children and the efficacy of psychoactive drugs as a treatment intervention. *American Journal of Orthopsychiatry, 46,* 335–352.

Landisberg, S., & Snyder, W. (1946). Nondirective play therapy. *Journal of Clinical Psychology, 146,* 203–214.

Lane, B. A. (1980). The relationship between learning disabilities to juvenile delinquency: Current status. *Journal of Learning Disabilities, 13,* 20–30.

Lang, P. J. (1968). Fear reduction and fear behavior: Problems in treating a construct. In J. M. Schlien (Ed.), *Research in psychotherapy* (Vol. 3). Washington, DC: American Psychological Association.

Lang, P. J., & Lazovick, A. D. (1963). Experimental desensitization of a phobia. *Journal of Abnormal and Social Psychology, 66,* 519–525.

Lang, P. J., & Melamed, B. G. (1969). Case report: Avoidance conditioning therapy of an infant with chronic ruminative vomiting. *Journal of Abnormal Psychology, 74,* 1–8.

Langer, E. J., & Abelson, R. P. (1974). A patient by any other name . . . Clinician group differences in labeling bias. *Journal of Consulting and Clinical Psychology, 42,* 4–9.

Lapouse, R., & Monk, M. A. (1958). An epidemiologic study of behavior characteristics in children. *American Journal of Public Health, 48,* 1134–1144.

Lapouse, R., & Monk, M. A. (1959). Fears and worries in a representative sample of children. *American Journal of Orthopsychiatry, 29,* 803–818.

Lapouse, R., & Monk, M. A. (1964). Behavior deviations in a representative sample of children: Variations by sex, age, race, social class, and family size. *American Journal of Orthopsychiatry, 34,* 436–446.

Lasegue, E. C. (1964). On hysterical anorexia (1874). Reprinted in M. R. Kaufman & M. Heiman (Eds.), *Evolution of psychosomatic concepts.* New York: International Universities Press.

Lashley, K. S. (1950). The problem of social order in behavior. In L. A. Jeffress (Ed.), *Cerebral mechanisms in behavior.* New York: Wiley.

Laufer, M. W., & Denhoff, E. (1957). Hyperkinetic behavior syndrome in children. *Journal of Pediatrics, 50,* 463–474.

Layzer, D. (1972). Science or superstition? A physical scientist looks at the IQ controversy. *Cognition, 1,* 265–299.

Layzer, D. (1974). Heritability analyses of IQ scores. Science or numerology? *Science, 183,* 1259–1266.

Lazarus, A. A. (1959). The elimination of children's phobias by deconditioning. *Medical Proceedings of South Africa, 5,* 261–265.

Lazarus, A. A. (1977). *In the mind's eye.* New York: Rawson.

Lazarus, A. A., & Abramovitz, A. (1962). The use of "emotive imagery" in the treatment of children's phobias. *Journal of Mental Science, 108,* 191–195.

Lazarus, A. A., & Rachman, S. (1957). The use of systematic desensitization in psychotherapy. *South African Medical Journal, 31,* 934–937.

Leahy, A. M. (1935). Nature-nurture and intelligence. *Genetic Psychology Monographs, 17,* 235–308.

Lebo, D. (1953). The present status of research on nondirective play therapy. *Journal of Consulting Psychology, 17,* 177–183.

Lechtig, A., Delgado, H., Lasky, R., Yarborough, T., Klein, R., Habicht, J. P., & Behar, M. (1975). Maternal nutrition and fetal growth in developing societies. *American Journal of Diseases of Children, 129,* 434–437.

Lefkowitz, M. M., & Burton, N. (1978). Childhood depression: A critique of the concept. *Psychological Bulletin, 85,* 716–726.

Leiderman, P. H. (1974). Mothers at risk: A potential consequence of the hospital care of the premature infant. In E. J. Anthony & C. Koupernik (Eds.), *The child in his family: Children at psychiatric risk.* New York: Wiley.

Leiter, R. G. (1969). *Examiner's manual for the Leiter International Performance Scale.* Chicago: Schoelting Co.

Lemkau, P., & Imre, P. D. (1969). Results of a field epidemiologic study. *American Journal of Mental Deficiency, 73,* 858–863.

Lenneberg, E. H. (1967). *Biological foundations of language.* New York: Wiley.

Leon, G. (1979). Cognitive-behavior therapy for eating disturbances. In P. Kendall & S. Hollon (Eds.), *Cognitive behavioral interventions: Theory, research and procedures.* New York: Academic Press.

Leon, G., & Dinklage, D. (1983). Childhood obesity and anorexia nervosa. In T. H. Ollendick & M. Hersen (Eds.), *Handbook of child psychopathology.* New York: Plenum.

Leon, G. R., Kendall, P. C., & Garber, J. (1980). Depression in children: Parent, teacher and child perspectives. *Journal of Abnormal Child Psychology, 8,* 221–235.

Lerner, E. A. (1972). *The projective use of the Bender Gestalt.* Springfield, IL: Charles C Thomas.

Lesser, L. C., Ashenden, B. J., Debuskey, M., & Eisenberg, L. (1960). Anorexia nervosa in children. *American Journal of Orthopsychiatry, 30,* 572–580.

Lester, D. (1978). Idiot savants: A review. *Psychology, 14,* 19–23.

Levant, R. F. (1978). Family therapy: A client-centered perspective. *Journal of Marriage and Family Counseling, 4,* 35–42.

Levant, R. F. (1984). *Family therapy: A comprehensive overview.* Englewood Cliffs, NJ: Prentice-Hall.

Levenstein, P. (1972). *Verbal interaction project.* Mineola, NY: Family Service Association of Nassau County.

Levitt, E. E. (1957). The results of psychotherapy with children: An evaluation. *Journal of Consulting Psychology, 21,* 189–196.

Levitt, E. E. (1963). Psychotherapy with children: A further evaluation. *Behavior Research and Therapy, 21,* 326–329.

Levitt, E. E. (1971). Research in psychotherapy

with children. In A. E. Bergin & S. L. Garfield (Eds.), *Handbook of psychotherapy and behavior change*. New York: Wiley.

Levitt, E. E., & Truumaa, A. (1972). *The Rorschach technique with children and adolescents*. New York: Grune & Stratton.

Levy-Agresti, J., & Sperry, R. (1968). Differential perceptual capacities in major and minor hemispheres. *Proceedings of the U.S. Academy of Sciences, 61*, 1151.

Lewinsohn, P. M. (1974). A behavioral approach to depression. In R. J. Friedman & M. M. Katz (Eds.), *The psychology of depression: Contemporary theory and research*. Washington, DC: Winston.

Lewis, D. O. (1985). Juvenile delinquency. In D. Shaffer, A. A. Erhardt, & L. L. Greenhill (Eds.), *The clinical guide to child psychiatry*. New York: The Free Press.

Lewis, H. (1954). *Deprived children*. London: Oxford University Press.

Lieberman, R. (1970). Behavioral approaches to family and couples therapy. *American Journal of Orthopsychiatry, 40*, 106–118.

Liberman, R. P., Ferris, C., Selgado, P., & Selgado, J. (1975). Replication of the Achievement Place model in California. *Journal of Applied Behavior Analysis, 8*, 287–299.

Lipowski, Z. J. (1977). Psychosomatic medicine in the seventies: An overview. *American Journal of Psychiatry, 134*, 233–244.

Lipowski, Z. J. (1984). What does the word "psychosomatic" really mean? A historical and semantic inquiry. *Psychosomatic Medicine, 46*, 153–169.

Litrownik, A. J., McInnis, E. T., Wetzel-Pritchard, A. M., & Filipelli, D. L. (1978). Restricted stimulus control and inferred attentional deficits in autistic and retarded children. *Journal of Abnormal Psychology, 87*, 554–562.

Litt, I. F., Cuskey, W. R., & Rudd, S. (1980). Identifying children at risk for noncompliance with contraceptive therapy. *Journal of Pediatrics, 96*, 742–745.

Loney, J. (1980). Hyperkinesis comes of age: What do we know and where should we go? *American Journal of Orthopsychiatry, 50*, 28–42.

Loney, J. (1983). Research diagnostic criteria for childhood hyperactivity. In S. B. Guze, F. J. Earls, & J. E. Barrett (Eds.), *Childhood psychopathology and development*. New York: Raven.

Loney, J., Kramer, J., & Kosier, T. (1981). *Medicated vs unmedicated hyperactive adolescents: Academic, delinquent and symptomatological outcome*. Paper presented at the annual meeting of the American Psychiatric Association, Los Angeles.

Loney, J., & Ordona, T. (1975). Using cerebral stimulants to treat minimal brain dysfunction.

American Journal of Orthopsychiatry, 45, 564–572.

Loony, J. G., Lipp, M. R., & Spitzer, R. L. (1978). A new method of classification for psychophysiological disorders. *American Journal of Psychiatry, 135*, 304–307.

Lopez, R. R. (1965). Hyperactivity in twins. *Canadian Psychiatric Association Journal, 10*, 421.

Lotter, V. (1966). Epidemiology of autistic conditions in young children. I. Prevalence. *Social Psychiatry, 1*, 124–137.

Lotter, V. (1967). Epidemiology of autistic conditions in young children. II: Some characteristics of the parents and children. *Social Psychiatry, 1*, 163–173.

Lotter, V. (1974). Factors related to outcome in autistic children. *Journal of Autism and Childhood Schizophrenia, 4*, 263–277.

Lotter, V. (1978). Childhood autism in Africa. *Journal of Child Psychology and Psychiatry, 15*, 231–244.

Lovaas, O. I. (1977). *The autistic child: Language development through behavior modification*. New York: Irvington.

Lovaas, O. I., Koegel, R. L., & Schreibman, L. (1979). Stimulus overselectivity in autism: A review of research. *Psychological Bulletin, 86*, 1236–1254.

Lovaas, O. I., Schaeffer, B., & Simmons, J. Q. (1965). Building social behavior in autistic children by use of electric shock. *Journal of Experimental Research in Personality, 1*, 99–109.

Lovaas, O. I., & Simmons, J. Q. (1969). Manipulation of self-destruction in three retarded children. *Journal of Applied Behavior Analysis, 2*, 143–157.

Lovaas, O. I., Young, D. B., & Newsom, C. D. (1978). Childhood psychosis: Behavioral treatment. In B. P. Wolman (Ed.), *Handbook of treatment of mental disorders in childhood and adolescence*. Englewood Cliffs, NJ: Prentice-Hall.

Lovibond, S. (1964). *Conditioning and enuresis*. New York: Pergamon.

Lovibond, S. H., & Coote, M. A. (1970). Enuresis. In C. G. Costello (Ed.), *Symptoms of psychopathology*. New York: Wiley.

Lowery, L. G. (Ed.). (1948). *Orthopsychiatry 1923–1948. Retrospect and prospect*. New York: American Orthopsychiatry Association.

Lubar, J. F., & Shouse, M. N. (1977). Use of biofeedback in the treatment of seizure disorders and hyperactivity. In B. Lahey & A. Kazdin (Eds.), *Advances in clinical child psychology*. (Vol. 1). New York: Plenum.

Lubin, B., Wallis, R. R., & Paine, C. (1971). Patterns of psychological test usage in the United States 1935–1969. *Professional Psychology, 2*, 70–74.

Lukeman, D. (1975). Conditioning methods of treating childhood asthma. *Journal of Child Psychology and Psychiatry, 16,* 165–168.

Lumsden, C. J., & Wilson, E. O. (1983). *Promethean fire.* Cambridge, MA: Harvard University Press.

Lupton, M., Simon, L., Barry, V., & Klawans, H. L. (1976). Biological aspects of anorexia nervosa. *Life Sciences, 18,* 1341–1348.

Luria, A. R. (1965). Neuropsychological analysis of focal brain lesions. In B. B. Wolman (Ed.), *Handbook of clinical psychology.* New York: McGraw-Hill.

Lynn, D. J., Mirkin, I. R., Lanese, D. M., Schmidt, H. S., & Arnold, L. E. (1983). Correspondence between DSM-II hyperkinetic reaction and DSM-III attention deficit disorder. *Journal of the American Academy of Child Psychiatry, 22,* 349–350.

MacFarlane, J. W., Allen, L., & Honzik, M. P. (1954). *A developmental study of the behavior problems of normal children between twenty-one months and fourteen years.* Berkeley and Los Angeles: University of California Press.

MacGregor, R., Ritchie, A., Serrano, A., & Schuster, F. (1964). *Multiple impact therapy with families.* New York: McGraw-Hill.

Machover, K. (1949). *Personality projection in the drawing of the human figure.* Springfield, IL: Charles C Thomas.

Machover, K. (1960). Sex differences in the developmental pattern of children as seen in human figure drawings. In A. I. Rabin & M. R. Haworth (Eds.), *Projective techniques with children* . New York: Grune & Stratton.

Macmillan, D. L. (1977). *Mental retardation in school and society.* Boston: Little Brown.

Macmillan, D. L., & Semmel, D. I. (1977). Evaluation of mainstreaming programs. *Focus on Exceptional Children, 6,* 8–14.

Madden, R., Gardner, E. F., Rudman, H. C., Karlsen, B., & Merwin, J. C. (1973). *The Stanford Achievement Tests,* (6th ed.). New York: The Psychological Corporation.

Madsen, C. H., Hoffman, H., Thomas, D. R., Korpsak, E., & Madsen, C. K. (1969). Comparisons of toilet training techniques. In D. M. Gelfand (Ed.), *Social learning in children.* Belmont, CA: Brooks/Cole.

Magidson, J. (1978). Reply to Bentler and Woodward: The .05 significance level is not all-powerful. *Evaluation Quarterly, 2,* 511–520.

Mahler, M. (1968). *On human symbiosis.* New York: International Universities Press.

Mahoney, M. J. (1977). Reflections on the cognitive-learning trend in psychotherapy. *American Psychologist, 32,* 5–13.

Makita, K. (1966). The age of onset of childhood schizophrenia. *Folia psychiatrica et Neurologica Japonica, 20,* 111–121.

Maletzky, B. M. (1974). D-amphetamine and delinquency. *Diseases of the Nervous System, 35,* 543–547.

Maloney, M. J. (1980). Diagnosing hysterical conversion reactions in children. *The Journal of Pediatrics, 97,* 1016–1020.

Maloney, M. J., & Farrell, M. K. (1980). Treatment of severe weight loss in anorexia nervosa with hyperalimentation and psychotherapy. *American Journal of Psychiatry, 137,* 310–313.

Maloney, M., & Klykylo, W. M. (1983). An overview of anorexia nervosa, bulimia, and obesity in children and adolescents. *Journal of the American Academy of Child Psychology, 22,* 99–107.

Marks, I. M. (1969). *Fears and phobias.* New York: American Press.

Marks, P. A., Seeman, W., & Haller, D. L. (1974). *The acturarial use of the MMPI with adolescents and adults.* Baltimore, MD: Williams & Wilkins.

Mash, E. J., & Dalby, J. T. (1979). Behavioral interventions for hyperactivity. In R. L. Trites (Ed.), *Hyperactivity in children: Etiology, measurement and treatment implications.* Baltimore: University Park Press.

Matarazzo, J. D. (1972). *Wechsler's measurement and appraisal of adult intelligence* (5th ed.). Baltimore, MD: Williams & Wilkins.

Matson, J. E. (1983). *Philosophy and care of mentally retarded: A worldwide status report.* New York: Pergamon.

Matson, J. L., & DiLorenzo, T. M. (1984). *Punishment and its alternatives.* New York: Springer.

Matson, J. L., & Mulick, J. A. (1983). *Handbook of mental retardation.* New York: Pergamon.

Matson, J. L., & Ollendick, T. H. (1977). Issues in toilet training normal children. *Behavior Therapy, 8,* 549–553.

Mattison, R., Cantwell, D. P., Russell, A. T., & Will, L. (1979). A comparison of DSM II and DSM III in the diagnosis of childhood disorders. *Archives of General Psychiatry, 36,* 1217–1222.

Mattsson, A. (1972). Long term physical illness of childhood: A challenge to psychosocial adaptation. *Pediatrics, 50,* 801.

Maurer, R. G., & Stewart, M. A. (1980). Attention deficit disorder without hyperactivity in a child psychiatry clinic. *Journal of Clinical Psychiatry, 41,* 232–233.

McAdoo, W. G., & DeMyer, M. K. (1978). Personality characteristics of parents. In M. Rutter & E. Schopler (Eds.), *Autism: A reappraisal of concepts and treatment.* New York: Plenum.

McCall, R. B., Hogarty, P. S., & Hurlburt, N. (1972). Transition in infant sensorimotor development and the prediction of childhood IQ. *American Psychologist, 27,* 728–748.

McCandless, B. R. (1976). The socialization of the individual. In E. Schopler & R. J. Reichler

(Eds.), *Psychopathology and child development: Research and treatment* (pp. 185–202). New York: Plenum.

McCann, B. S. (1981). Hemispheric asymmetries and early infantile autism. *Journal of Autism and Developmental Disorders, 11*, 401–411.

McCarthy, D. (1970). *McCarthy Scales of Children's Abilities.* New York: The Psychological Corporation.

McCary, J. L. (1973). *Human sexuality.* New York: Van Nostrand.

McCord, J., & McCord, W. (1969). A follow-up report on the Cambridge-Sommerville Youth Study. *Annals of the American Academy of Political and Social Science, 332*, 89–96.

McCorkle, L., Elias, A., & Bixby, F. (1958). *The Highfields story: A unique experiment in the treatment of juvenile delinquency.* New York: Holt, Rinhart, & Winston.

McDonald, J. D., & Shephard, G. (1976). School phobia: An overview. *Journal of the American Academy of Child Psychiatry, 14*, 291–308.

McElhaney, M. (1969). *Clinical psychological assessment of the human figure drawing.* Springfield, IL: Charles C Thomas.

McGuffin, P., & Reich, T. (1984). Psychopathology and genetics. In H. E. Adams & P. B. Sutker (Eds.). *Comprehensive handbook of psychopathology.* New York: Plenum.

McKay, H., Sinisterra, L., McKay, A., Gomes, H., & Lloreda, P. (1978). Improving cognitive ability in chronically deprived children. *Science, 200*, 270–278.

McMahon, R. C. (1980). Genetic etiology in the hyperactive child syndrome: A critical review. *American Journal of Orthopsychiatry, 50*, 145–149.

McMahon, R. J. (1984). Behavioral checklists and rating scales. In T. Ollendick & M. Hersen (Eds.), *Child behavioral assessment.* New York: Pergamon.

Mednick, S. A. (1978). Berkson's fallacy and high risk research. In L. C. Wynne, R. Cromwell & S. Matthysse (Eds.), *The nature of schizophrenia: New approaches to research and treatment.* New York: Wiley.

Mednick, S. A., & Schulsinger, F. (1968). Some premorbid characteristics related to breakdown in children with schizophrenic mothers. *Journal of Psychiatric Research, 6*, 267–291.

Mednick, S. A., Schulsinger, F., & Garfinkel, R. (1975). Children at high risk for schizophrenia: Predisposing factors and intervention. In M. L. Keitzman, S. Sutton, & J. Zubin (Eds.), *Experimental approaches to psychopathology.* New York: Academic Press.

Mednick, S. A., Schulsinger, F., Higgins, J., & Bell, B. (1974). *Genetics, environment and psychopathology.* New York: American Elsevier.

Mednick, S. A., & Witkin-Lanoil, G. H. (1977).

Intervention in children at high risk for schizophrenia. In G. W. Albee & J. M. Joffe (Eds.), *Primary prevention of psychopathology: Vol. 1. The issues.* Hanover, NH: University Press of New England.

Meeks, J. E. (1975). Group delinquent reaction. In A. M. Freedman, H. I. Kaplan, & B. J. Saddock (Eds.), *Comprehensive textbook of psychiatry. Vol. 2.* Baltimore: Williams & Wilkins.

Meichenbaum, D. (1977). *Cognitive behavior modification.* New York: Plenum.

Meichenbaum, D. (1979a). Teaching children self-control. In B. Lahey & A. Kazdin (Eds.), *Advances in clinical child psychology* (Vol. 2). New York: Plenum.

Meichenbaum, D. (1979b). *Cognitive behavior modification: An integrative approach.* New York: Plenum.

Meichenbaum, D., & Goodman, J. (1971). Training impulsive children to talk to themselves: A means of developing self-control. *Journal of Abnormal Psychology, 77*, 115–126.

Melamed, B. G. (1979). Behavioral approaches to fear in dental settings. In M. Hersen, R. M. Eisler, & P. M. Miller (Eds.), *Progress in behavior modification* (Vol. 7). New York: Academic Press.

Melamed, B. G., & Johnson, S. B. (1981). Behavioral assessment of chronic illness: Asthma and juvenile diabetes. In E. Mash & L. Terdal (Eds.), *Behavioral assessment of childhood disorders.* New York: Guilford.

Melamed, B. G., & Siegel, L. (1975). Reduction of anxiety in children facing hospitalization and surgery by use of filmed modeling. *Journal of Consulting and Clinical Psychology, 43*, 511–525.

Melamed, B. G., & Siegel, L. J. (1980). *Behavioral medicine.* New York: Springer.

Mendelson, I. S., Casey, R. E., Christie, E. J., Das, I., Zaleski, W. A., & Sugarman, R. (1981). Metabolic, endocrine, and nutrition profiling for high risk pregnancies as a preventive approach to disorders in growth and development of children. In P. J. Mittler & J. M. deJong (Eds.), *Frontiers of knowledge in mental retardation: Biomedical aspects.* Baltimore, MD: University Park Press.

Mendelson, W., Johnson, N., & Stewart, M. A. (1971). Hyperactive children as teenagers: A follow-up study. *Journal of Nervous and Mental Diseases, 153*, 273–279.

Merton, R. K. (1957). Social structure and anomie. In R. K. Merton (Ed.), *Social theory and social structure.* New York: Free Press.

Mesibov, G., & Schopler, E. (Eds.). (1983). *Autism in adolescents and adults.* New York: Plenum.

Michelson, L., Sugai, D. P., Wood, R. P., & Kazdin, A. E. (1983). *Social skills assessment and training with children.* New York: Plenum.

Mikkelsen, M., & Stene, J. (1970). Counseling in Down's syndrome. *Human Heredity, 20*, 457–464.

Miklich, D. R., Creer, T. L., Alexander, A. B., & Nichols, L. (1972). Three case histories in the use of self-modeling as a behavior therapy technique. *Children's Asthma Research Institute Bulletin, 2*(4).

Milby, J. B., Wendorf, D., & Meredith, R. L. (1983). Obsessive-compulsive disorders. In R. J. Morris & T. R. Kratochwill (Eds.), *The practice of child therapy*. New York: Pergamon.

Miller, H., & Baruch, D. A. (1950). A study of hostility in allergic children. *American Journal of Orthopsychiatry, 20*, 506–519.

Miller, L. C. (1983). Fears and anxieties in children. In E. Walker & M. Roberts (Eds.), *Handbook of clinical child psychology*. New York: Wiley.

Miller, L. C., Barrett, C. L., & Hampe, E. (1974). Phobias of childhood in a prescientific era. In A. Davids (Ed.), *Child personality and psychopathology*. New York: Wiley.

Miller, L. C., Barrett, C. L., Hampe, E., & Noble, H. (1972a). Factor structure of childhood fears. *Journal of Consulting and Clinical Psychology, 39*, 264–268.

Miller, L. C., Barrett, C. L., Hampe, E., & Nobel, H. (1972b). Comparison of reciprocal inhibition, psychotherapy, and waiting list controls for phobic children. *Journal of Abnormal Psychology, 79*, 269–279.

Miller, P., Champelli, J., & Dinello, F. (1968). Imipramine in the treatment of enuretic school children. *American Journal of Diseases in Children, 115*, 17–20.

Miller, R. T. (1974). Childhood schizophrenia: A review of selected literature. *International Journal of Mental Health, 3*, 3–46.

Millon, T., Green, C., & Meagher, R. (1982). *Handbook of clinical health psychology*. New York: Plenum.

Minde, K., Lewis, D., Weiss, G., Lavigueur, H., Douglas, V., & Sykes, E. (1971). The hyperactive child in elementary school: A 5 year, controlled follow-up. *Exceptional Children, 38*, 315–322.

Minuchin, S. (1974). *Families and family therapy*. Cambridge: Harvard University Press.

Minuchin, P., Biber, B., Shapiro, E., & Zimiles, H. (1969). *The psychological impact of school experience*. New York: Basic Books.

Minuchin, S., Rosman, B. L., & Baker, L. (1978). *Psychosomatic families*. Cambridge: Harvard University Press.

Mishler, E. G., & Waxler, N. E. (1968). *Interaction in families: An experimental study of family processes and schizophrenia*. New York: Wiley.

Mitchell, K. M., Bozarth, J. D., & Krauft, C. C. (1977). A reappraisal of the therapeutic effectiveness of accurate empathy, nonpossessive warmth, and genuineness. In A. S. Gurman & A. M. Razin (Eds.), *Effective psychotherapy: A handbook of research*. New York: Pergamon.

Mittler, P. J., & deJong, J. M. (Eds.). (1981a). *Frontiers of knowledge in mental retardation: Vol. I. Social, educational and behavioral aspects*. Baltimore: University Park Press.

Mittler, P. J., & deJong, J. M. (Eds.). (1981b). *Frontiers of knowledge in mental retardation: Vol. II. Biomedical aspects*. Baltimore: University Park Press.

Montenegro, H. (1968). Severe separation anxiety in two preschool children successfully treated by reciprocal inhibition. *Journal of Child Psychology and Psychiatry, 9*, 93–103.

Moore, D. R., & Arthur, J. L. (1983). Juvenile delinquency. In T. Ollendick & M. Hersen (Eds.), *Handbook of child psychopathology*. New York: Plenum.

Moore, K. L. (1959). Sex reversal in newborn babies. *Lancet, 1*, 217.

Morgan, C. D., & Murray, H. A. (1935). A method for investigating fantasies: The Thematic Apperception Test. *Archives of Neurology and Psychiatry, 34*, 289–306.

Morgan, H. G., & Russell, G. F. M. (1975). Value of family background and clinical features as predictors of long-term outcome in anorexia nervosa: Four year follow up study of 41 patients. *Psychological Medicine, 5*, 355–372.

Morgan, W. P. (1896). A case of congenital word blindness. *British Medical Journal, 2*, 137–138.

Morowitz, D. A., & Kirsner, J. B. (1969). Mortality in ulverative colitis, 1930–1966. *Gastroenterology, 57*, 481–490.

Morris, R., & Kratochwill, T. R. (1983). *Treating children's fears and phobias*. New York: Pergamon.

Morrison, F. J., Giordani, B., & Nagy, J. (1977). Reading disability: An information processing analysis. *Science, 196*, 77–79.

Morrison, J. R., & Stewart, M. A. (1971). A family study of the hyperactive child syndrome. *Biological Psychiatry, 3*, 189–195.

Morrison, J. R., & Stewart, M. A. (1973). The psychiatric status of the legal families of adopted hyperactive children. *Archives of General Psychiatry, 28*, 888–891.

Mowrer, O. H. (1956). Two-factor learning theory reconsidered, with special reference to the concept of habit. *Psychological Review, 63*, 114–128.

Mowrer, O. H., & Mowrer, W. M. (1938). Enuresis: A method for its study and treatment. *American Journal of Orthopsychiatry, 8*, 436–459.

Munsinger, H. (1975). The adopted child's IQ: A critical review. *Psychological Bulletin*, *82*, 623–659.

Murdoch, J. C. (1981). Hypothalamopituitary target organ function in adults with Down's syndrome. In P. J. Mittler & J. M. deJong (Eds.), *Frontiers of knowledge in mental retardation: Vol. II. Biomedical aspects*. Baltimore: University Park Press.

Murphy, L. B., & Frank, C. (1979). Prevention: The clinical psychologist. *Annual Review of Psychology*, *30*, 173–207.

Murphy, L. B., & Krall, U. (1960). Free play as a projective tool. In A. I. Rabin & M. R. Haworth (Eds.), *Projective techniques with children*. New York: Grune & Stratton.

Murphy, G. H., & Wilson, B. (1981). Long-term outcome of contingent shock treatment for self-injurious behavior. In P. J. Mittler & J. M. deJong (Eds.), *Frontiers of knowledge in mental retardation: Vol. II. Biomedical aspects*. Baltimore: University Park Press.

Murray, C. A. (1976). *The link between learning disabilities and juvenile delinquency: Current theory and knowledge*. Washington, DC: Law Enforcement Assistance Administration.

Myers, P. I., & Hammill, D. D. (1976). *Methods for learning disorders* (2nd ed.). New York: Wiley.

Naeye, R. L. (1981). Influence of maternal cigarette smoking during pregnancy on fetal and childhood growth. *Obstetrics and Gynecology*, *57*, 18–21.

Nash-Weber, B. (1975). The role of semantics in automatic speech understanding. In D. B. Bobrow & A. Collins (Eds.), *Representation and understanding*. New York: Academic Press.

Nathan, P. E. (1979). Diagnostic and treatment services for children: Introduction. *American Psychologist*, *34*, 967–968.

National Institute of Mental Health, Research Task Force. (1975). *Research in the service of mental health*. Rockville, MD: Author.

Naylor, H. (1980). Reading disability and lateral asymmetry: An information-processing analysis. *Psychological Bulletin*, *87*, 531–545.

Neal, D. H. (1963). Behavior therapy and encopresis in children. *Behavior Research and Therapy*, *1*, 139–149.

Neal, J. M., & Oltmanns, T. (1980). *Schizophrenia*. New York: Wiley.

Neisworth, J., Madle, R., & Goeke, K. (1975). "Errorless" elimination of separation anxiety: A case study. *Journal of Behavior Therapy and Experimental Psychiatry*, *6*, 79–82.

Neisworth, J. T., & Smith, R. M. (1978). *Retardation: Issues, assessment and intervention*. New York: McGraw-Hill.

Nelson, W. M., & Finch, A. J. (1978). *The Children's Inventory of Anger*. Unpublished manuscript, Xavier University.

Nemiah, J. C. (1967). Obsessive compulsive reaction. In A. M. Freedman & H. I. Kaplan (Eds.), *Comprehensive textbook of psychiatry*. Baltimore: William & Wilkins.

Neuhaus, E. C. (1958). Personality study of asthmatic and cardiac children. *Psychosomatic Medicine*, *3*, 181–186.

New York State Department of Mental Hygiene. (1955). A special census of suspected and referred mental retardation in Onondaga County, New York. *Technical Report of the Mental Health Research Unit*. Syracuse: Syracuse University Press.

Newman, H. H., Freeman, F. N., & Holzinger, K. J. (1937). *Twins: A study of heredity and environment*. Chicago: University of Chicago Press.

Ney, P. G., Palvesky, A. E., & Markley, J. (1971). Relative effectiveness of operant conditioning and play therapy in childhood schizophrenia. *Journal of Autism and Childhood Schizophrenia*, *1*, 377–349.

Nicol, A. R. (1985). *Longitudinal studies in child psychology and psychiatry*. New York: Wiley.

Nihira, K. (1978). Factorial descriptions of the AAMD adaptive behavior scale. In W. A. Coulter & H. W. Morrow (Eds.), *Adaptive behavior concepts and measurements*. New York: Grune & Stratton.

Nihira, K., Foster, R., Shellhaas, M., & Leland, H. (1974). *AAMD adaptive behavior scales* (rev. ed.). Washington, DC: American Association on Mental Deficiency.

Nihira, K., & Shellhaas, M. (1970). A study of adaptive behavior: Its rationale, method and application in rehabilitation programs. *Mental Retardation*, *8*, 11–16.

Nolan, J. D., & Pence, D. (1970). Operant conditioning principles in the treatment of a selective mute child. *Journal of Consulting and Clinical Psychology*, *35*, 365–368.

Nowicki, S., & Strickland, B. R. (1973). A locus of control scale for children. *Journal of Consulting and Clinical Psychology*, *40*, 148–154.

Noyes, A. P., & Kolb, L. C. (1968). *Modern clinical psychiatry*. Philadelphia: Saunders.

O'Connor, N., & Tizard, J. (1956). *The social problem of mental deficiency*. New York: Pergamon.

O'Connor, R. D. (1969). Modification of social withdrawal through symbolic modeling. *Journal of Applied Behavior Analysis*, *2*, 15–22.

O'Dell, S. (1974). Training parents in behavior modification: A review. *Psychological Bulletin*, *81*, 418–433.

Oden, M. H. (1968). The fulfillment of promises: Forty-year follow-up of the Terman gifted group. *Genetic Psychology Monographs, 7,* 3–93.

O'Donnell, C. R., Lydgate, T., & Fo, W. S. (1979). The buddy system: Review and follow-up. *Child Behavior Therapy, 1,* 161–169.

Offord, D. R., & Cross, L. A. (1969). Behavioral antecedents of adult schizophrenia. *Archives of General Psychiatry, 21,* 267–283.

Offord, D. R., & Jones, M. B. (1983). Skill development: A community interaction program for the prevention of antisocial behavior. In S. B. Guze, F. J. Earls, & J. E. Barrett (Eds.), *Childhood psychopathology and development.* New York: Raven.

Ojemann, R. H. (1967). Incorporating psychological concepts in the school curriculum. *Journal of School Psychology, 5,* 195–204.

O'Leary, K. D. (1980). Pills or skills for hyperactive children? *Journal of Applied Behavior Analysis, 13,* 191–204.

O'Leary, K. D., & Becker, W. C. (1967). Behavior modification in an adjustment class. *Exceptional Children, 9,* 637–642.

O'Leary, K. D., & Wilson, G. T. (1975). *Behavior therapy: Application and outcome.* Englewood Cliffs: NJ: Prentice-Hall.

Ollendick, T. H. (1979). Behavioral treatment of anorexia nervosa: A five-year study. *Behavior Modification, 3,* 124–135.

Ollendick, T. H., & Cerny, J. (1981). *Clinical behavior therapy with children.* New York: Plenum.

Ollendick, T. H., & Gruen, G. E. (1972). Treatment of a bodily injury phobia with implosive therapy. *Journal of Consulting and Clinical Psychology, 38,* 389–393.

Ollendick, T. H., & Hersen, M. (1979). Social skills training for juvenile delinquents. *Behavior Research and Therapy, 17,* 547–554.

Ollendick, T. H., & Hersen, M. (1984). *Child behavioral assessment.* New York: Pergamon.

Ollendick, T. H., & Matson, J. L. (1978). Overcorrection: An overview. *Behavior Therapy, 9,* 1–13.

Ornitz, E. M., & Ritvo, E. R. (1976). The syndrome of autism: A critical review. *American Journal of Psychiatry, 133,* 605–621.

Orris, J. B. (1969). Visual monitoring performance in three subgroups of male delinquents. *Journal of Abnormal Psychology, 74,* 227–229.

Orton, T. S. (1966). "Word-blindness" in school children and other papers on strephosymbolia (specific language disability-dyslexia). *Orton Society Monographs,* No. 2.

Overton, W. F. (Ed.). (1983). *The relationship between social and cognitive development.* Hillsdale, NJ: Erlbaum.

Owen, D. R. (1972). The 47 XYY male: A review. *Psychological Bulletin, 78,* 209–233.

Palmer, J. O. (1983). *The psychological assessment of children* (2nd ed.). New York: Wiley.

Parks, S. L. (1983). The assessment of autistic children: A selective review of available instruments. *Journal of Autism and Developmental Disorders, 13,* 255–267.

Paschalis, A. P., Kimmel, H. D., & Kimmel, E. (1972). A further study of diurnal instrumental conditioning in the treatment of enuresis nocturna. *Journal of Behavior Therapy and Experimental Psychiatry, 3,* 253–256.

Patterson, G. R. (1965). A learning theory approach to the treatment of the school phobic child. In L. P. Ullmann & L. Krasner (Eds.), *Case studies in behavior modification.* New York: Holt, Rinehart, & Winston.

Patterson, G. R. (1974). Interventions for boys with conduct problems: Multiple settings, treatments, and criteria. *Journal of Consulting and Clinical Psychology, 42,* 471–481.

Patterson, G. R., & Brodsky, G. (1966). A behavior modification programme for a child with multiple problem behaviors. *Journal of Child Psychology and Psychiatry, 7,* 277–295.

Patterson, G. R., Cobb, J. A., & Ray, R. S. (1973). A social engineering technology for retraining the families of aggressive boys. In H. E. Adams & I. P. Unikel (Eds.), *Issues and trends in behavior therapy.* Springfield, IL: Charles C Thomas.

Patterson, G. R., & Fleischman, M. J. (1979). Maintenance of treatment effects: Some considerations concerning family systems and follow up data. *Behavior Therapy, 10,* 168–185.

Patterson, G. R., & Guillon, M. E. (1968). *Living with children.* Champaign, IL: Research Press.

Patterson, G. R., Jones, R., Whittier, J., & Wright, M. A. (1965). A behavior modification technique for the hyperactive child. *Behavior Research and Therapy, 2,* 217–226.

Patterson, G. R., Ray, R. S., & Shaw, D. A. (1968). Direct intervention in families of deviant children. *Oregon Research Institute Bulletin, 8,* No. 9.

Paykel, E. S. (1974). Life stress and psychiatric disorder: Application of the clinical approach. In B. S. Dohrenwend & B. P. Dohrenwend (Eds.), *Stressful life events: Their nature and effects.* New York: Wiley.

Pearce, J. (1977). Depressive disorder in childhood. *Journal of Child Psychology and Psychiatry, 18,* 74–82.

Pedrini, B. C., & Pedrini, D. T. (1971). Reinforcement procedures in the control of encopresis. *Psychological Reports, 29,* 937–938.

Perry, M. A., & Furukawa, M. J. (1980). Modeling methods. In F. H. Kanfer & A. Goldstein (Eds.), *Helping people change* (2nd ed.). New York: Pergamon.

Pestalozzi, J. H. (1895). *Leonard and Gerard*. Boston: Heath.

Peterson, L., & Shigetomi, C. (1981). The use of coping techniques to minimize anxiety in hospitalized children. *Behavior Therapy, 12*, 1–14.

Petti, T. A. (1983). *Childhood depression*. New York: The Haworth Press.

Pfeffer, C. R. (1981). Suicidal behavior of children: A review with implications for research and practice. *American Journal of Psychiatry, 138*, 154–160.

Phillips, D. L. (1964). Rejection of the mentally ill: The influence of behavior and sex. *American Sociological Review, 29*, 679–687.

Phillips, E. L. (1968). Achievement Place: Token reinforcement procedures in a home-style rehabilitation setting for "pre-delinquent" boys. *Journal of Applied Behavior Analysis, 1*, 213–223.

Phillips, E. L., Phillips, E. A., Fixsen, D. L., & Wolf, M. M. (1971). Achievement Place: Modification of the behaviors of pre-delinquent boys within a token economy. *Journal of Applied Behavior Analysis, 4*, 45–59.

Phillips, E. L., Phillips, E. A., Fixsen, D. L., & Wolf, M. M. (1973). Behavior shaping for delinquents. *Psychology Today, 7*, 74–79.

Phillips, J. S., & Ray, R. S. (1980). Behavioral approaches to childhood disorders. *Behavior Modification, 4*, 3–34.

Piaget, J. (1963). *The origins of intelligence in children*. New York: International Universities Press.

Piaget, J., & Inhelder, B. (1969). *The psychology of the child*. New York: Basic Books.

Piazza, E., Carni, J. D., Kelly, J., & Plante, S. (1983). Group psychotherapy for anorexia nervosa. *Journal of the American Academy of Child Psychiatry, 22*, 276–278.

Piazza, E., Piazza, N., & Rollins, W. (1980). Anorexia nervosa: Controversial aspects of therapy. *Comprehensive Psychiatry, 21*, 177–191.

Pierce, M. L. (1971). A behavior modification approach to facilitating a disturbed child's reentry by teaching time-out procedures to the child's classmates. *School Applications of Learning Theory, 2*, 1–61.

Piggott, L. R. (1979). Overview of selected basic research in autism. *Journal of Autism and Developmental Disorders, 9*, 199–218.

Pinneau, S. R. (1961). *Changes in intelligence quotient: Infancy to maturity*. Boston: Houghton Mifflin.

Pirozzolo, F. J. (1979). *The neuropsychology of developmental reading disorders*. New York: Praeger.

Plachetta, K. E. (1976). Encopresis: A case study utilizing contracting, scheduling, and self-charting. *Journal of Behavior Therapy and Experimental Psychiatry, 7*, 195–196.

Plomin, R. (1983). Childhood temperament. In B. Lahey & A. Kazdin (Eds.), *Advances in clinical child psychology*. New York: Plenum.

Poznanski, E. O. (1983). Controversy and conflicts in childhood depression. In T. A. Petti (Ed.), *Childhood depression*. New York: Haworth Press.

Poznanski, E. O., Krahenbuhl, U., & Zrull, J. P. (1976). Childhood depression: A longitudinal perspective. *Journal of the American Academy of Child Psychiatry, 15*, 491–501.

Poznanski, E. O., & Zrull, J. P. (1970). Childhood depression: Clinical characteristics of overtly depressed children. *Archives of General Psychiatry, 23*, 815–829.

President's Committee of Mental Retardation. (1976). *Mental retardation: Century of decision*. Washington, DC: Author.

Price, G. G. , Walsh, D. J., & Vilberg, W. R. (1984). The confluence model's good predictions of mental age beg the question. *Psychological Bulletin, 96*, 195–200.

Prior, M. R. (1979). Cognitive abilities and disabilities in infantile autism: A review. *Journal of Abnormal Child Psychology, 7*, 357–380.

Prior, M., Boulton, D., Gajzago, C., & Perry, D. (1975). The classification of childhood psychoses by numerical taxonomy. *Journal of Psychology and Psychiatry, 16*, 321–330.

Prior, M., & Macmillan, M. B. (1973). Maintenance of sameness in children with Kanner's syndrome. *Journal of Autism and Childhood Schizophrenia, 3*, 154–167.

Proctor, J. T. (1958). Hysteria in childhood. *American Journal of Orthopsychiatry, 28*, 394–407.

Prout, H. T. (1977). Behavioral intervention with hyperactive children: A review. *Journal of Learning Disabilities, 10*, 141–146.

Psychological Corporation (1978). *The Metropolitan Achievement Tests* (5th ed.). New York: Psychological Corporation.

Purcell, K. (1963). Distinctions between subgroups of asthmatic children: Children's perceptions of events associated with asthma. *Pediatrics, 31*, 486–494.

Purcell, K. (1975). Childhood asthma: The role of family relationships, personality, and emotions. In A. Davids (Ed.), *Child personality and psychopathology* (Vol. 2). New York: Wiley.

Purcell, K., Bernstein, L., & Bukantz, S. C. (1961). A preliminary comparison of rapidly remitting and persistently "steroid dependent" asthmatic children. *Psychosomatic Medicine, 23*, 305–310.

Purcell, K., Brady, K., Chai, H., Muser, J., Molk, K., Gordon, N., & Means, J. (1969). The effects of asthma in children of experimental separation from the family. *Psychosomatic Medicine, 31,* 144–164.

Purcell, K., Weiss, J., & Hahn, W. (1972). Certain psychosomatic disorders. In B. Wolman (Ed.), *Manual of child psychopathology.* New York: McGraw-Hill.

Quay, H. C. (1964). Dimensions of personality in delinquent boys as inferred from factor analysis of case history data. *Child Development, 35,* 479–484.

Quay, H. C. (1965). *Juvenile delinquency.* New York: Van Nostrand.

Quay, H. C. (1972). Patterns of aggression, withdrawal and immaturity. In H. C. Quay & J. S. Werry (Eds.), *Psychopathological disorders of childhood.* New York: Wiley.

Quay, H. C. (1977). Measuring dimensions of deviant behavior. The Behavior Problem Checklist. *Journal of Abnormal Child Psychology, 5,* 277–287.

Quay, H. C. (1979a). Residential treatment. In H. C. Quay & J. S. Werry (Eds.), *Psychopathological disorders of childhood* (2nd ed.). New York: Wiley.

Quay, H. C. (1979b). Classification. In H. C. Quay & J. S. Werry (Eds.), *Psychopathological disorders of childhood* (2nd ed.). New York: Wiley.

Quay, H. C. (1984). *A critical analysis of DSM-III as a taxonomy of psychopathology in childhood and adolescence.* Unpublished manuscript, University of Miami.

Rachman, S. (1976). The modification of obsessions: A new formulation. *Behavior Research and Therapy, 14,* 437–443.

Rachman, S., DeSilva, P., & Roper, G. (1976). The spontaneous decay of compulsive urges. *Behavior Research and Therapy, 14,* 445–453.

Rae, W. A. (1977). Childhood conversion reactions: A review of incidence in pediatric settings. *Journal of Clinical Child Psychology, 6,* 66–72.

Ramondo, N., & Schwartz, S. (1981). Diagnosing early infantile autism. *Current Psychological Reviews, 1,* 3–16.

Rao, B. S., Subhash, M. N., & Narayanan, H. S. (1981). Inborn errors of metabolism associated with mental retardation detected at the National Institute of Mental Health and Neurosciences, Bangalore, India. In P. J. Mittler & J. M. deJong (Eds.), *Frontiers of knowledge in mental retardation: Vol. II. Biomedical apects.* Baltimore: University Park Press.

Rapin, I. (1982). *Children with brain dysfunction.* New York: Raven.

Rapoport, J. L. (1983). Stimulant drug treatment of hyperactivity: An update. In I. B. Guze, F. J. Earls, & J. E. Barrett (Eds.), *Childhood psychopathology and development.* New York: Raven.

Rapoport, J. L. (1985). Childhood obsessive-compulsive disorder. In D. Shaffer, A. A. Ehrhardt, & L. Greenhill (Eds.), *The clinical guide to child psychiatry.* New York: The Free Press.

Rapoport, J. L., Buchsbaum, M. S., Zahn, T. P., Weingartner, H., Ludlow, C., & Mikkelsen, E. J. (1978). Dextroamphetamine: Cognitive and behavioral effects in normal prepubertal boys. *Science, 199,* 560–563.

Rapoport, J., Elkins, R., Langer, D. H., Sceery, W., Buchsbaum, M., Gillin, C., Murphy, D., Zahn, T., Lake, R., Ludlow, C., & Mendelson, W. (1981). Childhood obsessive-compulsive disorder. *American Journal of Psychiatry, 138,* 1545–1554.

Rapoport, J. L., & Ferguson, H. (1981). Biological validation of the hyperkinetic syndrome. *Developmental Medicine and Child Neurology, 23,* 667–682.

Rapoport, J. L., & Ismond, D. R. (1982). Biological research in child psychiatry. *Journal of the American Academy of Child Psychiatry, 21,* 543–548.

Ratcliff, S. G., & Field, M. A. (1982). Emotional disorder in XYY children: Four case reports. *Journal of Child Psychology and Psychiatry, 23,* 401–406.

Ratner, B., & Silberman, A. E. (1953). Critical analysis of the hereditary concept of allergy. *Journal of Allergy, 24,* 371–378.

Redl, F. (1944). Diagnostic group work. *American Journal of Orthopsychiatry, 14,* 53–67.

Rees, L. (1964). The importance of psychological, allergic, and infective factors in childhood asthma. *Journal of Psychosomatic Research, 7,* 253–262.

Reichler, R. J., & Schopler, E. (1976). Developmental therapy: A program for providing individualized services in the community. In E. Schopler & R. J. Reichler (Eds.), *Psychopathology and child development: Research and treatment.* New York: Plenum.

Reid, D. K., & Hresko, W. P. (1981). *A cognitive approach to learning disabilities.* New York: McGraw-Hill.

Reid, J. B. (1978). *A social learning approach to family intervention: Observation in home settings* (Vol. 2). Eugene, OR: Castalia Publishing Co.

Reisinger, J. J., Ora, J. P., & Frangia, G. W. (1976). Parents as change agents for their children: A review. *Journal of Community Psychology, 4,* 103–123.

Reitan, R. (1964). *Manual for administering and scoring the Reitan Indiana Neuropsychological Battery for Young Children.* Indianapolis: Indiana University Medical Center.

Rekers, G. A. (1977). Assessment and treatment of gender problems. In B. Lahey & A. Kazdin (Eds.), *Advances in clinical child psychology* (Vol. 1). New York: Plenum.

Reynolds, G. S. (1975). *A primer of operant conditioning.* Glenview, IL: Scott Foresman.

Riesen, A. (1960). Effects of stimulus deprivation on the development and atrophy of the visual sensory system. *American Journal of Orthopsychiatry, 30,* 23–36.

Rimland, B. (1964). *Infantile autism: The syndrome and its implications for a neural theory of behavior.* New York: Appleton-Century-Crofts.

Rimland, B. (1971). The differentiation of childhood psychoses: An analysis of checklists for 2,218 psychotic children. *Journal of Autism and Childhood Schizophrenia, 1,* 161–174.

Rimland, B., Callaway, E., & Dreyfus, P. (1978). The effect of high doses of vitamin B_6 on autistic children: A double-bind crossover study. *American Journal of Psychiatry, 155,* 472–475.

Rimm, D. C., & Masters, J. C. (1979). *Behavior therapy: Techniques and empirical findings.* New York: Academic Press.

Risley, T. R. (1968). The effects and side effects of punishing the autistic behaviors of a deviant child. *Journal of Applied Behavior Analysis, 1,* 21–34.

Ritter, N. (1968). The group desensitization of children's snake phobias using vicarious and contact desensitization procedures. *Behavior Research and Therapy, 6,* 1–6.

Ritvo, E. R. (1983). The syndrome of autism: A medical model. *Integrative Psychiatry, 1,* 103–109.

Ritvo, E. R., Freeman, B. J., Geller, E., & Yuwiler, A. (1983). Effects of fenfluramine on 14 outpatients with the syndrome of autism. *Journal of the American Academy of Child Psychiatry, 22,* 549–558.

Ritvo, E. R., Ritvo, E. C., & Brothers, A. M. (1982). Genetic and immunohematologic factors in autism. *Journal of Autism and Developmental Disorders, 12,* 109–114.

Robbins, D. M., Beck, J. C. Pries, R., Jacobs, D., & Smith, C. (1983). Learning disability and neuropsychological impairment in adjudicated, unincarcerated, male delinquents. *Journal of the American Academy of Child Psychiatry, 22,* 40–46.

Roberts, M. C., Maddux, J. E., Wurtele, S. K., & Wright, L. (1982). Pediatric psychology: Health care psychology for children. In T. Millon, C. Green, & R. Meagher (Eds.), *Handbook of clinical health psychology.* New York: Plenum.

Robins, E., & O'Neal, P. (1953). Clinical features of hysteria in children. *Nervous Child, 10,* 246–271.

Robins, L. N. (1966). *Deviant children grown up.* Baltimore: Williams & Wilkins.

Robins, L. N. (1979). Follow-up studies. In H. C. Quay & J. S. Werry (Eds.), *Psychopathological disorders of childhood* (2nd ed.). New York: Wiley.

Robinson, D. (1982). Early warning for Down's syndrome. *Health, 14,* 19–20.

Robinson, E. A., Eyberg, S. M., & Ross, A. W. (1980). The standardization of an inventory of child conduct problem behaviors. *Journal of Clinical Child Psychology, 9,* 22–29.

Robinson, N. M., & Robinson, H. B. (1976). *The mentally retarded child* (2nd ed.). New York: McGraw-Hill.

Robson, J. M., Sullivan, F. M., & Smith, R. L. (1965). *Embryopathic activity of drugs.* London: Churchill.

Rock, N. L. (1971). Conversion reactions in childhood: A clinical study of childhood neurosis. *Journal of the American Academy of Child Psychiatry, 10,* 65–93.

Roen, S. R. (1967). Primary prevention in the classroom through a teaching program in the behavioral sciences. In E. Cowen, E. A. Gardner & M. Zax (Eds.), *Emergent approaches to mental health problems.* New York: Appleton-Century-Crofts.

Rolf, J. E. (1976). Peer status and the directionality of symptomatic behavior: Prime social competence predictors of outcome for vulnerable children. *American Journal of Orthopsychiatry, 46,* 74–88.

Romanczyk, R. G., Kistner, J. A., & Crimmins, D. B. (1980). Institutional treatment of severely disturbed children: Fact, possibility or nonsequitur? In B. Lahey and A. Kazdin (Eds.), *Advances in clinical child psychology* (Vol. 3). New York: Plenum.

Rose, S. D. (1972). *Treating children in groups: A behavioral approach.* San Francisco: Jossey-Bass.

Rosenberger, P. B., Wheeldeen, J. A., & Kalotkin, M. (1976). The effect of haloperidol on stuttering. *American Journal of Psychiatry, 133,* 330–334.

Rosenn, D. W. (1982). Suicidal behavior in children and adolescents. In E. Bassuk, S. C. Schoonover, & A. D. Gill (Eds.), *Lifelines: Clinical perspectives on suicide.* New York: Plenum.

Rosenthal, D. (1975). Heredity in criminality. *Criminal Justice and Behavior, 2,* 3–21.

Rosenthal, D., & Kety, S. (Eds.). (1968). *The transmission of schizophrenia.* New York: Pergamon.

Rosenthal, T., & Bandura, A. (1978). Psychological modeling: Theory and practice. In S. L. Garfield & A. Bergin (Eds.), *Handbook of psy-*

chotherapy and behavior change (2nd ed.). New York: Wiley.

Rosenzweig, M. R. (1976). Effects of environment on brain and behavior in animals. In E. Schopler & R. J. Reichler (Eds.), *Psychopathology and child development: Research and treatment* (pp. 33–50). New York: Plenum.

Rosenzweig, S. (1960). The Rosenzweig picture frustration study. In A. I. Rabin & M. R. Haworth (Eds.), *Projective techniques with children*. New York: Grune & Stratton.

Rosman, B. L., Minuchin, S., Baker, L., & Liebman, R. (1977). Input and outcome of family therapy in anorexia nervosa. *Adolescent Psychiatry* (Vol. 5). New York: Jason Aronson.

Ross, A. O. (1976). *Psychological aspects of learning disabilities and reading disorders*. New York: McGraw-Hill.

Ross, A. O. (1981). *Child behavior therapy*. New York: Wiley.

Ross, A. O., & Pelham, W. E. (1981). Child psychopathology. *Annual Review of Psychology, 32,* 243–278.

Ross, D. M., & Ross, S. A. (1976). *Hyperactivity: Research theory and action*. New York: Wiley.

Ross, L. E., & Ward, T. B. (1978). The processing of information from short-term visual store: Developmental and intellectual differences. In N. R. Ellis (Ed.), *International review of research in mental retardation. Vol 9.* New York: Academic Press.

Rothenberger, A. (1982). *Event-related potentials in children*. New York: Elsevier.

Rotter, J. B., & Rafferty, J. E. (1950). *Manual: The Rotter Incomplete Sentence Blank*. New York: Psychological Corporation.

Rourke, P. B., Bakker, D. J., Fisk, J. L., & Strang, J. D. (1983). *Child neuropsychology: An introduction to theory, research, and clinical practice*. New York: Guilford.

Routh, D. K., Schroeder, C. S., & O'Tuama, L. A. (1974). Development of activity level in children. *Developmental Psychology, 10,* 163–168.

Rubin, R., & Balow, B. (1971). Learning and behavior disorders: A longitudinal study. *Exceptional Children, 38,* 293–299.

Rumelhart, D. E. (1977). Toward an interactive model of reading. In S. Dornic (Ed.), *Attention and performance. Vol. 6.* Hillsdale, NJ: Erlbaum.

Rutter, M. (1968). Concepts of Autism: A review of research. *Journal of Child Psychology and Psychiatry, 9,* 1–25.

Rutter, M. (1972a). Childhood schizophrenia reconsidered. *Journal of Autism and Childhood Schizophrenia, 2,* 315–537.

Rutter, M. (1972b). Parent-child separation: Psychological effects on children. *Journal of Child Psychology and Psychiatry, 12,* 233–260.

Rutter, M. (1974). The development of infantile autism. *Psychological Medicine, 4,* 147–163.

Rutter, M. (1978a). Diagnosis and definition. In M. Rutter & E. Schopler (Eds.), *Autism: A reappraisal of concepts and treatment*. New York: Plenum.

Rutter, M. (1978b). Language disorder and infantile autism. In M. Rutter & E. Schopler (Eds.), *Autism: A reappraisal of concepts and treatment*. New York: Plenum.

Rutter, M. (1978c). Diagnosis and definition of childhood autism. *Journal of Autism and Developmental Disorders, 8,* 135–161.

Rutter, M. (1979). Language, cognition and autism. In R. Katzman (Ed.), *Congenital and acquired disorders*. New York: The Association for Research in Mental Disease.

Rutter, M. (1982a). Syndromes attributed to minimal brain dysfunction in childhood. *American Journal of Psychiatry, 139,* 21–33.

Rutter, M. (1982b). *Temperament: Concepts, issues and problems*. In Ciba Foundation Symposium Number 89. London: Pitmann Books Ltd.

Rutter, M., Bartak, L., & Newman, S. (1971). Autism — A central disorder of cognition and language? In M. Rutter (Ed.), *Infantile autism: Concepts, characteristics and treatment* (pp. 148–171). London: Churchill-Livingstone.

Rutter, M., & Giller, H. (1983). *Juvenile delinquency: Trends and perspectives*. New York: Guilford.

Rutter, M., & Lockyer, L. A. (1967). A five to fifteen year follow-up study of infantile psychosis. I. Description of sample. *British Journal of Psychiatry, 113,* 1169–1182.

Rutter, M., & Shaffer, D. (1980). DSM-III. A step forward or back in terms of the classification of child psychiatric disorders? *Journal of the American Academy of Child Psychiatry,* 371–394.

Rutter, M., Tizard, J., & Whitmore, K. (1970). *Education, health, and behavior*. New York: Wiley.

Ryback, D., & Staats, A. W. (1970). Parents as behavior therapy technicians in treating reading deficits (dyslexia). *Journal of Behavior Therapy and Experimental Psychiatry, 1,* 109–119.

Sandberg, A. A., Koepf, G. F., Ishihara, T., & Hauschka, T. S. (1961). XYY human male. *Lancet, 2,* 488–489.

Sandberg, S. T., Wieselberg, M., & Shaffer, D. (1980). Hyperkinetic and conduct problem children in a primary school population: Some epidemiological considerations. *Journal of Child Psychology and Psychiatry, 21,* 293–310.

Sandifer, M. G., Pettus, C., & Quade, D. (1964). A study of psychiatric diagnosis. *Journal of*

Nervous and Mental Disease, 139, 350–356.

Sandler, I. N., Duricko, A., & Grande, L. (1975). Effectiveness of an early secondary prevention program in an inner-city elementary school. *American Journal of Community Psychology, 3,* 23–32.

Sands, H., & Minters, F. C. (1977). *The epilepsy fact book.* Philadelphia: F. A. Davids.

Sarason, I. G. (1968). Verbal learning, modeling and juvenile delinquency. *American Psychologist, 23,* 245–266.

Sarason, I. G. (1978). A cognitive social learning approach to juvenile delinquency. In R. D. Hare & D. Shalling (Eds.), *Psychopathic behavior: Approaches to research.* New York: Wiley.

Sarason, I. G., & Ganzer, V. J. (1971). *Modeling: An approach to the rehabilitation of juvenile offenders.* Washington, DC: U.S. Department of Health, Education and Welfare.

Sarason, I. G., Johnson, J. H., & Siegel, J. M. (1978). Assessing the impact of life changes: Development of the Life Experiences Survey. *Journal of Consulting and Clinical Psychology, 46,* 932–946.

Sarason, S. B., & Lorentz, E. (1979). *The challenges of the resources exchange network: From concept to action.* San Francisco: Jossey Bass.

Sarbin, T. R., & Mancuso, J. C. (1980). *Schizophrenia: Medical diagnosis or moral verdict?* New York: Pergamon.

Satir, V. (1967). *Conjoint family therapy.* Palo Alto, CA: Science and Behavior Books.

Satterfield, J. H. (1978). The hyperactive child syndrome: A precursor of adult psychopathy. In R. D. Hare & D. Shalling (Eds.), *Psychopathic behavior: Approaches to research.* New York: Wiley.

Satterfield, J. H., Cantwell, D. P., & Satterfield, B. T. (1974). The pathophysiology of the hyperkinetic syndrome. *Archives of General Psychiatry, 31,* 839–844.

Sattler, J. M. (1982). *Assessment of children's intelligence* (2nd ed.). Philadelphia: W. B. Saunders.

Scarboro, M. E., & Forehand, R. (1975). Effects of two types of response-contingent time out on compliance and oppositional behavior in children. *Journal of Experimental Child Psychology, 19,* 252–264.

Schacht, T., & Nathan, P. E. (1977). But is it good for psychologists? Appraisal and status of DSM III. *American Psychologist, 32,* 1017–1025.

Schaefer, C. (1976). *Therapeutic use of child's play.* New York: Aronson.

Schaefer, C. E. (1979). *Childhood enuresis and encopresis.* New York: Van Nostrand.

Schaefer, C., & O'Connor, K. J. (1983). *Handbook of play therapy.* New York: Wiley.

Schaffer, H. R., & Emerson, P. (1964). The development of social attachments in infancy. *Monographs of the Society for Research in Child Development, 29* (3, Whole No. 94).

Scheiner, L. C., Musetto, A. P., & Cordier, D. C. (1982). Custody and visitation counselling: A report of an innovative program. *Family Relations, 31,* 99–107.

Scherer, M. W., & Nakamura, C. Y. (1968). A fear survey schedule for children (FSS-FC): An analytic comparison with manifest anxiety. *Behavior Research and Therapy, 6,* 173–182.

Schiff, M., Duyme, M., Dumaret, A., Stewart, J., Tomkiewicz, S., & Feingold, J. (1978). Intellectual status of working class children adopted early into middle class families. *Science, 200,* 1502–1504.

Schiffer, M. (1977). Activity-interview group psychotherapy: Theory, principles, and practice. *International Journal of Group Psychotherapy, 27,* 377–388.

Schiffer, M. (1984). *Children's group therapy.* New York: The Free Press.

Schlesier-Stropp, B. (1984). Bulimia: A review of the literature. *Psychological Bulletin, 95,* 247–257.

Schmidt, H. O., & Fonda, C. P. (1956). The reliability of psychiatric diagnosis: A new look. *Journal of Abnormal and Social Psychology, 52,* 262–267.

Schneider, G. E. (1979). Is it really better to have your brain lesion early? A revision of the "Kennard principle." *Neuropsychologica, 17,* 557–583.

Schneidman, E. S., (1975). Suicide. In A. M. Freedman, H. Kaplan, & B. J. Sadock, (Eds.), *Comprehensive textbook of psychiatry. Vol. 2.* Baltimore: Williams & Wilkins.

Schnurer, A., Rubin, R., & Roy, A. (1973). Systematic desensitization of anorexia nervosa seen as a weight phobia. *Journal of Behavior Therapy and Experimental Psychiatry, 4,* 149–153.

Scholom, A., Zucker, R. A., & Stollack, G. E. (1979). Relating early child adjustment to infant and parent temperament. *Journal of Abnormal Child Psychology, 7,* 297–308.

Schonhaut, S., & Satz, P. (1983). Prognosis for children with learning disabilities: A review of follow up studies. In M. Rutter (Ed.), *Developmental neuropsychiatry.* New York: Guilford.

Schopler, E., Andrews, C. E., & Stropp, K. (1979). Do autistic children come from upper-middle class parents? *Journal of Autism and Developmental Disorders, 9,* 139–152.

Schopler, E., Reichler, R. J., DeVellis, R. F., & Daly, K. (1980). Toward objective classification of childhood autism: Childhood autism rating scale. (CARS). *Journal of Autism and*

Development Disorders, 10, 91–103.

Schover, L. R., & Newsom, C. D. (1976). Overselectivity, developmental level and overtraining in autistic and normal children. *Journal of Abnormal Child Psychology, 4,* 289–298.

Schreibman, L. (1975). Effects of within-stimulus and extra-stimulus prompting on discrimination learning in autistic children. *Journal of Applied Behavior Analysis, 8,* 91–112.

Schreibman, L., Charlop, M. H., & Britten (1983). Childhood autism. In R. J. Morris & T. R. Kratochwill (Eds.), *The practice of child therapy.* New York: Pergamon.

Schroeder, C. S., Gordon, B. N., & Hawk, B. (1983). Clinical problems of the preschool child. In E. Walker & M. Roberts (Eds.), *Handbook of clinical child psychology.* New York: Wiley.

Schuckit, M. A. (1984). *Drug and alcohol abuse* (2nd ed.). New York: Plenum.

Schulsinger, F. (1974). Psychopathology: Heredity and environment. In S. Mednick, F. Schulsinger, J. Higgins, & B. Bell (Eds.), *Genetics, environment and psychopathology.* New York: American Elsevier.

Schwartz, S. (1981). Language disabilities in infantile autism. A brief review and comment. *Applied Psycholinguistics, 7,* 25–31.

Schwartz, S. (1982). Is there a schizophrenic language? *Behavior and Brain Sciences, 5,* 599–626.

Schwartz, S. (1984). *Measuring reading competence.* New York: Plenum.

Schwartz, S., & Kirsner, K. (1982). Laterality effects in visual information processing: Hemispheric specialization of the orienting of attention. *Quarterly Journal of Experimental Psychology, 34A,* 61–77.

Schwartz, S., & Kirsner, K. (1984). Can group differences in hemispheric asymmetry be inferred from behavioral laterality indices? *Brain and Cognition, 3,* 47–76.

Schwartz, S., & Wiedel, T. C. (1978). Individual differences in cognition: Relationship between verbal ability and memory for order. *Intelligence, 2,* 363–379.

Schwitzgebel, R. R. (1964). Delinquents with tape recorders. In F. Riessman, J. Cohen, & A. Pearl (Eds.), *Mental health of the poor.* New York: Free Press.

Sears, R. R. (1977). Sources of life satisfaction among the Terman gifted men. *American Psychologist, 32,* 109–128.

Seay, B., Hansen, E. W., & Harlow, H. F. (1962). Mother-infant separation in monkeys. *Journal of Child Psychology and Psychiatry, 3,* 123–132.

Seay, B., & Harlow, H. F. (1965). Maternal separation in the rhesus monkey. *Journal of Nervous and Mental Diseases, 140,* 434–441.

Segal, J. (1975). *Research in the service of mental health.* Washington, DC: National Institute of Mental Health.

Seguin, E. (1866). *Idiocy and its treatment.* New York: William Wood.

Selfe, L. (1977). *Nadia: A case of extraordinary drawing ability in an autistic child.* London: Academic Press.

Sells, S. B., & Simpson, D. D. (1980). The case for drug abuse treatment effectiveness based on the DARP research program. *British Journal of Addictions, 75,* 117–131.

Seligman, M. E. P. (1974). Depression and learned helplessness. In R. J. Friedman & M. M. Katz (Eds.), *The psychology of depression: Contemporary theory and research.* Washington, DC: Winston.

Seligman, M. E. P. (1978). Comment and integration. *Journal of Abnormal Psychology, 87,* 165–179.

Selye, H. (1956). *The stress of life.* New York: McGraw-Hill.

Selye, H. (1979). The stress concept and some of its implications. In V. Hamilton & D. B. Warburton (Eds.), *Human stress and cognition: An information processing approach.* London: Wiley.

Semel, E. M., & Wiig, E. H. (1980). *Clinical evaluation of language function. Diagnostic battery examiner's manual.* Columbus, OH: Charles Merrill.

Sever, J. L. (1970). Infectious agents and fetal disease. In H. A. Waisman & G. R. Kerr (Eds.), *Fetal growth and development.* New York: McGraw-Hill.

Shaffer, D. (1985). Nocturnal enuresis: Its investigation and treatment. In D. Shaffer, A. A. Ehrhardt, & L. Greenhill. (Eds.), *The clinical guide to child psychiatry.* New York: The Free Press.

Shaffer, D., Costello, A., & Hill, I. (1968). Control of enuresis with imipramine. *Archives of Disease in Childhood, 43,* 665–671.

Shapiro, A., & Shapiro, E. (1982). Tourette syndrome: History and present status. In A. J. Friedhoff & T. N. Chase (Eds.), *Gilles de la Tourette Syndrome.* New York: Raven.

Shapiro, A. K., Shapiro, E. S., Brown, R. D., & Sweet, R. D. (1978). *Gilles de la Tourette Syndrome.* New York: Raven.

Shaw, C. R., & McKay, H. D. (1969). *Juvenile delinquency in urban areas.* Chicago: University of Chicago Press.

Shepherd, M., Oppenheim, A. N., & Mitchell, S. (1966). Childhood behavior disorders and the child guidance clinic: An epidemiological study. *Journal of Child Psychology and Psychiatry, 7,* 39–52.

Shepherd, M., Oppenheim, B., & Mitchell, S.

(1971). *Childhood behavior and mental health.* New York: Grune & Stratton.

Shields, J. (1967). *Monozygotic twins brought up apart and brought up together.* London: Oxford University Press.

Shirley, M. M. (1933). The first two years. *Institute of Child Welfare Monograph. No. 7.* Minneapolis: University of Minnesota Press.

Shore, M. F. (1979). Legislation, advocacy, and the rights of children and youth. *American Psychologist, 34,* 1017–1019.

Sidman, M., & Stoddard, L. T. (1967). The effectiveness of fading in programming a simultaneous form discrimination for retarded children. *Journal of the Experimental Analysis of Behavior, 10,* 3–15.

Siegel, D. M., & Hurley, S. (1977). The role of the child's preference in custody proceedings. *Family Law Quarterly, 11,* 1–58.

Siegel, L. (1981). Unpublished data. University of Florida.

Siegel, L. J. (1983a). Hospitalization and medical care of children. In E. Walker & M. Roberts (Eds.), *Handbook of clinical child psychology.* New York: Wiley.

Siegel, L. J. (1983b). Psychosomatic and psychophysiological disorders. In R. J. Morris & T. R. Kratochwill (Eds.), *The practice of child therapy.* New York: Pergamon.

Siegel, L. J., & Peterson, L. (1981). Effects of coping skills and sensory information on the maintenance of children's response to repeated dental procedures. *Behavior Therapy, 12,* 530–535.

Simeonsson, R. J., Cooper, D. H., & Scheiner, A. P. (1982). A review and analysis of the effectiveness of early intervention programs. *Pediatrics, 69,* 635–641.

Simon, N. (1976). Echolalic speech in childhood autism. In S. Chess & A. Thomas (Eds.), *Annual progress in child psychiatry and child development.* New York: Brunner/Mazel.

Singer, M., & Isralowitz, R. (1983). *Adolescent substance abuse: A guide to prevention and treatment.* New York: The Haworth Press.

Singer, M., & Wynne, L. (1965). Thought disorder and family relations of schizophrenics. *Archives of General Psychiatry, 12,* 201–212.

Skeels, H. M., & Dye, H. B. (1939). A study of the effects of differential stimulation on mentally retarded children. *Proceedings and Addresses of the Sixty-Third Annual Session of American Association on Mental Deficiency, 44,* 114–130.

Skinner, B. F. (1957). *Verbal behavior.* New York: Appleton-Century-Crofts.

Skodak, M., & Skeels, H. M. (1949). A final follow-up study of one hundred adopted children. *Journal of Genetic Psychology, 75,* 85–125.

Skrzypek, G. J. (1969). Effects of perceptual isolation and arousal on anxiety, complexity preference, and novelty preference in psychopathic and neurotic delinquents. *Journal of Abnormal Psychology, 74,* 221–229.

Slaughter, D. T. (1983). Early intervention and its effects on maternal and child development. *Monograph of the Society for Research in Child Development, 48,* 4.

Slavson, S. R. (1943). *An introduction to group therapy.* New York: The Commonwealth Fund.

Slavson, S. R., & Schiffer, M. (1975). *Group psychotherapies for children.* New York: International Universities Press.

Sluckin, A. (1977). Children who do not talk at school. *Journal of Child Care, 3,* 69–79.

Sluckin, W., Herbert, M., & Sluckin, A. (1983). *Maternal bonding.* Oxford: Basil Blackwell.

Smart, M. S., & Smart, R. C. (1977). *Children: Development and relationships.* New York: Macmillan.

Smith, M. L. (1982). *How educators decide who is learning disabled.* Springfield, IL: Charles C Thomas.

Smith, R. E., & Sharpe, T. M. (1970). Treatment of a school phobia with implosive therapy. *Journal of Consulting and Clinical Psychology, 35,* 239–243.

Smith, S. L. (1970). School refusal with anxiety: A review of sixty-three cases. *Canadian Psychiatric Association Journal, 15,* 257–261.

Solanto, M. V. (1984). Neuropharmacological basis of stimulant drug action in attention deficit disorder with hyperactivity: A review and synthesis. *Psychological Bulletin, 95,* 387–409.

Sommer, R., & Sommer, B. A. (1983). My story in Milwaukee: Early intervention, IQ and psychology textbooks. *American Psychologist, 38,* 982–988.

Spache, G. D. (1972). *Diagnostic reading scales.* New York: CTB/McGraw-Hill.

Spache, G. D. (1981). *Diagnosing and correcting reading disabilities* (2nd ed.). Boston: Allyn & Bacon.

Spano, B. J. (1965). *Causal thinking, adjustment and social perception as a function of behavioral science concepts in elementary school children.* Unpublished doctoral dissertation, University of Florida.

Sparrow, S. S., Balla, D. A., & Chicchetti, D. V. (1984). *Vineland Adaptive Behavior Scales: Manual.* Circle Pines, MN: American Guidance Services.

Speck, R. V., & Attneave, C. L. (1971). Social network intervention. In J. Haley (Ed.), *Changing families.* New York: Grune & Stratton.

Speers, R. W., & Lansing, C. (1964). Some genetic-dynamic considerations in childhood psychosis. *Journal of the American Academy of Child Psychiatry, 1,* 328–344.

Spielberger, C. D. (1973). *State-Trait Anxiety*

Scale for Children. Palo Alto, CA: Consulting Psychologists Press.

Spinetta, J. J. (1982). Psychosocial issues in childhood cancer. In M. Wolraich & D. K. Routh (Eds.), *Advances in development and behavioral pediatrics* (Vol. 3). Greenwich, CT: JAI Press.

Spitz, R. A. (1945). Hospitalism: An inquiry into the genesis of psychiatric conditions in early childhood. *Psychoanalytic study of the child. Vol. 1*. New York: International Universities Press.

Spitz, R. A. (1946). Anaclitic depression. *The Psychoanalytic Study of the Child, 2*, 313–347.

Spitz, R. A. (1947). Hospitalism: A follow-up report. *Psychoanalytic study of the child. Vol. 2*. New York: International Universities Press.

Spitzer, R. L., Forman, J. B., & Nee, J. (1979). DSM III field trials: I. Initial interrater diagnostic reliability. *American Journal of Psychiatry, 136*, 815–820.

Spitzer, R. L., Skodol, A. E., Gibbon, M. & Williams, J. B. W. (1981). *DSM-III case book*. Washington, DC: American Psychological Association.

Spitzer, R. L., Williams, J. B., & Skodol, A. E. (1980). DSM III: The major achievements and an overview. *American Journal of Psychiatry, 137*, 154–163.

Stampfl, T. G., & Levis, D. J. (1967). Essentials of implosive therapy: A learning theory based on psychodynamic behavioral therapy. *Journal of Abnormal Psychology, 72*, 496–503.

Stampfl, T. G., & Levis, D. J. (1968). Implosive therapy: A behavioral therapy. *Behavior Research and Therapy, 6*, 31–36.

Stanley, L. (1980). Treatment of ritualistic behavior in an eight-year-old girl by response prevention. *Journal of Child Psychology and Psychiatry, 21*, 85–90.

Stanovich, K. E. (1978). Information processing in mentally retarded individuals. In N. R. Ellis (Ed.), *International review of research in mental retardation. Vol. 5*. New York: Academic Press.

Starr, R. J. (1979). Child abuse. *American Psychologist, 34*, 872–878.

Steele, B. F., & Pollock, C. B. (1974). A psychiatric study of parents who abuse infants and small children. In R. E. Helfer & C. H. Kempe (Eds.), *The battered child*. Chicago: University of Chicago Press.

Steffen, J. J., & Karoly, P. (Eds.). (1982). *Autism and severe psychopathology: Advances in child behavioral analysis therapy. Vol. II*. New York: Lexington Books.

Stein, M. I. (1947). The use of a sentence completion test for the diagnosis of personality. *Journal of Clinical Psychology, 3*, 46–56.

Stein, Z., Susser, M., Saenger, G., & Marolla, F.

(1972). Nutrition and mental performance. *Science, 178*, 708–712.

Stern, J. (1981). Brain dysfunction in some hereditary disorders of amino acid metabolism. In P. J. Mittler & J. M. deJong (Eds.), *Frontiers of knowledge in mental retardation: Vol. II. Biomedical aspects*. Baltimore: University Park Press.

Stern, L. W. (1930). *Psychology of early childhood up to the sixth year of age*. New York: Holt.

Sticht, T. G. (1979). Applications of the audread model to reading evaluation and instruction. In L. B. Resnick & P. A. Weaver (Eds.) *Theory and practice of early reading (Vol. 1)*. Hillsdale, NJ: Erlbaum.

Sticht, T. G., & Beck, L. J. (1976). *Experimental Literacy Assessment Battery (LAB)* (AFHRL-TT-76-51). Lowery Air Force Base, CO: Air Force Human Resource Laboratory/Technical Training Division.

Stover, L., & Guerney, B. G. (1967). The efficacy of training procedures for mothers in filial therapy. *Psychotherapy: Theory, Research and Practice, 4*, 110–115.

Stover, L., Guerney, B. G., & O'Connell, M. (1971). Measurements of acceptance, allowing self-direction, involvement and empathy in adult-child interaction. *Journal of Psychology, 77*, 261–269.

Strain, P. S., & Fox, J. J. (1981). Peers as behavior change agents for withdrawn classmates. In B. Lahey & A. Kazdin (Eds.), *Advances in clinical child psychology* (Vol. 4). New York: Plenum.

Strain, P. S., & Kerr, M. M. (1981). Modifying children's social withdrawal: Issues in assessment and clinical intervention. In M. Hersen, R. Eisler & P. Miller (Eds.), *Progress in behavior modification* (Vol. 11). New York: Academic Press.

Strauss, A. A., & Kephart, N. C. (1955). *Psychopathology and education of the brain-injured child: Vol. 2. Progress in theory and clinic*. New York: Grune & Stratton.

Strauss, C. C., Rubinoff, A., & Atkeson, B. M. (1983). Elimination of nocturnal headbanging in a normal seven-year-old girl using overcorrection plus reward. *Journal of Behavior Therapy and Experimental Psychiatry, 14*, 269–273.

Streissguth, A. P. (1976). Maternal alcoholism and the outcome of pregnancy: A review of the fetal alcohol syndrome. In M. Greenblatt & M. Schuckit (Eds.), *Alcoholism problems in women and children*. New York: Grune & Stratton.

Strober, M. (1981). The significance of bulimia in juvenile anorexia nervosa: An exploration of possible etiologic factors. *International Journal of Eating Disorders, 1*, 28–43.

Strober, M. (1984). Stressful life events associated

with bulimia in anorexia nervosa. *International Journal of Eating Disorders*, 3, 1–13.

Strother, C. R. (1973). Minimal cerebral dysfunction: An historical overview. *Annals of the New York Academy of Sciences*, 205, 6–17.

Stuart, R. B. (1974). Teaching facts about drugs: Pushing or prevention. *Journal of Educational Psychology*, 66, 189–201.

Sturgis, E. T. (1984). Obsessional and compulsive disorders. In H. E. Adams & P. B. Sutker (Eds.), *Comprehensive handbook of psychopathology*. New York: Plenum.

Suiter, M. L., & Potter, R. E. (1978). The effects of paradigmatic organization on verbal recall. *Journal of Language Disabilities*, 11, 217–250.

Sundberg, N. D. (1977). *Assessment of persons*. Englewood Cliffs, NJ: Prentice-Hall.

Susser, M., & Stein, Z. A. (1981). Human development and prenatal nutrition: An overview of edpidemiological experiments, quasi experiments, and natural experiments during the past decade. In P. J. Mittler & J. M. deJong (Eds.), *Frontiers of knowledge in mental retardation. Vol. II. Biomedical aspects*. Baltimore: University Park Press.

Sutherland, E. H., & Cressy, D. (1978). *Principles of criminology*. Philadelphia: Lippencott.

Swanson, H. L. (1979). Developmental recall lag in learning-disabled children: Perceptual deficit or verbal remediation deficiency? *Journal of Abnormal Child Psychology*, 7, 199–210.

Sylvester, C. E., Burke, P. M., McCauley, E. A., & Clark, C. J. (1984). Manic psychosis in childhood. *Journal of the American Academy of Child Psychiatry*, 172, 12–20.

Szasz, T. S. (1965). *Psychiatric justice*. New York: Macmillan.

Tager-Flusberg, H. (1981a). On the nature of linguistic functioning in early infantile autism. *Journal of Autism and Developmental Disorders*, 11, 45–56.

Tager-Flusberg, H. (1981b). Sentence comprehension in autistic children. *Applied Psycholinguistics*, 2, 5–24.

Tanguay, P. E., & Edwards, R. M. (1982). Electrophysiological studies of autism: The whisper of the bang. *Journal of Autism and Developmental Disorders*, 12, 177–183.

Tansley, P., & Panckhurst, J. (1981). *Children with specific learning difficulties*. Oxford: NFER-Nelson.

Tarjan, G., Wright, S. W., Eyman, P. K., & Keeran, C. V. (1973). Natural history of mental retardation: Some aspects of epidemiology. *American Journal of Mental Deficiency*, 77, 365–379.

Tasto, D. L. (1969). Systematic desensitization muscle relaxation and visual imagery in the counterconditioning of a four-year-old phobic child.

Behavior Research and Therapy, 7, 409–411.

Taylor, E. (1979). Food additives, allergy and hyperkinesis. *Journal of Child Psychology and Psychiatry*, 20, 357–363.

Teitelbaum, L. E., & Ellis, J. W. (1978). The liberty interest of children: Due process rights and their application. *Family Law Quarterly*, 12, 153–202.

Temerlin, M. K. (1968). Suggestion effects in psychiatric diagnosis. *Journal of Nervous and Mental Disease*, 147, 349–353.

Terman, L. M. (Ed.). (1925–1959). *Genetic studies of genius: Vol. I–V*. Stanford: Stanford University Press.

Terman, L. M., & Merrill, M. A. (1937). *Measuring intelligence*. Boston: Houghton Mifflin.

Terman, L. M., & Merrill, M. A. (1960). *Stanford-Binet Intelligence Scale*. Boston: Houghton Mifflin.

Terman, L. M., & Merrill, M. A. (1973). *The Stanford-Binet intelligence scale* (3rd rev. ed., with 1972 tables by R. L. Thorndike). Boston: Houghton Mifflin.

Terman, L. M., & Oden, M. H. (1959). *The gifted group at mid-life: Vol. 5. Genetic studies of genius*. Stanford: Stanford University Press.

Teuber, H. L. (1975). Recovery of function after brain injury in man: Outcome of severe damage to the central nervous system. *Ciba Foundation Symposium*, 34, 159–190.

The world almanac and book of facts. (1983). New York: Newspaper Enterprise Assoc., Inc.

Thomas, A., & Chess, S. (1977). *Temperament and development*. New York: Brunner/Mazel.

Thomas, A., & Chess, S. (1984). Genesis and evolution of behavioral disorders: From infancy to early adult life. *American Journal of Psychiatry*, 141, 1–9.

Thomas, A., Chess, S., & Birch, H. (1968). *Temperament and behavior disorders in children*. New York: New York University Press.

Thorne, F. (1944). The incidence of nocturnal enuresis after age 5. *American Journal of Psychiatry*, 100, 686–689.

Thrasher, F. M. (1963). *The gang* (rev. ed.). Chicago: University of Chicago Press.

Tinbergen, N., & Tinbergen, E. A. (1983). *Autistic children: New hope for cure*. London: Allen & Unwin.

Tinklenberg, J. R. (1975). Assessing the effects of drug use on antisocial behavior. *Annals of the American Association of Political and Social Science*, 417, 66–75.

Tomlinson, J. (1981). *Education subnormality*. London: Routledge & Kegan Paul.

Tomlinson, J. R. (1970). The treatment of bowel retention by operant procedures: A case study. *Journal of Behavior Therapy and Experimental Psychiatry*, 1, 53–85.

Torgersen, A. M. (1982). Influence of genetic factors on temperament development in early childhood. In Ciba Foundation Symposium Number 89, *Temperamental differences in infants and young children*. London: Pitman Books Ltd.

Treffert, D. A. (1970). Epidemiology of infantile autism. *Archives of General Psychiatry*, 22, 431–435.

Trites, R. L., Dugas, E., Lynch, G., & Ferguson, H. B. (1979). Prevalence of hyperactivity. *Journal of Pediatric Psychology*, 4, 179–188.

Trites, R. L., & Laprade, K. (1983). Evidence for an independent syndrome of hyperactivity. *Journal of Child Psychology and Psychiatry*, 24, 573–586.

Trojanowicz, R. C., & Morash, M. (1983). *Juvenile delinquency: Concepts and control* (2nd ed.). Englewood Cliffs, NJ: Prentice-Hall.

Truax, C. B., & Mitchell, K. M. (1971). Research on certain therapist interpersonal skills in relation to process and outcome. In A. E. Bergin & S. L. Garfield (Eds.) *Handbook of psychotherapy and behavior change*. New York: Wiley.

Tsai, L. Y., & Stewart, M. A. (1983). Etiological implication of maternal age and birth order in infantile autism. *Journal of Autism and Developmental Disorders*, 13, 57–65.

Tsai, L., Stewart, M. A., Faust, M., & Shook, S. (1982). Social class distribution of fathers of children enrolled in the Iowa autism program. *Journal of Autism and Developmental Disorders*, 12, 211–221.

Tuma, J. M., & Pratt, J. M. (1982). Clinical child psychology practice and training: A survey. *Journal of Clinical Child Psychology*, 11, 27–34.

Tuma, J. M., & Sobotka, K. R. (1983). Traditional therapies with children. In T. H. Ollendick & M. Hersen (Eds.), *Handbook of child psychopathology*. New York: Plenum.

Turner, J. S., & Helms, D. B. (1983). *Lifespan development* (2nd ed.). New York: Holt, Rinehart & Winston.

Turner, S. M., & Hersen, M. (1984). *Adult psychopathology and diagnosis*. New York: Wiley.

Turner, S. M., Jacob, R. G., & Morrison, R. (1984). Somatoform and factitious disorders. In H. E. Adams & P. B. Sutker (Eds.), *Comprehensive handbook of psychopathology*. New York: Plenum.

Tyler, V. O., & Brown, G. D. (1967). The use of swift, brief isolation as a group control device for institutionalized delinquents. *Behavior Research and Therapy*, 5, 1–9.

Ullmann, L. P., & Krasner, L. A. (1969). *Psychological approaches to abnormal behavior*. Englewood Cliffs, NJ: Prentice-Hall.

Ullmann, L. P., & Krasner, L. (1975). *A psychological approach to abnormal behavior* (2nd ed.). Englewood Cliffs, NJ: Prentice-Hall.

Ungerer, J. A., & Sigman, M. (1981). Symbolic play and language comprehension in autistic children. *Journal of the American Academy of Child Psychiatry*, 20, 318–337.

United Nations General Assembly. (1973). United Nations declaration of the rights of children. In A. Wilkerson (Ed.), *The rights of children: Divergent concepts in law and society*. Philadelphia: Temple University Press.

United States Department of Commerce (1983). *Statistical abstract of the United States (1982–83)*. Washington, DC: Author.

U.S. Department of Criminal Justice (1978). *Sourcebook for criminal justice statistics-1977*. Washington, DC: U.S. Government Printing Office.

U.S. Department of Health and Human Services. (1980). *Infant care*. Washington, DC: U.S. Government Printing Office.

Vaillant, G. E., & Vaillant, C. D. (1981). Natural history of male psychological health, X: Work as a predictor of positive mental health. *American Journal of Psychiatry*, 138, 1433–1440.

Valentine, G. H. (1966). *The chromosome disorders*. London: Hineman.

Van Buskirk, S. S. (1977). A two-phase perspective in the treatment of anorexia nervosa. *Psychological Bulletin*, 84, 529–538.

Vandenberg, S. G. (1971). What do we know about the inheritance of intelligence and how do we know it? In R. Canero (Ed.), *Intelligence: Genetic and environmental influences*. New York: Grune & Stratton.

Van Den Berghe, H., Fryns, J. P., Parloir, C., Deroover, J., & Keulemans, M. (1981). Genetic causes of severe mental handicaps: Preliminary data from a University of Leuven study. In P. J. Mittler & J. M. deJong (Eds.), *Frontiers of knowledge in mental retardation: Vol. II. Biomedical aspects*. Baltimore, MD: University Park Press.

Van Hasselt, V. B., Hersen, M., Whitehill, M. B., & Bellack, A. S. (1979). Social skill assessment and training for children: An evaluative review. *Behavior Research and Therapy*, 17, 413–437.

Van Riper, C. (1978). *Speech correction: Principles and methods* (6th ed.). Englewood Cliffs, NJ: Prentice-Hall.

Varble, D. L. (1971). Current status of the Thematic Apperception Test. In P. McReynolds (Ed.), *Advances in psychological Assessment* (Vol. 2). Palo Alto, CA: Science and Behavior Books.

Vaughn, V. C., & McKay, P. J. (1975). *Nelson's textbook of pediatrics*. Philadelphia: Saunders.

Vaz, E. W. (1967). *Middle class delinquency*. New York: Harper & Row.

Vitello, S. J., & Soskin, R. M. (1985). *Mental re-*

tardation: Its social and legal context. Englewood Cliffs, NJ: Prentice-Hall.

Volk, B. W. (1964). *Tay-Sachs disease.* New York: Grune & Stratton.

Wahler, R. G. (1969). Oppositional children: A quest for parental reinforcement control. *Journal of Applied Behavior Analysis, 2,* 159–170.

Wahler, R. G., House, A. E., & Stambaugh, E. E. (1976). *Ecological assessment of child problem behavior.* New York: Pergamon.

Wahler, R. G., Leske, G., & Rogers, E. S. (1979). The insular family: A deviance support system for oppositional children. In L. Hamerlynck (Ed.), *Behavioral systems for the developmentally disabled: I. School and family environments.* New York: Brunner/Mazel.

Wald, I. (1969). Epidemiology of low-grade mental deficiency in Poland: Organisation of the study and method of sampling. *Epidemiological Review, 27,* 245–247.

Waldrop, M. F., & Goering, J. D. (1971). Hyperactivity and minor physical anomalies in elementary school children. *American Journal of Orthopsychiatry, 41,* 602–607.

Waldrop, M. F., Pederson, F. A., & Bell, R. Q. (1968). Minor physical anomalies and behavior in preschool children. *Child Development, 34,* 391–400.

Walker, J., Kaufman, M. R., & Deutch, F. (1940). Anorexia nervosa: A psychosomatic entity. *Psychosomatic Medicine, 2,* 3–16.

Wallender, J., & Conger, J. (1981). Assessment of hyperactive children: Psychometric, methodological and practical consideration. *Progress in behavior modification* (Vol. 11). New York: Academic Press.

Wallerstein, J. S., & Kelly, J. B. (1974). The effects of parental divorce: The adolescent experience. In E. J. Anthony & C. Koupernik (Eds.), *The child in his family: Vol. 3. Children at psychiatric risk.* New York: Wiley.

Wallerstein, J. S., & Kelly, J. B. (1975). The effects of parental divorce: Experience of the preschool child. *Journal of the American Academy of Child Psychiatry, 14,* 600–616.

Wallerstein, J. S., & Kelly, J. B. (1976). The effects of parental divorce: Experience of the child in later latency. *American Journal of Orthopsychiatry, 46,* 256–269.

Wallerstein, J. S., & Kelly, J. B. (1977). Divorce counseling: A community service for families in the midst of divorce. *American Journal of Orthopsychiatry, 47,* 4–22.

Wallick, M. M. (1979). Desensitization therapy with a fearful two-year-old. *American Journal of Psychiatry, 136,* 1325–1326.

Walsh, K. (1978). *Neuropsychology: A clinical approach.* Edinburgh: Churchill-Livingstone.

Ward, A. J. (1970). Early infantile autism: Diag-nosis, etiology and treatment. *Psychological Bulletin, 73,* 350–367.

Watson, J. B. (1913). Psychology as the behaviorist views it. *Psychological Review, 20,* 158–177.

Watson, J. B. (1924). *Behaviorism.* New York: People's Publishing Company.

Watson, J. B. (1928). *Psychological care of infant and child.* New York: Norton.

Watson, J. B., & Raynor, R. (1920). Conditioned emotional reactions. *Journal of Experimental Psychology, 3,* 1–14.

Webb, J. T., & Mecksworth, B. (1982). *Guiding the gifted child.* Columbus: Ohio Psychology Publishers.

Webster-Stratton, C., & Eyberg, S. M. (1982). Child temperament: Relationship with child behavior problems and parent-child interactions. *Journal of Clinical Child Psychology, 11,* 123–129.

Wechsler, D. (1958). *The measurement and appraisal of adult intelligence* (4th ed.). Baltimore, MD: Williams & Wilkins.

Wechsler, D. (1967). *Manual for the Wechsler Preschool and Primary Scale of Intelligence.* New York: Psychological Corporation.

Wechsler, D. (1974). *Manual for the Wechsler Intelligence Scale for Children — Revised.* New York: Psychological Corporation.

Weeks, H. (1958). *Youthful offenders at Highfields.* Ann Arbor: University of Michigan Press.

Wehman, P., Abramson, M., & Norman, C. (1977). Transfer of training in behavior modification programs. *Journal of Special Education, 11,* 217–231.

Weinberg, W. A., Rutman, J., Sullivan, L., Penick, E. C., & Deitz, S. G. (1973). Depression in children referred to an educational diagnostic center: Diagnosis and treatment. *Journal of Pediatrics, 83,* 1065–1072.

Weiner, I. B. (1982). *Child and adolescent psychopathology.* New York: Wiley.

Weiss, B. (1982). Food additives and environmental chemicals as sources of childhood behavior disorders. *Journal of the American Academy of Child Psychiatry, 21,* 144–152.

Weiss, G., Minde, K., Werry, J. S., Douglas, V., & Nemeth, E. (1971). Studies on the hyperactive child: VIII. Five-year follow-up. *Archives of General Psychiatry, 24,* 409–414.

Weiss, J. H. (1974). The current state of the concept of a psychosomatic disorder. *International Journal of Psychiatry in Medicine, 5,* 473–480.

Wells, K. C., Forehand, R., & Griest, D. L. (1980). Generality of treatment effects from treated to untreated behaviors resulting from a parent training program. *Journal of Clinical Child Psychology, 9,* 217–219.

Wells, R. A., & Dezen, A. E. (1978). The results of family therapy revisited: The non-behavioral methods. *Family Processes*, *17*, 251–274.

Wenar, C. (1982a). Developmental psychopathology: Its nature and models. *Journal of Clinical Child Psychology*, *11*, 192–201.

Wenar, C. (1982b). *Psychopathology from infancy through adolescence*. New York: Random House.

Wender, P. H. (1971). *Minimal brain dysfunction in children*. New York: Wiley.

Werner, C., Ruttenberg, B. A., Dratman, M. L., & Wolf, E. G. (1967). Changing autistic behavior: The effectiveness of three milieus. *Archives of General Psychiatry*, *17*, 26–35.

Wernicke, C. (1874). *Der aphasische symptomenkomplex*. Breslau: Cohn & Weigart.

Werry, J. S. (1972). Psychosomatic disorders. In H. C. Quay & J. S. Werry (Eds.), *Psychopathological disorders of childhood*. New York: Wiley.

Werry, J. S. (1978). Measures in pediatric psychopharmacology. In J. S. Werry (Ed.), *Pediatric psychopharmacology: The use of behavior modifying drugs in children*. New York: Brunner/Mazel.

Werry, J. S. (1979a). Family therapy: Behavioral approaches. *Journal of the American Academy of Child Psychiatry*, *18*, 91–102.

Werry, J. S. (1979b). Psychosomatic disorders, psychogenic symptoms and hospitalization. In H. C. Quay & J. S. Werry (Eds.), *Psychopathological disorders of childhood* (2nd ed.). New York: Wiley.

Werry, J. S. (1979c). Organic factors. In H. C. Quay & J. S. Werry (Eds.), *Psychopathological disorders of childhood* (2nd ed.). New York: Wiley.

Werry, J. S. (1979d). Psychosomatic disorders, psychogenic symptoms, and hospitalization. In H. C. Quay & J. S. Werry (Eds.), *Psychopathological disorders of childhood* (2nd ed.). New York: Wiley.

Werry, J. S., Methven, R. J., Fitzpatrick, J., & Dixon, H. (1983). The inter-rater reliability of DSM III in children. *Journal of Abnormal Child Psychology*, *11*, 341–354.

Werry, J. S., & Quay, H. C. (1971). The prevalence of behavior symptoms in younger elementary school children. *American Journal of Orthopsychiatry*, *41*, 136–143.

West, D. J., & Farrington, D. P. (1973). *Who becomes delinquent?* London: Heinemann Educational.

Whalen, C. K. (1982). Hyperactivity and psychostimulant treatment. In J. R. Lachenmeyer & M. S. Gibbs (Eds.), *Psychopathology in childhood*. New York: Gardner Press.

Whalen, C. K., & Henker, B. (1976). Psychostimulants and children: A review and analysis. *Psychological Bulletin*, *83*, 1113–1130.

Whalen, C. K., & Henker, B. (Eds.). (1980). *Hyperactive children, the social ecology of identification and treatment*. New York: Academic Press.

Whaley, D. L., & Tough, J. (1968). Treatment of a self-injuring mongoloid with shock-induced suppression and avoidance. Michigan Department of Mental Health.

White, J. H., Hornsby, L. G., Boylston, W. H., & Gordon, R. (1972). The treatment of Little Fritz, a modern-day Little Hans. *International Journal of Child Psychotherapy*, *15*, 2–23.

Wiedel, T. C., & Schwartz, S. (1983). Verbal ability and memory processing speed. *Current Psychological Research*, *2*, 247–256.

Wiesen, A. E., & Watson, E. (1967). Elimination of attention seeking behavior in a retarded child. *American Journal of Mental Deficiency*, *72*, 50–52,

Willerman, L. (1973). Activity level and hyperactivity in twins. *Child Development*, *44*, 288–293.

Williams, C. D. (1959). The elimination of tantrum behavior by extinction procedures. *Journal of Abnormal and Social Psychology*, *59*, 269.

Williams, R. H. (1958). Anorexia nervosa (A somatic disorder). *British Medical Journal*, *2*, 190–194.

Williams, R. L. (1972). *The Butch-100: A culture specific test*. Paper presented at the annual meeting of the American Psychological Association, Honolulu.

Williamson, D. A., Sewell, W. R., Sanders, S. H., Haney, J. N., & White, D. (1977). The treatment of reluctant speech using contingency management procedures. *Journal of Behavior Therapy and Experimental Psychiatry*, *8*, 151–156.

Wilson, D. R., & Lyman, R. D. (1983). Residential treatment of emotionally disturbed children. In E. Walker & M. Roberts (Eds.), *Handbook of clinical child psychology*. New York: Wiley.

Wilson, E. O. (1975). *Sociobiology: The new synthesis*. Cambridge, MA: Harvard University Press.

Wing, L. (1969). The handicaps of autistic children: A comparative study. *Journal of Child Psychology and Psychiatry*, *10*, 1–40.

Wing, L. (1976). *Early infantile autism* (2nd ed.). Oxford: Pergamon.

Wing, L. (1981). Language, social and cognitive impairments in autism and severe mental retardation. *Journal of Autism and Developmental Disorders*, *11*, 31–44.

Wing, L., Yeates, S. R., Brierly, L. M., & Gould, J. (1976). The prevalence of early childhood autism: Comparison of administrative and epidemiological studies. *Psychological Medicine*, 6, 89–100.

Wingfield, J. C. (1983). The interplay between environmental and neuroendocrine factors in the integration of seasonal reproductive behavior. Paper presented at the 18th annual International Ethological Conference, Brisbane, Australia.

Winick, M. (1970a). Fetal malnutrition and growth processes. *Hospital Practice*, 5, 33–41.

Winick, M. (1970b). Nutrition and nerve cell growth. *Proceedings of the Federation of American Societies for Experimental Biology*, 29, 1510–1515.

Winick, M. (1976). *Malnutrition and brain development*. New York: Oxford University Press.

Winick, M. (1979). *Human nutrition: A comprehensive treatise: Vol. I. Pre- and postnatal development*. New York: Plenum.

Wirt, R. D., & Briggs, P. F. (1965). The meaning of delinquency. In H. C. Quay (Ed.), *Juvenile delinquency*. New York: Van Nostrand.

Wirt, R. D., & Lachar, D. (1981). The Personality Inventory for Children. In P. McReynolds (Ed.), *Advances in psychological assessment* (Vol. 5). San Francisco: Jossey-Bass.

Wirt, R. D., Lachar, D., Klinedinst, J. K., & Seat, P. D. (1977). *Multidimensional evaluation of child personality: Manual for the Personality Inventory for Children*. Los Angeles: Western Psychological Services.

Wolfenstein, M. (1953). Trends in infant care. *American Journal of Orthopsychiatry*, 23, 120–130.

Wolff, P. H., Waber, D., Bauermeister, M., Cohen, C., & Ferber, R. (1982). The neuropsychological status of adolescent delinquent boys. *Journal of Child Psychology and Psychiatry*, 23, 267–279.

Wolpe, J. (1958). *Psychotherapy by reciprocal inhibition*. Stanford, CA: University Press.

Woltman, A. G. (1960). Spontaneous puppetry by children as a projective method. In A. I. Rabin & M. R. Haworth (Eds.), *Projective techniques with children*. New York: Grune & Stratton.

Woodcock, R. W., & Johnson, M. B. (1977). *Woodcock-Johnson Psycho-educational Battery, Part II: Tests of achievement*. Hingham, MA: Teaching Resources Corp.

Word, P., & Rozynko, V. (1974). Behavior therapy of an eleven-year-old girl with reading problems. *Journal of Learning Disabilities*, 7, 551–554.

Wright, D. M., Moelis, I., & Pollack, L. J. (1976). The outcome of individual child psychotherapy: Increments at follow-up. *Journal of Child Psychology and Psychiatry*, 17, 275–285.

Wright, H. T. (1971). Prenatal factors in causation (viral). In R. Koch & J. Dobson (Eds.),

The mentally retarded child and his family: A multidisciplinary handbook. New York: Brunner/Mazel.

Wright, L. (1973). Handling the encopretic child. *Professional Psychology*, 5, 137–144.

Wright, L. (1975). Outcome of a standardized program for treating psychogenic encopresis. *Professional Psychology*, 6, 453–456.

Wright, L., Schaeffer, A. B., & Solomons, G. (1979). *Encyclopedia of pediatric psychology*. Baltimore: University Park Press.

Wulbert, M., & Dries, R. (1979). The relative efficacy of methylphenidate (ritalin) and behavior modification techniques in the treatment of a hyperactive child. In B. B. Lahey (Ed.), *Behavior therapy with hyperactive and learning disabled children* (pp. 237–246). New York: Oxford University Press.

Wynne, L. C., Cromwell, R. L., & Matthysse, S. (1978). *The nature of schizophrenia: New approaches to research and treatment*. New York: Wiley.

Yates, A. (1970). *Behavior therapy*. New York: Wiley.

Young, A. W., & Ellis, A. W. (1981). Asymmetry in cerebral hemispheric function in normal and poor readers. *Psychological Bulletin*, 89, 183–190.

Young, G. (1965). Personality factors and the treatment of enuresis. *Behavior Research and Therapy*, 3, 103–105.

Young, G., & Morgan, R. T. (1972). Overlearning in the conditioning treatment of enuresis. *Behavior Research and Therapy*, 10, 147–151.

Young, I. L., & Goldsmith, A. D. (1972). Treatment of encopresis in a day treatment program. *Psychotherapy: Theory, Research and Practice*, 9, 231–235.

Young, S. W. (1983). *Nuclear magnetic resonance imaging: Basic principles*. New York: Raven.

Zajonc, R. B., & Bargh, J. (1980a). The confluence model: Parameter estimation for six divergent data sets on family factors and intelligence. *Intelligence*, 4, 349–361.

Zajonc, R. B., & Bargh, J. (1980b). Birth order, family size and the decline of SAT scores. *American Psychologist*, 35, 662–668.

Zajonc, R. B., & Markus, G. B. (1975). Birth order and intellectual development. *Psychological Review*, 82, 74–88.

Zajonc, R. B., Markus, H., & Markus, G. B. (1979). The birth order puzzle. *Journal of Personality and Social Psychology*, 37, 1325–1341.

Zentall, S. (1975). Optimal stimulation as theoretical basis of hyperactivity. *American Journal of Orthopsychiatry*, 45, 549–563.

Zentall, S. S., & Zentall, I. R. (1976). Activity and task performance of hyperactive children as a function of environmental stimulation. *Jour-*

nal of Consulting and Clinical Psychology, 44, 693–697.

Zucker, R. A. (1976). Parental influences on the drinking patterns of children. In M. Greenblatt & M. Schuckit (Eds.), *Alcoholism problems in women and children.* New York: Grune & Stratton.

Zuckerman, M. (1974). The sensation seeking motive. In B. Maher (Ed.), *Progress in experimen-* *tal personality research* (Vol. 7). New York: Academic Press.

Zuckerman, M. (1979). *Beyond the sensation seek-* *ing motive.* Hillsdale, NJ: Erlbaum.

Zusman, J. (1975). Secondary prevention. In M. Freedman et al. (Eds.), *Comprehensive text-* *book of psychiatry: Vol. 2.* Baltimore: Williams & Wilkins.

AUTHOR INDEX

SUBJECT INDEX

ABOUT THE AUTHORS

Steven Schwartz received his doctorate from Syracuse University in 1971. He has taught at several universities, including the University of Texas and the University of Western Australia. Presently he is Reader in Psychology and Director of Clinical Psychology Training at the University of Queensland, Australia. Dr. Schwartz is the author of five books dealing with schizophrenia, decision making, and the history of psychology. He serves on the editorial board of *The Journal of Research in Personality*, *Applied Psycholinguistics*, and *Current Psychological Reviews*. His research areas of cognition, psychopathology, and decision making has been supported by the National Institutes of Mental Health, the Educational Research and Development Committee, and the Australian Research Grants Committee.

James H. Johnson received his PhD from Northern Illinois University in 1976. He has previously served on the faculty of the University of Texas Medical Center at Galveston (Division of Child Psychiatry) and as Assistant Professor of Psychology, University of Washington–Seattle. At present he is an Associate Professor of Clinical Psychology at the University of Florida, where he is Director of Training in the clinical-child area.

Dr. Johnson is presently Associate Editor of the *Journal of Clinical Child Psychology* and is President-elect of the American Psychological Association's Section on Clinical Child Psychology. He has published over three dozen articles dealing with areas such as assessment, stress, child abuse, child behavior therapy, and issues related to clinical-child training. He is also senior author of a forthcoming text dealing with approaches to child treatment.